Probing the Reformed Tradition

Princeton Theological Seminary

Probing the Reformed Tradition

Historical Studies in Honor of Edward A. Dowey, Jr.

Edited by
Elsie Anne McKee
and
Brian G. Armstrong

Westminster/John Knox Press
Louisville, Kentucky

Book design by Gene Harris

First edition

Published by Westminster/John Knox Press
Louisville, Kentucky

PRINTED IN THE UNITED STATES OF AMERICA

9 8 7 6 5 4 3 2 1

Library of Congress Cataloging-in-Publication Data

Probing the Reformed tradition: historical studies in honor of Edward A. Dowey, Jr. / edited by Elsie Anne McKee and Brian G. Armstrong.—1st ed.

p. cm.
Bibliography: p.
ISBN 0-664-21916-0

1. Reformed Church—Doctrines—History. 2. Calvin, Jean 1509–1564. 3. Presbyterian Church—Doctrines—History. 4. Dowey, Edward A. I. Dowey, Edward A. II. McKee, Elsie Anne. III. Armstrong, Brian G.
BX9422.5.P75 1989
230′.42—dc20 89-31961
CIP

Contents

Abbreviations

CCL	*Corpus Christianorum, series Latina* (Turnhout: Brépols, 1953–)
CO	*Ioannis Calvini opera quae supersunt omnia,* ed. W. Baum, E. Cunitz, and E. Reuss (Braunschweig and Berlin: Schwetschke, 1865–1900)
CR	*Corpus Reformatorum* (Berlin and Leipzig, 1834–)
CSEL	*Corpus scriptorum ecclesiasticorum Latinorum* (Vienna: F. Tempsky, 1866–)
DThC	*Dictionnaire de théologie catholique,* ed. A. Vacant et al., 15 vols. (Paris: Letouzey & Ané, 1908–50)
E.T.	English translation
LCC	*Calvin: Institutes of the Christian Religion,* 2 vols., ed. J. T. McNeill, tr. F. L. Battles, Library of Christian Classics (Philadelphia: Westminster Press, 1960)
OS	John Calvin, *Opera selecta,* ed. P. Barth, W. Niesel, et al. (Munich: Chr. Kaiser, 1926–52)
PL	*Patrologiae cursus completus . . . series Latina,* ed. J.-P. Migne, 221 vols. (Paris: J.-P. Migne, 1844–64)
SC	*Supplementa Calviniana* (Neukirchen Kreis Moers: Neukirchener Verlag, 1936–)
ST	Thomas Aquinas, *Summa Theologiae*
WA	*Martin Luther, Werke, kritische Gesamtausgabe* (Weimar: Hermann Bohlau, 1883–)
Z	*Huldreich Zwinglis sämtliche Werke,* ed. Emil Egli et al. in cooperation with the Zwingli Verein (Zurich, 1905–)

List of Contributors

Brian G. Armstrong
Associate Professor of Early Modern History, Georgia State University, Department of History, Atlanta, Georgia
†Mihály Bucsay
Emeritus Professor of Theology, Reformierte Theologische Akademie Budapest; General Director of the Raday College, Budapest, Hungary
Mark S. Burrows
Assistant Professor of Church History, Wesley Theological Seminary, Washington, D.C.
Fritz Büsser
Professor of Church History, Institut für schweizerische Reformationsgeschichte, Zurich, Switzerland
Gary B. Deason
Associate Professor of History, Religion, and Philosophy and Senior Tutor of the Paracollege, St. Olaf College, Northfield, Minnesota
Akira Demura
Professor of Church History, Tohoku Gakuin University, Sendai, Japan
Karlfried Froehlich
Benjamin B. Warfield Professor of Ecclesiastical History, Princeton Theological Seminary, Princeton, New Jersey
Ulrich Gäbler
Professor of Church History, University of Basel, Basel, Switzerland
Alexandre Ganoczy
Ordentlicher Professor für Dogmatik, Katholisch-Theologische Fakultät der Universität, Würzburg, Germany

B. A. Gerrish
John Nuveen Professor, University of Chicago, The Divinity School, Chicago, Illinois
Otto Gründler
Professor of Religion and Director of the Medieval Institute, Western Michigan University, Kalamazoo, Michigan
Robert M. Kingdon
Hilldale Professor of History and Member of the Institute for Research in the Humanities, University of Wisconsin, Madison, Wisconsin
John H. Leith
Pemberton Professor of Theology, Union Theological Seminary in Virginia, Richmond, Virginia
Elsie Anne McKee
Associate Professor of Church History, Andover Newton Theological School, Newton Centre, Massachusetts
Wilhelm Neuser
Professor of Church History, Willems-Universität, Münster, Westfalia, Germany, and Secretary of the International Congress for Calvin Research
José C. Nieto
Mary S. Geiger Professor of Religion and History, Juniata College, Huntingdon, Pennsylvania
Jean-Loup Seban
Assistant Professor of Church History, Princeton Theological Seminary, Princeton, New Jersey
Willem van 't Spijker
Professor in Church History, Theological University of the Christian Reformed Churches, Apeldoorn, Netherlands
Terrence N. Tice
Professor of Philosophy, School of Education, and Research Scientist in Urban, Technological, and Environmental Planning, University of Michigan, Ann Arbor, Michigan
Thomas F. Torrance
Emeritus Professor of Christian Dogmatics, University of Edinburgh, Edinburgh, Scotland
David Willis-Watkins
Charles Hodge Professor of Systematic Theology, Princeton Theological Seminary, Princeton, New Jersey
David F. Wright
Dean of the Faculty of Divinity, University of Edinburgh, New College, Edinburgh, Scotland

Preface

The Reformed tradition of the Christian faith: These words probably evoke a wide variety of ideas and feelings. For some, it is the great names which first spring to mind: Ulrich Zwingli, John Calvin, Heinrich Bullinger, Martin Bucer, Katharine Zell, John Knox, Jeanne d'Albret, Gaspard de Coligny, William of Orange, John à Lasco, Oliver Cromwell. Or perhaps it is Michael Servetus. Perhaps it is the notorious Supper Strife, the arguments of Separatists in the Church of England, the French and English civil wars. Perhaps for some the Reformed tradition stands for the source of social activism and reform or for tyrannical legalism, for world-transforming faith or for the forerunner of individualism and rationalism, for Christian freedom or for repressive discipline. Or it may bring to mind a host of other historical developments rightly or wrongly associated with the fire of sixteenth-century Christians burning with a new vision of *ecclesia reformata semper reformanda.* One thing is sure: Probing the Reformed tradition is never a dull experience!

Any extensive investigation of Reformed Christianity as a movement brings to the fore several of its distinctive characteristics. Universality is one of these. The Reformed church was the sole Protestant group in the sixteenth century to develop a program to support its claim to be the true "catholic" Christian church designed to replace the Roman church. This meant that it would be a missionary faith, with a program for establishing churches in all areas of the world and a developed organizational structure that would be adaptable and versatile, permitting the churches' survival in even the most hostile settings. From small beginnings, the Reformed faith spread rapidly along the major arteries of communication: along the Rhine to the north and south and west, along the Danube to the east, and along the Loire west toward the Atlantic. Branches of the Reformed family were first scattered across Europe; then, in the decades and centuries following the death of the first Reformers, they found their way, inter alia, to the Americas, Africa, the South Sea Isles, and the Far East.

A second distinctive trait of Reformed Christianity is the emphasis on integration of faith and life, the insistence that each of its members must work out an informed application of the principles of the faith to every detail of life. This meant that adherents of the Reformed heritage would become involved in the reformation of every institution of society, attempting to bring everything from politics and war to farming and leisure time into conformity with the principles of God's message to humankind found in Holy Scripture. Although not always wisely directed, the insistence that what is believed has inescapable implications for what is done has shaped both faith and practice. The Reformed Christian has never been a passive spectator in life. To a greater or lesser degree, with more or, regrettably, less generosity to those who differed, Reformed Christians have felt called to be instruments of transformation in a fallen world.

In a remarkable way, Edward A. Dowey, Jr., stands as a notable representative of the ecumenical and socially active traits of the Reformed tradition. Continuously involved in confessional and theological concerns of the church, he has maintained the openness to the wider Christian community characteristic of the Reformed conviction that doctrine matters intensely but that no one part of the body of Christ has the final word or can cease to listen to others within—and even without—the faith. Academic, yet anything but an "ivory tower" professor, Dowey the teacher almost unconsciously impressed on each generation of students his own deep-rooted conviction that the theology of which he spoke has present relevance. For Edward Dowey, the implications of belief for practice have found expression in a sturdy and consistently voiced opposition to institutional as well as personal manifestations of human sinfulness, even—or especially—among the regenerate. In keeping with his heritage, Edward Dowey exemplifies its strong tradition of *semper reformanda,* as for example in his determination to learn about and speak out against the injustices done to ethnic minorities and women and in his advocacy and practice of equal respect and equal responsibility for people of color as well as those who have long held power, for women as well as men.

Although no single book could illustrate the fullness of the tradition, in this volume honoring Edward A. Dowey, Jr., both Reformed characteristics have found some expression, especially in human terms, though also to some extent in the individual writers' subject matter. Something of the breadth of the Reformed tradition is visible in the spread of geographic and national origin of the contributors to this collection. Something of the recognition of the implications of faith for practice has been evident behind the scenes in the respect of senior colleagues for their junior woman editor—in spite of the endless correspondence she inflicted on them in the course of this project! Something of the passion for and pitfalls of ecumenism, of the desire for coherence without systematic uniformity, something of the consciousness of the claims of prophetic challenges to unjust authorities or the strength to face oppression, of the integration of religion and science, can be appreciated in particular essays.

As every historical movement is born in a particular context, so some of the critical contributing factors in the shaping of the Reformed tradition were questions of grace and sin, of how to read the Bible or use Renaissance humanism in the service of Christ. Part One explores some of these questions. Princeton professor Karlfried Froehlich devotes a dense but illuminating chapter to the investigation of justification, that doctrine which became central in Protestantism, as it developed in the later Middle Ages. Scottish theologian Thomas F. Torrance follows this with a discussion of another primary point, the matter of biblical interpretation as practiced by the prince of the humanists, Erasmus of Rotterdam.

No volume dedicated to Edward A. Dowey, Jr., could entirely omit the reformer John Calvin, and Part Two of this collection provides six varied studies of the renowned Genevan reformer. The first four articles focus on specific details of Calvin's teaching, especially—though not exclusively—as found in the *Institutes of the Christian Religion.* Wilhelm Neuser, the secretary of the International Congress for Calvin Research, casts new light on a small but neglected facet of Calvin's teaching on the doctrine of the true church, with exciting results. Roman Catholic Calvin expert Alexandre Ganoczy points to a fascinating and revisionary Trinitarian emphasis in the Genevan reformer's teaching on grace. The focus of Otto Gründler's study is Calvin's teaching on the *semen fidei,* an investigation which leads to the question of whether this may indeed have been the root of later Reformed orthodox developments. David Willis-Watkins moves us from the *Institutes* to Calvin's 1563 Samuel sermons, published in the

Supplementa Calviniana series, to explore new possibilities of the prophetic emphases in Calvin's later delineation of true kingship.

The final two contributions on Calvin are more broadly conceived as proposals for a more comprehensive picture of the theologian at work. Brian G. Armstrong enters the debate on the structure of Calvin's theology, summarizing the current state of the question and offering a clear suggestion for approaching the major themes that give shape to the *Institutes.* The essay of Elsie Anne McKee turns this methodological quest in a slightly different direction, drawing on extensive investigations of Calvin's context in exegetical history to hypothesize about the interrelationship between biblical interpretation and the development of the Genevan reformer's theology, particularly ecclesiology.

Calvin was certainly not the only Reformed leader of the Protestant Reformation, much less the sole reformer of importance. Some of the colleagues, opponents, and other contemporaries of the confessional age who shared the sixteenth-century scene with him are treated in Part Three. Zurich historian Fritz Büsser studies Ulrich Zwingli's work as an exegete, noting the influence of Erasmus and discussing the character of the first great Reformed pastor's biblical interpretation. The importance of Reformed studies in Japan, though often forgotten by Western writers, is brought to the fore by Akira Demura's exploration of the "father and son" relationship of Ulrich Zwingli and Karl Barth, especially as these theologians reflected on sacramental teaching and practice. Some of Calvin's Strassburg colleagues, Wolfgang Capito and Martin Bucer, are the focus of Willem van 't Spijker's study of one struggle of the Reformed tradition to define itself against the attractions of Anabaptist attitudes toward the importance of the external structures of the church. The role of Calvin's successor Theodore Beza and the influence of Zurich's Heinrich Bullinger in Reformed ecumenism in the sixteenth century are the subject of social historian Robert M. Kingdon's thought-provoking reminder to modern ecumenists of the possibilities and pitfalls which have faced this movement in the past. This section on the wider spread of the Reformed tradition in the sixteenth century concludes with a short piece by the late great churchman Mihály Bucsay on the Christianization and spread of the Reformation in Hungary.

The second section of Part Three moves from the sixteenth-century Reformed tradition to different ideas of reform and different approaches to religious questions. David F. Wright of

Edinburgh provides the first publication of a variant manuscript version of the early pages from the *Christianismi Restitutio* of Calvin's opponent Michael Servetus and supplies this Latin text with appropriate introductory and critical apparatus. The final two essays in this section touch on the boundaries between faith and Renaissance art, religion, and science. José C. Nieto, a specialist in St. John of the Cross, reveals his discovery that the great mystical poem the "Dark Night" was indeed most probably a secular love song, perhaps the finest in contemporary Spanish Renaissance literature. Gary B. Deason, known for his interest in the interdisciplinary study of early modern science and the Reformation, points out intriguing ways in which the actual relationship between Copernicanism and biblical interpretation in Reformed and Roman Catholic writers differs from the stereotypes.

The sixteenth and seventeenth centuries by no means marked the end of the Reformed tradition, and Part Four glances briefly at the later working out of some different features of the Reformed ethos and history. As we move into the late eighteenth century, the only descendant of the French Reformed tradition in this collection, Jean-Loup Seban, introduces a new perspective and style to the investigation of the intricacies and tessellations of the writings of various students of Kant who explored and interpreted the great philosopher's usefulness for questions of the possibility and perfectibility of Christian revelation. Perhaps best known for his fine studies of Reformation theology, B. A. Gerrish here presents a clear and intriguing picture of a Kantian-influenced writer, Friedrich Karl Forberg, a man concerned with that characteristic Reformed topic, practical belief, however uncharacteristic his development of that idea might have seemed to sixteenth-century Calvinists. One of the greatest Reformed figures of this later period, Friedrich Schleiermacher, is the subject of the versatile Terrence N. Tice's sensitive essay examining some of the typical and highly valued Reformed traits of this outstanding representative of the later German Reformed tradition.

Two historical studies of nineteenth-century Reformed leaders conclude Part Four. Ulrich Gäbler, long involved in the study of Zwingli and Bullinger, here turns his attention to exploring the archives of the Swiss city of Chur, with rather startling discoveries about the birth and childhood of the outstanding transatlantic Reformed leader, Philip Schaff. Though his scope was geographically more limited, James Henley Thornwell's influence is ably and clearly presented by John H. Leith, whose scholarly faithfulness does not obscure his Christian awareness of the faults of his subject even as he shows the development of one very important strand of the American Reformed heritage.

The volume includes an appendix devoted to Edward A. Dowey's life and work. First there is a brief biographical sketch by Elsie Anne McKee, followed by a bibliography of published and unpublished writings compiled by Mark S. Burrows.

In the course of collecting a series of essays from busy as well as gifted scholars from all around the world, one incurs a number of debts of gratitude. The editors wish to thank all the contributors who joined in this tribute to our friend and colleague, Edward A. Dowey, Jr. Special thanks go to Karlfried Froehlich, Charles West, and Bruce McCormack, who initiated this project. We would like to acknowledge with great appreciation the generous support of Princeton Theological Seminary and particularly its president, Thomas W. Gillespie, whose graciousness in every way has made this volume possible and whose encouragement has made the task of its editors so much more pleasant. The translators of the German texts, Mark Burrows, Keith Crim, Victoria Huizenga and Fred Klooster, and Bruce McCormack, deserve our warm thanks, as do the patient secretaries, Elizabeth Adams and Dee-Dee Walters of the History Department of Georgia State University, and Kay Coughlin of Andover Newton Theological School, who helped produce the manuscript in good order. To our publishers at Westminster/John Knox Press, particularly Keith Crim and Cynthia Thompson, our thanks are especially fervent at this ending of the collection process. The skill and accuracy of the Westminster/John Knox staff are finally responsible for the pleasure readers will find when taking this volume in their hands. To our families and colleagues who have borne with us in this lengthy process, our thanks are personal. Last but most certainly not least, both editors want to express their deep gratitude to their professor and mentor, honored colleague, and dear friend, Edward A. Dowey, Jr.

E.A.M.
Newton Centre, Massachusetts

B.G.A.
Atlanta, Georgia

PART ONE

Pre-Reformation and Reform

Justification Language and Grace: The Charge of Pelagianism in the Middle Ages[1]

Karlfried Froehlich

The patristic and medieval tradition did not develop a separate treatise *De iustificatione.* Lutheran historians of the nineteenth century regarded this fact as supporting the impression of a "dark" Middle Ages and pointed with pride to the rediscovery of the doctrine by the Reformers. Catholic historians, on the other hand, used the minor role of the theme of justification during the Middle Ages as an indication that it was not central to the church's doctrinal stance until the sixteenth-century challenge by the Protestants made an official definition necessary. The absence of formal interest in the topic should not deceive us, however. Today theologians generally agree that justification language points to vital concerns of the Christian faith which have been discussed in countless ways from the very beginning. Justification focuses attention on the fundamental structure of the relationship between God and human beings; it speaks of the role of each side in this relationship and determines the very definition of salvation. Over the centuries the major themes of soteriology underwent considerable development[2] in which the language of justification played an important part, opening up ever new aspects of depth and meaning through the peculiar accents of its semantic field.

Of course, "justification" never was a household word among Christian believers even after the Reformation. Yet if we were to consider the term exclusively as part of the technical parlance of school theology and trace the reasons for shifts of meaning and new emphases only in the professional world of the theologians, the picture would be incomplete. Much was at stake for *all* Christians in the discussion of soteriological themes, and school theologians did not always take the lead when it came to shaping the ascetic and sacramental piety of the age. Medieval theology had to reckon with the aspirations and convictions of a popular Christian piety which, while perhaps less articulate, was certainly equally tenacious in pursuing its own agenda. It is no surprise that medieval theologians took seriously the pastoral dimensions of their theologizing as it affected the life of the ordinary Christian.[3] In this respect, as well as in their theory and doctrinal orientation, they followed the example of the most influential among the Western Fathers, Augustine of Hippo.

The last remark certainly applies to the use of justification language in the West. This language bears the stamp everywhere of Augustine's theological and pastoral concerns, which grew out of his daily experience as a bishop among his people. These concerns, while not always fully clarified and harmonized, permeate his vast homiletical corpus as well as the polemical writings of his later years, especially during the Pelagian controversy. Much of this literature was available to medieval theologians.[4] For them, Augustine remained the classical authority in questions of soteriology. His authority was never doubted, and the elements contributed by him to this field, often reflecting his particular stance in the changing polemics of his own day, provided the basic material for medieval attempts at coming to terms with the biblical concept of justification.

Thanks to Augustine, the tradition of justification language never lost its connection with the terminology of Paul, in whose epistles this tradition had its roots. The importance of the Pauline epistles for Augustine's own development is well attested.[5] Under his influence a continuous flow of Pauline commentaries, serving the *lectio divina* of the monasteries and later the curricular requirements of the high medieval schools, kept the language of the apostle and its Augustinian reading constantly before monks, priests, and theologians. The form of this commentation varied.[6] During the Carolingian period the chain of patristic quotations still dominated. In the eleventh century it was gradually replaced by the glosslike *apparatūs* of the schools, the predecessors of the later standard glosses. From the twelfth century on we have an increasing number of discursive commentaries which reflect the needs of a new generation of monastic and academic audiences. They shared certain presuppositions, the most important of which was a deep, though not uncritical, respect for the patristic tradition. While little use was made of the Eastern Fathers, the corpus of Augustine's writings, with its many references to

Paul, remained a primary resource.[7] An equally important source, already known to the Bishop of Hippo, was "Ambrose," a pseudepigraphic commentary on the Pauline epistles from the fourth century, which today goes by the name "Ambrosiaster."[8] The two sources were supplemented by "Jerome" and "Primasius," under whose names revised versions of Pelagius' Pauline commentaries were circulating.[9] As we shall see, this heterogeneous combination of patristic authorities was not without serious consequences.

With very few exceptions, medieval commentaries on Paul did not use the standard fourfold sense of scripture (literal, allegorical, tropological, anagogical) or other multiple senses. We probably must attribute this fact to the special place Paul occupied in the thinking of medieval theologians.[10] On the one hand, he was regarded as the "last" of the inspired apostolic writers; on the other, he was the "first" *doctor evangelii* who explained openly the scriptural mysteries which had been hidden before. His text, therefore, constituted *manifesta expositio,* fully formulated Christian theology which did not require additional spiritual interpretation. This attitude may explain why Paul's terminology played such a decisive role in the medieval formulation of doctrine. Paul had formulated the normative *doctrina* which a later doctor could clarify but not alter or reformulate. Even the epistle of James was no more than a "clarification" of Paul's justification doctrine in a specific context which called for the correction of antinomian tendencies.[11] There could be no real contradiction between the two apostles. Paul and James must be read together, just as the Old Testament was needed in order to understand exactly which mysteries Paul was opening up.

It is important to remind ourselves that the norm for justification language in the Middle Ages was the Pauline terminology in its Latin Vulgate form. In and of itself, Paul's scriptural teaching was not deliberately distorted or misread by embarrassed fanatics of works righteousness, as Protestant prejudice has frequently assumed. Rather, the very real problem of ascertaining the "manifest doctrine" of Paul in this secondary linguistic form, Latin, together with its various canonical "clarifications" such as the epistle of James, gave rise to honest and highly sophisticated efforts at synthesizing the disparate evidence. Paul has never been easy to read and to systematize. Moreover, for the medieval mind the apostle himself was less important than his doctrine, his message. This message, however, in addition to the problems mentioned, came filtered through a Latin Augustinian reading with its own linguistic, practical, and polemical concerns. In the delicate interaction of all these factors, it was still the appropriation of Pauline thought and teaching that became the natural starting point for all medieval speculation on soteriological themes, including the topic of justification.[12]

It would be a fascinating task to follow in detail the history of the various elements of medieval justification theology as the history of a Latin Augustinian Paulinism. Such a project would have to discuss themes such as sin, original sin, Christology, grace, faith, good works, merit, predestination, sacraments, and eschatology. A number of general surveys of the development of the doctrine of justification which try to integrate these elements are available today.[13] In the present study I will limit myself to the one element which brings the shifting emphases in the medieval appropriation of the Pauline-Augustinian heritage into focus most sharply: the doctrine of grace. If one considers the fervor of the Pelagian controversy of the fifth century and its outcome, one should expect that the patristic directives were nowhere more outspoken and clear than at this point, even in their polemics against a specific heresy and its rejected doctrinal options. The historical reality was different. It seems that precisely the doctrine of grace was surrounded by the greatest ambiguity during the Middle Ages, an ambiguity that eventually led to a Reformation which made the theological meaning of the Pauline justification language the center of its own polemics—this time, however, on the basis of the original, the Greek Paul. It remains one of the ironies of the history of medieval theology that, while the defense of grace was on everyone's agenda, the very meaning of the patristic watchwords such as "Augustinian" and "Pelagian," and thus the dividing line between orthodoxy and heresy, shifted with the changes in theological climate and preoccupation. We have to understand the broader context of these changes in order to understand the confusion and to appreciate its intimate connection with both the agenda of the popular piety of the age and the theology of the schoolmen and their pastoral concerns.

I

According to the apostle Paul, justification is fundamentally the justification of the ungodly (*iustificatio impii,* Rom. 4:5). In Peter Lombard's *Collectanea* of c.1158/59, which became the standard *glossa ordinaria* on the Pauline epistles, the topic of original sin is first mentioned in connection with Rom. 3:23.[14] The comment begins with a seemingly Augustinian phrase pointing to Rom. 5:12: "All have sinned either by themselves or in Adam." When the phrase is explained, however, there is a disturbing mixture of Augustinian and Pelagian key terms: "They are not without sin either because they contracted sin from their origin, or added to it by bad habits" (1361A). Still, the underlying assumption is fully in tune with Augustine: Sinfulness is a universal phenomenon and is physically inherited: "From one sinner all are born sinners" (ibid.). While the Greek Fathers would not concur, Western exegetes regularly read Rom. 5:12 in this way, at least after Augustine.[15] Peter Lombard is no exception: "Through Adam's sin we as his posterity are shackled as if by hereditary evils" (1387C). For him as for others, biblical texts such as Eph. 2:3, Ps. 51(50):5, and Job 14:4 provided further proof. As a consequence of sin we die. But what we receive from Adam is not just the certainty of physical death. It is the dreadful legacy of punishment and guilt: "From him we have received damnation and guilt together" (1361A). The distinction of these two aspects of sin, punishment *(poena)* and guilt *(culpa* or *reatus),* goes back to Augustine, who probably thought of biblical texts such as Ps. 31(30):5.[16] It remained central for the medieval theology of baptism and penance.

Anselm of Canterbury, even before Peter Lombard, had turned in a new direction. He applied Augustine's Neoplatonic view of evil as "defect" to the notion of original sin as well. According to Anselm, original sin must be defined first and foremost in the negative, as the absence of a required original righteousness.[17] From this angle, concupiscence, misery, and death are but the penal consequences of the defect. Anselm's new definition acquired prominence only after the twelfth century, during which the universal experience of death and concupiscence was still related to the guilt and punishment of original sin in a variety of ways.[18] A widespread compromise defined the lack of righteousness as guilt and the presence of concupiscence as punishment.[19] During the later Middle Ages the persistent identification of original sin with concupiscence as its *poena* and *culpa* was regarded as indicating adherence to an old-fashioned Augustinianism for which Peter Lombard served as the prime example.[20]

This development points to the increasing importance in the discussion of the term "concupiscence," which Augustine had used in a great variety of contexts. In Peter Lombard's *Collectanea* it draws an extensive comment at Rom. 4:7, clarifying the technical sense of the term: "Iniquities here refer to original sin, that is, the tinder of sin *(fomes peccati),* also called concupiscence or concupiscibility, or the law of the members, or the indolence of nature, or other such names" (1369A–C).[21]

In Rom. 6:12 where Paul himself uses the term, the Lombard's note interprets the plural *(concupiscentiae)* as combining three internal acts: initial impulse, delight, and consent. Paul, he suggests, does not forbid the first but only the two others, which constitute "active" concupiscence. The comment, however, begins with the primary definition which we met already: Concupiscence is the "tinder of sin" (1407C–D). The term *fomes peccati* had a long patristic history in the Latin church, going back at least to Rufinus' translation of Origen's *Homilies on the Book of Numbers.*[22] Similar combinations such as *fomes peccandi* or *libidinis fomes* occur even earlier in Cyprian, Ambrose, and Ambrosiaster.[23] As a consequence of his reading of Paul (Rom. 7:13–25), Augustine understood the experience of concupiscence, to him most evident in sexual desire, as the sickness of a disordered will which seriously affects both body and soul.[24] The concept of sickness dominated the earlier Middle Ages, but Anselm's new definition began to change the picture.[25]

Scholars in the late Middle Ages recognized the school-forming impact of Anselm's new formula. When Gabriel Biel described three contemporary opinions on original sin at the beginning of the fifteenth century, he mentioned first the stricter Augustinianism of Peter Lombard and his followers, who identified original sin as a "morbid quality of the soul" with the "vice of concupiscence."[26] His second group is formed by the followers of Anselm; it includes John Duns Scotus and William of Ockham. These theologians focus on the absence of original righteousness, the unfulfillable obligation to have this righteousness *(debitum iustitiae originalis habendae)* being its primary consequence, concupiscence a distant second.[27] The third group advocates a compromise; Alexander of Hales, Bonaventure, and Aquinas are classified under this rubric. As is well known, Aquinas interpreted concupiscence as the matter, the lack of original righteousness as the form of original sin.[28] Biel saw himself somewhere in this camp and was probably closer to the great masters of the thirteenth century at this point than to the Anselmian "school." Other moderate Augustinians, however, tried to avoid the compromise. They expanded the notion of concupiscence again to mean *all* inordinate desire, equating the term with the Augustinian terminology of self-love, *amor sui.*[29] Nevertheless, the conclusion that this would automatically qualify all concupiscence as "sin" was rarely drawn. One obstacle was a theology of baptism which insisted that only the *fomes* aspect of concupiscence, not the *reatus,* remained in the baptized.[30] Another was the widespread "Abelardian" tendency to make an act of the will—that is, consent—the prerequisite for any full concept of sin. A third was the Anselmian logic that concupiscence as a *habitus* was not a "power" but strictly a lack of supernatural assistance. Under these circumstances the idea of a progressive overcoming of concupiscence as an evil inclination by a good one—that is, the infused *habitus*[31] of grace—seemed a natural alternative to the simple equation of concupiscence and original sin. Augustine, who took his cue from Paul's medicinal language, had already pointed in this direction: The more grace takes control, the more the remaining concupiscence must diminish.[32]

II

Peter Lombard's *Collectanea* praise Paul's language of grace time and again.[33] Already the general preface to the Pauline epistles hails the apostle as the "advocate of grace" (1279C). Paul's greeting of Rom. 1:7 ("Grace be to you") leads to the same theme. The Lombard explains: "This is the grace by which the ungodly person is justified and sins are forgiven" (1316B). In this connection two Augustinian key phrases are quoted, both themselves derived from Paul: "By grace the one who was a sinner is made righteous" (*gratiā fit iustus qui fuerat impius;* cf. Rom. 4:5); and: "Grace would not be grace unless it be given gratuitously" (*nec ista esset gratia si non daretur gratuita;* cf. Rom. 11:6).[34] The first became a medieval summary definition of justification; it was intended to safeguard God's absolute priority in initiating justification as the transformation of the sinner. The second represented a classical formulation of the anti-Pelagian argument in the Middle Ages; it stressed the free, totally undeserved nature of grace as a gift. This latter point appears again at Rom. 3:24 ("justified by his grace freely," *gratis per gratiam*): "Gratis, that is, without preceding merits; through his grace, that is, through gratuitous gifts; for the grace of God is God's gift, but the greatest gift is the Holy Spirit himself" (1361BC). The last phrase here introduces the Lombard's famous assertion on the basis of Rom. 5:5 ("God's love has been poured into our hearts through the Holy Spirit which has been given to us"; cf. 1381C), that the gift of the infused love of God and neighbor is not only a virtue but the Holy Spirit himself.[35] The commentaries on Peter Lombard's *Sentences* reflect the excitement of the later debates over this point which led to the rejection of his position by the great theologians of the thirteenth century; on the other hand, it encouraged the new distinction between created and uncreated grace at a time when all grace was understood in an

Aristotelian vein as supernatural form, not just as a transforming power "operating" and "cooperating," as Augustine had said.[36]

Drawing his terms from Phil. 2:13 and Rom. 8:28, Augustine expressed his distinction forcefully during the later years of the Pelagian controversy, i.e., the so-called semi-Pelagian phase.[37] This polemical context suggests a major problem with any reading of Paul: It is notoriously difficult to determine the contribution of God and humankind to the process of salvation. Paul had posed the issue in terms of faith and grace against the works of the law; Augustine described it in terms of the complementarity of God's grace and a human nature endowed with free will. But in Paul's letters the indicative of God's saving act in Christ regularly leads to the imperative, the appeal to turn from the old ways and live out the new calling. This ethical appeal was of central significance for the Christian message to the nations, and it was very much a part of the message of Augustine the preacher. In contrast to God's act of creating the world *ex nihilo,* his act of justifying the ungodly involved both sides: "He who created you without you, does not justify you without you."[38] Along with the patristic tradition, Augustine saw human participation primarily as a matter of the will. "God created him who did not know; He justifies him who wills; yet it is He who justifies."[39] But how free is the human will after the Fall? What can the ungodly contribute? Augustine's insistence on the impotence of the fallen will, and therefore on the absolute priority of God's helping grace *(auxilium gratiae),* did not fully answer the question. It established the indispensability of grace; but there was room for new thought about the extent to which human nature was left intact, or "wounded" (Luke 19:30, 34),[40] capable of participating, starting the process, or at least preparing itself for God's gracious intervention, just as matter must be disposed to form. Medieval theologians discussed these problems in a new climate of growing confidence in the potential of the human intellect even after the Fall, a fervent desire for perfection through ascetic and monastic life-styles, and a sophisticated academic theology.

Nevertheless, the historical presuppositions of the discussion could not be changed. The official victory of Augustinianism and the rejection of "Pelagianism" as a heresy was a clear given. No medieval theologian could desire to be a "Pelagian"; at least in this sense everyone thought of himself as an "Augustinian."

Modern research has shown, however, that both designations had an extremely complicated history during the Middle

Ages, owing to several factors.[41] First of all, there was the problem of sources. Knowledge of the official decisions in the Pelagian controversy was incomplete. The canons of the North African synod of 418 remained accessible through their inclusion into standard collections of canon law; an important document such as Pope Zosimus' *Epistola tractoria,* however, was unavailable.[42] Most astonishing is the lack of awareness of the semi-Pelagian or Massilian controversy, which continued in Gaul after Augustine's death. Here, the issues of predestination, the irresistibility of grace, and especially the *initium fidei,* the beginning of the justification process, were discussed and finally decided along moderately Augustinian lines: An otherwise unknown presbyter, Lucidus, was forced to recant any teaching of double predestination, determinism was rejected, and, in regard to the *initium fidei,* even the very desire to be saved was attributed to divine grace.[43] The Middle Ages knew, but made little use of, the so-called *Indiculus Coelestini,* a collection of ten brief anti-Massilian chapters drawn up by Prosper of Aquitaine and endorsed by Pope Coelestine.[44] The famous canons of the so-called Second Council of Orange, however, submitted to a regional gathering of bishops by Caesarius of Arles in 529 and endorsed by Pope Boniface II in 531, were simply forgotten.[45] They appeared in some Gallican manuscripts of the seventh and eighth centuries but, as they were not copied for any major collection, remained unknown until Peter Crabbe published them in his edition of councils in 1538, just in time for use at the Council of Trent.[46] Thomas Aquinas was one of the exceptional minds who, on the basis of a close reading of the late Augustine and the *Indiculus,* became aware of the semi-Pelagian issues and their doctrinal consequences.[47]

Another source problem was posed by the circulation of numerous Pelagian and Massilian writings under orthodox names. Jerome's authority alone covered several major works of Pelagius, including the *Letter to Demetrias, De divina lege,* and *Libellus fidei,* as well as the Pauline commentary.[48] Even Augustine was claimed as the author of Pelagian literature; a most interesting case is the influential *Hypomnesticon* or *Hypognosticon.*[49]

Under these circumstances, the understanding of the historical situation and the precise meaning of "Pelagian" remained vague and confused. Since the medieval view of the error derived almost exclusively from Augustine's polemic, an author's definition of Pelagianism was not only biased but simply reflected the measure of his appropriation of the Augustinian tradition. The early Middle Ages read Augustine in an imprecise and random manner, using the major writings only and quoting without care. We mentioned that Thomas Aquinas read him in greater depth, with the result that he "discovered" semi-Pelagianism. In his Treatise on Grace in *II Sent. d.28 c.1–3,* Peter Lombard had summarized the traditional picture, giving a full complement of standard Augustine quotations but showing no awareness of issues surrounding the *initium fidei.*[50] After Aquinas, the scholarly attention paid to the full Augustinian corpus emboldened some theologians of the fourteenth century (Thomas Bradwardine, Gregory of Rimini[51]) to launch a vigorous protest against "modern Pelagians," teachers in the Ockhamist school whose semi-Pelagian leanings may indeed have been nourished by ignorance as much as by their theological agenda. It was common knowledge that Pelagians denied original sin; even the Lombard's *Collectanea* mention them in connection with this point (1388B). But the setting of *II Sent. d.28* proves that the main error was perceived as concerning the doctrine of grace. Pelagians were "enemies of grace." They denied the necessity of grace for salvation, asserted the need of preceding merits, and exalted the ability of free will to fulfill God's commandments on its own without the help of grace. The weapon against this self-elevation of the creature was an unrelenting insistence on our utter dependence on God, creator and redeemer. Peter Lombard summed up the accepted doctrine: "Let us maintain unflinchingly and unhesitatingly that free will without prevenient and assisting grace is not sufficient to obtain righteousness and salvation, nor can God's grace be called down by preceding merits."[52]

Given the absolute need for grace, however, how does grace "cooperate" as Augustine had said? What is the proper view of a human nature able and prepared to receive this grace? The Lombard already spoke of the human mind's "natural aptitude for believing and loving" which is activated by God's prevenient grace.[53] Landgraf attributed the basic progress of the anti-Pelagian argument to the growing ability of thirteenth-century theologians to distinguish between nature and the supernatural. The goal of the human journey lies beyond our natural capacity. Thus, the argument against Pelagius came to rest on a simple premise: "No creature can reach beyond itself by its own power."[54] Supernatural help is indispensable to attain a supernatural goal. Where does this leave nature? Medieval theologians could not conceive of it as "independent" in the modern sense. But as the subject of the process of salvation, human nature had its own honor and power, regardless of its present state. Thus, a context emerged which stressed the primacy of grace and, at the same time, allowed a more positive evaluation of the human contribution; *gratia cooperans* has its counterpart in *natura cooperans.* A growing anthropological optimism, together with the traditional assertion of God's absolute priority, dominated the late medieval discussions about grace before first grace, merit as disposition, and the state *ex puris naturalibus.*[55] The question was no longer how little human nature was able to contribute, but how much.

Thomas Aquinas developed his doctrine of grace against the background of these emerging concerns with the help of Aristotelian concepts.[56] His anti-Pelagian argument emphasized that nothing in a human being itself can be the cause of its own salvation; justification as a motion from sinner to saint must have an outside mover. Using the notion of grace as form, he also shared an interest in the beginning of the process, the "preparation" or "disposition" for grace as the issue now appeared to him. The earlier Thomas followed the Dominican tradition, making considerable allowance for the self-preparation of the human will. "Man can prepare himself to receive justifying grace by his free will alone."[57] This sounds like inadvertent semi-Pelagianism, though a careful reading of the context does provide safeguards. After his discovery of the actual historical precedent, however, Thomas was able to draw a much more accurate picture of Pelagianism than he found in the Lombard; he even distinguished the error of Pelagius from that of the later "Pelagians," noting that for the latter the issue was the *initium fidei;* they claimed that "the beginning of our justification is from us, the consummation from God."[58] His own formulations now enforced the Pauline-Augustinian argument, insisting that God's grace must be seen as the sole cause of *any* step in the process, even the remotest preparation. Human nature on its own is in no position to contribute. Grace, however, does not abolish nature but perfects it.[59] Thus, "graced" nature—i.e., the justified person who has received the infused habit of grace *(gratia gratum faciens)* and its virtues—is properly disposed toward the goal and the reception of further grace in the way which Thomas described with Augustine as *gratia subsequens* and *cooperans.*[60] Its merits do count, precisely because they are God's own work.

Later medieval theologians like William of Ockham suspected this general position as dangerously close to Pelagianism.[61] Can justification depend on the necessary bestowal of a special habit of grace? Is God unable to accept anyone without it? Is he forced to accept anyone because of it? God's freedom seemed to be jeopardized, and the Pelagian specter of a natural capacity of graced human nature to claim its own salvation seemed to raise its head.[62] These advocates of God's absolute freedom, however, themselves had problems with Pelagian tendencies when they stressed human freedom in the realm of God's ordained power. Biel criticized Gregory of Rimini for "attributing too little to free will."[63] Special attention to the human contribution in the process of justification was characteristic of the entire *via moderna,* not just its Ockhamist faction. Of course, all were eager to exclude Pelagianism. Recent scholarship has made the case not only for anti-Pelagian intentions of Ockham and Biel but also for an underlying "anti-Pelagian structure" in the thought of the Scotist school as well as nominalism in general.[64] But the picture of Pelagianism in these circles was ill informed and often highly idiosyncratic; these theologians attempted to interpret the Lombard's simplistic formulae without firsthand knowledge of the sources.[65] Invariably, they excluded the errors concerning the *initium fidei,* i.e., any mention of the Massilian danger, even though the preparation for grace was the central theme in the discussions.

Ockhamists readily admitted that in God's established order *(de potentia Dei ordinata)* the final salvation of the *viator* requires God's gift of infused grace.[66] But in the auxiliary speculation about God's absolute power, the question of human nature's potential as such, *in puris naturalibus,*[67]—that is, without special grace—seemed more intriguing. Can the human person with unaided natural powers elicit a morally good act, perhaps even the highest one possible—i.e., loving God above everything else? Ockham saw no logical or theological reason for a negative answer, though he pointed out that the meritoriousness of such acts would still depend on God's acceptance alone.[68] A good act is a good act; it is the better the more freely it is elicited. Hypothetically, therefore, "God could decree that, if someone committed a mortal sin and afterward repented of his misdeed *ex puris naturalibus* without a supernatural form, his sin would thereby be remitted, and he would receive eternal life after death."[69] In the context of *III Sent. d.27,* Biel proposed five theses, the first of which reads: "The will of the human *viator* can love God above everything *ex suis naturalibus.*"[70] Statements like these certainly sound semi-Pelagian, if not blatantly Pelagian, and several scholars conclude that they are.[71] One could and should explain them in their context, which might expose the author's orthodox intentions. One could argue that Ockham's *pura naturalia* are an anthropological construct parallel to the theological one of God's *potentia absoluta,* guarding against the "Pelagianism" of subjecting God to necessity. Similarly, Biel's subsequent theses qualify the bold assertion of initial human freedom by declaring the reaching of the goal to be dependent on God's grace alone and rejecting Pelagius by name with an appropriate authority from canon law.[72]

All this hedging, however, could not satisfy the suspicion of colleagues who knew Augustine better or were less enamored of the philosophical thrust of the *via moderna.* Gregory of Rimini expressly rejected as false certain "modern" interpretations of what "Pelagian" meant; for him, the widespread opinion that naturally good acts can merit first grace *de congruo* "favors the condemned error of Pelagius."[73] "Augustinians" were unimpressed by the contention that no special grace is needed to prepare for justifying grace; Biel, for example, spoke of the *concursus* or *influentia generalis,* the universal presence of God's grace in the order of creation, as a sufficient presupposition for his talk about *pura naturalia.*[74] Gregory of Rimini was well aware of the Pelagian argument that sight is a gift of God but that seeing remains our responsibility. To declare that our natural powers, given by God, are sufficient for right willing and right acting is worse than the error of Pelagius, who at least maintained that grace facilitates our willing and doing.[75] Thomas Bradwardine had similar complaints. He too saw the Ockhamist teaching about human self-preparation as the most blatant evidence of the heresy; its point seemed to be that God gives his grace not *gratis* but on the basis of preceding merits. For Bradwardine, God's causality allows no cocausality.[76]

Both scholars, in fact, reacted to a new reading of a well-known Scholastic axiom, "To those who do what is in them, God does not deny his grace *(facientibus quod in se est Deus non abnegat gratiam)":* We begin the process; God then completes it.[77] The phrase probably goes back to Abelard's circle or the Porretan school, where it expressed the apparent quid pro quo logic of biblical verses such as Zech. 1:3: "Turn to me, says the Lord, and I will turn to you."[78] It was soon applied to the discussion about the preparation for grace, which was generally carried on without awareness of a semi-Pelagian danger. As a Dominican and an Aristotelian, Thomas Aquinas argued for the need of proper human disposition and a prepared free will but clearly interpreted the axiom in an Augustinian sense, maintaining the primacy of grace: "When a man is said to do what is in him, this is said to be within his power moved by God."[79] Biel, however, confident that the very notion of God's free acceptance excluded any Pelagian danger, could press the moral synergism implicit in the statement much further: Citing a host of Bible verses which had come to be associated with it (Zech. 1:3; James 4:8; Rev. 3:20; Luke 11:9; Jer. 29:3; Ps. 22:27), he concluded that God gives grace to everyone who does what is in him—namely, removing the obstacle of consent to sin and initiating the act of turning to God by the power of free will.[80] For Augustinian experts, this was Pelagianism. Bradwardine poured his contempt on this view of Jesus' "knocking at doors" (Rev. 3:20) and offering his grace like a vendor waiting for takers.[81] For Bradwardine, as for Gregory of Rimini, it was precisely the Ockhamist anti-Pelagianism which constituted the Pelagian heresy in its most insidious form.[82]

Whether a particular position was indeed "Pelagian" or not can obviously not depend on the polemical fervor of its opponents. As we have seen, the label and the fervor were clearly in evidence in the later Middle Ages. The name-calling indicates at least that the Pauline-Augustinian framework of justification language and its anti-Pelagian bias were very much alive throughout the period. Interest in *sola gratia* in the sense "never without grace" remained a shared concern. On the other hand, under the dominance of the Aristotelian form/matter distinction, theologians in every camp had to pay more attention to the human contribution in the process of salvation. How far the shifts to new modes of expression actually led away from the traditional framework must remain a matter for debate.

NOTES

1. This essay represents revised sections of an essay written for the U.S. National Lutheran–Roman Catholic Dialogue on Justification and subsequently published in a much abbreviated version in *Justification by Faith,* Lutherans and Catholics in Dialogue, 7, ed. H. G. Anderson, T. A. Murphy, and J. A. Burgess (Minneapolis: Augsburg Publishing House, 1985), pp. 143–161, 348–350.

2. See G. Greshake, "Der Wandel der Erlösungsvorstellungen in der Theologiegeschichte," in *Erlösung und Emanzipation,* ed. L. Scheffzcyk, Quaestiones Disputatae, 61 (Freiburg/Basel/Vienna: Herder, 1973), pp. 79–101.

3. An early example of this concern is provided by the circle around Peter the Chanter in Paris in the late twelfth century. See J. W. Baldwin, *Masters, Princes, and Merchants: The Social Views of Peter Chanter and His Circle,* 2 vols. (Princeton, N.J.: Princeton University Press, 1970). Beginning with Heiko Oberman's groundbreaking study of Gabriel Biel in *The Harvest of Medieval Theology: Gabriel Biel and Late Medieval Nominalism* (Cambridge,

Mass.: Harvard University Press, 1963), scholarly work on the so-called nominalists of the fifteenth century has increasingly given prominence to this aspect. See most recently the important study by Mark S. Burrows, "Jean Gerson and *De Consolatione Theologiae* (1418): The Consolation of a Biblical and Reforming Theology for a Disordered Age" (Ph.D. diss., Princeton Theological Seminary, 1988).

4. The manuscript tradition and its geographical distribution can now be studied in the series, *Die handschriftliche Überlieferung der Werke des hl. Augustinus* (edited by Austrian Academy of Sciences, Vienna, since 1969). An even more important source for the Middle Ages were florilegia and encyclopedic collections. The situation was complicated by a vast corpus of Pseudo-Augustinian writings often at variance with the authentic Augustine; see M. de Kroon, "Pseudo-Augustin im Mittelalter: Entwurf eines Forschungsberichts," *Augustiniana* 22 (1972), 511–530. Good general surveys of Augustine's impact on the Middle Ages are: F. Cayré, "Augustinisme (developpement de l')," *DThC, Tables generales,* vol. 1 (1951), 314–324; H.-I. Marrou, *St. Augustine and His Influence Through the Ages* (New York: Harper & Brothers, Harper Torchbooks, 1957), pp. 147–180; G. Leff, "Augustinismus im Mittelalter," *Theologische Realenzyklopädie* 3 (1979), 699–717.

5. See *Confessiones* 7.21.27; 8.6.14; 8.7.29f., etc. For Romans, see P. Platz, *Der Römerbrief in der Gnadenlehre Augustins,* Cassiciacum, 5 (Würzburg: Rita, 1938).

6. B. Smalley, *The Study of the Bible in the Middle Ages* (Oxford: Blackwell, 1952), pp. 37–52.

7. Especially important for Augustine's interpretation of Paul prior to the Pelagian controversy are several writings from his first years in Hippo: Two fragmentary commentaries on Romans (394/95), *CSEL* 84, ed. Divjak (1971), pp. 1–52, 143–181 (E.T., Paula Fredriksen Landes, *Augustine on Romans: Propositions from the Epistle to the Romans; Unfinished Commentary on the Epistle to the Romans,* SBL, Texts and Translations, Early Christian Literature Series, 6 [Chico, Calif.: Scholars Press, 1982]); a commentary on Galatians (395), *CSEL* 84, ed. Divjak (1971), pp. 55–141; *De diversis quaestionibus octoginta tribus* (388/95), *CCL* 44:1, ed. Mutzenbecher (1975), pp. 11–249 (qq. 66–74); *De diversis queastionibus ad Simplicianum* (397), *CCL* 44, ed. Mutzenbecher (1970). Some Pauline commentaries of the Middle Ages were little more than excerpts from Augustine's writings; an example is Florus Diaconus (ninth century) on the Pauline epistles, Migne *PL* 119:279–420. For other such compilations see H. Denifle, *Die abendländischen Schriftausleger bis Luther über Justitia Dei (Rom.1,17) und Justificatio (Quellenbelege zu Denifles Luther und Luthertum),* I/2, 2nd ed. (Mainz: F. Kirchheim, 1905), pp. 22–25.

8. The critical edition is available in *CSEL* 81:1–3, ed. H. J. Vogels (1966–69).

9. The text of Pelagius' original commentary was identified and edited by A. Souter, *Pelagius' Exposition of Thirteen Epistles of St. Paul,* Texts and Studies, 9, 3 vols. (Cambridge: Cambridge University Press, 1922–31); the two revisions were printed by Migne in *PL* 30:669–746 (Pseudo-Jerome), and 68:413–686 (Pseudo-Primasius). A Ph.D. dissertation by David W. Johnson, in progress at Princeton Theological Seminary, will demonstrate the extent to which Pseudo-Primasius, the "orthodox" revision attempted by Cassiodorus and his monks, perpetuated major tenets of Pelagian doctrine despite the clearly expressed intention to purge the text of Pelagianism. The revisers' theological acumen was not equal to the task.

10. Cf. H. de Lubac, *Exégèse médiévale. Les quatre sens de l'Ecriture* (Paris: Aubier, I/2, 1959), pp. 668–681; O. H. Pesch, "The Image of the Apostle in St. Thomas' Theology," *The Thomist* 38 (1974), 584–605.

11. On Augustine's attitude see P. Bergauer, *Der Jakobusbrief bei Augustinus und die damit verbundenen Probleme der Rechtfertigungslehre* (Vienna: Herder, 1962).

12. The problem which is signaled here can easily be grasped when one considers the implications of the Latin translation of the Greek word *dikaioun* as *justificare.* Different from the Greek, the Latin etymology suggests quite naturally the fundamental understanding of justification as a divinely initiated transformation. In Augustine's words: "What else are justified people but people who have been made righteous *(justi facti),* that is, by him who justifies the ungodly so that the ungodly becomes a righteous person?" (*De Spiritu et littera* 26.45, *CSEL* 60, ed. Urba and Zycha, p. 199:10–12). The legitimacy of this transformationist model as an interpretation of the biblical, especially the Pauline, teaching on justification remains one of the major issues between Roman Catholic and Lutheran theologians according to the recent common statement; see *Justification by Faith* (n. 1 above), paras. 20, 91, 96, 103, 154, 157; pp. 22, 48, 52, 70, 72.

13. Only a few can be mentioned here. They show the traditionally strong interest in this area on the part of German scholars. On the Roman Catholic side: J. Rivière, "Justification," *DThC* 8 (1924), 2042–2227; J. Auer, *Das Evangelium der Gnade,* Kleine katholische Dogmatik, vol. 5, ed. J. Auer and J. Ratzinger, 2nd ed. (Regensburg: Pustet, 1970); P. Fransen, "Dogmengeschichtliche Entfaltung der Gnadenlehre," in *Mysterium Salutis* IV/2 (ed. J. Feiner and M. Löhrer; Einsiedeln: Benziger, 1973), pp. 631–765; G. Greshake, *Geschenkte Freiheit. Einführung in die Gnadenlehre* (Freiburg/Basel/Vienna: Herder, 1977). A substantial introduction to the pertinent issues was written jointly by a Roman Catholic and a Lutheran theo-

logian: O. H. Pesch and A. Peters, *Einführung in die Lehre von Gnade und Rechtfertigung* (Darmstadt: Wissenschaftliche Buchgesellschaft, 1981). On the Protestant side, the comprehensive volume of A. Ritschl, *Die christliche Lehre von der Rechtfertigung und Versöhnung,* vol. 1: *Die Geschichte* (Bonn: Marcus & Weber, 4th ed., 1908), served for a long time as the standard treatment of the subject. See also J. Baur, *Salus Christiana. Die Rechtfertigungslehre in der Geschichte des christlichen Heilsverständnisses,* vol. 1: *Von der christlichen Antike bis zur Theologie der deutschen Aufklärung* (Gütersloh: Mohn, 1968); G. Müller, *Die Rechtfertigungslehre. Geschichte und Probleme,* Studienbücher Theologie (Gütersloh: Mohn, 1977). In English we now have the penetrating analysis of the development in Alister E. McGrath, *Iustitia Dei: A History of the Christian Doctrine of Justification,* vol. 1: *From the Beginnings to 1500* (Cambridge: Cambridge University Press, 1986), a book that has been in the making for many years. Since the present essay was written before McGrath's study became available, I was unable to take full account of his research and insights. The author modestly describes his study as "a bibliographical essay which records, correlates, and where possible extends, the present state of scholarly work on the development of the Christian doctrine of justification" (p. ix); its true merit, however, lies in the thoroughgoing synthesis and careful reevaluation of an impressive range of primary and secondary sources.

14. See I. Brady, *Magistri Petri Lombardi . . . Sententiae in IV libris distinctae.* Tom. I, Pars I (Grottaferrata: Editiones Collegii S. Bonaventurae, 1971), 62*–93*. On the place of the work in the development of the Gloss, see Smalley, *Study* (n. 6 above), p. 64. The *textus receptus* of the Romans commentary was reprinted from Josse Bade's Paris edition of 1535 in a usable, though not always reliable, form by Migne in *PL* 191:1298–1534. The title *"Collectanea"* is not original. The Migne edition will be cited in the text of the article by column and section. The history of the theme of original sin is surveyed in two excellent fascicles of the *Handbuch der Dogmengeschichte:* L. Scheffczyk, *Urstand, Fall und Erbsünde von der Schrift bis Augustin* (II/3a, part 1, 1981), and H. Köster, *Urstand, Fall, und Erbsünde in der Scholastik* (II/3b, 1979). Other important literature includes Landgraf, *Dogmengeschichte* I/2 (1953), pp. 204–281; IV/1–2 (1955–56); J. N. Espenberger, *Die Elemente der Erbsünde nach Augustin und der Frühscholastik (Forschungen zur christlichen Literatur und Dogmengeschichte,* 5/1; Mainz: F. Kirchheim, 1905); R. M. Martin, *La controverse sur le péché originel au début du XIVe siècle* (Louvain: Louvain University, 1930); J. Gross, *Geschichte des Erbsündendogmas. Ein Beitrag zur Geschichte des Problems vom Ursprung des Übels,* 3 vols. (Munich/Basel: Reinhardt, 1960–71); L. Hödl, "Theologische Neuansätze zum Verständnis des peccatum originale im 12.

Jahrhundert," *Sapientiae Doctrina. Mélanges . . . offerts a Dom H. Bascour OSB* (Louvain: Abbaye de Mont-César, 1980), pp. 119–136. One of H. Rondet's comprehensive studies is available in English: *Original Sin: The Patristic and Theological Background* (Shannon, Ireland: Ecclesia Press, 1972).

15. See K. H. Schelkle, *Paulus, Lehrer der Väter. Die altkirchliche Auslegung von Römer 1–11* (Düsseldorf: Patmos, 1956), pp. 162–178.

16. E.g., "In duobus tuis malis una est culpa, altera est poena; culpa est quod injustus es, poena est quia mortalis es" (*Sermo* 171.3.3, in Migne *PL* 38:934C); "Sustinendo sine culpa poenam Christus et poenam solvit et culpam" (*Sermo* 240.3.3, in Migne *PL* 38:1131D).

17. "Hoc peccatum quod originale dico aliud intelligere nequeo in eisdem infantibus nisi ipsam quam supra posui factam per inoboedientiam Adae iustitiae debitae nuditatem per quam omnes filii sunt irae," *De conceptu virginali et de originali peccato,* c.27 (ed. Schmitt, II, p. 170). For other instances of *nuditas, absentia, privatio (debitae iustitiae)* see Köster, *Urstand* (n. 14 above), 129 n. 47.

18. See the comprehensive studies by O. Lottin, "Les théories sur le péché originel de Saint Anselme à Saint Thomas d'Aquin," *Psychologie et morale au XIIe et XIIIe siècle,* IV/1 (Gembloux: Duculot, 1954), pp. 11–305.

19. *Summa Halensis, Inq. 2, tr. 3 q.2, 221:* "culpa est carentia debitae iustitiae sive deformitas quaedam . . . , concupiscentia vero est ipsa poena quae in parvulis dicitur concupiscibilitas, in adultis vero dicitur concupiscentia actu" (ed. Quaracchi, pp. 236–237).

20. "Ex his datur intelligi quid sit originale peccatum, scilicet concupiscentia, quod in omnes concupiscentialiter natos per Adam intravit eosque vitiavit" *(II Sent. d.30 c.10).*

21. The same list of equivalents appears in *II Sent. d.30 c.8;* "concupiscibility" was the technical term for latent concupiscence, especially in infants (cf. n. 27).

22. Origen, *Hom. in Num. XX.5* (Griechische christliche Schriftsteller 30, *Origenes Werke* 7, ed. Baehrens, p. 198:20).

23. The instances are cited in *Thesaurus Linguae Latinae* (Leipzig: Teubner; VI/1, 1926), p. 1021. Very important for Augustine was the triad of sins in 1 John 2:16 (Vulgate: *concupiscentia carnis, concupiscentia oculorum, superbia vitae*); here, too, sexual lust is first. See *Hom. in I Joann.* 2.10–14, in Migne *PL* 35:1994–1997.

24. E.g., *Confessiones* 8.5.11f.; 8.8.2O–21; *De Civitate Dei* 13.15; 14.2–3, etc. Cf. A. Vanneste, "Saint Paul et la doctrine augustinienne de péché originel," *Analecta Biblica,* 18 (Rome: Pontifical Biblical Institute, 1963), II, pp. 512–522.

25. See, for instance, Hugh of St. Victor, *De sacramentis christianae fidei* 1.7.28, in Migne *PL* 176:299A: "Si ergo quaeritur quid sit originale peccatum in nobis, intelligitur corruptio sive vitium

quod nascendo trahimus per ignorantiam in mente, per concupiscentiam in carne."

26. Gabriel Biel, *In II Sent. d.30 q.2 a.1 (1A);* see H. A. Oberman, *The Harvest of Medieval Theology: Gabriel Biel and Late Medieval Nominalism*, rev. ed. (Grand Rapids: Wm. B. Eerdmans Publishing Co., 1967), pp. 120–131, esp. 122f.

27. In fact, Duns Scotus kept concupiscence out of the definition altogether: "ad istum peccatum concurrunt duo, carentia iustitiae ut formale et debitum habendi eam ut materiale" *(In II Sent. d.32 q.1 n.3, Op. Oxon.).* The consequence was that original sin meant the loss of the *additional* gift of original righteousness only; thus, while human nature no longer functions at maximum efficiency, its essence and potential are intact.

28. Thomas Aquinas, *In II Sent. d.30 and 31; ST 1-2 q.82 a.3 c.; De Malo 4.2,* etc.

29. Köster, *Urstand* (n. 14 above), pp. 135f., mentions Peter John Olivi, Hugolinus of Orvieto, and Dionysius of Montina.

30. Cf. Peter Lombard's comment on Rom. 4:8: "Dimittitur ergo concupiscentia carnis in baptismate, non ut non sit, sed ut non imputetur peccatum; hoc enim est non habere peccatum, non esse reum peccati" (Migne *PL* 191:1369B). Augustine is cited in support.

31. The term *habitus* replaced the older language of *qualitas* which, however, was still important in the doctrine of grace, e.g., for Aquinas. It seems to have been used in a systematic manner first by Philip the Chancellor (twelfth century); cf. Landgraf, *Dogmengeschichte* I/1 (1952), pp. 214–219; Fransen, "Dogmengeschichtliche Entfaltung" (n. 13 above), pp. 672–679.

32. See *Ad Simplicianum* 1.1.7 (Rom. 7:7–25), in *CCL* 44, ed. Mutzenbecher (1970), pp. 12f.; somewhat different is *Enchiridion* 31.117: "Regnat carnalis cupiditas ubi non est Dei caritas" (*CCL* 46, ed. Evans [1966], p. 112:21f.).

33. In addition to the literature mentioned in n. 13 above, and Landgraf, *Dogmengeschichte* I/1–2 (n. 14), the important studies on grace include: J. Schupp, *Die Gnadenlehre des Petrus Lombardus,* Freiburger Theologische Studien, 35 (Freiburg: Herder, 1932); J. Auer, *Die Entwicklung der Gnadenlehre in der Hochscholastik,* 2 vols. (Freiburg: Herder, 1942–51); E. Iserloh, *Gnade und Eucharistie in der philosophischen Theologie des Wilhelm von Ockham* (Wiesbaden: F. Steiner, 1956); B. Lonergan, *Grace and Freedom: Operative Grace in the Thought of St. Thomas Aquinas* (New York: Herder & Herder, 1971); B. Hamm, *Promissio, Pactum, Ordinatio: Freiheit und Selbstbindung Gottes in der scholastischen Gnadenlehre* (Tübingen: J. C. B. Mohr [Paul Siebeck], 1977). McGrath, *Iustitia Dei,* pp. 100–108.

34. The phrases are derived from *De Spiritu et littera,* for example

9.15: "iustitia Dei, non qua Deus iustus est, sed qua induit hominem cum iustificat impium" (*CSEL* 60, ed. Urba and Zycha, p. 167); 9.16: "nam et iniustus, ut iustificetur, id est, ut iustus fiat, legitime lege uti debet" (p. 168); "per ipsam quippe iustificatur gratis, id est nullis suorum operum praecedentibus meritis, alioquin gratia iam non est gratia" (ibid.).

35. *I Sent. d.17 c.1:* "Quod Spiritus Sanctus est caritas qua diligimus Deum et proximum," and c.6. See Landgraf, "Caritas und Heiliger Geist," *Dogmengeschichte* I/1 (1952), pp. 220–237; P. Kaufmann, *"Charitas non est nisi a Spiritu Sancto:* Augustine and Peter Lombard on Grace and Personal Righteousness," *Augustiniana* 30 (1980), 209–230. Augustine already used the underlying biblical material against Pelagius; cf. *De Spiritu et littera* III.5: "Ut autem diligatur, caritas Dei diffunditur in cordibus nostris, non per arbitrium liberum quod surgit ex nobis sed per Spiritum Sanctum qui datus est nobis" (*CSEL* 60, ed. Urba and Zycha, p. 157).

36. The distinction between created and uncreated grace appears first in the Sentences commentaries as a criticism of the Lombard, who had denied that the infused love of Rom. 5:5 could be a created virtue; see Auer, *Entwicklung* (n. 33 above) 1:86–123, and Landgraf, "Caritas" (n. 35 above), pp. 225ff. The reasons for this criticism are clearly spelled out by Bonaventure, *In II Sent. d.28 a.1 q.1 concl.:* "Quoniam nec est possibile nec decens Deum esse formam perfectivam alicuius creaturae, ideo praeter donum increatum quod comparatur ad hos actus tanquam principium effectivum, conveniens est et opportunum ponere donum creatum, per quod anima informetur" (Quaracchi ed., II, p. 635). Later commentators on d.17 are discussed by P. Vignaux, *Luther, commentateur des Sentences (Livre I, Distinction XVII)* (Etudes de Philosophie Médiévale, 21; Paris: Vrin, 1935). For lists of rejected opinions of the *Magister Sententiarum* in the thirteenth and fourteenth centuries see J. De Ghellinck, *DThC* 12:2 (1935), 2014–2015.

37. "ipse ut velimus operatur incipiens, qui volentibus cooperatur perficiens," with references to the two verses, *De gratia et libero arbitrio* 17:33, in Migne *PL* 44:901C. The term "semi-Pelagians" is of modern origin; it was first used in the Lutheran Book of Concord.

38. *Sermo* 169.11 (Migne *PL* 38:923); cf. P. Brown, *Augustine of Hippo* (Berkeley: University of California Press, 1967), pp. 244–258.

39. Ibid. 169.13.

40. Augustine already interpreted the parable as an allegory of Christ, the good Samaritan, who restores human nature; cf. D. Sanchis, "Samaritanus ille: L'exégèse augustinienne de la parabole du Bon Samaritain," *Recherches de Science Religieuse* 49 (1961), 406–425. Medieval exegetes used the distinction in the text that the man was "despoiled" and "wounded" for the *donum superadditum* and the essence of human nature.

41. The problem with the term "Pelagianism" is well stated by H. A. Oberman: "Here we touch on one of the most difficult, as yet insufficiently explored, aspects of medieval thought: the flavor of the accusation, 'Pelagian,' and its concomitant verb, 'to pelagianize' shifted from author to author, just as opinions varied considerably with regard to the position Pelagius actually took" *(Forerunners of the Reformation: The Shape of Late Medieval Thought Illuminated by Key Documents* [New York/Chicago: Holt, Rinehart & Winston, 1966], p. 126). In addition to Oberman's various studies and Landgraf, *Dogmengeschichte* I/1 (1952), pp. 144–148, see also H. McSorley, *Luther: Right or Wrong? An Ecumenical-Theological Study of Luther's Major Work, The Bondage of the Will* (Glen Rock, N.J.: Newman Press; Minneapolis: Augsburg Publishing House, 1966), pp. 7–215, for an instructive and well-documented survey of Pelagianism in the Middle Ages. The understanding of medieval "Augustinianism" is in great flux today. Special interest concentrates on a *schola moderna Augustiniana* and its place in late medieval thought; see D. Trapp, "Augustinian Theology of the Fourteenth Century: Notes on Editions, Marginalia, Opinions, and Book Lore," *Augustiniana* 6 (1956), 146–274; A. Zumkeller, "Die Augustinerschule des Mittelalters: Vertreter und philosophisch-theologische Lehre (Übersicht nach dem neuesten Stand der Forschung)," *Analecta Augustiniana* 27 (1964), 167–262. Zumkellers detailed studies of individual theologians of the Augustinian order have shed considerable light on the internal developments, especially in the order. For an assessment, cf. H. A. Oberman, "Augustinrenaissance im späten Mittelalter," *Werden und Wertung der Reformation* (Tübingen: J. C. B. Mohr [Paul Siebeck], 1977), pp. 82–140. A. E. McGrath, "Augustinianism? A Critical Assessment of the So-Called 'Medieval Augustinian Tradition' on Justification," *Augustiniana* 31 (1981), 247–267, concludes that the diversity of combinations defies any neat classification; see also his *Iustitia Dei,* pp. 172–179. Other scholars concur. See Chr. Ocker, "Augustinianism in Fourteenth Century Theology," *Augustinian Studies* 18 (1987).

42. Denziger-Schönmetzer, *Enchiridion symbolorum* 222–230, 231 (hereafter DS). The canons of Carthage were included in Ivo of Chartres' collection of canons, part 12, c.30 (Migne *PL* 161:978), and Gratian's *Decretum* (see Friedberg I, Index p. xx), though under the name of a council of Mileve. Three fragments of the *Epistola Tractoria* are printed in Migne *PL* 20:693f.

43. See DS 330–342, 373–375, 379–393.

44. DS 238–249, 237.

45. See DS 398–400 (endorsement) and 370–397 (text) with the introductory note. On the issues at Orange, see E. Amman, *DThC* 14 (1941), 1796–1850.

46. Eight manuscripts are listed in the critical edition, *Concilia*

Galliae, CCL 148A (1963), p. 53. Crabbe's edition, *Concilia omnia tam generalia quam particularia* (Cologne: Quentel) I, pp. 339–341, was used by the Council fathers; see H. Jedin, *A History of the Council of Trent,* vol. 2 (London: Thomas Nelson, 1961), p. 142 n. 1.

47. We owe the reconstruction of this discovery to H. Bouillard, *Conversion et grace chez S. Thomas d'Aquin,* Théologie, 1 (Paris: Aubier, 1944), pp. 99–123; see further: M. Seckler, *Instinkt und Glaubenswille nach Thomas von Aquin* (Mainz: Matthias-Grünewald-Verlag, 1961), pp. 90–133; briefly also Pesch-Peters, *Einführung* (n. 13 above), pp. 64–68; McGrath, *Iustitia Dei,* pp. 74f.

48. See E. Dekkers, *Clavis Patrum Latinorum,* Sacris Erudiri, 2nd ed. (Brugge/Den Haag: St. Pietersabdij, 1961), nos. 737, 740, 731, and 738, 739, 741–744. The real author of *Ad Demetriadem,* Pelagius, was already recognized by Thomas Bradwardine and Gregory of Rimini; cf. Oberman, *Werden und Wertung* (n. 41 above), p. 87. But Erasmus still edited the Pauline commentary under Jerome's name in 1516.

49. Dekkers, *Clavis,* no. 381; cf. J. E. Chrisholm, *The Pseudo-Augustinian Hypomnesticon Against the Pelagians and Celestians,* Paradosis, 16 and 21, 2 vols. (Fribourg: Université de Fribourg, 1967–80).

50. Cap. 1: "De haeresi Pelagiana"; c.2: "Quomodo Pelagiani dictis Augustini utuntur . . ."; c.3: "Quomodo Augustinus illa verba determinet in Retractationibus" (Quaracchi ed., II, pp. 452–456).

51. On Bradwardine: McSorley, *Luther* (n. 41 above), pp. 193–195; Oberman, *Werden und Wertung,* pp. 83–93; also: Oberman, *Archbishop Thomas Bradwardine: A Fourteenth Century Augustinian* (Utrecht: Drukkerij en Uitgevers, 1958); G. Leff, *Bradwardine and the Pelagians* (Cambridge: Cambridge University Press, 1957). On Gregory, who is at the center of attention today, see the recent volume, *Gregor von Rimini. Werk und Wirkung bis zur Reformation,* ed. H. A. Oberman, Spätmittelalter und Reformation, Texte und Untersuchungen, 20 (Berlin/New York: W. de Gruyter, 1981), with essays by V. Marcolini, C. P. Burger, M. Schulze et al. Under the leadership of D. Trapp, a critical edition of Gregory's Sentences commentary is under way.

52. *II Sent. d.28 c.1:* "Id vero inconcusse et incunctanter teneamus, liberum arbitrium sine gratia praeveniente et adiuvante non sufficere ad iustitiam et salutem obtinendam; nec meritis praecedentibus gratiam Dei advocari sicut Pelagiana haeresis tradidit" (Quaracchi ed., II, p. 452); c.3: "Quod vero dicunt sine gratia hominem per liberum arbitrium omnia iussa implere . . ." (p. 453).

53. *II Sent. d.28 c.3:* "Quod non ita dictum est, tanquam ex libero arbitrio valeat haberi fides vel caritas, sed quia aptitudinem naturalem habet mens hominis ad credendum vel diligendum, quae Dei gratia praeventa credit et diligit" (p. 456).

54. "Nulla creatura ex se potest supra se," quoted from Richard Fishacre by Landgraf, *Dogmengeschichte* I/1 (1952), p. 147. On the issue, see also the entire section V (ibid., pp. 141–201), and H. de Lubac, *Surnaturel: Etudes historiques* (Paris: Aubier, 1946).

55. On this discussion see below, pp. 33–34.

56. For this section, cf. especially Pesch and Peters, *Einführung* (n. 13 above), pp. 55–107; McSorley, *Luther* (n. 41 above), pp. 138–182; McGrath, *Iustitia Dei,* pp. 78–83.

57. "Et ideo aliis consentiendo dicimus quod ad gratiam gratum facientem habendam ex solo libero arbitrio se homo potest praeparare" (*In II Sent. d.28 q.1 a.4 c,* ed. Mandonnet, p. 729); cf. *In II Sent. d.5 q.2 a.1 c.; In IV Sent. d.17 q.1 a.2,* and especially the answer to the question, "Utrum homo sine gratia possit se ad gratiam praeparare" (*De Veritate,* q.24 a.15, Parma ed., 9, pp. 208f.).

58. "Respondeo dicendum quod in hac quaestione cavendus est error Pelagii qui posuit quod per liberum arbitrium homo poterat adimplere legem et vitam aeternam mereri nec indigebat auxilio divino nisi quantum ad hoc quod sciret quid facere deberet . . . postmodo Pelagiani posuerunt quod initium boni operis est homini ex se ipso dum consentit fidei per liberum arbitrium; sed consummatio est homini a Deo. Praeparatio autem ad initium boni operis pertinet. Unde ad errorem Pelagianum pertinet dicere quod homo possit se ad gratiam praeparare absque auxilio divinae gratiae; et est contra Apostolum . . . (Phil. 1:6)" (*Quodlibetum* 1.7 q.4 a.2); "excluditur error Pelagianorum qui dicebant . . . quod iustificationis nostrae initium ex nobis sit, consummatio autem a Deo" (*Summa contra Gentiles* 3.149); "Per hoc autem excluditur error Pelagianorum qui dicebant quod initium fidei in nobis non erat a Deo, sed a nobis" (ibid. 3.152). In *De articulis et sacramentis ecclesiae* 1, he cites the Pelagian position and the Pauline rebuttal: "Tertius est error Pelagianorum qui quidem primo negaverunt peccatum originale esse in parvulis contra id quod dicit Apostolus ad Rom. 5:12 et in Ps. 50:7; secundo dicunt quod principium boni operis inest homini a seipso, sed consummatio est a Deo, contra id quod dicit Apostolus ad Phil. 2:13; tertio dicunt gratiam dari homini secundum sua merita contra id quod dicitur Rom. 11:6 . . ." (Parma ed., 16, p. 116).

59. "Gratia non tollat naturam sed perficiat," *ST* 1 q.1 a.8 ad 2; cf. J. Beumer, "Gratia Supponit Naturam. Zur Geschichte eines theologischen Prinzips," *Gregorianum* 20 (1939), 381–406, 535–552; B. Stöckle, *Gratia Supponit Naturam. Geschichte und Analyse eines theologischen Axioms,* Studia Anselmiana, 49 (Rome: Herder/Orbis Catholicus, 1962).

60. See *ST* 1-2 q.111 a.2–3. The term *gratia gratis data* here means the Pauline *charisma,* a special gift in service of others (a.1). The Franciscan tradition used it for a preparatory grace, later called "actual," by which God moves a person initially to take action.

61. A major study of grace in Ockham is E. Iserloh, *Gnade und Eucharistie* (n. 33 above), whose discussion partner often is P. Vignaux, *Justification et prédestination au XIVe siècle: Duns Scot, Pierre d'Auriole, Guillaume d'Occam, Gregoire de Rimini* (Paris: Presses Universitaires de France, 1934), pp. 97–175. In the new critical edition, important volumes for our purposes have already appeared: *In I Sent. d.4–17* (*Opera Theologica* 3, ed. Etzkorn; St. Bonaventure, N.Y: Franciscan Institute, 1977); *Reportatio in II Sent.* (*Opera Theologica* 5, ed. Gal and Wood; 1981); *Quodlibeta* (*Opera Theologica* 9, ed. Wey; 1980).

62. This is Ockham's argument against Peter Aureoli: "Haec opinio [i.e., Aureoli's] ponit quod est aliqua forma causata in anima que ex natura rei incitat Deum ad acceptandum actum talem et naturam in qua est. . . . Igitur haec opinio ponit sicut opinio Pelagii quod homo potest naturaliter elicere actum qui necessitat Deum ad acceptandum naturam cuius est" (*In III Sent. q.5,* Iserloh, *Gnade und Eucharistie,* p. 103; cf. *Quodlibetum* VI q.4, ed. Wey, pp. 588f.; *In I Sent. d.17 q.1,* ed. Etzkorn, p. 454).

63. "Nam est opinio Gregorii de arimino qui parum attribuens libero arbitrio . . ." (*In II Sent. d.28 q.1* (A), quoted in Oberman, *Harvest* [n. 3 above], p. 50 n. 63).

64. Ockham: cf. Vignaux, *Justification* (n. 61 above); Biel: cf. W. Ernst, *Gott und Mensch am Vorabend der Reformation. Eine Untersuchung der Moralphilosophie und -theologie bei Gabriel Biel,* Erfurter Theologische Studien, 28 (Leipzig: Benno, 1972); L. Grane, *Contra Gabrielem: Luthers Auseinandersetzung mit Gabriel Biel in der Disputatio contra Scholasticam Theologiam 1517,* Acta Theologica Danica, 4 (Gyldendal: Aarhuus Stiftsbogtrykkerie, 1962); Duns Scotus: cf. W. Dettloff, "Die antipelagianische Grundstruktur der scotistischen Rechtfertigungslehre," *Franziskanische Studien* 48 (1966), 266–270. Nominalism more generally: A. E. McGrath, "The Anti-Pelagian Structure of 'Nominalist' Doctrines of Justification," *Ephemerides Theologicae Lovanienses* 57 (1981), 107–119. See also his *Iustitia Dei,* pp. 76–78, 166–172

65. In the interpretation of *II Sent. d.28,* Ockham's main point is that Pelagians maintain that "man can merit his salvation *ex puris naturalibus";* Biel simply charges that they advocate salvation *"sine gratia";* cf. also his sermon *De circumcisione Domini:* "If grace could come from the creature, a grace which would suffice unto salvation, then any creature would be able to save himself by his own natural powers, that is, do what only grace can do. That is the error of Pelagius," Oberman, *Forerunners* (n. 41 above), p. 168.

66. Ockham, *Quodlibetum* VI q.4: "Secundo dico quod numquam salvabitur homo, nec salvari poterit, nec umquam eliciet vel elicere poterit actum meritorium secundum leges a Deo nunc ordinatas sine gratia creata. Et hoc teneo propter Scripturam sacram et dicta sanc-

torum" (ed. Wey, p. 588; cf. 598). Biel shared this position; see n. 72 below.

67. In the polemical context of the Ockhamist tradition, the term meant human nature without the habit of grace; this was a hypothetical transitional state between guilt and grace as it occurs, for example, in the process of conversion. Adam's status in paradise was similar. Cf. Ockham, *Quodlibetum* VI q.4: "Homo existens in puris naturalibus nec est gratus Deo speciali acceptatione nec reprobatus. Et ideo Deus posset peccatori remittere peccatum et reducere eum ad statum innocentiae sive ponere eum in puris naturalibus" (ed. Wey, p. 599); "Qui est in puris naturalibus nec est in gratia nec in culpa; igitur non includit contradictionem quod peccatori remittatur culpa sine gratiae infusione" (p. 597). For Biel, see Oberman, *Harvest,* pp. 46–49.

68. *In I Sent. d.17 q.2:* "Voluntas potest ex se in actum demeritorium, ergo non includit contradictionem voluntatem ex puris naturalibus ferri in actum meritorium. Non tamen erit ille actus meritorius ex puris naturalibus, sed ex sola gratia Dei, non formaliter voluntatem informante, sed illum actum ex puris naturalibus elicitum gratuite acceptante" (ed. Etzkorn, p. 470); ibid., q.1: "Praeterea, actus diligendi Deum super omnia . . . magis ex natura sua habet quod faciat aliquem libere et sponte elicientem talem actum esse acceptum Deo quam quaecumque forma quae non est in potestate habentis, sed tantum recipit eam" (p. 451); ibid., q.2: "Nec actus meritorius, nec etiam actus caritatis, excedit totam facultatem naturae humanae. Quia omnis actus caritatis quem secundum communem cursum habemus in via, est eiusdem rationis cum actu ex puris naturalibus possibili, et ita ille actus non excedit facultatem naturae humanae. Verumtamen, illum actum actum esse meritorium non est in potestate naturae humanae—sive habeat caritatem sive non habeat—, sed est in libera Dei acceptatione" (p. 472). Biel concludes in the same vein: "Liberum hominis arbitrium ex suis naturalibus sine gratia elicere potest actum moraliter bonum" (*In II Sent. d.28 q.1 a.2 conc. 1,* ed. Werbeck and Hofmann, p. 538).

69. "Posset enim Deus statuere quod quicumque post peccatum mortale ex puris naturalibus doleret de peccato suo sine omni forma supernaturali, quod eo ipso remitteretur sibi peccatum suum, et quod ipse post mortem esset recepturus vitam aeternam" (*In I Sent. d.17 q.1,* ed. Etzkorn, p. 460).

70. Gabriel Biel, *In III Sent. d.27 q.1 a.3 dub.2; propositio* 1: "Viatoris voluntas humana ex suis naturalibus potest diligere Deum super omnia." The statement is supported by an appeal to right reason: "Omni dictamini rationis rectae voluntas ex suis naturalibus se potest conformare; sed diligere Deum super omnia est dictamen rectae rationis; ergo . . . ;" and by inference from the contrary: "Homo errans potest diligere creaturam super omnia et frui ea ex

puris naturalibus; ergo pari ratione potest diligere Deum ex suis naturalibus super omnia et frui eo. Mirum enim valde esset quod voluntas posset se conformare dictamini erroneo et non recto" (ed. Werbeck and Hofmann, pp. 504f.).

71. E.g., Iserloh for Ockham; Oberman for Biel. McSorley, *Luther,* charges "Semipelagianism" in both cases.

72. E.g., thesis two: "Actus amoris Dei amicitiae super omnia non potest stare in viatore de potentia Dei ordinata sine gratia et caritate infusa" (ibid.; n. 70 above); thesis three: "Quamvis dilectio Dei ex naturalibus quae dicta est, sit prior natura caritate et gratia infusis in esse naturae, caritas tamen prior est in meriti ratione." Biel concludes the entire argument: "Et hoc est quod multi doctores dicunt, quod homo potest implere praeceptum quantum ad substantiam facit . . . , non tamen ad . . . intentionem praecipientis. Et ad hoc est determinatio ecclesiae De consecr. d. IV cap. ultimo: 'Qui dixerit quod sine gratia possumus mandata Dei implere per liberum arbitrium, anathema sit.' Contrarium enim fuit haeresis Pelagiana" (ed. Werbeck and Hofmann, p. 507).

73. See Gregory of Rimini, *In II Sent. d.26/28 q.1 a.2* (ed. Trapp et al.), p. 22; the quotation is from *a.1:* "Faventque cuidam errore Pelagii condemnato"; cf. Oberman, *Harvest,* p. 197 n. 23.

74. *In II Sent. d.28 q.1 a.1 (2):* "Cum loquimur de puris naturalibus, non excluditur generalis Dei influentia quae ut causa prima concurrit cum agente secundo" (Oberman, *Harvest,* p. 47 n. 53); ibid., *II Sent. d.28, Pref.:* "Quia removendo obicem qui est consensus in peccatum, et eliciendo per liberum arbitrium motum in Deum, bonum facit quod in se est. Ultra enim ex se non potest, supposita semper generali influentia Dei sine qua omnino nihil potest."

75. "Quorum sententia (i.e., Pelagian teaching) . . . in hoc consistit quod ex nobis non habemus posse bene agere, sed ex deo qui potentiam dedit et adiuvat . . . , sicut posse videre habemus a deo, videre autem a nobis. Certe ab hoc non discordant qui dicunt quod per liberum arbitrium vel vires naturales, quas constat nos a deo habere, sufficimus absque alio auxilio recte velle et agere, nisi forte in hoc quod non dicunt vires nostras iuvari auxilio gratiae, quod dixit Pelagius. Et in hoc peius errant ipsi quam ipse" (*In II Sent. d. 26/28 q. 1,* ed. Trapp et al., p. 59).

76. "Deum nulli beneficium gratis dare, sed tantum pro merito praecedente" (Bradwardine, *De causa Dei,* I, c.3 (ed. Savile; London, 1618, p. 23). In chs. 36–39 (ed. Savile, pp. 309–329), Bradwardine exposes four specific forms of this overarching heresy. According to the first, Pelagians maintain, "Quod etsi merita non sunt causa collationis gratiae principalis, sunt tamen causa sine qua non confertur" (p. 312).

77. In Bradwardine's list, this is the second form of the heresy: "Sunt adhuc alii opinantes quod homo non potest ex se mereri pro-

prie gratiam; potest tamen se debite praeparae, et tunc Deus sibi dabit gratiam suam gratis," c.37 (ed. Savile, p. 316). On the history of the axiom, see Landgraf, *Dogmengeschichte* I/1 (1952), pp. 249–263; McSorley, *Luther,* pp. 165–179; Oberman, *Harvest,* pp. 132–135; McGrath, *Iustitia Dei,* pp. 83–91.

78. "Magister Petrus Abaelardus ait quod (philosophici ethnici) erant digni salute, id est ut daretur eis unde salvarentur, quia si fecissent quantum possent, numquam permitteret eos Deus transire sine fide" (*Quaestiones super Epp. Pauli,* on Rom. 1:21, in Migne *PL* 175:440C); "Facite quod pertinet ad vos, quia facio quod pertinet ad me. Ego facio quod amicus, animam meam pro vobis ponendo; facite et vos, quod amici, me diligendo et mandata mea faciendo" (Radulph Ardens, *Hom. 2 de sanctis,* on John 15:14, in Migne *PL* 155:1496B). Cf. Landgraf, *Dogmengeschichte* I/1 (1952), p. 251.

79. "Et ideo cum dicitur homo facere quod in se est, dicitur hoc esse in potestate hominis, secundum quod est motus a Deo" (*ST* 1-2 q.109 a.6 ad 2; cf. q.112 a.2–3; *De Veritate* q.24 a.15).

80. "Quia secundum legem ordinatam cuilibet facienti quod in se est, et per hoc sufficienter disposito ad gratiae suceptionem Deus infundit gratiam secundum illud prophetae: Convertimini ad me, et ego convertar ad vos (Zach. 1) . . ." (Biel, *In III Sent. d.27 q.1 a.3 dub.2, propos.2*). See also the text from *In II Sent. d.28, Pref.,* quoted in n. 74 above.

81. "Dicunt enim eum sicut mercatorem pauperculum clamare et pulsare ad ianuas et ad ostia singulorum; aperienti vero pro sua apertione gratiam suam dare, quod tamen verius commutare seu vendere diceretur" (Bradwardine, *De causa Dei,* I, c. 38, ed. Savile, p. 319). This is the third form of the Pelagian heresy (cf. nn. 76f. above).

82. "Sed quis non videat istos et eorum similes haeresim Pelagianam tantum vocaliter declinare, et ipsam realiter praedicare? Mutant vocem propter horrorem nominis haeretici euitandum, ut sic eandem pravitatis sententiam sophistice palliatam et larvatam fallaciter, cautius introducant . . . Vox quidem vox Iacobi est, scil. viri fidelis Deoque dilecti, sed manus iniquam sententiam inserentes manus sunt Esau, viri scil. infidelis et Deo odibilis" (ibid., c. 36, ed. Savile, p. 314).

The Hermeneutics of Erasmus

Thomas F. Torrance

While it cannot be claimed that Erasmus was the father of Greek as Reuchlin was of Hebrew studies in the Western church, he was without doubt the ablest and the most influential humanist scholar of his age, who made immense contributions to biblical interpretation. In fact, it was he more than any other who laid the foundations of modern scholarship in the investigation and handling of the text of the New Testament. He was not such a great Greek scholar as Budaeus or such a careful and profound commentator as Calvin, but it was largely owing to him that the dialectical and (as he called it) "barbarous" treatment of the scriptures by the later Schoolmen was brought into disrepute, and a new approach was initiated in which all the available knowledge of the original languages and the cultures to which they belonged was utilized in the aid of sober and patient exegesis.[1] He owed a great deal to others, most of all—apart from the ancient scholars to whom he constantly appealed—to Lorenzo Valla and John Colet. From Valla he learned much in the appreciation and use of "good letters" and in a critical approach to the Latin text of the New Testament,[2] and from Colet he learned not a little how to bring humanist studies to serve the elucidation of the Holy Scriptures, and their liberation from the sterile legalisms and syllogisms of the Schoolmen, through a pure devotion to Jesus and his teaching.[3] "Huc discuntur disciplinae, huc philosophia, huc eloquentia ut Christum intelligamus, ut Christi gloriam celebremus. Hic est totius eruditionis et eloquentiae scopus."[4]

Two basic factors appear to determine all of Erasmus' work of biblical interpretation.

1. From an early age in his career, apparently during his studies in Paris, Erasmus revolted sharply against the subtleties and cavilings of the "neoteric theologians." He detested the way in which they *played* with biblical statements and convictions, distorting them to quite alien meanings through notions derived from the peripatetic philosophy or simply out of their own proud ingenuity. He derided their habit of elaborating subtle distinctions and frivolous questions, and then projecting their conclusions into God, thus thinking of him in a quite worldly way, instead of respecting his majesty and deity. One of Erasmus' outstanding contributions in this period was his successful attack on the nominalist notions of grammar and syntax, which he stigmatized as barbarous, for these involved a radical separation of language from culture and so abstracted the interpretation of biblical statements from the living context of meaning in the civilization in which they were expressed that they gave rise to an arid and frigid theology which could have no real relevance to the spiritual and human life of people.[5]

Although he never rejected a proper use of dialectic, especially if it were kept subordinate to the proper aim *(scopus)* of theology, Erasmus thoroughly distrusted all speculation and could never bring himself to agree that the kind of logical connections Scholastic theologians employed in their disputations were apposite to "Christian philosophy," which was essentially spiritual rather than intellectual.[6] The *Logos* with which we are concerned in Christian studies is not Reason but the divine Speech *(Sermo),* i.e., not a word of our own devising which we project into God in order to make him speak our language and think our thoughts, but a word that derives through the prophets and apostles and which is the expression of the Spirit or Mind of Christ.[7] On the other hand, Erasmus was never able to develop a proper answer to the false dialectical theology of the "Scotists," for he never managed to penetrate far behind organized language to the inner connection of the realities denoted—that had to wait for the Reformers and their development of a positive theology on the ground of biblical exegesis. Erasmus was content merely to develop narrations of the biblical teaching, and to imbibe "the Spirit of Christ" and work it out in the moral connections of human life. Thus for Erasmus interpretation was essentially a descriptive and paraphrastic science, and its results were ethical and social rather than evangelical and theological.

2. Erasmus took over the theory of Valla that language and culture belong inseparably together—decay in letters reflects the general decline in civilization. He was convinced that the

converse was equally true, that progress in culture must come about through an advance together of good letters and liberal arts. Indeed, Erasmus was so forcibly seized with that conviction that the whole of his life was devoted to its embodiment and achievement.[8] Applied to the question of biblical studies, this resulted in the realization that, for the Bible to be made perspicuous, it required a new context in which to reflect its meaning, a new civilization which could be employed to serve its interpretation and implement its teaching. Erasmus felt that the interpretation of the Bible in the Middle Ages corresponded to the barbarity of men's attitude to good letters, for how could the Bible reflect its meaning properly in the arid dialecticism of the Schools or in the crudity and illiteracy of the monks? He longed for a recovery of the old culture of Greece and Rome, and a new appreciation of the old theologians and interpreters who used classical culture to reflect the meaning of the Bible and who at the same time Christianized the ancient culture by the philosophy of Christ.[9] Hence he made it the task of his life to work for the recovery of purity and eloquence in language, and in and through that medium to let "evangelical truth" subdue the barbarity and crudity of men and recreate humanity in a new civilization. It was Erasmus' stand for a Christian humanism that gave direction to his many activities and even lent a real consistency to many of his most contradictory statements. He aimed at a reconciliation of the culture of classical antiquity with the Christian spirit and was convinced that it would result in the elevation of humanity in an era of tolerance, wisdom, peace, and progress.[10] Judged from the perspective of the late eighteenth and the nineteenth centuries, he was essentially "modern."[11]

Like Reuchlin and his friend Sir Thomas More,[12] Erasmus reacted against Aristotelian philosophy even in its classical form, preferring, as he said, with the great majority of philosophers and poets, to follow the teaching of Plato.[13] It was Plato, moreover, who had influenced some of the old theologians and expositors whom Erasmus most admired, such as Origen, Ambrose, and Augustine, so that it is not surprising that he too should revive the old Hellenic distinction between the *mundus sensibilis* and the *mundus intelligibilis.* "The intelligible world, which we may also call the angelical world, is that in which God dwells with blessed minds; the visible world comprises the celestial spheres and all that they involve. Then let us imagine man as a sort of third-world participant in both, in the visible in respect of his body, in the invisible in respect of his soul. In the visible world we are strangers *(peregrini)* and ought never to be at rest, but whatever we experience through our senses we must refer by some apt analogy *(apta quadam collatione)* to the angelical world, or (which is more profitable) to the morals of man and that part of him that corresponds to it. What this sun is in the visible world, the divine Mind is in the intelligible and in that part of you which is most akin to it, I mean, the spirit."[14]

Erasmus also took over the teaching of the Platonic Socrates that man's highest wisdom is to know himself,[15] and so he held that, when our eyes are directed inward to self-understanding, they are directed upward to the intelligible world to which we are akin in our spiritual natures. Under the influence of Origen, however, Erasmus thought of man's constitution as threefold: flesh and soul and spirit. The flesh is the vile part of us, the spirit that part in which we are in the similitude of God and are united to him, while the soul occupies a place midway between the flesh and the spirit, and which may be carnal or spiritual according as it yields to the influence of the flesh or the spirit.[16]

This combination of Platonic philosophy and Origenistic anthropology had an important influence on Erasmus' hermeneutics, for it directed him to look for the meaning in an inward and purely spiritual experience. He shows some evidence of having studied Plato's *Cratylus* and having adopted from it the notion that words are naturally and mimetically related to the things they signify. But he developed that in his own way. Thus he insisted that even if no likeness between some word and the thing it signified could be discerned, there must be some invisible reason for it other than mere convention, and he tended regularly in his interpretation of letters, whether profane or Christian, to interiorize the meaning—that is, to look not so much to the language as significant of things or events but as expressive of mental states and moral attitudes.[17]

Typical of this whole approach is Erasmus' work *On the Use and Abuse of the Tongue,*[18] for throughout he emphasizes the fact that it is the moral personality of the speaker that is determinative in the use of language. God alone perceives what is hidden in man's heart. But the tongue has been given to man for this purpose, that man may get to know the mind and spirit of man through its internuncial function. It is fitting, therefore, that the image should correspond to the archetype. Mirrors reflect *bona fide* the image of the objective reality, but what are called "lying mirrors" are held up for ridicule. Hence the Son of God who came to earth in order that we might get to know the Mind of God through him, wished to be called the Speech of the Father *(Sermo Patris),* and likewise the Truth

(Veritas), because it is extremely base that the tongue should differ from the spirit. God in heaven, how rare among Christians is fidelity of speech *(linguae fides).*[19] Two points may be noted here.

1. Erasmus prefers the Augustinian translation *Sermo* to *Verbum* for the Greek *Logos* applied by the Fourth Gospel to the Son of God, for it does not lend itself easily to a misinterpretation in a rational direction. But by *Sermo* Erasmus means something rather different from the divine Speech which interested Anselm so deeply, the objectivity of God's eternal Word behind the revealed Word. That is not altogether lacking in Erasmus, but with him *Sermo* bears a connotation which quickly passes over into *Letters.* That is the slant He gives to the classical doctrine of the Incarnation of the Word. "God speaks very rarely and sparingly, but His speaking is supremely true and efficacious. The Father spoke once, and begot His eternal Word. He spoke again, and by His omnipotent Word He founded the whole fabric of this universe. Again He spoke through His prophets through whom He handed on to us sacred books, concealing under a few simple words the immense treasure of divine wisdom. Finally in sending His Son, that is the Word clothed with flesh, He brought forth His Speech in a succinct form upon the earth, drawing everything together as if in one epilogue."[20] The peculiar slant that Erasmus gave to this doctrine comes out particularly clearly in one of the most significant of all his works, his little biography of Jerome,[21] the patristic authority who more than any other was for him the epitome of Christian humanism and sober scholarship. In Jerome, Erasmus found a theological account of the Christian faith which was essentially undogmatic and was mediated through pure and eloquent speech, *bonae litterae,* rather than through the elaboration of sophisticated arguments and definitions such as one finds among the Scholastics, be they Thomist, Scotist, or Occamist. If *dialectica* is needed for the exposition of the Christian faith, what could be better than that of Augustine? But Erasmus himself preferred the *eloquentia* of Jerome, for it is nearer to the kind of speech handed down to us from the apostles.[22]

2. True and healthy speech is that which faithfully reflects the mind of the speaker—hence, both in speaking and in interpreting, it is the relation of the tongue to the heart that is all-important. "What the Father is in divine things, who produces His Son out from Himself, the mind is in us, for it is the source of our thoughts and speech. As the Son is born of the Father, so in us speech proceeds from our spirit. The Son is said to be the Image of the Father, so that he who knows one or the

other knows both. In us speech is the mirror of the spirit—hence the famous saying of Socrates, 'Speak that I may see you.' A handsome youth was brought before him, whose appearance bespoke natural ability. But Socrates did not see the youth as long as he was silent, for the spirit does not shine out in the face so much as in the speech. It is not so much from the face as from the tongue that physicians detect the signs of disease. But the surest signs of a healthy spirit, or of a sick spirit, are in the tongue which is the face of the mind."[23] Erasmus was convinced that speech, whether in its written or spoken form, derives from the inner depths of the personal being, so that its power for good or evil depends on the veracity or mendacity of the relation between the word and the inward state which it expresses. Thus speech can be corrupted in two ways, either through a false or insincere relation between outward expression and inward conviction, or through inner impurity defiling speech at its source. The Scholastics corrupted biblical speech in the first way, forcing it by their depraved interpretations to lie, and the monks corrupted it in the second way through the impurity of their living.[24] It is the recovery of divine Speech through faithful attention to good letters that will allow the healing virtue of God's Word to operate effectively among men. The tongue of man may be a source of poison, but (Erasmus cites from Prov. 12:18) "the tongue of the wise man is sanity." What is needed is a *lingua medica* to cure those infected with a pestilent tongue. That can come only from God: *Emisit sermonem suum et sanavit eos,* as the psalmist declares.[25] It is the function of the biblical expositor to mediate that divine Speech to his generation, so that through it men may become assimilated in their inward thoughts and spirits to the divine Mind and the divine Spirit as imaged in Jesus Christ. It is in him that God has tempered the sublimity of his celestial Speech to us and spoken to us more within our capacities, so that through hearing and imitating him we may obtain eternal salvation.[26]

We are fortunate in having from Erasmus several works on method (in this too, he was decidedly modern) which help us not a little in understanding the principles of his hermeneutics. In addition to the *Enchiridion militis Christiani* of 1503, in which he set forth his program for the recovery of the philosophy of Christ, there are the *De ratione studii ac legendi interpretandique auctores* of 1511, the *Ratio seu compendium verae theologiae* of 1519, and the *Ecclesiastes sive de ratione concionandi* of 1535. We can hardly do better than look at them in that order, drawing from the *Enchiridion* at relevant points.

I. *De ratione studii*

The *De ratione studii* is particularly instructive, for it sets forth for the ordinary student what Erasmus considered to be the proper method of reading and interpreting authors, without having Christian authors particularly in mind—although not all that he has to say here is relevant for us.[27]

The work opens with an important distinction between the knowledge of things *(cognitio rerum)* and the knowledge of words *(cognitio verborum).* If the former is thought to be preferable, it must be remembered that the latter comes first in time and must not be neglected. Since things are known only through verbal signs *(per vocum notas),* he who does not have an expert knowledge of the power of language will be blind in his judgment of things and cannot but suffer delusions. None are more likely to fall into captious arguments anywhere than those who boast that they are concerned with things themselves and not with words.[28] However, when we ask Erasmus what the *cognitio rerum* is, he appears to point only to factual information such as can be acquired from ancient writers on geography or natural science or medicine, and all that is useful for the understanding of classical literature, he says, but he seems to have little understanding of what "real studies" are. This is characteristic of Erasmus, for all through his works, and not least in his exegetical writings, he stops short of penetrating through language to an objective knowledge of the realities denoted. That in turn radically affects his interpretation.

Erasmus makes it clear, then, that grammar must have the first place in the order of our studies (in this he includes Greek and Latin). He insists, in contrast to the medieval grammarians, that the proper method of mastering grammar is not through rules and definitions but through reading the classical authors themselves. Only grammar acquired in that way will be appropriate for their interpretation. The rules of grammatical structure, of prosody and rhetoric, are important because they help us to appreciate the styles of the authors and to develop a precision in the study of their characteristic use of expressions, archaisms, and figures of speech. Logic, of course, has its place, but dialectic is no guide to the understanding of style. What is important is that the interpreter must steep himself in the literature he is studying—and there is no better way to become acquainted with it than to teach it, for then we discover how much we really do and do not know.[29]

In turning to the content of the ancient literature, Erasmus lays stress on the study of history[30] and of proverbs or adagia.[31] What Erasmus has to say about these sheds not a little light on his fundamental approach to literature and its interpretation. Erasmus' attitude to history is highly ambiguous. He is deeply committed to the movement of return to the sources of Western civilization in the classical culture of Greece and Rome, and he applies that throughout to his understanding of Christianity—i.e., by probing into its historical origins, as one can see very clearly by the way in which he treats the problems of the text of the New Testament.[32] He was capable of writing a historical biography of Jerome in which he insisted in using only original sources and allowing them to call into question the tradition about Jerome that had become overlaid with legend and fictitious story.[33] But when Erasmus comes to speak of *historia* itself, he reveals what W. H. Woodward has called "an entire absence of historical perspective."[34] Historical writing is looked on only as a form of literature, to be included, in fact, under the general umbrella of *grammatica*[35] and to be valued mainly for the fact that historical narratives illustrate moral and spiritual truth.[36] That is to say, the importance of historical narrative lies not in its direct but in its oblique sense.

That is why Erasmus laid such great stress on proverbs, parables, allegories, and myths, for it is in the tropical turns of speech that not only natural phenomena but profane and even crude narratives may be made to yield "something divine," i.e., timeless truth or a moral or spiritual nature.[37] He applied this method of interpretation not only to the classical authors such as Homer and Vergil but also to the historians and philosophers. To cite Woodward again:

> Unfortunately Erasmus did not confine himself to considering the particular "allegorical" interpretations which may have been intended by Plato or Vergil, he opened the door to floods of arbitrary glosses and moral lessons such as the mediaevalists had applied to all departments of thought. On the other hand this should be said. The allegorical method is the intermediate stage between a conscious antinomy and its historical solution. . . . The historical attitude being impossible, the Allegory was the only instrument of reconciliation. But such allegories rested upon no critical basis, they were at the disposal of the ingenious mind, and could take any form which the exigencies of the argument required. Hence to the neutral inquirer, with no specific cause to advance, such a method served to bring to light, rather than to solve, the problem to which it was applied.[38]

We shall have to return later to Erasmus' use of allegory in the interpretation of the biblical documents, but our interest at the moment lies in his idea that attention must be directed to the style and form of the author's diction, to his use of language, his elegance of phrase, rhetorical devices, and above all to his use of metaphorical or tropical turns of speech in order to let them serve as clues to guide our intuitive penetration into the mind and individuality of the author. "Postremo ad philosophiam veniat et poetarum fabulas apte trahat ad mores, vel tanquam exempla, ut Pyladis et Orestis, ad amicitiae commendationem, Tantali fabulam ad avaritiae detestationem."[39]

A more succinct account of how Erasmus advises study of some classical piece of writing is given in the *De conscribendis epistolis,* where he suggests a fourfold reading.[40] An initial reading is necessary in order to inform oneself of the general point of view. A second reading should follow in which care is taken to examine grammatical structure and individual words and sentence forms. Then the third reading ought to be directed to an investigation of the rhetorical devices and characteristic features of the composition. The interpreter must inquire into the author's mind and his reasons for the language used; but if he finds himself deeply moved, he must keep his feet on the ground and calmly assess his emotional reaction to find out what is the occasion for it and why he has not reacted in the same way to others. If he comes across some adage or proverb or anything similar, let him appropriate it and make use of it for himself. In a final reading, however, consideration must be given to anything that admits of practical or philosophical use, and especially to any instance that can serve a moral end. But, further, discussion of the text with others will help the interpreter to revise his judgment and correct his understanding.

Quite clearly this method of interpretation is fraught with serious danger, for in spite of the fact that it requires such a serious and thorough examination of what is actually said, the concentration on the style and the aesthetic form, and the employment of the interpreter's prior intent as the ultimate guide to understanding, can lead only too easily to a reading out of the author what the interpreter wants to find in him. That is particularly apparent when Erasmus seizes on the adages or myths as the instrument through which to open up the inner meaning of what is written. He takes the myth of Narcissus as an example, for it is a striking parable of the truth that supreme love goes together with the greatest similarity or affinity. Narcissus caught sight of himself in a fountain of limpid water and was immediately inflamed with love for what he saw. "What is more like ourselves than our image?" Erasmus asks. "Therefore when one man of learning loves another man of learning, he loves nothing else but his own image in the other, yet in another sort of way. So it is also with the sober, the modest, or the upright man, each is attracted to his own kind."[41]

Although Erasmus had profane authors in mind here, it is his own extremely sympathetic study of Jerome that provides about the best example of this method of interpretation. Quite clearly he was attracted to Jerome by the reflection of himself in him. What he had to say of him and of his method was important for Erasmus, therefore, as a sort of *apologia pro vita sua.* One can certainly appreciate that in the interpretation of Jerome, but what about the application of this method to Paul or John or Peter? Erasmus' views of the right way in which to apply this approach to the scriptures were set forth initially in the *Enchiridion,* to which we must now turn to supplement what he had to say in the *De ratione studii.*

Three things guide his handling of biblical texts.

1. Erasmus has a profound reverence for the sacred scriptures; they come from God and must be handled with humility. It is like the manna that came down from heaven and was given in small quantities—that is to say, the scriptures have come by inspiration from God, but divine truth is communicated to us through them in a humble and lowly way, for under the homeliness, under rude words, are included great mysteries. This is not the doctrine of mortals, which is vitiated by error, but the teaching of Christ, which is altogether pure and bright and clean.[42] "Therefore you must always remember that the divine letters are not to be handled except by cleansed hands, that is, with the greatest purity of spirit, lest that which is given to you as an antidote may be turned into poison, and the manna start to putrify if you do not take it into your innermost affections. First of all, then, you must have a high regard for the scriptures, thinking of them as the very oracles that have come out from the sanctuary of the divine Mind. You will then feel yourself moved by divine power, formed and carried away, and changed in an indescribable way, if you approach the scriptures religiously, with veneration and humility."[43]

2. Because the teaching of Christ which we hear in the scriptures is essentially simple and unsophisticated, we must bring to the reading of the text the simple and bright eye, the purity of heart and faith of which the gospel speaks; that is to say, we must govern our life by the rule and pattern of the love of Christ if we are to hear what he has to teach us, letting him always occupy the central point in all our relations with him and with others.[44] This means that we have to renounce the

sophistications which we are tempted to bring to the text, for they can only corrupt our understanding of it—they derive either from false dialectics or from false affections, in which we seek to wrest the scripture to serve our own ambition and to bolster up our own aims. Erasmus admits that the teaching of the scriptures in this way is a perilous undertaking, for it cuts across so many interests and concerns to which others have given themselves, and rouses their hostility.[45]

3. Essentially simple though the divine teaching or the philosophy of Christ is, it is hidden in the Gospels and epistles of the apostles behind strange and extremely difficult forms of expression, figures and oblique turns of speech *(figurae tropique obliqui),* so that we often have the utmost difficulty with what is actually written before we can perceive the real meaning. This sends us to study the most approved interpreters of the scriptures, to aid us in acquiring a brief and simple summary of Christ's philosophy to serve as a regular guide in interpretation. Study and read again and again, Erasmus says, chiefly the old doctors and expositors, and choose especially those who go farthest from the letter of the scripture, such as Origen, Ambrose, Jerome, and Augustine.[46]

The chief conviction that appears to determine Erasmus' handling of the scriptures is that "the Spirit of God has His own tongue and His own figures of speech which you must get to know above all through diligent observation. The divine Wisdom prattles to us like some obliging mother, accommodating His words to our infancy. He gives milk to infants in Christ, soft food to the weak. Do you therefore hurry on with your growth, and advance to solid food. God's Wisdom has stooped down to your lowliness, but you must rise up to His sublimity."[47] The way to do that, Erasmus goes on to say, is to break the shell and dig into the marrow—that is to say, to break through the "letter" or the "flesh" into spiritual knowledge, for the "letter" kills but the "spirit" quickens and gives life. Spiritual things must be compared with spiritual things. "Do you therefore who are endowed with a productive mind *(ingenio tam felici praeditus)* resolutely refuse to linger in the sterile letter, but hasten on to more hidden mysteries, and as a help to your constant endeavour add frequent prayers until He who has the key of David opens for you the book sealed with seven seals—He who shuts up the secrets of the Father which no man opens, for no one knows the Father but the Son and he to whom the Son has willed to reveal Him."[48]

It is worth noting that Erasmus considers this to be only an adaptation of the method which is to be adopted in the interpretation of profane literature. What is basic to both is the distinction between the body and the soul, the letter and the spirit, so that interpretation must advance beyond the literal sense to the inward or oblique meaning. This applies, he says, to all poets and philosophers, and principally to the followers of Plato, but most of all to Holy Scripture, which like the Silenus of Alcibiades under a rude and foolish exterior presents divine and holy things—but they are to be interpreted therefore as allegorical statements.[49] The scripture and even the gospel have their flesh and their spirit, and it would be folly to stick in the flesh and not penetrate beyond to the spirit. "What is the difference then between your reading the book of Kings or of Judges in the Old Testament and your reading of Titus Livy, if you pay no attention to the allegory in either? In the latter there is much that amends common behaviour, and in the former there are some things which appear quite absurd, but which if understood superficially, will hurt behaviour, such as David's theft, adultery with homicide, etc. Therefore, despising the flesh of the Scripture, especially of the Old Testament, make it your point to search out the mystery of the spirit."[50]

Erasmus is aware, however, that this kind of investigation must be controlled, else it will become quite arbitrary, and so he insists that "in digging for mysteries, you must not follow the conjectures of your own mind, but you must learn the method and the art which Dionysius has handed down in his book *De divinis nominibus* and St. Augustine in his *De doctrina Christiana.* After Christ it was St. Paul who opened up certain sources of allegory, and it was He whom Origen followed, and in that part of theology is easily supreme."[51] The medieval theologians certainly concerned themselves with allegorical interpretation, but they treated it quite unfruitfully, because they lost the art of eloquence and were content to follow only Aristotle, throwing out the followers of Plato and Pythagoras although they were preferred by Augustine.[52]

When Erasmus applies the same procedure to the New Testament, he insists that even there a distinction must be drawn between the flesh of the gospel and the spirit—the body without the spirit, he says, can have no being, but the spirit of the body is in need of nothing. It is Paul who teaches us to have no confidence in the flesh.[53] This cannot be taken to mean that Erasmus despised the historical acts of the Incarnate Son, in the life, death, and resurrection of Jesus, but rather that we must seek to be assimilated to the inward revelation of God mediated to us in that way—learning to hear inwardly God's

Word *(intus audire verbum Dei),* for the Lord speaks His Word inwardly *(Dominus intus dicit verbum).*[54] Another way he has of expressing this is to speak of it as the image of the divine Mind, or the image of Christ's mind to which we must be assimilated if we are to interpret the Gospels properly. "You honour the image of Christ's face formed in stone or wood, or portrayed with colours. Much more religiously ought you to honour the image of His Mind which by the operation of the Holy Spirit is expressed in the language of the Gospels."[55] That is the essential thing for Erasmus, the interiorizing of the gospel, the contemplation of the beauty and serenity of the Spirit of Christ as it is represented in the simplicity of the evangelical truth, and through that contemplation the assimilation of the mind of the interpreter to "the spirit and pattern of His divine mind."[56] He thinks of that movement as parallel to that which Plato had in mind when he spoke of the wings which spring up in our spirits through love of the truth. "Move upward, then, from the body to the spirit, from the visible world to the invisible, from the letter to the mystery, from sensible things to intelligible realities, from complicated things to simplicities, raise yourself upward as with the certain steps of Jacob's ladder. If you draw near in that way, the Lord in His turn will draw near to you. If you try with all your strength to rise up out of your darkness and the confusion of your senses, He will accommodate Himself to you and come to meet you out of His inaccessible light and unthinkable silence in which not only all the tumults of the senses but the images of all the intelligible realities cease and become silent."[57]

In view of statements like this, which are by no means isolated, it is impossible to agree with many writers who declare that Erasmus had little or no mystical side to his nature or his faith. The influence of Dionysius and Augustine on him was immense, although he kept it in control—or, to use his own expression, he kept his feet on the ground. The problem is rather how far he allowed this Origenist and Augustinian notion, that we must transcend even the flesh or "carnal history" of Jesus in order to attain to the heights of divine revelation, to affect his exegesis of the evangelical records and his interpretation of the gospel itself. Certainly, in the debate over his use of *sermo* to interpret the Johannine *logos* he made it clear that the divine speech which was made flesh and which we hear in the Gospels is not something passing or transient—"sermo non est temporarius quemadmodum noster, sed aeternus."[58] For a fuller answer to the problem we have to turn to the other two main works of Erasmus which we have selected for discussion.

II. *Ratio seu methodus compendio perveniendi ad veram theologiam*

This was originally written as a short statement on method *(Ratio seu compendium verae theologiae)* to act as a preface for Erasmus' edition of the New Testament in 1516. But it was greatly enlarged for the second edition of 1519 et seq. (with the extended title given above) and really became one of his most important works, if only because it initiated a series of works on theological method from Reformed and Lutheran theologians later on in the century. Although it can stand alone, and has been published separately, much of its significance lies in its immediate relation to the text of the New Testament and its explication.[59]

Erasmus recalls right away the works of Augustine, *De doctrina Christiana,* and of Dionysius, not only the *De divinis nominibus* but the *De mystica theologia* and the *De significativa theologia,* but without wishing to contradict them; he has other things to put forward. The first thing he demands is a tranquil and quiet spirit in order that the image of the eternal truth may shine more distinctly in the interpreter as in a placid stream or in a smooth and clean mirror. No admission to divine colloquy may be gained without cleansing and purification. The eye of faith must be single and characterized by simplicity if it is to discern celestial things. The only entrance into the royal secrets of heaven is through a lowly door; all that is inimical to the truth, such as the love of fame, arrogance, or impious curiosity, must be left behind. Far from trusting his own judgment, the interpreter must allow himself to be formed and shaped by what he learns.[60] Every human discipline has its own aim which it must disentangle from those of others if it is to be carried out properly. Likewise with theological studies: "This is your first and only aim, this is your commitment, this is the one thing you are to do, to be changed, to be carried away, to be fashioned, to be transformed into what you learn."[61]

This requires discipline as well as prayer and great diligence. First of all, it is necessary to learn the three languages—Hebrew, Greek, and Latin—for without languages we cannot read and understand what we read; but it also requires incessant study of the ancient expositors and doctors and a copious supply of information drawn from the classical cultures, without the distortion of foolish questions and problems elaborated in disjunction from the actual subject matter we are investigating. There can, of course, be no Christian theology without grammar and dialectic; but once we have mastered all these tools, we have to put them to proper use within the perspective and objective of theological study, and then to that we must bend all our powers like some athlete in the games.[62]

It is certainly the question of aim or objective, the *scopus,* that Erasmus makes primary in this treatise, for everything depends on getting the perspective right and developing the kind of method appropriate to the nature of the subject matter. The one and only objective is Jesus Christ, and that must be considered objectively and subjectively. He is himself our frame of reference, so that everything in theological studies and in Christian things must be referred to him as the one center of all *(omnium unicum centrum).* We ourselves have to be directed to him so that it belongs to our objective to be assimilated to him, to grow up in him into the measure of his fullness.[63] It is characteristic of Erasmus that these two aspects should be held together. The devotion of the exegete to Christ in the center carries with it the renunciation of all alien philosophies, the shedding of our own unreality and hypocrisy, the readiness to live in accordance with what is learned from Christ, and throughout all a passionate devotion to the subject, sacred letters and in and through them Christ himself.

As Erasmus sees it, the determination and clarification of the *scopus* are essential to proper interpretation, but interpretation is needed to clarify and determine the *scopus.* These two activities have to proceed side by side. After the initial clearing of the ground, and the preparation of a brief summary *(summa,* or *compendium)* of the general trend of the teaching of the New Testament, that can be used as a working guide for the longer task of drawing out in fuller detail the main elements that form the contents of the Christian message.[64]

In the initial activity of clarifying and determining the *scopus,* particular attention must be paid to what is actually said, by whom it is said, to whom it is said, by what words and at what time, and on what occasion, to what precedes and to what follows each passage elucidated.[65] Note must be taken of "the distinction of times" if we are not to run into confusion, especially in the relation of the teaching of the Old Testament to that of the New.[66] But it is as we are able to develop our narration of the contents in series of expositions that we will find that the more obscure passages and doctrines have light thrown on them from others which are clearer. It often happens that, when we try to explicate the meaning of the words, we clarify the meaning of the sentences, but the reverse is also true.[67] But it is as the *scopus* becomes clearer to us that we will find obscurity vanishing.[68] Thus a certain order of authority or importance in the unity and variety of the books of the Bible will become apparent if they are looked at from a center in Christ, their *scopus*. Erasmus considers, for example, that Isaiah should be set before Esther, and that Matthew should have precedence over the Apocalypse, and Paul's epistle to the Romans over the epistle to the Hebrews, and so forth. In this way the variety does not lead to confusion but ministers rather to fullness of understanding.[69]

The major bulk of the *Ratio seu methodus* is given over to the task of drawing out the main teaching of the New Testament insofar as it affects the procedure to be adopted in exposition and interpretation; that is to say, Erasmus is keenly aware of the fact that the actual subject matter must be allowed to influence the method to be used in its elucidation. But far from taking the form of a *summa* of dogmatic principles, this summary takes the form of an unfolding through narration of the essential teaching of the New Testament. This is for Erasmus primarily a descriptive rather than an explicatory task. Divine things, as he has said elsewhere, are more to be indicated than explained ("magis indicanda sunt quam explicanda").[70]

Along with this, however, goes the problem of bringing out the inner spiritual meaning of the New Testament, and since "almost the whole speech of Christ is oblique with figures and tropes" ("totus sermo Christi sarmo figuris ac tropis obliquus est"), care must be given to allegorical interpretation as the instrument through which the oblique sense is drawn out.[71] This does not mean that Erasmus despises the historical sense, for he regards it rather as the foundation for allegory.[72] No allegorical interpretations can be allowed which are only a pretext for the accommodation of scripture to some philosophy, but only those which are in accordance with the demands of the subject matter.[73] On the other hand, Erasmus insists once again that the truth is to be found in allegories which make up almost the whole of scripture through which the divine wisdom prattles with us, as it were ("per quam aeterna sapientia nobiscum veluti balbutit"). Quite often the open meaning is quite false—indeed ridiculous and absurd—if the sense of the words is accepted in a straightforward way.[74] Allegorical interpretation, however, is not to be used to develop fantastic doctrines but rather to help us penetrate beneath the common sense to a deeper meaning ("a communi sensu ad sensum penitiorem") which is the truest and the most salubrious.[75]

A disciplined treatment of allegory will follow the rules laid down by the classical interpreters, such as the seven rules of Tychonius as expounded by Augustine.[76] Every passage must be examined carefully for itself, no biblical testimony is to be torn out of its context and distorted in order to justify some extraneous notion, and the meaning which is taken out of obscure words must answer to the whole orb of Christian doctrine, to the Christian life and to natural equity. If we use the sacred writings in this way, they will minister salvation. Nothing is worse than playing with divine scripture or abusing the mystical words in scurrilous jokes.[77] Erasmus is convinced that a great deal of misinterpretation and distortion can be avoided if the interpreter is himself a man of moral integrity and sincerity who puts his investigation of the Holy Writings to a spiritual and ethical end, and keeps in front of him the true *scopus* to which the whole of the scripture is directed.[78]

III. *Ecclesiastes sive de ratione concionandi*

This work was written not so much for the scholar as for the preacher of the gospel *(concionator evangelicus)* and must be taken to represent Erasmus' mature views, for it appeared in 1535 not long before his death.[79] There is much here that we have already discussed and need not repeat, and much more that does not concern us, which we must leave aside. We single out three principal elements that have a contribution to make to our study.

1. The whole work is prefaced with a discussion of the relation between the Incarnate Word and the incomprehensible Speech *(Sermo)* of God, for Erasmus is aware that it is the mighty power that lies behind faithful preaching of the gospel. Christ is the sole Word of God who expounds him and reveals him. He is the omnipotent Speech of God who is without beginning and without end, and who eternally proceeds from the heart of the Father. Through him the Father has made all things, governs all things; through him the fallen race of man is restored and the church is united to himself. Through him in a wonderful and indescribable way he wished to make known to the world, that through him he would quicken the dead, pour out the gifts of the Holy Spirit, add his secret energy to the sacraments of the church; through him he will judge the world, separating the goats from the sheep, and make a new heaven and a new earth, and inspire the citizens of the Heavenly Jerusalem, and fill them with his riches. He is the incomprehensible Speech of God, the surest Expositor of the divine Mind; at no point is there any discrepancy between him and the Archetype of the *Summa Veritas.* It is through him that the eternal divine Mind has miraculously spoken to the created world, and in manifold ways to us by the prophets. Through him he has spoken to us most distinctly, in his mission on earth,

as man born of man, so that now he may not only be heard but perceived with our senses and handled with our hands.

Just as the speech of man is the truthful image of his mind and does not proceed from man apart from his spirit—for as his speech is so is his spirit—so Christ the Incarnate Word proceeds from the Father as his omnipotent Speech, revealing the divine Mind that transcends all that we can think or imagine. He is the *Sermo* of God, his image and his voice. He it is who dwells with us by his Spirit and speaks himself to us. Hence the tongue of the preacher has no other efficacy than that which derives from the Spirit of Christ dwelling in his heart, governing his speech and adding to his uttered words hidden power. The voice of the preacher reaches the ears of the hearers, but it is God alone who by his secret force transforms men's minds. Jesus Christ is the Way, the Truth, and the Life, God speaking through his Son, Christ himself speaking to liberate the world from error.[80]

That would appear to be as exalted a view of the proclaimed Word as one can find anywhere in the Reformation. In spite of his opposition to what he regarded as the more tumultuous aspects of the movement for reform, and his failure to think out the profound implications of what he himself narrated of the gospel, Erasmus was gripped by the power of the living, active Word of God and realized that that was the power and reality with which we have to do in the interpreting and proclaiming of the evangelical message. It is not surprising that Erasmus as well as Luther should leave his mark on John Calvin, who published the first edition of his *Institutio* in the year following the *De ratione concionandi.*

2. In this work Erasmus shows more evidence of taking seriously the relation of speech to the realities it is employed to denote. Thus he insists that the meaning of words, even in their transferred sense, is not to be taken from the words themselves considered as names (in the Platonic sense) but rather from their relation to the realities which they denote.[81] He is apparently aware, too, that words may denote more than they can express, as we can see in the use of emphasis.[82] But more important is the suggestion that, in expounding the scriptures, the preacher should expound the scriptures in accordance with the order *(ordo, consequentia, tenor consequentium)* which the scripture itself supplies, which reminds us of the insistence of Athanasius that in interpretation it is the sequence or connection of the actual content of a passage, rather than that manifested by the words, that must be followed.[83] Elsewhere Erasmus insists that while words and meanings are related to one another like body and soul, it is the sequence of

meaning *(sententia)* that must be brought out in a translation rather than the word-for-word sequence of the original text.[84] That is well illustrated by his *Paraphrases* on the New Testament, where he insists, as he says, in bringing his own thoughts to the rule of what is revealed in the text rather than the other way around.[85] The paraphrase is thus a method of bringing out the meaning of the text through constructing an amplified sequence of thought that brings out as fully as possible the sequence lying behind the grammatical sense of the scriptures.

Yet this remains the great weakness of Erasmus' hermeneutics, for he cannot get beyond a descriptive, paraphrastic interpretation. As soon as he comes up against the realities denoted by the language of the New Testament, he tends to draw back and take refuge in a purely literary exposition. Thus his spiritual and theological judgments are never very profound. He was content as an interpreter to present the evangelical narrative as far as he could freed from the glosses which had obscured it in the Dark and Middle Ages, with the confidence that the inherent power and truth of God's Word would leave their impact on the reader. To the end he rejects dialectic as useless in biblical exposition.[86]

3. Erasmus offers here a more careful and critical account of the relation between the historical sense and the spiritual sense of Holy Scripture. As in the *Ratio verae theologiae,*[87] he accepts the fourfold sense that was held by the Fathers and the Schoolmen, the grammatical or historical, the tropological, the allegorical, and the anagogical, although he related the allegorical or parabolic more to doctrine. But he clearly prefers the simpler twofold distinction by the ancient Fathers, between the grammatical, or literal, or historical, and the spiritual.[88]

It is the natural or direct sense *(germanus sive rectus sensus)* of scripture that is the primary one, and therefore it is to it first of all that attention must be directed. It is the foundation for everything else and must not be subverted in the slightest. If the basis is crooked, everything else will be distorted. But the scriptures do not just have a human sense, and they are seriously distorted if their meaning is reduced to that. They have a spiritual sense, which, so far as the language used is concerned, is tropical or allegorical; but if this spiritual sense is to be grasped and expounded aright, it cannot be torn away from the natural sense, for it serves the natural sense. If it does not serve it, it is to be rejected; but if it does serve it, it cannot be rejected. The direct sense taken by itself may well be quite absurd, and therefore needs the spiritual sense even to be an acceptable direct sense. It is adherence to the direct or natural sense that prevents us from being "lords of the Scripture" and checks our use of allegorical interpretation, so that it does not become a violent instrument in our hands with which we make the scriptures say what we want them to say. When we do that, we convert divine authority into human authority.[89]

Erasmus points out that frequently the scriptures use words which have a natural meaning in the profane world or in ordinary life, but when they are applied to divine things their meaning necessarily undergoes a modification. It is that change from the ordinary natural sense *(germanus sensus)* that he has in mind when he speaks of the spiritual sense. To use these terms as if there were not that change or modification in their meaning would be quite abhorrent. It is the true sense of the scripture *(verus Scripturae sensus)* that we must seek to elucidate.[90] But biblical statements have a depth of meaning into which we must probe, and that is the purpose of the fourfold sense. Rightly taken, that does not bring confusion but reveals the fertility of the scripture, i.e., that it is always pointing out to us far more than can be expressed directly in human speech.[91] Holy Scripture has an inexhaustible depth of meaning.[92]

Erasmus is clearly more anxious than ever to point out the dangers of tropical exegesis, for it lends itself so easily to *violent* treatment. Even Jerome, he points out, was sometimes violent in his interpretation of the scriptures, forcing passages to bear a meaning that were not germane to them and were not properly indicated by them.[93] What we must try to disentangle is the metaphorical element in scriptural statements, for metaphor, he says, is the source of all allegorical and tropical meanings, and if we can discern how the allegorical moment arises necessarily out of the actual sense, we have a method in which to check and control allegorical interpretation.[94] It is for this reason that Erasmus likes the simplicity of the twofold sense *(geminus sensus)* which we treat in such a way that we allow the underlying reality *(alētheia)* to break through into manifestation *(dēlōsis)*.[95] Although he does not say so, that stands much nearer to the analogical understanding of biblical language advocated by Thomas.[96] He insists, however, on drawing a firm line at the anagogical sense, for at the point where our human speech in the Bible points up to what utterly transcends us, it breaks off, and it is impossible—indeed, irrational—to attempt to go farther.[97] We must keep to a *sobria mediocritas* in all determination of allegorical or typical meanings.[98] The art of allegorical interpretation is a gift of the Spirit called *prophecy,* but it must be kept in control.[99]

But there are the other tests and checks which we must apply. Everything must be made to point to Christ as the center and scope of the biblical revelation, and nothing can be derived from this or that passage by allegorical interpretation that in any way conflicts with the doctrines established from the whole body of the biblical teaching.[100] Every statement which we deduce by this means which conflicts with the dogmas of the faith must be rejected.[101]

Toward the end of the work Erasmus makes a distinction which once again recalls the teaching of Athanasius. In Christ there are three natures, he says, body and soul according to his human nature, and his divine nature.[102] When we understand the meaning of the Holy Scripture on that basis, we have to distinguish between a bodily sense and a spiritual sense and, over against them, the divine sense to which both the bodily and the spiritual senses of the scripture point. Although this is not the way in which Erasmus used to think, his point of view might be expounded by saying that what he was concerned to reject here was an Apollinarian exegesis of the scriptures, i.e., the elimination of the human mind in it which is assimilated to the divine Mind without vanishing into it. That may well be the element of truth for which Erasmus was constantly fighting in his championing of a Christian humanism in the interpretation of sacred letters. But if so, he should have gone further in his doctrine that God prattles to us in our human speech,[103] by saying that the human speech with which God's Word is clothed is so united to the divine Speech that it is, so to speak, the most powerful sacramental reality and force in the life of the church. That is to say, he might have gone on to relate the doctrine of the consubstantiality of the human nature of Christ in an applied form to the Word of God heard in the Holy Scripture, but that was precisely the explosive thing about Luther's doctrine of the Word which shook Erasmus and made him hesitate and draw back. He was not prepared for the full consequences that the Reformation doctrine of the Word contained.

But it must be said that Erasmus did not appreciate the problems in their real depth, for he failed entirely to see that the tropical exegesis which he advocated in deflecting the direct sense of the New Testament message could not but lead to a tropical theology of the acts of God in Christ—that is, to the menacing error which appeared in so many different forms in the early church and which Athanasius, whom Erasmus appreciated so much, had to contend with throughout his whole life, against Arians and semi-Arians, against Macedonians and Tropici. Now a form of this same error was raised again by Erasmus through a tropical exegesis that was detached from the dialectical control imposed on it by the Thomists. The ancient battles had to be fought all over again. That is why, when Calvin came upon the theological scene, he rigorously opposed all forms of allegorical and tropical exegesis and championed the *homoousion* in its application to the communication of divine Revelation and Grace.

How, then, are we to assess Erasmus' contribution to the development of biblical hermeneutics?

There can be no doubt that he did immense service in clearing the ground of the rank growth of gloss, invention, and sophism which derived from the mixture of mystical sense and irrelevant dialectics. He turned the eyes of Christendom back to the ancient scholars of the church and through them forced the church to look again at its historical origins. He uncovered the text of the New Testament and at the same time supplied the tools of exegesis, and he took at least the first major steps toward its elucidation. The importance of his annotations on the text of the Gospels, Acts, and the epistles can hardly be exaggerated; for centuries they continued to force scholars to face up to what the text actually said, and by comparing the views of the classical interpreters brought some real measure of objectivity into the judgment of the serious reader. In this work he opened up the avenues of historical criticism and reconstruction, at least so far as the establishing of the original text was concerned, and so called in question the habit of interpreting through adding layer on layer of ecclesiastical opinion to the biblical documents. His rigid adherence to the descriptive or narrative and paraphrastic method of elucidation helped considerably to enable the church to interpret the scriptures out of themselves, without forcing them into alien molds in order to make their meaning relevant to the ongoing life of the church and the world around it.

At the same time Erasmus realized the problems involved in translation, for all translation is inevitably involved in interpretation, if only because it is the meaning that has to be transferred and not the word connections or sentence connections from one language to another. Language thus constitutes an interpretative medium through which the material contents of documents are translated out of one historical or cultural context into another. This was brought home to Erasmus when his annotations on the New Testament were attacked by Edward Lee for being more than translations, and for involving *inventions.* Erasmus replied that, far from being inventions, they were extended forms of translation which brought out the real meaning and did not simply give a word-for-word or sentence-for-sentence translation as if there were no difference in the essential nature of the languages concerned. But there was a deeper problem here. How can translation be truly effected unless at the same time something of the essential culture in which the original language is embedded and has its basic meaning is also translated into the new context? It was one of Erasmus' greatest contributions to the modern world that he discerned this and set about his task of classical and biblical studies in such a way that he took account of it, i.e., in a resolute refusal to separate language from culture or to interpret written documents in abstraction from the civilizations out of which they were produced and in which their language had the original orientation which gave it meaning. It was false abstraction between language and culture, Erasmus held, together with the nominalist notions of grammar and syntax and "Scotist" terminism to which it gave rise that had led to the degeneration of culture and created a generation of "barbarians." Hence he bent all his energies to achieve a new synthesis between *bonae litterae* and Christian tradition in which he hoped that the great inheritance of the classical cultures could be recovered and combined in a purified form with evangelical truth to form the basis of a new civilization. The rejection and refutation of linguistic barbarianism became all the more important to Erasmus when, under the influence of Colet, he turned to devote himself especially to biblical studies. He realized that since the scriptures are records of the Speech of God to man, are therefore the communication of the Word of God in human form *(humano more),* they cannot be investigated and understood in abstraction from the human life and human understanding to which they are addressed. To become perspicuous in each generation, the divine scriptures must be allowed to create for themselves a human way of life which in turn will be the continuing medium through which their meaning is reflected in the understanding and life of men. Thus Erasmus combined human studies with spiritual understanding of the gospel and used every tool he could find in the classical cultures to enable him to carry that out. Precisely because he sought in the scriptures more than human documents, he insisted that a way of interpreting them must be found which would allow that other and twin sense to be brought to light. The tool universally used for that purpose in profane and Christian literature alike was some form of allegorical hermeneutic, and he set himself to shape that into an instrument that would suit his purpose; but he failed to see that it could only lead back into the same or at least similar entanglements from out of which he had done so much to extricate the scriptures.

Hence over against his great positive achievements we must set some fundamental failures. He failed to discern adequately the relation of biblical language to the acts of God in history, and therefore failed to penetrate very far beyond a merely literary activity in the interpretation of the scriptures. When it came to essential meaning, to doctrine, his understanding of history was superficial. Although he did discern, as few of his immediate contemporaries, the need for historical research and historical understanding, when it came to the actual point he turned aside from it through his assessment of history as having merely illustrative value. At the same time this oblique approach to history helped him to face the challenge of breaking through language to the realities it is intended to denote, and therefore of understanding language from its objective relation to the independently real as well as its subjective relation to the realities of the speaker and his spiritual and mental experiences. But behind this there was a deeper failure. He had very little sense of the conflict between the truth and the mind of the natural man. In some respects this is surprising, for he was constantly in conflict with others who objected to his devotion to "Hebrew and Greek truth" and who saw their way of life and thought menaced by his exposure of the errors in the received and authorized Latin text of the Bible. But he tended too easily to put that down to barbarity and ecclesiastical dogmatism or false dialectics, and he had too easy a view of the power of the truth once revealed to eliminate error. That is why Luther felt that Erasmus was so superficial—at heart Erasmus was a humanist not only in the literary sense but in the theological sense. He never had the struggles that Luther had in suffering the attack of the truth on his preconceptions, and the exposure by the truth of man's own profound enmity to it. This failure to see the epistemological relevance of the cross which was one of Luther's greatest insights into the gospel, to understand the profound meaning of repentance as the radical change of mind and heart that comes from reconciliation with Christ, meant that interpretation involved no struggle, no battle with the self, no facing up to the objection of the divine Truth to the interpreter as one whose innermost being distorts what he hears and understands. Hence it was comparatively easy for Erasmus to fuse together evangelical truth and profane classical culture into a new Christian philosophy. But this meant, and could not but mean, that he failed finally to interpret the scriptures objectively, out of the depth of their saving message, but interpreted them as he was able to build out of them a new way of life, or, as we might say today, a new ideology.

The fact is that Erasmus stopped short of serious interpretation of the scriptures out of their own objective depth. He only went halfway in letting them reshape his mind and fashion habits of thought with which to appreciate them—and so brought to them habits of thought and attitudes of mind that were alien to them. There can be no question about the fact that it was his passion for the oblique sense of the scripture and for allegorical exegesis that contributed to this immensely. Instead of letting the message of the scriptures call the traditional forms of thought and the habits of mind he brought with him into question, he interiorized them, stripped them of their crudities and intellectual rigidities, and spiritualized them so that they would serve a placid way of life. Thus he substituted for the casuistical ethic of the Middle Ages a new psychological ethic concerned with the development and adornment of the human personality. But it was ultimately Pelagian and served to deflect the full force of the biblical message, and so inhibited serious exegesis and theological penetration. The whole problem of preconception and presupposition had to be raised more openly and faced more courageously before the great contributions of Erasmus to biblical interpretation could be fully utilized. But as he stood, Erasmus was the great forerunner of liberal and romantic hermeneutics.

NOTES

1. See especially Erasmus, *Antibarbari (Opera Omnia* 10:1691–1744).
2. L. Valla, *Elegantiae Linguae Latinae,* 1471 (edited by Erasmus, *Opera Omnia* 1:1069ff.). Cf. Erasmus, *Opus Epistolarum* (ed. P. S. and H. M. Allen, and H. W. Garrod), 1.23, and *De ratione studii ac legendi interpretandique auctores* 4; and L. Valla, *In Latinam Novi Testamenti interpretationem ex collatione Graecorum exemplarium adnotationes* (published by Erasmus in 1505).
3. See the discussion of W. Schwarz, *Principles and Problems of Biblical Translation: Some Reformation Controversies and Their Background,* 1955, pp. 108ff., and J. H. Lupston, *A Life of Dean Colet,* ch. 5, pp. 59ff.
4. *Opera Omnia* 1:1026.
5. This is a theme that runs throughout the *Liber Antibarbarorum* (*Opera Omnia* 10).

6. See *Enchiridion militis Christiani,* prefatory epistle (CCCXXIX); and *Ratio seu methodus compendio perveniendi ad veram theologiam* (*Opera Omnia,* 1703, vol. 5), pp. 126f., 136.

7. *De ratione concionandi* I (*Opera Omnia* 5:771f.; and *Paraclesis, id est, Adhortatio ad Christianae philosophiae studium* (*Opera Omnia* 5:137–144).

8. See again the fine account of Schwarz, *Principles,* pp. 94f.

9. This is vividly clear throughout the *Enchiridion militis Christiani.*

10. See W. H. Woodward, ed., *Desiderius Erasmus, Concerning the Aim and Method of Education* (New York: Columbia University, Teachers College Press, 1964), pp. 35ff., 39ff.

11. In some respects Erasmus is the forerunner of Herder and Dilthey, especially in his view of the relation of language to the expression of the culture to which it belongs.

12. See the *Moriae Encomium Declamatio,* 1511 (cf. *Bibliotheca Erasmiana,* 122f.).

13. *Enchiridion* 13 (*Opera Omnia* 5:29).

14. *Enchiridion* 13, p. 27.

15. *Enchiridion* 3, p. 12, and 5, p. 16.

16. *Enchiridion* 4, pp. 11f., and 7, pp. 19f.

17. *De pronunciatione* (*Opera Omnia* 1:930); *De ratione concionandi* III (*Opera Omnia* 5:852, 958).

18. *Lingua, sive de linguae usu atque abusu* (*Opera Omnia* 4:657ff.).

19. *Lingua,* p. 691.

20. *Lingua,* p. 696. See also *De ratione concionandi* (*Opera Omnia* 5:771f.).

21. *Hieronymi Stridonensis Vita,* ed. by W. K. Ferguson, *Erasmi Opuscula, A Supplement to the Opera Omnia,* 1933, pp. 134–190.

22. *Hieronymi Stridonensis Vita,* pp. 178ff.

23. *Lingua,* p. 698.

24. *Lingua,* pp. 700ff.

25. Ps. 107:20; *De ratione concionandi* I (*Opera Omnia* 5:836).

26. *Lingua,* p. 748.

27. *Opera Omnia* 1:522–530. See Woodward, ed., *Desiderius Erasmus . . . Education,* pp. 162ff.

28. *De ratione studii,* p. 522.

29. Ibid.

30. *De ratione studii,* p. 523.

31. *De ratione studii,* p. 525. The immense importance of this for Erasmus' conception of literature is apparent from his own laborious collections of proverbs published in the different editions of his *Adagia,* of 1500 and after, to which the entire vol. III of the *Opera Omnia* is devoted.

32. Cf., for example, the discussion of the opening verses of the Acts of the Apostles, *Opera Omnia* 6:433.

33. *Erasmi Opuscula,* pp. 134ff. Cf. the remarks of Ferguson, pp. 129f.

34. Woodward, ed., *Desiderius Erasmus . . . Education,* p. 130. Cf. *De rerum copia* II (*Opera Omnia* 1:106), where Erasmus points out that historical writers are allowed to invent speeches, for nothing is more admirable for their purpose—but he doubts whether Christians may do this.

35. *De ratione concionandi* II, p. 853.

36. *De ratione studii,* p. 523. Hence he can even say: "Sunt qui Novi Testamenti historiam ad allegoriam trahunt: quod ego sane vehementer approbo" (*Ratio verae theologiae* V, p. 125).

37. *De ratione concionandi,* pp. 865, 1028f.

38. Woodward, *Desiderius Erasmus . . . Education,* pp. 49f.

39. *De ratione studii,* p. 527.

40. *Opera Omnia,* xxx I, pp. 447f.

41. *De ratione studii,* pp. 527f.

42. *Enchiridion militis Christiani* (*Opera Omnia* 5:6f.).

43. *Enchiridion,* prefatory epistle (CCCXXIX) (*Opera Omnia* 3:340f.).

44. *Enchiridion,* prefatory epistle, pp. 339f.

45. *Enchiridion,* prefatory epistle, p. 339.

46. *Enchiridion* II, p. 8.

47. *Enchiridion* II, p. 8. Cf. *Responsio ad notationes Eduardi Lei in Mattaeum* (*Opera Omnia* 4:140).

48. *Enchiridion,* p. 9.

49. *Enchiridion* 13, p. 29.

50. Ibid.

51. Ibid.

52. Ibid.

53. *Enchiridion,* p. 30.

54. *Enchiridion* 13, pp. 37f.

55. *Enchiridion* 13, pp. 31f.

56. *Enchiridion,* p. 32.

57. *Enchiridion,* pp. 38f.

58. *Apologia pro in Principio erat Sermo* (*Opera Omnia,* 9:117).

59. *Opera Omnia* 1:75–138.

60. *Ratio seu methodus,* p. 76.

61. *Ratio seu methodus,* p. 77: "Hic primus et unicus tibi est scopus, hoc votum, hoc unum age, ut muteris, ut rapiaris, ut affleris, ut transformeris in ea quae discis."

62. *Ratio seu methodus,* pp. 77–84.

63. *Ratio seu methodus,* pp. 84, 88.

64. *Ratio seu methodus,* p. 84.

65. *Ratio seu methodus,* pp. 85, 128.

66. *Ratio seu methodus,* pp. 86–88; *De ratione concionandi* IV, pp. 1075f.

67. *Novum Testamentum* i (*Opera Omnia* 6).

68. *Ratio seu methodus,* pp. 85, 89, 131.

69. *Ratio seu methodus,* pp. 91f.

70. *Apologia ad Jacobum Fabrum* (*Opera Omnia* 9:51).

71. *Ratio seu methodus,* pp. 85f.

72. See *De ambili ecclesias concordia* (*Opera omnia* 5:470: "Nec oportet historicum sensum reiicere, quo locus fiat allegoriae, quum ille sit huius basis et fundamentum, qui cognitus facit, ut aptius tractetur intelligentia retrustior ac mystica."

73. *Ratio seu methodus,* p. 126.

74. *Ratio seu methodus,* p. 124.

75. *Ratio seu methodus,* p. 119.

76. See also *De ratione concionandi* III, pp. 1058ff.

77. *Ratio seu methodus,* pp. 131ff.

78. *Ratio seu methodus,* pp. 134f.

79. *Opera Omnia* 5:770–1100.

80. *De ratione concionandi* I, pp. 772f.

81. *De ratione concionandi* I, pp. 796f.; II, p. 852; III, p. 958.

82. *De ratione concionandi* III, p. 1005.

83. *De ratione concionandi* III, pp. 953, 1019, 1026f., etc.; of the *Apologia,* xx2, to the *Novum Testamentum* (*Opera Omnia* 6).

84. *Contra morosos quosdam ac indoctos* (*Opera Omnia* 6, xx6).

85. *Tomus primus paraphraseum in Novum Testamentum,* 1523, p. a5.

86. *De ratione concionandi* II, p. 906.

87. *Ratio seu methodus,* pp. 127f.

88. *De ratione concionandi* III, pp. 1034f.

89. *De ratione concionandi* II, p. 906.

90. *De ratione concionandi* III, pp. 1019f.; 1028f., cf. *Lingua* IV, pp. 700f.

91. *De ratione concionandi* III, pp. 1020, 1026.

92. *De ratione concionandi* III, pp. 1026f.

93. *De ratione concionandi* III, pp. 1029, 1031. He points to Origen as a good example of an interpreter. "He did not derive his allegories from the philosophers, or from the Talmud or the Cabala, or out of the dreams of his own head, but out of the scriptures themselves, comparing passage with passage." *I. Origenes Libros censuriae* (*Opera Omnia* 8:440).

94. *De ratione concionandi* III, pp. 1033ff.

95. *De ratione concionandi* I, p. 796.

96. *De ratione concionandi* III, p. 1061, where Erasmus refers to Augustine's distinction between the *aetiological* and *analogical* treatment of scripture in the *De utilitate credendi,* 5–8.

97. *De ratione concionandi* III, pp. 1037f.

98. *De ratione concionandi* III, p. 1043.
99. *De ratione concionandi* I, p. 825.
100. *De ratione concionandi* III, pp. 1043ff., 1047f., 1056.
101. *De ratione concionandi* III, p. 1054.
102. *De ratione concionandi* III, p. 1057.
103. *De ratione concionandi* IV, pp. 1072f.

PART TWO

John Calvin

Calvin's Teaching on the *notae fidelium:* An Unnoticed Part of the *Institutio* 4.1.8

Wilhelm Neuser

Translated by Mark S. Burrows

Previous studies of Calvin's ecclesiology have neglected his discussion of the *notae fidelium.* In general, studies devoted to this topic begin with the famous discussion of the *notae ecclesiae* and skip over the short introductory section devoted to the *notae fidelium* (4.1.8). These characteristics are mentioned briefly but are not given any closer consideration. Indeed, earlier commentators on this section of the *Institutes* have argued that Calvin's discussion of the invisible church obviates any authentic characteristics; the "judgment of neighborly love" (i.e., *judicium charitatis* of 4.1.8) decisively curtails the value of such possible characteristics. For this reason the studies of Th. Werdemann,[1] P. Wernle,[2] P. Barth,[3] J. Bohatec,[4] W. Kolfhaus,[5] W. Niesel,[6] H. Quistorp,[7] W. Krusche,[8] and A. Ganoczy[9] do not pursue the matter any further. Yet, while Calvin on this point takes over in scarcely changed form the teaching of the *Confessio augustana* (Art. 7) on the *notae ecclesiae,* his thoughts on the marks of the true Christian are theologically original and significant in the historical development of piety. What is at stake here is the question, What are the visible signs of the elect? or, Who are the members of the true church?

His teaching on the *notae fidelium* (4.1.8) stands between sections devoted to the true and visible church (4.1.7), on the one hand, and to the *notae ecclesiae* (4.1.9ff.) on the other. Because these two sections—i.e., on the *notae fidelium* and the *notae ecclesiae*—have as their abiding concern the theme of the visible church, it appears appropriate to include 4.1.7 in this general discussion and, further, to analyze carefully Calvin's pattern of thought in this and the following section (4.1.8). In 4.1.7 we find a description of the true and visible church, which also names the characteristics to be found in members of the visible church. In 4.1.8 it is the visible marks which are the subject of Calvin's attention. In order to grasp Calvin's thoughts on this point in its context, this study will examine the passage piece by piece as it is found in the final text of 1559.

I. The Description of the True and Visible Church (4.1.7) [10]

> How we are to judge the church visible—which falls within our knowledge—is, I believe, already evident from the above discussion. For we have said that Holy Scripture speaks of the church in two ways.

Calvin here turns his attention to the matter of the visible church. Its relationship to the true church of Christ is the theme of the ensuing discussion. The emphasis he places on the recognizability of the visible church suggests the conclusion that the true church is not perceptible from a human vantage point. Yet Calvin himself does not draw this conclusion; quite the contrary. In developing section 4.1.8, he treats the characteristics of the faithful and builds on the premise that the true church and recognizable church are by no means opposites and so do not preclude one another. If, in fact, the true church were by no means recognizable, there could be no possible consideration of the *notae fidelium.*

1. *The True Church of Jesus Christ*

> For we have said that Holy Scripture speaks of the church in two ways. Sometimes by the term "church" it means that which is actually in God's presence, into which no persons are received but those who are children of God by grace of adoption and true members of Christ by sanctification of the Holy Spirit. Then, indeed, the church includes not only the saints presently living on earth, but all the elect from the beginning of the world. (4.1.7, *ad init.*)

The true church, then, is not completely invisible: in addition to adoption as children of God, Calvin mentioned the sanctification through thc Holy Spirit, which is visible to human eyes. The fact that the true church is expressly understood as the number of the elect, and thus consists of identifiable individuals, considerations of its recognizability are for Calvin fundamentally admissible. Calvin calls them, therefore, "the saints who live on earth" (4.1.7).

2. *The Visible Church*

> Often, however, scripture uses the term "church" to designate the whole multitude of persons spread over the earth who profess to worship one God and Christ. By baptism they are initiated into faith in him; by partaking in the Lord's Supper they attest their unity in true doctrine and love; in the Word of the Lord they have agreement, and for the preaching of the Word the ministry instituted by Christ is preserved. (Ibid.)

Calvin describes the visible church not as the creation of Christ and the recipient of Christ's gifts but as the body constituted according to the observable behavior of Christians. He names five such activities: the honoring of God and of Jesus Christ; being initiated into faith through baptism;[11] participation in the Supper as a meal of confessional and charitable character; unified understanding of the word of Christ; and the preservation of the preaching office. Apparently Calvin is here specifying those characteristics belonging to Christians in the church, and it is this enumeration which establishes the foundation for his discussion of the *notae fidelium* in the following section (4.1.8). The description of Christians in the visible church introduces this matter, such that in the ensuing discussion Calvin considers whether there exist any characteristics of the faithful which are at the same time marks of the true church. The objection to such a conclusion follows immediately:

> In this church are mingled many hypocrites who have nothing of Christ but the name and outward appearance. There are very many ambitious, greedy, envious persons, evil speakers, and some of quite unclean life. Such are tolerated for a time either because they cannot be convicted by a competent tribunal or because a vigorous discipline does not always flourish as it ought. (4.1.7)

There follows a description of the visible church as the *ecclesia permixta;* that is, among the members of the church are to be found hypocrites and immoral persons. The latter include four groups: the ambitious *(ambiosi),* greedy *(avari),* envious *(invidi),* and revilers or "evil speakers" *(maledici).* Otto Weber's translation of the last group as "blasphemers" is incorrect: those *blasphemi* who slander God are precisely those who are not intended; rather, Calvin insists in direct terms that the *maledici* are those who speak "against the brethren."[12] Luther translates this term as "slanderers" *(Afterredner).* For the evaluation of the immoral members of the church it is important to note that Paul mentions two groups in 1 Cor. 5:11: namely, the *avari* and *maledici,* mentioning in the same passage harlots, the greedy, idolaters, revilers, drunkards, and thieves. With such persons one should not have any table fellowship. Calvin discusses this particular biblical citation (1 Cor. 5:11) eight sections later (4.1.15) in his discussion of church discipline. "Paul establishes the principle when he declares that it is against the divine law *(nefas)* even to partake of bread with a person of offensive character."[13] The characteristics named in 4.1.7 are also to be placed, apparently, under the category of church discipline: such persons, as he here puts it, exemplify a "quite unclean life" *(impurior vita),* a characterization which he elsewhere calls an "offensive life-style" *(probrosa vita).* Calvin uses these terms interchangeably.[14]

The phrase he here uses, "because they cannot be convicted by a competent tribunal," refers to the matter of church discipline. In his commentary on 1 Cor. 5:11 Calvin explains the term *legitimo iudicio convinci;* in the *Institutes* we do not find it again. Calvin also rejects the translation of this passage as "if a brother is judged to be a lecher." It rather means, "No one is able to be restored by the church's judgment if that one's sins are not acknowledged."[15] This interpretation contradicts, he contends, the intention of Paul. The meaning should be: "If anyone is to be a brother among you but conducts himself in a shameful manner unbefitting to a Christian, hold no table fellowship with such a one."[16] According to Calvin, this is an occasion for church discipline. Yet he also adds to this the qualification that "Paul does not name any other offenses than those which are brought to public attention; the inner piety and that which is hidden is not to be judged by the congregation."[17] Yet when later in the section "The Purpose of Church Discipline" (4.12.5) Calvin cites 1 Cor. 5:11, he omits mentioning "thieves," because these do not belong to church discipline proper but to the civil jurisdiction.

As clear as it is that "the immoral" mentioned in 4.1.7 must be submitted to church discipline—a point which the context itself demonstrates—it is apparent that Calvin does not name the severe cases from 1 Cor. 5:11 but rather the lighter ones, viz., the ambitious, greedy, envious, and slanderers. These are the vices which can be subjected to public scrutiny and which are at the same time passions of the heart. He explains ambition in the *Institutes* (3.7.2) as "to hanker after human praise" and counts this among the *"hidden* pestilence."[18] Ambition, together with greed *(avaritia),* belongs to those vices which are referred to by the admonition to self-denial *(abnegatio sui).*[19] Ambition and greed are passions which lead to sin, in such a way that "the saints are as yet so bound by that disease of concupiscence that they cannot withstand being at times tickled and incited either to lust *(libido)* or to avarice *(avaritia)* or to ambition *(ambitio),* or to other vices *(vitia).*"[20] Envy *(invidia)* also belongs among the other vices.[21] It is thus clear that Calvin's reference to passions refers at the same time to those vices which Christians themselves are to resist through self-denial. Only in the case of public manifestation do these fall under the category of church discipline. Hence, the phrase "because they cannot be convicted by a competent tribunal" is clarified by Calvin's definition of vice in Book 3 of the *Institutes.*

In a positive sense, then, Calvin characterizes the visible church through five activities of church membership, while he sets forth this conception in a negative sense through describing the hypocrites and immoral persons. The latter, of which he delineates four examples, include those who struggle with their own passions as well as those who need the warning of authorities responsible for church discipline because their vices have become public. This discordance characterizes the visible church.

3. *The Visible and Invisible Church*

> Just as we must believe, therefore, that the former church, invisible to us, is visible to the eyes of God alone, so we are commanded to revere and keep communion with the latter, which is called "church" in respect to men.

It is incorrect to speak of Calvin, as is always the case in the literature, as having a doctrine of the visible and invisible church. The term *ecclesia invisibilis* appears in the *Institutes* only in this single passage. The title for 4.1.7 in Otto Weber's translated text [as in the English edition of Ford Lewis Battles] should read instead: *True and Visible Church.* We have earlier established that the true church of the elect is not completely invisible, a point which W. Krusche has rightly recognized in noting that "the church which to us is hidden, invisible and only recognizable to God's eyes is not another entity alongside that which we call 'church.' "[22] In Calvin's lecture on Deuteronomy 12:1 we find the distinction made between the "hidden," "true" church and the "outer" church,[23] a delineation which transcends the Augustinian visible/invisible dichotomy. The point to be made here is that the true church is to be sought in the "outer" rather than the "invisible" church. Hence, the title for 4.1.7 should read *True and Visible Church.*

The final sentence of this section (4.1.7) returns to the theme articulated at the outset: Calvin's interest focuses on the visible church. He is intent on explicating these characteristics, and for this reason he turns his attention next to the theme of the *notae fidelium.*

II. The Characteristics of the Faithful *(notae fidelium)*

Section 4.1.8 begins as follows: "Accordingly, the Lord by certain marks (*certae notae*) and tokens (*symbola*) has pointed out to us what we should know about the church." Calvin imbeds his teaching on the *notae fidelium* within the context of his treatment of the *notae ecclesiae,* such that the characteristics of the church stand as the final thrust of his discussion. He does not, however, wish to speak about the church without first speaking about individual Christians. The church is the congregation [Gemeinde], and the congregation is made up of individual Christians. At the same time, the church is more than the sum of its individual members; it is the mother of the believers. Nonetheless, Calvin does not pass over the question of the characteristics of these believers. Section 4.1.8, incorrectly entitled "The Limitation of Our Judgment" in Weber's [as in Battles'] translation, has but a single theme, even though it is articulated under the broad rubric of "characteristics of the church"; namely, "the characteristics of the believers."

1. *The Unrecognizability of True Christians*

Calvin continues in this passage:

> To know who are His is a prerogative belonging solely to God. Steps were indeed thus taken to restrain men's undue rashness; and daily events themselves remind us how far his judgments surpass our comprehension. For those who seemed utterly lost and quite beyond hope are by his goodness called back to the way; while those who more than others seemed to stand firm often fall. Therefore, according to God's secret predestination (as Augustine says), "many sheep are without, and many wolves are within" [*Sermons on John's Gospel* 45]. For he knows and has marked those who know neither him nor themselves. Of those who openly wear his badge, his eyes alone see the ones who are unfeignedly holy and will persevere to the very end—the ultimate point of salvation.

It is clear enough that those persons are true Christians who are elected through God's predestination. Calvin unmistakably underscores the point about the hiddenness of the elect through his comment on predestination and reference to Augustine. But is the "true" church to be defined as the "invisible" church? Calvin does not draw this conclusion, even though it appears to be a logical if not inevitable one. Calvin himself only derives from the theme of the hiddenness of predestination the conclusion that God alone recognizes the elect. This conclusion does not, however, contradict the assertion that God furnishes other Christians with characteristics *(notae)*, marks *(symbola)*, and visible signs *(signatos habere, palam signum ferre)* which stand in contrast to those who are of the elect. First, God reminds those despisers of the faith "daily through events" which occur in a public manner that they do penance, while ardent Christians fall into serious sins. Second, there are those persons who "know neither [God] nor themselves"; on such God places an invisible mark, one which remains hidden since these do not yet believe and cannot be recognized by others as elect. God's mark is in this sense invisible; only in the next sentence does Calvin come to speak of a "public" sign (or "badge"). These elect, however, do not remain unrecognizable in a permanent manner: at some point in the future their faith comes to the fore, such that they "know God and themselves." The true Christians (and the true congregation) cannot remain in any lasting way invisible; the invisible church is *at present still* the invisible church. Third, there are those who "openly wear [God's] badge." Once again it becomes evident that election and faith for Calvin remain inseparable, so that God's hidden election and the mark of faith are intertwined with one another. Calvin does not, of course, wish to say that election and the *notae fidelium* stand in an unwavering correlation, since he admits that there are also those bearing God's public "badge" who are hypocrites. But he does insist that election and the "life of faith" are indissoluble. Occasionally in the *Institutes* Calvin mentions such signs of election. For example, in the chapter on predestination (3.21) he concludes:

> Now among the elect we regard the call as a testimony *(testimonium)* of election. Then we hold justification another sign *(symbolum)* of its manifestation, until they come into the glory in which the fulfillment of that election lies.[24]

Again, in the *Institutes* 4.2.4 Calvin teaches: "For this [i.e., the hearing of the word of God] is the abiding mark *(nota perpetua)* with which our Lord has sealed *(signavit)* his own."[25] The hearing and taking to heart which accompanies this proclamation, progress in justification, and the salvation of life are all "signs" of election.

We must here also take account of Calvin's explication of 2 Thess. 2:13, which reads, "Brethren chosen by God, because

God chose you from the beginning to be saved through sanctification by the Spirit and belief in the truth." Calvin interprets this passage as follows:

> But because it is not our affair to meddle into the secret decisions of God, in order that we might find certainty of our salvation, God has established signs or characteristics of election *(signa vel tessera electionis),* and these must suffice in giving us trust in God's election. . . . Paul intends nothing other than this, identifying for us more specific signs *(propriora signa)* of election; these signs unveil for us what remains in itself an unrecognizable election, and stand in an indivisible relation *(individuo nexu)* with it. Therefore, in order that we might know that we are elected by God we should not examine what God has done before the beginning of the world, but rather we should search within us for a true verification *(legitima probatio)* whether God has saved us through his Spirit and whether he has enlightened us in faith in his gospel.[26]

Here, too, Calvin manifests first of all his reticence: we must be content with these signs, since we ultimately have nothing other than these signs. There is no [human] knowledge per se regarding election. But he also underscores here with more emphasis than in the *Institutes* that these signs stand in an indivisible relation to election. This introspective knowledge does not mean, however, that the signs are not discernible in an external manner; holiness of life and belief in the truth are true forms by which election finds verification.

2. *The Recognizability of True Christians*

When Calvin mentions the members of the congregation who bear the sign of Christ, it is clear that he is speaking of Christians in the visible church. It is these persons whom he described with such detail in 4.1.7, on the basis of the activity of their faith and their susceptibility to hypocrisy. Description and evaluation of these characteristics follow one another, as we have already pointed out. Indeed, Calvin directs his attention in the following section to this question. "But on the other hand, because [God] foresaw it to be of some value for us to know who were to be counted as his children, he has in this regard accommodated himself to our capacity" (4.1.8). The phrase "of some value" or "to some extent" *(aliquatenus)* qualifies the quality of our knowledge of who the children of God are; that is, this qualification arises from the singular nature by which God recognizes the elect. Nonetheless, Calvin's intent is to identify a human knowledge or perception of those belonging among the truly faithful. This knowledge is expedient.

The restriction implied through this phrase *aliquatenus* stands over against the declaration that the *notae fidelium* are established through God's providence *(Deus providebat)*. These *notae fidelium,* Calvin notes, are grounded in God's will. God's hidden decision regarding predestination determines those who are elected to eternal life and those who are rejected; indeed, God's providence establishes that the election will become visible through a particular behavior manifested by the elect in the congregation. These "signs" originate with God.

Calvin makes it quite clear at the same time that this insight into the divine will derives from an encounter with God, who alone allows this to be known. God's decision is even now hidden from the church, though God has "accommodated himself," through providence, "to our capacity." This term "accommodate" *(accommodare)* occurs with frequency in Calvin's writing.[27] In the opening sentences of Book 4 of the *Institutes* he writes that it is God who has engaged the external means of salvation *(externa subsidia)*—viz., preaching of the gospel, the office of the pastor and teacher, and the sacraments. With these means of salvation, "God has accommodated himself to our capacity, and has directed us through his wonderful providence [!] how it is that we should approach him."[28] It also belongs to God's concession toward us that he has granted to us the *notae fidelium,* and thereby meets us in our own capacity. The phrase "in terms of our capacity" implies no restriction. "Accommodating language and the truth to which it points are really a unity."[29] The *accommodatio* is an expression of God's compliance; Calvin often joins this notion with the idea of God's condescension.[30]

The words "to be of some value . . . to know" contain a reservation and at the same time a concession in relation to the *notae fidelium.* Calvin specifies both of these in what follows: "And, since assurance of faith was not necessary, [God] substituted for it a certain charitable judgment whereby we recognize as members of the church those who, by confession of faith, by example of life, and by partaking of the sacraments, profess the same God and Christ with us." The "assurance of faith" is for Calvin the highest aspect of faith (here see 3.2.15–41), something which God grants only to the elect.[31] In point of fact, a reference to this "assurance of faith" is "not necessary," and this for the simple reason that such an ultimate assurance is not ascertainable—with the exception of those martyrs for the faith. Assurance of faith is no sign. Clearly there is hidden in this claim a renewed proviso concerning both the ability and the desirability of making any pronouncement on election. Yet despite this, Calvin articulates signs by which people might be recognized as belonging to the *true* church, by which he does not mean membership in the external church. This assertion thus raises many questions: What are these characteristics? How is it possible to name characteristics of the faithful if all inferences to the divine decisions regarding election are ruled out? Calvin's answer to these questions is startling in two respects. First, he names as one measure the *judicium charitatis;* and, second, he draws on the characteristic of the *visible* church as elaborated in 4.1.7. Since it is in this section that we find Calvin's full answer to the question of the *notae fidelium,* we must pause to consider it more carefully.

When Calvin finally mentions the *notae fidelium,* we should not be completely surprised. As earlier mentioned, Calvin has already described those persons who bear in a public fashion the sign of Christ; i.e., the hearing of the word of God, the calling, justification, and sanctification are, following Calvin's pronouncement in the *Institutes,* these signs. Even here he does not mention any other signs, though his remarks are more concrete. "Professing the same God and Christ with us" through the confession of faith, example of life, and participation in the sacraments stands apparently as the bridge to his description, in the preceding section, of which members ultimately constitute the visible church. Here, as there, it is the relation to the church which is presupposed, such that the Christian is such through participating in the congregation. The concurrence with other Christians receives emphasis in both cases.

But there are also distinctive differences to be noted. It is true that the premise in both cases identifies the place which "confession" plays in this matter. But the true characteristic [Wesenszug] of Christians lies solely in the worship of God and Christ, while the mark [Kennzeichen] includes the confessional acknowledgment of God and Christ. In other words, the distinguishing features of true Christians are more inclusive and point toward a believing confession (i.e., "with us"); the description of church membership places the beginning of Christian identity in the foreground, whereas the marks identify the breadth of Christian life. This latter finds expression through "the worship of God and Christ," the initiation in the faith through baptism, the Lord's Supper as the meal of fellowship (rather than as a granting of fellowship with Christ), the emphasis of the presence of the preaching office, and the emphasis on hypocrites in the church. The confession of faith (which means for Calvin a confession before baptism and the Lord's Supper), an exemplary life, and a full participation in the sacraments only set forth Christian activities, since these marks must be made visible and perceptible. All of these are to lead toward the concrete manifestation of the faith.

Does the *judicium charitatis* thus represent a diminution of these characteristics of the faithful and their role within the true church? The principle that God alone knows the identity of the elect remains intact as a qualifying clause of his argument. But this assertion is for Christians immaterial, since these are oriented toward the "judgment of neighborly love." It is this which obligates them to recognize those as believers and members of the true church who bear the signs of the faithful. And here we must once again recall that Calvin introduced in the immediately preceding sentence divine providence as the validating characteristic. Furthermore, it should be noted that love of neighbor is not to be identified either with the love which understands all or that which drapes the mantle of forgetfulness over all that is wrong. On the contrary, these signs are conditions which are difficult to fulfill, such that only mature Christians are among those who carry this sign. The judgment of neighborly love has no relation to the weakness of the faith or to the minimal progress in sanctification. Nor is there any ultimate measuring tool for the "example of life." Nonetheless, Calvin abandoned in later versions of the *Institutes* the continuation of this discussion regarding the *notae fidelium* as expounded in the 1536 edition. There he had argued as follows:

> Even if there remains an incompletion in a person's morals (just as we can find no one who is fully perfect in this life), that person should not be pleased or take delight in these vices, and one should rather expect from him something good. In the future such persons, guided by God, should progress to a better state to the point that all imperfection is put aside and they attain to the eternal blessedness of the elect.[32]

Calvin apparently later came to disapprove of this strong emphasis on the imperfection of the faithful. Indeed, he excised this passage from later editions of the *Institutes.* This suggests how decisive he intends his later discussion of the *notae fidelium* to be. The theme of *judicium charitatis,* which he had taken from Augustine and which is also to be found in Luther's writings,[33] is for him no act of mercy but rather a measured judgment about the eternal welfare of Christians reached on the basis of his view of neighborly love.

In light of the relative paucity of source material on this question, it is worthwhile and instructive to draw on Calvin's exegetical handling of Phil. 4:3. In this context Calvin raises the question whether Paul has not appropriated the theme of God's kingdom in proclaiming the secret will of God, in that he mentions with regard to Clement and others that their names stand "in the book of life." In answering this question, he notes:

> We can only judge according to the signs *(signa)* through which God announces his elections, though we can only make this judgment in accord with our capacity. In this sense we acknowledge that certain persons radiate the characteristics *(notae)* of offspring, and these we reckon for the time being [einstweilen] as children of God until that book will be opened which reveals all things. Until then it is a matter belonging to God alone, who recognizes his own and finally separates the sheep from the goats. Nonetheless, it is our responsibility to hold all those persons as sheep who in obedience subject themselves to the shepherd Christ, and who attach themselves to his flock and remain continually in it. Our duty is to value the gifts of the Holy Spirit which God distributes to his elect so highly that they appear to us as seals of the hidden election.[34]

The phrase "for the time being" [einstweilen] appears to restrict the meaning of *judicium charitatis.* But over against this qualification Calvin sets his discussion of the Holy Spirit's rich gifts in the elect, gifts which must be visible even in the outward life of the faithful. Calvin's exegesis here corresponds to that of the *Institutes,* though there the three instances of the *notae fidelium* are less concrete because they emerge in the language of metaphor.

3. *The "Plainer Marks"*

Section 4.1.8 of the *Institutes* closes with this affirmation: "[God] has, moreover, set off by plainer marks the knowledge of his very body [i.e., the church] to us, knowing how this is a greater necessity for our salvation." Calvin here makes a transition in 4.1.9 to speak of the marks of the church. The reason why he accords to this theme "a greater necessity for our salvation" can be determined only from the ensuing discussion. The *notae ecclesiae* concern the means through which God effects salvation. The *notae fidelium* reflect, similarly, the product of this effect; viz., faith and works, which always remain behind this hidden purpose. Faith lives on the basis of God's gifts and not from one's self-perception, although Calvin insists on emphasizing progress in faith. When he underscores, in 4.1.9, the "different basis for judgment" which exists between "individuals and churches," he goes on to conclude that with regard to the means of salvation "it is certain that such things are not without fruit." He does not intend to say this in terms of the individual person; in this sense, these means of salvation are "more certain characteristics" *(certiores notae).* With this clarification Calvin clarifies the final thrust of his discussion: The *notae fidelium* are *certain* characteristics by which the members of the true church might be recognized.

III. Conclusion

1. *The Result*

The most penetrating consideration of the theme we have here considered is that of W. Krusche, whose analysis of this topic in his study entitled *The Church as the Community of the Holy Gathered Through Word and Spirit* has the advantage of using a rich spectrum of source materials. Krusche devotes a section of this work to the theme of "church and election";[35] in this discussion he reaches noteworthy conclusions, such as the suggestion that Calvin's teaching on ecclesiology posits not two but a single model of the church:[36] "The invisible church is thus both manifest *in* the visible church and hidden *within her.*"[37] Nonetheless Krusche denies himself, through his use of the concept "invisible church" which Calvin only utilizes a single time in the *Institutes,* any access to the critical theme of the *notae fidelium.* "Because the Holy Spirit works in secret," he concludes, "there can be no marks by which we might recognize with certainty who belongs to the invisible church, the so-called *turba electorum.* It is for the Lord, and not for us, to recognize his own."[38] This claim, as we now see, works from premises foreign to Calvin's thought, above all the assertions "works in secret" and the theme which is a consequence of this, "not for us." The Holy Spirit works also in a perceptible manner—it is the recognition of this which is the difficulty—and gives us the *certae notae fidelium.* Krusche goes on to place the judgment of love regarding the members of the church over against the judgment of faith regarding the true church; the former, and not the latter, represents for him an "unmistakable, certain" judgment.[39] Calvin, however, argues in a way which avoids this alternative: he goes further to perceive in the *notae fidelium* an instance of God's providence, a useful knowledge for Christians to have, an accommodation of God *(accommodare)* to our limited capacities, a "sign" of the Spirit's work with which we are obliged to reckon.

As a consequence of his approach Krusche cannot incorporate any individual instances of judgment within Calvin's ecclesiology. This also brings him to argue, in opposition to P. Barth and W. Niesel, that Calvin describes the visible church also *from the human perspective* (4.1.7!), and that Calvin's logic moves from the *notae* of the visible church to the *true* (invisible) church on the basis of his conviction that "the preached word never remains without fruit."[40] On the basis of such observations, Krusche might easily have realized the connection to Calvin's teaching on the *notae fidelium,* but he ultimately fails to do so.

Without doubt Calvin treats the *notae fidelium* in 4.1.8 with reservation. In this regard he wishes to avoid suggesting that the God who stoops down to humanity in condescension might thereby lose his majesty, or that faith might be identified with "sight," or that the body of Christ is simply identified with the visible church. To put this another way: Calvin holds to his claim that while God "begins [sanctification] in his elect," justification "occurs not piecemeal, but in such a way that the faithful are immediately clothed with Christ's purity and appear with free hearts in heaven."[41] At the same time, however, Calvin emphasizes the point that salvation *is* begun and must become visible. His mediating position between both extremes defies a short explanation, though we might conclude that he is here intent on articulating an eschatological tension between the "already" and the "not yet."

The terse language of 4.1.8 is not easily comprehensible. Yet there is no question that Calvin wishes to treat the *notae fidelium* or *electorum* before he turns to discuss the *notae ecclesiae.* In 4.1.7 he prepares us for this teaching, while in 4.1.8 he sets it forth. Any reader tempted to skip over this section (i.e., 4.1.8) will neglect his instruction regarding a cluster of related themes, including: the progress in faith and in sanctification, the work and efficacy of the Holy Spirit, the righteousness of both faith and works, and the *syllogismus practicus.* And, as a result of such neglect, Calvin's role as a theologian of sanctification will receive insufficient attention.

2. *The History of Influence* [Wirkungsgeschichte]

The influence of this facet of Calvin's theology has not yet been explored in the scholarship. We can say in a preliminary way, however, that it is certain that Calvin did not himself teach—nor did he wish to teach—a pietistic *ordo salutis.*[42] Yet his teaching on the *notae fidelium* was apparently taken up by the *Confessio belgica.* In Article 29 of that confession, entitled

"On the Marks of the True Church," we find following a treatment of the marks of the church the following argument:

> With respect to those who are members of the church, they may be known by the marks of Christians, namely, by faith; and when they have received Jesus Christ the only Savior, they avoid sin, follow after righteousness, love the true God and their neighbor, neither turn aside to the right or left, and crucify the flesh with the works thereof. But this is not to be understood as if there did not remain in them great infirmities; but they fight against them through the Spirit all the days of their life.[43]

The meaning of these marks as explicated in this later confession, however, has shifted when viewed alongside Calvin's earlier treatment. For Calvin, as we have pointed out, these marks are the outer, visible signs of the Christian life, while this later creed applies them in a pastoral vein. In other words, this later document considers these marks as representing faith as a whole, rather than functioning as the outward manifestation of faith as Calvin interpreted them. Faith as here described is not finally to be visible, but it should be decisive, deeply rooted, and powerful; with Calvin, on the other hand, these marks represent the characteristics of the Christian within that church which uses the means of salvation, and they hence serve for other Christians as a visible example for Christian living.

NOTES

1. Th. Werdemann, *Calvins Lehre von der Kirche in ihrer geschichtlichen Entwicklung* (1909), pp. 262, 268ff.

2. P. Wernle, *Der evangelische Glaube nach den Hauptschriften der Reformatoren,* vol. 3, *Calvin* (1919), p. 360.

3. P. Barth, "Calvins Verständnis der Kirche," *Zwischen den Zeiten* 8 (1930), 230. See also his "Wesen und Gestalt der Kirche nach Calvin," *Evangelische Theologie* 3 (1936), 318ff., 326ff.

4. J. Bohatec, *Calvins Lehre von Staat und Kirche mit besonderer Berücksichtigung des Organismusgedankens* (1937), pp. 286ff.

5. W. Kolfhaus, *Christusgemeinschaft bei Calvin* (Neukirchen, 1939), pp. 86ff.

6. W. Niesel, *Die Theologie Calvins* (Munich, 1939), pp. 182ff. (E.T., *The Theology of Calvin* [Philadelphia: Westminster Press, 1956].)

7. H. Quistorp, "Sichtbare und unsichtbare Kirche bei Calvin," *Evangelische Theologie* 9 (1949/50), 95.

8. W. Krusche, *Das Wirken des Heiligen Geistes nach Calvin* (Göttingen, 1957), pp. 312ff.

9. A. Ganoczy, *Ecclesia ministrans. Dienende Kirche und kirchlicher Dienst bei Calvin* (Freiburg/Basel/Vienna, 1968), pp. 143, 148ff.

10. In most cases we follow Otto Weber's translation of Calvin's *Institutes:* Johann Calvin, *Unterricht in der christlichen Religion,* 3 vols. (Neukirchen, 1938). [*Translator's note:* Whenever possible I have used Ford Lewis Battles' translation of the *Institutes of the Christian Religion,* 2 vols. (Philadelphia: Westminster Press, 1960). I have amended this translation to follow Weber's only where Neuser's argument depends upon a particular German formulation.]

11. See the French text: "a la baptesme pour tesmoignage de sa Foy," *OS* 5:12.34.

12. *Commentary on James* 3.10, *CO* 55:411.

13. *OS* 4:18.36–37.

14. This phrase does not recur in the *Institutes.* In the *Commentary on 1 Cor.* 5.11, *flatigiosae vitae; CO* 49:385.

15. *CO* 49:385.

16. Ibid.

17. Ibid.

18. *OS* 5:152.13–15 *(secretiores pestes).*

19. *Inst.* 3.7.2 (*OS* 4:152.24) and elsewhere.

20. *Inst.* 3.3.10, *OS* 4:65.20–23.

21. This is mentioned in another sense again in *Inst.* 4.20.16, *OS* 5.489.2.

22. Krusche, *Das Wirken,* p. 313.

23. Text: *CO* 41:289. Cf. Krusche, *Das Wirken,* p. 312 n. 1080.

24. *OS* 4:379.3–6.

25. *OS* 5:35.18–20.

26. *CO* 52:205. Cf. Krusche, *Das Wirken,* p. 253.

27. Cf. Battles, "God Was Accommodating Himself to Human Capacity," *Interpretation* 31 (1977), 19–38.

28. *Inst.* 4.1.1, *OS* 5.1.22–24.

29. Battles, "God Was Accommodating," p. 37.

30. E. A. Dowey, Jr., "The Structure of Calvin's Thought as Influenced by the Twofold Knowledge of God," in *Calvinus Ecclesiae Genevensis Custos,* ed. W. H. Neuser (Frankfurt: Peter Lang, 1984), pp. 139ff.

31. W. H. Neuser, "Theologie des Wortes—Schrift, Verheissung, Evangelium bei Calvin," in *Calvinus Theologus,* ed. W. H. Neuser (Neukirchen: Neukirchener Verlag, 1976), pp. 28ff.

32. *OS* 1:89.

33. *WA* 2:456.

34. *CO* 52:59.

35. "Die Kirche als durch Wort und Geist versammelte Gemeinschaft der Heiligen," Krusche, *Das Wirken,* pp. 311–316.

36. See n. 22.

37. Krusche, *Das Wirken,* p. 313; our emphasis.

38. Ibid., p. 314.

39. Ibid.

40. Ibid., pp. 315ff.

41. *Inst.* 3.11.11, *OS* 4:193.33ff., 36ff.

42. Cf. C. Graafland, "Hat Calvin einen Ordo salutis gelehrt?" in *Calvinus Ecclesiae Genevensis Custos,* ed. Neuser (1984), pp. 221–244.

43. W. Niesel, *Bekenntnisschriften und Kirchenordnungen der nach Gottes Wort reformierten Kirche* (Zollikon-Zurich, 1938), pp. 131, 23ff. [*Translator's note:* The translation of the Belgic Confession is from *The Creeds of Christendom,* ed. Philip Schaff, vol. 3: *The Evangelical Protestant Creeds* (Grand Rapids: Baker Book House, 1985), p. 420.]

Observations on Calvin's Trinitarian Doctrine of Grace

Alexandre Ganoczy

Translated by Keith Crim

An investigation of the passages in the *Institutes* in which Calvin discusses the grace of God[1] indicates that to a surprising and significant extent these discussions are found in a Trinitarian context. I do not use the word "Trinitarian" here in the sense of speculation about the inner nature of the secrets of God's being, as, for example, Augustine and Richard of St.-Victor used it. Rather, this adjective is used to indicate simply the explicit or implicit mention of the Father, the Son, and the Holy Spirit with the intention of showing that the reality of grace and the efficacy of grace are the common work of the Trinity.[2]

I would even go so far as to say that to a certain degree the mystery of the activity of the triune God constitutes the comprehensive systematic framework of what Calvin says about God's will for salvation, and especially of the unfolding of this will in history. Thus we may assume that the eternal community of the three persons with one another is the condition for the possibility of, and the creative support for, all the human community in Christ which constitutes the essence of the relationship of grace.

If we understand "grace," as the concept is found in the Old Testament, in terms of the benevolent basic attitude of the Creator toward humankind, or as the Creator's "being present for humankind,"[3] and if we understand the redeeming and consummating Creator as Trinitarian, in the sense of the New Testament revelation, it becomes clear why for Calvin the Trinity was the basis for all grace, and grace was the source of all other means for God's saving acts: justification, church, sacrament, social service *(diakonia).* Or, to put it in other words, just as the "Trinity" encompasses "grace," so "grace" encompasses all other relationships between God and humankind.

This concentric view of the matter seems to me to supply the explanation as to why Calvin understood the relationship between the doctrine of justification and the doctrine of grace in a manner different from that of Luther. For Calvin the justification of sinners was not the all-dominant theological theme, so that grace would be assigned the role of merely one aspect or one function. Quite the contrary. For Calvin the theme of grace in its Trinitarian definition was the point at which any talk about the justification of sinners first becomes meaningful. To be sure, he agrees in part with Luther, his great forerunner, and more than just verbally, when he states that justification is the "main hinge on which religion turns."[4] Nonetheless, Calvin has already written ten chapters about God's grace and its implications before he comes to this statement, and he devotes only four chapters explicitly to justification among the twenty-four chapters of Book 3 on the grace of God.

For me that is more than a statistical observation. It permits us to interpret the material as follows: The decisive factor is the theocentric view of the triune God, who is love. No concern with human sinfulness should be permitted to obscure this. But because the triune God is love, he bestows grace on human beings, and where this grace is bestowed (grace that is more than a judicial pardon or reprieve!), God also justifies sinners, in that they can become holy, pray aright, receive Word and sacraments in a worthy manner, and be useful members of the church and of society. Those who live thus in the grace of God also act with that socially effective love which can come alone from the gracious God. Beginning in the Trinitarian community of the Godhead, the Calvinist doctrine of grace results in the establishment of community and in usefulness for the community. In this way it escapes a one-sided concentration on sin found in individualistic views of salvation that are hardly worthy of the name of Christian.

All this sounds theoretical, almost hypothetical, like much that systematic theologians write. Still I believe that I can verify what I am saying by the texts themselves.

I

Calvin speaks of the grace of God[5] as the "grace of Christ"[6] or, even more significantly, as the "grace of the Holy Spirit."[7] The latter formula takes on its whole dogmatic significance when we remember that Book 3 begins in an unmistakably pneumatological manner. To be sure, we receive through

God's grace the "communion with Christ which is offered through the gospel,"[8] but this does not take place without "the secret energy of the Spirit," thanks to which "we come to enjoy Christ and all his benefits."[9] Following on this statement, Calvin, in good Pauline and Johannine manner, develops a direct correlation of "Christ–Holy Spirit," by which, however, in a manner significant for this methodological procedure, he approaches the relationship of grace more from the pneumatological than from the Christological pole. "The Holy Spirit is the bond *(vinculum)* by which Christ effectually unites us to himself."[10] Moreover, "Christ came endowed with the Holy Spirit in a special way,"[11] just as he, as the completion of his incarnation, was resurrected by the power of the Holy Spirit.[12] This soteriological and Christological uniting function of the Spirit of God also has a direct Trinitarian counterpart: The "eternal word of God is joined in the same Spirit with the Father."[13] Correspondingly, it holds that without the power of the Holy Spirit, Christ "would have come to us in vain" *(frustra),*[14] and we must receive him, unless we wish that Christ's coming for us be "unprofitable" *(otiosum)*.[15] Christ "unites himself to us by the Spirit alone" *(solo spiritu),*[16] which is for me a typically Calvinist echo of the Lutheran formula of exclusivity, *"solo Christo," "sola gratia," "sola scriptura."*

The correlation, however, would not be biblically "symmetrical" if it were not balanced by a clearly Christocentric aspect. Calvin goes on to say that "the gifts of the Spirit" "have been laid up" with Christ, and that Christ will "bestow" them "upon his people."[17] He has also not only promised his disciples the "Spirit of truth" (John 14:17) but "as the proper office of the Spirit, he assigned the task of bringing to mind what he had taught by mouth."[18] Finally, at the consummation the kingdom of Christ will be characterized by "a richer outpouring of the Spirit."[19]

Just as Calvin avoided any hint of subordinationism and unwaveringly held fast to the unity of being of the three persons in the Godhead, it follows that he ascribes the same titles and functions to Christ and to the Holy Spirit. Thus, for example, in almost the same breath he calls the Holy Spirit "the inner teacher" *(internus doctor),*[20] and the exalted Christ, "the inner Schoolmaster" *(interior magister).*[21] On the basis of 1 Cor. 6:11 he ascribes the work of cleansing and justification to both.[22] In this way the two ambassadors whom the Father has sent reveal their deep sharing of common functions while still distinguished as persons. The *one* work of God's grace results from the convergence in operation and the complementary nature of the sending of the Son and the Holy Spirit. To be sure, in this both maintain their distinctiveness, without confusion, without change. Only the Son became incarnate, the one crucified, risen, and sitting at the right side of the Father. As such he imparts himself from the "heights" of heaven (we know how Calvin conceived of Jesus' ascension and exaltation in a quasi-spatial sense) through the Holy Spirit, who moves within us, and who unceasingly testifies to Christ, and who is the guarantor of his work. Similarly, the Holy Spirit is manifest as the spirit of the exalted Christ in a nearness that can be conceived of in a temporal and spatial sense with a fitting immediacy. This seems to me to explain well why Calvin unites so closely the grace of God; that is, God's concrete offer of the power of salvation to each person, and his pneumatology.

II

The community that exists between the Father, who imparts his grace, and a grace-filled community, is now an eternal community in *agapē,* which constitutes its essence. Those who have received grace were incorporated into this community. Here too Calvin places the Holy Spirit in the foreground. He quotes the well-known apostolic blessing in 2 Cor. 13:13 and comments as follows: Paul "asks 'the grace of . . . Christ and the love of God' for believers, at the same time coupling with it 'participation in the . . . Spirit,' without which no one can taste either the fatherly favor of God *(paternum Dei favorem)* or the beneficence *(beneficentiam)* of Christ."[23] This does not mean that the Spirit functions as the one who enables us to taste the benefits of Christ; that is, in a quasi-instrumental manner. Rather, the third person of the Trinity brings the being of God into the heart of the human person. Where God's grace is made manifiest, there *agapē*—that which God is and not merely what God has—comes into the depth of the human reality. This is shown by Rom. 5:5, a favorite passage of Augustine's, and one that Calvin liked to cite in this context: "The love *(charitas)* of God has been poured into our hearts through the Holy Spirit, who has been given to us."[24] To be sure, "The Spirit is sometimes called the 'Spirit of the Father,' sometimes the 'Spirit of the Son.' "[25] But these genitive constructions are not to be understood in the sense of an instrumental, possessive concept. The Holy Spirit is not described thus because of being simply a divine power, but because the Spirit is the personal "minister" of all complete relationships of grace: "God the Father gives us the Holy Spirit for his Son's sake, and yet has bestowed the whole fullness of the Spirit upon the Son to be the minister and steward of his liberality *(ut suae liberalitatis minister esset ac dispensator).* For this reason, the Spirit is sometimes called the 'Spirit of the Father,' sometimes the 'Spirit of the Son.' "[26]

The Spirit of God is by no means revealed as a "bundle of energy" that emanates from God and Christ, but rather as a being that "dwells" in those who believe (Rom. 8:11). Thus there are actually three givers where the grace of God is bestowed on human beings (according to the motto *"opera ad extra communia"*) and none of them is subject to another. "For there is nothing absurd in ascribing to the Father praise for those gifts of which he is the Author, and yet in ascribing the same powers to Christ, with whom were laid up the gifts of the Spirit to bestow upon his people."[27] The one and the same grace of God, together with the gifts that are the concrete expression of that grace, come equally from all three who bestow them upon us.

The entire bestowing of gifts receives from the third person of the Trinity its confirmation and completion. Calvin gave an exegesis of 1 John 5:6–8 that is characteristic of his Trinitarian doctrine of grace: "For as three witnesses in heaven are named—the Father, the Word, and the Spirit—so there are three on earth: the water, the blood, and the Spirit. There is good reason for the repeated mention of the 'testimony of the spirit,' a testimony we feel engraved like a seal upon our hearts."[28] What is sealed in this way is the bestowal of grace, which is expressed by the Pauline symbolic expression "adoption." In this alternative expression we see the expression of the fatherhood of God the Father as it applies to us and makes us God's adopted daughters and sons. But as the subject of the activity that leads to this result, again in reference to Rom. 8:15–16, we find the Spirit: "First, he is called the 'spirit of adoption' because he is the witness to us of the free benevolence of God with which God the Father has embraced us in his beloved only-begotten Son to become a Father to us."[29] The metaphor of embracing is possibly derived from Augustine, who saw those who received grace as surrounded on all sides by God's eternity, which transcends all space, as in a mother's womb.[30] Calvin did not hesitate to compare the union with Christ that is enjoyed by those who have received grace with the sexual union of man and wife in one flesh: "The same purpose is served by that sacred wedlock through which we are made flesh of his flesh and bone of his bone (Eph. 5:30), and thus one with him. But he unites himself to us by the Spirit alone. By the grace and power of the same Spirit we are made his members, to keep us under himself *(ut nos sub se contineat)* and in turn to possess him."[31] The bestowing of grace on human beings is a Trinitarian activity in the power of the Holy Spirit, who draws near to us.

III

Calvin would not be a true disciple of Paul, John, Augustine, and Luther if he did not stress the function of faith in this connection. That faith which makes a sinner just in God's eyes is for Calvin unambiguously a gift of grace, or more precisely the creation of Christ and his Spirit in human hearts. Christ is the object and instructor of faith; that is, of the basic human attitude which is compatible with grace; but "faith itself has no other source than the Spirit."[32] The motivation by which a nonbeliever becomes a believer comes from the infinite goodness of the Father, insofar as persons place their basic trust in it: "Accordingly, we need the promise of grace, which can testify to us that the Father is merciful; since we can approach him in no other way, and upon grace alone the heart of man can rest."[33] Here too it is possible to discover echoes of Augustine, especially when we consider further the statement immediately preceding the one just quoted, "that we are attracted to seek him *(ad Deum quaerendum allicimur).*"[34] According to the Bishop of Hippo, humans come to faith because God plants in them the eros, the desire, the delight by which he draws them with gentle power to himself.[35] Attracted by the goodness of the Father, taught by the Son, made fruitful by the Holy Spirit, people come to the faith that can be defined by a Trinitarian formula: It is "a firm and certain knowledge of God's benevolence toward us, founded upon the truth of the freely given promise in Christ, both revealed to our minds and sealed upon our hearts through the Holy Spirit."[36] There is also a variant description of the attitude of faith that is centered in Christ: "Christ was given to us by God's generosity, to be grasped and possessed by us in faith. By partaking of him, we principally receive a double grace: Namely, that being reconciled to God through Christ's blamelessness, we may have in heaven instead of a Judge a gracious Father; and secondly, that sanctified by Christ's spirit we may cultivate blamelessness and purity of life."[37] Here too the statement is triadic in form.[38]

IV

On the basis of this faith sinners are made righteous through God's grace. Justification, or the forgiveness of sins, is not, however, the end but rather the beginning of the process in which grace is bestowed. What begins here finds its lifelong continuation in sanctification. There are two foci of this process, and the second develops the first. The act of justification anticipates a corresponding history of sanctification. For Calvin, both are as inseparable as are the light and the warmth of the sun.[39] "Whomever, therefore, God receives into grace *(in gratiam recipit),*[40] on them he at the same time bestows the spirit of adoption, by whose power he remakes them to his own image,"[41] which is par excellence identical with Christ.

Righteousness and sanctification are therefore inseparable *(inseparabilia esse haec duo),*[42] but they must not on that account be confused with each other, just as little—I would like to say by way of analogy—as the three persons of the Godhead, who together, and yet in their constitutive differentiation, accomplish this two-dimensional work. Calvin expresses this differently. "For Paul's statement is not redundant: that Christ was given to us for our righteousness and sanctification (1 Cor. 1:30). And whenever he reasons—from the salvation purchased for us, from God's fatherly love, and from Christ's grace—that we are called to holiness and cleanness, he clearly indicates that to be justified means something different from being made new creatures."[43] Insofar as Calvin accepts a theory of appropriation (which in comparison with the principle *opera ad extra communia* seems for him to have a secondary significance), he ascribes the process of sanctification to the Holy Spirit. This occurs, however, more in relationship with New Testament pneumatology, which is employed throughout in the sense of the divine economy, rather than in Trinitarian speculations.

V

The resurrection from death is the consummation of a sanctified life. When Calvin deals with this aspect of the doctrine of grace, he links the individual-eschatological theme, which is characteristic for him, with its ecclesiological context. He speaks again of the three persons of the Godhead when he writes, "God raised his Son from the dead, not to make known a single example of his power, but to show toward us believers the same working of the Spirit."[44] The work of grace is depicted here as ecclesial, even ecclesiological. Christ underwent the Easter event as the one who was already "head of the church."[45] This was an action of the Father through his Son in the power of the Spirit,[46] so that that which "was begun" in Christ the Head might be completed "in all the members."[47]

VI

That which is said at the end of Book 3 anticipates the theme of Book 4. Here the church, as the multitude of those chosen by grace, brought together and united in one body, becomes the center of attention. The concept of grace, for obvious reasons, makes its appearance with God's gracious choice that separates the "elect" from the "reprobate." "All those who, by the kindness *(clementia)* of God the Father, through the working of the Holy Spirit, have entered into fellowship with Christ *(in Christi participationem),* are set apart as God's property and personal possession; and that when we are of their number we share *(consortes)* that great grace."[48] This involves a genuine *consortium gratiae,* a solidarity of union of those who believe with the grace of God, as it has been revealed, in the One who was crucified and is now risen. The elect participate even now in the eternal life of their Head. This holds them together in such a way that the church which they comprise can only be the one catholic church. Calvin also bases this catholicity of the body of Christ, which exists in unity, on Trinitarian doctrine. "The church is called 'catholic,' or 'universal,' because there could not be two or three churches unless Christ be torn asunder. . . . But all the elect are so united in Christ that as they are dependent on one Head, they also grow together into one body. . . . They are made truly one since they live together in one faith, hope, and love, and in the same Spirit of God. For they have been called not only into the same inheritance of eternal life but also to participate in one God and Christ."[49]

This community stands, therefore, just as does every individual believer, according to the example of Jesus Christ and under the guidance of the Spirit of God, in the presence of the eternal Father, their faces turned to him, the Lord's Prayer on their lips. "But because the narrowness of our hearts cannot comprehend God's boundless favor, not only is Christ the pledge and guarantee of our adoption, but he gives the Spirit as witness to us of the same adoption, through whom with free and full voice we may cry, 'Abba, Father' (Gal. 4:6)."[50]

VII

Entry into this ecclesial community is granted through baptism. Calvin emphasized only slightly the function of this sacrament for wiping away sin, but ascribes to it much more clearly the role of giving entry into the *communio Christi.* Thus here too his ecclesiology of the body of Christ finds full expression. Baptism is for Calvin "regeneration," so that we might say that through baptism one is born into the body of Christ. It goes without saying that he comments on this "incorporation" of those who are baptized "into grace"[51] in terms of the Trinitarian baptismal formula in Matt. 28:19. Then he adds: "But we obtain regeneration by Christ's death and resurrection only if we are sanctified by the Spirit and imbued with a new and spiritual nature. For this reason we obtain and, so to speak, clearly discern in the Father the cause, in the Son the matter, and in the Spirit the effect, of our purgation and our regeneration."[52] The differentiation among the three persons of the Trinity is reflected thus in the gift of grace conferred by our baptism.

In this respect, both sacraments, baptism and the Lord's Supper, have an identical structure. The triune God makes use of this structure in order to bear witness to his grace and to enable those who believe to experience his blessing. According to Paul, nothing can prevent the sacraments "(wherever and whenever it pleases God) from bearing true witness to the communication of Christ, and the Spirit of God himself also from revealing and fulfilling what they promise. We have determined, therefore, that sacraments are truly named the testimonies of God's grace and are like seals of the goodwill that he feels toward us."[53]

VIII

Calvin's doctrine of grace, which implicitly, but clearly enough, expresses the connection between the ecclesial community and the relationship among the three persons of the Trinity, does not stop at the boundary to that which is purely human and secular. God's grace is at work not only in the church but in society as well. The features of a "humanistic" assurance are not lacking here, for the *agapē* of God is, as Karl Rahner once said, expressed "anthropocentrically." Thus Calvin writes, "Yet whatever earthly miseries and calamities await those whom God has embraced in his love *(complexus est),* these cannot hinder his benevolence from being their full happiness. Accordingly, when we would express the sum of blessedness *(summam beatitudinis),* we have mentioned the grace of God; for from this fountain every sort of good thing flows to us."[54]

"Every sort of good thing," both the spiritual and the material, has its creative source in the grace of the triune God. Thus in the logic of the Calvinist doctrine of grace there is a social ethic to be found. By virtue of this ethic it is self-evident that the rich are to be ready and willing to share their possessions with the poor. God's grace sets an example that humans are to follow and imitate. So for those who believe there is a demand for self-denial that is analogous to the self-emptying of the One who became incarnate. This is not an end in itself, but has the common good of our fellow human beings as its goal: "Those talents *(dotes)* which God has bestowed upon us are not our own goods but the free gifts of God *(gratuita Dei dona).*"[55] They are to be shared with others, or used in a manner appropriate to the justice of God. The sharing of what we have received is to be done according to that principle of *agapē* which Paul established in 1 Cor. 13 for the gifts of God, and so to further brotherly unity amid diversity. In the Scholastic manner[56] Calvin termed these gifts *gratiae* (note the plural), and adds, "And therefore the lawful use of all benefits consists in a liberal and kindly sharing of them with others. . . . We are taught that all the gifts we possess have been bestowed *(deposita)* by God and entrusted to us on condition that they be distributed for our neighbors' benefit."[57]

In this context the Trinity is not explicitly mentioned. But I like to assume that the final condition for the possibility of this social ethic that is rooted in Calvin's understanding of grace is nothing else than the Trinity, certainly in their threefold openness to humankind, but perhaps also in their intimate life, which is an incomparable community in *agapē.* In a corresponding manner, human community, insofar as it is truly Christian, takes on the form of a vine in the hands of the divine vinedresser, the *agricola Trinitas,* as Augustine said,[58] and is conformed to his image.

NOTES

1. This is discussed principally in Book 3 of the edition of 1559, which has as its title "The Way in Which We Receive the Grace of Christ: What Benefits Come to Us from It, and What Effects Follow."

2. The Augustinian principle *opera Trinitatis ad extra communia* (cf. *On the Predestination of the Saints* 8.13, *PL* 44:970) clearly involves for Calvin also the entire scope of divine grace. The "attribution" of specific actions to one or the other of the persons of the Trinity seems not to be exclusive.

3. Cf. A. Ganoczy, *Gnadenlehre* (Düsseldorf, 1989). The Creator's "being present for humankind" is a major theme of this book.

4. *Institutes* 3.11.1, *OS* 4:182.15f.: "et ita discutienda ut meminerimus praecipuum esse sustinendae religionis cardinem." Cf. the *Apol-*

ogy for the Augsburg Confession 4.2, in *Die Bekenntnisschriften der evangelisch-lutherischen Kirche* (Göttingen, 1930, 1959), 159, 1f.: "praecipuus locus doctrinae christianae."

5. I intentionally use the possessive construction "grace of God," rather than simply "grace," much less "graces" in the plural, in order to avoid from the outset any appearance of Scholastic reductionism to the *gratia creata,* whether *habitualis* or *actualis,* although these expressions, as used by Aquinas, could be a help in clarifying, for example, the ways in which the *one* grace is expressed (cf. *ST* 1-2, q.3, a.2, ad 4).

6. For example, in the title of Book 3 of the *Institutes, OS* 4:1.3–5; 3.1.2, *OS* 4:3.4f.; 3.11.6, *OS* 4:188.1.

7. Mentioned with emphasis three times in succession in *Inst.* 3.1.3 (*OS* 4:4.25 and 5.12f.): "By the grace and power of the same Spirit we are made his members, to keep us under himself and in turn to possess him."

8. *Inst.* 3.1.1, *OS* 4:1.21.

9. 3.1.1, *OS* 4:1.21–24. I am using the German translation by O. Weber, which I correct frequently from the *OS* text.

10. 3.1.1, *OS* 4:2.5f.

11. 3.1.2, *OS* 4:2.9f.

12. 3.25.3, *OS* 4:436.9f.

13. 3.1.2, *OS* 4:2.37f.

14. 3.1.2, *OS* 4:2.39.

15. 3.1.3, *OS* 4:5.2f.

16. 3.1.3, *OS* 4:5.10f.

17. 3.1.2, *OS* 4:2.32f.

18. 3.1.4, *OS* 4:6.2–4.

19. 3.1.2, *OS* 4:2.15f.

20. 3.1.4, *OS* 4:5.27.

21. 3.1.4, *OS* 4:6.10.

22. Cf. 3.1.1, *OS* 4:2.2–4.

23. 3.1.2, *OS* 4:3.4–8. Note the term *communicatio,* by which Calvin, following the Vulgate, translates the Greek word *koinōnia.* This term, as indicated above at note 8, plays an important role in Calvin's Christology, and also in his soteriology and his doctrine of the Lord's Supper. (Cf. *Inst.* 4.17.5–9, 11, *OS* 5:347.28; 348.7, 14, 28; 349.5, 36; 350.14f., 33; 354.15 and passim.)

24. *Inst.* 3.1.2, *OS* 4:3.8f.

25. 3.1.2, *OS* 4:2.24f.

26. 3.1.2, *OS* 4:2.22–25.

27. 3.1.2, *OS* 4:2.30–33; cf. Augustine, *On the Trinity* 15.18.32, *PL* 42:1082f.

28. *Inst.* 3.1.1, *OS* 4:1.27–31.

29. 3.1.3, *OS* 4:3.12–14.

30. We need only recall Augustine's statement, "Habitas in Deo,

sed ut contineari" (*Ep. Ioan. ad Parthos* 8.14, *PL* 35:2044). Compare Calvin's statement at the end of 3.1.3, "to keep us under himself . . ."

31. *Inst.* 3.1.3, *OS* 4:5.9–13.
32. 3.1.4, *OS* 4:5.31f.; cf. the whole of section 4.
33. 3.2.7, *OS* 4:16.1–4.
34. 3.2.7, *OS* 4:15.36f.
35. Cf. Augustine, *Confessions* 6.5.7; 13.7.8, *PL* 32:722f., 847f.: "pondus meum amor meus, eo feror quocumque feror"; *Contra duas Ep. Pel.* 2.8.17, *PL* 44:583f.: *cupiditas boni;* see also *De pecc. mer. et rem.* 2.17.26, *PL* 44:167.
36. *Inst.* 3.2.7, *OS* 4.16.31–35.
37. 3.11.1, *OS* 4:182.3–7.
38. A more fully developed triadic matrix may be recognized in *Inst.* 3.2.31–33, where the faith story of a believer is traced back, first to the power of the Father (*OS* 4:41.16ff.); second to the promises in Christ (42.24); and third to illumination by the Spirit, without which the word alone is of no benefit (44.9f.).
39. *Inst.* 3.11.6, *OS* 4:187.24f.
40. The Latin accusative construction "in gratiam recipit" evokes better than my translation *(in Gnaden annimmt)* the movement of acceptance into and inclusion in the fellowship with God, which Calvin, in my opinion, again and again places in relationship with God's grace.
41. *Inst.* 3.11.6, *OS* 4:187.22–24.
42. 3.11.6, *OS* 4:187.20f.
43. 3.11.6, *OS* 4:187.36–188.3.
44. 3.25.3, *OS* 4:435.27–436.1.
45. 3.25.3, *OS* 4:436.8f.
46. 3.25.3, *OS* 4:436.8–10.
47. 3.25.3, *OS* 4:435.14f.
48. 4.1.3, *OS* 5:6.26–7.4.
49. 4.1.2, *OS* 5:4.6–14.
50. 3.20.37, *OS* 4:347.36–348.4.
51. 4.15.6, *OS* 5:289.23f.
52. 4.15.6, *OS* 5.289.25–30.
53. 4.14.7, *OS* 5.264.25–31.
54. 3.2.28, *OS* 4:38.18–23.
55. 3.7.4, *OS* 4:154.39–40.
56. Cf. *ST* 1-2, q.3, a.1, resp., where 1 Cor. 12:7 is cited as an example of the category *gratia gratis data.*
57. 3.7.5, *OS* 4:155.30–32, 34–36.
58. Augustine, *In Ioan. tr.* 80.2, *PL* 35:1839f.

From Seed to Fruition: Calvin's Notion of the *semen fidei* and Its Aftermath in Reformed Orthodoxy

Otto Gründler

I. Introduction

The two anchors of the doctrine of salvation in the history of Calvinist theology are the doctrine of predestination and its corollary, the doctrine of the perseverance of faith in the elect. This is true both of Calvin himself and of Calvinist Orthodoxy. Yet, while the doctrine of predestination has been the subject of numerous studies during the last 150 years, its close correlation to the Reformed doctrine *de perseverantia sanctorum in fide* has found relatively little scholarly attention, with the notable exception of Jürgen Moltmann's monograph on the subject.[1] What was at stake in this issue for Calvin and his orthodox successors was nothing less than the assertion, roundly condemned by the Council of Trent, of the believer's certainty and assurance of his salvation. As Heinrich Heppe remarks, "certainty and assurance of the state of grace is the most essential sign of faith and the most direct effect produced by it in the consciousness of the elect person. And this certainty of salvation . . . is not a conviction based upon reflection (not a *Certitudo coniecturalis*), but a direct *Certitudo absoluta* given with faith itself. The believer is certain not only of the truth of the object of faith, but also of the fact that his subjective faith is real faith and that by it he really possesses salvation and enjoyment of the covenant of grace."[2]

At issue, therefore, is the question of the very nature of faith itself and its continuity or perseverance in the elect. Orthodox Calvinists of the late sixteenth and of the seventeenth century (with the exception of the school of Saumur—especially Moïse Amyraut—and of the "Covenant theologians" Kaspar Olevianus and Johannes Cocceius) answer the question by reintroducing the Thomistic-Aristotelian *habitus* concept: True faith perseveres in the elect since it is a supernatural substance or virtue infused by God in his elect through the Holy Spirit. The infallibility of faith in the elect is the necessary consequence of the infallibility of divine predestination. While the Synod of Dort refers to this supernatural quality by which the elect have been born again and are preserved from falling into mortal sin as an "immortal seed" *(semen immortale),* orthodox writers before and after Dort interpret the biblical image of the seed as *habitus infusus.*

Calvin's answer to the question of faith's continuity is that faith will persevere in the elect, no matter what doubts befall them, because the believer is held by God, who is faithful to his promise. Hence the continuity of faith, according to Calvin, consists in this, that God himself, through the constant intercession of Christ on behalf of the elect, is the guardian of the believer's faith, even in the midst of sin and temptation. Ultimately, it is the intimate relationship between the believer and Christ, this "sacred marriage" as he calls it, which for Calvin guarantees the perseverance of the elect in faith. This strictly Christocentric orientation of Calvin's teaching seems to place him in sharp contrast with both medieval and reformed Scholasticism. Yet Calvin's position is not without ambiguity, which emerges at the point where he introduces (with reference to 1 John 3:9) the image of the *semen fidei,* planted in the elect by the Holy Spirit, which prevents them from ever lapsing *finaliter* or *totaliter* into mortal sin. Even in the face of obvious sin committed by the elect, this seed of faith remains in them like a "secret root" *(occulta radix),* or a "glowing coal beneath the ashes" *(carbo vivus sub cineribus)* which endures forever and cannot be extinguished.[3] Moreover, the *semen fidei* also exists in infants, as far as they belong to the elect, and in due time grows into mature faith.[4]

Thus the question arises as to whether Calvin's doctrine of faith already contains the seed of the habitualism which came to fruition a generation later in the orthodox doctrine *de perseverantia sanctorum in fide.*

II. The Nature and Constancy of Faith According to Calvin

As knowledge of God's will toward us, faith is received from God's revelation in his Word. However, "the Word accomplishes nothing without the illumination of the Holy Spirit."[5] Calvin describes this illumination alternately as the renewal of the mind,[6] enabling it to hear and understand the preaching of Christ, the "interior" and "effectual" call,[7] by which the "word preached" is caused to sink into our hearts.[8] Illumination is the inward gift of the Spirit enabling the elect to accept and receive the external manifestation of revelation through scripture and preaching. But for Calvin faith is more than mere knowledge of God's promise in Christ, more than assent to the objective truth and abstract certainty of revelation. The true nature of faith's certainty is seen by Calvin as the believer's personal appropriation of God's promise, in personal assurance of salvation, as the "assurance and trust *(fiducia)* of the heart" in God's mercy.[9]

> This is the chief axis on which faith turns, that we should not think of God's promises of mercy to be true apart from us *(extra nos)* and not in us *(in nobis)*, but rather make them ours by embracing them inwardly. From this arises that trust *(fiducia)* which [the apostle] in another place calls peace.[10]

Faith for Calvin is a firm and certain conviction of one's own personal salvation in Christ.[11] Both elements, knowledge as well as the personal assurance of salvation, describe the nature of faith as Calvin understands it. Both are the work of the Holy Spirit, as Calvin's formal definition of faith makes clear: "Faith is a firm and certain knowledge of the divine benevolence toward us which, founded upon the truth of the gratuitous promise in Christ, is both revealed to our minds and sealed in our hearts by the Holy Spirit."[12]

Yet even experience shows that faith is of little value unless it is accompanied by perseverance, which is not the lot of all.[13] But Christ dispels all doubt and anxiety by his intercession on our behalf.

> There can be no doubt that Christ, when he prays for all the elect, asks the same for them that he asked for Peter, namely that their faith should never cease. From this we may gather that they are in no danger of defection, since the Son of God has prayed for the constancy of their piety, and has not been repulsed.[14]

Here the constancy or continuity of faith consists in that God himself, through Christ's intercession, is the preserver of faith. Faith will persevere in the elect no matter what doubts befall them, because they are held by God, who is faithful to his promise. By faith we are indissolubly connected with the body of Christ into which we have been implanted through the secret work of the Holy Spirit. For "through the grace and power of that same Spirit we are made his members, so that he keeps us under him and we, in turn, possess him."[15]

Thus far it seems that Calvin clearly avoids any habitual interpretation of the perseverance of faith in the elect by placing the certainty of perseverance *extra nos,* in God's faithfulness to his promise. However, Calvin goes beyond this by also insisting on the continuity of faith *in nobis,* for "God regenerates the elect forever with incorruptible seed *(semen incorruptibile)* so that the seed of life *(semen vitae)* never perishes."[16] This seed is the Word of God which "produces fruit similar to itself, whose germ never entirely *(nunquam in totum)* perishes."[17]

This fruit or effect of the Word of God in the elect leads to Calvin's assertion of the continuity of faith *in nobis.* He compares the incorruptible seed to "the glowing coal beneath the ashes" or to a "secret root" *(occulta radix)* which "is never eradicated from a pious heart, but continues firmly fixed however it may be shaken and seem to bend this way or that."[18]

Clearly, the *perseverantia electorum* through God's faithfulness to his promise and the effective intercession of Christ now find a highly significant supplement in the images of the "secret root" and the "living seed" of the Holy Spirit in the pious heart of the believer. In the same passage Calvin quotes Augustine: "Whatever powerful enigmas the devil erects against us, when he possesses not the heart, which is the residence of faith, he is kept at a distance."[19]

The implication seems to be that here the perseverance and continuity of faith is located *in nobis,* in the pious heart of the elect, invincible against the assaults of temptation and the devil. In keeping with his teaching that God's eternal election becomes effective in vocation and regeneration, Calvin vehemently rejects Bucer's notion of a *semen electionis* implanted in the elect at birth by the Holy Spirit which makes them inclined toward piety and faith.[20] On the other hand, Calvin also concedes a *conservatio electorum ante conversionem:* "Those whom the Lord has determined to rescue from this gulf of perdition, he defers till his appointed season; before which he only preserves them from falling into unpardonable blasphemy."[21]

With the introduction of the *semen* image one notices an unmistakable shift of focus from the divine promise *extra nos* to the "pious heart" *in nobis,* in which God has planted an incorruptible seed, in which the Word has generated "a fruit similar to itself," i.e., not subject to corruption. One cannot help but get the impression that Calvin shows at least a tendency toward a habitual understanding of *semen fidei,* an impression which is further strengthened by Calvin's use of the term in connection with infant baptism. While it is true, he argues, that for all who are able to hear and comprehend it the Word of God is the only "seed of regeneration," it is also true that God has called many "in an internal manner . . . without the intervention of any preaching."[22] Likewise, God has the freedom to regenerate his elect at any age, even in infancy, by means other than preaching. Indeed, infants are "baptized into future repentance and faith; for though these graces have not yet been formed in them the seeds of both are nevertheless implanted in their hearts by the secret operation of the Spirit."[23] Here the implanting of the seed precedes regeneration. Bypassing the Word, the Holy Spirit plants the *semen fidei futuri* in the infant elect.

It is true that Calvin nowhere equates *semen fidei* with the Scholastic concept of *habitus infusus* or *virtus infusa.* Nevertheless, his use of such images as *carbo vivus, occulta radix, semen incorruptibile,* and, above all, *semen fidei futuri* seemed sufficiently similar to the traditional concept of a supernatural, divinely infused *habitus fidei* to blunt the sharpness of Calvin's polemics against the medieval Scholastics and to pave the way for the reemployment of the *habitus* concept by the majority of the orthodox Calvinist theologians who followed.

III. The Nature of Faith in Orthodox Calvinism

During the same year (1559) that saw the publication of the final edition of Calvin's *Institutes,* Girolamo Zanchi (1516–1590) wrote his *De perseverantia sanctorum in fide, Confessio,* which includes an extensive treatise on the nature of faith. Zanchi defines faith as follows:

> True and justifying faith, which is common in all the elect, is of a twofold nature. On the one hand, it is the habit *(habitus)* of faith itself, or the power *(vis)* and virtue infused by the Holy Spirit into the hearts of the elect, out of which (habit) the act, by which we actually believe in Christ, is born and—as the schools say—elicited. For faith is, as will be shown, a virtue and quality infused by the Holy Spirit. On the other hand, faith is the act of faith by which we believe.[24]

The distinction between habit and act of faith is clearly taught in scripture, according to Zanchi. While it is impossible to be justified and receive remission of sins without actual faith, the Bible also demonstrates faith to be a "habit adhering and remaining in the hearts of the elect" when it says that "the just shall live by his faith" or that "without faith it is impossible to please God." Surely the just must be said to live by their faith even while they sleep, Zanchi argues. And who can deny that in infants, too, in whom there is yet no act of knowledge, no act of trust *(fiduciae),* dwell the "spirit and power of faith itself"?[25]

Zanchi notes that he is in agreement with Scholastic doctrine on this issue:

> What the scholastics refer to as a habitual gift of grace is precisely what the Apostle calls the inner man *(internum hominem).* And who will deny that faith is a gift of God, a faculty infused by the Holy Spirit by which we believe? That faith is thus to be understood on the one hand as an act and on the other hand as a habit—a habit that is infused but not acquired—is therefore beyond all controversy.[26]

It is precisely the infused *habitus fidei* to which Zanchi ascribes perpetuity and continuity. He points to Abraham as the biblical example of perpetual faith that cannot be extinguished even in sin and temptation. If the apostle teaches that we are justified by no other faith than the one exhibited by Abraham, this means that no other faith is justifying than the faith that has the quality of perpetuity.[27] To make his position quite clear, Zanchi declares at the end of his treatise that he has not followed the definition of those "who define faith as trust *(fiducia)* in the promise of mercy through the Son of God." While one cannot separate true trust from faith, it is not the same as faith, but rather an effect of it.[28]

It is clear that Zanchi's view represents a deliberate and conscious reiteration of the Thomistic-Aristotelian distinction between habit and act. Faith is a divinely infused, supernatural *habitus* or virtue, a perpetual and persevering quality or faculty freely infused by the Holy Spirit into all the elect, including infants. The *habitus fidei* is a gift of God that makes the act of faith possible. "For there is a distinction between the gift by which we believe and the act of believing."[29]

Girolamo Zanchi and the leading reformed orthodox theologians after him directly translate the biblical relationship of promise and fulfillment, which Calvin seeks to maintain, into the relationship of cause and effect. Hence the faith of the elect is no longer understood as the fulfillment of God's promise but as a necessary effect of predestination, and the biblical image of the seed of faith is equated with the Scholastic notion of the *habitus infusus* inherent in the elect since birth. Franciscus Junius explicitly refers to the *semen fidei* of 1 John 3:9 as *habitus seminalis* already present in infants.[30]

The same equation of *semen fidei* and *habitus fidei* occurs in the *Synopsis purioris Theologiae* of Leiden (1624) with reference to the state of grace of newborn infants.[31] William Perkins repeats almost verbally Zanchi's definition: Saving faith must be considered as act and as habit. While acts of faith can cease temporarily, the habit of faith cannot perish. Thus even after his fall into sin there remained in David *"fidei et regenerationis semen."*[32]

The same point is maintained by Johannes Wollebius in Basel: While faith can lapse with respect to its acts, the *habitus* of faith can never be lost.[33]

IV. Conclusion

Calvin's doctrine of faith and its perseverance in the elect would be far removed, indeed, from the *habitus* doctrine of Calvinist orthodoxy had he not gone beyond the *extra nos* of faith's perseverance, i.e., the faithfulness of God to his promise. But by introducing the notion of a *semen fidei in nobis,* a seed that is incorruptible—a seed, even, of future regeneration and faith—Calvin himself seems to invite the subsequent orthodox equations of *semen* and *habitus,* of *fructus* and *actus,* of promise and cause, and of fulfillment and effect. To draw such equations not only made better sense to the reformed Scholastics; it also made clear the necessary relationship between election and perseverance. Nor would it have seemed fair to them for anyone to accuse them of restricting God's freedom. For, as Calvin says, the seed of faith is the Word of God, which, *in nobis,* produces fruit similar to itself, a fruit incorruptible and forever imperishable.

NOTES

1. J. Moltmann, *Prädestination und Perseveranz* (Neukirchen: Verlag der Buchhandlung des Erziehungsvereins, 1961); "Erwählung und Beharrung der Gläubigen nach Calvin," *Calvin-Studien 1959,* ed. J. Moltmann (Neukirchen: Verlag der Buchhandlung des Erziehungsvereins, 1960).

2. Heinrich Heppe, *Reformed Dogmatics,* rev. and ed. Ernst Bizer, tr. G. T. Thomson (London: G. Allen & Unwin), 1950, p. 536.

3. John Calvin, *Institutes of the Christian Religion,* tr. John Allen, 8th American ed., rev. and corr., 2 vols. (Grand Rapids: Wm. B. Eerdmans Publishing Co., 1949), 3.2.21.

4. *Inst.* 3.16.31.

5. 3.2.33.

6. 2.2.20.

7. 3.24.1–2.

8. 3.24.8.
9. 3.2.33.
10. 3.2.16.
11. 3.2.16.
12. 3.2.7.
13. 3.24.6.
14. 3.24.6.
15. 3.1.3.
16. 3.2.11–12.
17. 3.2.21.
18. 3.2.21.
19. 3.2.21.
20. 3.24.10–11.
21. 3.24.10–11.
22. 4.16.19.
23. 4.16.20.
24. *Hieronimi Zanchii Operum Theologicorum* (Geneva, 1613), 7.1.347ff.
25. Ibid.
26. Ibid.
27. Ibid.
28. Ibid.
29. Ibid.
30. Fr. Junius, *Opuscula theologica selecta,* ed. A. Kuyper (1882), p. 208.
31. *Synopsis purioris Theologiae,* ed. H. Bavink (1881), p. 306.
32. W. Perkins, *Opera Omnia,* vol. 1 (1618), p. 152.
33. Joh. Wollebius, *Compendium Christianae Theologiae* (Basel, 1626), ch. 22.

Calvin's Prophetic Reinterpretation of Kingship

David Willis-Watkins

Francis I had inherited the awesome title "Most Christian King." In dedicating the first edition of the *Institutes* to Francis, Calvin reminds the king of the implications of his office.

> This consideration makes a true king: to recognize himself a minister of God in governing his kingdom. Now, that king who in ruling over his realm does not serve God's glory exercises not kingly rule but brigandage. Furthermore, he is deceived who looks for enduring prosperity in his kingdom when it is not ruled by God's scepter, that is, his Holy Word; for the heavenly oracle that proclaims that "where prophecy fails the people are scattered" [Prov. 29:18] cannot lie. And contempt for our lowliness ought not to dissuade you from this endeavor.[1]

In fact, the true church, Calvin argued, is the one marked by poverty, not pomp. The true church bears the prophetic Word necessary to the well-being of Francis' realm. Calvin offered the "little handbook" both to guide the faithful in the interpretation of scripture and to identify the faith of those—the true church—who are being persecuted in the realm of the "Most Christian King."

The reason for placing the Letter to Francis I as a preface to the *Institutes* in 1536 is clear enough,[2] as is, perhaps, the reason for keeping it there in the subsequent editions of the *Institutes* which appeared while Francis was still king. But the kings who followed Francis were not the encouragers of reform in the realm as Francis had originally been. The evangelicals who were being persecuted for their faith had increasingly to look elsewhere than to the king for protection, and many of them were forced to flee the harsh measures taken against them. Nonetheless, Calvin retains the original dedicatory letter to Francis I in every subsequent edition of the *Institutes,* right on through 1559 and 1560. In doing so, he is making a forceful statement about the office of king; whoever the incumbent, whoever claims that office, is accountable before God for the well-being of the people, and whoever neglects or betrays his trust will not long remain king.

Through the successive editions of the *Institutes* Calvin also makes a distinction between the civil obligations of private individuals and the civil obligations of "popular magistrates constituted for restraining the willfulness of kings."[3] This section was not, however, expanded as other parts of his treatment of the problem of civil government grew. The final chapter of the *Institutes* grew as Calvin struggled with the problem posed for society as a whole and the true church within it by the persecution of the church and the encouragement of its enemies. Calvin does not move to the point of imagining that a Christian king may not have as one of his highest tasks the encouragement of the true church, nor does he entertain the idea that every citizen has a responsibility to take up arms against a tyrant. In fact, the bulk of the chapter on civil government (Book 4, section 20) in the final edition of the *Institutes* is still an encouragement for Christians to suffer even the outrages of an unjust government, confident that the conscience cannot be invaded by those who harm the body and confident that sooner or later God will overthrow unjust and cruel rulers.

Measured by the bulk of this rather passive attitude toward political power exercised by others, Calvin's envisioning of the obligation of constituted magistrates to resist an unjust king may seem minimal. In fact, however, this apparently slight concession represented a large step in legitimating—*in extremis*—taking up arms against a tyrant.[4] For the identity of the "popular magistrate," thus validated as armed resisters, became a matter for the intense competition, conflict, and realignment of the various political powers competing for dominance in France.

The present study is part of a larger assessment of Calvin's treatment of kingship in the changed political situation following the final editions of the *Institutes.* His sermons on 2 Samuel belong to this period. He preached right on through the book from May 23, 1562, to February 3, 1563. These sermons are an important source for identifying Calvin's mature understanding of the office of king—its derivation, legitimacy, and limitations. In this preaching we find many of the fundamentals of Calvin's political thought expressed: God's free choice (not blood lineage) as the source of the true ruler's authority; the kind of care which the real ruler exercises (and which a tyrant does not); and the distinction and yet overlapping (but not complete separation) between transient realms and the reign of Christ.

When Calvin treats human and divine governance (what they are and are not, how they are related positively and negatively), his teaching comes with a richness of metaphor too often lost in subsequent theocratic political theories and movements. His language is replete with corresponding woes and benedictions, warnings and affirmations. These are not so much descriptions of qualities of government, which have to be balanced out, as they are descriptions of dynamics of power which are dialectically related. They are the ways God is faithful, also through and over against and in the political realm, to his covenants with the people. They are, at one level, descriptions of the conditions that must prevail for an earthly government to remain in power for long. They are, however, also warnings and affirmations in which "king" is given radically transposed meanings when used as one of several analogical hinges on which our language about the sovereignty of God swings.

We will pay special, but not exclusive, attention to the sermons on David's last words, 2 Sam. 23:1–7.[5] Calvin preached these in January 1563. That is the year after the Massacre of Vassy and the first of the so-called four wars of religion, and the year of the final session of the Council of Trent, and the year before Calvin's death.[6] These sermons help us see what, if any, different nuances of interpretation emerged when he preached on texts which themselves contain explosive material about kingship—and when he did so to congregations which included many refugees who were vitally affected by contemporary political developments in France.

The Figure of David

Referring to what David has to say about his ruling justly because the Spirit of the Lord is on him (2 Sam. 23:2–3), Calvin says that David is pointing beyond himself to the one of whom "anointed" primarily speaks, Jesus the Anointed. David's own experience of ruling justly by the Spirit was (we know because we have experienced its fulfillment and can look back at David's experience) partial when compared with that which was to come. The words "righteous ruler, ruler in the fear of God" apply, says Calvin, to David as *figure.*

> Therefore let us take this declaration as referring to David as figure, and above all as referring to our Lord Jesus Christ where the truth was accomplished. In this way David here shows that the entire good of the people depends on this condition—that Jesus Christ rule. This is just the same as when the prophets want to show a true restoration of the people of God and his Church, which had been scattered, they say "They shall follow their king" and then "They will have their head, king David." For David had already been dead and rotted for a long time. But when David is spoken of [by them] the reference is to the one who is going to come from his race.
>
> Therefore we see that these things are inseparable, namely that God governs his people and that there is a ruler ordained for us by him.[7]
>
> Hence whatever good things God had lavished on David would have been earthly and crumbly and the memory of them lost, had not the foundation been firm—firm because it was founded on the promise of God that there would be a perpetual kingdom in this people which he had elected. And that is why David notes all the particular goodnesses by which God had declared himself father to him, of which this is the main thing: this kingdom which had been temporal for a time, until the coming of the truth and the substance. The truth and substance is the kingdom of our Lord Jesus Christ in whom all our salvation consists and on whom depend all the goodnesses which God lavishes on us so that they will be beneficial to our salvation.[8]

This way of treating the grace David experienced is typical of the weight Calvin gives to the Old Testament.[9] Of course, it could be argued that sufficient justice is hereby done to the uniqueness and individuality of David on his own terms, and the Old Testament—or Hebrew literature—on its own terms. That is a serious point whenever a person or event is taken as a "figure" for someone or something else. In the case of Calvin's treatment of David, at any rate, it is clear that treating David as a figure of Christ is not to diminish David's weight or importance or uniqueness: in fact, for Calvin it is a very gracious thing that David is not just taken "on his own terms," or that other members of the church—whose history, for Calvin, begins with the Old Testament—are taken "on their own terms." The uniqueness of David and the other saints is not diminished by their being seen in relation to Jesus Christ—indeed, as sharing already in Christ's benefits, either under a figure or in substance. David and the other Old Testament saints, under their own conditions, share in an anticipatory way in the benefits of Jesus Christ, the one Mediator, from the beginning to the end, between God and humanity.

When he comes Jesus is able to be identified as the Christ partly because of the way God already worked with David as a figure of the substance Who was to come. However, David's own experiences of God's mercy, including the way God visits him with Nathan's prophetic word, is of a whole—belongs to the same reality under another and earlier form—with the one way God is merciful and just, namely, through Jesus Christ. That is why Calvin's treatment of the Psalms is such a rich harvest for those who, day in and day out, struggle to live the Christian life. The Psalms are not interesting glimpses into the piety of an ancient people displaced by something greater. They are the most enduring articulation of the piety of the community which experiences God's merciful judgment and judging mercy, which experiences, in short, growth in repentance, forgiveness, regeneration. David's personal cries to God—songs, confessions, lamentations—are his own; but they are those which the faithful community prays and sings and repeats for instruction as their own.

David is in this sense also a figure of the forgiven sinner with whom each member of the community identifies when the Psalms are repeated. This is integral to the topic primarily before us—notably, Calvin's interpretation of kingship. That is because David's experiences of God's grace, as a forgiven sinner who lives by grace and who exercises his vocation by grace, is integral to David's being the king over all Israel.[10] Choosing this one to be king, and keeping this one king through the prophetic intervention and providential care, is how God remains faithful to Israel—exactly by not letting the people of Israel have, after all, the kind of king they thought they wanted and which they chose to have (1 Sam. 8). David is dealt with by the Word and thereby becomes a servant of the Word in his dealings with the people. This is the order—grace, therefore service in one's office—that we see to be a consistent teaching in these sermons.

The relationship between unmerited choice and the nature of the offices which flow from it is clearly expressed in Calvin's treatment of 2 Sam. 23:1. "Now as to the second part [the first being that David was freely chosen], he says that God, the God of Jacob, anointed him, and that he is the gracious singer in Israel. Here he attributes two offices to himself, as they were his, and the entire thing is founded on the free goodness of God."[11] David the shepherd is freely chosen and anointed king; David rightly exercises the kingly office as a shepherd; David rightly exercises the kingly office by exercising the office of prophet. We shall consider these three parts of Calvin's treatment in that order.

The King by God's Choice

> When he [David] is called the son of Jesse, it is not by honor or dignity but in speaking of his condition which was previously contemptible. He intends to give all the more attention to the grace of God; and at the same time he wishes that we focus more on the charge which had been committed to him than on where he came from. . . . Now the intention of David is to show that he was chosen by God, not because he merited to be taken. For in declaring that his beginnings were in a stable and that he was subsequently his father's herdsman, he shows that he has nothing that ought to be considered excellent from a human point of view.[12]

Far from understanding a supposed arbitrariness on God's part, Calvin's treatment of God's dealings with Israel through David underlines the true God's trustworthiness. God's covenantal trustworthiness means not letting them go the way of the other nations and their predictable kings. God sticks to his Word and keeps sending that Word to the people, through prophets and even through the one anointed to serve as king prophetically. God does what seems to be the extraordinary thing—passing by the obvious choices according to worldly standards and choosing the young sheepherder son of Jesse—precisely to remain faithful to his promises to Israel that he would be their God and would keep them his people.

> For it is certain that the kingdom, first of all, came to him because God, contrary to the opinion of everyone, put his hand out to him. Even his father did not think him worth presenting when Samuel came to choose him—as we have seen; he was there kept back like an abortion! If he was treated with such contempt in his father's house, what would all the people and all the country think of him? So it was certainly necessary for God to deploy his grace when he ordained David to be the anointed one in Israel.[13]

David's experience of God's initiative is not just focused on how David comes to be king. It all really has to do with how God, through others and through the office of king, among other ways, is reminding Israel of God's free choice of them by which they become God's people in the first place. The choice of David from among the ranks of the least likely candidates corresponds to the larger and prior choice of a wandering band of nonpeoples to become God's people. Whatever else the king of this people may or may not be, his office will serve to call

Israel forward to becoming what God has called them into being.

That is why the public anointing of David as king over "all Israel" involves, in Calvin's interpretation, an alliance—a covenant—on the part of the people with the ruler before God and on the part of the ruler with God before the people and God.[14] At least that is the way it seems to be treated. There is an alliance, but the alliance is not equal in all directions. The manner of the ruler in caring for the people—how the right ruler exercises his office—is like that of a shepherd.

The Shepherd King

God's choice of David is a reminder to Israel of its identity in the free selection of God. But David's choice is also a warning against the criteria by which the nations identify a king and choose to be ruled. The utterly surprising character of God's choice is integral to how God remains faithful to his covenant, namely, by making a king out of someone so unlike what the other nations look for in a person to be king. The criteria drawn from faithful shepherding are judgments on wealth and armor and blood lineage as criteria for kingship. God's choice of a shepherd boy to be king means that he was fitted for the office by the way he was raised and trained: He knew on whom to rely, and he knew what it means to be responsible for a flock by protecting them from outside dangers and by feeding and guiding them.

In an earlier sermon (on 2 Sam. 5:1–5, June 29, 1562), Calvin summarized under the title of shepherd *(pasteur)* what it means to be a good king,

> . . . namely that he should take care of his subjects as a shepherd takes care of his flock. For there are two things which are required of a shepherd: first, that he provide the flock good pasturage, and then, that he defend the flock against all robbers and wolves and every peril. That, I say, is what princes ought to get done, if they think they must account to God for the charge which has been committed to them. That charge is that they take care that their subjects live and be maintained in peace, and then that they defend their subjects against all threats. But that is not what is happening, for those who call themselves shepherds are not just asking for the wool; they are no longer content with it. They slaughter their poor subjects, cut their throats to sop up their blood. We see today that the princes have no regard or consideration of what it is to keep their subjects in a good pasture. They ought to take care of them; but instead, they are like lions. They inflate themselves

with pride; they suppose the world is only created for them, and they have no scruples whatsoever about gulping down and eating the substance of poor people. And when they will have consumed their poor subjects, then ambition pushes them to make war. It is all the same to them whether people are burned, whether people are killed, whether the earth be full of orphans and widows. And why? They are princes, they say, and they have the power to make war! There you have it. But, as the Psalmist says, God is seated in the midst of them and orders them with this charge for which one must give account, and they will be like one of the very least, little ones.[15]

In the beginning of his sermon on 2 Sam. 23:2, Calvin points to Psalm 72 for a description of the benefits of the king for the people, that for which a ruler is accountable. The imagery there reinforces the imagery of the kind of care and protection and nourishment which God wills for his people by anointing this kind of king instead of the king the people demand in 1 Samuel 8.[16]

The Prophet King

There is already a sharp reminder and correction of what it means to be king. But, as Calvin interprets David's last words, David points to the other office that goes with that of his being king: the office of prophet. That, says Calvin, is what David means when he refers to his having been made the gracious singer of Israel, the psalmist. The office of prophet is integral to David's being the kind of king—the shepherd king—God sustained and corrected him into being.

Although it seems as if he is here only talking about his harp and melody, he is in fact looking at the main thing when he uses the name "gracious singer." He means by it the gift of prophecy. For it would not have been a great honor for a king to know how to play some musical instrument. That would not even have been worthy of a person of his estate. But when it is an accessory to such an excellent gift—that God had constituted him organ of his Spirit—then that is what David had in mind when he is called the gracious singer of Israel.

Wherefore we are supposed to attend to that melody, there, and to take all our delight in it—instead of having itchy ears that we want soothed with vanity and folly, a vice which is too common to the world and one to which we are all too attached. Let us rejoice, I say, to seek this melody, wherein is all our pleasure: that we be taught by the goodness and grace of God, that we be drawn to him, that we be given an overture to call upon him, that we have that

> with which to be consoled in our affliction, that we be able to confront our enemies knowing that the victory is assured us, provided God support our cause and be our defense.[17]

David is a special case because, as prophet, he is the one who supplies Israel—and the church—with the songs of delight and instruction. David not only hears the Word addressed to him, and restates it as other prophets do, but his songs become part of God's Word to move us with delight to hear and do God's promises.

The main way this kind of king rules in this kind of way is by the law of God. This is not by imposing God's law as something to be done to escape punishment (which is only to govern the people with servile fear) but by moving the people to take the kind of delight in the law by which they obey it and embrace it as given for their well-being. That is what it means for David to be called a gracious singer! And as descriptive of what taking delight in the law means, Calvin—obviously—points to David's song on exactly that subject, Psalm 119.

> Every time . . . we see this word—that David was the gracious singer of Israel—let us practice what he says in Psalm 119, namely that the law had been for him sweeter than honey. In this way let us appreciate such a sweetness in its teaching that it draw us to God and make us stick there. And let us appreciate such a sweetness in its teaching that, while we have many painful disappointments in this world which might well make us bitter, we never stop, right in the midst of such sadness and anguishes, coming to this joy which is given us in such a fashion.[18]

The shepherd king rules by persuasion of the truth and goodness—the sweetness—of what he teaches and does.[19] This is what it means to be the people of a shepherd king—to know and take delight in his voice, to be moved by the Spirit to free and willing obedience. The delight David takes in the law, and moves us to take in the law, points even more powerfully to what it means to be governed by the one king above all who rules by the scepter of his word, Christ. He is the shepherd king whose voice we are to hear with delight and obedience. That is what the freedom of the church and of the believer is: to be ruled *sponte* by the Word and the Spirit. Freedom is the life of a citizen of this kingdom of Christ. This is the same point that Calvin made in his treatment—in the *Institutes* right through the final edition—of the civil powers, that they could not destroy the freedom of the conscience.

To be ruled by the "scepter of the Word"—that is what it

means to be governed by God who works through God's appointed servants. One who is truly king is a willing servant of this God who sends the Word—indeed, who is the Word. That is why one who is most responsible as ruler is governed by the one who is most unlike the kings all the nations have as substitutes for being ruled by God. The scepter of the Word—that both describes which one is the ultimate ruler and what it means to "rule." Jesus Christ as the ruler is a gracious judgment on kingship which substitutes itself for God's governance, and is a gracious judgment because the way he rules is so utterly different from what is otherwise understood by ruling.

The continuity of the prophetic Word is indispensable to being selected king, to being anointed king, to being continually judged and therefore continually renewed in the office. Conversely, when one who bears the title of king chooses to ignore or disobey this prophetic Word, God overthrows and replaces the pretender with a newly anointed one who hears and obeys the prophetic Word. This is the central issue behind the intrigues and battles by which Saul is replaced by David. The king comes to his office rightfully only because he is identified and named by the Word sent to, and then respoken by, the prophet. Moreover, the continued identity of a person as king is dependent on the prophetic Word's being spoken and obeyed in the realm. The Word sustains the king's identity as one who has forgotten neither the shepherd's dependence on God nor the shepherd's job of feeding, guiding, and protecting the flock assigned him.

That is what is so serious about a kingdom in which the Word cannot be freely preached, and why Calvin always insisted that the true church—far from being out to destroy France or being against the king's own task—was necessary to the prosperity of the people whom the king is to serve. Without the presence of the prophetic Word the king of France cannot be what he—let us assume—intends to be. Without that prophetic Word, passed on and respoken by the true church, the king behaves and becomes indeed the kind of king Israel chooses to have instead of God. That is why Calvin's original plea to Francis I is not a self-serving bit of propaganda to ensure the perpetuation of one religious group—the "evangelicals"—instead of another by the state. What is at stake when the true church which continues to preach the prophetic Word is persecuted and driven out from a nation is also the political well-being and future of the entire populace. Christ's rule is not finally thwarted by a ruler who refuses the scepter of the

Word, for eventually God will raise up servants of his providential will to bring to naught those who practice brigandage under the name of ruling.

The threat which accompanied Calvin's words of encouragement to Francis I was not just a rhetorical device. Calvin's view of the inclusiveness and benevolence of God's providence obviously extended to his interpretation of political history. He counts on God's intervention against brigands who usurp the name of ruler because presumably Francis I, having been formed in a tradition in which Augustine's views of the history of the two cities was so influential, would take seriously such a warning. The providential rule of Christ is integral to Calvin's view of how God wills to order the political affairs of persons. God's rule is not restricted to how he reigns over the faithful. Besides that, there is his "universal operation by which he conducts everything according to the condition and uniqueness he gave each creature in making it";[20] and there is the rule according to which he makes all creatures serve "his goodness, justice and judgment, according to which he now helps his servants, now punishes the evil, now tests the patience of his faithful or chastens them paternally."[21]

The Prophetic Figure of David and Resistance to Tyrants

Calvin's treatment of David functions prophetically as a mirror for the Christian ruler. As figure, David has his own relative function and particularity which, for Calvin, is summarized by his being treated in the books of Samuel as the shepherd king, who, in David's case, also fills the office of prophet. God's dealing with David shows us not just the relation of figure to substance, David to Christ; it also shows whence earthly rulers derive their relative authority, and for what, and to whom, they are accountable. Central to that dealing is God's choosing a person to bear rule. That choice, its public and private acknowledgment, the continual equipment and correction of the ruler and the people in that choice—all this is a function of the prophetic Word which God freely chooses to send, out of God's sheer good pleasure, to have and to keep Israel his people. Where that word is heard and obeyed by a people and ruler, there one has the overlapping of Christ's spiritual rule and providential rule.

It was not uncommon, especially for Christian humanists, to write handbooks to remind Christian rulers of the responsibilities of their office and to provide advice on how to reform society. In one way it is surprising that Calvin did not supply such a handbook exclusively devoted to the office of ruler.[22]

On the other hand, it is not at all surprising. For one thing, the *Institutes* began as just such a handbook: to alert the king to the fact that he was persecuting not some seditious sect but the true church in his realm, and to supply the king and evangelicals with a summary of the piety being unjustly persecuted. Calvin was so much a part of the political process himself that he reflected on the nature of rule, and the Christian magistrate, from the standpoint of one thrown into sharing responsibilities for the reform not just of the church but of society at large. One can look at his commentary on Seneca's *De clementia* as a work to gain prominence among the circle of humanists in France or as a serious effort to effect change with a tract in the form of a commentary on such a pressing topic. At any rate, he treated the office of the ruler over several years in different formats: the Seneca *Commentary,* the chapters on the magistrate in successive editions of the *Institutes* and the dedicatory letter to Francis I, and the commentaries on those passages of scripture most drawn on and debated in political theory. Add to these the practical decisions embodied in the reform of Geneva and his diplomatic and pastoral correspondence on political matters.[23]

According to his own view of offices with the church, Calvin—in these various writings—was exercising the office of teacher. He also, in his preaching, exercised the office of evangelist, which included the prophetic office.[24] Calvin's preaching on the figure of David was a major way Calvin was functioning prophetically. Developing a political theory, even spelling out a vision of the ideal ruler, would not be a prophetic reinterpretation of kingship. It is exactly the characteristic of the true prophet that he or she not speak his or her own word on a given subject but that he or she respeak, as a mouthpiece through which God accommodates himself, the Word of God which befalls him or her—which, Calvin argued, occurs in these times through scripture. That means that what is prophetic about Calvin's treatment of David as king is not just the content of the sermons. It is also prophetic that such content was proclaimed by a refugee pastor to congregations in a city which trained and supplied servants to the Word for France and elsewhere. That is, the hope for France, the hope for the fulfillment of the conditions envisioned in the admonition to Francis I, was the continuity of the prophetic Word being taught and preached in this French-speaking city. The prophetic reutterance of the Word from the pulpit cannot be dissociated from the effort to embody it in the reforming ordinances of Geneva or from the system of regional synods which it legitimated as a better approximation of ruling than a centralized, monarchical one. The prophetic word could not be just equated with the preaching of the Word. That preaching, however, was both the necessary condition for the continuity of a Christian magistrate and the index of whether or not God would uphold a ruler who would be a willing servant of the Word, or would providentially send some to overthrow a royal brigand.

The transition from Calvin's preaching on the figure of David to a full-fledged theory of resistance, including participation in military action involving ordinary citizens, is not just due to the content of his sermons. In them we find new proportions given to themes which were already present in his earlier work, and we find sharp sets of warnings about the consequences for rulers who are like brigands; but there is no hint of a call to anything like active rebellion on the part of ordinary citizens. The transition to subsequent political theory might be accounted for as a repudiation of a fundamental cautious or regressive feature of Calvin's thought. However, it is more likely that what we see at work is a critical buildup, a certain reaching of a critical mass, of hope which is grounded in exactly this kind of prophetic office or reuttering the Word in its freedom and power. As the much-hoped-for ideal held up to Francis I goes thwarted well into the seventh decade of the century, response to the Word increasingly takes the form of active resistance to unjust rulers. Continuity of prophetic word, and continuity of efforts to stamp out the conditions in which that word can be heard—these two are the spark and the tinder which proved to be explosive. For the combination of these two reshaped how Christian freedom was to be exercised—that is, reshaped what the believer could engage in as political action with a good conscience.[25] There is a shift in the demands of piety: from piety which expresses itself in the legality of submission even to unjust rulers to piety which expresses itself in the legality of resistance to tyrants who have the name but not the covenantal accountability of rulers.[26]

The pressure to work out a political theory fit for the new times after 1562, and especially after 1572, is there only if the conscience of the believer—be that of the constituted popular magistrate or of the ordinary citizen—is freed to resist a tyrant. That involves redefining who indeed is the ruler against whom one cannot take up arms and who is the ruler one cannot refuse to obey when he calls on the citizen for support against the wolves, the forces which would destroy the realm. That redefinition primarily involved drawing out the implications of the nature of the covenant by which a person is made a ruler and is held accountable for the well-being of the whole people.

Violation of that covenant undercut a person's claim to be the true ruler and opened the way—made necessary—to a replacement of the pretending ruler by the true ruler newly appointed and ordained by God.

All the material for such a political development is in place in Calvin's thought, but it takes the crucible of the political events from 1562 onward for these elements to become fused into the thought and action characterized by the writings and career of a person like Philip Mornay.[27] It is not just the course of political developments which is the crucible, however. It is equally the shift of hope and attendant piety which is involved with the longevity of the persecution and the failure of successive efforts to end the religious wars with peaces which would guarantee the evangelicals' freedom of worship, if not equal exercise of civil power. The warning to the "Most Christian King" had been on record since 1536, and the warnings about what happens to kings who continue to persecute the true church had been issued for all this time. Trust in God's provident intervention and trust in Christ who will not be thwarted in his promises to provide for the continuity of his Word are part of the piety not just of the minor magistrate but of the ordinary believer.

Taking up arms in obedience to the magistrate immediately over one was one way the ordinary believer's conscience was freed for resistance to a tyrant, for even more significant was the conviction that one was thereby sharing in Christ's providential rule. By this the ordinary believer's conscience was freed for a new expression of legal piety: freedom not just to submit to the lessons of living under an unjust tyrant, but freedom to share in the right ordering of human life, which is what the law was given for in the first place. Christ's providential ordering in which the believer was thereby sharing included replacing long-warned persecutors of the true church with a magistracy which would at least more closely approximate the narrative of God's rule through the shepherd king, prophet king.

NOTES

1. *Calvin: Institutes of the Christian Religion,* ed. J. T. McNeill, tr. F. L. Battles, Library of Christian Classics (Philadelphia: Westminster Press, 1960), p. 12 (hereafter LCC); J. Calvin, *Opera Selecta,* ed. P. Barth (Munich: Chr. Kaiser), vol. 1, p. 23 (hereafter *OS*).

2. See F. L. Battles, tr. and annot., 1536 edition of Calvin's *Institutes* (Atlanta: John Knox Press, 1975), introduction; and D. Willis,

"The Social Context of the 1536 Edition of Calvin's *Institutes,*" in *Papers from the 1986 International Calvin Symposium, McGill University,* ed. E. J. Furcha (Montreal: McGill University), pp. 133–153. Although the final edition of the *Institutes* was also dedicated to Francis I, it is noteworthy that the lectures on Daniel, 1561, were dedicated to "all faithful servants of God who desire that Jesus Christ's kingdom should be rightly established in the kingdom of France" (*Ioannis Calvini opera quae supersunt omnia,* ed. W. Baum, E. Cunitz, and E. Reuss [Braunschweig and Berlin: Schwetschke, 1865ff.], vol. 18, p. 619 [hereafter *CO*]).

3. 1536 edition, ch. 6 (*OS* 1:279); 1559 edition, 4.20.31 (LCC, p. 1519).

4. H. Höpfl, *The Christian Polity of John Calvin* (Cambridge: University Press, 1982), points out that while the tendency of Calvin's views was to strengthen legal propriety among his followers, the demands of the *pietas* of godly magistrates could be greater than what was defined as legal under a regime which was relentlessly destructive; in this sense Calvin left some unfinished business which was taken up by subsequent Huguenot writers who could claim they were only elaborating on the provision Calvin made but left undeveloped (pp. 213–217). W. Bouwsma notes this provision in Calvin for active resistance to those who go beyond the limits of their office. Bouwsma also, however, quite correctly calls attention to the weight Calvin also gave to another way unjust rulers were to be curbed—that is, according to God's providential guiding of history, as when the Persians defeated Israel's Babylonian captors (W. Bouwsma, *John Calvin: A Sixteenth-Century Portrait* [New York: Oxford University Press, 1988], pp. 208–210). See also J. T. McNeill, "John Calvin on Civil Government," ch. 2 of *Calvinism and the Political Order,* ed. G. L. Hunt and J. T. McNeill (Philadelphia: Westminster Press, 1965), esp. pp. 38–42; LCC, p. 1518 n. 53 (at *Inst.* 4.20.31); and John Leith, *Introduction to the Reformed Tradition* (Atlanta: John Knox Press, 1977), pp. 202–207. W. F. Graham, *The Constructive Revolutionary: John Calvin and His Socio-Economic Impact* (Richmond, Va.: John Knox Press, 1972), attends mostly to Calvin's dealings with the Genevan magistrates and from these speaks of "Calvin's political blinders" and minimizes Calvin's influence on subsequent Huguenot political theory (pp. 158–173).

5. J. Calvin, *Predigten über das 2. Buch Samuelis,* ed. H. Rückert, *Supplementa Calviniana* (Neukirchen Kreis Moers: Neukirchener Verlag, 1962) pp. 696–715 (hereafter *SC*). On Calvin's theology as seen from his preaching, see H. Scholl, *Reformatio und Politik: Politische Ethik bei Luther, Calvin und den Frühhugenotten* (Stuttgart: W. Kohlhammer, 1976), pp. 48–65; W. Niesel, "Der theologische Gehalt der jüngst veröffentlichten Predigten Calvins," in *Regards contemporaines sur Jean Calvin* (Strasbourg, 1964; Paris: Presses

Universitaires, 1965), pp. 6–16; W. H. Neuser, "Theologie des Worts," in *Calvinus Theologus,* ed. W. H. Neuser (Neukirchen: Neukirchener Verlag, 1976), pp. 17–37; R. Stauffer, *Interprètes de la Bible,* Théologie historique, 57 (Paris: Editions Beauchesne, 1980), pp. 167–248; B. Farley, ed. and tr., *John Calvin's Sermons on the Ten Commandments* (Grand Rapids: Baker Book House, 1980), pp. 13–33; R. Peter, "Genève dans la prédication de Calvin," in *Calvinus Ecclesiae Genevensis Custos,* ed. W. H. Neuser (Frankfurt: Peter Lang, 1984), pp. 23–48; E. Mülhaupt, *Die Predigt Calvins* (Berlin: W. de Gruyter, 1931) and *Der Psalter auf der Kanzel Calvins* (Neukirchen Kreis Moers: Neukirchener Verlag, 1959); and T. H. L. Parker's treatment of Calvin's preaching in relation to his commentaries and lectures: *Calvin's Old Testament Commentaries* (Edinburgh: T. & T. Clark, 1986), pp. 1–42.

6. For the political and diplomatic developments, see R. Kingdon, *Geneva and the Coming of the Wars of Religion in France, 1555–1563* (Geneva: Droz, 1956), ch. 11; J. H. M. Salmon, ed., *The French Wars of Religion* (Boston: Heath, 1967), pp. 1–48; J. L. Gray, *The French Huguenots* (Grand Rapids: Baker Book House, 1981), pp. 94–120; D. Nugent, *Ecumenism in the Age of the Reformation: The Colloquy of Poissy* (Cambridge, Mass.: Harvard University Press, 1974); A. Dufour, "Das Religionsgespräch von Poissy," in *Die Religionsgespräche und der Reformationszeit,* ed. G. Müller (Gütersloh, 1980), pp. 117–126; and M. Prestwich, "Calvinism in France, 1559–1629," in *International Calvinism,* ed. M. Prestwich (Oxford: Clarendon Press, 1985), pp. 71–107. For recent debates on these early years of French Protestantism, see B. Armstrong's treatment of the historical background to Pierre du Moulin, "The Changing Face of French Protestantism: The Influence of Pierre du Moulin," in *Calviniana,* ed. R. Schnucker, Essays and Studies (Kirksville, Mo.: Sixteenth Century Journal Publishers, 1988), vol. 10, pp. 131–149, esp. pp. 131–134.

7. *SC* 1:703–704.

8. Ibid., p. 696.

9. E. A. Dowey correctly treats his doctrine of Calvin under the heading "The Changing Forms of Historical Revelation," in *The Knowledge of God in Calvin's Theology* (New York: Columbia University Press, 1952), pp. 164–167. This is the subject dealt with in Book 2, chs. 9–11, of the *Institutes.* See also M. E. Osterhaven, "Calvin on Covenant," in Donald McKim, ed., *Readings in Calvin's Theology* (Grand Rapids: Baker Book House, 1984), pp. 89–106; J. Hesselink, "Law and Gospel or Gospel and Law? John Calvin's Understanding of the Relationship," in R. Schnucker, ed., *Calviniana,* pp. 13–32.

10. This addresses the importance of Calvin's treatment of God's twofold acceptance, whereby not only are sinners freely justified but

the works of forgiven sinners are also justified (*Inst.* 3.17.4–6). See J. Boisset, "Justification et sanctification chez Calvin," in *Calvinus Theologus,* ed. Neuser, pp. 131–148; F. Wendel, *Calvin* (New York: Harper & Row, 1963), pp. 233–263.

11. *SC* 1:699.

12. Ibid., p. 698.

13. Ibid., p. 699.

14. See his earlier sermon (June 29, 1562) on 2 Sam. 5, where he describes the reciprocal nature of the covenant made at Hebron when David is anointed king over all Israel. The people promise to be subject to the ruler, and the king promises to fulfill faithfully the charge committed to him. "For this covenant which David makes is a solemn pledge by which he proclaims that he will not employ tyranny on the people, and that it will be for the common health that he will reign" (*SC* 1:103). See also J. Bohatec, *Calvins Lehre von Staat und Kirche* (Breslau: Marcus, 1937), pp. 239–266.

15. *SC* 1:102.

16. Ibid., p. 697.

17. Ibid., p. 699.

18. Ibid., p. 700.

19. The attention Calvin gives to the converting delight of the Word is partly an expression of his location within the rhetorical tradition of the Christian humanists. See Bouwsma, ch. 7, and his "Calvin and the Renaissance Crisis of Knowing," *Calvin Theological Journal* 17 (1982), 190–211; D. Willis, "Rhetoric and Responsibility in Calvin's Theology," in *The Context of Contemporary Theology,* ed. A. J. McKelway and D. Willis (Atlanta: John Knox Press, 1974), pp. 43–63; F. Wendel, *Calvin et l'humanisme* (Paris: Presses Universitaires, 1976), esp. pp. 77ff.; B. Gerardin, *Rhétorique et Théologique* (Paris: Editions Beauchesne, 1979), esp. ch. 4.

20. Calvin, "Contre la secte phantastique," *CO* 7:186.

21. Ibid., p. 187. On the relation between providential ordering and natural law, see J. Bohatec, *Calvins Lehre,* pp. 12–35; M.-E. Chenevière, *La pensée politique de Calvin* (Geneva: Labor et Fides, 1937), pp. 61–77; D. Little, "Calvin and the Prospects for a Christian Theory of Natural Law," *Norm and Context in Christian Ethics,* ed. G. Outka and P. Ramsay (New York: Charles Scribner's Sons, 1968), pp. 175–197; A. Cochrane, "Natural Law in the Teachings of John Calvin," *Church-State Relations in Ecumenical Perspective,* ed. E. Smith (Pittsburgh: Duquesne University Press, 1966), pp. 176–217; Dowey, *Knowledge of God,* pp. 62–68; D. Willis, *Calvin's Catholic Christology* (Leiden: E. J. Brill, 1966), esp. ch. 4 and the section on "Christ's Reign *etiam extra Ecclesiam,"* pp. 144–152; G. Vincent, "Discours et doctrine: modalités de l'affirmation Calvinienne de la Providence," in Neuser, ed., *Calvinus Ecclesiae Genevensis Custos,*

pp. 197–207; C. Partee, "Calvin on Universal and Particular Providence," in McKim, ed., *Readings in Calvin's Theology,* pp. 69–88.

22. Höpfl, *Christian Polity,* pp. 149–151.

23. See A. Biéler, *La pensée économique et sociale de Calvin* (Geneva: Labor et Fides, 1959); E. McKee, *John Calvin on the Diaconate and Liturgical Almsgiving* (Geneva: Droz, 1984); R. Kingdon, "Calvin and the Government of Geneva," in Neuser, ed., *Calvinus Ecclesiae Genevensis Custos,* pp. 49–67; J. Leith, "Polity and the Reformed Tradition," in his *Introduction to the Reformed Tradition,* pp. 137–162; W. Bouwsma, *John Calvin,* ch. 13; W. F. Graham, *The Constructive Revolutionary,* chs. 6–8; O. Weber, "Competence de l'Eglise et compétence de l'Etat d'après les Ordonnances Ecclésiastiques de 1561," in *Regards contemporaines sur Jean Calvin,* pp. 74–85.

24. See R. Stauffer, "Les discours à la première personne dans les sermons de Calvin," *Interprètes de la Bible,* pp. 183–223.

25. On conscience, law, and political action, see Chenevière, *La pensée politique de Calvin,* pp. 78–90; Dowey, *Knowledge of God,* pp. 64–72; D. Willis, "Persuasion in Calvin's Theology: Implications for His Ethics," in *Calvin and Christian Ethics,* ed. P. de Klerk (Grand Rapids: Calvin Study Society, 1985), pp. 83–94; D. Foxgrover, "Scrap of Bread and a Right Conscience," in ibid., pp. 125–144; P. Lehmann, *Ethics in a Christian Context* (New York: Harper & Row, 1963), ch. 14. Lehmann, especially in ch. 3 ("What God Is Doing in the World," which corresponds to the providential rule of Christ described above), and ch. 4 ("Christian Ethics and a Theology of Messianism," which includes the threefold office of Christ), identifies a theological foundation for political engagement very much in the tradition of Reformed political theology. The effort to bring this prophetic tradition to bear in subsequent contexts is apparent in the formulation of the Barmen Declaration and the struggle of the Confessing Church, in the inclusion of the paragraph on the misuse of weapons and nationalism in the Confession of 1967 of The United Presbyterian Church U.S.A., and in the confrontation with apartheid in South Africa. What is being tested in each of these cases is not just ripeness for political action, but the theological and legal foundations and indicatives for such political engagement. See A. Cochrane, *The Church's Confession Under Hitler* (Philadelphia: Westminster Press, 1962); E. A. Dowey, *A Commentary on the Confession of 1967 and an Introduction to The Book of Confessions* (Philadelphia: Westminster Press, 1968), esp. pp. 39–42, 126–140; C. Villa-Vicencio and J. De Gruchy, *Resistance and Hope: South African Essays in Honor of Beyers Naudé* (Grand Rapids: Wm. B. Eerdmans Publishing Co., 1985); A. Boesak, *Black and Reformed: Apartheid, Liberation and the Calvinist Tradition* (Maryknoll, N.Y.: Orbis Books, 1984).

26. See B. Gerrish, "Theology Within the Limits of Piety Alone: Schleiermacher and Calvin's Doctrine of God," *Reformatio Perennis,* ed. by B. Gerrish (Pittsburgh: Pickwick Press, 1981), pp. 67–87; F. Battles, *The Piety of John Calvin* (Grand Rapids: Baker Book House, 1978).

27. See P. Fuhrmann, "Philip Mornay and the Huguenot Challenge to Absolutism," in Hunt and McNeill, eds., *Calvinism and the Political Order,* pp. 46–64; J. Gray, *The French Huguenots,* pp. 120–211; J. Chambon, *Le protestantisme français* (Geneva: Labor et Fides, n.d.), ch. 4; H. Clavier, *The Duty and the Right of Resistance* (Oxford: Blackwell, 1956); R. Kingdon, *Geneva and the Consolidation of the French Protestant Movement, 1564–1572* (Geneva: Droz, 1967).

Duplex cognitio Dei, Or? The Problem and Relation of Structure, Form, and Purpose in Calvin's Theology[1]

Brian G. Armstrong

Edward A. Dowey, Jr.'s *The Knowledge of God in Calvin's Theology,* first published in 1952,[2] was a watershed event in Calvin studies in the English-speaking world. It not only introduced to the English reader the considerable German research on the question of the structure of Calvin's thought in the *Institutes* but also made a lasting contribution to that discussion. Dowey's attention to the unquestionably dialectical structure of Calvin's thought lifted much of the research on Calvin to a new level of analysis. By stressing that the theme of the *duplex cognitio Dei (De cognitione Dei creatoris* and *De cognitione Dei redemptoris)* defines the basic structure of the *Institutes,* and especially by underlining that the *former depends on the latter,* and that faith is always the unspoken fount from which Calvin writes, Dowey reshaped scholarly perspective on Calvin's theology. Further, the subtheses of his study have become the "givens" for an understanding of Calvin's theology: the accommodated nature of all knowledge of God, the correlative character (i.e., the constant interplay of the two poles, God and self) of all knowledge of God, the existential (that is, based on saving faith) character of all knowledge of God, and the clarity and comprehensibility of all revelation of God.

Since the publication of Dowey's work, a great many books and articles dealing with the problem have been forthcoming, many proposing modifications or alternatives to his argument.[3] Because the debate over the structure of Calvin's thought continues, it is obvious that Dowey's thesis has not been universally accepted, and certainly not regarded as the last word, although I believe that the central elements of the thesis have remained essentially unchanged. Perhaps more than anything else, the reason for the continuance of, and diversity of opinion in, the debate lies in the confusion which Calvin himself contributed to the matter of the nature, structure, and unity of his thought. That confusion may have its basis, inter alia, in findings such as that of William Bouwsma in his recent, fascinating *John Calvin: A Sixteenth-Century Portrait*,[4] when he argues that, in fact, there are "two Calvins, coexisting uncomfortably within the same historic personage."[5] While I have grave difficulty applying this idea to the problem of the nature and structure of Calvin's thought in the *Institutio,* Bouwsma has highlighted the fact that there are elements of Calvin's theology which are not easily integrated by the modern mind.

The intent of this paper is to provide new perspectives on the problem of the structure of Calvin's thought, hoping thereby to rescue the debate from some of the stalemate which it seems to have reached. Primarily I will be looking at Calvin's thought as found in the *Institutio,* with only occasional reference to his exegetical, catechetical, and polemical writings. As one surveys the literature relating to the matter, there are several considerations which I feel have received too little attention, considerations I hope will help to bring the debate into better focus.

In the first place, I am convinced that the issue of the structure of Calvin's thought cannot be separated from careful consideration of the nature of his theology. Much of the literature on the question has centered too closely on the problem of structure per se. This has often been accompanied by the assumption that Calvin was a systematic theologian. He was not; his activity was one of pastor, not theological professor. The primary intent of his labors was always the practical, not logical or speculative formulations of theological truth. Although many have pointed this out, the idea of a systematician seems to die slowly, largely, one suspects, because the majority of interpretations of Calvin's thought have come from the pens of professional theologians. Perhaps the freshness of Bouwsma's approach and the force with which he drives the point home will help to overcome the traditional assumptions and approach. Unhindered by theological baggage, Bouwsma has been able to see clearly that Calvin not only was not a systematic thinker, he did not even aspire to the construction of a system.[6]

Closely related to the assumption that Calvin was writing formal, academic theology has been the attempt to find a *Centraldogma* in Calvin. Indeed, nowhere is the old "systematic" idea more evident than in this attempt, for it is predicated on the assumption that a system must have a center and that this center must be a *dogma.* There is no central dogma because he is not primarily interested in, nor is he writing, dogmatics. Since Hermann Bauke's suggestion that there is a certain *complexio oppositorum* which defines the structure of Calvin's thought,[7] scholars have increasingly recognized this feature, but it has not led to the abandonment of the search for the central dogma.[8]

In the second place, the structure of Calvin's thought needs to be investigated in the light of the conflict between Renaissance and Reformation. I have argued elsewhere that these two movements are fundamentally at odds, though some of their basic programs could be successfully integrated. In his study of Calvin's Romans commentary, B. Girardin has, I believe, identified a fundamental element in Calvin's thought by his brilliant delineation of the constant interplay of Renaissance rhetoric and Reformation theology,[9] while, among others, Willis and Bouwsma have highlighted Calvin's commitment to the rhetorical tradition and suggested some ways it shapes the structure of his thought.[10] I would contend that Calvin is located precisely in that tension and conflict which existed between the Renaissance and Reformation movements and in the conflicting ideals which these two movements represent.[11]

Among the interests in these two movements which did not conflict completely was the emphasis on rhetoric. Rhetoric, basic to the Renaissance mind-set, could be accommodated relatively well into the Protestant (Reformation) mind-set because of the emphasis on the preached Word. But as a basic element of a thought system, the Renaissance rhetorical interest did not accord well with the fundamental, overriding theological interest of the new Protestant movement. Calvin lived intimately in the two worlds of Renaissance and Reformation, and he never was able to resolve the conflict of fundamentally different ideologies. Consequently, his theology was accommodated to conflicting ideologies in such a way that there will always be two poles, two aspects, two dialectical and conflicting elements in each theological topic which he discusses. At bottom, this dialectical structure of each element of his thought not only responds to the conflict between Renaissance and Reformation programs but is also fundamentally based in a broad, general philosophical dialectic between the ideal and the real. This fundamental perspective on the relationship between God and human beings lies at the basis of the division of the *Institutio* into four books, and permeates and informs every topic covered within each book. It means that the *In-*

stitutio should be read not from the perspective of the topics which Calvin discusses, for these are arranged, he tells us, only according to an *ordo docendi.* Rather, the material should be read and evaluated on the basis of the large themes which run through all the material from the first page until the last like so many threads through an intricate tapestry.

The Nature of Calvin's Theology: Its Spiritual Purpose

Long ago E. Harris Harbison called attention to the strong predilection of Calvin for dealing only with what is "useful and profitable." Many since that time have reiterated the observation, with Bouwsma recently arguing boldly that such utilitarianism is the basis of Calvin's program of reform.[12] And this impression is hard to miss as one reads Calvin. He constantly cautions that we should avoid curious questions, that we should remain within the bounds of sobriety, that the best answer for those who pursue such curious questions as "What was God doing before he created the world?" is that "he was creating Hell for the curious" (*Institutes* 1.14.1).[13] Repeatedly, he admonishes us to stay within our bounds and to seek only to know the useful: "Let those who dearly love soberness, and who will be content with the measure of faith, receive in brief form what is useful to know" (1.14.1). When he introduces his ideas on the meaning of the knowledge of God in Book 1, that discussion is strictly limited to what is profitable, to "what it is to our advantage to know of him" (1.2.1). In point of fact, he tells us, "It is our duty willingly to renounce those things which are unprofitable" (1.14.3). The critical question, of course, is: "Useful for what? Profitable for what?" If the goal of theology is intellectual or academic, why would knowledge of any sort be unprofitable? The answer is that any kind of knowledge, whether or not directly or immediately applicable, would be profitable. Since Calvin clearly says that some things are not useful to know, we must conclude either that he is not particularly astute, or that he is anti-intellectual, or that his theology is something other than a repository of a set of propositions which serve in an intellectual forum and endeavor.

It is this latter option which must be carefully recognized and, even more importantly, then incorporated into a thoroughgoing and cohesive interpretation of Calvin's thought. When we ask, "What positive statement can we make about the nature of Calvin's theology which will be helpful as we try to understand its essential character?" I would contend that the most obvious and appropriate response is that his theology is simply for the spiritual purpose of providing for the nurture of the saints. Because this has seemed too simplistic, too "pious," too unsophisticated and unworthy of a great thinker, it appears that we have shied away from the obvious. Indeed, we have drawn back from Calvin's own often-repeated position that his theology is intended for exclusively spiritual ends, for spiritual edification. "The theologian's task," he tells us, "is not to divert the ears with chatter, but to strengthen consciences" (1.14.4). Any other program will serve only to distort the nature and purpose of theology:

> Let us remember here, as in all religious doctrine, that we ought to hold to one rule of modesty and sobriety: not to speak, or guess, or even to seek to know, concerning obscure matters anything except what has been imparted to us by God's word. Furthermore, in the reading of Scripture we ought ceaselessly to endeavor to seek out and meditate upon those things which make for edification. Let us not indulge in curiosity or in the investigation of unprofitable things. (1.14.4)

Or again, he contends that "we see that the Lord's purpose was to teach nothing in his sacred oracles except what we should learn to our edification" (1.14.16). Hence we conclude that theology according to Calvin must be understood as solely and exclusively for believers, for the people of faith. Faith provides a new dimension by which the believer is able to penetrate to a deeper, a spiritual level. For example, as he introduces his discussion of "providence," Calvin argues that "faith has its peculiar way of assigning the whole credit for Creation to God" (1.16.1). True, he will concede that "carnal sense thinks there is an energy divinely bestowed from the beginning, sufficient to sustain all things," but only the believer will be able to penetrate to the truly spiritual dimensions:

> But faith ought to penetrate more deeply, namely, having found him Creator of all, forthwith to conclude he is also everlasting Governor and Preserver—not only in that he drives the celestial frame as well as its several parts by a universal motion, but also in that he sustains, nourishes, and cares for everything he has made, even to the least sparrow (cf. Matt. 10:29). (1.16.1)

So it is notable that those who seek to define a primary aspect of Calvin's theological formulations by calling attention to his spirituality, to his piety, are pointing in the proper direction. A failure to give careful and due regard to this spirituality is simply a failure to understand the nature and purpose of Calvin's theology. Now it is true that it has often been recognized that *pietas* for Calvin is prerequisite to knowledge, but the implications of that recognition have not been developed into a comprehensive interpretive principle, particularly as relates to the nature and role of *pietas.*

Early in Book 1 Calvin makes clear his position that "God is not known where there is no religion nor piety" (1.2.1). The sense of God's power is, he contends, "an appropriate instructor in piety for us, which issues in religion"; he then proceeds to define piety as "that awe combined with love of God which comes from knowing [experiencing] his benefits" (1.2.1). Thus it is the pious mind which alone is able to fulfill the proper role and function of human existence. The pious mind does not attempt to exceed its bounds because

> [it] always exercises the utmost diligence and care not to wander astray, or rashly and boldly to go beyond his will. It thus recognizes God because it knows that he governs all things; and trusts that he is its guide and protector, therefore giving itself over completely to trust in him. Because it understands him to be the Author of every good, if anything oppresses, if anything is lacking, immediately it betakes itself to his protection, waiting for help from him. Because it is persuaded that he is good and merciful, it reposes in him with perfect trust, and doubts not that in his loving-kindness a remedy will be provided for all its ills. Because it acknowledges him as Lord and Father, the pious mind also deems it meet and right to observe his authority in all things, reverence his majesty, take care to advance his glory, and obey his commandments. (1.2.2)

Animated not by fear but rather by a lively sense of the goodness and grace of God, the pious mind "restrains itself from sinning not out of dread of punishment alone, but, because it loves and reveres [him] as Father, it worships and adores him as Lord" (1.2.2).

It is at this point that we can properly address the end or purpose of theology—viz., the worship and adoration of God. Worship is our highest calling as human beings, our highest good, our proper and necessary response to the knowledge or experience of God. In Book 1 Calvin teaches us that "we cannot conceive him in his greatness without being immediately confronted by his majesty, and so compelled to worship him." In fact, Calvin will contend that "it is worship of God alone which renders men higher than the brutes" (1.3.3). Even more to the point, Calvin urges us to recognize that "the first foundation of righteousness is the worship of God. . . . We call worship of God the beginning and foundation of righteousness. When it is removed, whatever equity, continence, or temperance men practice among themselves is in God's sight empty and worthless" (2.8.11). Or, in other terms, Calvin explains that "the knowledge of God set forth for us in Scripture is destined for the same goal as the knowledge whose imprint shines in his creatures, in that it invites us first to fear God, then to trust in him. By this we can learn to worship him both with perfect innocence of life and with unfeigned obedience, then to depend wholly upon his goodness" (1.10.2).

Worship and adoration of God are for Calvin the end of theology, of our knowledge of God, precisely because of his conviction that men and women were created to be in a vital, necessary, and dependent relationship or communion with God. The human race is totally dependent on God, whether viewed from the perspective of our original existence or from the perspective of our continuing day-to-day existence. If there is one fundamental assumption which underlies the whole of Calvin's theology, it is found, I believe, in the dictum of Augustine that we are created for fellowship or communion with God and are restless until we find our rest in that God. The relationship or communion with God which is necessary for spiritual life, and therefore for women and men to be what God created them to be, is most consistently described by Calvin as being in a veritable "union with the Maker." "As it was the spiritual life of Adam to remain united and bound to his Maker," Calvin tells us, "so estrangement from him was the death of his soul" (2.1.5). Thus, sin's primary effect was the severance of that necessary bond, that union with God, and so it brought spiritual death, alienation, and bondage in its train. The entire message of the gospel is that God in Christ is seeking to restore men and women to spiritual life, to a healthy and trusting relationship with God, and thus to the freedom to be whole and healthy persons. The benefits of the redemptive work of Christ accrue to us only as we are united to Christ. Christ "makes us, ingrafted into his body, participants not only in all his benefits but also in himself" (3.2.24).

It is the Holy Spirit, Calvin teaches, who is "the bond by which Christ effectually unites us to himself" (3.1.1), and it is this "union alone [which] ensures that, as far as we are concerned, he has not unprofitably come with the name of Savior" (3.1.3). Throughout Book 3 Calvin continually repeats that every aspect of salvation is ours only as we are participants in Christ. "Therefore," he says, "that joining together of Head and members, that indwelling of Christ in our hearts—in short, that mystical union—are accorded by us the highest degree of importance, so that Christ, having been made ours, makes us sharers with him in the gifts with which he has been endowed. We do not, therefore, contemplate him outside ourselves from afar in order that his righteousness may be imputed to us but because we put on Christ and are engrafted into his body—in short, because he deigns to make us one with him" (3.11.10). All of this sounds really very mystical, and indeed it is. The piety of Calvin which is crucial to any proper interpretation of his theology is a mystical piety.

Now it is not my purpose to try to develop a fully integrated and cohesive statement on the spiritual nature and purpose of Calvin's theology, but rather to argue that this is the direction which we must travel if we are to characterize his religious thought satisfactorily. We must avoid the assumption and natural practice of trying to understand his theology in terms of topoi or loci. What give his theology its richness and uniqueness are instead the pervasive themes of relationship/communion with/in God, the human response which consists of a trusting worship, adoration and obedience, and similar "subjective" and "applied" emphases which permeate Calvin's theology from beginning to end, not just in one particular, discrete section. Calvin simply does not understand theology to be partly theoretical and partly practical. It is always at once practical and edifying. Indeed, his theology cannot properly be understood as consisting of discrete topics or theological doctrines but, rather, must be seen from the perspective of the practical spiritual themes which run like so many threads of a tapestry through all the ideas basic to his understanding of the Christian message.

The introduction of the concept of sin as the cataclysmic event which has destroyed the possibility of worship and adoration, and which interrupts the relationship with God for which we were created, provides a natural transition from the nature of Calvin's theology to the structure which provides its setting. For the happy and ideal original condition must now be accommodated to the harsh realities of sin's effects, including preeminently disharmony or dissonance, alienation and bondage, in all our endeavors. It is this constant tension, interplay, and interrelationship between the ideal world of God's goodness and the "real" world where evil triumphs over good which provides an important key to understanding the structure of Calvin's thought.

The Hypothetical Structure of Calvin's Thought

Hypothetical Elements in Book 1

In Book 1 of the *Institutes,* as is well known, Calvin sets forth his understanding of the nature and sources of the knowledge of God the Creator. In the opening chapters he introduces, and sometimes develops, most of the large and controlling themes which will pervade and inform his theology throughout. At the same time he also addresses the more discrete topics within which are included the sources of the knowledge of God the Creator. These sources are identified as creation itself (i.e., the entirety of the created order, including humankind), and scripture.[14]

The discussion of humanity and of the created order as sources of the knowledge of God the Creator is contained in the first five chapters. Calvin makes abundantly plain his belief that God has clearly revealed himself in creation. In Dowey's words, "he never for a moment doubts the objective clarity of God's revelation";[15] that is to say, God has so clearly left his mark on every detail of his creation that the human race can find therein a manifestation of the nature of God which is sufficient for their needs. Furthermore, this revelation is accommodated to our capacity. But, both at the outset and at the conclusion of his presentation, Calvin also makes clear the hypothetical or conditional character of the material he develops. To use his words: "I speak only of the primal or simple knowledge to which the very order of nature would have led us *if* Adam had remained upright" (1.2.1; my emphasis). But therein the problem resides: Adam did not remain upright and thus the availability of this objective revelation is canceled. At the end of the section Calvin repeats the idea: "And here again we ought to observe that we are called to a knowledge of God: not that knowledge which, content with empty speculation, merely flits in the brain, but that which will be sound and fruitful if we duly perceive it, and if it takes root in the heart" (1.5.9). Of course, because of sin we cannot duly perceive it, nor can it take root in the heart. Again, then, we are faced with the purely hypothetical character of the discussion. What is to be carefully noted at this point is that this pattern which is established at the outset is the one which will be followed throughout; that is to say, Calvin always develops what might have been if sin had not occurred, of what God has perfectly done, as over against that disruption and distortion which has been brought about by sin.

One may well object to this interpretation of the purpose of Calvin's theology by asking the question, If sin has made the revelation of God in the created order no longer available to us, why, then, does Calvin spend time developing the topic? Why would he risk the misunderstanding, which has in fact occurred, that he is here espousing a form of natural theology? The answer to questions of this nature points us, I believe, to at least one of the reasons, if not *the* reason, behind his hypothetical formulation; namely, since the end of theology is that we are led to the worship and adoration of God, it is essential that we apprehend what we can about the marvelous goodness of God in accommodating himself to our finitude by investing his mark on creation and so providing a point of contact with his creatures. God's greatness and goodness, his fatherly care and concern, are bountifully displayed in this great theater. A full appreciation of God's goodness, even after saving faith, is impossible without an integration of one's experience of grace with the understanding of God's objective revelation. The knowledge of God the Redeemer will be incomplete and unfulfilled unless it is linked with the understanding of the nature of God which comes from the knowledge of God the Creator. Moreover, Calvin is concerned to show that God has always manifested himself as a God of grace and love, and that his redemptive plan is not a new manifestation but rather a continuum with the revelation of himself in the created order. But alas! The benefits of the revelation of God the Creator are only hypothetically possible because of the derangement brought by sin.

The "if clause" which governs the opening section of Book 1 has been generally recognized, but that similar conditional clauses carry through the book has not been seen. In chapter 6 Calvin moves to a discussion of God's revelation in scripture. He first establishes that there is a complication in proceeding as he had done in the opening chapters. Now we must see that God has "added the light of his Word, to make Himself known unto salvation" (1.6.1). There can be no doubt that "Adam, Noah, Abraham . . . with this assistance penetrated to the intimate knowledge of Him" (ibid.). The language here reflects the topics of faith and redemption, but he quickly inserts that he is not yet speaking of the "proper doctrine of faith" but of "that kind of knowledge by which one is permitted to grasp who that God is who founded and governed the universe" (ibid.). In words which reveal the pragmatic rationale for the ordering of the material, he adds, "because we have not yet come to the fall of the world . . . I shall now forego discussion of the remedy" (ibid.). Here, then, we have a parallel to his declaration of purpose in chapter 2. There he limited himself to "the primal and simple knowledge" which would have been available had not sin occurred. Here he limits himself to the knowledge of God which informs us of the creation and governance of the world—as if the knowledge of God the Redeemer were not present. This is all purely hypothetical, for the function of the scripture as "spectacles" which "clearly show us the true God" is, in fact, inoperative without the work of the Spirit, which must be present for the Word to have effect. Or, said otherwise, the same condition is operating here as in chapter 2, for he is here speaking of the knowledge of God the Creator which would be possible from the scripture had sin not occurred.

Calvin's attempt to exclude redemptive knowledge while speaking of the revelation in scripture is artificial and unrealizable. He is constantly on the horns of a dilemma, often mixing references to knowledge of God the Creator and God the Redeemer. In chapter 7, when addressing how the authority of scripture is established, it is the reception by *believers* which is crucial: "The Scriptures obtain full authority *among believers* only when they are regarded as having sprung from heaven" (1.7.1; my emphasis). He also argues that it is the secret, or inner, testimony of the Spirit which convinces the conscience that scripture is assuredly the Word of God. In this context Calvin again has recourse to conditional language: *"If* we desire to provide in the best way for our consciences . . . we ought to seek our conviction in . . . the secret testimony of the Holy Spirit" (1.7.4; my emphasis); that is, if there is no work of the Spirit, an edifying confrontation with scripture is impossible. So, while he does not wish to say that scripture is the Word of God independent from the "existential" conviction which comes from the Spirit, it is a necessary implication of Calvin's argument that he does regard scripture as having that quality. But this "Word of God" quality is only potential, only hypothetical, unless the Spirit works within to make it part of our experience: "The Word will not find acceptance in men's hearts before it is sealed by the inward testimony of the Spirit" (ibid.).

Also in this material is the idea that confrontation with the scripture will immediately show us God's nature and render us obedient to his will. But again it is only a potential or hypothetical matter, for it is only "if we read it with pure eyes and sound minds, [that] we shall immediately perceive the majesty of God, which will subdue our audacious contradictions, and compel us to obey Him" (1.7.5; Allen translation).

In chapter 8 Calvin concedes that there are certain "proofs" which can be brought forth to establish the credibility of scripture. Yet it would be wrong to conclude that someone can use such proofs to establish that the Bible is the Word of God. No, once again there is here a hypothetical situation. It is only if the Holy Spirit, through an inner witness, has confirmed the scripture to be the Word of God that such "proofs" have any value. At the outset of the chapter Calvin had declared that "unless this certainty, higher and stronger than any human judgment, be present, it will be vain to fortify the authority of Scripture by arguments . . . unless this foundation is laid, its authority will always remain in doubt" (1.8.1).

Calvin concludes Book 1 with sections on the Trinity, on Creation, and on Providence. In each discussion one finds examples of the hypothetical motif, but because of the complexity of the argument, I will not address them here. It does need to be noted, however, that in his teaching on the Trinity, with its stress on the discrete roles of the Father, Son, and Spirit, lies one of the keys to the comprehension of the hypothetical motif. If one misses the argument that the Spirit is the power and efficacy of the divine activity, one will have difficulty comprehending much of what he says in the realm of redemption, and it is probably commonplace that his entire theology is conditioned by his understanding of redemption through Christ.

Hypothetical Elements in Book 2

In Book 2, the "Knowledge of Ourselves," the same hypothetical character is immediately established. Just as in Book 1 the knowledge of God the Creator must be built on an understanding of the marvelous fabric of the original creation, so here "knowledge of ourselves lies first in considering what we were given at creation and how generously God continues his favor toward us, in order to know how great our natural excellence would be *if only* it had remained unblemished" (2.1.1). The entire discussion of what has been called his "doctrine of man" is permeated by a constant reference from the "natural excellence" of humanity to the frightful deformity which characterizes its actual, fallen state.

Similarly, Calvin's discussion of the law which follows immediately in Book 2 is developed with this hypothetical motif, both as regards "that inward law . . . written, even engraved upon the hearts of all" (2.8.1), and the written law graciously provided for the Israelites. Both of these manifestations of the divine law would, in their natural excellence, have been sufficient to lead women and men to the worship and adoration of God if there had been no fall. More specifically, with regard to the written law Calvin asserts, "We cannot gainsay that the reward of eternal salvation awaits complete obedience to the law, as the Lord has promised" (2.7.3). But such complete obedience is not possible for sinful humanity. Thus we must phrase it, to use his words, "If our will were completely conformed and composed to obedience to the law, its knowledge alone would suffice to gain salvation" (2.7.7). This hypothetical quality of Calvin's understanding of the law enables him to view the law not primarily in a negative sense—not as a "killer," as Luther had done—but as a positive, gracious provision of God to lead us to worship. Indeed, in the discussion of the first table of the law we encounter Calvin's most frequent references to the worship motif which is central to his theology, perhaps the most dramatic evidence of his positive view of the law as originally given by God. But, of course, only potentially does the law have a positive function, for in humankind's present state of sin the law serves only as a judge or condemning agent. So, like Luther, Calvin is forced to conclude that, for all practical purposes, the law's function is as a "killer" because of the fact of sin. However, Calvin's category of the hypothetical dimension does not permit him to be categorically negative, and so he must (and does) develop a positive function for the law in God's redemptive plan.

Calvin concludes Book 2 with a full description of the nature and work of Christ. The work which Christ accomplished for the redemption of humankind is set forth without explicit reference to its hypothetical quality. That it is governed by a hypothetical motif is, however, explicitly asserted in Book 3, and we turn to that discussion.

Hypothetical Elements in Book 3

In Book 3 Calvin's teaching on the knowledge of God the Redeemer has its proper location, even if frequently it has been alluded to in earlier sections. Here we find his soteriological teaching directly addressed, including, of course, his teaching on election or predestination. One might well argue that only here will it matter if the hypothetical or conditional character of his teaching is to be found. While I would not agree with such a position, since I view his theology as essentially one piece, the problem really does not arise, since again right at the outset of his presentation we encounter the hypothetical framing of the argument. All that which Christ accomplished, all the benefits of his life and work, all the activity which makes it possible for humankind to be restored to the original state of union with God, remains only potential until the work of the Holy Spirit, in bringing men and women to faith, establishes the bond or union of the believer and Christ. F. Wendel previously made this observation but did not go on to make any thorough application of the idea to Calvin's theology of grace.[16] Already in Book 2 Calvin had foreshadowed the hypothetical motif which would control the material in Book 3. In 2.2.20 we read: "Did not Christ descend to earth in order to reveal the Father's will to men? And did he not faithfully carry out his mission? This is obviously so. But nothing is accomplished by preaching him if the Spirit, as our inner teacher, does not show our minds the way."

As he develops the argument proper in Book 3, Calvin begins by arguing that first we must "understand that as long as Christ remains outside of us, and we are separated from him, all that he has suffered and done for the salvation of the human race remains useless and of no value for us" (3.1.1). Or again, "all that he possesses is nothing to us until we grow into one body with him" (ibid.). We are reminded that it is the Holy Spirit who "is the bond by which Christ effectually unites us to himself" (ibid.), which "union alone ensures that, as far as we are concerned, he has not unprofitably come with name of Savior" (3.1.3). Thus the mystical union with Christ, highlighted in our discussion of the nature of Calvin's theology, is also central and crucial to the fabric of the hypothetical structure of his thought. Indeed, I believe that the nature and force of his use of the hypothetical motif as it relates to his teaching on grace is best perceived and understood when serious attention is given to the role and importance in his theology of the mystical union of the believer with Christ. The entire discussion of soteriology is a working out of the mystical union principle. In Christ we have restored to us the spiritual life which was lost in Adam. When it comes to our restoration to righteousness, "we possess it only because we are partakers in Christ: indeed with him we possess all its riches" (3.11.23).

Now it is certainly possible for one to quarrel with the above interpretation of Calvin's material. I can well imagine that one who wishes to do so would wish to ask, Is there in the material in Book 3 a conditional clause such as those which have been cited from Books 1 and 2 in support of this interpretation? The answer is yes, there is such an explicit passage. In the introductory chapter of Book 3 Calvin has established that the material to be discussed in this book falls under the rubric of the doctrine of the Holy Spirit, and he has briefly set forth the nature and effect of the secret work of the Spirit. As he turns to his discussion of the doctrine of faith, the first of the soteriological topics which he presents, he establishes the context in which the material in Book 3 is to be understood by providing an overview of the main points of his discussion in books 2 and 3:

> At this point it is important to recall what we have already taught: First, that God sets down for us in His law what we ought to do, and that if we fail in any single part of it then the dreadful judgment of eternal death which it threatens will rest on us; secondly,

that since it is not only difficult, but even far beyond our strength and abilities to meet the requirements of the law, if we look only to ourselves and consider that of which we are deserving, then no parcel of good hope remains and, forsaken by God, we exist in eternal death; thirdly, that there is only one means of deliverance through which we can be rescued from this terrible calamity, namely, the appearance of Christ the Redeemer, via whose hand our Heavenly Father, out of his infinite mercy and goodness, has been pleased to come to our rescue, provided that we, with firm faith, embrace this mercy and rest in it with steadfast hope. (3.2.1)

Thus, the teachings of Book 3, the soteriological doctrines, are to be understood as conditioned by our exercise of faith. Little attention has been given in the past to this passage, but it seems to serve the same role for the discussion which follows in this book as do the "if clauses" which are pivotal for the understanding of the material in both books 1 and 2. Of course, if that is true, then all the topics which follow and which "depend" on faith are governed by the hypothetical motif.

There are a good many aspects of Calvin's teaching on the individual topics in Book 3 which substantiate the conclusion that the conditional motif governs the discussion of all the material therein. I shall give only one instance. The hypothetical and actual, the ideal and the real, structure which characterizes Calvin's theology is nowhere more clearly seen than in the discussion of the doctrine of justification by faith and its relationship to the doctrine of sanctification. The position he sets forth here is a fundamental distinction made by the Protestant Reformers; namely, that viewed from the perspective of justification (i.e., viewed in Christ) the individual is pure and holy, accepted and forgiven. On the other hand, viewed from the perspective of sanctification (i.e., viewed in themselves and from the perspective of their actual condition and performance), all believers are still enmeshed in sin, impure, and in need of constant forgiveness. As this works itself out in Calvin's theology, one is constantly reminded that what is said about the believer's experience in Christ must always be conditioned by the fact that in Luther's phrase each one is *simul iustus et peccator.*

Hypothetical Elements in Book 4

Finally, a brief look at Book 4 and Calvin's teaching on the church. Here again we find the same structure and conditional motif to be central and basic. Calvin begins his discussion by establishing that it is by "faith in the gospel that Christ becomes ours and [that] we are made partakers of the salvation and eternal blessedness brought by him" (4.1.1) and that the church is God's gracious provision of "outward helps" to nourish and sustain that faith. The attention to the church as providing "outward helps" means that almost exclusively Calvin's discussion will center on the visible church, and especially on the practical functions of the visible church, not on its makeup. But, although the discussion focuses on the visible church, from the first it is clear that all that Calvin says hereon is conditioned by the more powerful and more pervasive idea that the true church, the true body of Christ, is invisible, not identical with the visible church, and, in fact, not to be limited to or confused with the visible church. "We must leave to God alone the knowledge of his church, whose foundation is his secret election," he tells us (4.1.2).

What this means for our present discussion is that Calvin's entire teaching on the church takes on a conditional quality. This is true even with regard to the invisible church. The invisible church, for example, is appropriately expressed in the phrase "the communion of the saints," but only according to this condition: "If truly convinced that God is the common Father of all and Christ the common Head, being united in brotherly love, they cannot but share their benefits with one another" (4.1.3). But the knowledge/experience of the members of the invisible church cannot be known with certitude by us because it "belongs to the realm of faith" and therefore its identification "is for God alone, not for us, to do" (4.1.3). This means that, in the area of the church, the only topic we can address is the visible church. And, as Calvin does this specifically, the hypothetical element is again controlling.

In the first place, no statement can be made about the visible church which must not be qualified by the recognition that the members of the true church cannot be known with certitude in this earthly life. Calvin then discusses the "marks" of the church—those features which must be present if we are to say a visible church exists: "*If* it has the ministry of the Word and honors it, *if* it has the administration of the sacraments, it deserves without doubt to be considered a church" (4.1.9; emphasis added). In 4.1.11 Calvin discusses the problem of knowing when it is lawful to leave a local assembly and again has recourse to the use of "if clauses."

Finally, in 4.3 Calvin eloquently and forcefully discusses the importance of the ministry as the "chief sinew by which believers are held together in one body." But, he says, the church can be held together "*only if* it be upheld by the safeguards in which it pleased the Lord to place its salvation," i.e., the exercise of the human ministry (4.3.2; emphasis added). Thus, "the renewal of the saints is accomplished; thus the body of Christ is built up (Eph. 4.12); thus we grow up in every way in him who is the Head (Eph. 4.15) and grow together among ourselves; thus we are all brought into the unity of Christ, if prophecy flourishes among us, if we receive the apostles, if we do not refuse the doctrine administered to us" (4.3.2).

Conclusion

I hope to have shown that the practical theology of Calvin is intended first and foremost for the spiritual purpose of edifying the saints, and that it must be understood and analyzed from that perspective. Second, I hope to have shown that an indispensable element in ascertaining the structure of Calvin's thought in the *Institutes* is the hypothetical motif which one finds throughout the material. That motif is, if anything, even more prominent in his sermons and commentaries, but space has not allowed attention to these sources. My suggestions and arguments should be understood as one attempt to understand some of the key elements of Calvin's theology; they are not presented as having solved the problem but will, I hope, provide a stimulus for new perspectives and research.

NOTES

1. An earlier version of the paper was published in *John Calvin's Institutes: His Opus Magnum* (Potchefstroom: PUCHE, 1986). I am grateful to Director B. J. van der Walt for the permission to publish this reworked version.

2. E. A. Dowey, Jr., *The Knowledge of God in Calvin's Theology* (New York: Columbia University Press, 1952; repr. 1965).

3. I will not attempt a complete list here. Some of the major studies prior to 1965 are analyzed by Dowey himself in the preface of the reprint edition of his book. Then again Dowey brings the analysis up to 1982 in his address to the Third International Congress for Calvin Research (see *Calvinus Ecclesiae Genevensis Custos,* ed. W. H. Neuser [Frankfurt: Peter Lang, 1984], pp. 135–148). I would single out the following, among many others, as representative of the state of affairs:

Ford Lewis Battles, "Calculus Fidei," in *Calvinus Ecclesiae Doctor,* ed. W. H. Neuser (Kampen: J. H. Kok, 1979), pp. 85–110. Battles' article, prepared for the Second International Congress for Calvin Research (and to be found in much longer form in typescript at the Meeter Center for Calvin Studies in Grand Rapids), has not received the attention it may merit. He fastens on the antithetical structure of Calvin's logic and shows convincingly that in developing his material Calvin always moves between two poles in a series of near-infinite regressions. Battles tries to relate this to the theory of limits of the mathematical sciences. The result, he avers, is that Calvin is always seeking the *via media.* I am unsure about the use of the mathematical model, but readily agree that Calvin's formulations always must be seen as the result of a dynamic interplay of dialectical pairs. "Knowledge of God" and "knowledge of self," e.g., is a pairing which is constantly applied in every single formulation of his thought in the *Institutio.* The main problem with Battles' proposal, as I see it, is that it comprehends *only* structure and does not lead beyond that to *what it means* for Calvin's theology.

Alexandre Ganoczy has made major contributions to the debate in his several learned books and articles. Especially in *Ecclesia Ministrans* (Wiesbaden, 1968), in the first section dealing with the *Grundzüge* or basic concepts of Calvin's theology, he accepts the principle of a fundamental dialectic and argues that the dialectic is located in the infinite-God/finite-human pairing, complicated by the problem of sin, and concludes that it does not mean a unitive *via media,* as Battles contends, but that it produces disharmony, especially as regards the union of the faithful with Christ. Ganoczy begins to address the problem of what it means for Calvin's theology, but only in a negative way.

Edward Dowey's reexamination of the problem in 1982 (in *Calvinus Ecclesiae Genevensis Custos,* ed. Neuser) suggestively posits that "the soteriological center of Calvin's thought, expressed in the two-fold knowledge of God, structures the basic dialectic of his thinking" (p. 146). While this appears on the face of it to offer both a central principle and an application to theological formulation, he does not go on to illustrate this at any length, and thus one is not too sure how he would apply it to specific teachings such as the doctrine of the church, for example.

The work of **B. Girardin** and **E. David Willis**, among others, on Calvin and the rhetorical tradition deserves special mention. See notes 9 and 10 below.

4. W. Bouwsma, *John Calvin: A Sixteenth-Century Portrait* (New York: Oxford University Press, 1988).

5. Ibid., p. 230.

6. Ibid., p. 5; cf. also Bouwsma's reminder on p. 226 that for Calvin neither brilliance nor education is helpful when it comes to spiritual teaching, and that theology should in no way be the preserve of specialists.

7. Hermann Bauke, *Die Probleme der Theologie Calvins* (Leipzig, 1922).

8. Richard Muller's learned discussion of *Christ and the Decree:*

Christology and Predestination in Reformed Theology from Calvin to Perkins (Durham, N.C.: Labyrinth Press, 1986) takes seriously the old idea that predestination was Calvin's central teaching, and juxtaposes predestination to Christology, opting for a Christological center. At times he speaks more broadly of a central soteriological emphasis, but this is not consistent. The juxtaposition Muller pursues suggests a dialectical motif, but on a narrow theological scale and totally from within the theological program.

Dowey's recent suggestion (n. 2 above) that Calvin's thought has a soteriological center seems too simplistic at first blush (what Christian theologian does not have a soteriological center?) but on reflection has much to commend it. It breaks the pattern of looking for a specific *Centraldogma.* It also accords better with the nature of Calvin's theology, which is characterized by attention to a few broad themes, not attention to specific theological topics.

9. B. Girardin, *Rhétorique et Théologique* (Paris: Editions Beauchesne, 1979).

10. E. D. Willis, "Rhetoric and Responsibility in Calvin's Theology," in *The Context of Contemporary Theology: Essays in Honor of Paul Louis Lehmann,* ed. A. J. McKelway and E. D. Willis (Atlanta: John Knox Press, 1964), pp. 43–63. Also, "Persuasion in Calvin's Theology: Implications for His Ethics," in *Calvin and Christian Ethics,* ed. P. De Klerk (Grand Rapids: Calvin Studies Society, 1987), pp. 83–94. Cf. also Bouwsma, *John Calvin,* pp. 113–127, and p. 14, where he avers that "the rhetorical culture of Renaissance humanism left a profound mark on every aspect of Calvin's mature thought."

11. Cf. B. G. Armstrong, *Calvinism and the Amyraut Heresy* (Madison: University of Wisconsin Press, 1969), pp. 31ff. and 121ff.

12. Bouwsma, *John Calvin: A Sixteenth-Century Portrait,* pp. 17, 159–160, 192–203.

13. Except for one or two instances when I have supplied my own translation or had recourse to Allen's older work, I have used the McNeill edition of the *Institutes,* translated and indexed by Ford Lewis Battles (Philadelphia: Westminster Press, 1960).

14. It is important to observe that the role of the created order and of scripture as deposits of the revelation of God is that of confirming or clarifying the subjective *sensus divinum* which is part of the makeup of every individual. But while this point is very important in the context of defining the nature of the knowledge of God, it is not directly germane to the point at hand.

15. Dowey, *The Knowledge of God in Calvin's Theology,* p. 32.

16. F. Wendel, *Calvin: The Origins and Development of His Religious Thought,* tr. P. Mairet (New York: Harper & Row, 1963), p. 234.

Exegesis, Theology, and Development in Calvin's *Institutio*: A Methodological Suggestion

Elsie Anne McKee

I. Context and Hypothesis

It is taken for granted that John Calvin was one of the great theologians of the Christian tradition, and his *Institutes of the Christian Religion* is frequently cited as probably the single most influential book of the Protestant Reformation. Many scholars remind their readers that Calvin was also a great exegete, whose commentaries on almost the entire Bible comprise a remarkable shelf full of books which can still be read with profit in the post-Enlightenment world. Too often, however, these two aspects of the reformer's work are treated separately, and the exegetical (and other) works are neglected in favor of the orderly and comprehensive textbook, the *Institutes.* A number of scholars have noted this problem, but relatively little attention has been devoted to probing how the bifurcation might be overcome. The object of the present discussion is one proposal, based on studies of the interrelationship of exegesis and theological development in Calvin's ecclesiology, for moving beyond this perceived split in treatments of the Genevan reformer's thought.[1]

First it is useful to see why Calvin's thought is so often treated as adequately represented by the *Institutes* alone. Calvin is himself partly responsible for the divided approach to his thought. Before beginning his own biblical commentaries, the humanist-turned-reformer carefully examined current exegetical practices. After passing in appreciative but critical review some of his most prominent contemporaries, Calvin decided to publish his biblical expositions and his *loci com-*

munes, understood as an introduction to scripture, in distinct writings. Hence the commentaries and the *Institutes* were neatly separated.[2] The conceptual links between the two were, however, preserved by cross-references. In the commentaries these references are occasional and explicit;[3] in the *Institutes* they are frequent and implicit, and have apparently usually been accorded only cursory notice or even misconstrued.

The links between the *Institutes* and the commentaries have been obscured not only by Calvin's choice of method but also by the changing climate of theological discourse, especially the modern distrust for proof texts. It is well known that Calvin shared the sixteenth-century Protestant determination to be a faithful teacher of scripture, eschewing all human invention.[4] Nonetheless, modern scholars often find it difficult to take seriously Calvin's claim that the *loci* of the *Institutes* were indeed based on scripture, and so they tend to look elsewhere for the "real" if unconscious influences on the reformer's thought.[5] It is just possible, however, that the modern dislike for hiding behind "authorities" may obscure our understanding of how hermeneutics and biblical theology functioned in the sixteenth century. At all events, such a conjecture suggests an angle of approach to the apparent bifurcation in Calvin's thought.

If one takes seriously Calvin's claim that his theological textbook is an introduction to scripture, to be read in tandem with the commentaries, and if one hypothesizes that the biblical references in the *Institutes* are in fact at least partially cross references to the exegetical writings, some interesting possibilities are suggested. The first of these is a rather untraditional way of analyzing Calvin's theological method. The second and derivative benefit is a new means of testing the legitimacy with which Calvin could claim that his theology was that of scripture, as judged by the best scholarship of his day. Most simply stated, the thesis of this paper is that a study of the development of the biblical citations in the *Institutes* illustrates the truth of the *loci communes* theory. One aspect of Calvin's theological method was a concerted, ongoing effort to present (or construct) a biblical theology by organizing exegesis in an orderly and comprehensive way. Nor was the relationship between exegesis and theology static or one way. Although undoubtedly theological (as well as social, political, and other) convictions influenced Calvin's interpretation of scripture, setting the biblical passages he cites in the *Institutes* in historical context demonstrates the rich exegetical justification for Calvin's claim to be a faithful interpreter of God's Word. It also reveals the Genevan reformer's gifts as a consummate master of biblical commonplaces.

The following comments are based on two presuppositions. The first is that a chronological examination of Calvin's biblical references as they appeared over the course of time, especially, though not exclusively, in the *Institutes* and commentaries, can offer clues about the reformer's theological method. Perhaps because the *Institutes* is usually read in its final 1559 form, perhaps because the biblical citations are commonly skipped as arbitrary proof texts, almost no attention has been given either to the lifetime development of Calvin's scripture references or to what such an analysis might contribute to an understanding of the development of his theology. The history of a text in Calvin's thought is only part of the story, however.

The second premise of this discussion is that a fair assessment of Calvin's integrity in claiming to teach scripture faithfully can be made only when the Protestant reformer's interpretation is understood in the context of exegetical history. Although outstanding in many ways that make his commentaries useful even to modern biblical scholars, Calvin was also a man of his own times. His exegesis and theology can be rightly understood and evaluated only when one knows the "mental furniture" of a sixteenth-century commentator and theologian. Setting the biblical texts he cites in the *Institutes* in historical perspective illustrates both the conditions and the resources Calvin had for the interpretation of the passages on which he based his thought. This background may also reveal what possibilities existed for the development of particular ideas as the reformer's own conceptual grasp of the Bible became ever more refined and focused on practical application.

The balance of this paper is devoted to fleshing out the hypothesis that some of the developments in the *Institutes of the Christian Religion* from 1536 through 1559 can be best explained if one takes seriously Calvin's advice to read this book as an introduction to the Bible and a companion to his own commentaries. To put this another way, is it possible to understand better both Calvin's theological method, and what his claim to be faithful to scripture meant in concrete practice, if the biblical citations in successive editions of the *Institutes* are read as cross-references to the reformer's ongoing study of scripture and its expositors? Was the theologian really, as he himself believed, an exegete continuously working not to innovate but to reform Christian teaching and practice in conformity with the best possible interpretation of the sole authority, the Bible?

II. A Test Case—Aspects of Ecclesiology

Providing conclusive evidence for the thesis that development in the *Institutes of the Christian Religion* can in part be explained as a function of Calvin's own growth as a biblical exegete would be a herculean task. It is possible, however, to examine a small and relatively self-contained portion of the reformer's thought to discover whether the hypothesis can uncover a fruitful approach to his method and/or a plausible justification for his claim to teach only what he found in the Bible.

Aspects of the doctrine of the church, especially the canons for worship, discipline, and the ministry, offer a good test case for Calvin's ongoing organizing of exegesis into biblical theology. In the first place, these elements of ecclesiology, "second level" teachings by comparison with such doctrines as soteriology, were given distinctive shape by the Calvinist Reformed tradition. How Calvinists explained the biblical bases for ecclesiastical organization distinguished them both from medieval theologians and from many Protestants who did not try to find their church polity only in the Bible. Thus, because Calvin's discussions of worship, discipline, and the ministry are arguably some of the more extreme instances of applied exegesis, these passages provide some of the clearest possibilities for tracing his method. For much the same reasons, Calvin's use of scripture to establish his understanding of church order is one of the areas in which his integrity as an exegete has been most sharply contested. Therefore, an analysis of the way his understanding of these texts fits into the exegetical traditions of the passages is a useful example of the historical legitimacy of Calvin's interpretation.

In taking ecclesiology as the test case for examining the interplay between Calvin's exegesis and his theology, a caveat is in order. Focusing on this more extreme instance has the advantage of making the reformer's hermeneutical procedure clearer by contrast with other writers, but it also imposes the obligation of caution in drawing conclusions regarding what Calvin might have "read into" a verse. The organizing of exegesis into coherent teaching, like the practical implementation of any theory, tends to narrow its expression; of the possible interpretations, usually only one can be acted on. Criticism for choosing at all must be distinguished from evaluation of the particular choice made; one or both may be at fault, but they are not the same problem. For the purposes of this discussion, the legitimacy of attempting to create a practicable theology out of scripture is assumed, and therefore, by extension, so is the theologian's right to choose a particular interpretation of any given text.[6] This article will concentrate on the reasonableness with which Calvin could claim that he was not inventing his interpretation of scripture, i.e., the agreement of his exegesis with the best scholarship of his day. This focus makes it apparent that Calvin's theology (as summarized in the *Institutes*) gives an impression of novelty primarily because of the completeness and coherence of its organization of exegesis, rather than for any real innovation in the content of the interpretation. And thus one comes full circle, to the problems of constructing a theology out of exegesis—a topic for another occasion!

To conclude, it seems fair to say that Calvin's teaching on church order offers one of the outside limits for the influence of nonbiblical factors on exegesis, and, conversely, perhaps the best evidence for the real (if not sole) role of scripture in the formulation and development of the theology set out in the *Institutes.*

III. Exegesis and Development in the *Institutes*

One of the simplest ways to begin an investigation of the relationship between exegesis and theology in Calvin's thought is by a schematic examination of the lifetime development (addition, modification, omission) of biblical texts cited in successive editions of the *Institutes of the Christian Religion.*[7]

In the first edition of the *Institutes* in 1536, a remarkable number of positions, many of them reactions against Roman theology, are already clear. The key text for defining right worship in the Reformed tradition (as in much of Christian history) is Acts 2:42. Calvin's mature view of the elements of corporate Christian worship is plainly stated in 1536. Word, sacraments, prayer (including praise), and fellowship (summarized as *caritas,* expressed concretely primarily in almsgiving) are necessary parts of New Testament and therefore rightly Reformed worship.[8] Discipline is also clearly introduced and based, traditionally, on Matt. 18:15–18. In typical Protestant fashion, Calvin emphasizes that this ecclesiastical reproof is committed to the church, not to the clergy alone.[9] The teaching on the ministry in 1536 includes references to two offices, those of the preacher-pastor and the deacon. One of the several texts on the pastoral ministry, which becomes the cornerstone in later editions of the *Institutes,* is Eph. 4:11. Calvin's Protestant concern is preaching, in reaction against a priesthood which concentrated on sacraments to the neglect of the Word. The traditional pericopes, 1 Tim. 3:8–13 and especially

Acts 6:1–6, are, for Calvin as for other Protestants, the basis for rejecting a liturgical definition of the diaconate and insisting that the true function of deacons is care for the poor and sick.[10]

Among the biblical texts which later play significant roles in Calvin's ecclesiology, several others also appear in 1536. The Old Testament pericope 2 Chron. 19:6ff. and the New Testament verse Rom. 12:8 are two of the passages cited in support of the religious duties of Christian rulers. 1 Tim. 5:17 is cited to support ministerial salaries, and 1 Cor. 5:1ff. is paraphrased in the discussion of the purposes of excommunication.[11]

Early in January 1537 Calvin produced the "Articles" to which he wanted the Genevans to subscribe as a basis for his ministry. In this brief document there is reference to Matt. 18:15–18 as the form of correction established by Christ. The bishops of the medieval church are rebuked for stealing this power from the faithful, and so Calvin asks that there be elected "certain people of good life and witness from among all the faithful."[12] It is clear that these are not clergy, although they report to the pastors, but it is also certainly not explicit that these people are magistrates. The fact that they bring their observations on the behavior of the faithful (or unfaithful) to the pastors and not to the city council is significant. Apart from the Matthew passage, which may or may not be relevant,[13] there is, however, no biblical reference to explain Calvin's choice of this agency for discipline.

The biblical basis for electing certain members of the laity to help with discipline is the key addition to the *Institutes* of 1539. Calvin's discussion of civil rule in 1536 included a citation of Rom. 12:8. Now this same passage is expanded by the addition of a reference to 1 Cor. 12:28, while the interpretation of Rom. 12:8 is slightly but significantly modified. Although the context is an aside in the discussion of civil government, Calvin says that both these verses originally described a council of elders who handled discipline in the early church.[14] Calvin also repeats the emphasis on discipline in connection with Matt. 18, again saying that excommunication is by the vote of the believers, but now explicitly naming this power of the keys a necessary and permanent part of church life.[15]

The Romans commentary of 1540 is notable in terms of Calvin's ecclesiology for two passages in particular. The pericope Rom. 12:6–8 is explained as a list of ordinary, permanent offices in the church. Although the distinction between pastors and teachers (doctors) and pastors and elders is only hinted at, some other clarifications are made. "Those who preside" are the council of elders for discipline, while "the liberal" and "the merciful" are two kinds of deacons. Calvin explains the liberal as deacons of the church (Acts 6 and 1 Tim. 3 are in his mind, as the 1536 and 1543 editions of the *Institutes* make plain). Calvin sees the merciful as widows and other ministers. The exposition of Rom. 16:1–2 explains this last peculiar identification. Paul calls the woman Phoebe a "deacon." Deacons are a permanent ministry in the church, but what does one do with a woman deacon? In Acts 6 and 1 Tim. 3 only men are mentioned, and in sixteenth-century terms a woman had to be subordinate to men. However, because Calvin saw scripture as unified and normative, he could not ignore Phoebe, so he molded the interpretation of Rom. 12:8 to account for Rom. 16:1. This also permitted an acceptably Reformed understanding of another problem text, 1 Tim. 5:9–10, a traditional Roman basis for women's religious orders and vows of celibacy. In good Protestant fashion Calvin denies the traditional interpretation of the widows and reads the latter as a second sort of deacon, those like Phoebe who are merciful and care personally for the poor and sick. The Calvinist Reformed teaching on the diaconate thus reaches full development first in the commentary remarks on Rom. 12:8 and 16:1.[16]

In 1541 Geneva received an ecclesiastical constitution, the *Ordonnances ecclesiastiques.* Pastors, teachers, elders, and two kinds of deacons are presented in a bald statement. Brief allusion is made to biblical bases for the pastoral and diaconal offices and ecclesiastical discipline (1 Tim. 3:1–13; Titus 1:5–9; Matt. 18:17, with Rom. 12:8 probably implicit),[17] but elder and teacher receive no special support, perhaps because of the genre of the work, in which biblical references are minimal and not usually explicit. At least Calvin's views of 1 Cor. 12:28 and "those who preside" in Rom. 12:8, stated parenthetically in the 1539 *Institutes,* are not called into play.

Although it is commonly acknowledged that the edition of the *Institutes* published in 1543 marks the high point for the doctrine of the church, it is not so often recognized that this can be clearly documented also by the biblical citations and what they represent. Developments from the Romans commentary are incorporated into the *Institutes'* discussions of the ministry, and earlier remarks are refined. Pastors and teachers (doctors) in Eph. 4:11 are now distinct and "permanent" offices, while apostles, prophets, and evangelists are "temporary." This development of the first undifferentiated use of Eph. 4:11 is perhaps influenced by the treatment of the more limited list of offices of the Word in the commentary on Rom. 12:6–8.[18] The latter passage certainly shapes the treatment of deacons and elders. The double diaconate of the commentary on Rom. 12:8 is added to the *Institutes* text to link Acts and 1 Timothy.[19] The addition of Rom. 12:8, however, alters the Timothy reference. The 1 Tim. 3:8ff. citation is replaced by an appeal to the widows of 1 Tim. 5:9–10, although it is clear that the earlier passage is still considered part of the "diaconal system." (Phoebe of Rom. 16:1 is never mentioned in the *Institutes,* but this verse is still part of the normative diaconal texts through the naming of the widows.) The passage on the diaconate is not the only place 1 Tim. 5:9ff. is added in 1543; this verse is also used elsewhere in an extended argument against monastic vows.[20]

Not only does Rom. 12:8 link Acts 6 and 1 Tim. 5, but it also now serves as a basis for the office of elder, as a structural part of church order and not merely an incidental comment as in 1539. Unlike the diaconal usage, however, this is not simply a transfer from the Romans commentary. When Rom. 12:8 and 1 Cor. 12:28 are now made a practical part of polity in the permanent office of lay elders charged with discipline, another nuance and another text are added to this teaching. For the first time, 1 Tim. 5:17 is explained as two kinds of presbyters, some of whom preach and rule while others only rule.[21] This interpretation provides a way to distinguish pastors and elders, not hitherto clearly demarcated. Perhaps influenced by 1 Tim. 5:17, in this passage of the *Institutes* Calvin also clarifies the ambiguous status of "those who preside" in Rom. 12:8 by insisting that the office of elders is purely ecclesiastical, not civil, since there were no Christian magistrates at the time Paul was writing. The interplay between the *Institutes* and commentaries is evident in the fact that this comment about the magistracy was added to the exposition of Rom. 12:8 when the commentary was revised in the 1550s.[22]

Links between the elders and discipline are made explicit by a development in the interpretation of Matt. 18:15–18. No longer does this pericope leave the definition of the "church" vague. To the insistence that lay Christians are included in the "church" which exercises the power of the keys, there is now added the refinement that "church" here means the tribunal of the elders. Another citation of this passage in Matthew affirms clearly that discipline is an office of the church plainly distinguished from the authority of civil rulers, even Christian ones, and Calvin here says that Christ was appealing to the "custom . . . of his people."[23] Almost the same points are juxtaposed to one of the new references to 1 Cor. 5:1ff. The "church" which excommunicates is here a *legitimum consessum,* a "lawful assembly" as opposed to one man (the pope or priest) alone, although this assembly is not explicitly identified with the elders. Similarly, it is flatly stated in connection with the citation of 1 Cor. 5:1ff. that the spiritual power of discipline is completely separate from the power of the sword.[24]

By 1543, therefore, the development in the *Institutes'* teaching on discipline and the ministry is virtually complete. A few more touches are added in commentaries on the key verses understood to establish discipline. In 1546 the discussion of 1 Cor. 5:4 explains that in the ancient church the power of investigating and judging questions of excommunication was entrusted to a college of elders because crowds do not act moderately without guidance.[25] Calvin does not say that this passage refers to the office of elders, as some of the exegetical tradition would certainly have allowed, and in the *Institutes* he never reads the text as supporting his teaching on that office. His words in the commentary also are not dogmatic but provide a way to harmonize this pericope with other biblical passages such as Matt. 18:15–18. The commentary on the latter passage, in 1554, explains at length how "church" in verse 17 is rightly understood as the assembly of elders, since Christ was speaking before the establishment of his church and accommodated his words to the custom of his people. Here Calvin adds the note that this Jewish custom was the election of the Sanhedrin.[26] In the *Institutes* of 1559 this one last touch from the commentary is introduced into the explanation of Matt. 18:17; the "church," i.e., the council of elders which exercises discipline in the church, is the Christian version of the Sanhedrin.[27]

IV. Exegetical Context and Calvin's Method

It is clear from the foregoing that, at least in ecclesiology, an ever richer network of biblical citations accompanies the generally acknowledged development or expansion in the *Institutes* discussion. One might well ask, however, how this multiplication or refinement of references challenges the notion that Calvin merely made his proof texts more sophisticated. Some of the development appears to post-Enlightenment eyes to be reading into the text what one wishes to find.

As is well known, there are certain precritical assumptions about scripture and its role(s) which color the picture. Prior to modern times, theologians, like ordinary Christians, took it for granted that the New Testament church and its ministry were intended by Christ to be permanent institutions, with some relationship to the writer's own ecclesiastical context. Exactly what that relationship was varied with the view of scriptural authority, of course. To the common notion that the New Testament church was a generally unified and permanent institution, Reformed Protestants added the idea that scripture is the sole authority for church order as well as doctrine. Thus they drew the conclusion that the task of the exegete-theologian is to ferret out not only doctrinal coherence but also the paradigmatic ecclesiastical pattern, and to determine how both are applicable to the church of all ages; that is, the theologian must discover how the apparently fragmented glimpses of New Testament church life fit together and which, if any, were applicable only in certain circumstances (and thus need not be factored into contemporary practice). The longer one studies the Bible, and the more one knows about what the best commentators have said, the more refined can be one's picture of what scripture means for the faithful in one's own day.

Among other things, the Reformed conviction that *"sola scriptura"* is intended to be applied also to church order explains two major differences between Calvin's formal exegesis and his comprehensive theology. First, some points the teacher discusses in the commentaries are not taken into the *Institutes,* or appear only tangentially, because, while true, they do not serve contemporary application. The second, more theological justification for selectivity tacitly recognizes the limits of biblical uniformity, and thus by extension the fact that interpretation and application, exegesis and theology, are two different genres. Calvin affirms that more liberty may be allowed in biblical exposition than in "the teachings of religion."[28] Essentially this seems to mean that for Calvin, while a passage may legitimately bear several interpretations, the one emphasized in the *Institutes* is determined by coherence with the primary themes of the gospel. If there is dispute, the space for disagreement is narrowed in proportion to the relationship with the central themes of scripture as a whole.[29]

Presuppositions about biblical unity and authority were not the only things Calvin shared with traditional theologians. He was also heir to the exegetical teachings of centuries which are scarcely known to commentators on this side of the great divide of the Enlightenment. The weight given to the *Institutes* and the relative neglect of the commentaries predispose scholars to see the effect of Calvin's theology on Calvin's exegesis. Only a knowledge of the Genevan reformer's context in the history of interpretation can provide documentation of the influence of the exegesis on the theology.

An examination of the traditional interpretation of some of Calvin's key biblical references reveals an amazing amount of support for the reformer's explanations. Never does Calvin create his exegesis out of whole cloth; what the twentieth century may regard as his most outrageous ideas are almost invariably a selective appropriation of the exegetical materials available in his day.

Ecclesiology provides examples of Calvin's adoption of traditional interpretations which modern writers consider unacceptable. Finding in 1 Tim. 5:17 a double presbyterate was common to Roman Catholics and Protestants alike in the sixteenth century; it was the idea of a lay presbyter of discipline which distressed some of Calvin's contemporaries, and this lay elder's autonomy vis-à-vis the civil power which upset others.[30] Reading Rom. 12:6–8 as a list of ecclesiastical offices was fairly traditional, though including "temporal business" as the primary responsibility of an ecclesiastical ministry was indeed too much for some people.[31] Distinguishing between temporary and permanent offices in Eph. 4:11 and 1 Cor. 12:28 was surprising only when stated as a consistent and explicit theory; as tacit assumption it had been operative for centuries.[32] Explaining the *gubernationes* of 1 Cor. 12:28 or "those who preside" in Rom. 12:8 as Christian leaders other than the pastors, i.e., as laity who aided the pastors with ecclesiastical discipline, was an early Protestant (especially Zwinglian) development of medieval tradition, readily available for Calvin's use.[33] Determining the number and definitions of the elements of worship named in Acts 2:42 was primarily simply an adoption of Erasmus' improved Greek text, based especially on the authority of Chrysostom.[34] To restrict "church" in Matt. 18:17 to something less than the whole congregation was to be as orthodox as possible; almost every voice in the history of the text explained "church" in some such fashion, and Protestants indeed broadened this by including laity with clergy.[35]

Calvin exercised judgment in his borrowing. For example, where a portion of the tradition would have allowed an interpretation of a text which Calvin could have used, as in 1 Cor. 5:1ff., the Genevan reformer restrains himself. He does not cite this pericope to support his office of elders, though it does of course contribute to the question of discipline.[36] The different usages of Matt. 18:17 and 1 Cor. 5:1ff. indeed illustrate Calvin's careful reasoning in the organizing of exegesis. The Matthew passage occurs in the context of Christ's ministry among the Jews, when reference to the Sanhedrin was logical; Paul's words to the Corinthians are written after the establishment of the (separate) church. Calvin recognizes this difference by affirming the equation "church-Sanhedrin-council of elders" but not "congregation-elders." In his discussion of the

Corinthians passage, the "council of elders" is noted only as an institution of the early church.

To discover that points in Calvin's exegesis which most shock the twentieth century are found in the traditional interpretation may absolve him from the indictment of pure invention, but it does not explain the impression of real creativity as a theologian made by the *Institutes.* What distinguishes Calvin's organization of exegesis into theology is the broad vision of scriptural unity which guides the selection of interpretations in accord with his purpose of revealing the coherence among the various discrete texts. Although Calvin's architectonic gifts are also evident in the commentaries, they are most clearly seen in the *Institutes,* where the biblical citations are crafted together in what generations of readers found a very satisfying way. Tracing the way Calvin selected from the tradition the explanations with which, over time, he built up a coherent and ever more complex exegetical pattern illustrates the functioning of his theological method.

Examining some of the constructive patterns in the *Institutes'* use of biblical texts reveals that theological development from exegesis might work in a variety of ways. One of the simplest is the appearance of a new nuance when a text previously not cited is added. This common occurrence is seen in the addition of 1 Cor. 12:28 in 1539, the first time a "council of elders" is clearly mentioned. Recent works by Heinrich Bullinger and Martin Bucer may have suggested this interpretation to Calvin.[37]

A more interesting form of development in biblical citations is the qualifying effect that the addition of one text may have on the interpretation of another. When 1 Cor. 12:28 is included in 1539, juxtaposed to a reference to Rom. 12:8 carried over from 1536, the meaning of the latter is slightly but significantly modified. Both the first (1536) civil usage of "those who preside" in Rom. 12:8 and its new, ecclesiastical interpretation had roots in the exegetical tradition. Without denying his previous position, Calvin picks up a second, traditional, explanation to correct the difficulties encouraged by the first.[38] The alteration in emphasis, from prince to lay elder, seems to have been partially occasioned, or at least influenced, by the new perception of the *gubernationes* of 1 Cor. 12:28.

A more subtle form of development in the scripture network can perhaps be inferred from the negative usage of biblical references. A second possible reason for the way Calvin altered the interpretation of "those who preside" in Rom. 12:8 in 1539 may be implied by what he does *not* do with 2 Chron.

19:6ff. This Old Testament pericope is found in the same paragraph as Rom. 12:8 in the 1536 *Institutes,* where the latter verse is used to support the religious functions of the Christian ruler. According to Zwinglian commentators, this association of "those who preside" in Rom. 12:8, with Jehoshaphat in Chronicles, carries with it the idea that the magistracy exercises discipline. When in 1539 Calvin alters the emphasis of "those who preside" from a civil application to its (original) ecclesiastical meaning, he is tacitly rejecting the Zwinglian preference for reading Rom. 12:8 through the lens of 2 Chron. 19:6ff. The elders of discipline in the New Testament were not magistrates and should not be equated with Jehoshaphat.[39]

A shift in interpretation may take the form of picking up a strand of the tradition which Calvin had previously not used. The elders in Rom. 12:8 are one example; a slightly different kind is found in 1 Tim. 5:17. In 1536 this verse is cited, very traditionally, to establish the obligation to support the ministry materially. In 1543, 1 Tim. 5:17 is called on to account for the distinction between pastors and elders.[40] The latter is, in fact, simply a variation of another aspect of the exegetical tradition which found a double presbyterate in this verse. Calvin's particular expression of the theme is perhaps the first (though Bucer may have had a similar idea), and it is certainly far more self-consciously chosen than the way the two kinds of presbyters were previously distinguished, but it was plainly a development of the tradition and not an invention.

Sometimes development in the use of a text may follow the broad lines of Protestant thought but be given a particular theological twist for what appears to be an exegetical reason. As in many other cases, Calvin's first use of Matt. 18:17 is in reaction against Rome; the "church" which disciplines is not only the clergy but includes laity. By 1543, Calvin had adopted the common Protestant idea that the "church" here is represented by a council of elders. Bullinger argues for this position on the grounds that Christ was using synecdoche, but Calvin attempts to determine the historical context of the words and says that Jesus was appealing to the "custom . . . of his people," a custom later named explicitly as the Sanhedrin.[41] Thus Calvin's development of Matt. 18:17 follows the common Protestant stages of reaction and definition, but the definition is refined by the Genevan reformer's effort to explain the text in context. One important result of this exegesis is that theologically Calvin refuses to identify the elders of the church with the magistracy because the Sanhedrin was not a civil authority. The association of Matt. 18:17 with the office of elders may also have suggested the comment that "those who preside" (Rom.

12:8) were not civil rulers because there were no Christian magistrates when Paul wrote.

Two of the most striking and important factors in Calvin's development of theology from exegesis were the need for internal biblical coherence and external defense against wrong interpretations. Development in scriptural interpretation might serve the purpose of explaining the relationship between two or more passages, or justify a revision of traditional exegesis. The Matthew passage on discipline is one illustration of rejection of a "false" clerical interpretation of "church" and a way of coordinating this general commandment on discipline with the various verses on "rulers" (Rom. 12:8; 1 Cor. 12:28; 1 Tim. 5:17).

Calvin's doctrine of the double diaconate reveals even more fully what could happen when particular verses were (to the sixteenth-century mind) apparently incompatible, or the teaching was (to a Protestant) obviously false. Unlike many exegetes, Calvin did not feel free to skip passages of scripture. However, he also shared in practice, if not in theory, the general sixteenth-century objection to women's having authority over men in the church.[42] Thus Phoebe, the deacon in Rom. 16:1, presented real problems for a biblical church order. So too, for different reasons, did the widows of 1 Tim. 5:9–10, commonly read by the tradition as nuns under a vow of celibacy. Therefore when Calvin published his commentary on Romans in 1540, he had to explain how a woman deacon was consistent with the rest of the scriptural evidence, especially Acts 6.[43] Consideration of Phoebe's function suggested a properly Protestant way to explain both her and the widows, and a hint in Bucer's commentary on Rom. 12:8, which Calvin had perhaps previously neglected, offered a way to relate those women to the men in Acts 6 and 1 Tim. 3. The liberal and merciful whom Bucer had identified as two kinds of church officers charged with charity could be identified as the liberal male administrators of Acts and the merciful, subordinate nurses, Phoebe and the widows. The doctrine born of Calvin's attempt to solve exegetical problems—how to understand in what sense Phoebe was a deacon and what the election of the widows meant—has seemed to modern scholars invention pure and simple. In fact, however, it illustrates the reformer's creative effort to be faithful to the whole of scripture, however awkward. It also shows how much influence exegesis could have on the development of theology, since the double diaconate in Rom. 12:8 was at least in part born of the problem of reconciling Phoebe and the widows with the rest of Protestant diaconal teaching.

V. Conclusions

What conclusions can be drawn from this examination of part of Calvin's teaching on the church in the *Institutes*? First, it is apparent that Calvin's statement that the *Institutes* and the commentaries were intended to complement each other expresses a symbiotic relationship which should be taken more seriously than has been common, and that this mutuality deserves more attention. It is also clear that at least *some* of the development in the comprehensive theology was brought about by struggle with the biblical texts themselves. In this sense, some (if not all) of the scripture passages cited in the *Institutes* are not merely proof texts for a position reached by another route. Political, social, and especially theological influences were also present, but they do not tell the whole story; sometimes an exegetical problem determined a doctrinal conclusion.

The third and perhaps most interesting thing which becomes apparent from an examination of the exegetical histories of the biblical citations is that Calvin's genius lay in his theological perspective on exegesis. Very little in the content of Calvin's interpretation is new. What is novel is the vision which informed the way the Protestant biblical scholar read scripture in the light of other scripture, and his drive to provide a coherent and practicable view of biblical teaching. It is undoubtedly this coherence as an exegete which contributed in good measure to the impact of the *Institutes* on the biblically oriented world of the sixteenth century. Calvin's gift for making sense of scripture, his skill in painting a convincing picture of interrelationships among apparently discrete texts so that these could be practiced, is also perhaps one of the most abiding impressions the reformer's exegetical theology leaves with the modern scholar. Without inventing an entirely new interpretation, Calvin consistently used the exegetical resources available to him in ways others did not, to build an introduction to the Bible as comprehensive and coherent as possible.

Before any definitive conclusions can be drawn about the relationship of exegesis and theology in Calvin's thought, other areas besides ecclesiology would have to be explored. Nonetheless, twentieth-century students of sixteenth-century religious thought might well reconsider the nature and complexity of the interrelationship of exegesis, theology, and development in the *Institutes*, if the present investigation is representative of Calvin's biblical hermeneutics and theological methodology.

NOTES

1. See a few English examples of reservations about exclusive focus on the *Institutes:* John Dillenberger, *John Calvin: Selections from His Writings* (Missoula, Mont.: Scholars Press, 1975), pp. vii, 11–12; J. K. S. Reid, ed., *Calvin: Theological Treatises* (Philadelphia: Westminster Press, 1954), p. 13; T. H. L. Parker, *Calvin's New Testament Commentaries* (London: SCM Press, 1971), pp. vii–x, 1–2 and esp. chs. 2–3; Edward A. Dowey, Jr., "The Structure of Calvin's Thought as Influenced by the Twofold Knowledge of God," in *Calvinus Ecclesiae Genevensis Custos,* ed. W. Neuser (Frankfurt: Peter Lang, 1984), p. 141. T. H. L. Parker, "Calvin the Exegete," in *Calvinus Ecclesiae Doctor,* ed. W. Neuser (Kampen: J. H. Kok, 1980), p. 41, points to a general lack when he says that, to his knowledge, "the relationship of the 1540 Romans commentary as part of an expository development with the 1539 *Institutio* as part of a dogmatic development has not been explored." The present study was inspired primarily by a desire to summarize in relatively brief and coherent form the conclusions I have reached over a number of years of study of Calvin's ecclesiology in the context of exegetical history.

2. Calvin, dedication to Romans commentary, *Iohannis Calvini Commentarius in Epistolam Pauli ad Romanos,* ed. T. H. L. Parker (Leiden: E. J. Brill, 1981), pp. 1–3 (hereafter *Romanos*). Calvin here discusses Melanchthon, Bullinger, and Bucer, weighing the merits of different ways of commenting and explaining his own purpose of *"perspecua brevitas"* in biblical commentaries. For the purpose of the *Institutes* as an introduction to scripture, as his *loci communes,* see Preface to the Reader, *Institutio Christianae Religionis 1559,* in *OS* 3:6–7. For the reformers' adoption of the humanists' *loci* method, with its *inventio* or gathering of leading concepts from a document, see the summary discussion in Parker, *Calvin's New Testament Commentaries,* chs. 2–3, esp. pp. 29ff.

3. A rapid survey of the New Testament commentaries gives fourteen instances: Acts 6:3; Rom. 3:21; 3:28; 1 Cor. 1:1; 3:9; 3:14; 5:5; 9:5–6; 2 Cor. 4:17; 5:10; Eph. 3:18–19; 1 Tim. 2:6; 3:8; 1 Peter 1:20. Most cases concern issues of dispute between Rome and Protestants.

4. Calvin, "Discours d'Adieu," *OS* 2.402–403.

5. Examples on the diaconate: R. H. Henderson, "Sixteenth-Century Community Benevolence," *Church History* (1969), 427; J. K. S. Reid, "Diakonia in the Thought of John Calvin," *Service in Christ,* ed. J. I. McCord and T. H. L. Parker (London: Epworth Press, 1966), p. 106; R. M. Kingdon, "Was the Protestant Reformation a Revolution? The Case of Geneva," *Transition and Revolution,* ed. R. M. Kingdon (Minneapolis: Burgess Publishing Co., 1974), p. 73. On discipline, Harro Höpfl, *The Christian Polity of John Calvin* (Cambridge: University Press, 1982), pp. 111 and passim.

6. The interpretation of biblical texts becomes more "narrow" or precise in the sixteenth century, especially among Protestants, apparently because of the need or desire to apply scripture, the sole authority. It would perhaps be interesting to investigate this impression to discover how far it is true and what factors influenced its development.

7. For purposes of finding Calvin's cross-references, the biblical citations are restricted to those he notes himself. Fuller indices are found in the *Opera Selecta,* while the McNeill-Battles English edition (*Calvin: Institutes of the Christian Religion;* Philadelphia: Westminster Press, 1960) provides still more detailed notes of biblical allusions. The latter are useful in showing that the interplay between theology and scripture/exegesis is even more extensive than the reformer himself explicitly marked. For example, in 2.8.57 the McNeill-Battles edition indicates a conflation of Matt. 18:17 and Luke 6:32, in addition to Matt. 5:46–47, which Calvin cites, in a passage where it is strongly denied that monks can be considered all the "sons of God," to the exclusion of the rest of the church. In 2.8.32 the English points to a paraphrase of Acts 2:42, which the editors of the *Opera Selecta* missed. Sometimes, as with Matt. 18:18, Calvin himself will add biblical references in later editions for texts he has used in earlier ones. A fuller study of biblical allusions might well reward the effort.

8. Calvin, *Christianae religionis Institutio 1536,* ch. 4, *OS* 1:149. See Elsie Anne McKee, *John Calvin on the Diaconate and Liturgical Almsgiving* (Geneva: Droz, 1984), chs. 3 and 10.

9. Calvin, *Institutio 1536,* chs. 2, 5, 6 (bis), *OS* 1:89, 187, 239, 244 for Matt. 18:15–17.

10. Calvin, *Institutio 1536,* discusses presbyters in chs. 1 and 5 (*OS* 1:52–53, 212–213). Reference to Eph. 4[?] and 4:11 in ch. 6 (*OS* 1:52, 243). Deacons and Acts 6 and 1 Tim. 3 in ch. 5 (*OS* 1:218–219). Calvin, like all other Protestants, turned the medieval interpretation of the diaconate upside down by reading 1 Tim. 3:8–13 through the lens of Acts 6:1–6. This reinstating of the "religious" vocation of "serving tables" and consequent rejection of a (purely or primarily) liturgical definition of the diaconate is a case of exegetical revision of doctrine which Calvin inherited, but it is among the clearest instances of the influence of exegesis on theology. See McKee, *Calvin on the Diaconate,* chs. 6–7.

11. Calvin, *Institutio 1536,* ch. 6 (Rom. 12:8 and 2 Chron. 19), chs. 1 and 6 (2 Chron. 19), ch. 1 (1 Tim. 5:17), ch. 2 (1 Cor. 5:1–5, bis); *OS* 1:261, 52, 262, 53, 89, 90.

12. Calvin, "Articles concernant l'organisation de l'église," *OS* 1:372–373.

13. See Elsie Anne McKee, "Calvin, Discipline, and Exegesis: Matt. 18:17 and I Cor. 5:3–5 in the Sixteenth Century: A Summary,"

in *Théorie et pratique de l'exégèse: Actes du troisième colloque international sur l'histoire de l'exégèse biblique au seizième siècle,* ed. F. Higman and I. Backus (Geneva: Droz, forthcoming in 1990).

14. Calvin, Institutio 1559, 4.20.4, *OS* 5:475. See Elsie Anne McKee, *Elders and the Plural Ministry: The Role of Exegetical History in Illuminating John Calvin's Theology* (Geneva: Droz, 1988), pp. 40–43, 61–62.

15. Calvin, *Institutio 1559,* 4.12.4, *OS* 5:214–215.

16. Calvin, *Romanos,* pp. 271–272 for Rom. 12:8, pp. 322–323 for Rom. 16:1–2. See McKee, *Calvin on the Diaconate,* ch. 9, and n. 42 below.

17. Calvin, "Les ordonnances ecclesiastiques," *OS* 2:328ff., esp. pp. 328, 329, 340, 341, 358; p. 363 adds a 1561 reference to Matt. 18:17, but this is not concerned with agents of discipline.

18. Calvin, *Institutio 1559,* 4.3.4, *OS* 5:45–46. See other references in McKee, *Elders and the Plural Ministry,* pp. 133–136, 214–215, for a possible relationship in the development of Romans and Ephesians.

19. Calvin, *Institutio 1559,* 4.3.9, *OS* 5:50–51.

20. Calvin, *Institutio 1559,* 4.13.18–19, *OS* 5:255–257.

21. Calvin, *Institutio 1559,* 4.11.1, *OS* 5:195. See McKee, *Elders and the Plural Ministry,* esp. pp. 87–88, 97ff.

22. Calvin, *Romanos,* pp. 272.

23. Calvin, *Institutio 1559,* 4.12.2, 4.11.1, *OS* 5:213, 195. Jewish custom but no carryover of Jewish civil law, 4.11.4, *OS* 5:199–200. See McKee, "Calvin, Discipline, and Exegesis" (n. 13 above).

24. Calvin, *Institutio 1559,* 4.11.5, *OS* 5:200.

25. Calvin, *CO* 49:379–380. See McKee, "Calvin, Discipline, and Exegesis."

26. Calvin, *CO* 45:514.

27. Calvin, *Institutio 1559,* 4.11.1, *OS* 5:196.

28. Calvin, dedication to Romans commentary, *Romanos,* p. 4.

29. See the revised explanation of Rom. 12:8 at nn. 14, 22, 38, 39 for one example of Calvin's shift in interpretation (downplaying civil and emphasizing ecclesiastical) because of his broadening perspective on New Testament conditions.

30. See McKee, *Elders and the Plural Ministry,* pp. 91ff.

31. Ibid., pp. 172–175, 181–185, 190–197.

32. Ibid., pp. 142ff., 185–190.

33. Ibid., pp. 47–50, 72–76.

34. See McKee, *Calvin on the Diaconate,* ch. 3, esp. pp. 70–75.

35. See McKee, "Calvin, Discipline, and Exegesis."

36. Ibid.

37. See McKee, *Elders and the Plural Ministry,* esp. pp. 51, 72–76.

38. Ibid., ch. 2, esp. pp. 40–41, 52–53.

39. Ibid., ch. 2, esp. pp. 49–50, 53–54.

40. Ibid., ch. 4, esp. pp. 88, 97–103.

41. See McKee, "Calvin, Discipline, and Exegesis."

42. See Jane Dempsey Douglass, *Women, Freedom, and Calvin* (Philadelphia: Westminster Press, 1985), esp. ch. 3, for Calvin's theoretical openness.

43. See Elsie Anne McKee, "Calvin's Exegesis of Romans 12:8: Social, Accidental, or Theological?" *Calvin Theological Journal* (1988), 6–18, for full discussion.

PART THREE

Reform and Reformers in the Sixteenth Century

Zwingli the Exegete: A Contribution to the 450th Anniversary of the Death of Erasmus

Fritz Büsser

Translated by Bruce McCormack

Zwingli's life and work were completely devoted to serving the reform of church and society. If one were to ask what the center of his reforming activity was, which sustained all the rest, there can be only one answer: the proclamation of God's Word. Zwingli's work in Zurich began on January 1, 1519, with a continuous exposition of the Gospel of Matthew; likewise, the Zurich reformation began on the occasion of the so-called "First Zurich Disputation" on January 29, 1523, with the historic resolution of the political authorities (mayor and councils) that only the gospel was to be preached in all parts of the canton. This resolution led on the one hand to well-known reforming measures (dissolution of the monasteries, removal of images, reform of the service of worship, and the creation of new arrangements for the poor, for marriage, and for morals). On the other hand, it led to the founding of the "Prophezei" and thereby to scientific engagement with the Holy Scriptures, to Bible translations, and to commentaries on the Bible.[1]

I. A Grotesque Gap in Zwingli Research

As was just stated, the sustaining center of Zwingli's life, as of the Zurich reformation, was the Holy Scriptures. Zwingli understood himself as a prophet; i.e. (in accordance with 1 Cor. 14:29), as an expositor of the scriptures, and his coworkers also saw him in this light.[2] Accordingly, his exegetical and homiletical work have been recognized since the sixteenth century, and there is scarcely a presentation of Zwingli and the Zurich reformation which has not referred to the "Prophezei," the oldest Reformed academy, in which the exposition of scripture stood at the center of attention.[3]

Nevertheless, the truly central theme announced by the title of the present essay, "Zwingli the Exegete," has been treated in an extremely perfunctory manner up until now. Apart from Walther E. Meyer's 1976 essay on "The Genesis of Huldrych Zwingli's New Testament Commentaries and Written Sermons,"[4] there are only two works of importance: Ernst Nagel wrote generally on "Zwingli's Attitude Toward Scripture" (1896),[5] and Edwin Künzli published in 1950–51 a portion of his dissertation on "Zwingli as Expositor of Genesis and Exodus."[6] This lacuna in research is as inexplicable as it is deplorable. It stands in no relationship to the significance of Zwingli as exegete. As will be shown in the following pages, Zwingli's exegetical works occupy a significant place, both quantitatively and qualitatively.

I begin with some statistical evidence: (1) a brief quotation from Zwingli concerning the beginning of his preaching activity in Zurich; (2) an overview of the relative space devoted to exegetica in the three editions of the collected works of the Zurich reformer, which have appeared up to now; and (3) a chronological table of Zwingli's exegetical work in the years 1525–1531.

1. In the sense of a statement of accounts, Zwingli said the following with respect to his preaching activity on the occasion of the Second Zurich Disputation on October 26, 1523:

> As soon as I had arrived in Zurich [on January 1, 1519], I began for my part to preach the holy Gospel according to Matthew, without any admixture of human ornamentation. I openly declared to the prior and to the chapter that I planned to do that. . . . Afterwards, I preached on the Acts of the Apostles, the Letter of Paul to the Galatians, the two letters to Timothy, the two letters of Peter, the Letter to the Hebrews; and now, on Luke.[7]

2. That Zwingli's work on the Bible (preaching, exposition) occupies a significant place from a purely statistical point of view is demonstrated most impressively by the three editions of Zwingli's collected works.

The first edition of the complete works, which Zwingli's son-in-law Rudolf Gwalther saw to in 1544–45 (and which was "reprinted" in 1581), comprised four volumes and divided the works into three groups. Volume I contained the dogmatic works ("partim quidam ab ipso Latino conscripta, partim vero e vernaculo sermone in Latinum translata"); volume II, the polemical; and volumes III and IV, the exegetica.[8] The significance of the exegetica, which had already been documented externally, was underscored by Gwalther through three interesting supplements. In the foreword to volume III (Old Testament) he placed Zwingli in a series with the tradition of the early church and the Church Fathers.[9] At the beginning of volume IV he placed a foreword by Leo Jud,[10] which to my knowledge has scarcely been taken notice of to this day, as well as a poem of his own: "Concerning the Five Most Preeminent Restorers of the Doctrine of the Gospel."[11] The five were Reuchlin, Oecolampadius, Erasmus, Luther, and Zwingli.

A second edition of the complete works appeared in Zurich in 1828–1842 in eight volumes, with a supplement added in 1861.[12] Its editors, Melchior Schuler and Johannes Schulthess, described it correctly as the "first complete edition." They arranged Zwingli's texts according to the languages in which the texts were written. Thus, volumes I and II (1–3) brought forth the German writings and volumes III–VI, the Latin writings. Volumes VII and VIII contained Zwingli's letters (of which a selection had already been published once in 1536 in Basel, together with selected letters of Oecolampadius[13]). Schuler and Schulthess naturally subsumed the exegetical writings under the Latin writings. As was already the case with Gwalther, here too they occupy an impressive amount of space. Whereas the German writings (vols. I and II) fill 1,830 pages (30.42 percent) and the Latin writings (vols. III and IV) 984 pages (16.36 percent), the exegetical writings (vols. V and VI) comprise 1,894 pages (31.48 percent). The letters (vols. VII and VIII) contain 1,308 pages (21.74 percent).

These numbers may be approximately confirmed by the third edition, the so-called "critical" edition, *Huldreich Zwinglis sämtliche Werke.*[14] Begun in 1905 by Emil Egli and Georg Finsler and carried forward under the supervision of the Zwingli Verein in Zurich, the "critical" edition today contains next to the works (hitherto, vols. I–VI.3), the letters (vols. VII–XI) and marginal glosses (vol. XII), already Zwingli's exegetica on the Old Testament (vols. XIII and XIV). An edition of New Testament exegetica, on the other hand, was first begun in 1986. It may one day occupy no less space than in the earlier editions.

3. How great is the editorial task yet to be solved is shown in an impressive way by an overview of Zwingli's exegetical works written in the years 1525–1531. Walther E. Meyer has reconstructed this on the basis of the most minute investigations, in his already mentioned essay "The Genesis of Huldrych

Zwingli's New Testament Commentaries and Written Sermons."[15]

Without going into detail, the results of Meyer's study show that in the years 1525–1531, Zwingli gave two lecture series concurrently (mornings in the "Prophezei" at the Grossmünster on the Old Testament, and afternoons, at the Fraumünster on the New Testament). He further shows that Zwingli made these two series of lectures useful for a series of sermons which ran parallel to them. Incomparably more important, however, is the fact that if Zwingli occupied himself in these years, the last phase of his life—which was marked on the one hand by the great theological conflicts with Rome over the Mass, with Luther over the Lord's Supper, and with the Anabaptists, and, on the other hand, by the political struggle for carrying through the Reformation in the Swiss Confederation—with this kind of intensive exegesis of the Old and New Testaments, then he must himself have assigned the greatest relevance to his exegetical work. The recognition of that fact raises a number of questions—first of all, the question of the background, the root of this activity.

II. The "Theology" of Erasmus

In order to anticipate the necessarily provisional, fragmentary answer: It was not simply the quantity of Zwingli's exegetical work (its external compass) which had its roots in humanism. It was especially the quality of this work (the nature, kind, and way of theologizing; in short, the scientific method) and the content of Zwingli's reforming activity which had its roots there. To put it even more clearly and concretely, it was fundamentally Erasmus' conception of a theology derived from the Bible alone which decisively stamped Zwingli's theological work, not a theology determined by any (Scholastic) system or a central viewpoint (e.g., Luther's use of law and gospel). Or, to express it in another, provocative way: In his reforming theology Zwingli simply took up what Erasmus sketched out, desired, and suggested as biblical theology. To be sure, Zwingli then further developed and completed what Erasmus had envisioned in a way that was just as independent of Erasmus as it was consistent with the latter's basic intentions.

This contention may seem bold, perhaps even exaggerated. In order to understand it, however, there are two facts which need to be considered. The first is that humanism in general and Erasmus in particular had much more than a mere propaedeutic significance for the Reformation. Zwingli, and after him

Bullinger and Calvin, remained humanists as reformers throughout their entire lives.[16] And a second factor is closely connected with the first. Many modern scholars no longer see in Erasmus merely a humanist who aspired to a renewal of society through educational reform (practically through a revival of the spirit and virtues of classical antiquity); but, rather, a prominent Christian theologian who contributed de facto essential elements to the reform of church and society in the sixteenth century through a single-minded integration of humanistic scholarship into theology.[17] Such scholars proceed from the fact that in the center of Erasmus' life's work stood his work on the Bible: his Greek and Latin translation of the New Testament and, closely connected to it, his introductions to the study of the Bible (*Paraclesis, Methodus, Apologia,* and above all a *Ratio seu methodus compendio perveniendi ad veram theologiam,* which should be valued as a summary of his theology); his *Annotationes* to and *Paraphrases* of the New Testament; and, in addition, numerous theological editions of Church Fathers and Scholastic authors. According to H. Holeczek, these works, "taken by themselves, amount to an imposing theological library."[18]

To be sure, the significance of Erasmus the theologian is not yet exhausted by this achievement. At least as important, precisely for Zwingli, are three fundamental elements which, according to Augustijn, circumscribe more closely the integration of humanistic learning into theology effected by Erasmus. "The first element is Erasmus' consistent acceptance of the *philological methods* of humanists, employed in studying ancient texts, for biblical sciences and the study of Church Fathers."[19] Combined with this first element in Erasmus is a second: the *desire* for a new *scientific method for theology.* "The rule of systematic theology would be broken and in its place, exegesis would receive the place of honor. . . . Theology would no longer be carried out in accordance with the laws of a strict logic, the whole of the scholastic method would be endangered; it would have to quit the field for the humanist method of science in which dialectic and rhetoric would be united."[20] "A third and final element is the *program of reform* which Erasmus wanted to put into effect. The study of the New Testament and the Church Fathers was not simply a technical affair; it should lead to a new *spirituality,* a contemporary piety. In this program, Erasmus turned against the externalization of the church and its means of grace . . . and against scholasticism" in favor of a Christocentric faith and, flowing out of that, an ethically determined act-Christianity which is authenticated in private and public everyday life.[21]

Erasmus—the Key to the Theology of Zwingli

How did the influences just described work themselves out in the Reformation generally and in Zwingli in particular? In answering this fundamental question, I take as my starting point the most important preface of Erasmus to his editions of the New Testament. In the preface, *Theological Methodology or Procedure, How One Can Attain to a True Erudition in Things Divine* (which was mentioned above in its Latin title), Erasmus first brings forward an impressive confession of Christ as the source and centerpiece of the Christian faith (in the framework of extensive discussions of faith and love where he even adduces a doctrine of justification which is completely in keeping with the spirit of the Reformation). Then, however, he writes the following statements, which read like *the* recipe for Zwingli's reforming theology and, therefore, deserve to be printed not with small but with great golden letters.

> *You should either compile some theological themes for yourself or take them over from someone who has already worked them out.* Then everything which you read should be collected under these themes, as in certain nests. By this means, it should be much more easily evident what you want to borrow and save. In this manner (in order to bring forward only a few viewpoints by way of example): concerning faith, fasting, enduring evils, concerning aid for the sick, how to put up with godless holders of office, concerning the avoidance of stumbling-blocks for the weak, *concerning the study of Holy Scripture,* concerning the obligations of piety toward parents or children, concerning Christian love, how one must honor the nobility, concerning envy and jealousy, concerning chastity and other things of this kind. Many other categories could be thought of. When they have been ordered according to the congruity and incongruity of the objects considered, then one must arrange in accordance with them everything of decisive importance which is found in the books of the Old Testament, in the Gospels and in the epistles of the apostles, everything which agrees with or contradicts them (as we have already declared in our "Copia"). If it now seems good to someone, he can also bring together here that which he is able to regard as useful from early interpreters and finally, even from the books of the heathen.[22]

III. Zwingli as Dogmatician

Now, to what extent is Erasmus de facto the key to the work of Zwingli? A first and, in its way, especially impressive answer is given by the dogmatic (including polemical) writings of the reformer. It is precisely these writings that show Zwingli to be a teachable pupil of Erasmus. In that they all, without exception, employ the just-described *loci* method, they prove themselves to be the execution, the fulfillment of the methodological and scientific-theoretical wishes of Erasmus, "either to compile some theological themes for yourself or to take them over from someone who has already worked them out." Above all other dogmatic and polemical writings of Zwingli, it is the two great outlines of dogmatics—the *Auslegen und Gründe der Schlussreden* (1523), the first Reformed dogmatics in the German language, and the *Commentarius de vera et falsa religione* (1525) which show themselves to be independent, well-considered compilations of theological *loci.* On the other hand, the later confessional writings are of the other type, "taken over from others," insofar as the *Credo-sermon* (1528), the *Fidei ratio* (1530) and the *Fidei expositio* (1531) conform to the articles of the Apostles' Creed, while also bringing further *loci* to expression in all kinds of excursus. Moreover, it is interesting in this connection to make a comparison of the number of theological themes treated from one time to the next. The number declines from the sixty-seven *Schlussreden* to the twenty-nine chapters of the *Commentarius* and then returns to the twelve of the Apostles' Creed.

The table of contents of the *Commentarius* may serve to provide a view of the whole. It treats the following themes.

> 1. On the concept "religion"; 2. Subject and object of religion; 3. On God; 4. On humankind; 5. On religion; 6. On the Christian religion; 7. On the gospel; 8. On repentance; 9. On the law; 10. On sin; 11. On the sin against the Holy Spirit; 12. On the keys; 13. On the church; 14. On the church against Emser; 15. On the sacraments; 16. On marriage; 22. On vows; 23. On the invocation of the saints; 24. On merit; 25. On prayer; 26. On purgatory; 27. On the magistracy; 28. On scandal; 29. On statues.[23]

Zwingli follows the directions of Erasmus with no less consistency when he is occupied with a particular theological theme. We choose as an example the *locus* on purgatory, a theme which had been especially hotly contested since the first years of the Reformation. Zwingli devoted to it Articles 57 to 60 of the *Schlussreden* and *Locus* 26 of the *Commentarius.*[24] Particularly instructive is the exposition of Article 57 of the *Schlussreden,* insofar as already, in the article itself, Zwingli lays down his method with the greatest clarity and conciseness. First comes Article 57 itself: "The true Holy Scriptures know nothing of a purgatory after this life." The interpretation which then follows (just as directly following Erasmus) collects and investigates everything pertaining to the theme from the Bible and the Church Fathers, everything which agrees with it or contradicts it.[25] How does that look in practice? Zwingli begins his exposition with a confession of the scripture principle. "The true Holy Scriptures know nothing of a purgatory after this life. Here I said, first of all, 'The true Holy Scriptures'; from this I exclude the Apocrypha, i.e., the unknown writings. Then I said that the untainted, sure, divine scriptures know nothing of purgatory" (Z II 414:2–11; *Huldrych Zwingli: Writings,* I, p. 335 [see note 24]). Immediately connected to these statements, there follows a disposition. "This may appear strange to everyone, not to the papists alone, but to some scholars also who in our day expound scripture earnestly and faithfully. It will be necessary therefore to look, first, at the passages of scripture from which they tried to prove purgatory. And after we have shown that they always do violence to scripture with regard to this matter, we shall then state our understanding, which is, that after death we know nothing except either heaven or hell. Nor shall I be sidetracked by the fact that several prominent teachers have sought to prove purgatory by reference to their scripture, but not from divine scriptures" (Z II 414:12–20; *Huldrych Zwingli: Writings,* I, p. 335). This disposition corresponds, then, to the actual arrangement.

In a first round, Zwingli handles the classical passages adduced in support of the traditional doctrine of purgatory: Matt. 12:32; Matt. 5:25f.; Matt. 18:34; 2 Macc. 12:44–46; 1 Cor. 3:10–15 (Z II 414:21–425:20; *Huldrych Zwingli: Writings,* I, pp. 335–342). Especially instructive is his treatment of the last two named passages. As for using 2 Macc. 12:44–46 (prayer for the dead) as proof for purgatory, Zwingli's response is brief and to the point. The passage is not to be found in the canon. "The fourth instance, read in the temple from the Book of Maccabees, I consider, just as it is, apocryphal; since the origin of said book is uncertain, we cannot support any argument from it." Farther on, he adds, "The Book of Maccabees has about as much authority with me as John Mandeville or Hildebrand. Look at Josephus, by contrast, who also wrote a history of the Jews. Jews, Greeks and Latins use him too, though he is not canonized. You will soon see how much faith you should put in the greedy inventor of fables who rhymed together the Book of Maccabees" (Z II 419:22–24; 420:5–10; *Huldrych Zwingli: Writings,* I, p. 339).

With respect to 1 Cor. 3:10–11 (the trial of buildings in the fire), Zwingli remarks that here one must proceed on the basis of the sense of passage. The passage has to do not with purgatory but with Christ and believers. From the context we learn that Paul preached Christ to the Corinthians. "This rock and foundation is Christ." The superstructure refers, according to 1 Cor. 3:9, to believers. "For we are fellow-workers for God; you are God's field, God's building." And then, in Zwingli's words: "And 'fire' means 'persecution' [*Verfolgung, Anfechtung; adflictio*], as in Isa. 43:1f., 'Though you walk in fire, you shall not be consumed.' Thus Paul intends to say in the last quoted passage, 'What anyone has built upon the foundation, which is Christ Jesus, shall be revealed in the persecution' " (Z II 423:8–12; *Huldrych Zwingli: Writings,* I, pp. 340–341).

In the second place, Zwingli wants to express his opinion. "At this point I shall indicate my own opinion also and the reasons for believing that there is no purgatory of the kind the theologians speak of. I bank on the fact that God said nothing to us about purgatory" (Z II 425:21–23; *Huldrych Zwingli: Writings,* I, p. 342). That is to say, Zwingli grounds his rejection of purgatory first of all on the fact that God has said nothing about it. Returning to biblical proofs, he immediately continues: "Indeed, he [God] expressed an opinion which completely contradicts it, for he spoke of no other dwelling place after this world than heaven and hell, Luke 16 [22–26]" (Z II 425:23–26; *Huldrych Zwingli: Writings,* I, p. 342). On the other hand, for Zwingli, "the purgatory of which the theologians speak is against the power of faith. For one who believes has already been saved; he need not wait for any calamity or condemnation" (Z II 426:19–21; *Huldrych Zwingli: Writings,* I, p. 343). As proof texts, Zwingli here depends on Heb. 11:6; 1 Cor. 1:30; John 3:16–18; 5:24. He appeals as well to the conception of the last judgment in Matt. 25: 31–46 and 2 Cor. 5:10 or, alternatively, on the immediate transition from this time into eternity: 1 Cor. 15:23; Luke 23:43; Phil. 1:23f.; 2 Cor. 5:4–6.

In passing, it may be observed that Zwingli argues in a very similar fashion in the *Commentarius* as well as in the *Fidei expositio* (although without biblical proof texts in the latter). In the *Commentarius* he also supports his argument by appeal to some Church Fathers.

IV. Zwingli the Exegete: The Annotationes in Evangelium Lucae[26]

The stimuli provided by Erasmus are naturally reflected all the more in Zwingli's exegetical work, not only in a qualitative or formal respect but, rather, in view of a stronger integration of the results of the exposition into Zwingli's work as a whole. That here a source exists of which too little use has been made may be demonstrated by one example. Walther Meyer, in his already cited essay on Zwingli's New Testament exegetica, had this to say about the "Expositions of Luke" in 1531—Zwingli's "exegetical and homiletical swan song":

> It unites in itself the entire spectrum of Zwinglian theology from its beginnings to its last out-working. It is especially fascinating to find here that Zwingli, at the end of his life's work and under the sign of a dogmatic reflection which has been thought through to the end in terms of a consistent ontology, returns to the dynamic beginnings of his reforming activity, just as we also find traces of this procedure in Zwingli's latest work, the *Expositio fidei.*[27]

As the editor of the *Fidei expositio* for the critical edition of Zwingli's works, I can not only confirm these fundamental remarks of Meyer's; I can also supplement them and illustrate them. In doing so, I must limit myself to just a few aspects and examples, fully conscious of the fact that it is a matter here only of provisional observations.

1. I begin with a pair of "technical" remarks. As was also the case with his exegetica on the Old Testament, the *Annotationes in Evangelium Lucae* does not provide a thoroughgoing commentary in the modern sense but simply notes (here again, following Erasmus). These are sometimes made with respect to particular expressions, sometimes to particular verses, sometimes to entire pericopes, and, finally, to entire chapters as well. Frequently in this connection, evidence of the use of Hebraisms is given,[28] as well as of the employment of rhetorical devices.[29] Also conspicuous is the number of so-called *digressiones,*[30] i.e., excursus, to which belong not only the sections so designated by Zwingli himself but many other examples. Zwingli expressly designates as *digressio* the excursus on Luke 2:11 ("Digressio per gradationem, in qua ostenditur summa et tota Evangelii ratio," S VI/I, pp. 553f.); Luke 7:16 ("Digressio: Quomodo, quando, et quibus benefaciendum, ut bene collocetur beneficium," pp. 594f.); and Luke 9:47 ("modestia et humilitas," pp. 619f.). Moreover, Zwingli's explanations of the following are also typical examples of excursuses: Luke 3:3 (baptism and repentance, pp. 558f.); 3:14 (the question of the soldiers: What shall we do? pp. 561–565); 3:12f. (concerning publicans, pp. 565f.); 6:27f. (love of the enemy, pp. 585f.); 6:29 (retaliation, pp. 586–589); 6:43f. (image of the tree and its fruit, pp. 590–592); 10:1 (on the usefulness and necessity of the apostolate, pp. 622f.).

2. The just-cited passages lead to a second observation. In the exegetica, Zwingli has favorite themes—themes in which he reaches back to previous treatments. To give an example, his

explanation of prophecy is simultaneously a proof of the fact that the *Annotationes in Evangelium Lucae* completes his *Fidei expositio*—or, to put it another way, it is simultaneously a proof of the fact that this confession requires completion and explanation through corresponding sections of his exegetica.

As is well known, Zwingli treats prophecy in the *Fidei expositio* very concisely, only at the end of chapter 7 on "Governments."

> To sum up, in the Church of Christ government is just as necessary as preaching, although this latter occupies the first place. For as a man cannot exist except as composed of both body and soul, however much the body is the humbler and lower part, so the Church cannot exist without the civil government, though the government attends to and looks after the more material things that have not to do with the spirit. Since then, two particularly bright lights of our faith, Jeremiah and Paul, bid us pray to the Lord of our rulers that they may permit us to lead a life worthy of God, how much more ought all in whatever kingdom or people to bear and to do all things to guard the Christian peace! Hence we teach that tribute, taxes, dues, tithes, debts, loans, and all promises to pay of every kind should be paid and the laws of the state in general be obeyed in these things.[31]

The editor, W. J. Hinke, remarks on this passage, "Zwingli was probably thinking of Jer. 29:7 and 1 Tim. 2:2. He discusses the latter passage in his treatise 'De vera et falsa religione,' see Zwingli's *Werke,* Vol. III, 1914, p. 873f."

More important and going farther than the *Commentarius* (which had already appeared in 1525) are, however, precisely in relation to the function of the prophet, Zwingli's *Annotationes in Evangelium Lucae,* especially a pair of passages in Luke 1 (Zechariah) and Luke 3 (John the Baptist). On Luke 1:76, Zwingli writes, "Tam necessaria est prophetia, ut si nullus esset magistratus, verus propheta erigere et constituere magistratum possit: ubi vero propheta nullus est, nihil efficiet magistratus, nec pius unquam erit populus" (p. 550). Especially informative, then, is Luke 3, a chapter which Zwingli introduces with the following words: "Prophetarum omnium limes et finis est Ioannes Baptista, qui ante Christum tanquam aurora ante solem praecedit, digitoque eum praesentem monstrat, non porro futurum praedicit" (p. 558). Here Zwingli remarks in detail with respect to the already mentioned verse Luke 3:3:

> Remissio peccatorum periphrasis est evangelii; alias Paulus iustificationem vocat more Hebraico pro absolutione et remissione pec-

> catorum. Nemo enim iustus est, nisi qui credit in Christum, et qui credit sibi per Christum remissa esse peccata, idem studebit se Christo conformare (pp. 559f.).

Zwingli's sigh over the Isaiah quotation in Luke 3:4 is a clear allusion to the circumstances of his times—or, to be even more precise, it can be understood only against the background of Zwingli's own experience.

> Hodie proh dolor pauci aut nulli sunt Ioannes: praedicamus omnes evangelium suaviter, et quantum sine periculo vitae fieri potest; qui vero consceleratis pro dignitate resistant, pauci sunt, aut fere nulli. Evangelium enim plausibile est cunctis, at si non perpetuo lex simul inculcetur pessimi fiunt homines. Non recipiunt homines Christum, neque gratiam eius avide amplexantur, quin nec eis gratia praedicanda est, nisi prius morbos suos agnoscant, et peccatorum suorum agnitione quasi desperent. Tales enim avidi sunt gratiae, et sitientes iustitiae (p. 560).

However, the question of the soldiers to the Baptist in Luke 3:14, "What shall we do?" becomes for Zwingli the real high point of this chapter. In a clearly constructed excursus covering no less than three and a half pages, the reformer comes to terms with the questions of the sword and of just war, which had been raised by the Anabaptists (but also through the resistance of the five central cantons of Switzerland to the Reformation). We cite here only two passages:

> Bella suscipere, ut in pace et tranquillitate liceat vivere, Christianis etiam licet, quamlibet reclament Catabaptistae. . . . Ad repellendum ergo malum, et ut impii et perduelles compescantur, in tutoque sint pii et boni, opus est manu domini, omnipotentis regis et summi principis, qui ministris suis (nam vicem dei in terris gerunt magistratus) gladium praebet ad resecanda et comprimenda mala. Hic iam magistratus gladio utitur, sed per eos qui fidei suae commissi sunt, quibus si ferire praecipit et interficere sontes, quid hoc aliud erit quam bellum, sed iustum, legitimum, divinum? Qui hoc geri posse negat, simul omnem iustitiam pessumdat. Bellum ergo quaeritur, ut in pace et iustitia sine iniuria bonis vivere liceat. Habet ergo magistratus milites suos atque cohortes, quibus arma ferre, ferire hostes, adeoque defendere cives ex mandato magistratus licet, qui aliquando in praesidiis et regionibus ad cavendas seditiones, et comprimendos motus collocati publicam tuentur tranqillitatem. Quales hi fuerunt qui ad Ioannem discendi gratia venerunt, qui dum officio suo bona fide invigilant, non solum magistratibus, sed deo quoque serviunt. Est ergo bellum iustum, ubi iuxta leges et ordinem magistratus milites iussa

exequuntur, ubi magistratus pro defensione suorum armis utitur in eos, qui vel religionem vel pietatem violare moliuntur, aut publicam labefactare tranquillitatem. Quod bellum scriptura sacra non solum probat, sed docet quoque, ut ex libris veteris testamenti manifeste colligi potest. Illic enim ordinationem magistratus, legum, bellorum, rerumpublicarum graphice depictam videre licet. Nec desunt exempla in Mose, Iosua, Ezechia, Iosaphat, Iosia etc. (pp. 561–562).

To be sure, with these statements Zwingli's remarks on the prophet and prophecy in the *Annotationes in Evangelium Lucae* are far from being exhausted. Such remarks are found, among other places, at Luke 3:19f. (the imprisonment of John, pp. 567f.); 4:24 ("no prophet is acceptable in his home country," pp. 572f.); 6:20a ("And he lifted up his eyes on his disciples": "For these words are the arms of all those who preach the Word of God, who like shepherds go before their sheep and expose themselves to danger," p. 583); Luke 10 ("On the usefulness and necessity of the apostolate," pp. 622–623), especially 10:4 ("The chief office of the apostolate is to teach, to warn, to cry out against wickedness," p. 623).

3. Naturally, obviously, parallels to others of Zwingli's writings are to be found in the *Annotationes in Evangelium Lucae.* I limit myself here to comparisons with the *Fidei expositio,* which was drawn up at approximately the same time (it was first published in 1536). Meyer, too, refers to it. To be sure, a direct relationship is found only once. In a long note on Luke 2:21 (the circumcision of Jesus), Zwingli comes to speak on the sacraments.

Exemplum huius in Hieremia habetur, qui cum iussus esset ligneam catenam collo appendere, regibusque ostendere, multo significantius captivitatem denunciavit, quam si solum verbis hanc insonuisset. Denique plus metus illis incussit, quum non audirent solum, sed viderent etiam futuram poenam. Sic fit in Eucharistia, ubi non auditus solum verbis promissionum, sed et caeteri sensus omnes suo quodam modo afficiuntur, ut in alio libello satis indicavimus (p. 555).

Without doubt, Zwingli alludes to the corresponding passage on "The Virtue of the Sacraments" in the *Fidei expositio.*[32]

In no way does the matter rest there. If one proceeds in a reverse direction, starting from the *Fidei expositio* in search of elucidations and completions of thought, one finds in the *Annotationes in Evangelium Lucae* a wealth of parallels. I refer in the following only to a very small selection of especially interesting examples, and I lay down as a premise that, as a rule, it is a matter of an excursus (a theme) in both works which was very important to Zwingli.

S IV	LW II	(Exposition)	S VI/I	Annotations
49	244	On the Lord Christ	553–554	(Luke 2:11)
56–58	256–260	What the power of the sacraments is	555	(Luke 2:21)
60–61	263–264	The forgiveness of sins	558–561	(Luke 3:3)
61–64	265–269	Faith and works	590–592	(Luke 6:43–45)
			629–630	(Luke 10:25)
63–64	269	On the Law	586–589	(Luke 6:29)
64–66	269–272	Life eternal	575	(Luke 5:1)
			608	(Luke 8:52)
66–67	272–276	On the Catabaptists	561–565	(Luke 3:14)

4. New themes which have scarcely been noticed before in Zwingli research appear in the *Annotationes in Evangelium Lucae.* By way of example, I think here of an aspect of theological anthropology to which my Zurich colleague Gerhard Ebeling has called attention recently: "the coram-relation as the ontological key to anthropology."[33] It is a question here of the determination of humankind always and in all relations to stand before God.

If one looks through the Luke *Annotationes* for this coram-relation, the first thing that strikes one's attention is that it appears fairly frequently. It is found in relationship to two theological themes which are central for Zwingli. It is used as a paraphrase for the covenant and true faith. Once again, Zechariah and John the Baptist serve as examples. The first passage in which the expression [*ambulare*] *coram Deo* appears, concerns Zechariah (and Elizabeth): "But they were both righteous before God, walking in all the commandments and ordinances of the Lord blameless" (Luke 1:6). Zwingli's remarks here:

> Torquent se hic multi quomodo coram deo iusti fuisse dicantur, quum coram eo nemo mortalium iustus esse possit. . . . Hic nodus facile dissolvi potest, si simpliciter intelligamus Hebraicae loquutionis formulam, quae *lipne 'adonai* eos iustos dicit, qui metu dei et amore iustitiae, innocentiae et sanctitati student, qui bona conscientia et sincera, quasi in conspectu dei omnia videntis, versantur. Sic deus Abrahae dicit: Ambula coram me, et esto integer! Sic

Henoch dicitur ambulasse, et Noe iustus fuisse coram domino, hoc est, metuentes et reverentes dei fuerunt. Coram deo ergo iustum esse, est timorem dei habere (p. 542).

Yet that is certainly not sufficient! Zwingli knows well that before God no one is righteous, and therefore he concludes the paragraph with these words: "Iustum ergo esse coram deo, est fidem in Christum coniicere, esurire et sitire iustitiam. Fide enim iustitia piorum constat" (p. 543).

Zwingli points in the same direction when he explains Luke 1:15 ("John will be great in the sight of the Lord").

Hic iam tertio ponitur Coram domino, tamen aliter atque aliter. Hic coram domino est in ministerio et negotio domini. Neque enim in se magnus erat, sed ideo dicitur magnus, quod magnam rem nunciaret, quod magni domini et regis praecursor erat, quod magnum haberet officium, magnus vitae innocentia et sanctitate. In Ioanne typus austerae et gravis vitae praebetur mundo, ut est Matthaei undecimo et tertio cap. Quamlibet vero austerus et gravis fuerit, caeteros tamen populariter viventes nequaquam damnat, sed fert. Deinde agnoscit imbecillitatem suam, humilitatem et gratiam, se indignum profitetur qui vel corrigiam calceamentorum Christi solvat. Hoc exemplo discant Catabaptistae, caeteros etiamsi ipsi sint sanctissimi, non despicere, seque non minus peccatores esse, quam caeteros. Exemplo quidem argutae apis per omnes virtutum flores curramus, et e singulis excerpamus, quae vitae prosint Christianae. Vera enim pietas studium innocentiae est, et iustitiae, sed simul lux est, quae interim nobis ostendit quantum adhuc a lege dei absimus, quantumvis legis et iustitiae fuerimus observantes et studiosi. Ostendit enim lapsus et errata quibus etiam in ipsa legis observatione sumus obnoxii, ostendit iustitiam nostram esse pollutam et contaminatam, ut ita nemo suae iustitiae, nemo suae innocentiae fidere possit. Oportet ut agnoscamus nos esse peccatores, quibus ex pura gratia et misericordia dei conferatur iustitia et salus. Quae gratia nobis per Christum (qui pignus est gratiae) certo obsignata est (p. 543).

I will pass quickly over the next three passages in which Zwingli treats the coram-relation and refer only to the fundamental features. On Luke 3:21 (the baptism of Jesus) he remarks that all the works of God are directed to bringing it about that men and women recognize God as their creator and Father and encounter him in trust, love and reverence him,

ut coram hoc clementissimo patre suo integre et innocenter ambulet, nempe iuxta voluntatem eius. In hoc pendent omnes prophetae, omnia sanctorum omnium scripta. Hoc urgent omnes sancti ab initio mundi. At considerata nostra imbecillitate et impotentia, deus filium suum nobis promisit et dedit, per quem delerentur peccata nostra. Summa ergo utriusque testamenti in hoc sita est, ut deum cognoscamus, amemus, fide et innocentia vitae colamus, ei toto pectore fidamus: ubi vero in his labi contingit, ut certi simus filium nobis datum et pro nobis in mortem expositum, expiationem nostram esse et reconciliationem coram deo (p. 568).

The step to covenant theology (Gen. 17:1f.) is truly not a great one. That faith and love provide its contents, Zwingli remarks on Luke 8:27 (healing of the possessed Gerasene) with the words: "Haec ergo fides vera est, quae sic deum cognoscit, quae sic coram eo ambulare studet, voluntati eius obsequitur, eum amat, colit, observat, ei fidit ac firmiter adhaeret" (p. 605).

5. We come now to the main point. As has already been intimated by the comparison between the *Annotationes in Evangelium Lucae* with the *Fidei expositio* (number 4) and the reference to the coram-relation (number 5), for Zwingli, the exegetica are not simply a "technical affair." Rather, precisely here Zwingli shows himself to be a student of Erasmus in that the study of the Bible "[ought to] lead to a new spirituality, a contemporary piety." To speak once more with Augustijn: "Erasmus wanted to reach a point where the church transformed itself from a power apparatus and a purely sacral fellowship to a fellowship which helped men and women to break through to the kernel, to intercourse with God."[34]

It was precisely this goal which Zwingli's reformation of church and society pursued. Corresponding proof texts (which are just as numerous as they are impressive and convincing) are not found in the systematic and polemical works of Zwingli, which up to now have been the center of interest (and in which the same themes have always been advanced, to the point of insensibility!). They are found rather in the letters and above all in the exegetica—and not last of all in the *Annotationes in Evangelium Lucae,* as a few examples from chapter 6 may help to illustrate. In the sequence of texts:

Luke 5:33ff.: Pulchris parabolis et allegoriis mediocritatem summam (ut etiam philosophi testantur) virtutem docet Christus, sine qua caeterae virtutes vitia sunt non virtutes. . . . Homo perfectus esse non potest (p. 578).

Luke 5:34: Fides vero et spiritus docent pios ubi sit ieiunandum, ubi edendum, ubi orandum, ubi rursus ab oratione ad opera charitatis redeundum. Quod Paulus dicit: Non estis sub lege, sed sub gratia, idem est cum hoc dicto Christi (p. 579).

6 (Introduction): Subinde clarius elucescit quae vera quaeque falsa et hypocritica sit religio. . . . Nos fere omnes similes sumus pharisaeis, videri enim volumus quales haudquaquam sumus. Si studeremus id esse quod videri volumus, plus esset religionis verae et solidae pietatis (p. 580).

6:19: Christus vero lux est totius mundi. . . . Christus ergo non in hoc duntaxat venit ut nos morte sua redimeret, sed ut totum hominem intus et extra renovaret ac sanctificaret, ut novae vitae exemplar in se proponeret. Conari igitur debemus, ad optima quaeque et praestantissima; ubi vero quid deest, Christus hoc sarciet (p. 583).

6:36: Bonitas dei includit in se misericordiam et iustitiam. Iustitia sal est, misericordia butyrum aut aqua: ex his duobus, si misceas, sapidus fit cibus: alterum si des, cibus non est, sed gustum laedit. Miscenda ergo utraque, et simul condienda. Misericordia sine iustitia esse non potest: nam si est sine iustitia, misericordia non est, sed mollities. Si iustitia est sine misericordia, non est iustitia, sed crudelitas et tyrannis. Summum enim ius summa est iniuria (p. 589).

Taken as a whole, the themes of Zwingli's reforming spirituality all circle around the imitation of Christ. In all their sinfulness, men and women should hold themselves to the words and deeds of Christ, on the basis of faith. That means that we are to do his works of love unhypocritically and in trust in the power of the Spirit of God. In this comprehensive framework are found extraordinarily personal remarks, i.e., remarks which can be understood only on the basis of the threatening circumstances of Zwingli's life. I think here, for example, of his interpretation of Luke 6:46ff. (the parable of the house built on rock, pp. 592f.); 9:23 (on the imitation of Christ, pp. 613f.); 12:19 (the parable of the rich fool, pp. 651f.).

Conclusions

On the basis of our consideration of the influence of Erasmus on Zwingli, a pair of conclusions force themselves on us which, I think, merit further reflection. First of all, Zwingli's oft-repeated assertion that he had already discovered the gospel (i.e., become a reformer) in 1516—and not first under the influence of Luther—acquires greater weight. To his subjective remembrance is added an objective confirmation: the influence of Erasmus on Zwingli through the whole of his life may have exercised an effect not only on the methodological and scientific-theoretical elements but rather also on the shape and content of Zwingli's theology. No less a witness than the Strassburg reformer Martin Bucer stated in 1528 (!): "What is useful for a Christian man or woman or necessary to know, that Erasmus of Rotterdam did not teach, even to the point of superfluity, long before Luther?"[35] And Zwingli himself wrote in a letter concerning his originally cordial, later tension-filled, but always gratitude-filled relationship to Erasmus, that the latter had said, after reading his *Commentarius:* "O good Zwingli! What have you written which I have not already written earlier?"[36] Thereby, the question (which is raised again and again) of a so-called "reformational turn" in Zwingli's life is rendered superfluous. It is a boring question, ultimately determined by the biographies (i.e., the conversion experiences) of Luther and Calvin, and, above all, it is one dimensional.

Finally, in place of those essays on "Erasmus and Zwingli" which trade in generalities, the concrete task which urges itself on us is that of undertaking a point-by-point comparison of the theologies of Erasmus and Zwingli. Such a study could easily lead to the recognition that, although that learned "citizen of the world," Erasmus, rejected the citizenship of the city of Zurich, he was brought in by Zwingli through a back door to become the secret reformer of Zurich, if not the father of Reformed *theology* generally. Certainly, we would have to observe carefully the fact that Erasmus was already fifty years old in 1516, and sixty in 1526, and that therefore it required a Zwingli, who was a generation younger, to realize the reforms in theology, church, and society desired by his "teacher." It also required a politically experienced and engaged pastor, together with a united citizenry.

NOTES

1. G. R. Potter, *Zwingli* (Cambridge: Cambridge University Press, 1976); G. W. Locher, *Die Zwinglische Reformation im Rahmen der europäischen Kirchengeschichte* (Göttingen, 1979); U. Gäbler, *Huldrych Zwingli, His Life and Work* (Philadelphia: Fortress Press, 1986).

2. F. Büsser, *Huldrych Zwingli, Reformation als prophetischer Auftrag* (Göttingen, 1973). "Der Prophet—Gedanken zu Zwinglis Theologie" and "De prophetae officio," in Büsser, *Wurzeln der Reformation in Zürich* (Leiden, 1985), pp. 49–59, 60–71. "In Defense of Zwingli: 1536" in *Prophet, Pastor, Protestant,* ed. E. J. Furcha and H. W. Pipkin (Allison Park, Pa.: Pickwick Publications, 1984), pp. 1–21.

3. Locher, *Zwinglische Reformation,* pp. 161–163. Büsser, "Reformierte Erziehung in Theorie und Praxis," in *Wurzeln der Reformation in Zürich,* pp. 199–216.

4. W. E. Meyer, "Die Entstehung von Huldrych Zwinglis neutestamentlichen Kommentaren und Predigtnachschriften," *Zwingliana* 14 (1976), 285–331.

5. E. Nagel, *Zwinglis Stellung zur Schrift* (Freiburg and Leipzig, 1896). Nagel treats here: I. The genesis of Zwingli's view of scripture in the context of his education (with express emphasis on the role of Erasmus!); II. The general characteristics of Zwingli's attitude toward scripture as it appeared in the struggle with Rome [Scripture and authority, the essence of the Word of God]; III. The modification of Zwingli's attitude toward scripture as a consequence of the controversy over rebaptizing [scripture and Spirit]; IV. The modification of Zwingli's original standpoint in the course of the controversy with Luther and his followers [here more extensively: the method of interpreting scripture in detail].

6. E. Künzli, "Zwingli als Ausleger von Genesis und Exodus" (diss., University of Zurich, 1951; typescript of xiv + 254 p.). From this dissertation was published: *Zwingli als Ausleger von Genesis und Exodus* (Teildruck Diss. theol. Zurich, 89 pp. [Zurich, 1950]), and "Quellenproblem und mystischer Schriftsinn in Zwinglis Genesis- und Exoduskommentar," *Zwingliana* 9, no. 4 (1950), 185–207; 9, no. 5 (1951), 253–307. It might also be pointed out that Edwin Künzli contributed in a decisive way to the edition of Zwingli's Old Testament works in volumes 13 and 14 of the critical *Huldreich Zwinglis sämtliche Werke,* ed. Emil Egli, Georg Finsler, Walther Köhler, Oskar Farner, Fritz Blanke, Leonhard von Muralt, Edwin Künzli, Rudolf Pfister, Joachim Städtke, and Fritz Büsser in cooperation with the Zwingli Verein (Zurich, 1905–) (hereafter Z). In this framework he published some smaller works; cf. Z VI/III, Zurich, 1983, pp. xi f.

7. Z II 707:31–708:6. Cf. Heinrich Bullinger, *Reformationsgeschichte,* vol. 1, ed. J. J. Hottinger and H. H. Vögeli (Frauenfeld, 1838), p. 31.

8. Cf. the bibliographical description by Georg Finsler, ed., *Zwingli-Bibliographie: Verzeichnis der gedruckten Schriften von und über Zwingli* (Zurich, 1897), p. 75.

9. "Operum D. Huldrychi Zuinglii tomus tertius; ea, quae in Genesim, Exodum, Esaiam et Ieremiam prophetas, partim ex ore illius excepta, partim ab illo conscripta sunt, una cum Psalterio Latinitate donato, contenens" (Zurich, 1544), pp. 2r–3r. The critical edition of Zwingli's exegetica on the Old Testament contains only Zwingli's prefaces to the reader (Z XIII 5:1–6:9; 294:1–295:10; XIV, 5–14; 417–425). These merit publication, but space constraints prohibit that in the present essay.

10. "Quartus tomus operum D. Huldrychi Zuinglii, qui annotationes in Evangelistarum et Apostolorum scripta aliquot ex ore eiusdem per Leonem Iudae exceptas continet" (Zurich, 1544–45), pp. AA2r–AA3r.

11. Ibid., AA3v–AA4r.

12. Finsler, *Zwingli Bibliographie,* p. 75 No. 105c (hereafter S).

13. Ibid., p. 105 No. 206. This first selected edition of letters of Zwingli and Oecolampadius contains four parts. It then brings that "Scriptorum Io. Oecolampadii et Huldrichi Zuinglii *Purgatorio,* per Theodorum Bibliandrum . . . conscripta," to which the present writer has referred in his "In Defense of Zwingli:1536," in *Prophet, Pastor, Protestant* (n. 2 above).

14. See n. 6 above. The translations of the Zwingli editions into other languages contain no exegetica.

15. Meyer, "Entstehung," pp. 330f. For a somewhat more detailed plan, corresponding extensively with the printing, I refer to the Appendix by Hans Rudolf Lavater to the reprint of the so-called "Froschauer Bible of 1531" (Zurich, 1983), p. 1385.

16. Cf. James D. Tracy, "Humanism and the Reformation," in *Reformation Europe: A Guide to Research,* ed. Steven Ozment (St. Louis: Center for Reformation Research, 1982), pp. 33–57. This essay offers a rich bibliography: (1) Bibliographies and Libraries; (2) Modern Editions and Translations; (3) Secondary Literature.

17. C. Augustijn, *Erasmus on de Reformatie* (Amsterdam, 1962); *Erasmus von Rotterdam, Leben-Werk-Wirkung* (Munich, 1986). R. H. Bainton, *Erasmus of Christendom* (New York: Charles Scribner's Sons, 1969). M. Hoffmann, *Erkenntnis und Verwirklichung der wahren Theologie nach Erasmus von Rotterdam* (Tübingen, 1972); "Erasmus and Religious Toleration," *Erasmus of Rotterdam Society Yearbook* II (1982), pp. 80–106; "Erasmus on Church and Ministry," ibid., VII (1987), pp. 1–30; "Faith and Piety in Erasmus' Thought" (lecture at Sixteenth Century conference, Tempe, Ariz., 1987). H. Holeczek, *Humanistische Bibelphilologie als Reformproblem bei Erasmus von Rotterdam, Thomas More und William Tyndale* (Leiden, 1975); *Erasmus Deutsch* I (Stuttgart-Bad Cannstatt, 1983); "Erasmische Reform und Reformation," in *Erasmus von Rotterdam* (Basel: Katalog des Historischen Museums Basel—Ausstellung in der Barfüsserkirche 20. April bis 7. Sept. 1986), pp. 58–62. E. W. Kohls, *Die Theologie des Erasmus* (Basel, 1966). J. B. Payne, *Erasmus: His Theology of the Sacraments* (Richmond, Va.: John Knox Press, 1970). R. Stupperich, *Erasmus von Rotterdam und seine Welt* (Berlin and New York, 1977). G. W. Winkler, *Erasmus von Rotterdam und die Einleitungsschriften zum Neuen Testament* (Münster, 1974).

18. Holeczek, "Erasmische Reform und Reformation," p. 59.

19. Augustijn, *Erasmus von Rotterdam,* p. 168. The whole of this section, "Erasmus und sein Einfluss," pp. 162–176, is relevant.

20. Ibid., p. 169. Augustijn refers in this context on the one hand to various long excursus in the *Annotationes* as well as "the best example," *De libero arbitrio.*

21. Ibid., pp. 169f.

22. Erasmus, *Opera omnia,* ed. Leclerc (Leiden, 1703–06), V, pp. 130f. The "Copia" mentioned in the text quoted here refers to the writing "De duplici copia verborum ac rerum" (*Opera omnia* 1:3–110) and esp. Book II (*Collected Works of Erasmus* 24 [Toronto, 1978], pp. 279–659). The "Copia" first appeared in Paris in 1512. On this entire question, see Augustijn, *Erasmus von Rotterdam,* pp. 82–91.

23. *Z* III 638:1–16.

24. *Z* I 464:16–23; II 414:1–438:11; III 855:11–867:3. For an English translation of the *Exposition and Basis of the Conclusions* see *Huldrych Zwingli: Writings,* ed. E. J. Furcha and H. W. Pipkin, vol. 1 (Allison Park, Pa.: Pickwick Publications, 1984).

25. See n. 22 above.

26. S VI/I, pp. 539–681. It is to be noted that the *Annotationes* break off with Luke 16:18, clearly immediately before the reformer's departure to Kappel on 11 October 1531. In what follows, we will give all the citations in the text itself.

27. Meyer, "Entstehung," p. 320.

28. On Luke 3:2: *"Factum est verbum domini.* Hebraica est loquutio, pro eo quod Latinus diceret: Manifestavit aut mandavit dominus verbum suum Ioanni, iussit Ioannem praedicare, revelavit Ioanni verbum suum, ut caeteris annunciaret . . ." (S VI, p. 558); on Luke 3:3: *"Baptismum poenitentiae.* Hebraismus est. Ioannes praedicavit ut homines resipiscerent, ut vitam immutarent" (ibid.); on Luke 3:4: *"Vox clamantis.* Hebraismus est pro voce clamante, ut Vir iustitiae, id est, vir iustus" (p. 560).

29. In the same chapter (Luke 3), Zwingli mentions the rhetorical concept of periphrasis (p. 559: "Remissio peccatorum periphrasis est evangelii"), allegory (p. 560: "Omnis mons humiliabitur"), simile (p. 361: "Securis est admota radicibus"), synecdoche (p. 568: "poenitentiam denique capi pro Evangelio, per Synecdocham, quum poenitentia altera sit pars evangelii, altera remissio peccatorum").

30. Cf. Erasmus, "Copia II, Method 6," *Collected Works* 24, pp. 289f.

31. Zwingli, *The Latin Works of Huldrich Zwingli,* ed. W. J. Hinke (Philadelphia, 1922), p. 263.

32. Ibid., pp. 255–260. Cf. my commentary in the soon-to-be-published edition of the *Fidei expositio,* Z VI/IV.

33. G. Ebeling, *Dogmatik des christliche Glaubens,* I: *Der Glaube*

an Gott den Schöpfer der Welt (Tübingen, 1979), pp. 334f. This is taken from paragraph 14, "Der Mensch coram Deo."

34. Augustijn, *Erasmus von Rotterdam,* pp. 169f.

35. M. Bucer, *Deutsche Schriften,* ed. R. Stupperich, vol. 2 (Gütersloh, 1962), p. 379.

36. *Z* VIII 333:26–334:3.

Zwingli in the Writings of Karl Barth—with Special Emphasis on the Doctrine of the Sacraments

Akira Demura

I

More than thirty years ago Jaques Courvoisier contributed an essay to Karl Barth's seventieth birthday Festschrift, *Das Antwort,* under the title "Zwingli et Karl Barth."[1] Several years later, Courvoisier was invited to Princeton Theological Seminary as the speaker of the celebrated Warfield Lectures of the year 1961. The contents of the lectures, in much expanded form, were published in 1963 as *Zwingli: A Reformed Theologian.*[2] So far as his article in *Das Antwort* is concerned, however, it does not seem that it drew much attention from Reformation scholars. Neither is it known how Karl Barth himself appraised the article at the time of its publication.

Clarifying that his own fundamental interest was focused more on Zwingli than on Barth, Courvoisier still contended that a man in the twentieth century who, knowing Karl Barth, reads Zwingli, has a "curious feeling" that the acquaintance with Barth has assisted him in having a better and deeper understanding of Zwingli. According to Courvoisier, there is definitely "a certain family tie" between the reformer of the sixteenth century and the theologian of the twentieth century beyond the obvious fact that they both belong to the same ecclesiastical tradition.[3]

Courvoisier further asserts that there is a distinct and unmistakable parallelism between the two, not only in their common endeavor to construct their theology on the very basis of Christology but also in many other theological loci. For example, Zwingli's "despised" symbolic interpretation of the Lord's Supper, often depicted as "a rationalist caricature," is nothing but an expression of his firm determination to deny any concept of the "analogy of being" such as Luther accepted and to stick insistently to the "analogy of faith" which is the logical outcome of the principle of *sola fide.* Also, one should not fail to recognize a clear similarity between Zwingli's determined *"Nein"* on the occasion of the famous Marburg Colloquy and Karl Barth's *"Nein"* in his confrontation with his theological opponents.[4]

Furthermore, Zwingli's stern refusal to side with the sacramental teachings of the Lutherans, the Roman Catholics, or the Anabaptists, and his continuous efforts to develop his own sacramental doctrine on the ground of ecclesiology, have much to do with Karl Barth's theological struggles. Finally, Courvoisier takes up Zwingli's view of the essence and the task of a Christian community and comes to the conclusion that its Christocentric orientation has much in common with Karl Barth's point of view as reflected, for instance, in his book, *Christengemeinde und Bürgergemeinde* (1946), in which Barth contends that the civil community is nothing other than "the instrument of the divine grace in view of its struggle against human nature."[5] In this sense, so says Courvoisier, one cannot deny that "Zwingli and Karl Barth move in the same thought world."[6] To round off the entire discussion, both Zwingli and Karl Barth are faithful sons of the Swiss Confederation, both cherishing the idea of armed neutrality as the preferable alternative for the national safety, both with a profound love of their native country and a decisive commitment *(engagement)* to the cause of the fatherland. They are both "authentically Swiss"![7]

While conceding that he had only made a beginning and the study would need to be extended to other major theological *loci* such as the doctrines of creation, original sin, election, or ecclesiology, Courvoisier strongly maintained that there is a distinct theological harmony between Zwingli and Karl Barth. Originally, so confides Courvoisier, he planned to entitle his essay "Zwingli, precurseur de Karl Barth." He rejected the idea because he was afraid that this expression might imply a value judgment, since in general a precursor is less important than the one who follows, or his life is significant only in relation to the one that comes later. "I did not want to say this. It is not my business to say whether one is greater than the other." The final phraseology was, therefore, "Zwingli et Karl Barth," with a coordinate conjunction, the implication being Zwingli "the Ancestor or Grandfather of Karl Barth." Courvoisier is convinced that Zwingli, the ancestor, would have felt much affection for and pride in his theological grandson, Karl Barth.[8]

II

As was mentioned above, the scholarly responses to this article, including Karl Barth's own, cannot be ascertained. It may safely be said, however, that Courvoisier's essay of the year 1956 now calls for a fresh appraisal in view of the fact that, some ten years later, in 1967, Barth seems to have further drastically revised his sacramental teaching. The doctrine of baptism, in particular, which had formerly been expounded in his noted Gwatt Lectures, *Die kirchliche Lehre von der Taufe*, 1943[9] and, as such, world-shaking enough, was now to be reexamined and reexpressed in his *Kirchliche Dogmatik* IV/4.[10] Barth has gone so far as to say: "I might not, therefore, so strongly object, if someone comes to label the baptismal teaching which is herein proposed as 'Neo-Zwinglian,' either in praise or accusation, although the stimulation from Zwingli has in no case played any role for its origination." Barth hurries, however, to add that "it is in so far as Zwingli is to be better understood than he understood himself, or, at any rate, better than he was able to make himself understood."[11]

We must say that this statement by Barth is quite noteworthy, because Barth himself names his own sacramental position as "Neo-Zwinglian" even though, admittedly, Barth goes far beyond the concept and terminology of Zwingli down into the very core of Zwingli's theological thinking. Our natural question is, therefore: Can we possibly conclude that Barth would admit his father-and-son relationship with the Zurich reformer, even if he denies his immediate indebtedness to Zwingli? In truth, however, the problematic seems to be much more complicated because of the elapse of time. To put it in the following way: Is Barth's avowed acknowledgment of his "Neo-Zwinglian" position in his 1967 *Kirchliche Dogmatik* IV/4 founded on the same theological bases which Courvoisier had counted up in his 1956 essay as well as his 1963 monograph? That is, was Barth, as Courvoisier believed, moving in "the same thought world" as Zwingli? In our attempt to answer these questions, even tentatively, a few more preliminary discussions appear to be in order.

First of all, the very interpretation of Zwingli by Courvoisier may be reexamined. His fundamental view of Zwingli as a "théologien christologique"[12] appears to be supported by such a Zwingli specialist as the Bern church historian Gottfried W.

Locher,[13] especially with the publication of the latter's gigantic monograph on the life and thought of Zwingli in which Locher reaffirms his own view expressed in earlier works.[14] Nevertheless, we must say that the question still remains open, basically because the theological framework of "Christological" or "Christocentric" is yet unfixed and still under much discussion. It is obvious that the theme is far beyond the scope of this small essay, however.

Second, one might equally call into question the adequacy of Karl Barth's interpretation of Zwingli. The difficulty on the side of Barth seems, however, to consist more in the question as to whether or not there had been a "displacement," to borrow Eberhard Jüngel's expression,[15] in Karl Barth from his earlier position, expounded, for example, in his 1943 Gwatt Lectures, to his later stance, predominantly in his *Kirchliche Dogmatik* IV/4. To sum up: The matter here concerned seems double, indeed: exegetical or hermeneutical, and factual. Exegetically, it is concerned with the accuracy with which either Courvoisier or Barth read Zwingli and/or Courvoisier read Karl Barth. Needless to add that the problem of accuracy includes the one with which we ourselves read Zwingli, Barth, or Courvoisier. Factually, the matter concerned is whether there had been a shift or change in Barth's sacramental or baptismal teaching noticeable enough to require his readers to take another look at him.

III

In order to answer these questions more or less appropriately, let us now take a quick look at Barth's 1943 Gwatt Lectures, with special attention to his references to Zwingli. Eberhard Jüngel, in his thoroughgoing critical study of Barth's baptismal doctrine, summarizes the epoch-making significance of these lectures in the following way.

> The book, *Die kirchliche Lehre von der Taufe* . . . was no more nor less than a frontal attack against the ecclesiastical practice of baptism as well as against the baptismal teaching which had until then legitimated this practice as valid and justifiable. On the ground of a better, certainly the first ecclesiastically legitimatizable doctrine of baptism, Karl Barth demanded the reinstitution of the order of baptism in the sense of "a baptism for which there is accountability also on the side of its recipients." The one who receives baptism "must . . . not merely be a passive object of the rite but must become again a free partner of Jesus Christ in the sense that the

recipient freely makes up his mind, freely confesses and freely testifies to his own willingness and readiness."[16]

From this point of view of "responsible baptism" *(Verantwortlichkeitstaufe),* the prevailing infant baptism is no other than a "half baptism" *(Halbtaufe* or *halbe Taufe),* which is utterly unjustifiable.[17] In this respect, the baptismal teaching of all the outstanding confessions, including those of the Reformed tradition, has not only a chasm but a gross defect. Insofar as the doctrine of baptism is concerned, that of both Luther and Calvin, along with their successors, is incredibly unsatisfactory because of its hopeless confusion.[18]

In his discussion of the sixteenth-century Reformers, Karl Barth says that Zwingli would have spoken correctly if he had been content to say that baptism was the symbol of the faith of the church as well as that of each individual church member, and that, consequently, the baptismal rite was the act of remembrance—namely, the act of confessing and confirming this faith. Regrettably, however, Zwingli did speak otherwise, precisely because he thought that the efficacy of baptism depended on the power of faith which was to be fortified by the use of this symbol.[19] Hence comes the extraordinary dullness and frigidity of his baptismal teaching, as in the case of his eucharistic teaching. It lacks a "sacramental" dimension, and the relationship to the New Testament references is problematic.[20]

This is Barth as he looked on Zwingli in the year 1943 and the Barth in whom Courvoisier would very much like to recognize a "father-and-son" relationship with Zwingli. After all, was not Courvoisier somewhat premature in reaching the above-mentioned conclusion, which was no other than his own wishful thinking? Could he by any chance have reached a fairer conclusion if he had read Barth's *Kirchliche Dogmatik* IV/4? Interesting though these questions may well be, we need not go into them any further in this connection. In the light of our theme, "Zwingli in the Writings of Karl Barth," Courvoisier's work need detain us no longer.

IV

Fully aware that the cardinal issue of the *Kirchliche Dogmatik* IV/4 is not the problem of so-called infant baptism, let us now restate our question in the following way. Karl Barth, as we will see in somewhat greater detail below, represents much the same theological position in the *Kirchliche Dog-*

matik IV/4 as Zwingli—a common denial of the "Mysterium"; namely, the sacramental character of baptism. Why, then, did they reach different and opposite conclusions as to the validity of infant baptism? Is it not that Zwingli, or, at any rate, Zwingli as Barth would like to interpret him, should and could have reached the rejection of infant baptism if he had remained theologically consistent? Is it right to say that Zwingli compromised with the reality of the sixteenth-century Zurich situation because of his insistence on the medieval concept of *corpus Christianum* at the price of theological integrity?

In a sense, these questions center around the very problem of the much debated "turning point" of the Zurich reformation. At which point should the turning point be sought? Needless to say, this is one of the fundamental issues in modern Zwingli studies.[21]

As far as Zwingli's own writings are concerned, it is true that there are scattered statements that seem to support the possibility that Zwingli changed his earlier and theologically more consistent position to a more "realistic" but theologically unjustifiable stance. For example, in one of his most representative writings on the problem of baptism, *Von dem touff, vom widertouff und vom Kindertouff* (1525), Zwingli confesses explicitly: "For some time I myself was deceived by the error and I thought it better not to baptize children until they came to years of discretion."[22] In view of the fact, however, that there are not many parallel passages leading in this direction to be found in Zwingli, one may rightly doubt to what extent this was his definite and decisive position.

It is equally true, nevertheless, that Zwingli's contemporary opponents did not assume that this utterance of Zwingli's was only casual and accidental. Balthasar Hubmaier is an example. Formerly a close associate of Zwingli in the evangelical reformation of the town of Waldshut, yet later one of the most virulent controversialists against him, Hubmaier would like to remind Zwingli of the date and place. According to Hubmaier, on the day of Philip and Jacob (May 1) he had a chance to confer with Zwingli on the street in Zurich on the matter of baptism.[23] The conversation took place a few months after the First Zurich Dispute when Zwingli had pressed the Vicar of Constance, Johann Faber, so hard for the faithful adherence to the scriptural truth. Hubmaier recalls Zwingli as saying that man should not baptize children until they are educated in the matters of faith. If this was the case, one can hardly deny Zwingli's later "about-face" from his purer position. Was it caused by the fatal shortcoming among the sixteenth-century Reformers as regards their view of the local and Christian community, to cite Karl Barth again?[24]

On the other hand, while the sixteenth-century Anabaptists had gone so far as to reject infant baptism in a wholesale way and to administer adult or faith baptism, how is it that Karl Barth himself, despite his repeatedly expressed sympathy not only with the Baptists but also with the Mennonites,[25] still insisted on the once-for-all-ness of baptism and refused to practice the second baptism—i.e., the responsible baptism—in addition to the "halfway" infant baptism? Are we forced to say that Karl Barth is not theologically consistent in this respect, as some of his critics avow? Even though Barth admits that an "anabaptism" which had been postulated by some hotheaded fanatics, such as the Anabaptists in the Reformation, was not executed in an utterly invalid and ineffective way in spite of the fact that it was extremely annoying and full of problems because of its disorderliness, he nonetheless rejects the warrantableness of a second baptism. Here Edmund Schlink, for instance, rightly sees a theological *Unkonsequenz* in Barth and tries to seek the reason for this inconsistency somewhere else than in the purely theological baptismal doctrine.[26]

So much for the preliminary comments on the general theme of this essay. We now come to the central part of the paper. In the pursuit of our topic, we are going to make use of two approaches. One is the analysis of Barth's writings by cutting crosswise, so to speak; another method is that of cutting lengthwise. The former is going to be a more careful study of Barth's *Kirchliche Dogmatik* IV/4, with special emphasis on his sacramental teaching in general and the doctrine of baptism in particular. This will be carried out always with cross-reference to the writings of Zwingli. The second approach will be an attempt to follow Karl Barth in chronological sequence in order to discover the traces of his theological dialogue with Zwingli from the beginning of his pastoral and professional activities.

V

According to Karl Barth, Zwingli was and remains "a lonely man" in terms of his understanding and teaching of baptism. Zwingli's baptismal teaching, expounded in his *Commentarius (De vera et falsa religione)*, *Von dem Taufe*, *Antwurt über Balthasars touffbüchlin* or *Elenchus in Catabaptistarum strophas* (all 1525) as well as in *Quaestiones de*

Sacramento Baptismi, written against Schwenckfeld (1530), falls definitely outside the traditional doctrine, Roman Catholic, Lutheran, or Calvinist Reformed, in the sense that "he wanted to keep his distance from every 'sacramentalist' interpretation of baptism, including the one which he thought, not without proper reason, he could detect even in his Anabaptist opponents."[27] The following passages of Zwingli seem to endorse Barth's view.

Zwingli says that a grave misunderstanding of baptism has been prevalent since the time of the apostles, a misunderstanding on the very basis of misinterpreted scriptural passages such as John 3:5, as if the poured water as such had had some cleansing and forgiving power. To quote Zwingli himself:

> The controversy has shown us that it is not the pouring of water which washes away sin. And that was what we once believed, although without any authority in the Word of God. We also believed that the water of baptism cleanses children from a sin which they never had, and that without it they would be damned. All these beliefs were erroneous, as we shall see later. Water-baptism cannot contribute in any way to the washing away of sin.[28]

At first glance, it seems that the parallelism between the baptismal teaching of Karl Barth and that of Zwingli can hardly be questioned. Of course, we are quite aware that the usage of the word "baptism" in Zwingli is extremely complex and multiple—so labyrinthine as to cause confusion among his readers. Nonetheless, his claim for a fundamental clear-cut distinction between the baptism of the Spirit, which includes "inward teaching, calling, and cleaving to God," and the baptism of water, which implies "the external instruction and immersion in water,"[29] can rightly be subscribed by Karl Barth, whose basic assertion is that the Christian life should be built on the ground of "the baptism with the Holy Spirit" and not of the "baptism by water."[30]

At a deeper level, however, the discrepency between Barth and Zwingli seems equally evident. In the first place, Barth points out the latent Neoplatonism in Zwingli in the latter's criticism of sacraments. Zwingli's contention that the external cannot and should not stand for the internal and that the material does not reveal the spiritual is grounded more on philosophical or metaphysical than on theological bases.[31] This, of course, is exactly the focus of much controversy among Zwingli scholars. Had there been only Neoplatonic dualism behind Zwingli's denial of the saving efficacy of the sacraments, Zwingli could have agreed with Thomas Müntzer or Hans Denk in their overall rejection of the baptismal rite, administered either in infancy or adulthood. According to Karl Barth, however, Zwingli went to the other extreme and reached an uncritical and "unscrupulous" acceptance of infant baptism because he thought it was a matter of indifference, at any rate as long as it was administered with the external pouring of water. Baptism, thus stripped of its sacramental character and nullified in its redemptive effect, can seek its theoretical ground only in the concept of a Christian community. Needless to add that in Zwingli there is no idea, such as is unique in Karl Barth, that the incarnate Christ himself is the subject and the substance of the baptism of the Spirit, solely because Christ is *the* sacrament.[32] We must say that this point of view is utterly missing in Zwingli.

In the second place, we notice the difference between the two in their attempts at characterizing the water-baptism itself. Barth defines it as a responsible act on the human side, in full appreciation of and deep gratitude for the prevenient divine grace which prepares the person as a whole for Christian living. The water-baptism is the first expression of a person's determination to respond to God's calling, which is the pouring of the Holy Spirit on him.[33] Far from abolishing and excluding the water-baptism, therefore, the baptism of the Spirit rather makes it possible and indispensable, according to Barth. On the other hand, one can scarcely find any passages in Zwingli in which he tries to characterize the water-baptism as an act of joyful and grateful response to God. From whence, then, comes this divergence? Does it come from Zwingli's alleged Neoplatonic dualism or from his insistence on the parallelism between baptism and circumcision (seen in the following paragraphs)?

In brief, how is it that, whereas there is a fundamental harmony between Zwingli and Karl Barth in their common rejection of the sacramental efficacy of the water-baptism, the latter comes to a strong emphasis on the responsible character of baptism and, accordingly, to the negation of infant baptism, while the former ends up in ready and willing acceptance of infant baptism? Barth asserts emphatically that baptism is not a *signum instrumentale* but a *signum cognitivum*.[34] This is evidently true for Zwingli, too. Nevertheless, in the former the one who "cognizes" is each individual believer; in the latter, the subject of cognition is the believing community—namely, the church as a whole. Which of these two is inconsistent? When Barth defines his own position as "*neo*-Zwinglian," does he do so because he recognizes this fatal inconsistency in Zwingli?

VI

As another illustration of the difference between Barth and Zwingli, we now turn to their views of the significance of the baptism of John the Baptist in salvation history. As is well known, Zwingli's basic apology for infant baptism was grounded on the oneness of God's covenant through the Old and the New Testaments. How often he repeats the continuous identity of the circumcision in the Old Testament and the baptism in the New—as circumcision in the Old, so infant baptism in the New. The attempt, therefore, to trace the origin of federal theology back in Zwingli may not be entirely groundless. On the other hand, so far as the *Kirchliche Dogmatik* IV/4 is concerned, the concept of the divine covenant does not seem to be the constructive principle in Barth's discussions.[35]

It may not be too much to say that the whole history of Christian thinking can be divided into two camps in terms of the interpretation of John the Baptist and his salvation-historical significance. The discussion centers around the question as to whether John the Baptist *still* stands in the Old Covenant or *already* in the New.[36] In the prolonged controversy between Zwingli and Hubmaier, one of the cardinal issues was precisely this. In the second and the third chapters of his *Von dem christlichen Tauff der gläubigen* (1525), Hubmaier deals with this problem intently and comes to the conclusion that John was no more than a "gsatzprediger," just like other Old Testament prophets, the only difference being that his predecessors had proclaimed the coming Christ, while John pointed out the "gegenwertigen Christum."[37] Christof Windhorst, in his excellent study of Hubmaier's theology, mentions: "[The Johannine preaching] did not bring the forgiveness of sin but only pointed out where it was to be found."[38]

According to Hubmaier, the Baptist did advocate the essential necessity of spontaneity on the side of the recipients, and this automatically excluded the possibility of infant baptism.[39] The baptism of John the Baptist and of the disciples of Jesus which were administered prior to the resurrection, however, did not bring the internal rebirth and the remission of sin, simply because these were all nothing but water-baptism.[40] Hubmaier further expounds this point in his *Gesprech* (1526), and says that the baptism of John "erkelet, erfrort, erschreckt, todtet, fiert in die Hell," whereas the baptism of Christ "erhitzget, erkuchet [erquickt], trostet, macht lebendig, fiert wider aus der Hell."[41] It is manifest that for Hubmaier the genuine turning point of salvation history is to be sought at the resurrection.[42]

In sharp contrast, Zwingli is positively convinced of the identity of the Johannine baptism with that of Christ. He claims that the origin of Christian baptism is looked for not in the Dominical command of the world mission, recorded in Matthew 28, but in the very baptism of John.[43] According to Zwingli, those who deny infant baptism are identical with all the *theologi*—i.e., the medieval Schoolmen—for both groups separate the two baptisms. The implication is that the baptism-refusers (Anabaptists) have fallen into the same error as the papists. Both assert that the Johannine baptism is no more than a *"vorbedutnus" (typus et figura)* of the baptism of Christ; both do injustice *(gwalt und unrecht)* to John and Christ alike. John the Baptist was by no means "a shadow under the Old Testament" but, rather, "an initiator of the good news out of God's order." To quote Zwingli's refutation of Hubmaier (*Antwurt,* 1526), the assertion by Hubmaier that John the Baptist and the apostles prior to the resurrection preached only *"das ruch gsatzt"* is "a gross and unthinkable blasphemy"; it is "an unashamed and unbearable statement."[44]

As was suggested before, Hubmaier was keenly conscious that he had support not only from the scripture but also from such Church Fathers as Origen, Cyril, Theophylactus, Chrysostom, and Jerome.[45] On the contrary, Zwingli knew that he stood in an entirely different position in the appraisal of the redemptive efficacy of the Johannine baptism, although it remains rather uncertain whether he included the Church Fathers of the ancient time, as Hubmaier did, among the *theologi.* He may have thought only of the medieval Schoolmen.[46]

As to the background of Zwingli's alleged uniqueness in the history of Christian thinking,[47] the interpretations among Zwingli specialists diverge quite widely. Windhorst, for example, would see in Zwingli a spiritualist tendency that ended up in the separation of *Wort* and *Geist,*[48] under the overall influence of humanism and Erasmus, in particular; while Hubmaier, under the guidance of Luther, determinedly resisted such a perilous ontological dualism. John Yoder, one of the most trenchant Anabaptist "in-group" criticizers of Zwingli, smells out the fundamentally Platonic and metaphysical worldview in Zwingli. Yoder says Zwingli's theological thinking always tended to be *"geschichtslos-intellektualistisch,"* and to center around the "überzeitlich" beyond time and space, whereas the Anabaptist proponents stood against him with their *"geschichtlich-eschatologisch"* understanding of salvation history.[49] In contradistinction, Jack W. Cottrell tries to prove that the Zwinglian theology has a solid salvation-historical framework with its "promise-fulfillment motif," which naturally leads to the assertion of the oneness of both covenants and to the identification of the baptisms of John and Christ.[50] For our present purposes, this is sufficient discussion of this aspect of the Zwinglian research.

VII

The apparent digression in the preceding paragraphs was needed in order to make a brief comparison between Karl Barth's and Zwingli's views of the efficacy and significance of the baptism of John. By and large, like Zwingli, Barth admits that the Johannine baptism is fundamentally a Christian baptism and different from that in Judaism or heathenism, exactly because both John's and Christ's baptisms contain similar significance and point to the divine judgment and grace; those who are baptized into these baptisms confess their faith in God and the church.[51]

Nevertheless, Barth emphasizes that Christian baptism after Pentecost has become something different from the baptism of John as well as from that of the apostles prior to Pentecost. Barth counts up six points where he recognizes these differences.[52] (1) In Christian baptism "the relation can be described only in comparatives—a more urgent and threatening, but also a more promising imminence of the . . . kingdom of God among men." (2) It "derives from the outpouring and impartation of the Holy Spirit which took place for the first time at Pentecost, but which has taken place repeatedly since." (3) It "carries a heightened emphasis on God's judgment inasmuch as it now takes place in retrospect of the Judge who had come and the judgment which he had executed." (4) "Not in contradiction but in marked contrast thereto we must add that after Pentecost Christian baptism . . . is orientated predominantly *a parte potiori* and with much stronger emphasis to the remission of sins. It is thus decisively and predominantly an affirmation of God's act as an act of salvation." In John the imperative comes first, to be underlined by the indicative, while in Jesus the indicative comes first to dominate and control the imperative. (5) Whereas the Johannine baptism must be characterized essentially as individualistic, Christian baptism has become community-centered and community-formative. (6) Christian baptism is to be administered in the name of the One who is the Messiah of Israel and the *Sōtēr* of the whole world. Despite this observation on the differences between the Johannine baptism and the post-Pentecostal Christian baptism, Barth still emphasizes that these two baptisms are one and the same in terms of their objective and substance.

As seen above, Hubmaier had come to the conclusion that the two covenants were discontinuous, and he had in a wholesale way rejected the salvific efficacy of infant baptism. According to Hubmaier, this theme of discrepancy and discontinuity had been the traditional understanding since the age of the Church Fathers. From this standpoint, Zwingli had to be looked upon as having deviated glaringly from this traditional view. Although it cannot be known whether or not Barth had this much knowledge of Hubmaier, it would be an amusing conjecture to imagine Karl Barth's going along with Hubmaier.

Because Barth himself does not seem to be so carefully attentive to the question of Zwingli's inner development, our comparative study of Zwingli and Barth has unavoidably been restricted to the Zwingli of 1525 and the Barth of the *Kirchliche Dogmatik* IV/4. To sum up, the question has been: how it is that, out of the same root of the Zwinglian (or neo-Zwinglian) baptismal doctrine, two mutually exclusive fruits—reconfirmed infant baptism and the assertion of responsible adult baptism—have been brought forth? Was Zwingli's insistence on infant baptism an unexpected bad mutation, so to speak, quite heterogeneous and incoherent to his sacramental doctrine, as Barth pungently points out? In that case, the blame of "Unkonsequenz" is to be laid on Zwingli. Or did Barth misunderstand Zwingli after all?

In order to elucidate these points, we now turn to the chronological study of Karl Barth's encounter with Zwingli. We depend mostly on Barth's rather scattered references to Zwingli in his earlier letters, sermon notes, and lecture syllabi. The great handicap in this connection is that Barth's lectures on Zwingli given in the winter semester of 1922–23 in Göttingen, which would no doubt be of incomparably great help toward our objective, are not yet published in the *Gesamtausgabe.* At all events, however, it would be the Barth of 1922–23 and prior to his "displacement," to borrow again Eberhard Jüngel's term. The following, therefore, is nothing but a tentative sketch within the above-mentioned limitation.

VIII

As a pastor ordained into the Reformed church, it was but natural that Karl Barth had long been interested in Zwingli. As early as 1913 or 1914, some scattered references can be found in his sermon manuscripts. These, however, are only casual and occasional and do not reflect any specifically theological concern with the Zurich reformer.[53] While Barth was engaged in pastoral work in Safenwil, there was published in connection with the four hundredth anniversary of the Protestant Reformation a semipopular biographical sketch of Zwingli by a church historian of Zurich, Oskar Farner, under the title *Huldrych Zwingli, der schweizerische Reformator.*[54]

In a letter dated October 28, 1917, Eduard Thurneysen wrote to Karl Barth from his parsonage in Leutwil, saying: "I have read Farner's booklet with pleasure. I could not help deliberating upon why nothing goes well with us. Of course, it is not true that everything went well with Zwingli, either. In general, the Reformation history tells us ten times more than the historians and churchmen can well see. I have no doubt about it."[55] Five months later, Barth wrote back to Thurneysen on the same subject. In this letter of March 25, 1918, Barth refers to a ministerial conference where there was an occasion to review the above-mentioned Zwingli booklet. Barth says:

> Our president distanced himself from Zwingli with open aversion [to the latter]; and here it has become clear to me that this prototype of a Reformed pastor (that is, a liberal pastor) is also quite alien to me. I would very much like to hear from you something about what you, in your catechetical series, have discovered that is interesting about him. At any rate, his commentary on Romans also belongs to the feebler things written on Romans. For example, the Holy Spirit equals for him, obviously, piety [*Frömmigkeit*], just as it is treated in Wernle and like-minded fellows. And that Ragaz quotes him so frequently after all throws a strange light on him. Some sinister parallels become apparent. Our speaker followed strictly Zwingli's *life* and deeds with a layman's simplicity, and I did not know enough about the background in order to cast a better light on this ghastly portrait which slowly emanated. Perhaps we would request you to come to one of our meetings and to accomplish that which I am really not very good at. In our next session, Calvin will be dealt with, where the circumstances are, however, different. But for the task of "justifying" such a man, I am just not the happiest choice. Oh, what misfortune![56]

It is needless to add that Barth was diligently working on his *Römerbrief* at this time. The *Gesamtausgabe* enumerates some fifteen or more references to Zwingli in this work, among which one of the most important seems to be a comment on Rom. 2:25. Barth mentions: "Zwingli and liberalism receive justice, under the wrath of God. The sacrament *is* no longer the fellowship with God; it only *signifies* it and it will soon signify it no longer, because it has by and large lost its object."[57] This is said in the course of Barth's discussion of the spiritualization of Christian faith, which will finally end up by making out of Christianity one of the religions, or one of many other viewpoints. It is obvious that Barth had Zwingli's *In Epistolam ad Romanos annotationes* close by him.

Evidently, Barth's assessment of Zwingli is rather ambivalent. Out of around one dozen quotations, some are casual and cursory; some are affirmative, as in the understanding of sin as "mangel und prasten";[58] some are negative, as in the reference to the interpretation of Zwingli as the prototype of "freethinking" pastors.[59] This ambivalence on the side of Barth and his close associate Thurneysen is well suggested in the latter's letter to the former, dated June 24, 1918. Enclosing a copy of Hans Baur's book review of *Suchet Gott* which had appeared in the *Protestantenblatt,* Thurneysen writes:

> This friend of Gottfried Traub's and true sole heir of Zwingli testifies that we are religious Bolsheviks. He praises us for "great concepts in general," and warns that we are dangerous to those who are not independent in their thinking. The Zwingli on whom Baur calls becomes suspect. It may be asked if this Zwingli is indeed the real Zwingli. This will become a burning question in 1919, when Zwingli's appearance in Zurich will be celebrated. Then we will see all kinds of things.[60]

From this Barth-Thurneysen correspondence it can be seen that they were both somewhat suspicious of the popular and conventional image of Zwingli and yet, despite vigorous efforts, were unable to free themselves from it.

IX

On February 11, 1922, Barth wrote a long letter to Thurneysen. Barth had already moved to Göttingen as professor of Reformed theology in the university there and was then lecturing on both the Heidelberg Catechism and Ephesians. Barth says, "On my side, I am pleased with the way in which the old Reformed theologians saw the longitudinal pattern in history and they called that the gospel: the saving truth which was *ab initio mundi usque ad ejus consummationem.*"[61] He then quotes Calvin as regards the latter's special doctrine that the Israelites had been baptized while crossing the Red Sea. He refers to Zwingli's teaching, which included in the kingdom of heaven, along with Adam, Abel, Enoch, and others,

Hercules, Theseus, Socrates, and others, not to mention some of the obscure kings of the Carolingian French dynasty. Barth refers to these ideas not without sympathy because they do not mythologize history.

As professor of Reformed theology, it was only natural that Barth was devoted to Calvin. The March 26 letter reports his firm determination to start from a solid background of medieval Scholasticism, move to Luther and Zwingli, and eventually reach Calvin.[62] A circular letter by Barth with the date of April 2 reveals that, faithful to his commitment to the medieval Schoolmen, he was working on Bonaventura's *Breviloquium*—that is, the famed *Itinerarium mentis in Deum*—since he was eager "to learn the medieval period even in an off-hand sample, but not out of excerpts only." Barth then continues: "Then there still wait Augustine, Meister Eckhart, Luther and Zwingli, of course, naturally everything only in samples as usual! And only then comes a new attempt at scaling Calvin himself. Finally comes the 'point of view' and the beginning of the manuscript for the four hours of lecture I must march into, so that I may not feel so hotly pursued as in this [past] winter."[63]

Barth had already made up his mind to give lectures on the theology of Zwingli in the winter semester of 1922–23 and had begun preparing for them even before the summer. In the May 22 personal letter to Thurneysen, Barth adds: "Last evening I had with Stange, Wobbermin, and Hirsch a lengthy discussion on Zwingli, who is now rapidly growing in my view."[64] The letter may suggest that Barth was increasingly interested in Zwingli.

Lamenting over his "feeble Latin and a chaotic kind of apperception,"[65] Barth spent the whole summer of 1922 in preparation for his scheduled lectures on *"Die Theologie Zwinglis."*[66] His struggle with Zwingli continued on through the fall months. In his circular letter dated December 18, just before the Christmas vacation, Barth confides to his friends: "At long last I am finished. I have just given my last lecture, in which I commented on that noteworthy passage in Zwingli's *Werke* I, 232f. [Zwingli's exposition of the eighteenth article of his 67 *Schlussreden*]; I ascertained the date of Hoen's letter as 1523; I shared the remarkable prayer of Zwingli out of *Epicheresis* [*De canone missae epicheresis*]. . . . In fact, since the beginning of this semester, there has been no restful hour for me. Always Zwingli, Zwingli, James [the letter of James], Zwingli."[67] Needless to point out, of course, the eighteenth article is where Zwingli had decisively rejected the sacrificial character of the Mass and emphasized its symbolic significance. Neither is it necessary to add that the letter of Hoen here mentioned has been alleged to be the eye-opener for Zwingli toward his "symbolic" interpretation of the Lord's Supper. It is indeed a great regret that we have to wait until the publication of Barth's lecture notes before we learn of Barth's own comments on the Zwinglian sacramental doctrine at that moment. Barth's general impression on Zwingli, however, can well be surmised from his second reference to Zwingli in the same circular letter. He says:

> Besides, I had to read a great quantity of Zwingli, in whom up till now I have just been rummaging around. C[Calvin?] has posed for me a question as to what actually is the matter with Zwingli and not unjustly is scenting the closeness [of Zwingli] to the "Reformers." In a sense, he is a gigantic, unsentimental, unhysterical non-anti-intellectualizing Ragaz. The noisy proclamation, then, that humanism intends to partake in the God of the Reformation, and indeed is equal to it, is correct. It is given to father Luther (and all those "purely religious ones") as a barbed hook at just the moment when he, at the height of his "belief," broke out in a somewhat premature ridiculing laughter about the good Karlstadt. Thus it really constitutes the break in the euphoria of the reformation, the moment when arguments returned again to Socrates and Seneca, but also when they used allegories from rural life, and when one had to counter all those little religious illusions again with a tough "the flesh is no good," repeated ad nauseam. This unfortunate "bit of cinnamon" of remembrance—which Luther understandably greeted with disgust—that the picture book of the world, even in its most beautiful places, which had just been looked into again with renewed zeal, only represented the picture book of God, and that one could do nothing else in that situation than to grit one's teeth—just like the Romans—in the midst of these difficulties and afflictions of this world.[68]

Puzzling and enigmatic as many of Barth's remarks in this letter may be, the latter seems to convey Barth's growing fretfulness caused by his sense of failure to discover something in Zwingli. Barth's word *stobern* (to hunt around, to rummage, to search everywhere) is quite symbolic. It may reflect his own inner impatience with Zwingli. He asks if after all Zwingli was one of those *"Reformpfarrer."*

X

The long-awaited winter vacation was soon gone, and Barth resumed his lectures again. Everyday was with Zwingli, Zwingli, James, and Zwingli again. His January 23 circular letter indicates that his Zwingli lectures were entering into the critical stage. He writes:

> I am treating the Eucharistic controversy with the most extensive apparatus. It is quite likely that the lecture will get bogged down there. Of course, the description of the Battle of Kappel I certainly do not want to leave out. What is painful for me to admit yet impossible to deny is that the image of Zwingli is more and more unfavorable. There is no doubt that he was not a great spirit. His only significance in the context of the entire Reformation rests upon the fact that he was the man who raised the (albeit necessary) objection against Luther, and did so loudly, if not with the most substantial arguments. Other than that, he was one competent representative of that humanistic-Christian type, quite lovable and thoroughly *probus,* with its urgent stressing of monotheism and ethics. As a "religious personality," for the use of the German-speaking Swiss, he may certainly have been agreeable and adequate; as "a reformer," however, he could demand, fundamentally, no more right to be so designated than Sebastian Hofmeister or Guillaume Farel. And as "a theologian"! My dear brothers, I have for years been reading in those Schuler und Schulthess volumes. As Eduard is my witness, last fall I started this with my best intentions. But it really is impossible.[69]

As a matter of fact, what Barth had found in Zwingli was "the well-known modern Protestant theology under the thin egg-shell of the ancient church." It was that old stale and pathetic spiritualism, the notorious reconciliation of faith and reason, religion as experience, an ostentatious juggling away of miracles, a total exchange of knowledge and enlightenment. "The riddle of Luther's anger toward him is no more a riddle to me, very fortunately. . . . Luther's Eucharistic doctrine is incomparably better than Zwingli's. It has become clear to me even through the study of his earlier writings only, in which it is still on its way to formation." Barth goes even so far as to say that the total significance of the Zwinglian theory has to be brought into the daylight. "It was truly lucky that Calvin arrived afterward and put the carriage, which had been stuck in 'undialectic,' again onto the right track."[70]

Deep and grave was Barth's disappointment. He could keep on moving only out of a sense of duty. He anxiously waited for the termination of this winter semester. He would sit up the whole night perusing Zwingli's *De vera et falsa religione.* He perceived that the family was waking up in the next room. He had only time enough to change his clothes and hurry to the lecture hall of the university. Despite such an immersion in Zwingli, "I have found *no* fruit on this fig tree."[71] With these nights with Zwingli, Barth had become increasingly skeptical. His conclusion was:

> Unless I shall be proved wrong by future research, the lines in Reformation history have to be drawn entirely otherwise than I daringly assumed a year ago. Hopelessly, Zwingli has come to stand at the head of the ranks of Schwenckfeld, Sebastian Franck, Karlstadt, and the like, just as some of the most important Lutheran quasi-historians of dogma have long since assumed him to be. Calvin was the only figure who grasped what was at stake—Zwingli failed to comprehend it—and was the only one to advance in a respectable manner against Luther.[72]

The February 16, 1923, letter indicates that Barth was lecturing on Zwingli's doctrine of providence. Anticipating the end of the term, he says: "It will be good since I have certainly lost some of the pleasure in [reading] Zwingli. *De providentia* and the battle of Kappel will bring a rapid end of [the term]."[73] In less than two weeks, he reports that he has finished with the Zwingli and James lectures. Barth's final evaluation of Zwingli at this point was that "he is irremediably Aristotelian, to be put in a line with Thomas in the rear and Schleiermacher ahead." Zwingli's meaningfulness in Reformation history consists merely in his being a "guard over against the presumption of religion," as Ernst Stähelin liked to put it. It was because of this presumptuousness that, from 1525 on, Luther began to set aside the paradoxes. The same presumptuousness had set Luther's attitude to Zwingli in a fatal direction.[74]

Barth would, however, reserve the ultimate judgment on Zwingli precisely because "what is so evident to me now is that we cannot form a decisive opinion of someone else. . . . Later on, I will surely read more about this impossible Zwingli again when I shall have gained wider perspectives. There is certainly much to take notice of in this figure. In this connection, beware of that book by Wernle, in which everything becomes a children's lesson, though [this book] has often been an external crutch for my feeble Latin."[75]

Unfortunately, we cannot know whether or not Barth ever had another occasion to study Zwingli with equal or greater intensiveness. A hasty glance at the indices to the *Kirchliche Dogmatik* I/1 through IV/3, or to the recent *Gesamtausgabe,* shows not a small number of references to Zwingli. It is a matter of question, however, if they reflect the results of his continued dialogue with Zwingli from the new and wider perspective.

This essay must come to an end in an exceedingly inconclusive way. The question as to whether there was a "turning point" or "displacement" in Karl Barth's interpretation and appreciation of Zwingli still remains open for various reasons. Undoubtedly, the question calls for more intensive and careful reading in both Zwingli and Karl Barth.

NOTES

1. Jaques Courvoisier, "Zwingli et Karl Barth," *Antwort. Karl Barth zum siebzigsten Geburtstag* (Zollikon-Zurich: Evangelischer Verlag, 1956), pp. 369–387.

2. Jaques Courvoisier, *Zwingli: A Reformed Theologian,* The Annie Kinkaid Warfield Lectures of 1961 (Richmond, Va.: John Knox Press, 1963).

3. Courvoisier, "Zwingli et Karl Barth," p. 369.

4. Ibid., pp. 378–380.

5. Ibid., pp. 382–384. See Karl Barth, *Christengemeinde und Bürgergemeinde* (Zollikon-Zurich: Evangelischer Verlag, 1946), pp. 9–10. (Japanese translation by Kazuo Hasumi [Protestant Publisher, 1954], esp. p. 75.) Courvoisier seems to overlook Barth's pungent criticism of the Reformation parallelism of church and state as in, for example, *Rechtfertigung und Recht* (Zollikon-Zurich: Evangelischer Verlag, 1948), pp. 9ff. (Japanese translation by Yoshio Inoue [Protestant Publisher, 1954], pp. 4–8.)

6. Courvoisier, "Zwingli et Karl Barth," p. 382.

7. Ibid., pp. 384–386.

8. Ibid., pp. 385–387.

9. Karl Barth, *Die kirchliche Lehre von der Taufe* (Zollikon-Zurich: Theologischer Verlag, 1943). (Japanese translation by Tatsu Shishido [Protestant Publisher, 1971]; E.T., *The Teaching of the Church Regarding Baptism,* Ernest A. Payne [London: SCM Press, 1948]. Hereafter *Teaching Regarding Baptism.*)

10. Karl Barth, *Die kirchliche Dogmatik,* vol. IV: *Die Lehre von der Versöhnung,* part 4 (Zurich: EVZ Verlag, 1967). (Hereafter *KD.*) (E.T., *The Christian Life,* tr. G. W. Bromiley [Edinburgh: T. & T. Clark, 1969].)

11. Barth, *KD* IV/4, p. 142.

12. Courvoisier, "Zwingli et Karl Barth," p. 382.

13. Gottfried W. Locher, *Die Theologie Huldrych Zwinglis im Lichte seiner Christologie,* vol. 1 (Zurich: Zwingli Verlag, 1952).

14. Gottfried W. Locher, *Die Zwinglische Reformation im Rahmen der europäischen Kirchengeschichte* (Göttingen and Zurich: Vandenhoeck & Ruprecht, 1979), ch. 11, "Zwinglis Theologie," pp. 206ff.

15. Eberhard Jüngel, *Karl Barths Lehre von der Taufe. Ein Hin-*

weis auf ihre Probleme, Theologische Studien, 98 (Zurich: EVZ Verlag, 1968), p. 42.

16. Jüngel, *Karl Barths Lehre von der Taufe,* p. 5.

17. Barth, *Teaching Regarding Baptism,* p. 48.

18. Ibid., pp. 48ff.

19. Ibid., pp. 20f.

20. Ibid., p. 28.

21. Representative of the Anabaptist "in-group" scholars, John Yoder can be cited here. See his "The Turning Point in the Zwinglian Reformation," *Mennonite Quarterly Review (MQR)* 32 (1958), 128–140. Also *Taufertum und Reformation in der Schweiz,* vol. 1: *Die Gespräche zwischen Täufern und Reformatoren 1523–1538* (Karlsruhe: H. Scheider, 1962). Over against this, for example, "out-group" scholar Robert C. Walton in his *Zwingli's Theocracy* (Toronto: University of Toronto Press, 1967), pp. 217–226, asserts that the Zwinglian reformation was consistent through and through and consequently there could be no "turning point." Hans J. Hillerbrand, as an "in-group" scholar, admits the difficulty of regarding Anabaptism as the "radicalization" of the evangelical reformation. See his "Anabaptism and the Reformation: Another Look," *Church History* 29 (1960), 404–423. Also see " 'The Turning Point' of the Zwinglian Reformation: Review and Discussion," *MQR* 39 (1965), 309–312.

22. Zwingli, *Huldreich Zwingli sämtliche Werke* (*Corpus Reformatorum*), vol. 4. See the English translation, "Of Baptism," by G. W. Bromiley, in *Zwingli and Bullinger* (Philadelphia: Westminster Press, 1953), p. 139. (Hereafter "Of Baptism.")

23. Balthasar Hubmaier, "Ein gesprech . . . auf Mayster Vlrichs Zwinglens . . . Tauffbuchlen von dem Kindertauff," in *Balthasar Hubmaier Schriften,* ed. G. Westin and T. Bergsten (Gütersloh: Gütersloher Verlagshaus Gerd Mohn, 1962), p. 186. (Hereafter "Ein gesprech" and *Schriften.* Japanese translation by Akira Demura [The Jordan Publisher, 1972], p. 209.)

24. See for example, Barth, *Teaching Regarding Baptism,* pp. 52f.

25. Barth, *KD* IV/4, p. 212.

26. Edmund Schlink, *Die Lehre von der Taufe,* in *Leiturgia,* vol. 5 (Kassel: Johannes Stauda Verlag, 1969), pp. 759–760. (Japanese translation by Tatsu Shishido [Protestant Publisher, 1988], pp. 261, 271.)

27. Barth, *KD* IV/4, p. 141.

28. Zwingli, "Of Baptism," p. 153; see p. 130.

29. Ibid., p. 133.

30. Barth, *KD* IV/4, pp. 33, 45 and passim.

31. Ibid., p. 141.

32. Ibid., pp. 112, 117.

33. Ibid., pp. 110f.

34. Ibid., pp. 115, 132f., 134ff., 171, 190f.

35. Ibid., pp. 4ff., 24, 66, 69, 71, 179f., 215. Needless to say, much discussion is in order on this subject.

36. Akira Demura, "Zwingli and Hubmaier: Their Views on the Salvation-Historical Significance of John the Baptist," "Bulletin of Tohoku Gakuin University," *Church and Theology* 11 (1980).

37. Hubmaier, "Von dem christlichen Tauff der gläubigen," *Schriften,* pp. 123f. (Hereafter "Tauff.")

38. Christof Windhorst, *Täuferisches Taufverständnis: Balthasar Hubmaiers Lehre zwischen traditioneller und reformatorischer Theologie* (Leiden: E. J. Brill, 1976), p. 55.

39. Hubmaier, "Tauff," *Schriften,* p. 125.

40. Ibid., p. 127.

41. Hubmaier, "Ein gesprech," *Schriften,* p. 197.

42. Other expressions by Hubmaier: "Vnderschaid zwischen dem Tauff Johannis vnd Christi," in "Ein gesprech," *Schriften,* p. 197 margin. "Gott furt durch Johannen hyab inn die hell, vnnd durch Christus wider auffher," and "der klare, lautere vnd helle vnderscheyd," in "Tauff," *Schriften,* pp. 127, 131.

43. Zwingli, "Of Baptism," pp. 160ff.; *Zwingli Werke* 4 (*CR* 91), pp. 258ff.

44. Zwingli, "Über doctor Balthazars touffbuchlin waarhaffte grundte antwurt," *Zwingli Werke* 4 (*CR* 91), 596–599.

45. Hubmaier, "Ein gesprech," *Schriften,* p. 197.

46. This point has much to do with the philosophy of history or the interpretation of salvation history both in Hubmaier and Zwingli. See Hans Hillerbrand, "Anabaptism and History," *MQR* 45 (1971), 107–122. Gottfried W. Locher, "Das Geschichtsbild Huldrych Zwinglis," *Theologische Zeitschrift* 9, no. 3 (July 1953), and *Huldrych Zwingli in neuer Sicht* (Zurich: Zwingli Verlag, 1969), esp. pp. 94–96. Hubmaier's thoroughgoing knowledge of both Church Fathers and medieval Schoolmen is seen in his "Der Vralten vund gar neuen Leerern Vrteil . . . 1526," *Schriften,* pp. 227–255. See Rollin S. Armour, *Anabaptist Baptism: A Representative Study* (Scottdale, Pa.: Herald Press, 1966), pp. 49–54. Extremely illuminating is David C. Steinmetz's article "Scholasticism and Radical Reform: Nominalist Motifs in the Theology of Balthasar Hubmaier," *MQR* 45 (1971), 123–144.

47. See Franz Lau, "Luther und Balthasar Hubmaier," *Humanitas-Christianitas,* ed. K. Beyschlag et al. (Witten: Luther Verlag, 1969), pp. 63–73. According to Lau, Luther in the disputation of 1520 takes more notice of the difference between the two baptisms than the identity. Armour, *Anabaptist Baptism,* p. 156 n. 188, quotes the official Tridentine anathema on those who say that the two baptisms are the same in efficacy (Sessio VII, Canon 1).

48. Windhorst, *Taufverständnis* (n. 38 above), pp. 64–68, 102, 185.

49. John H. Yoder, *Täufertum und Reformation in Gespräch* (Zurich: EVZ Verlag, 1968), pp. 33, 42.

50. Jack W. Cottrell, "Covenant and Baptism in the Theology of Huldreich Zwingli," unpublished Ph.D. dissertation, Princeton Theological Seminary, 1971, pp. 282ff.

51. Barth, *KD* IV/4, pp. 76–79, 94–98.

52. Barth, *The Christian Life*, pp. 75–84.

53. Barth, *Gesamtausgabe, Predigten 1913; Predigten 1914* (Zurich: Theologischer Verlag, 1976, 1974).

54. Oskar Farner, *Huldrych Zwingli* (Emmishofen: Johannes Blanke, 1917).

55. Barth, *Gesamtausgabe: Karl Barth-Eduard Thurneysen Briefwechsel*, vol. 1: *1913–1921* (Zurich: Theologischer Verlag, 1973), p. 239.

56. Ibid., p. 270.

57. Barth, *Der Römerbrief*, 1st ed., 1919 (Zurich: Theologischer Verlag, 1985), pp. 62f.

58. Ibid., p. 498 n. 38.

59. Ibid., pp. 420f.

60. Barth, *Briefwechsel* 1:283.

61. Barth, *Gesamtausgabe: Karl Barth-Eduard Thurneysen Briefwechsel*, vol. 2: *1921–1930.* (Zurich: Theologischer Verlag, 1974), p. 37.

62. Ibid., p. 60.

63. Ibid., p. 66.

64. Ibid., p. 79.

65. Ibid., p. 81. To Thurneysen, June 8, 1922.

66. Ibid., p. 110 n. 5.

67. Ibid., p. 120. Barth always quotes from the edition of Melchior Schuler and Johannes Schulthess, *Huldreich Zwinglis Werke. Erste vollständige Ausgabe.*

68. Ibid., pp. 123–124.

69. Ibid., pp. 131f.

70. Ibid., pp. 132f.

71. Ibid., p. 134.

72. Ibid.

73. Ibid., p. 143.

74. Ibid., pp. 150f.

75. Ibid., p. 151.

"Capito totus noster nunc est. Utinam fuissent semper." Capito's Return to the Reformed Camp

Willem van 't Spijker

Translated by Victoria Huizenga and Fred Klooster

On November 16, 1533, Martin Bucer wrote the words to A. Blaurer that report Capito's return to the Reformation camp: "Capito is completely ours; if only he had always been."[1] It is an interesting report in which he at the same time expressed his opinion of his colleagues. Hedio was a fine Christian, with his own possibilities, of course, which one ought not to infringe upon. Matthias Zell was a pious man, but he had too much of a tendency to listen to his wife. Bucer's view of himself was brief: *millies, millies miser.*

In this openhearted confession it becomes clear what Bucer's view was of the situation in Strassburg: "Things are not going badly for us in so far as it concerns the ministers."[2] They formed a working community which had the reformation of the city of Strassburg as its goal. Their programs were developed as a team project. They recognized the necessity of presenting a united front, at least to the outside world. Already in 1524 Bucer had his liturgical manifesto, *Grund und Ursache,* "signed by the other eight Strassburg ministers" because he considered a broad base necessary.[3] The Reformation could be carried out only by a team of theologians and ministers.

Therefore, it signaled a dangerous crisis when, during the years when Spiritualists and Anabaptists were agitating in Strassburg, Wolfgang Capito got into psychological, theological, and religious difficulties which threatened to disrupt the unity of the Reformation camp. Capito had a tendency to depression which was understandably aggravated by a somewhat uncertain personal situation, but even more by the unrest caused by the arrival of numerous charismatic prophets, dreamers, and enthusiasts. They intended to spread the radical

Reformation in Strassburg, the haven of justice. Capito had unlimited trust in people who were in trouble, a characteristic that Bucer termed *intempestiva in indignos beneficentia;*[4] this made it difficult for Capito to say no.

In addition, theological questions played their own role. There were questions concerning the ecclesiastical structure of the Reformation, questions which had their roots in exegesis and dogmatics. What was the significance of the old covenant for questions concerning church organization? Anabaptists had their opinions; the Spiritualists had theirs. And Capito leaned in a direction that was not entirely clear, at least not in those years. He became more or less uncertain after coming into contact with the sectarians. The result was that his views on the covenant and baptism became confused. He came mighty close to those who rejected the covenant of grace and infant baptism as they had been held for centuries. Behind that rejection lurked dogmatic uncertainties which concerned the most basic Reformation themes of freedom and the priority of grace. Luther's discovery of justification *sola fide* was also preached in Strassburg. The Strassburg ministers were actually the first ones who urged Luther to refute vigorously Erasmus and his view of the *liberum arbitrium.*[5] And linked to that was the fact that Capito, in distinction from Luther, saw the freedom of grace guaranteed, not first of all by justification *sola fide* but by the freedom of the Holy Spirit's work. That led to an extraordinary emphasis on sanctification in a spiritualistic sense. This pointed in a direction that would lead to a different construction of the dogmatic problem.

At the same time, occasioned by several factors, a religious crisis developed which brought everything into turmoil and deeply affected his faith. On January 26, 1532, after Capito had already come through the crisis, Bucer wrote to A. Blaurer:

> It was beneficial to Capito to see that everywhere those who have the Lord, who sincerely seek him, also have Christ. Although he in fact devoted himself to the founders of sects and strange dogmas beyond what was necessary and he did not succeed in what he attempted to do (because we were not able to share the truth about Christ with them), he began to be disgusted with the masses and at times agonized because he thought God had rejected him and that he was of no further use to the church.[6]

This religious despondency robbed him of the desire and courage to work. Bucer was right when he linked the seriousness of the crisis with a threatening estrangement, not only in personal relations but also with a schism in the Strassburg church. He gathered all his friends together in an effort to bring Capito back on the right track. And his zeal was rewarded; Capito not only changed his view of, and attitude toward, the sects; he also, like Bucer, gave in much less to spiritualism. Most of all, Bucer rejoiced to see that Capito discovered anew that God goes his own way as well as being reminded of what the Lord had done through him.[7] God works through us. When he uses us, we then have grounds for hope.

Capito's Relationship to the Anabaptists and Cellarius

Most of those who write about the events in Strassburg during the 1520s agree that Capito's difficulties were mainly related to his attitude toward Cellarius rather than to the Anabaptists. He clearly differed from Bucer. Gerbert tried to characterize the difference this way:

> Capito aimed to win over the individual subject and in this way to create the unity of the church; he was more of a pastoral counselor than a churchman. With Bucer it was the other way around. To him the objective concept of the *ecclesia* took precedence; the church must be preserved; whoever disrupts the unity must withdraw; therefore Bucer also turned much more quickly to the magistrate.[8]

It is clear that the differences involve different conceptions of the church. In 1524 both Bucer and Capito, in similar ways, had an eye for the unity of the church. Baptism is an "external matter" and therefore is to be left free.[9] The devil delights in dividing believers in regard "to external matters when he doesn't know how to divide them on major matters."[10] Baptizing of children "is for the better"; one dare not forbid it.

In those words we hear something about the struggle to maintain the unity of the church. Hence the tolerance toward the Anabaptists: "If anyone insists on baptism and wants it where he lives, in order not to destroy the body and to maintain unity we do not want to separate from them nor condemn them—to each according to his own conscience."[11]

Above all, one should avoid rebellion: "Nothing is to be done by way of revolt or rebellion."[12] Both Bucer and Capito agreed with those basic principles. But while Bucer valued infant baptism ever more positively, Capito maintained his spiritualist standpoint. In this he was also supported by his friendship with Cellarius.[13] Cellarius met the Zwickau prophets in Wittenberg in 1521, and through them he became alienated from the hierarchy of the church. He thought that infant baptism was not rationally defensible, and he was convinced of the necessity of establishing a visible community of saints on earth.[14] When he arrived in Strassburg in November 1526, he was warmly welcomed into Capito's home. He was also able to argue convincingly against free will in his disputation with Hetzer (December 1528).

On this point Capito and Cellarius agreed. When Cellarius published his *De operibus Dei* in July 1527, Capito wrote the introduction.[15] Cellarius' book was an important and solid defense of predestination in conjunction with a view of regeneration which excluded any mediation of salvation by means of Word or sacrament. The power of faith surpasses every natural power. Faith consists of the consciousness of the goodness of God which pervades everything: "(Fides) quae proprie experiens et vivus sensus bonitatis Dei est, in omnia se fundentis, omnia optime et sapientissime creantis et disponentis, et ex mera clementia praedestinationis suae filios regni salvantis."[16]

In this way faith became a "feeling of absolute dependence" in the predestinating God; thereby not only Word and sacrament lost their meaning but also theology, as a *theologia crucis,* completely disappeared.

The peculiarity of this spiritualistic viewpoint became evident in its unusual, uncomplicated connection between *praedestinatio* and *regeneratio.* Characteristic of Cellarius was his playing theologically with the idea of an internal sanctification which was already *in utero gliscit,*[17] and which is later strengthened. Sparks of the divine light are implanted in the *electi* by the grace of predestination. As they mature, the heart of the elect is moved by the goodness of God, and when sin wells up in our members, they cry to God: "Donec Dominus revelato Evangelio de Filio pleniore luce cor illuminet et in certam favoris spem crescentis spiritus testimonio obsignat."[18]

It is not surprising that in this view the sacraments have only symbolic meaning. They play as restricted a role as does the Word, which cannot be a *medium gratiae* since salvation was already actually given to the predestined *"a vulva," "in utero."*

In this view it is also impossible to make a proper distinction between the old and the new covenant. In connection with the sacraments Cellarius would not hear of any promise whereby weak consciences are strengthened.[19] God's grace works without mediation within one's consciousness. There the *experiens et vivus sensus bonitatis Dei* originates. Outward symbols are nothing: "currens aut volens ego nihil sum, liberalis electio tua ad vitam in Christo Iesu ad nullam creaturam se alligans, solum aliquid est."[20]

Cellarius argued as follows: "Hic cadit solicita ista infantium salutis cura et eorum anxia baptisatio."[21] But this understanding of baptism was similar to that of the Anabaptists. And that is where Bucer's doubts began.

Capito and Bucer

Cellarius' publication of his book would probably never have received as much attention if Capito had not written the introduction, and if Capito had not himself expressed similar views in the publication of his lectures on Hosea. Not only in Strassburg but also in Zurich, Basel, and Bern many were concerned about these developments.

Capito's sympathy for Cellarius was unalloyed. He expressed it in the following words of praise: "Martin Cellarius, a man of God with an extraordinary intellect, recently arrived here. When he heard about the situation in our church, and about what was being revealed here and how freely God's grace was flowing, he decided to talk with us about faith and certain doctrines."[22] Capito reports that they were willing to talk with one another. He lists the issues in discussion in detail: "de fide praedestinationis, de discrimine inter vasa electionis et reprobationis, de semine Dei et electis, de perseverantia sanctorum, de salutis certitudine, de spiritu sancto, de natura et ratione filiorum Dei, et id genus aliis."[23]

These were precisely the themes which lay not only on the boundary between Wittenberg and Zurich but also on the boundary of the Reformation and the enthusiasts *(Schwärmertum).* Yet in the way in which Capito reported these things, he made clear that he was taken in by Cellarius. God was manifestly present in all this. And Cellarius understood things as they were seen in Strassburg; he understood them even better than the Strassburgers themselves understood them.[24]

Capito had only praise for Cellarius' book, *De operibus Dei.* He claimed that, even from the first moment of meeting Cellarius, he had learned more and gained more insight than he had from months of painstaking study of books, of which he had many excellent ones, especially in the Hebrew language. Without hesitation he recommended the works of Cellarius in the same breath with those of Bucer, who lectured on Matthew, as well as with his own lectures on Hosea, Malachi, and Jonah.

When Capito's commentary on Hosea appeared in late March 1528, in which he gave his opinions on several critical issues of the day and in addition presented the main views of Cellarius as his own, Bucer felt abandoned. It seemed as though Capito was continuing Cellarius' thoughts and even developing them further. Capito also traced the whole of salvation back to predestination in a simplistic way: "Quicunque igitur Deo per Christum credis, persuasum habes quaecunque tibi contingunt, ex praedestinantis patris aeterna voluntate contingere, et in tuam contingere utilitatem."[25] He also knew about a seed that is planted in the *electi* at birth. It manifests itself as some sort of the fear of the Lord which resides in the heart as a small coal until, warmed by the Holy Spirit, it begins to glow. These coals do not die out because the calling of God and his counsel are eternal. In the *timor Dei,* Capito distinguished three *tempora.* The first is the time at which the *semen benedictionis* is implanted in the *utero.* The second is the time when the Lord, whether hidden or revealed, strengthens the power and motion of the heart through the faith of predestination. In Capito's view the third one is the time realized in the resurrection.[26]

It is not at all clear what role the Word of God can play in the whole history of the realization of predestination in a believer's life. Also, it should not be seen as an inconsistency that Capito refers to the scriptures only as a norm of doctrine or even only as a *regula affectum.*[27] Word and Spirit stand in complete independence next to each other. The Spirit goes his own way, the way of predestination. The Word of God comes up alongside, illuminating but not radically renewing. The real work occurs through divine power and action alone.

When Capito in addition was too friendly with the Anabaptists and their customs in his commentary, Bucer's doubts increased.[28] He complained to Zwingli.[29] Capito was too kind toward Cellarius' "homo vere spiritu catabaptistico correptus." Bucer was unsuccessful in his efforts to discuss the matter with Capito. And he suspected that Cellarius was behind it all. In his lectures Capito had expanded on the ideas of Cellarius, and for that reason Bucer had presented a detailed defense of infant baptism in his commentary on John's Gospel and explained his typological exegesis. Capito remained silent, and Bucer did not know how the two men judged the matter. To be sure, Cellarius publicly criticized Bucer in the presence of Capito for teaching *"blasphema."* In his commentary on Hosea, Capito even attacked Bucer's views *"verbatim"* but *"presso licet nomine."* Bucer wanted to challenge him to a debate; earlier they had discussed everything. Capito answered that he did not know how one could interpret the prophets if one did not take Cellarius' views into account. What could Bucer do further? "The book was published and one could only expect serious scandal to follow these quarrels."

Bucer had reconciled himself to Capito in the hope of distancing him from the Anabaptists and from Cellarius as well. But he would not have succeeded if Zwingli and Oecolampadius had not come to his aid.

From such reports one can see what the situation in Strassburg was. In spite of everything Bucer defended his friend who tried to assist the Anabaptists. Yet through it all they brought Capito to ruin. The good man suffered from long periods of sleeplessness as well as daily illness which did not improve because of his depression.[30]

Bucer presents a good picture of his friend. The situation was dangerous enough. And the friends in Zurich and Basel were troubled by the whole affair.

As early as April 22 Capito asked Zwingli for his evaluation of his Hosea commentary.[31] He had sent the commentary on March 29 with the comment that differences in detail should not encroach on the main thing, namely, love.[32] But now he was eager to know what Zwingli thought about the Hosea commentary. He wrote Zwingli that if he had spoken other than the truth, he should not blame that on evil intentions but on his weakness.[33] On June 17, Zwingli wrote to Capito and Bucer that he had learned from a third party that Cellarius had managed to bring about an estrangement between them.

Zwingli gave his opinion about Cellarius. If earlier someone would have said that Cellarius had changed, Zwingli would have answered as follows: "How can such a person be changed, one who seeks only himself so that his name may become famous. But he does it in such a clumsy way that no one can surpass his hypocrisy."[34]

Zwingli appealed to Capito and Bucer to carry on as David and Jonathan did, and to do nothing else: "Dissentiant alii; at vos iunctis viribus ad pacem omnes compelletis."

This suggestion helped. On June 24, Bucer wrote Zwingli that Capito had listened to his friendly advice, even though he could not yet think about infant baptism in the same way as they did. He did not want to lose the vision of a united church.[35] Yet he could not see his relationship to the sects differently than he did before.

Oecolampadius informed Zwingli that in Basel the Anabaptists rejoiced because of Capito's friendly attitude toward them:

> In Capitone nostro aliquid desidero. Catabaptistae enim multum hic gloriantur, quod ipsis faveat, quandoquidem aliquanto benignius eos tractat; tametsi non dubitem, quod nondum assentiatur eis, velim tamen et per te admoneri ipsum; at nolim, quod me

prodas; nam et ego monui, et adhuc constat rumor. Fortasse hoc Cellario debebimus.[36]

Oecolampadius was not mistaken in this. He had been drawn to Cellarius himself.[37] As he told Zwingli, he also sent a letter to Capito. And Capito did draw back. He did not want to tarnish his relationship to Zwingli and Oecolampadius.

But he maintained his stance toward the pious among the Anabaptists. On July 31 he gave an account of the matter in a detailed letter to Zwingli.[38]

> I see clear differences among the Anabaptists. One finds superiors and leaders among them. They are called *katechetas,* superintendents. They all avoid me as a dog avoids a snake. I don't like them. They are full of lies and deceit as far as I can see. But there are also others who appeal to me because of their admirable innocence.

Capito felt drawn to them. He was also "natura verus et a fuco et gloria abhorrens, ruri agresti vicinior, meaque vitia novi familiariter neque dissimulo magnopere."[39]

On August 6, 1528, Oecolampadius wrote Zwingli that Bucer had told him that Capito was becoming more and more convinced that the Anabaptists were wrong and that he daily came to trust them less and less. Also his relationship to Cellarius also became less intense. Capito also had no more difficulties with Bucer:

> Nihil habet dissidii cum Bucero, nec ab eo turba timenda est; tametsi paedobaptisma abolitum velit et alia quaedam Cellarii in Hoseam infarserit, nihilominus sinceritatem fidei probe contra eos tuetur; antesignanos et capita factionum eiiciendos censet, libertatem in externis, qua licet baptizare infantes, fortiter asserit. Nihil ultra exigimus ab illo.[40]

Strange to say, his standpoint was respected by Oecolampadius. Freedom *"in externis"* did not mean that one would not permit, or at least not reject, believer's baptism, but that infant baptism as something outward would not be forbidden. One can see that Capito retained his point of view from 1524 onward longer than Bucer did.

Behind all this was the spiritualistic view of the difference between the inner work of the Spirit and the external human work. In addition, the original view of predestination, with its predominant emphasis on regeneration as the expression of, or sign of, predestination had not yet lost its peculiar one-sidedness. From the theological perspective almost nothing had changed.

It is at least clear that Capito's attitude was not significantly different from his earlier views. A much more radical crisis was unquestionably needed to restore real unity in the Strassburg reformation. What Bucer contemplated was the unity of the church whereby the common good of the city contributed to the *Corpus Christianum,* church and state, ministers and magistrates, society and citizenry; everything would unite under the one Word of God and indeed in the Strassburg church of God.

What Capito had in mind was the spiritual unity of a community of love in which each individual, under the guidance of the Spirit, would experience God's omnipotence in election and which would then be shared with others. The truth did not lie in the middle. It could only be reached by way of a deep crisis; for Capito this meant a crisis of inwardness. For Bucer it was to be a crisis of "outwardness." Capito discovered his solution in the 1530s; Bucer discovered his in the 1540s when the empire and the city of Strassburg and its citizens saw their unity threatened. But were they solutions?

Capito's Crisis and the Solution

It is clear that the personal relationships in Strassburg, especially between Capito and Bucer, had been only superficially restored. In the years immediately following Zwingli's intervention, it seemed at first sight as if things remained as they had been. The sects were still active. When in March the ministers requested a public discussion with the Anabaptists, the council refused permission. It is noteworthy that Bucer, Hedio, and Zell together approached the council. Capito was not present. The ministers, "after working seriously for three years with the Anabaptists, reported that they all had one God and one kingdom of God. However, several serious errors were present: Some do not confess Christ as God, others ignore or do not let the Scriptures speak; they value more highly what they claim is inwardly revealed to them by the Holy Spirit."[41] For "valid reasons" the council decided not to permit a public hearing. That was on March 20, 1529. But on August 25 the first mention of baptism was included on the list of blasphemies which the council wanted to deal with.[42]

Gradually more severe disciplinary measures were enacted. On October 31, 1530, a decision of the council, made in reference to an imperial mandate, was aimed at the Anabaptists; it provided Capito and Bucer the opportunity to discuss matters with them.[43] The Anabaptists and their imitators "would now be imprisoned." Discipline against them became a serious matter.

Meanwhile, Capito maintained his previous views: "Et tamen fateor ingenue in plerisque extare signa timoris domini et veram deditionem adeoque zelum fuco nescium." When asked whether the Anabaptists endured martyrdom because of true faith or because of obstinacy or stubbornness, he had to admit that he did not know: "Testificor coram deo me non posse dicere amentia potius, quam divino spiritu vitam negligere hanc praesentem."[44]

When the magistrates had to deal with people who refused to take an oath, Capito wrote: "I do not have the time to address you personally, otherwise I would have come to you when appropriate. I have a heartfelt concern for these poor people who show a zeal for God."[45]

On September 17, 1531, Oecolampadius wrote Capito that he was deeply concerned about his excessive *familiaritas* with enemies of the church: "Adhuc tamen est quod anxium tenet ac sollicitum, nempe familiaritas ista quam cum hostibus ecclesiae habes, dum contubernales tibi sunt et prophanum panem tecum frangunt, qui nos indignos habent quibuscum sacrum fragant."[46]

With those words his friend from Basel rightly described the situation. In his zeal Capito went too far. He not only tolerated heresy but even went so far as to endure the sects. Bucer's attitude was completely different. For example, in his German Apology to the Tetrapolitan Confession (1530) he wrote: "Heresy [is] a sort of self-righteousness in matters that belong to our holy religion by means of which one presents something that seems better than the common faith of our Christian doctrine but which really separates from the church."[47]

We mentioned earlier that only a superficial healing of the troubled relations between Capito and Bucer had taken place and that only a personal crisis could really bring about a change. That crisis came near the end of 1531.[48] The two close friends, Zwingli and Oecolampadius, had died. In addition, Capito's wife, Agnes, died early in November 1531. Capito was already weak and had been sick for a long time. Sleeplessness robbed him of strength, and severe depression followed.

As noted earlier, Bucer wrote about this; Capito had the feeling that God did not help him—even worse, that he had rejected him and that he was of no further use to the church.

We have a report from Capito himself. In mid-December 1531 he wrote that

> the Lord has kept me under his severe fatherly punishment; my dear sister and wife who was a great help to me became ill and died quietly. His anger concerned my restlessness and temptations. I recognized the presence of God's wrath and my sin became unbearable. . . . I can not think of anything else anymore but that he also wants to end my life.[49]

During those difficult days Bucer showed himself a true friend to Capito. He organized a trip[50] which would take Capito to southern cities, Basel, Bern, Zurich, Konstanz, Lindau, Memmingen, Augsburg, Kempten, Ulm, and then back to Strassburg. Capito was absent from Strassburg from December 21 to early April 1532. On this trip Capito discovered that he not only had his place in the midst of the Reformation movement and among his friends but also, as Bucer wrote, that God had worked through him.

This is how the citizens of Bern experienced it: "Take note, in the midst of our troubles there came Capito, a true father of our church and sent by the Lord as we and the entire city testify!"[51] That is what Berchtold Haller wrote to Martin Bucer on January 16, 1532. Later Capito reported about this part of his life "which he himself viewed as under a certain providential indication: 'I am convinced that God sent me out.' "[52]

H. R. Lavater mentions Capito's "providential participation" in the Synod of Bern, a synod which clearly reflected his influence. At least that is also how Capito himself experienced it. Bucer and his friends also noticed that Capito again showed an interest in practical questions. In addition, Capito also changed his attitude toward the sects. It became clear to him at Bern that the church needed not only an inner unity but also a structural unity. His experiences under the difficult situation at Bern could now be put to good use in the work of the Synod of Strassburg which was held in 1533. He was now able, even driven, to "exchange his earlier subjective church work for the only realistic church political action, that of Bucer. From that point on Capito remained faithfully at Bucer's side."[53]

During those days and months Bucer was greatly concerned to find a wife for Capito, one who could also be a mother to his children.[54] Capito himself considered Sabina, the widow of an Anabaptist. Bucer feared that this possibility might only make matters more difficult. Therefore he did his best to interest Capito in Wibrandis Rosenblatt, Oecolampadius' widow. During his travels Capito had visited her, and on August 11, 1532, they were married. Through this marriage a new impetus was given to strengthen the Reformational circle of friends.

Oecolampadius had often been concerned about Capito's

views. Now the marriage of Capito and Wibrandis meant not only that Capito was responsible for the care of Oecolampadius' children, as well as of his many books and papers, but in addition that Capito considered it his moral responsibility to maintain the heritage of the Basel reformer. Thereby the complete return of Capito to the Reformation camp was guaranteed.

Capito totus noster nunc est

The 1532 Synod of Bern and the 1533 Synod of Strassburg, as well as subsequent measures, greatly influenced church life in Reformation regions. Its significance for Capito was especially great. An equally significant influence came by way of Capito's responsibility, as he saw it, to republish Oecolampadius' many writings, especially his commentaries.

Already in September 1533, Capito wrote the introduction to Oecolampadius' commentary on Jeremiah. Capito considered it necessary to write the "argumentum in hunc prophetam." But that was not all. He also filled in the blank spaces which were left in some of the manuscripts and therefore completed Oecolampadius' preparatory work in this edition.[55] The publisher of the work was even clearer than Capito was. Matthias Apiarius wrote that the commentary on Jeremiah has gotten a second author who in his own right has written as if it were his own work, "aut ex integro pleraque finxit aut inchoata suo penicillo quod aiunt, ad plenum formavit."[56] Oecolampadius' commentary on Ezekiel, also published in 1534, shows even more of Capito's influence. When it was decided to publish Oecolampadius' commentary on the prophets in Geneva in the 1550s, Bullinger wrote to Calvin "that he should make sure that nothing would be cut out or changed in *'huius viri sancti laboribus'* as had happened in Strassburg with the commentaries on Jeremiah and Ezekiel."[57]

Before this the commentary on Ezekiel showed the influence of Capito's pen. Contemporaries, however, simply considered it completely Capito's own work to which one could turn to learn his own views. Capito made sure that Simon Grynaeus' report of Oecolampadius' death was included. He himself wrote a biographical introduction to the commentary. Yet the book now became completely Capito's book. At the end of the work Capito wrote, "Habes hactenus, pie lector, quae nobis in hunc difficillimum prophetam annotare visum est."[58]

Capito looked upon the work as a sort of cooperative product. He did not doubt that Oecolampadius "explanatum calculo suo approbaturum fuisse largiter, si nobiscum suppresset," because Capito had no particular church in mind, "sed ad unicum Ecclesiarum caput collimavi." Thus Oecolampadius' work became Capito's. Nevertheless, in the commentary he referred more to conditions in Strassburg, as becomes clear from his marginal references to prophets and prophetesses: "Satanas contra Argentinensem Ecclesiam falsos prophetas excitavit."[59] And the index includes this: "Argentinensis Ecclesia incuriosior falsos prophetas habet," a reference that obviously does not come from the pen of Oecolampadius.

From all this it follows that it was rather easy for Capito to return to the Reformation camp. We do not mean to imply that he slipped back in as if he were ashamed. There was no place for that in one who was characterized by simplicity, honesty, and righteousness. "Sum natura verus et a fuco et gloria abhorrens," he wrote to Zwingli on July 31, 1528. The new edition of Oecolampadius' commentaries provided Capito with the opportunity to express his views in an appropriate way. He now wrote of the relationship of Word and Spirit in the same way as was done at the Synod of Strassburg. And it was precisely those pages in Oecolampadius' commentary which his contemporaries recognized as the expression of Capito's views.[60]

Capito undoubtedly had the Anabaptists in mind when he referred to the significance of the external Word. We must listen to every word:

> Vult autem eum esse debere attentum ad omnia verba, ut primum bene discat, ne sit doctor antequam discipulus, et nec partem audiat tantum, et aliam partem negligat, sicut hi faciunt, qui de solis operibus disserunt, et nihil de fide, et qui sola blanda narrant, et nihil asperum. Nam sine cruce promissio efficax esse non potest, et qui peccata illa interiora oculis conscientiae non exponit, is nullam remissionis gratiam poterit afferre.[61]

In spite of all that, one cannot say that Capito's attitudes had radically changed. If the Spirit's work does not precede, the sermon is quite useless. "Itaque auditio externa, quae quidem efficax esse debet, interiorem sermonem veluti praesupponit."[62]

That did not mean that a sermon had no significance at all. The Anabaptists contested "de ordine ex verbis." But that is not what the relationship between Word and Spirit is all about. If the *exterior auditio efficax* is to occur, it must begin with the Spirit. "Illud tamen nullus negarim temporis ordinem talem non esse necessarium."[63]

For Capito the *ordo in ministerio* had a particular ecclesiastical significance. The work of the Spirit has priority in the theological sense, not the temporal, since the external sermon precedes. People hear the Word inwardly "per verbum spiritus et vitae, externus autem per verbum literae, sive per praedicatum verbum. Nec separamus in ministerio nostro verbum interius ab exteriore, sed distinguimus, ut agnoscamus quatenus opus Dei in nobis procedit, ne pro divino humanum verbum arripiatur, et pro fide sit opinatio humana." In this way Capito means to praise God's grace, "quae datur aut cum verbo praedicato, aut ante, aut post illud, ut ipsi visum fuerit."[64]

By his public return to the side of Bucer, Capito held on to the foundations of the Strassburg reformation. The freedom of God's grace was endangered by Cellarius' view of the connection between predestination and regeneration. Capito's view of the relationship of Word and Spirit pointed out a way which Bucer also chose in his *Retractationen:* a stronger union which was to prove its worth ecclesiastically, so that in practical church questions the window remained open toward Wittenberg while at the same time it was clear that Strassburg—that means Capito and Bucer—retained their orientation to Zurich, Basel, and Bern.

Thus Capito's return was more than a personal event. It became significant for real unity in the Reformation movement.

NOTES

1. "Capito totus noster nunc est. Utinam fuisset semper." T. Schiess, *Briefwechsel der Brüder Ambrosius Blaurer und Thomas Blaurer 1509 bis 1567,* vol. 1 (Freiburg, 1908), p. 442.

Literature: J. W. Baum, *Capito und Butzer, Strassburgs Reformatoren* (Elberfeld, 1860); O. E. Strasser, *Capitos Beziehungen zu Bern* (Leipzig, 1928); B. Stierle, *Capito als Humanist* (Gütersloh, 1974); J. M. Kittelson, *Wolfgang Capito: From Humanist to Reformer* (Leiden, 1975); W. Locher, ed., *Der Berner synodus von 1532, Edition und Abhandlungen zum Jubiläumsjahr 1982* (Neukirchen, 1988); C. Gerbert, *Geschichte der Strassburger Sectenbewegung zur Zeit der Reformation 1524–1534* (Strassburg, 1889) (hereafter *Sectenbewegung*); A. Hulshof, *Geschiedenis van de Doopsgezinden te Straatsburg van 1525 tot 1557* (Amsterdam, 1905); G. H. Williams, *The Radical Reformation* (London, 1962).

2. Schiess, *Briefwechsel* 1:459.

3. *Martin Bucers Deutsche Schriften,* vol. 1, *Frühschriften 1520–1524,* ed. by R. Stupperich (Gütersloh, 1960), p. 189.

4. Schiess, *Briefwechsel* 1:442.

5. J. Rott, *Correspondance de Martin Bucer,* tome 1, *Jusqu'en 1514* (Leiden, 1979), pp. 295ff.: "Quare te per Christum obsecramus, carni et sanguini ne asquiescas, quod de Erasmo semel scripsisti, propter Christum etiam odiendos parentes, nunc omnium rhetorum consiliis praeferas. Christi enim verbum est; pereat latine linguae decor, pereat eruditionis miraculum, quo Christi gloria obscuratur. Huius verbo salvamur, aliorum magis perdimur," 23 Nov. 1524.

6. Schiess, *Briefwechsel* 1:320, no. 261; see Gerbert, *Sectenbewegung,* p. 184.

7. Schiess, ibid.: "Capito ipse eadem scripsit, sed ita ut decebat ea memorantem, quae per ipsum Dominus operatus est."

8. Gerbert, *Sectenbewegung,* p. 73.

9. *Grund und Ursach,* p. 260.

10. Ibid., p. 261.

11. Ibid., p. 262.

12. Ibid., p. 277.

13. *Bibliotheca dissidentium. Répertoire des non-conformistes religieux des seizième et dix-septième siècles,* édité par André Séguenny, Textes revus par Jean Rott, tome II, *Martin Borrhaus (Cellarius),* par Irena Backus (Baden-Baden, 1981).

14. Ibid., p. 12.

15. Gerbert, *Sectenbewegung,* pp. 66ff.; H. Krebs and H. G. Rott, *Quellen zur Geschichte der Täufer,* vol. 7: *Elsass;* part 1, *Stadt Strassburg 1522–1532* (Gütersloh, 1959), p. 90.

16. M. Cellarius, *De operibus Dei* (Strassburg, 1527), p. 2, recto.

17. Ibid., p. 6, recto.

18. Ibid.

19. Ibid., p. 49, recto: "Taceo eos qui hic in symboli huius usus promissionem praetexunt, unde imbecilles conscientiae confirmentur, sic agere quasi confirmatio magis symbolis per promissionis verbum tribui possit, quam iustificatio."

20. Ibid., p. 71, recto.

21. Ibid., p. 71, verso.

22. Krebs and Rott, *Elsass* 1:116ff.

23. Ibid., p. 116.

24. Ibid., p. 117: "Comperit revelante Domino, rem esse sicut nos proposueramus, imo dilucidius quam nos verum inspexit, persuasumque habuit ad gloriam Dei proferendam, eadem factura."

25. W. Capito, *In Hoseam Prophetam Commentarius* (Strassburg, 1527), p. 75, verso.

26. Ibid., pp. 76, verso–77, verso.

27. Against Gerbert, *Sectenbewegung,* p. 76.

28. Krebs and Rott, *Elsass* 1:152.

29. Bucer to Zwingli, 15 April 1528, in *Huldreich Zwingli sämtliche Werke* 9:426.

30. Ibid., p. 426: "Laboravit diu insomnia vir vere alioqui plus. Conflictatur eum cottidianis morbis: inde aucta atra bilis hominem turbat. Ita tame studet unitati ecclesiarum et te atque Oecolampadium observat, ut sperem, si moneres eum, et paulo gravius, ita tamen, ut te adhuc amicum suum agnosceret, te non parum apud ipsum profuturum."

31. Capito to Zwingli, 22 April 1528, in ibid., p. 442.

32. *Zwingli Werke* 9:406.

33. Ibid., p. 442: " 'Hoseam' nostrum, ut meas tentationes cognoscas, lege; nam si quae secus dico, quam vel res et veritas patitur vel hactenus tractata sunt, id tribue non animo et ingenio malo, sed infirmo, quod in veritatem inspiciens aliud non potuit. Observo te tuaque, ut mereris, reverenter, per quem dominus tanta praestitit."

34. Ibid., p. 487: "quomodo potest eum mutare, qui ad hoc unum incumbit, ut nomen magnum fiat, id autem tam expedita, attamen profunda hypocrisi, ut similem ipse nunquam viderim, sed hoc tamen viderim, non temere esse, qui ad eam profunditatem hominis penetrare possit."

35. Ibid., p. 492.

36. Ibid., p. 494.

37. E. Stählin, *Das theologische Lebenswerk Johannes Oekolampads* (Leipzig, 1939), pp. 390ff.

38. *Zwingli Werke* 9:516ff.

39. Ibid., pp. 516f.

40. Ibid., p. 526.

41. Krebs and Rott, *Elsass* 1:233.

42. Ibid., p. 247.

43. Ibid., p. 278.

44. Ibid., p. 285.

45. Ibid., p. 299.

46. Ibid., p. 344.

47. Ibid., p. 341.

48. For the following, see: Gerbert, *Sectenbewegung,* pp. 182–192; O. E. Strasser, *Capitos Beziehungen zu Bern,* pp. 67–77; *Der Berner synodus von 1532,* vol. 2: *Studien und Abhandlungen,* pp. 64ff., 354ff.

49. Krebs and Rott, *Elsass* 1:363f.; see also *Der Berner synodus,* p. 65.

50. Compare the itinerary established by H. R. Lavater in *Der Berner synodus,* pp. 363ff.

51. Ibid., p. 360.

52. Ibid., p. 362; cf. p. 354: "Ich weiss noch nit anders, dann (wie ich hievor geschriben), das mich gott ussgetriben hat, uff das bi den kirchen, da etwas evangelii gehort ist, ein besser grund gelegt und die zerbrochen hertzen durch Christum an got bestendig gewisen würden."

53. Gerbert, *Sectenbewegung,* pp. 188ff.

54. Ibid., pp. 185ff.; R. H. Bainton, *Women of the Reformation in Germany and Italy* (Minneapolis: Augsburg Publishing House, 1971), pp. 84ff.

55. E. Stähelin, *Briefe und Akten zum Leben Oekolampads,* vol. 2 (Leipzig, 1934), pp. 740ff.

56. E. Stähelin, *Das theologische Lebenswerk,* p. 407.

57. Ibid., p. 408.

58. E. Stähelin, *Briefe und Akten* 2:751ff. In the *Commentary,* p. 306, recto.

59. *In prophetam Ezechielem commentarius D. Ioan. Oecolampadii, per Wolfgangum Capitonem aeditus* (Strassburg, 1534), p. 90, verso.

60. E. Stähelin, *Das theologische Lebenswerk,* p. 408; *Briefe und Akten* 2:762.

61. Ibid., p. 16, verso.

62. Ibid., p. 17, recto.

63. Ibid.

64. Ibid., p. 17, verso.

Barriers to Protestant Ecumenism in the Career of Theodore Beza

Robert M. Kingdon

In this ecumenical age, scholars have naturally and laudably brought to our attention ecumenical initiatives in earlier ages, even ages as marked by confessional strife as the period of the Reformation, even within movements as often labeled intolerant as that founded by John Calvin. Thus John T. McNeill in his *Unitive Protestantism* pointed out the number of ways in which Calvin followed Luther and other early Protestant leaders in trying to bring their followers together into a single Reformed church.[1] Thus Willem Nijenhuis in his *Calvinus Oecumenicus* demonstrated that Calvin not only worked to secure unity with Lutherans but also supported the reforming bishops of England, and therefore can hardly be held responsible for later splits between Lutherans and Calvinists on the Continent or between Episcopalians and Presbyterians in Britain.[2] And thus Mario Turchetti delineated expertly the hopes and dreams of a sizable party of sixteenth-century intellectuals, nominally both Catholic and Protestant, who departed from the leadership of both Calvin and the Vatican in the hope of creating *concorde,* a religious middle way that would then be used to coerce Christian society into unity.[3]

If we are to understand the period of the Reformation in its entirety, however, and thus place ourselves in a position to draw from it lessons of contemporary benefit, we must not let ourselves be so carried away by our own ecumenical hopes that we ignore the powerful antiecumenical forces in the period, forces which in fact usually did prevail. A neat example of these conflicting forces, and of how they were resolved in an antiecumenical direction, can be found in the career of Theodore Beza, Calvin's successor as director of that branch of

Reformed Protestantism guided from Geneva. It can be found specifically in his relations with Jacob Andreae, a Lutheran leader of a slightly younger generation, and with Heinrich Bullinger, a Zwinglian leader of a distinctly older generation. The importance of Bullinger, Zwingli's successor as director of that branch of Reformed Protestantism guided from Zurich, has, of course, been brought to the attention of specialists on the Reformation by Edward Dowey. We all wait with considerable anticipation for the published products of his decades of research on this crucially influential leader of early Reformed Protestantism, whose many publications and astonishingly voluminous correspondence had an influence within the movement rivaled only by that of Calvin himself.

What happened in brief is this: Beza and Andreae, as brilliant and idealistic young leaders of the competing Reformed (Zwinglio-Calvinist) and Evangelical (Lutheran) branches of early Protestantism, met near the beginning of their careers in 1557 and fashioned a compromise that they hoped and believed made pan-Protestant unity at last possible. That compromise was immediately and viciously torpedoed by senior spokesmen for the two parties, preeminent among whom was Bullinger. Beza and Andreae continued their brilliant careers and completely fulfilled the high hopes held for them. They assumed positions of increasing importance in their respective churches and eventually became widely respected and honored leaders. But they never again attempted compromise. In fact, they became spokesmen for intransigent wings of their respective parties. They not only attacked each other's ideas, they excoriated each other in increasingly vicious and personal polemics. The patterns of development one finds in their parallel careers provide important and instructive, if discouraging, insights into the early history of Protestantism.

It will be some time before we can fully understand the complex relationships between Beza and Andreae and the influences of their elders on them. Much of the raw information that would make that possible is locked away in the as yet unpublished correspondence of the parties involved. But some of this correspondence is at last being published in critical editions of exemplary quality. Of these editions, the one with which I am personally best acquainted is the correspondence of Theodore Beza. Originally collected by Hippolyte Aubert, it was prepared for publication by teams of scholars in Geneva, at first directed by Henri Meylan and now by Alain Dufour, and published by the Librairie Droz. The account that follows, therefore, is based primarily on the volumes of the Beza correspondence that have already appeared. It will need to be complemented at some point with information drawn from later volumes, particularly involving the climactic confrontation between Beza and Andreae in Montbéliard. It will also need to be complemented with materials drawn from the Bullinger correspondence and from Lutheran sources. I hope that this sketch, nevertheless, will at least indicate some of the problems in this domain that deserve exploration.

When Theodore Beza arrived in Geneva from Paris in 1548 and announced his adherence to the Reformed cause, Protestants throughout Europe had reason to rejoice. As a member of the French provincial nobility, he had access to courtly circles and diplomatic skills rare among the intellectual leaders of the Protestant movement. As a scholar with training quite similar to Calvin's, he had also developed intellectual talents certain to impress the men who had formulated Protestant theology. He had secured a law degree from Orléans, with the same teachers who had trained Calvin. He had pursued studies in the humanities to an even more developed degree than Calvin, publishing a volume of Latin poems that revealed an exceptional literary talent and that displayed a formidable command of classical and biblical Greek. He had not, to be sure, pursued formal studies in theology, but neither had Calvin, and it was assumed that Beza would also be able to master Protestant theology simply through reading and correspondence. He was hired to teach Greek at the new Protestant Academy in Lausanne, then under the direct control of the Zwinglian Swiss city-state of Bern. He quickly and easily entered the circle of theologians directing the Reformation from Swiss cities. He soon began publishing works supporting their theological program, including a translation into French of Bullinger's *Perfectio Christianorum* in 1552 and a retort to Sebastian Castellio's critique of Geneva's decision to burn Servetus for heresy—his *De haereticis* of 1554.[4]

Given this background, it is not surprising that Beza was soon asked to use his talents on diplomatic missions for the Reformed cause. Of particularly crucial importance to his understanding of interconfessional issues were two he undertook in 1557. The first of these missions was to the Swiss Protestant cantons and to the German Protestant princes and cities of the Rhineland on behalf of the Waldensians of Piedmont.[5] These peasant proto-Protestants, living in valleys on both sides of the Alpine spine separating France from Savoy, were subject to increasingly ferocious persecution from the French monarchy. When Geneva and Lausanne became Protestant and hired leaders of the stature of Calvin and Viret, the Waldensians had quickly turned to them for guidance. They had raised funds to make possible publication of the first Protestant Bible in French and had offered support of other types. Calvin and Viret and their associates in the leadership of Protestantism in French Switzerland wanted very much to do whatever they could to spare the Waldensians from persecution. They resolved to send embassies to the Swiss and German Protestants to urge them to intercede with the French royal government on behalf of the Waldensians. The Swiss had traditionally supplied mercenaries to the French crown, and the German Protestants of the Rhineland had often been allies of the French in their struggles with the Holy Roman Emperor. Both thus possessed some leverage in dealing with the French government.

Beza and Farel, the fiery old prophet of the Protestant movement in French Switzerland, were selected to lead this embassy. They went first to Bern and Zurich, where Bullinger helped them in presenting their case, and were completely successful in persuading authorities there to intercede with the French for the Waldensians. They then went on to Germany. There they found their task complicated by the growing fears among German Protestant authorities that theological deviations, particularly in defining and interpreting the sacraments, could lead to dangerous types of religious radicalism. They found that they would have to present to these authorities some evidence that the French Waldensians for whom they spoke were sober Protestants like themselves and not wild-eyed religious radicals of the sort that had terrified governmental leaders all over Germany since the great peasants' rebellions of the 1520s. They needed to offer proof that the French Protestant party for which they spoke did not endorse any of the revolting heresies on matters of sacramental theology developed by the radicals. They did this by helping to draft and then signing two statements on eucharistic theology, one with Michael Diller, a preacher at the court of the Count Palatine of the Rhine in Heidelberg, the other with Jacob Andreae, then preacher in Göppingen and adviser to the Duke of Württemberg.[6] These draft statements were quickly copied and circulated among German Protestant intellectuals. They led hard-line Lutherans to crow that they had finally vanquished Zwinglianism and won the Swiss and French Protestants over to their theological point of view. A close look at these statements reveals that the Lutherans did indeed have something to crow about. The Göppingen statement which had been drafted primarily by Beza and Andreae was particularly offensive to Zwinglians. It contained an agreement to use the word "substance" in defining the mode in which Christ is present in the Eucharist.[7] It agreed that both the faithful and the unfaithful truly receive Christ in the sacrament, even if they do not both benefit from that reception.[8] Neither were opinions that any committed Zwinglian could accept.

When Beza and Farel reached Zurich on their way home, they reported with considerable pleasure to Bullinger and the other local leaders their success in reaching an agreement with the Lutherans, an agreement which had eluded Zwingli and Luther themselves. They did not, however, have the good sense to show the Zurichers copies of the agreements they had signed. When copies arrived there after Beza and Farel had returned home, Bullinger and his colleagues were furious. They felt that they had been betrayed and deceived. They held Beza particularly responsible for this disaster. They complained in angry letters to Beza himself, to Calvin, and to others. Bullinger wrote the angriest of these letters.[9] Peter Martyr Vermigli, who had recently moved to a teaching position in Zurich from one in Strassburg in order to escape Lutheran intolerance, also wrote.[10] Johannes Haller, leader of the Reformed church in Bern, before even seeing a copy of the agreement, complained bitterly about its content.[11]

This was an anger the French Protestant leaders really had to mollify. The Protestant regimes in both Lausanne and Geneva were directly dependent on the goodwill of Zwinglian powers. Lausanne and the surrounding *pays de Vaud* had become and remained Protestant only because it had been conquered and was still occupied by the troops of Zwinglian Bern. Geneva had won its independence from its bishop and Savoy only because of a formal military alliance with Bern. And Bern looked for intellectual leadership, as it had from the beginning of its commitment to Protestantism, to Zurich and its Zwinglian pastors. The political alliances between these Germanic and French areas, furthermore, had been reinforced with an intellectual alliance. From 1544 on, Calvin and Bullinger had with considerable care negotiated a common theological statement, finally given definitive wording in a personal meeting and signed as the Zurich Consensus in May of 1549.[12] This document had been accepted by most of the other Swiss Reformed churches, as a binding confession of faith. Bullinger and Haller looked upon the confessions drafted in part by Beza, particularly the one drafted in Göppingen, as flagrant breaches in this Swiss Consensus. That was one of the most specific reasons for their anger.

To disarm this anger, Calvin and Beza both quickly wrote a

number of letters to Bullinger and his colleagues seeking to mollify them in several ways. Both advanced as a defense Beza's relative youth and inexperience.[13] In so doing, they were almost certainly alluding to his rather obvious naïveté as a theologian. Both reminded the Zurichers that some kind of agreement with the Lutherans would be highly desirable for both tactical and religious reasons. Beza acknowledged openly and frankly that he had made a serious mistake in not showing the text of the Göppingen agreement to the Zurichers when he passed through their city on his return journey, and he promised never again to make a mistake of that sort. Bullinger, Vermigli, and Haller all finally agreed to pardon Beza for his imprudence.[14]

At that point, Beza set off on yet another diplomatic mission, again with Farel, and again to the Swiss Protestant cantons and the German Protestant princes. Once more they wanted to ask them to intercede for Protestants in France. This time it was for a group of socially prominent Parisians, including a number of nobles, who had been seized in a raid on a secret and illegal worship service on the rue St. Jacques in the French capital and had been thrown into jail. Again Beza and Farel had to reassure the Lutherans that they were interceding for sober and socially conservative Protestants, not wild-eyed religious radicals. This time they met with a group of Lutheran theologians of even greater prominence and diplomatic experience than Diller and Andreae, headed by Philip Melanchthon himself. Melanchthon, as a humanist of the same stripe as Beza, was particularly adroit in negotiating with him. Melanchthon flattered the young Calvinist considerably by offering him an ode composed in his honor. And he suggested that Beza, on behalf of the imprisoned French Protestants, simply agree to endorse the Augsburg Confession which he himself had drafted back in 1530, and had carefully revised several times in later years, as the definitive statement of Protestant belief. The 1540 version of this confession, generally known as the *variata,* had been warmly endorsed by Calvin, although it was never accepted by Bullinger.

Beza, having been stung once, was a little more careful this time. He and Farel and their associates drafted a confessional statement in Worms in which they did agree in substance to accept the Augsburg confession, but not in its entirety, making a special point of excepting the 1530 version of the clause defining the Eucharist, the object of greatest controversy between Lutherans and the Reformed.[15] Melanchthon and his colleagues understood Beza's position and were willing to accept this as a temporary compromise and to support their appeals to the German princes. Those appeals were successful, and the German princes did indeed send embassies of intercession to Paris.

Then Beza, as soon as he had returned home to Lausanne, sent Bullinger and his colleagues in Zurich a copy of the Worms confession and also wrote a long and careful letter explaining just what they had done.[16] Beza made it clear that he now understood the distinctions in eucharistic theology that were so important to the Zwinglians and that he had been careful to reject (1) the Lutheran definition of the real presence, (2) the Lutheran teaching that the unfaithful as well as the faithful receive Christ in the sacrament, and (3) the necessary deduction from Lutheran doctrine that the risen body of Christ must be ubiquitous.[17] He also developed with some passion the practical and religious arguments for seeking a full reconciliation with the Lutherans.

The Zurichers remained unimpressed. They sent to Beza a fairly detailed refutation of the Worms confession, arguing that they couldn't really believe Calvinists could accept all of it, given their support of the Zurich Consensus, and pointing out that there were significant differences between the Reformed and the Lutherans on issues other than the Eucharist.[18] This letter was a good deal more temperate in tone than the letters provoked by the Göppingen confession but was still resolute in its opposition to any accommodation with the Lutherans. It ended by advising Beza to stop writing confessions, implicitly suggesting that he still didn't really understand what he was doing. A copy of this letter, furthermore, was sent to Haller in Bern, and led him to send a letter of warning on behalf of the Bernese pastors to Beza, a warning that was particularly ominous, given Bern's control over Lausanne.[19] Bern, indeed, was soon to eject most of the Protestant pastors and teachers in Lausanne and the area around it for following Calvin's views too slavishly. Beza himself avoided dismissal only by resigning and moving to a new position in Geneva just before this crackdown.

Zwinglian pressure, however exercised, effectively ended Beza's attempts to be an agent of Protestant ecumenism. Never again did he try to negotiate in good faith with Lutheran leaders. More and more he tried to prove to the Zwinglians that he was committed to the alliance they had struck with the Calvinists. More and more he demonstrated that he could use his formidable talents in their common cause. More and more he became a leading opponent of Protestant ecumenism, lashing out in increasingly ferocious polemics against Lutherans and even against such other opponents of his point of view as the spokesmen for the emerging Anglican party in England. And throughout the rest of Bullinger's life, the older man kept reminding Beza of his youthful errors and of his obligation to defend without compromise the Reformed version of the true faith.

The next significant opportunity for Beza to display his diplomatic talents and prove his orthodoxy came at the Colloquy of Poissy in 1560.[20] This was arranged by the French government, then led by the Queen-Regent Catherine de Médicis, as an attempt to stem the rising tide of controversy provoked by the rapid spread of Calvinist Protestantism in France. It involved a formal discussion between the leaders of the French Catholic Church and leaders of the Calvinist party, in the presence of members of the royal family and the court. Beza was asked to lead the Protestant delegation to this colloquy. Preeminent among his associates was Peter Martyr Vermigli from Zurich, not only a highly sophisticated defender of the Zwinglian theological position but also a native of the home state of the Queen-Regent, Florence.

In his opening statement at Poissy, Beza infuriated many in the Catholic party. While much of his address was conciliatory, Beza's dramatic language in repudiating any version of the real presence of the body and blood of Christ in the elements of the eucharistic sacrament, by asserting that the body of Christ is "as far removed from the bread and the wine as is heaven from earth," so offended Catholic prelates in the audience that some were provoked to cry "blasphemy."[21] This extremism may have led the wily Cardinal of Lorraine, a senior member of the Catholic delegation, to a sly attempt to sever French Protestantism from German support. He professed a personal interest in the Confession of Augsburg and suggested that it might well serve as a ground for compromise between Catholics and Protestants in France. Following the colloquy, he and his brother, the Duke of Guise, even entered into negotiation with the arch-Lutheran Duke of Württemberg, Andreae's patron, on this possibility.[22]

It has usually been supposed that the Guises were bluffing, seeking to undercut the French Protestant cause and discredit it among Lutherans. It is intriguing to speculate, however, on what might have happened had Beza and Vermigli called their bluff and agreed to negotiate on this basis. A younger Beza, before his 1557 experiences with Bullinger, might have been inclined to enter into such a negotiation. In 1560, however, it was clearly impossible, particularly with Vermigli at his side. A stream of letters from Calvin in Geneva and Bullinger in Zurich kept warning Beza and Vermigli not to fall into this trap and to stand firm on a thoroughly Reformed theological platform. The Colloquy of Poissy ended in complete failure, and France was plunged within another year into nearly forty years of bloody religious wars. That was the melancholy consequence of this collapse of the best opportunity for religious reunion ever placed before the contending religious parties in sixteenth-century France.

Four years later, in 1564, Calvin died and Beza took his place as Moderator of the Geneva Company of Pastors and as the principal theological spokesman for that branch of the Reformed movement looking to Geneva for leadership. His prestige within the Reformed church in France, in particular, grew ever greater. Twice he attended meetings of national synods of that church, in 1571 at La Rochelle and in 1572 in Nîmes. In the La Rochelle Synod, sometimes called the "synod of princes" because of the considerable number of great Huguenot aristocrats in attendance, Beza even served as Moderator. But here again, at the height of his international reputation and powers, Beza ran into trouble with Bullinger. The principal accomplishments of the La Rochelle Synod were the drafting of a definitive confession of faith, with three official copies in parchment to be deposited in three separate places, and the drafting of a discipline, or constitutional ordinance, describing the proper organization of the French Reformed church. But the Synod also tried to resolve a number of disputes that had broken out among French Protestants. One of them involved an argument in eucharistic theology. The synod resolved this argument by condemning those who would not accept the use of the word "substance" in official descriptions of the ways in which the faithful communicate with Christ in the Lord's Supper.[23] Now this was precisely the position of the Zurich church. Peter Ramus, the brilliant rhetorician and a French Protestant who much resented Beza's leadership within his church, immediately wrote to Bullinger, bringing to his attention this decision.[24] Bullinger was furious all over again and wrote another of his angry letters to Beza. He acidly pointed out that Calvin himself had agreed to leave this offensive word out of the Zurich Consensus. He also raised questions about some of the other decisions taken at La Rochelle to which Ramus objected.[25]

Beza again took Bullinger's complaint very seriously and wrote a long and carefully constructed letter in response.[26] The attack on the use of the word "substance," he explained, was aimed against a group of Italian troublemakers in Lyon and was not intended in any way to criticize the position of Zurich. He then saw to it that the next national synod, in

Nîmes, took steps to appease Zurich. It adopted a resolution making clear that the earlier condemnation was intended only for domestic deviants and should in no way be construed to criticize "those foreign churches who, for reasons best known to themselves, do not use the word 'substance.'" And it adopted a fresh statement on the true presence in the Eucharist that, by emphasizing the "mystical and spiritual" nature of communion with Christ, was more nearly in agreement with the Zwinglian position.[27]

Meanwhile Beza had become a point man in formulating Reformed responses to attacks on their sacramental theology from hard-line Lutheran theologians. In this he was following a tradition established by Calvin late in his career with his polemical retorts to Joachim Westphal and Tileman Heshussius. Beza's first polemical attack on a Lutheran theologian, in fact, was a 1559 sequel to Calvin's exchanges with Westphal, and his second was a 1561 companion piece to Calvin's retort to Heshussius.[28]

After Calvin's death Beza's polemical attacks on Lutheran theologians became increasingly ferocious and frequent. One of his most important targets was Johannes Brenz, supervisor of the Protestant establishment in the duchy of Württemberg, a state in competition with the Reformed for control of much of southwestern Germany. Beza attacked Brenz particularly for teaching ubiquitarianism, the doctrine that Christ's risen body can be in many places at once so that it can participate corporally in the eucharistic elements as the sacrament is celebrated at the same time in many different localities. Brenz was the explicit target of an attack on ubiquitarianism Beza published in 1565, under the title *Ad D. Io. Brentii argumenta quibus carnis Christi omnipraesentiam nititur confirmare.*[29] Beza also ripped into Matthias Flacius Illyricus, the chief spokesman for the Gnesio-Lutherans, that particularly conservative branch of the Lutheran movement formed in opposition to the influence of Melanchthon. Beza also attacked Martin Chemnitz, the theologian who took the lead in defending the Lutheran position against the strictures of the Council of Trent. But Beza reserved his greatest polemical ferocity for the friend of his youth, Andreae. Polemics against these and other Lutherans are scattered through a variety of treatises,[30] prefaces, and open letters. One piece in which Beza attacks all four of these particular targets is an open letter to the Landgraf of Hesse appended as a preface to a book by the moderate Lutheran Nuremberg lawyer Christopher Hardesheim titled *Refutatio dogmatis de fictitia Christi omnipraesentia* and published in Geneva in 1571.[31]

The only Lutheran leaders of prominence for whom Beza had any kind words were Philip Melanchthon and some of his disciples. That support, of course, simply confirmed the orthodox Lutherans in their view that the Philipist followers of Melanchthon were really crypto-Calvinists.

Andreae responded in kind to Beza's attacks. Their exchanges became very nasty and personal. Each accused the other, for example, of embracing the heresy of the Nestorians. Andreae began this exchange by charging Beza with reviving this ancient heresy. Beza replied that Andreae was the real Nestorian. This retort, documented in some detail, makes up a major part of his letter to the Landgraf of Hesse preceding the Hardesheim treatise.[32]

At every point in this running polemical war with the Lutherans, Beza was egged on by Bullinger. There are constant references in Bullinger's letters to Lutheran books that must be refuted and constant urgings to Beza to hurry up with the job of preparing specific refutations.[33] There are nasty characterizations of specific Lutheran leaders. Thus, for example, Bullinger describes Andreae as a man who is "garrulus, vanus et ambiciosissimus, avaritia et inani gloria turgidus."[34] There are even occasional rather pointed reminders in these letters of how naive Beza had been back at Göppingen.[35] Bullinger was clearly using Beza's talents in his own lifelong vendetta with the people who kept tarnishing the memory of his beloved Zwingli and who kept challenging the authority of his Zurich. He may have shared a common Swiss suspicion of all forms of power emanating from Germanic lands. In any case union with the Protestants of Lutheran Germany was not a goal to which he gave high priority.

Sometimes Beza even went beyond Bullinger in his hostility to religious deviance among Protestants. He could not stand Peter Ramus, his lay rival within the French Reformed church, and warned Bullinger about him.[36] He engaged in a sharp, if at first unpublished, exchange with Thomas Erastus over the decision of the government of the Palatinate to adopt consistorial excommunication, to use in this way the powers of the church for social control.[37] Erastus, who was personally close to Bullinger, was defending the position of Zurich in this debate, for Zurich had consistently refused to use ecclesiastical powers to control human behavior, leaving social control in the hands of secular government. To avoid increasing tensions between Zurich and Geneva, Erastus and Beza agreed to avoid exposing this dirty linen to the general public by going into print. They stated their points of view on this issue only in letters and in manuscripts limited to private circulation. Years later, after Erastus had died, his widow permitted publication of his treatise attacking the rigors of Calvinist ecclesiastical discipline. Only then did Beza publish his attack on the Erastian position.[38]

Beza also willingly supported English Puritans in their early campaign against the Anglican establishment, despite warnings from Bullinger against accepting all the charges made by these wild men. Beza, however, not only believed their charges but gave them powerful support. He agreed, most notably, to assist Andrew Melville's campaign against bishops in Scotland by sending to that country for distribution and eventual publication a slashing attack on the very notion that episcopacy is a system of church government approved by God and permitted by scripture.[39] Calvin had never gone that far. Neither had Bullinger.

In 1585, Beza met Andreae once more. They were no longer young neophytes still in the shadow of older theological giants. Vermigli, Calvin, and Bullinger on the Reformed side had all died. Luther, Melanchthon, and Brenz on the Lutheran side had all died. Beza and Andreae were now at the peak of their powers and influence. They were clearly among the most prominent intellectual leaders of their respective parties. Andreae had recently completed successful negotiations to persuade Lutherans of every faction to accept a Formula of Concord as the basic statement of their belief, thus ending decades of bitter intra-Lutheran strife. As the text of the Formula makes obvious, however, Lutheran unity had been achieved only by including in its definitions of belief savage repudiations of Zwinglian and Calvinist points of view. Beza, since Bullinger's death in 1575, had become the most prominent single spokesman for the non-Lutheran Reformed churches in all of Europe.

This meeting between Andreae and Beza took place in Montbéliard, a French-speaking principality controlled by the Duke of Württemberg. The Duke, advised by Andreae and others, had insisted that his French subjects accept the same conservative Lutheran form of Protestantism as his German subjects and had forced several French Calvinist pastors to leave the area. A number of prominent French Protestant noblemen, however, had recently moved to Montbéliard, seeking refuge from Catholic pressure within their native country. They resented being forced to conform to Lutheranism. At their request, the Duke organized a colloquy between Calvinists and Lutherans. Beza led the Calvinist negotiating team; Andreae led the Lutheran one. They were now free to negotiate as their own consciences dictated. They were no longer subject to pressures from older and better established theologians in their respective parties. But there was no question at Montbéliard of returning to the goodwill and openness of Göppingen back in 1557. Both Beza and Andreae had risen to their positions of leadership in part by exploiting their followers' dislike for and distrust of the opposing Protestant party. Both of them were now passionately committed to different versions of theology, particularly on sacramental interpretations but increasingly on other matters as well. Years of mudslinging in print had deepened their animosity and made it very personal. Neither would budge from his fixed positions. At the end of the debate they would not even shake hands.[40]

In the end, therefore, Beza became a reigning champion of Protestant anti-ecumenism, insisting that only the form of the Reformed religion to which he was attached was true and that there must be no compromise with any other form. In this he had turned his back resolutely on the ecumenical dreams to which he had been open in his youth, to his original hopes of uniting all Protestants in a single purified church. We cannot be sure of what his motives had been in moving him to this unedifying conclusion, just as we cannot be sure of the inner motives underlying any decision by any leader of prominence either in the past or in the present. We can speculate that Beza became persuaded that he had been naive and now understood Protestant theology better. We can speculate that he was moved by sincere admiration for Calvin and Bullinger and wished to be taught by these erudite elders. Or if we are more cynical, we can suspect Beza of careerism and of being overly sensitive to political pressures. In any case, however, he does not provide us with a model of much contemporary use. His development from ecumenism to antiecumenism provides us rather with a warning of the difficulties still facing efforts to unite all Christians.

NOTES

1. John T. McNeill, *Unitive Protestantism,* rev. ed. (Richmond, Va.: John Knox Press, 1964).

2. Willem Nijenhuis, *Calvinus Oecumenicus: Calvijn en de eenheid der kerk in het licht van zijn briefwisseling* (The Hague: Nijhoff, 1959).

3. Mario Turchetti, *Concordia o tolleranza? François Bauduin (1520–1573) e i 'Moyenneurs'* (Geneva: Droz; Milan: Angeli, 1984).

4. For full bibliographic descriptions, see Frédéric Gardy, *Bibliographie des oeuvres théologiques, littéraires, historiques et juridiques*

de Théodore de Bèze (Geneva: Droz, 1960), nos. 58–61, pp. 32–34; nos. 80–82, pp. 44–47.

5. There is a useful narrative account of these two missions in Paul-F. Geisendorf, *Théodore de Bèze* (Geneva: Labor et Fides, 1949), pp. 82–94. See also McNeill, *Unitive Protestantism,* pp. 204–212.

6. For texts of these two confessions, see Théodore de Bèze, *Correspondance,* vol. 2, ed. by Henri Meylan and Alain Dufour (Geneva: Droz, 1962), pp. 243–248.

7. Ibid., p. 245.

8. Ibid., p. 244.

9. Ibid., p. 75. See also Bullinger to Calvin in *CO* 16:541–542, 567–568, 571–574.

10. Bèze, *Correspondance* 2:79–80.

11. Geisendorf, *Théodore de Bèze,* p. 86.

12. John T. McNeill, *The History and Character of Calvinism* (New York: Oxford University Press, 1954), p. 198.

13. Bèze, *Correspondance,* 2:86–94 (to both Bullinger and Vermigli), 98–103 (to Bullinger); *CO* 16:544–545 (to Vermigli), 564–566 (to Bullinger), 594–596 (to Bullinger).

14. Geisendorf *Théodore de Bèze,* p. 88; Vermigli to Calvin in *CO* 16:586.

15. Bèze, *Correspondance* 2:115–117.

16. Ibid., pp. 131–138.

17. Ibid., p. 133.

18. Ibid., pp. 145–152.

19. Ibid., pp. 157–159.

20. For a full account of this colloquy, see Donald Nugent, *Ecumenism in the Age of the Reformation: The Colloquy of Poissy* (Cambridge, Mass.: Harvard University Press, 1974).

21. Ibid., p. 100.

22. Ibid., p. 202.

23. For a text of this condemnation, see John Quick, *Synodicon in Gallia Reformata* (London, 1692), 1:92.

24. For an account of this exchange, see Robert M. Kingdon, *Geneva and the Consolidation of the French Protestant Movement, 1564–1572* (Geneva: Droz; Madison, Wis.: University of Wisconsin Press, 1967), pp. 102ff.

25. Bèze, *Correspondance* 12:206–209.

26. Ibid., pp. 215–227; also Kingdon, *Consolidation,* pp. 209–215.

27. Quick, *Synodicon* 1:104. See also Bèze, *Correspondance* 13:267–272, for the text of a formal letter from the Synod of Nîmes to the Pastors of Zurich.

28. For full bibliographic descriptions, see Gardy, *Bibliographie,* no. 96, pp. 59–60; nos. 135–137, pp. 81–84.

29. Ibid., no. 222, pp. 126–127.

30. See particularly in Gardy, *Bibliographie,* nos. 223 and 244, pp. 127–128, two editions of a set of three tracts, one aimed against Andreae, another against Flacius; nos. 291–295, pp. 157–160, against Andreae and Nicolas Selneccer of Leipzig; no. 344, p. 185, against Andreae and his colleague Wilhelm Holder.

31. Republished with very useful notes in Bèze, *Correspondance* 12:60–92.

32. For Beza's accusation, see *Correspondance* 12:67–71, *inter alia*. For reference to Andreae's accusation, see pp. 186–187.

33. E.g., Bullinger to Beza, 12 May 1564, in Bèze, *Correspondance* 5:64–66, urging a reply to Brenz.

34. Bèze, *Correspondance* 12:183.

35. Ibid. p. 247 and n. 38.

36. Ibid. pp. 220ff.

37. See Ruth Wesel-Roth, *Thomas Erastus: Ein Beitrag zur Geschichte der reformierten Kirche und zur Lehre von der Staatssouveränität* (Lahr and Baden: Schauenburg, 1954), esp. pp. 90–95, 112–118, for a useful if occasionally flawed account of this exchange.

38. Gardy, *Bibliographie,* no. 380, p. 204.

39. Titled *De triplici episcopatu* but published only in English in 1580 as an anonymous *Judgement of a most reverend and learned man from beyond the seas, concerning a threefold order of bishops.* For more on this piece, see Patrick Collinson, *The Elizabethan Puritan Movement* (London: Jonathan Cape, 1967), pp. 110 and 208.

40. For a brief narrative account of this colloquy, see Geisendorf, *Bèze,* pp. 351–356. Jill Raitt of the University of Missouri–Columbia is preparing a book-length study of this exchange.

The Benefits of Christianization and Reformation for the Hungarian People

Mihály Bucsay
Translated by Bruce McCormack

Although it is an unfinished piece, the editors are honored to include the following contribution by Mihály Bucsay, perhaps the one individual in Hungary most responsible for close and cordial relations between the Reformed Church of Hungary and the Reformed churches of the West and, indeed, throughout the world. On July 8, 1988, Dr. Bucsay passed from this world before he could put the finishing touches on his entry. Rather than edit it and risk changing the spirit of his material, we have chosen to publish it as it was at his death. We believe that it is an important contribution to scholarship as well as a fitting tribute to his many scholarly and ecclesiastical contributions.

At the time of his death Dr. Bucsay was Emeritus Professor of Theology at the Reformed Academy in Budapest, the General Director of the Raday College of the Danube District, Pastor of the German-speaking Reformed Congregation of Budapest, and a member of the Praesidium of the International Congress for Calvin Research. The convocation of scholars at the Fourth International Congress for Calvin Research held at Debrecen in 1986, an event of enormous importance in the development of cooperation between scholars of the East and the West, was made possible by the massive efforts of Dr. Bucsay. He was a gracious, giving, friendly man of great ability, conviction, and vision and was held in highest esteem by his colleagues in Hungary and throughout the world. A friend and colleague of Dr. Dowey on the International Praesidium, Dr. Bucsay eagerly accepted our request for a contribution. We are especially pleased to present it here and to record our pleasure by including Dr. Bucsay as one of our departed friends to whom this volume is dedicated.

One reckons correctly in distinguishing, among the benefits of Christianity, two forms of effect. These flow in both cases from the same source, and their separate products cannot be isolated from one another. The first of these is the blessing in the hearts of individual people; the other manifests itself in societies and institutions—viz., in nations and cultures—in which people live.

It is a well-known (although often unconvincingly challenged) fact that the Christian faith belongs to the most marvelous sources of strength which are capable of bringing about revolutionary transformations in human life. To be sure, this claim is not valid for a faith which degenerates into superstition or remains content with mere externalities or conventions. But it is certainly valid where faith reaches its truest expression in a personal relation to God. The benefits of the church for individual men and women are the more important of the two kinds of effects. These benefits usually have their effect as the result of the handing on of the Christian faith by the Fathers to those living today. Although this effect must be measured as an inner and personal one, it is not without its own means of transference. Such means must include the church's worship, with prayers and preaching, the sacraments of baptism and the Eucharist, and, in a most important sense, the Christian fellowship itself with confession and the diaconate. Yet not only through such external means are Christian people brought to an overpowering sense of praise, obedience, and communion with God—in a word, to personal faith itself; this occurs solely, on a deeper level, through the inner working of the Holy Spirit in the soul.

Although faith is something personal, its consequences do not leave undisturbed the social context in which individuals themselves live. These effects can be discerned within the arena of the changes in the moral life of communities and of the broader dimensions of intellectual culture. Perhaps this distinction between two forms of benefits which accrue from faith will be clearer if we distinguish from this second level two instances from the Hungarian church's history: the first of these is the process of Christianization, and the second the Reformation itself within Hungary.

The Christianization

The tenth century marks a fateful moment in the development of the Hungarian people. For it was at this juncture that they settled in their present location. They renounced marauding raids and grafted themselves instead onto the already settled Germanic and Slavic peoples, who had previously been reached by Christian missions. In this moment of transition, it was first and foremost the ruler Vajk who became the means of providence. Vajk was baptized and took as his new Christian name Stephan (or "István" in the Hungarian tongue). He was grasped by the personal saving effects of faith, becoming in the process a convinced adherent of the powerful movement of Christian renewal which spread outward from the monastic center of Cluny.

After the defeat of Merseburg in 937, the Magyars began to doubt the power and wisdom of their shamans, the so-called "táltos." The first step away from this dependence, and toward a new orientation, involved approaches to the Byzantine world, since the Hungarians had first encountered the Eastern church during their migrations from the extreme eastern sector of Europe to their later location in the lower stretches of the Danube and Theiss valleys. Byzantium also secured the benevolence of the militarily strong Hungarians through annual gifts which were given for several decades. Despite such efforts, however, the mission of the Eastern church among the Hungarians had no lasting or profound effect. And, when Hungary suffered a great defeat in 955 at Augsburg, the Byzantine church suspended these annual gifts altogether. The Magyars answered this interruption with a series of damaging military campaigns directed against Byzantium. Only after considerable effort were the armies of the Byzantine territories able to suppress the Hungarians. The Christian emperors of the East and West thereafter established a military alliance to protect themselves against the Magyars. István's father, the Grand Duke Géza, had to draw the necessary, if also painful, consequences: he opened his land to Christian missionaries—priests and monks, knights and their entourage, Germans, Slavs, and Italians. Géza's move was unmistakably political in strategy, since he wished to prevent Hungarian Christianity from being dominated by any single foreign church as a mission territory.

With István, however, the situation was entirely different. István was a convinced and enthusiastic Christian. The Bishop of Prague, Adalbert the Holy, who confirmed him, brought up this heir to the throne in the highly spiritual and strictly ascetic spirit of Cluny. Indeed, the bishop was himself a close friend of the abbot of Cluny, Majolus.[1] Another teacher and later friend of the king's, Bishop Gerardus-Gellért, who originally came from Venice, was a student in the northern Italian branch of this great movement for the reform of the church and monastic life. And, finally, Bishop Wolfgang of Regensburg—the teacher of Gisela of Bavaria, who was István's wife—also adhered to the noble and strict piety of the Cluniac cloister Gorze, located near Metz.

Thus, István's decision to align himself not with Byzantine but with Roman Christianity had little to do with political strategy. Rather, this move was the consequence of his close ties to Cluny, the great movement of church reform in the West. The religious and ethical standards which characterized Cluniac life became the dominant force influencing István in his political and diplomatic efforts. It was ultimately the personal fellowship with God's Son, who reigned in righteousness and love over all peoples, which determined István's loyalties, causing him to surrender the ideals and forms of pagan worship in his past. István's political decisions, therefore, were ultimately determined as self-consciously Christian deeds, and became a great blessing for his nation and people.

At this juncture Hungary quite quickly became a Christian nation. Mighty warriors learned from foreign priests who distributed the Eucharist how to bend their knees. István himself began to develop the church.[2] Every ten villages had to build a church. A tenth of all revenues was given over to the bishops, with a fourth going to the pastors of these village churches. The queen and the bishops provided the various objects needed for the sacred ceremonies—altar cloths and the splendid priestly vestments. Church attendance became obligatory. No longer were white horses sacrificed in forest meadows. The pagan cultic worship was strictly forbidden.

As the son of a people who lived in the narrow boundaries of their ethnic identity, István demonstrated a quite astonishing international and "ecumenical" spirit. He remained tolerant of the Eastern Christians. When in 1018 Bulgaria lost its independence, István secured a pilgrimage route from Hungary and those territories leading to the Holy Land. He also built hospices for pilgrims along this route, and not only in Byzantium and Jerusalem. But in addition to this he also guarded the pilgrimage routes to Rome, building comfortable lodgings for pilgrims in Ravenna and Rome. We know of a letter from the abbot Berno of Reichenau, one of the representatives of the Emperor, in which he thanks István and Gisela in effusive language for the warmhearted care of his monks during their pilgrimage to Jerusalem.

István also treated the priests of the earlier pagan worship with leniency, seeking ways to reeducate them in the Christian religion. István gave to a group of folksingers, known as the Igric, a village in every county and placed them under the supervision of officials from the local castle. They then continued to live peaceably in these villages (called "Igrici") and soon wrote new songs for the new era. The songs praised the heroic deeds that were achieved against enemy incursions into the country, which had already become Christian.

It certainly was not easy to win over a people to a heartfelt acceptance of Christianity when the majority of them had been baptized against their will. In 1046, eight years after István's death, a rebellion against the "new" religion claimed many victims. Bishop Gellért, too, died a martyr's death. It was the legendary and gallant figure of King László (1077–1095) who first succeeded in winning over broader stratas of society to a love and reverence for Christianity.[3]

The schism which occurred in the year 1054 had very little effect on Hungary's relationship to Byzantium and the Eastern church for over 200 years. The numerous Orthodox cloisters in Hungary remained unmolested until the invasion of the Mongols in 1241. It was only after the more tolerant house of Árpáden had died out and had been replaced by the Anjou kings that the viewpoint of Rome (according to which, Eastern Christians were schismatics and enemies of Christianity) prevailed in Hungary as well. Now, within the institution of more powerful civil mechanisms, the compulsory latinization of Christianity began. When King Lajos the Great (1342–1382) led victorious campaigns against the Balkans, Dominicans and Franciscans were put into action there to combat Eastern Orthodoxy.[4] The advance of the Turks, however, forced the Hungarian king, as well as the two orders, to evacuate this region around 1400. In the fifteenth century, the Franciscans set about trying to convert Hungarian Hussites, who had spread through southern Hungary. During these evangelistic actions, things took place in the church which one would prefer to remain silent about. The church as a whole was not active in this affair, however; rather, that portion of the church which relied on state power turned against the other part, which was deprived of this power.

The Reformation

The Reformation found Hungary in a situation in which church and state, people and culture were in the greatest danger. Through the assault of the Turks, Hungary had been confronted with the question of being or nonexistence. In this situation, the Christian faith—purified and activated through the Reformation—proved its salvific power for individual Christians as well as for collective society and the institutions of the Magyars. We would like now to investigate briefly these circumstances and changes.

Before 1526, the Hungarian people, represented by the provincial diets, turned decisively against the Reformation. The Reformation seemed to bring with it the danger of dividing the powers of Christianity at the most dangerous moment when the Turks were arming themselves for war against Hungary. Moreover, in the beginning, the Reformation seemed to be an all too German affair to a Hungary which judged it on the basis of external appearances. Before 1526, its first patrons, promoters, and adherents were the German queen Maria of Hapsburg and her court, as well as the German settlements in northern Hungary and Siebenbürgen. To be sure, Hungarians are not Germans, and they reacted to the audacious appearance of the "German prophet" Luther with disapproval and rejection in the beginning. Before 1526, the three provincial diets decreed heavy penalties for "Lutherans," up to and including burning at the stake. "Article IV," dated April 24, 1523, declared: "All Lutherans and their patrons" shall be punished with death and loss of property. "Article IV" of the year 1525 prescribed even more strictly: "Let all Lutherans be burned." István Báthori, the Palatine of the land, had three Lutherans burned.

This assessment changed radically after the total defeat of Hungarian troops at the battle of Mohács on August 29, 1526. Not only the young king but also the majority of the ruling class, both civil and clerical, died in battle. To this catastrophe was joined another: the election of two kings. Neither of the two new kings, Ferdinand of Hapsburg (1526–1564), who ruled in the west and north, and Johann von Szapolyai (1526–1540), the former Woiwode (ruler) of Siebenbürgen in the east, was able to bring order into state and church. Both had reason to fear that those over whom they ruled would desert and go over to the camp of the opposing king. Adding to the danger was the fact that the Turks sat in between the regions ruled by the two kings, thus splitting the country into three parts. Neither church nor state could do anything to counter the decline in morale. In this situation, the Reformation of Luther brought to the Magyars that new and strong hope which they desperately needed. This was due first of all to the fact that the

Reformation helped provide ethical and theological viewpoints which made it possible to understand the causes of the catastrophe. In this light, the disaster of Mohács and the domination of the Turks were interpreted as a deserved judgment of God. Repentance and conversion seemed to be urgent necessities. Numerous national poets gave expression to this thought at that time with their songs of lamentation, or "jeremiads." As the foremost cause of the national catastrophe, they set forth the deterioration of divine worship and morals. I quote the title of the song of an unknown poet, wherein the list of contritely recognized sins is enumerated: "Lamentation of Hungary, whose destruction and great ruin occurred because of the worship of idols, the transgression of the law, cruelty, falsehood and atrocious conduct." By worship of idols was understood the decay in divine worship which, according to the view of the Reformation, expressed itself in the lack of the gospel in the vernacular and in the luxuriant growth of the cult of the saints and of ceremonies.

There followed in the year 1541 a third catastrophe. The "upper" capital, Buda, fell into Turkish hands. This new shock initially traumatized the people but then was interpreted and explained just as Mohács had been: as a consequence of the sins of the people and their leader. Many talented young Hungarians decided at this time to go into the Turkish zone of occupation and to serve the subjugated peoples there with the comfort of the gospel as teachers and ministers. Among them were the aging cathedral canon and theology professor, Martin Kálmáncsehi Sánta; the likewise aging former court preacher, Mihály Sztári; and the university lecturer, István Szegedi Kis, who was now returning home from Cracow. From the younger generation we will mention only Mátyás Thury, who conducted a burgeoning school at Tolna in the occupied zone, and the learned Gregor Belényesi, who had decided to devote the rest of his life to "the victory of the cross of Christ" in the occupied zone after he had gotten to know Calvin personally in Geneva.

Life under Turkish rule was difficult to endure. We possess a description of the relationship between 1556 and 1558 in a circular letter which was published in 1613 in Karchau: "Idea Christianorum Hungarorum in et sub Turcismo Epistola, quondam a Paulo Thurio, Rectore Scholae Tholnensis ad amicos perscripta . . ." (*Altungarische Bibliothek,* II, 355). The circular letter appeared also in German translation in the "Hungarian Magazine" by Windisch (III, 1783, pp. 478–490). From the letter, we cite one passage.

When the Turks were defeated by the Hungarians in a battle, they poured out their rage against the head of the Christian community because in their view, it was the intercessory prayers of the ministers and the community which had caused their defeat. Our right reverend bishop (Michael Sztárai, one of the most successful reformers in the Turkish zone, a renowned lyricist and playwright) stood ready on three occasions to be beheaded by the Turks, but each time, God saved him in a marvelous way. The Turks racked their brains day and night to find a way to dispose of the Christian pastors and schools. They had come to the conclusion that the latter were to blame for the fact that the Hungarians had not become Turks.

The subjugated Hungarian people of the occupied zone, who had been deprived of all external means of support, found a new inner source of stability in the word of the Bible. Not only did they receive assurance of salvation from the sermon, but in many occupied villages, over a period of about a hundred years, the ecclesiastical and civil tasks of the communities (which were being built up from the grass-roots level) so passed over into one another that the Bible was used as a lawbook in civil jurisprudence.[5] Naturally, the forms of ecclesial and civil organization which arose in these occupied communities had very few features in common with the former system of government.

The same kind of spontaneous development from below can be confirmed in the area of church worship and piety.[6] All they had left was the Bible, and that is all they wanted to have. Postbiblical traditions and forms of worship from the medieval church, which had more aesthetic appeal, found little comprehension in these communities. It is no wonder that the Reformation in the Turkish zone soon went another way than did the conservative Lutheran reformation of free Hungary, which also made progress. The Christians in the occupied zone shaped their forms of worship in the most simple style, with the help of the Bible. Luther's words to the provost of Berlin, Buchholzer, would have seemed like a voice from another world to these communities under Turkish rule:

> If the gospel is purely preached and the sacraments are administered according to Christ's institution and masses for the dead and holy water have fallen out of usage, then go ahead in God's name and wear a silver or golden cross and a cowl or surplice of velvet, silk, or linen! And if your lord, the Elector, is not satisfied with the one cowl or surplice which you put on, then put on three, as Aaron, the high priest, put on three coats, one over the other, which were

> magnificent and beautiful (which is the reason why the papists call church clothing vestments).

If the Christians of the Hungarian occupation zone had allowed curious Turkish visitors to see silver or gold ornaments in their worship services, these riches would not have remained long in their possession.

In the long run, a conflict could not be avoided between the simple and grass-roots forms of worship and government in the occupied zone (for which the modest forms of the Swiss reformation in Zurich, Strassburg, and Geneva served as models) and the moderately conservative Wittenberg direction taken in free Hungary. At the center of the debate stood the doctrine of the Lord's Supper and forms of worship. When external circumstances permitted it (when the military power of the Roman Catholic bishop of Grosswardein was no longer to be feared), the more radical forms of worship and doctrine of the Lord's Supper which prevailed in the occupied zone spread like wildfire into eastern Hungary and were taken over by the Hungarian portion of the population in Siebenbürgen. Under the direction of theologians who had previously worked in the occupied zone, the Reformation in Hungary was carried through in the Swiss way. Martin Kálmáncsehi, Gregor Szegedi, and Peter Melius, through their repeated synods, their school, and their publishing house, developed Debrecen into a center which was able to ward off successfully the assaults of the antitrinitarian movement (which was emanating from Siebenbürgen with the support of nobility).

We are now in a position to provide a clear answer to our question regarding the benefits of the Reformation for the Hungarian people in the sixteenth century. One can say with complete confidence that, in spite of adverse circumstances in the turbulent sixteenth century, the piety and ethical life of the people—their readiness to make sacrifices for church, school, and literature—stood at a higher level than a century before. Through the Reformation, the gospel penetrated the broadest levels of society for the first time, because this was a movement "from below." It also brought rich fruit for cultural and social life. In union with humanism, the Reformers created a lively intellectual life in the vernacular. The Reformers authored the first Hungarian book of fairy tales (1536), the first Hungarian grammar (1539), the first Hungarian history of the world (1559), and the first Hungarian work on botany (1578).

It is small wonder that when, in the seventeenth century, the house of Hapsburg and the Roman Catholic hierarchy prepared to make Hungary once again a Roman Catholic state and a hereditary land of the Hapsburgs, it was the princes of Siebenbürgen (István Bocskay, Gabriel Bethlen, and George Rákoczi) who secured religious freedom for Protestants, as well as the independence of Hungary, through a series of battles. When Siebenbürgen could no longer provide this protection and Protestant ministers and teachers were sold as galley slaves in Naples, it was once again their Christianity, purified by the Reformation, which kept them in fidelity to their Savior and their congregation and thereby thwarted the intentions of the Counter-Reformation.

In conclusion, we would like to say a word about the way taken by the Hungarian Reformed Church after 1945. As we saw, already in the century of the Reformation, the church was strongly committed to social engagement. After 1945, too, in that new situation which was interpreted as a judgment of God on omissions of church and state, the voice of the gospel was raised as a call to repentance and new hope. Jeremiah was the most often read prophet. Through this biblical orientation, our church learned to shape its cooperative work in the life of the people in a positive way. This fact was recognized on the side of the state. The relationship between state and church in Hungary is a good one, full of trust on both sides; both social organizations and powers stand next to one another on the foundation of their own principles. In this respect too, however, the source of positive orientation on the part of believing Christians to the interests in life of their fellow men and women was, and remained, their personal relationship to God. A church which does not live out of this source is no church. On the other hand, a piety which, like a good tree, brings forth good fruit for the neighbor belongs to the nature of the church. Any other, sterile kind of piety is unchristian, in spite of its many religious words. The benefits of faith show themselves in the Hungary of today in sacrifices for church, nation, and humanity. This sacrifice is free and flows from the riches of the relationship to God.

To provide some conception of these sacrifices, we would mention one example from among hundreds of similar cases: 10 percent of all brain-damaged children in this country are housed and cared for in the diaconal homes of the Hungarian Reformed Church.

In our world today, there is still unfortunately much conflict and oppression. To bear the future of humankind in the heart as a secure hope (because Jesus Christ bears this future) is the privilege of all Christians, including Hungarian Christians. We know that the task which gives content and meaning to our lives is nothing other than to provide cooperative help there, where the Lord of the history of all peoples is working to create a single community of brotherhood and sisterhood. Steps of progress on this way are therefore our greatest joy because we are convinced that these Christian goals are not only the meaning of our own earthly existence but also the meaning of history.

NOTES

1. Albert Brackmann, "Die politische Wirkung der clunyazenser Reform," *Historische Zeitschrift* 139 (1928), 47–74.

2. Gyoergy Gyoerffy, "Dem Gedächtnis Stephans des ersten Königs von Ungarn," *Acta Historica Academiae Scientiarum Hungaricae* 17, nos. 1–2 (1971), pp. 1–11.

3. József Deér, *Heidnisches und Christliches in der Altungarischen Monarchie,* 2nd ed. (Darmstadt, 1969); Lajos Csóka, *Geschichte der Benedektinischen Mönchtums in Ungarn,* Studia Hungarica, 11 (Munich, 1980).

4. Gábor Patacsi, "Die ungarischen Ostkirchen," *Ostkirchliche Studien* 11, no. 4 (1962), pp. 273–305.

5. Ferenc Salamon, *Ungarn im Zeitalter der Türkenherrschaft* (Leipzig, 1887).

6. Béla Soeroes, *A magyar liturgia toerténete,* Geschichte der ungarischen Liturgie, vol. 1 (Budapest, 1904), p. 149.

The Edinburgh Manuscript Pages of Servetus' *Christianismi Restitutio*

David F. Wright

Few episodes of the Reformation have been as frequently told—and mistold—as the fateful condemnation and burning of Michael Servetus in Geneva in 1553. During his trial the prosecution extracted from him the admission that he was the author of the *Christianismi Restitutio,* which had been published all but anonymously at the outset of the year. After considerable difficulty Servetus had found a printer in the small town of Vienne, near Lyons in southern France, where Balthazar Arnoullet and his brother-in-law Guillaume Guérolt allowed their presses to produce around eight hundred or a thousand copies.

By the time of Servetus' arrest in Geneva on Sunday, August 13, most of the printing had been consigned to the flames that awaited the works of heretics and blasphemers. At Lyons, at Frankfurt, and perhaps also at Geneva major consignments were destroyed. Although the comprehensiveness and rapidity of its incineration may sometimes have been exaggerated,[1] the *Restitutio* soon became a very rare book. By the close of the sixteenth century very few, if any, copies may have survived beyond the three that are today to be found in Paris, Vienna, and Edinburgh. It is, however, becoming increasingly clear that manuscript copies compensated in part for the almost total elimination of the printed book. Most recently a copy made late in the sixteenth or early in the seventeenth century has come to light in Milan.[2]

The publication of the *Restitutio* and its early history have attracted close attention, not only from bibliographers and students of Reformation radicalism but also from historians of medicine, for it contains the first printed sketch of the pulmonary circulation of the blood. There is accordingly no need for this essay to repeat information readily available elsewhere.[3]

The singular interest of the copy now preserved in the Library of the University of Edinburgh (shelf mark Df.8.90)[4] lies in its having lost, perhaps not many months after publication in January 1553, the first sixteen pages of the printed text, and their replacement, probably not many moons later, by eighteen manuscript pages. The printed volume lacks the title page, the *Index* of contents on the next page, and the two-page *Prooemium* and first twelve pages of text of the first work of this compilation, *De Trinitate Divina . . . Libri Septem.* These pages are numbered continuously, 1–16. The manuscript pages, numbered 2 (recto) to 10 (verso), cover only pages 3 through 16 of the printed book. The text of *De Trinitate Divina* continues without a break from the end of the manuscript at the foot of f.10_v on the left side of the opening to the beginning of the print on the first line of page 17 on the right. Such a perfect match required the scribe to squeeze forty lines onto f.10_v (and at the last line to stray minimally into the margin). His earlier pages contain between 29 and 37 lines, averaging 33.5.

It has long been recognized that the manuscript text diverges to some extent from its printed counterpart, and at least since David Cuthbertson's *A Tragedy of the Reformation* was published in 1912 an explanation of the divergence has been ready to hand: The manuscript pages derive from Servetus' original draft of the work which he sent to Calvin probably in the year 1546.[5] We must return to this hypothesis. In the meantime, it is the main purpose of this study simply to give the text of the manuscript section in full, as a basis for further investigation of questions long considered but never pursued to a satisfactory resolution.[6] Although this occasion will not allow an extended discussion of these questions, the presentation of the text will be followed by some preliminary orientation, as well as by reference to its special appropriateness in a volume honoring a distinguished American interpreter of John Calvin.

This study does not set out to supply a critical edition of the manuscript's contents. That task, along with translation into English, still awaits the *Restitutio* as a whole. That will be the place to identify in full biblical quotations and allusions, provide cross-references to other works of Servetus, and pinpoint his patristic and other sources.

In transcribing the text, I have not reproduced its abbreviations and contractions, except in references to books of the Bible. They are in fact sparingly used in the manuscript, in marked contrast to the 1553 edition. The *apparatus criticus* is chiefly intended to record divergences between the manuscript and the text of the Paris and Vienna copies. Although it makes no difference, I have worked with the Vienna exemplar, since the Parisian one has suffered some damage. (At one very small point where both copies are, for different reasons, defective, the Edinburgh manuscript alone preserves the text.) A few minor misspellings or variant spellings in the manuscript have gone unnoticed in the *apparatus* (e.g., *monstabit; circoncisionis; quero,* for *quaero*), as have variant forms of biblical references. Nor does the *apparatus* preserve the abbreviations in the printed copies. I have followed the standard differentiation between "u" and "v." In the margin I have marked the page divisions both in the manuscript (e.g., f.3_V) and in the edition (p. 4). By Murr's design the latter serve also for his 1790 (1966) reprint. As an appendix to the Edinburgh manuscript text and its collation with the printed version, the inaccuracies of Murr's edition are also noted. Students of the *Restitutio* cannot wholly trust the Murr text, which is now widely available.

The siglum "E" refers to the readings of the Edinburgh manuscript; "P" and "V," respectively, to the complete copies at Paris and Vienna.

The Edinburgh Manuscript Text

Prooemium[
trinit[f. 2_r (p. 3)

Manifestationem Dei per verbum[ ]nem per
spiritum, utramque in so[ ]tialem, in solo
5 ipso nos discernemus,[ ]et spiritus deitas in
homine dignoscatur[ ]nem divinam a seculis expli-
cabimus, magnum[ ]controversiam pietatis mysterium,
quod sit Deus o[ ]verbo, nunc in carne manifestatus,
angelis[ ]minibus visus, visione olim velata, nunc

1-11 *lacunae ex chartae fragmento abscisso;* 1–2 *tit. in PV* DE TRINITATE / DIVINA, QUOD IN EA NON / sit invisibilium trium rerum illusio, sed / vera substantiae Dei manifestatio / in verbo, & communica/tio in spiritu, / LIBRI SEPTEM. / PROOEMIUM; 3 *ante* Manifestationem *suppl. PV* Qui nobis hic ponitur scopus, ut est maiestate sublimis, ita perspicuitate facilis, et demonstratione certus: res omnium maxima, lector, Deum cognoscere substantialiter manifestatum, ac divinam ipsam naturam vere communicatam; 3 Dei ipsius *PV;* 5 nos *E,* plane *PV;* 8 *post* manifestatus *add.* spiritu communicatus *PV.*

10 revel[ ]Modos veros aperte referemus quibus se nobis
e[ ]hibuit Deus externe visibilem verbo, et interne perceptibilem spiritu, mysterium utrinque magnum, ut Deum ipsum homo videat, et possideat. Deum antea non visum, nos nunc revelata facie videbimus et perspicue in nobis
15 ipsis intuebimur, si ostium aperiamus, et viam ingrediamur. Aperire iam oportet ostium ostium hoc, et viam hanc lucis sine qua nihil potest videri, sine qua nemo potest sacras literas le|gere, nec Deum cognoscere, nec Christianus (p. 4)
fieri. Haec est unica veritatis via nobis hic proposita,
20 certa, facilis, et syncera, qua si tu lector ingrediaris, secreta Dei tibi aperte monstrabit. Divinam Christi in verbo generationem, Spiritus sancti profectionem, et eandem utriusque in Deo substantiam, haec via tibi patefaciet. Haec te ad caelestia omnia perducet, et Deum verum ob ocu-
25 los ponet. Age igitur pie, lector, quisquis ad Christum suspiras, syncero erga ipsius veritatem affectu, ad hanc viam te nobiscum accinge, Christum tibi in omnibus scopum propone, ut eum cognoscas semper adnitere, eius honorem et gloriam in omnibus defende, te totum illi penitus com-
30 mitte, in eum intentus haec semper/[ ]t gratam f. 2_v
Christo ipsi, ac utilem[ ]ibus, nos hic operam non[ ]gessimus autem in quinque libris [ ]adiectis postea dialogis, ut quasi[ ]adus quosdam ad integram Christi cogni[ ]nem ascendamus. Pri-
35 mus liber continet[ ]de Christo ἀξιώματα, tres Phariseorum,[ ]odem sophistarum rationes, et improbationes, cum absurdissimis invisibilium illationibus. Secundus viginti scripturae locos exponet. Tertius erit de personae Christi in verbo praefiguratione, de visione Dei, et verbi hypostasi.
40 Quartus de nominibus, et essentia Dei, et de rerum omnium principiis. Quintus de spiritu sancto. Dialogus deinde primus post transactas legis umbras in omnibus complementum declarabit, angelorum, animarum, et inferni substantiam explorans. Secundus modum generationis Christi docebit, et ipsum
45 non esse creaturam, nec finitae potentiae, esseque vere adorandum, et vere Deum. O Christe Iesu ne me deseras servum tuum, in hac tua causa laborantem, hostium terroribus et afflictioni-

14 perspicue *E,* luculentem *PV;* 16 ostium ostium *E;* 18 literas *E,* scripturas *PV;* 18 cognoscere *E,* intelligere *PV;* 19 est unica . . . proposita *E,* veritatis est via *PV;* 20–21 qua si . . . monstrabit *om. PV;* 23–24 haec via . . . Deum verum *E,* integre sola patefaciens, Deumque ipsum nobis *PV;* 25 ponens *PV;* 25–32 Age igitur . . . operam non [ ] *om. PV* (Digessimus *PV*); 26 erga *correxi ex* ergo *E;* 30–36 *lacunae ex chartae fragmento abscisso;* 32 libros *PV;* 35 axiomata *PV;* 36 [ ]odem *E,* totidem *PV;* 46 et vere *E,* verumque *PV;* 46 *ab* O Christe *caput novum incip. PV.*

bus pressum. Boni tui spiritus consolationem, et robur petenti,
nunc tribue, mentem meam, et calamum dirige, ut divinitatis tuae
50 gloriam possim enarrare, et veram de te fidem exprimere. Causa
haec tua est, gloriam tuam explicans, et tuorum salutem, quae
mihi adolescentulo annos vix nato viginti, impulsu quodam divino
tractandam sese obtulit, cum de his nihil essem ab homine doctus.
Tractare tunc coepi, et (quae mundi est caecitas) mox ad necem
55 rapiendus sursum deorsumque petebar./Territus ob id, et in (f. 3_r)
exilium fugiens annos multos apud exteros delitui magno animi
maerore. Adolescentem me imbecillem, et ineloquentem cernens,
causam fere totam deserui, cum nondum essem satis instructus.
Sed euge o clementissime Iesu, ades tu denuo clienti afflicto
60 patronus consolationis plenus animum revocare ita iubes, ut iam
alacer pergam, multorum lectione munitus, et imprimis certissima
tuae veritatis fiducia. Testis horum tu es, ne quis me novatorem
existimet, inani aliqua cupiditate motum. Testem te iterum
invoco Deum, ob eam rem me distulisse et ob imminentem persecu-
65 tionem, ut cum Iona in mare fugere potius cuperem, aut in insulam
aliquam novam. Sed te iubente cuius agitur causa mihi non licet:
differre non amplius licet, quia tempus completum est, ut ex
signis temporum ostendam. Lucernam non esse abscondendam tu nos
docuisti, ut vae mihi sit nisi Euangelizem. Causa veritatis agitur
70 cui omnes tenemur. Superest lector ut te pro Christo benevolum
exhibeas, et rem totam audias sermone simplici, quo gaudet
veritas sine aliquo fuco.| (p. 5)

De homine Iesu Christo, et simul-
chris falsis.

75

Liber Primus.

Librum primum narrationis filii Dei, instar primae praedicationis
Apostolorum, a notioribus inchoabo, ab iis quae cordato cuique
sunt manifesta, et omnibus publice praedicata, ut haec nostra

46–48 ne me deseras . . . et robur *om. PV et suppl.* fili Dei, qui de caelo nobis datus, deitatem patefactam in teipso visibilem manifestas, teipsum aperi servo tuo, ut manifestatio tanta vere patefiat. Spiritum tuum bonum, et verbum efficax; 50 et *E,* ac *PV;* 51 *post* tua est *add. PV* et tuam a patre, et spiritus tui; 51 tuam *om. PV;* 51 et tuorum salutem *om. PV;* 52 mihi . . . viginti *om. PV;* 52 divino quodam impulsu *PV;* 53 mihi obtulit *PV;* 53 de his . . . doctus *E,* essem de tua veritate solicitus *PV;* 54 tunc *E,* aliquando *PV;* 54–66 et (quae . . .) . . . non licet *om. PV;* 67–68 differre . . . ostendam *E,* et nunc iterum tractare cogor, quia completum est vere tempus, ut ex rei ipsius certitudine, et ex signis temporum manifestis, sum nunc piis omnibus ostensurus *PV;* 69 veritatis *E,* communis Christianis omnibus *PV;* 70 post benevolum *add. PV* usque ad finem; 71 audies *PV;* 71–72 simplici . . . veritas sine *E,* veritatis absque *PV;* 76–77 apostolorum praedicationis *PV;* 78 sint *PV.*

via facile principium habeat. Ab ipso homine Iesu Christo prin-
80 cipium sumam, tum quia de ipso nunc agetur, tum ut sophistas
reprimam, qui ad / verbi speculationem, sine hoc fundamento f. 3_v
ascendentes, in alium filium traducuntur, et verum filium Dei
oblivioni tradunt. Quibus ego ad memoriam quis sit ille verus
filius reducere conabor, pronomine ad sensum demonstrante, ipsum
85 hominem verberibus caesum et flagellatum concedam haec tria
simpliciter vera esse. Primo. Hic est Iesus Christus. Secundo.
Hic est filius Dei. Tertio. Hic est Deus. Ecce ostium. Ecce
via, in qua sola est illuminatio cognitionis gloriae Dei, quae
relucet in facie Iesu Christi.

prima propositio

Principio hunc dici Iesum, quasi primum postulatum ex seipso
aperte patet. Nam illud est puero in circoncisionis die nomen
impositum sicut tibi Ioannes, et illi Petrus Luc. 1. et 2. Iesus
ut veteres docent, est nomen proprium viri, et cognomen Christus.
Iudaei eum esse Iesum omnes concedebant, sed Christum esse
95 negabant, interrogantes de Iesu qui dicitur Christus: et alienos a
synagoga faciebant illos, qui faterentur illum esse Christum.
Super qua re frequens erat Apostolorum contra ipsos disputatio,
An Iesus ille esset messias. Sed de Iesu nulla fuit unquam
dubitatio, nec quaestio, nec aliquis unquam hoc negavit. Per-
100 pende quo tendat ille ser|mo, et quo animo Paulus testificabatur (p. 6)
Iudaeis Iesum illum esse messiam Act. 9. 17. 18. Quo spiritus
fervore Apollos ille Alexandrinus Iudaeos revincebat, probans
hunc Iesum esse Christum. De homine ipso haec dicebantur sine
sophismate aliquo. Non sophistas, sed Iudaeos ibi cogita, pis-
105 catores cogita, et mulieres simplicitate pura credentes hunc
Iesum esse Christum. Caeci item cum quorundam relatione Iesum
Nazarenum transire audissent, mox clamarunt,/ Iesu filii David f. 4_r
miserere nostri. Qualem tu ibi existens transeuntem Iesum Nazarenum mente conciperes? Concedentes igitur hominem esse Iesum,
110 concedere deinde cogimur eum esse Christum, cum concedamus eum
esse a Deo unctum. Nam ipse est puer sanctus tuus quem unxisti,

79–80 Ab ipso . . . principium *E,* Ipse homo Iesus est ostium et via, a quo et merito exordium *PV;* 81 speculationem *E,* cognitionem *PV;* 84 conabor *E,* curabo *PV;* 87–89 Ecce ostium . . . Christi *om. PV;* 90–91 Principio . . . aperte patet *E,* Quod hic primo dicatur Iesus, postulatum est primum, ex seipso manifestum, quo certius nihil ostendere possis *PV;* 91 Nam *om. PV;* 92 Nomen Iesus *PV;* 96 illos *om. PV;* 96 illum *E,* eum *PV;* 99–100 Perpende *E,* Specta *PV;* 100 et *om. PV;* 105 credentes hunc *E,* concedentes *PV;* 106 *post* Christum *add. PV* Iesum hunc Nazarenum, Iesum filium David; 106–109 Caeci . . . conciperes? *om. PV;* 109–111 Concedentes . . . Deo unctum *E,* Concedentes vero, hunc esse Iesum, concedere cogimur, hunc esse Christum, a Deo vere unctum *PV, et caput novum a* Concedentes *incip.;* 111 ipse *E,* iste *PV;* 111 uxisti *E.*

Acto. 4. Iste est sanctus sanctorum, quem ungendum praedixit
Daniel. 9. Acto. insuper 10. tamquam rem cunctis prespicuam ait
Petrus. Ipsi nostis. Nam de Iesu sermo publice notus, ut scili-
115 cet Iesum illum Nazarenum unxerit Deus spiritu sancto et virtute.
Quoniam Deus erat cum illo, et ipse est a Deo iudex constitutus
vivorum et mortuorum. Et Acto. 2. Certissime sciat omnis domus
Israel quod hunc Iesum quem vos crucifixistis fecit Deus, et
dominum, et Christum, id est unctum. Non accipiebant ipsi vocem
120 Christus pro re quadam incorporea, sed erat corpus a Deo unctum,
et deitatis habens substantiam, ut videbis corpus hoc est spiritu
sancto unctum. Clemens, Iustinus, Ireneus, Tertullianus, et
reliqui seniores vocem hanc Christus naturae humanae vocabulum
esse affirmant. Vocabuli item ratio idipsum notat, nam esse
125 unctum non potest nisi ad humanam naturam referri. Quis igitur
negabit hominem esse unctum? Antichristus est qui negat hunc
Iesum esse Christum, et qui concedit illum esse unctum ex Deo
natus est. Ioan. 2. et 5. Praeterea in recognitionibus Clementis
libro primo rationem vocabuli exponit Petrus, quia reges solebant
130 vocari Christi, ideo iste ab excellentia unctionis prae ceteris
est rex Christus unctus. Nam sicut Deus angelis angelum, bestiis
bestiam, et syderibus sydus ita hominibus hominem principem fecit
Christum. Veteris quoque authoritate scripturae docemur hominem
dici Christum, cum et terrenus rex diceretur Christus. 1 Samu. 12.
135 et 24. et Esai. 45. Item Math. 1. Ex qua genitus est Iesus ille
qui dicitur Christus. Nota articulum, nota cognomen, intelligenda
sunt de generatione hominis haec, et pronomina rem sensu perceptam
ibi demonstrant. / Ho|mo est qui de spiritu sancto genitus est. f. 4_v
Hominem Christum aperte describit Lucas cap. 3 dicens, Et ipse (p. 7)
140 Iesus incipiebat esse triginta annorum et putabatur filius Ioseph.
Ille qui putabatur filius Ioseph erat Iesus Christus filius Dei.
Acto. quoque 13. Iudaeis ait Paulus, Deus iuxta promissionem
ex David semine eduxit Christum, hunc a vobis interemptum. Ibidem-
que et Ioan. 1. dixit Ioannes Baptista, Non arbitramini me esse
145 Christum. Quam ridicula esset Ioannis excusatio, si Christi
vocabulum ad hominem non referatur? Frivola esset Christi inter-
rogatio, et Petri responsio Math. 16. cum dixit Christus Quem
me dicunt homines esse? Et Petrus respondit, Tu es ille Christus,
tu es ille filius Dei viventis. Illum ipsum quem alii Eliam,
150 alii Ieremiam esse putabant, ait Petrus esse Christum filium Dei.

114 sermo est *PV;* 115 illum virum *PV;* 115 uxerit *E,* 116 a Deo iudex constitutus *E,* qui constitutus est a Deo iudex *PV;* 117 Certissime, inquit *PV;* 119–122 Non accipiebant . . . sancto unctum *om. PV;* 125 naturam humanam *PV;* 126–127 hunc Iesum negat *PV;* 127 illum *E,* ipsum *PV;* 128 Praeterea *om. PV;* 131 unctus *E,* vocatus *PV;* 133 scripturae authoritate *PV;* 133 aperte docemur *PV;* 136 Nota[1] *E,* Nota ibi *PV;* 136 nota[2] *E,* et *PV;* 136–138 intelligenda . . . demonstrant *om. PV;* 141 Ille ipse *PV;* 144 arbitremini *PV.*

Non dixit incorporeus ille filius in te est, sed tu es filius.
Et quum ibi iussit Christus, ne cui dicerent, quod ipse esset
Christus, quid per illud pronomen demonstrasse putas? Si ipse
Christus non est quomodo nos Christos facit? In hoc probando
155 quod est meridiana luce clarius, hic non diutius insisterem,
nisi corruptas viderem eorum mentes, qui mysterium incarnationis
non intelligentes, rem incorpoream Christum esse, et realem
filium putant, cum tamen omnibus seculis verus homo sit semper
dictus Christus. Audi testimonium ipsiusmet Christi se hominem
160 vocantis, Ioan. 8. Quaeritis me interficere hominem veritatem
vobis locutum. Et 1 Timoth. 2. Mediator Dei, et hominum homo
Christus Iesus. Quod si se ostendat illa vox homo, quam sophistae connotative sumendo adulterant, accipe illam vocem vir,
et audi Petrum dicentem Act. 2. Iesum Nazarenum fuisse virum
165 a Deo designatum. Et Luc. ultimo. De Iesu Naza/reno qui fuit — f. 5_r
vir propheta potens. Et Ioan. 1. Post me veniet vir, et Esai.
53. Novissimum virorum virum dolorum. Et Zach. 6. Ecce vir
germen nomen eius, et Acto. 17. Iudicaturus est Deus orbem per
eum virum scilicet Christum. Si sensus communes habeas lector,
170 et credas| naturae pronominis demonstrativi, cognosces manifeste — (p. 8)
hanc esse veram et originalem illius vocis significationem. Nam
eo ad oculum demonstrato passim conceditur hic est Christus,
Tu es Iesus, et quod loquitur, quaerit, respondet, esurit: et
quod videbant illum ambulantem super aquas. Quem quaeritis?
175 Iesum Nazarenum. Ego sum. Quemcunque osculatus fuero ipse
est tenete eum. Ego ipse sum palpate et videte. Ad Iudaeos
loquens Petrus ait, Hunc Iesum quem vos interemistis suscitavit
Deus, cuius omnes testes sumus. Quid per talia pronomina tu
cum Iudaeo disputans demonstrares? Apud eos nec de trinitate,
180 nec de filio invisibili erat unquam auditum. Nonne deterioris
sumus nos conditionis quam Samaritana mulier quae Ioan. 4 dixit
Venite et videte hominem, qui dixit mihi omnia quaecunque feci,
nunquid hic est ille Christus? Et mulieris mentem nihil de
rebus incorporeis scientem comprobavit Christus. Nam cum ipsa
185 quaereret messiam venturum qui dicitur Christus, respondit, ego
ipse sum qui loquor tibi. Ego quem vides loquentem, non res
alia incorporea, sed ego qui loquor sum verus et naturalis filius
Dei. Similem de ipso Iesu fidem conceperat caecus ille illumi-
nandus Ioan. 9. dicens: Ille homo qui dicitur Iesus lutum fecit.
190 Hanc de Christo fidem habens fuit tunc illuminatus, nec falsum

152 quum *E,* quando *PV;* 154–156 In hoc . . . eorum mentes *E,* Rei tam aperte non esset diutius insistendum, nisi corrupti essent eorum animi *PV;* 163 vocem illam *PV;* 164 Petrum audi *PV;* 176 Et acto. 2. ad Iudaeos *PV;* 180 invisibili filio *PV;* 180 erat aliquid *PV;* 180 An *E,* Nonne *PV;* 184 comprobavit Christus *E,* ipse tunc comprobavit *PV;* 185–186 ego ipse *E,* ipse, Ego *PV;* 187 alia *E,* aliqua *PV;* 188–189 illuminatus *PV.*

de Christo credidit. Praeterea de quo homine intelligis illud
Apostoli. Sicut unius delicto et rel. Ita per gratiam unius
hominis Iesu Christi: sicut per hominem mors ita, ita et per
hominem resurrectio mortuorum. Aut utrobique homo dicitur
195 absolute aut utrobique connotative, alioqui comparatio esset
nulla. Primus / Adam, et secundus ibi dicitur, ut nihil hic f. 5_v
sophistis prosit connotative sumere. Demum Ioan. 20. Signa
fecit, ut credamus quod Iesus est Christus filius Dei. Exped-
itum est de Iesu. Sed ut credamus quod Iesus ille sit a Deo
200 genitus, et mortuus pro salute nostra, Natanael ex eo quod
dixit: Vidi te sub ficu, infert, ipsum esse filium Dei.
Similem illationem alii faciunt Matth. 14. ex eo quod fugavit
ventum.| (p. 9)

Secunda propositio

Illationes istae aperte probant, quod secundo dixi hunc
ipsum quem Christum appello esse filium Dei. Nam ex signis
quae faciebat inferunt ipsum esse filium Dei. Probato quod
ipse est Iesus Christus, est hoc quoque probatum, cum scriptura
semper clamet Iesum Christum esse filium Dei. Palam ipse
monstratur esse filius Dei et eius respectu Deus dicitur pater,
210 vere pater, quia ab eo est substantialiter genitus, sicut tu a
patre tuo. Non est ex ipso Ioseph genitus Christus, sed de
spiritu sancto genitus est, de substantia Dei genitus est:
corpus hoc est vere, et naturaliter genitum ex Deo, sine aliquo
sophismate quem generationis modum in sequentibus aperte doce-
215 bimus. Id nunc obiter dicimus, quod verbum Dei instar nubis
obumbravit virginem, et fuit ros naturalis geniturae Christi,
instar nubis terram germinare facientis. Psal. 71. Esa. 45 et
55. Hac ratione dici filium docent Mattheus, et Lucas cap. 1.
In Luca ait angelus ipsi Mariae. Spiritus sanctus superveniet
220 in te, et virtus altissimi obumbrabit tibi, unde sequitur:
Quapropter et quod nascetur sanctum vocabitur filius Dei.
Eandem rationem tradit Matthe. dicens eam factam gravidam de
spiritu sancto, et quod in ea genitum est, de spiritu sancto esse.
Quod in ea genitum est filius est. Aperte loquitur non sophistice,
225 Ex Maria genitus est Iesus, ex substantia Mariae filius. Si

192 et rel. *om. PV;* 193 ita[1] *om. PV;* 196 secundus Adam *PV;* 197 prosit, hominem *PV;* 200 mortuus *E,* unctus *PV;* 202 alii *om. PV;* 204 aperte probant *E,* apertissime demonstrant *PV;* 206 ipsum hominem *PV;* 206–208 Probato . . . Palam *E,* Si constat ipsum hominem esse Iesum Christum, constat ipsum hominem esse filium Dei, cum scriptura semper doceat, Iesum Christum esse filium Dei. Constat vere, Deum patrem Iesu Christi esse Deum patrem hominis. Aperte ubique homo *PV;* 209 dicitur *E,* vere *PV;* 211 ex *E,* ab *PV;* 213 corpus hoc *E,* Hic Iesus *PV;* 213 genitus *PV;* 214 aperte *E,* perspicue *PV;* 216 virginem . . . Christi *E,* virgini. Egit in ea, ut ros geniturae *PV;* 217 nubis *E,* imbris *PV;* 221 vocabitur *E,* erit vere *PV;* 222 de *E,* a *PV.*

Maria est naturalis / mater, alicuius naturalis filii est ipsa mater, adnota quod dixit Lucas 15. cap. Filius in te genitus, quem tu concipies, et paries filius altissimi vocabitur: is erit magnus, et dabit illi Deus sedem David patris sui. Quare non dixit, filius primae personae vocabitur, et dabit illi prima persona sedem, sed filius altissimi Dei, et dabit illi Deus sedem. An secunda illa res incorporea est a spiritu sancto genita? An non quod a spiritu sancto genitum est vere filius est. Nihil ad rem facit quod plerique verba angeli pervertentes vocem sanctum ad alium filium detorquent, qua|si primogenitus Christus non sit ea dignus, praesertim cum ipsemet Lucas capite sequenti declaret, quare sanctum dixerat. Quia ipse est masculus aperiens vulvam. Omne autem masculum aperiens vulvam sanctum Domino vocabitur Exod. 13.34. et Nu. 8. Praeterea Dei virtutem seu fortitudinem altissimi, quae descendente spiritu obumbravit Mariae, metaphysicum, invisibilem filium esse volunt quia copulative ibi dicitur, spiritus, et virtus, spiritus, et fortitudo. Ad hoc nos docimus, quod Lucas eo virtutis seu fortitudinis nomine idipsum significat quod cap. 24. et acto. 1. Ubi idem Lucas refert, accipietis virtutem seu fortitudinem veniente in vos spiritu sancto. Eadem ratione dixit idem Luc Ioannem venturum, in spiritu, et virtute Eliae: et in hoc esse eum plus quam prophetam. Alii prophetae non habebant cum spiritu prophetiae virtutem faciendi miracula, sicut Elias, ob quam rem dicitur in eo spiritus et virtus seu spiritus et fortitudo. Virtutem quoque habuit Ioannes etiam ab utero: virtutem attingendi eum quem praedixerat, virtutem habuit convertendi impios ad Deum suum adhibito miracu/lo ut Elias. Sicut ad vocem Eliae in testimonio veritatis, descendit ignis de caelo, effusis aquis super altare. 3 reg. 18. Ita ad Ioannis aqueum baptismum in testimonium veritatis Christi miraculose descendit de caelo spiritus sanctus, Matth. et Luc. 3. Virtus ergo spiritui adiuncta potentiam aliquam significat, non res alias metaphysicas. Haec est inter spiritum, et virtutem differentia, quia non in quovis spiritu par virtus, seu par fortitudo. Hic ipse est ille duplex spiritus Eliae, quem petiit Elisaeus, scilicet spiritus prophetiae, et spiritus miraculorum. Hac eadem ratione acceperunt Apostoli spiritum sanctum, et virtutem, spiritum sanctum et fortitudinem, ut sic afflati potentia magna, et virtute miraculorum redderent testimonium resurrectionis Christi, Acto. 1. et 4. Copula illa aliquid addit, sicut quando dicitur spiritu sancto, et igne. Ignis adiectio vim addit,

(Margin: f. 6_r at line 226; 230; 235 (p. 10); 240; 245; 250; f. 6_v at line 253; 255; 260; 265)

227 dicit *PV;* 227 15. cap. Filius *E,* Is filius *PV;* 233 vere genitum *PV;* 239 Praeterea Dei virtutem *E,* Virtutem insuper *PV;* 246 in *E,* cum *PV;* 247 hoc quoque *PV;* 248 habuerunt *PV;* 249 sicut *E,* ut habuit *PV;* 251 etiam *om. PV;* 252 habuit *om. PV;* 253 testimonio *PV;* 259 non est *PV;* 261 scilicet *E,* videlicet *PV;* 261 spiritus[2] *E,* virtus *PV;* 266 *post* addit *repetit E* sicut quando dicitur spiritu sancto et, *sed cancellata.*

et expurgationis vehementiam. In Act cap. 6. exiguntur viri
pleni spiritu sancto, et sapientia, qui ultra commune spiritus
donum habeant sapientiam negotio commodam. Ex quibus praeclare
270 intelligitur quare| Lucas in Christo, et Apostolis dixerit (p. 11)
spiritum sanctum et virtutem, quod magis declaratur ex eo
quod dixit idem Lucas Iesum Nazarenum unxit Deus spiritu sancto,
et virtute, spiritu sancto, et fortitudine Acto. 10. Ubi illa
copula non facit virtutem metaphorice sumi, pro incorporeo filio,
275 sed quia spiritus Christi habet omnem fortitudinem: adde quod
Lucas non dixit fortitudinem illam vocari filium, sed id quod
virtute Dei in Maria genitum est, filius Dei ideo vocabitur,
quia virum non cognovit, et virtute Dei, in adumbratione illa
vicem seminis viri supplente efficitur ipsa gravida. / Ac eo f. 7_r
280 ipso dicetur ipsa facta gravida a spiritu sancto, et Christus
ipse a spiritu sancto genitus, missus, et unctus. Esa. 48. 61.
et Matth. 1. Non quod secunda illa res sit genita a tertia, sed
hic ipse, qui a spiritu sancto ex Maria genitus est, filius est.
Ita locum hunc intellexit Ireneus initio lib. 5. ex Maria dicens
285 genitum esse filium altissimi. Ita, coactus exponit Augustinus
in Ioannem tractatu. 99. Virtutem Dei dicens esse ipsummet
spiritum sanctum agentem in generatione Christi. Praeterea
hominem filium, dici filium, ipsa vocabuli ratio nos docet.
Nam sicut propria passio corporis est ungi, ita propria passio
290 carnis est nasci: Virtute quidem spiritus fit ut nascatur corpus,
tamen ipsum vere nascitur vere generatur, et corpus ipsum habet
vere participationem substantiae Dei, ut postea dicemus: Quis
quaeso est ille qui putabatur filius Ioseph? Quis est ille
ventris fructus? An non fructus ille est substantialis filius?
295 Quis est ille masculus aperiens vulvam? An non masculus ille
est proprie filius? Quis est ille puerulus de quo loquitur
Mattheus capite secundo, quem assumebat, ducebat, et reducebat
Ioseph? An non puerulus est ille ibi filius ex Aegypto vocatus?
Illius pueruli, illius corporalis filii, nullum alium patrem
300 invenies nisi Deum: nullum alium genitorem nisi Deum: aut dices
esse phantasma, et non carnem: Nam si caro est, ab aliquo
genita est, ergo alicuius genitoris filius est: eo magis

274 metaphysice *PV;* 276 fortitudinem *E,* virtutem *PV;* 278 obumbratione *PV;* 279 efficietur *PV;* 280 dicitur *PV;* 284 intelligit *PV;* 285 generatum *PV;* 285 altissimi Dei *PV;* 287–288 Praeterea . . . dici filium *E,* Quod insuper homo sit proprie filius *PV, et a* Quod *caput novum incip.;* 289 propria passio corporis *E,* proprium hominis *PV;* 289–290 propria passio carnis *E,* proprium eius *PV;* 290 *post* nasci *add. PV* proprium hominis est generari; 290 fit ut nascatur *E,* id fit *PV;* 292 ut postea dicemus *om. PV;* 293 quaeso *om. PV;* 294 fructus ventris *PV;* 296–297 loquitur *E,* fit mentio *PV;* 297 assumebat *PV;* 298 puerulus *om. PV;* 298 ille est *PV;* 299 puelli *PV;* 300 invenies *E,* reperies *PV;* 301 et *om. PV.*

quia Deus dicitur pater huius carnis, pater huius cibi. Ioan.
6.| Deus agricola, pater huius vitis. Ioannis. 15. Si ergo (p. 12)
305 corporalis vere hic est filius, et incorporalis est aliquis
alius realis invisibilis / filius, sunt iam duo reales filii, f. 7_v
quoquo modo eos in unum cumulum unias: quia duo sunt geniti,
et duo nati, duas duarum rerum generationes reales concedimus,
ergo duos reales genitos, et duos natos negare non possumus.
310 Quis non fascinatus, inter natos, genitos, et filios differ-
entias tales faceret? Scripturae sacrae de Iesu unico Dei
filio loquuntur, nec quicquam aliud ab homine filium dixerunt
realiter genitum. Ad hunc modum oportet Christianos omnes,
hunc Iesum Nazarenum esse Christum filium Dei agnoscere.
315 Christus ipse, et mulieribus, et rudibus plebeiis se esse messiam
filium Dei aperte praedicabat. Age, quaeso te, qualem messiam
ex simplici eius praedicatione tunc concipere debuit muliercula?
Eo magis quia nesciebantur in lege trinitariorum nostrorum
metaphisica figmenta. Metaphoricus alius, et invisibilis
320 filius postea excogitatus est, ex male intellecto Ioannis
verbo, ut evidenter ostendam. Alia certe tunc de filio Dei fides
erat, quam nunc, id quod familiari exemplo nunc collige. Deus
dixit Ioanni super quem videris spiritum descendentem, et man-
entem super eum, hic ipse est filius meus. Et ego, ait, vidi,
325 et testimonium perhibui, quod hic est filius Dei. Ioan. 1. Hoc
adverte primo, quod Ioannes aliquando nesciebat, quis esset
filius Dei. Deinde adverte manifestationem, et reliqua ibi
acta. Sophistarum sententia deceptus fuisset Ioannes, et
alios decepisset dicens, illum de quo vidit esse filium Dei.
330 Ego inquit nesciebam eum, sed externo signo dato, hunc esse
filium Dei est mihi monstratum / aperte, ut ita ipsum esse f. 8_r
filium Dei omnibus Iudaeis ostenderem dicens, Ecce agnus,
ecce filius. Quem tu mihi agnum hic facis? Hic quem vides
est agnus Dei, filius Dei. Hic oculis subiectus, manibus pal-
335 patus, et sensibus omnibus aliis perceptus: Fallax alioqui
fuisset caelestis vox dicens: Super quem videritis hic est
ille. Fallax fuisset, cum super re populis praesente descendens
dixit Hic est filius meus dilectus, vel, Tu es filius meus. Si
rem aliam laten|tem per illud pronomen demonstrabat, non erat (p. 13)
340 patens testimonium, seducebat populum, qui de invisibili filio
nihil unquam audierat. Item Ioannis. 9. Interrogatus a quodam
Iesus, quis esset ille filius Dei, respondit: Et vidisti eum,
et qui loquitur tecum ipse est. Hic ipse quem vides est filius

305 filius Dei *PV;* 309 pure non *PV;* 316 et filium *PV;* 319 Metaphoricus *E,* Metaphysicus *PV;* 321 nunc evidenter *PV;* 321–322 Alia . . . fides erat *E,* Alia tunc erat de filio fides *PV;* 322 nunc[2] *E,* ita *PV;* 331 aperte monstratum *PV;* 333 facies *PV;* 335 aliis omnibus *PV;* 336 videris *PV;* 338 dilectus *om. PV;* 340–341 qui de . . . audierat *om. PV.*

Dei. Eo ad oculum demonstrato dixit centurio. Vere hic homo
345 filius erat Dei. Pronomina illa rem sensu perceptam demonstrant:
Centurio non erat sophista, non est per communicationem idiomatum
locutus, nec connotative hominis voce usus. De vero homine dixit,
Hic homo iustus erat: hic homo filius Dei erat. Audi Paulum
qui illico atque visum recepit ingressus synagogam praedicabat
350 Iesum, quoniam hic est filius Dei, Acto. 9. De sophistarum
idiomatibus ne verbum quidem. Summus sacerdos nihil de secunda
illa incorporea re cogitabat dicens, Es tu filius Dei benedicti?
Et ad mentem eius respondit Iesus, Ego sum Mar. 14. Vos dicitis
quia ego filius Dei sum. Luc. 22. Ita simpliciter illi crede-
355 bant / dicentes, Ego credidi quod tu es filius Dei. f. 8_v

Obiiciat iam sophista, non videri rem magnam si ipse homo
Iesus dicatur filius Dei, cum et nos filii Dei nominemur.
Respondeo. Res maxima est esse filium Dei, et plura inde
sequuntur quam unquam intellexerit mundus, ut ostendam. Ipse
360 est verus, et naturalis filius, nos adoptivi. Ex eo ipso quod
nos filii Dei nominamur probatur ipse esse verus filius:
Quomodo homines filios faceret si ipse homo non esset verus
filius? Nos filii dicimur dono et gratia per ipsum nobis
facta. Ideo ipse huius nostrae adoptionis author, excellen-
365 tiore alio modo dicitur filius. Est ipse naturalis filius
ex vera Dei substantia genitus ut postea videbis. Alii non
sunt filii originis sed fiunt filii Dei. Per fidem Iesu
Christi nos efficimur filii Dei Galatas. 3. et Ioannis. 1.
Ideo per adoptionem dicimur filii Rom. 8. et Ephes. 1. Non
370 solum filius sed verus filius ipse dicitur, non communis filius
sed proprius filius. Sapi. 2. et Rom. 8. Aeque proprie Deus
dicitur pater Iesu Christi sicut terreni patres dicuntur patres
filiorum suorum. Alioqui Deus non posset dici causa pecu-
liariter efficiens, et productiva alicuius certi effectus. Si
375 prolem aliquam sibi singulariter eligat, et solus tantum opere-
tur ad generationem illius (etiam substantiam | suam illi (p. 14)
tribuendo) quantum potest, et plus quam potest terrenus pater
operari, quare non aeque merebitur proprie / dici pater? f. 9_r
Nunquid ego qui generationem aliis tribuo, ipse sterilis ero
380 dicit Dominus? Esa. 66. Imo potius dicitur ipse pater, quia
ab ipso omnis paternitas in caelo, et in terra nominatur Ephos.

345 Pronomina *E,* Cogita tu, per pronomina *PV;* 345–348 demonstrant . . . iustus erat *E,* demonstrari. Cogita deinceps, centurionem non fuisse sophistam, nec fuisse per communicationem idiomatum loquutum, nec connotative hominis voce usum. Verum hominem ostendens dixit *PV;* 348 erat Dei *PV;* 356 Obiiciat iam sophista *E,* At dices tu *PV, nec caput novum incip.;* 363–364 per ipsum nobis facta *E,* ipsius *PV;* 366 ut postea videbis *om. PV;* 367 sed fiunt filii Dei *E,* Fiunt filii Dei, non nascuntur filii Dei *PV;* 373 suorum filiorum *PV;* 378 operari *om. PV;* 378 proprie merebitur *PV.*

3. Eo magis quia non solum eum genuit, sed et deitatis substantia, luce, et plenitudine eum decoravit, ut in hoc assimiletur patri filius. Item alia ratione proprius quam homines dicitur
385 ipse pater quia ipse in aliorum generationibus operatur: alii vero in sui filii generatione nihil agunt. Ergo si proprius dicitur ipse pater propriissime ultra alios Christus dicetur esse filius: Sed sublimiora postea de hac filiatione dicemus si filiationem dici fas est. Argumentum iam retorqueri ita
390 potest. Nam filius Dei filiationem suam nobis communicat, at filiatio illius secundae rei nihil habet nobiscum commune, sed hominis filiatio. Ipse nos fratres vocat quia homo, homo est primogenitus fratrum, sicut primogenitus mortuorum. Ergo homo primogenitus est homo genitus filius. Sophistae sibiipsis
395 videntur ita magnifici ut non dignentur oculos ad hunc filium inclinare. Rem abiectam, et ridiculum putant hominem dici filium Dei. Ad filium oportere aiunt ut sit eiusdem speciei specialissimae cum patre. Sed unde hoc colligunt? Imo id fieri non potest, quando parentes sunt diversarum specierum.
400 Id iam improbat scriptura tota, improbat ipsemet / Christus, (f. 9_v) qui aliorum hominum comparatione se filium Dei ostendit Ioannis 10. Si alios inquit homines scriptura vocat Deos, et filios Dei, vos dicitis me blasphamare quia dixi filius Dei sum, cum pater ultra alios consortes, et participes meos, me sanctificavit.
405 Ecce illum qui sanctificatus est, esse filium Dei. Hic est ille sanctus filius Dei. Hic est ille de quo dicunt Apostoli: Sanctum filium tuum Iesum. Quis sanctus, nisi masculus aperiens vulvam, verus, et corporalis filius Dei?

Tertia propositio

Tertio istam dixi esse veram. Christus est Deus. Dicitur vere Deus, substantialiter Deus, cum in eo sit deitas corporaliter. Sed quia haec sunt in sequentibus apertissime aperienda sufficit nunc si di|catur Deus forma Dei, species Dei habens (p. 15) potentiam, et virtutem Dei, dicitur Deus per virtutem sicut homo per carnem: Data ipsi a patre ipsa deitatis potentia dicitur
415 ipse esse Deus fortis Esa. 9. Puer natus est nobis, vocabitur Deus fortis. Ecce Dei nomen et fortitudinem nato puero tributa, cui data est omnis potestas in caelo, et in terra. Ipse dicitur Deus Israelis Esaiae 45. Thomas Ioan. 20. eum appellat, Dominus meus, Deus meus. Paulo ad Romanos 9. dicitur Christus

388 sublimiora alia *PV;* 388 de hac filiatione postea *PV;* 390 suam filiationem *PV;* 394 *a* Sophistae *caput novum incip. PV;* 396 ridiculam *PV;* 397 ut *E,* quod *PV;* 398–399 id fieri non potest *E,* est penitus impossibile *PV;* 399 quando quando *E;* 400 Id iam *E,* Hoc etiam *PV;* 406 sanctus *E,* qui sanctus vocabitur *PV;* 407 Quis est ille sanctus, nisi ille masculus *PV;* 410 deitas corporaliter *ante* deitas *E, sed cancellata;* 411 apertissime *E,* perfectissime *PV;* 412 sufficit nunc *E,* sat nunc erit *PV;* 412 quia forma *PV;* 414 ipsi *E,* illi *PV;* 415 esse *om. PV.*

420 in omnibus, et super omnia Deus laudandus Deus / benedictus, f. 10_r
et benedicendus in secula. Multis aliis locis eius divinitas
ostenditur, quia exaltatus est ut acciperet divinitatem, et
nomen super omne nomen: Sophistae vero non solum negant hunc
esse Deum, sed et unctum esse negant. Imo quae sunt naturae,
425 ab eo usurpant, negantes esse filium Mariae. Denique negant
hunc esse hominem, sed humanitatem. Negant hominem esse
hominem, et concedunt Deum esse Asinum. An non isti sunt
Antichristi, et Christi calumniatores. Potest ne maior esse
calumnia quam si me loquentem dicas me non esse? aut si mihi
430 convenire neges ea quae mihi palam tribuuntur? Omnia haec
praedicata volunt calumniatores isti esse illius secundae rei
nomina: ad quod commentum communis schola sophisma quoddam
communicationis idiomatum adinvenit. Quandam novam impositionem
in illo termino homo fingunt, ut connotative sumatur et
435 aequipolleat huic orationi, sustentans naturam humanam. Ac
nunc per communicationem idiomatum concedunt hanc propositionem.
Filius Dei est homo, id est secunda persona sustinet naturam
humanam, et est illa connotativus homo. Ad eundem modum concedunt fieri posse, ut Deus sit asinus, et spiritus sit mulus,
440 sustentans mulum. Cogita lector. Si Christus aut eius discip-
ulus Paulus, aut alii discipuli praedicarent, tollerarent illi
haec hominum figmenta, et placitas vocum imposturas: Nonne
Christum sophistarum faciunt magistrum, dicentes vocem illam
Christus esse a prophetis et apostolis impositam ad significandum,
445 secundam personam in divinis, connotando quod sustinet | naturam (p. 16)
humanam? Sed quid si loco vocis Christus ponatur / ubique vox f. 10_v
unctus? An rem illam proprie unctam dicent, et eam accepisse
spiritum sanctum, et virtutem? An illa diceret, Omnia mihi
tradita sunt a patre meo? An sophistice de illa locutus esset
450 pater, dicens Ecce puer meus quem elegi, dilectus meus, ponam
spiritum meum super illum? Profecto ad hominem Iesum relatum

422–423 Ipse dicitur . . . Esaiae 45 *E,* Et Esa. 45. ego dominus vocans nomen tuum, Deus Israelis *PV;* 419 Christus dicitur *PV;* 421 in secula *om. PV;* 423 Sophistae . . . negant hunc *E,* Adversarii vero illum ita despiciunt, ut non solum *PV;* 424 negent *PV;* 424 ea quae *PV;* 425–426 Denique negant hunc *E,* negantes *PV;* 427 et concedunt Deum esse asinum *paene penitus deleta in V;* 428 veri Antichristi *PV;* 428 Potest ne maior esse *E,* Potest esse maior *PV;* 432 commentum *E,* figmentum *PV;* 436 nunc *E,* tunc *PV;* 437 sustentat *PV;* 438 et ita *PV;* 439–440 ut Deus . . . mulum *paene penitus deleta in V* (*et* 440 susten[tans] *defic. in lacunoso P*); 441 discipuli nobis denuo *PV;* 441–442 tollerarent illi haec *E,* an tolerare possent talia *PV;* 442 et placitas *E,* placitasque *PV;* 442 Nonne *E,* An non *PV;* 443 faciunt ipsi *PV;* 443 vocem illam *E,* eam dictionem *PV;* 445 sustentet *PV;* 446 Sed *om. PV;* 448–449 mihi tradita sunt *E,* sibi esse tradita *PV;* 449 meo *E,* suo *PV;* 451 id relatum *PV.*

invenies Matth. 12. Sicut quicquid unquam in bibliis scriptum
est ad ipsum refertur, ipsum omnia respiciunt, et per illum omnia
complentur. Quae vero, et qualis est illa communicatio praedi-
455 catorum? Nam illud praedicatum sustinens naturam humanam prius
non conveniebat homini. Qualiter ergo homo sua praedicata, si
non sunt sua Deo communicat? Quod in Christo sit duplex
natura divina, et humana nos certe fatemur, et apertissime doce-
bimus. In Christo vere coniunguntur Deus et homo, in unam
460 substantiam, unum corpus, et unum novum hominem. Eph. 2. Sed
quia haec divina natura, ex verbi arcanis pendet, pinguiore
minerva nunc dicamus, Deum posse homini deitatis plenitudinem
communicare, dare ei divinitatem, maiestatem, potestatem, et
gloriam suam. Dignus est agnus qui occisus est accipere
465 divinitatem, potentiam, sapientiam, honorem et gloriam.
Apocal. 5. Si Moses factus est Deus Pharaonis Exod. 7. Et
Cyrus Deus Israelis Esa. 45. multo fortius et excellentiore
longe modo factus est Christus Thomae, et omnium nostrum
Dominus, et Deus. Solomon quoque ad literam dicitur Deus
470 Psal. 44. At illi erant Dii non natura sed temporali dono.
Christus vero est naturali nativitate Deus, naturaliter
genitus de substantia Dei. Tota patris deitas, adoratio Dei,
et visio Dei, est in Christo vero Deo. Sicut pater est verus
Deus, ita veram suam deitatem unico filio suo unice tribuens
475 efficit, ut ille sit verus Deus.

Post tria de Christo ἀξιώματα tria quoque superest Phariseorum argumenta diluere, quae ipsemet Christus pro nobis diluet.

Si Christus est Deus, erunt etiam plures dii. Ad obiectionem
Ioan. istam Phariseorum qui Christum arguebant, eo quod se Deum
10 faciebat, respondet ipse. Quia ego dixi dii estis.

452 Sicut *om. PV;* 452 de filio scriptum *PV;* 453 illum *E,* ipsum *PV;* 454 communicatio illa *PV;* 455 sustentans *PV;* 456 ergo *E,* igitur *PV;* 457 sit *E,* fuerit, et sit *PV;* 458 certe fatemur, et *om. PV;* 461 divina Christi natura *PV;* 461–462 pinguiore minerva *E,* simpliciore via *PV;* 478 axiomata *PV;* 478 *ante* Si Christus *add. PV* Argumentum primum, *nec hic caput novum incip.;* 478 etiam *E,* iam *PV;* 476–478 *in mg. add PV* Argumentum primum pharisaeorum.

Editions Collated: Murr (1790/1966) and 1553

Since Murr's 1790 edition-cum-reprint of the 1553 *Restitutio,* itself photographically reprinted in 1966 (see above, n. 3), will be the only access to the work for most readers, I have recorded the points at which it inaccurately reproduces the text of the *editio princeps* for the section missing in the Edinburgh copy. I have not noted Murr's not infrequent departure from the original punctuation, or his occasional change of capitalization. Whereas the 1553 text abounds with contractions and abbreviations, Murr reproduced every word in full, in the process perpetrating several of his mistakes.

The page and line references are to Murr's edition, and the siglum *M* identifies his readings, and *PV* the 1553 text: p. 3, line 11: omnium *M,* res omnium *PV;* p. 4, line 3: cognationem *M,* generationem *PV;* line 3: perfectionem *M,* profectionem *PV;* lines 25–26: tractanda *M,* tractandam *PV;* p. 6, line 2: 27 *M,* 17 *PV;* line 27: ratione *M,* rationem *PV;* p. 7, line 7: 2 *M,* 1 *PV;* line 16: quoniam *M,* quando *PV;* line 25: locutum *M,* loquutum *PV;* line 32: 2 *M,* 1 *PV;* p. 8, lines 4 and 5: quia *M,* quod *PV;* p. 9, line 2: appello *M,* apello *PV;* p. 10, line 23: a *M,* de *PV;* p. 11, line 19: cognatione *M,* generatione *PV;* line 34: Nem *M,* Nam *PV;* p. 12, line 13: plebeis *M,* plebeiis *PV;* p. 13, line 32: filius *M,* filius, sed proprius filius *PV;* p. 14, line 9: cognationibus *M,* generationibus *PV;* p. 15, line 21: calumniatores *M,* calumniatores isti *PV;* line 5: aequepolleat *M,* aequipolleat *PV;* p. 16, line 29: est *M,* et² *PV;* line 32: *a* Post tria *caput novum non incipit M, sicut PV.*

Murr's list of Errata (p. 734) is his own, not that of the 1553 edition, but he records only the first one of those I have listed above. In the whole work he noticed only about twice the number extracted here from the first sixteen pages.

Servetus as Jonah, America as Nineveh

Alexander Gordon was the first to notice that in the manuscript, but not the printed, version of the *Prooemium* (f. 3r; cf. p. 4) a sentence occurs which shows, as Roland Bainton later put it, that "Servetus for the first time in history thought of America as a place of refuge for the religious exile."[7] In an intriguing autobiographical comment, Servetus admits to having long put off the task he now undertakes (i.e., the writing of the *Restitutio*), partly "because of the threat of persecution, which made me wish instead to flee, like Jonah, to the sea or to some new island *(in insulam aliquam novam)*" (lines 64–66). Gordon's translation is bolder: "to one of the New Isles."

In 1535 and again in 1541 Servetus had brought out editions of Ptolemy's *Geographia,* using as his starting point the new annotated Latin translation of Willibald Pirckheimer, the Nuremberg humanist, published at Strassburg in 1525. In one of his additions to Pirckheimer's commentary, Servetus insists that the territory discovered by Christopher Columbus must not be called "America," for "Americus" (i.e., the Italian navigator, Amerigo Vespucci) reached it much later than *(multo post)* Columbus—and in the service of Portugal, not Spain![8]

Alas for the Spanish Servetus; he was a born loser. He had no more success in influencing the naming of the new continent than in defying the fundamental creedal traditions of European Christendom. He might have stood a better chance of preventing "America" from catching on if he had offered an attractive alternative. With an uncharacteristic lack of imagination, he could do no better, in his edition of Ptolemy, than "new land" *(terra nova)* or "new islands" *(insulae novae)*.

As Gordon also pointed out (though without providing the references), Servetus mentions "the new islands" twice in the printed *Restitutio.* In the second book of one of its constituent treatises, *De Fide et Iustitia Regni Christi,* he opposes the belief that righteousness and salvation are to be found only where the biblical promises are heard. Appealing to Rom. 2:14–15 and a series of Old Testament precedents, he also cites "the new islands":

> Whatever kind of faith in God is to be found in the new islands *(in insulis novis),* it can be sufficient, provided a person acts correctly in accordance with conscience.[9]

He argues to similar effect in the tenth of his *Epistolae Triginta* to Calvin:

> In the new islands *(In insulis novis),* the ground of faith and righteousness is found solely in the testimony of conscience.[10]

In both these passages the case of Nineveh is advanced as a biblical support for Servetus' argument.

> The Ninevites' fasting was their righteousness, even though they had no promises there. . . . The Ninevites believed that God could avert the ruin of their city. . . . The Ninevites in believing the God of the prophet Jonah were justified, despite knowing neither the promises made by God nor the Law.[11]
>
> Those who shared the ship with Jonah and those who lived in Nineveh believed God, even though he promises nothing but threatened them with death. Christ bears witness that they were justified on account of their entrusting themselves to God with unwavering confidence, in the conviction that he could avert their death.[12]

Angel Alcala suggests a connection between Servetus' temptation to flee to "some new island" and his idealization of this new world, like some idyllic Nineveh—"un *locus* ideal de primitivismo regido por la conciencia y la razón natural."[13] Bainton's comment that "Jonah did not desert Nineveh, and under the assumed name of Villanovanus or Villeneuve went to France" confuses the picture, or rather reflects Servetus' versatile use of the biblical story.[14] The enticing allure of "the new islands" to Bainton's "hunted heretic" was that of a place where his message, like Jonah's at Nineveh, would be instinctively embraced by a conscience taught by nature, free of the overlay of the prejudiced and persecuting tradition of post-Constantinian Europe.

It is not known, adds Alcala, whether Servetus' "intención migratoria" manifested itself in any external action.[15] He did not yield to the temptation to take to flight, nor will I yield to quite a different temptation. It is not for a citizen of the United Kingdom to indulge in speculative reconstructions of America's religious history had Servetus actually done a Jonah and taken ship for "the new islands." But one is surely safe in believing that Ed Dowey is not sorry that Servetus remained on my side of the Atlantic, even though the author of *The Knowledge of God in Calvin's Theology* may not be quite so hostile to Servetus' epistemological notions about Nineveh as some other modern interpreters of Calvin are.

There is another, hitherto unnoticed, reference in Servetus to "the new islands" whose significance goes beyond this constellation of ideas. It occurs in a letter to Calvin first published by the editors of the *Corpus Reformatorum* in the *Prolegomena* to their dossier on the Servetus affair. Probably in 1546, Servetus addressed three questions to Calvin. The letter before us (unmentioned by Calvin, it seems) was Servetus' rejoinder to Calvin's second reply (i.e., his response to Servetus' rebuttal of his initial reply), in which Calvin had briefly answered seven additional questions which Servetus had attached to his rebuttal. The second of these was whether anyone can be justified without the divine promise.[16] Calvin grants *(concedo)* that this is impossible, but he immediately guards his flank against any inference therefrom debarring infants from baptism.[17] Servetus' letter ridicules Calvin's insistence that no one can believe in God except in response to his promise.

> I could adduce innumerable witnesses and examples to explode this statement of yours—of people who were justified both before the age of the law and during the age of the law and the age of grace, even in Nineveh and in the new islands *(etiam in Ninive et in insulis novis).*[18]

The added importance of this passage lies in the realm of chronology. It provides an invaluable connection between a letter that can be dated with some confidence to 1546 (or possibly 1547),[19] and the text of the Edinburgh manuscript, with its mention of fleeing like Jonah to "some new island." This link affords a timely transition to the last section of this study, which will consider in a preliminary fashion the broader questions raised by the Edinburgh manuscript pages.[20]

Manuscript and Printed Book

Ever since it came to light,[21] the manuscript section of the Edinburgh *Restitutio* has attracted scholarly speculation. David Cuthbertson, a librarian in the University Library, claimed that the book was Calvin's own copy and that the manuscript pages derived from the "original draft" of the work sent to Calvin by Servetus in 1546. The latter hypothesis remains more probable than the former, although even the former has some suggestive evidence in its favor.

On February 26, 1553, a close associate of Calvin's in Geneva, Guillaume de Trie, disclosed in a letter to his cousin, Antoine Arneys, in Lyons that the town of Vienne was host to an archheretic named Servetus, or "Villeneufve," who had succeeded in having his blasphemous books published there. As proof of this verdict on the man, de Trie enclosed "la premiere feuille" of what could only be the printed *Restitutio.*[22] T. H. L. Parker translates this as "page 1,"[23] but this can scarcely have been adequate for de Trie's purpose, whether it was the first page of the *Prooemium* (page 3) or of the treatise proper (page 5). For Bainton it was "the first folio," which meant "the first four leaves" of the book.[24] Bainton is here following Antoine Gachet d'Artigny, who in 1749 discovered and published de Trie's letters to Servetus in the Vienne archives and reported that the letter of February 26 was accompanied by the title and index and "des quatres premières feuilles" of the *Restitutio.*[25] This report in turn appears to rest not on Gachet d'Artigny's discovery of any pages of the printed *Restitutio* at Vienne, but on his combining a later accusation by Servetus with a reference to "quatre feuillets d'un Livre" in a submission made on March 16 by one of the Lyons officials charged with pursuing de Trie's disclosures.[26] It must be to this same sample of printed material that Servetus referred months later in Geneva when he accused Calvin of getting de Trie to send "la moytie du premier quayer du livre dudict Servetus, ou estoyt le titre, et indice ou table et quelque commancamant du dict livre, intitule Christianismi restitutio."[27]

For Cuthbertson (unaware, it seems, of the Vienne evidence of "quatre feuillets"), de Trie's "la premiere feuille," elucidated by Servetus' challenge to Calvin, could only be the first sheet, i.e., eight leaves or sixteen pages—exactly what the Edinburgh copy lacks. And whatever responsibility is laid at Calvin's door for de Trie's exposure of Servetus at Vienne, de Trie was close enough to Calvin for the copy of the *Restitutio* that lost "la premiere feuille" to be, not implausibly, Calvin's own.

More reliably Calvin is known to have had in his possession for some years before 1553 a manuscript version of at least a major part of what became the *Restitutio.* Calvin reported to Farel on January 13, probably in 1546,[28] that Servetus had recently *(nuper)* sent him a letter accompanied by a *longum volumen suorum deliriorum.* The letter was probably the first of the exchanges mentioned earlier, for in Servetus' second letter (i.e., his refutation of Calvin's reply to his three questions) he recommends that Calvin reread his (Servetus') *quartum librum de baptismo. Nam videris eum nondum legisse.*[29] This can refer only to Book 4 (*De Ordine Mysteriorum Regenerationis,* in the printed *Restitutio,* pages 525–576) of the treatise *De Regeneratione Superna, et de Regno Antichristi* (pages 355–576). Servetus apparently expected Calvin to return his handiwork, but in vain, it seems. In the letter whose mention of "the new islands" was noticed above, Servetus pleads *Remitte . . . scripta mea.*[30] When Calvin unilaterally abandoned the correspondence, Servetus tried other Genevans. At the end of his third letter to the minister Abel Poupin, he expresses his regret *quod per vos non licuit mihi emendare locos aliquot in scriptis meis, quae sunt apud Calvinum.*[31] Later, during Servetus' trial at Geneva on August 14, 1553, he was presented by the prosecutor with certain books both printed and handwritten. He admitted that the hand was his own, which he had sent to Calvin about six years ago "pour en avoir son iugement."[32] During his third cross-examination on August 17 reference was made several times to the manuscript rather than to the printed text.[33]

None of the information in the last few paragraphs is new to Servetan studies. Although it has been readily available for over half a century (at least since Doumergue's volume 6 appeared in 1926), some basic research tasks still remain to be undertaken.

1. The relationship between the Edinburgh manuscript's text and the manuscript in Paris, Bibliothèque Nationale lat. 18212, must be scientifically investigated. The latter contains a variant text parallel to the printed volume's pages 92–246 (but not in this order and with minor gaps).[34] Scholars have frequently asserted that both manuscripts derive from the first

version sent to Calvin in 1546 or so. The Paris manuscript can probably be traced back indirectly to Lausanne, where Calvin may have sent Servetus' draft for Viret's perusal.[35] The date of the Paris text has been keenly investigated, since Servetus' distinction as the first to discover the pulmonary circulation of the blood may rest on it. Gordon and Bainton claimed to show that when it was written, Servetus lacked access to the works of Clement of Alexandria (first published in Greek in 1550 and in Latin in 1551) and Philo (first Greek edition 1552) which the 1553 *Restitutio* uses, but Alcala has recently raised a question mark: the Paris manuscript contains one of the Greek words quoted from Philo. The issue awaits resolution.[36]

A comparison of the divergences between each manuscript and the corresponding printed text should throw some light on whether they derive from a single draft of the *Restitutio.* Gordon collated the Paris pages on the pulmonary circulation, and Bainton obviously did some collation himself, but the main labor lies ahead.[37] The recent Spanish translation has taken note of variants in both manuscripts, but far from exhaustively.[38] The two manuscripts are not in the same hand,[39] nor can the Edinburgh one be said to contain the "many obvious errors of transcription" that Gordon found in the Paris text.[40]

Gordon differentiated between "the original draft" retained by Servetus and the version sent to Calvin and believed to be represented by our two manuscripts. The latter was "the prepared text, that would have been published had Calvin returned the manuscript." As it was, Servetus had to work from his "original draft" in producing the published text.[41] In the light of the relatively minor differences so far disclosed between the manuscript texts and the 1553 edition (with the exception of four or five passages early in the Edinburgh pages), it is just as likely that Servetus retained a copy of what he sent to Calvin. The reason why he wanted his manuscript back was not that without it publication was a problem (as the edition proved in 1553) but that he wanted to revise it and was unhappy to have it circulating uncorrected. As he said to Poupin, he had been unable *emendare locos aliquot in scriptis meis, quae sunt apud Calvinum.*[42]

2. A further reason for carrying out the twofold collation urged above (first, of the full Paris manuscript text with the edition, and second, of the results with those emerging from my collation of the Edinburgh fragment) must be to determine the extent of the changes Servetus made prior to publication. If his regret addressed to Poupin was genuine, did his desire to "improve certain passages" owe anything to the correspondence with Calvin? It would not be surprising if these compari-

sons disclosed some evidence of the movement of Servetus' mind between approximately 1546 and 1552.

3. Also to be taken into account is another Paris manuscript, lat. 3676 chart., ff. 218–296, which contains a text of most of the *Epistolae Triginta* to Calvin which are included in the *Restitutio.* The *Corpus Reformatorum* editors collated a transcription of it with Murr's edition of the *Restitutio* for their edition of the *Epistolae.* But although they describe Murr's text as *satis mendose expressus,* the variants they record in the manuscript reveal minimal divergence.[43] But one would not expect Servetus to have revised the *Epistolae* like a first draft of a book.

4. Finally, when the time comes for a critical edition of the *Restitutio,* it may even be possible and appropriate to correct the 1553 text from one or other of the manuscripts. Alcala from time to time indicates his preference for variants in the manuscripts over the printed text.[44] Even in the short space of the Edinburgh pages a fairly obvious correction of the published version can be detected. At lines 119–122 the latter omits a whole sentence, probably by haplography, the typesetter's eye jumping from *unctum* at the end of one sentence to the same word at the end of the next. Since the following sentence, common to both texts, picks up the words *vocem . . . Christus* found also in the manuscript's sentence, an accidental omission seems indicated in the print. But whether, at line 261, the manuscript's *spiritus miraculorum* is a "better" or "more correct" reading than *virtus miraculorum* is more elusive.

The Manuscript and Printed Texts Compared

Attention has already been drawn to the extensive agreement between the two versions of this short section of the *Restitutio.* For lines on end they are identical (e.g., 261–274, 462–478), or virtually so (e.g., 156–179, 233–250, 322–340, 348–363). A fair proportion of the differences between them are little more than cosmetic, such as minor variations in word order, of which some twenty-five can be counted. A preference for *sat nunc erit* over *sufficit nunc* (412) is attributable only to taste or whim (cf. *perspicue* for *aperte,* 214, etc.).

If the manuscript is treated for comparative purposes as representing the draft from which Servetus prepared the work for publication, few obvious corrections are discernible, such as *obumbratione* (278), and probably *imbris* (217), *metaphysice, metaphysicus* (274, 319) and *vocatus* (131; *unctus* at 200 is more questionable). In cases like these, however, the divergence may be the fault of the copyist of the manuscript.

The most prominent difference is the absence from the 1553 text of most of the autobiographical material in lines 54–66 and parts of lines 52 (a reference to Servetus' youthful age) and 46–48, where, in place of the fraught prayer *ne me deseras . . . afflictionibus pressum,* the book offers a more conventional request for assistance *(teipsum aperi servo tuo).* The omission of the exhortation to the reader at lines 25–32 also softens the personal thrust of the preface, without removing it entirely (cf. 70–72). A similar interest may help to explain the omission of 106–109, with its question addressed to the reader.

A toning down is probably also to be recognized in the omission of two bold promises made in the manuscript preface: the way of truth "will openly display to you the secrets of God" (21), and "will lead you to all heavenly realities" (24). Yet a number of differences suggest a firmer decisiveness in the printed version. The time is "truly" fulfilled (67), as Servetus will demonstrate from "manifest" signs of the times (68). *Aperte* strengthens *docemur* (133), and on other occasions a higher degree of certainty or clarity is claimed for the exposition (e.g., 90–91, 204). Likewise *curabo* replaces *conabor* at line 84.

Indeed, once the preface is over and Servetus is launched on his subject, many of the changes, albeit minor in scope, are additions which serve to sharpen or clarify the force of the printed text. Thus at lines 206–208 the latter spells out the progression of thought more painstakingly, and the lucidity of 287–288 similarly improves on the manuscript. The omission of *Hic homo iustus erat* (348) leaves the argument more precisely focused on Jesus the *homo* being *filius Dei.* At line 221 the holy offspring of Mary "truly will be" the Son of God, rather than "will be called."

A few changes may more significantly preclude misunderstanding. At line 213 *Hic Jesus* replaces *corpus hoc* when Servetus is speaking of the one born of God in the incarnation. Similarly at 289–290, *propria passio corporis* in the manuscript gives way to *proprium hominis,* and likewise with *carnis.* Unhappiness with the draft's use of *corpus* with reference to the human Jesus may account for the omission of lines 119–122, which I have above attributed to haplography in the printed version.

Other variants reveal no *Tendenz.* At line 367 the printed text clearly recalls Tertullian's tag *Fiunt, non nascuntur Christiani* (*Apol.* 18.4), but Servetus had long been familiar with his works. The workmanlike *simpliciore via* replaces the classical *pinguiore minerva* at 461–462. *Concedentes* seems less appropriate for simple folk's acknowledgment of Jesus as Christ than the manuscript's *credentes* (105), but the published text's coherence is improved by the omission of lines 87–89. Not only are they out of place between the itemizing of the three heads and the beginning of the discussion of the first of them, but Servetus has already, in the printed version, presented Jesus as the *ostium* and *via* at line 79.

If we may judge from these few pages, Servetus seems to have made numerous but mainly minor changes to his first draft of the *Restitutio.* The effect was greater clarity and precision at many points rather than any detectable change of substance, although some concern to guard against being misunderstood may be present. Most obvious is the disappearance from the publication of 1553 of the historically invaluable autobiographical elements in the manuscript.

NOTES

1. Henri Tollin could identify 30 or 40 copies in the first years after publication (E. Doumergue, *Jean Calvin: Les hommes et les choses de son temps,* 7 vols. [Paris, 1899–1927], 6:272 n. 8). For early circulation in Italy, see Alexander Gordon, "Miguel Serveto-y-Revés. II," *Theological Review* 15 (1878), 412, 426n. Cf. also S. Kot, "L'influence de Servet sur le mouvement antitrinitaire en Pologne et en Transylvanie," in B. Becker, ed., *Autour de Michel Servet et de Sebastien Castellion* (Haarlem, 1953), pp. 72–115; M. Balázs, "Die osteuropäische Rezeption der Restitutio Christianismi von Servet," in R. Dán and A. Pirnát, eds., *Antitrinitarianism* (Leiden, 1982), pp. 13–23.

2. G. Ongaro, "La scoperta della circolazione polmonare e la diffusione della *Christianismi Restitutio* di Michele Serveto nel XVI secolo in Italia e nel Veneto," *Episteme* 5 (1971), 3–44. For a MS at Paris, see E. F. Podach, "De la diffusion du 'Christianismi Restitutio' de Michel Servet (1553) au XVIe siècle. MS 14 de la Bibliothèque du Protestantisme à Paris," *Bulletin de la Société de l'Histoire du Protestantisme français* 99 (1952), 251–264, and "Die Geschichte der 'Christianismi Restitutio' im Lichte ihrer Abschriften," in Becker, *Autour de M. Servet,* pp. 47–61. This MS includes both excerpts derived from another (lost) MS (copied from an exemplar of the 1553 edition attested in Cologne around 1580 but otherwise unknown), and an incomplete text of the *Restitutio* copied, perhaps not directly, from another MS in 1560–61.

3. For bibliography, J. F. Fulton, *Michael Servetus, Humanist and Martyr* (New York, 1953), pp. 84–92. The 1790 Nuremberg edition-cum-facsimile by C. G. von Murr (Fulton, p. 90) was photographically

reprinted by Minerva of Frankfurt in 1966. It is not free of faults (see below). On the MSS see also José Barón Fernández, *Miguel Servet: Su Vida y Su Obra* (Madrid, 1970), pp. 142–170, and the Spanish translation of most of the *Restitutio* by Angel Alcala and Luis Betes, *Miguel Servet: Restitución del Cristianismo* (Madrid, 1980), pp. 48–57. Alcala has translated the rest in *Miguel Servet: Treinta cartas a Calvino* (Madrid, 1981).

The fullest account of the publication is given by Doumergue, *Jean Calvin* 6:254–275.

4. Deposited in the library in 1695. (See David Cuthbertson, *A Tragedy of the Reformation: Being the Authentic Narrative of the History and Burning of the "Christianismi Restitutio" 1553* [Edinburgh and London, 1912], pp. 25–29. On the faults of this book see Gordon in *The Christian Life and Unitarian Herald,* May 18, 1912, p. 235.) R. Willis, *Servetus and Calvin* (London, 1877), p. 535, knew of only two copies, but in 1878 in *The Athenaeum,* no. 2635 (April 27), p. 541, reported the rediscovery of the Edinburgh copy (cf. Cuthbertson, *Tragedy,* pp. 23f.; Gordon, "M. Serveto-y-Revés. II," p. 412n.).

5. Cuthbertson, *A Tragedy of the Reformation,* pp. 38ff., citing a letter of 1910 from Alexander Gordon. Cuthbertson claims (pp. 29f.) to provide a transcription of the first page of the MS, but instead reprints the text of the equivalent printed pages.

6. R. H. Bainton, *Hunted Heretic: The Life and Death of Michael Servetus 1511–1553* (Boston, 1953), p. 221, recorded that E. Morse Wilbur made a complete transcription.

7. Gordon, "Servetus and America," *The Christian Life and Unitarian Herald,* Oct. 24, 1925, p. 360; Bainton, "The Present State of Servetus Studies," *Journal of Modern History* 4 (1932), 89 (cf. 75), and *Hunted Heretic,* pp. 73f., 88 (Servetus probably had South America in mind).

8. Cf. Bainton, *Hunted Heretic,* pp. 90f. E. Bullón y Fernández, *Miguel Servet y la geografía del Renacimiento,* 2nd ed. (Madrid, 1929), gives Servetus' account (pp. 199–203), partly translated by C. D. O'Malley, *Michael Servetus: A Translation of His Geographical, Medical and Astrological Writings* (Philadelphia and London, 1953), p. 37. For bibliography, see Fulton, *Michael Servetus,* pp. 60–65.

9. *Restitutio,* p. 333.

10. Ibid., pp. 603–604.

11. Ibid., p. 333.

12. Ibid., p. 603.

13. Alcala and Betes, *Restitución,* p. 533 n. 75; cf. p. 122 n. 14.

14. Bainton, "The Present State," p. 75. The same applies to the title, "Nineveh Unrepentant," of ch. 4 of *Hunted Heretic,* which

deals with the hostile reception of Servetus' antitrinitarian works of 1531–32.

15. Alcala and Betes, *Restitución,* p. 122 n. 14.

16. *CO* 8 (*CR* 36):486.

17. *CO* 8:495.

18. *CO* 8:xxxi.

19. Doumergue, *Jean Calvin* 6:257–261.

20. Another unnoticed point of contact between our MS and one of Servetus' additions to Ptolemy's *Geographia* deserves to be mentioned. In a section *De Hispania et eius ad Galliam comparatione* (Latin in Bullón y Fernández, *M. Servet,* pp. 189–196; English in O'Malley, *M. Servetus,* pp. 25–29), he says that the Spanish "infeliciter discunt, ut alibi potius quam in ipsa Hispania hispanum doctum invenias. Semidocti iam se doctos putant, sapientiam maiorem quam habeant simulatione et verbositate quadam ostentant" (p. 194). The autobiographical confession found only in the MS (lines 52–66) suggests that Servetus is here analyzing the Spanish mind from some painfully acquired self-knowledge. He was barely out of his teens when he first essayed to treat of such weighty wisdom "cum de his nihil essem ab homine doctus." Recognizing his tender youthfulness and ineloquence he almost abandoned the cause completely, "cum nondum essem satis instructus."

This parallel may add force to Gordon's surmise ("Servetus and America," p. 360) that Servetus began his first draft of the *Restitutio* "about 1541."

21. See n. 4 above.

22. *CO* 8:837. See Bainton, *Hunted Heretic,* p. 160, for a long-lasting confusion between these *Restitutio* pages and others from Calvin's *Institutio.* It goes back to Gachet d'Artigny, "Mémoires" (see n. 25 below), p. 98, and is found also in Weiss, "Calvin, Servet" (see n. 26 below), p. 400.

23. Parker, *John Calvin: A Biography* (London, 1975), p. 120.

24. Bainton, *Hunted Heretic,* p. 153.

25. Gachet d'Artigny, "Mémoires pour servir à l'histoire de Michel Servet," in his *Nouveaux mémoires d'histoire, de critique et de littérature,* vol. II (Paris, 1749), pp. 55–154 at p. 84. Cf. Doumergue, *Jean Calvin* 6:281f.; *CO* 8:838 n. 1 (where the reference to the *Index* being on the verso of the title page derives not from Gachet d'Artigny, as though he had inspected these pages, but from the *Corpus Reformatorum* editors).

26. Gachet d'Artigny, "Mémoires," p. 88 (cf. N. Weiss, "Calvin, Servet, G. de Trie et le tribunal de Vienne," *Bulletin de la Société de l'Histoire du Protestantisme français* 57 [1908], 397). Further references to these "quatre feuilles" appear at pp. 89, 90f., still on March 17, i.e., before any further material evidence was supplied

from Geneva. According to Bainton, *Hunted Heretic,* p. 258 n. 5, the documents found by Gachet d'Artigny were subsequently destroyed.

27. *CO* 8:805. Bainton, *Hunted Heretic,* p. 198, summarizes as "half of the first quire."

28. *CO* 8:283; Doumergue, *Jean Calvin* 6:260–261.

29. *CO* 8:486.

30. *CO* 8:xxxi.

31. *CO* 8:751; for the date cf. Doumergue, *Jean Calvin,* vol. 6, pp. 263–265, esp. 265 n. 2.

32. *CO* 8:734 n. 2.

33. *CO* 8:743–749.

34. See Bainton, "The Present State," pp. 90–92, for the page equivalence.

35. According to one reading of de Trie's third letter to Arneys in Lyons (last day of March 1553), the MS of the *Restitutio* had been in Lausanne for two years (*CO* 8:843; cf. 734 n. 2; Bainton, *Hunted Heretic,* pp. 158, 259 n. 14; Weiss, "Calvin, Servet," p. 399). See Bainton, "The Smaller Circulation: Servetus and Colombo," *Sudhoffs Archiv für Geschichte der Medizin* 24 (1931), 374, for the Paris MS's Lausanne link. The MS in Servetus' hand must have been back in Geneva by August 1553.

36. Gordon, "M. Serveto-y-Revés. II," p. 429n.; Bainton, "The Smaller Circulation," pp. 371–374; Alcala and Betes, *Restitución,* p. 53, referring to p. 377 (= *Restitutio,* p. 202), where just before the Greek quotation from Philo that the MS lacks, one of its words *(skia)* appears in Greek in the MS alone. Unfortunately the other Greek quotation from Philo occurs in a section of the *Restitutio* which the MS lacks altogether (p. 200, line 37, to p. 201, line 24; Bainton "Smaller Circulation," p. 374 n. 1).

37. Gordon, "M. Serveto-y-Revés. II," pp. 417–421; Bainton, "The Smaller Circulation," p. 373; *Hunted Heretic,* p. 153.

38. Alcala and Betes, *Restitución,* pp. 55, 109f., for an explanation of their methods. Variants in the Edinburgh MS are noted at pp. 120 n. 4, 121–123, 130 n. 24, 137 n. 50, 140 n. 66.

39. Facsimiles in Alcala and Betes, *Restitución,* facing pp. 145 and 272 (Edinburgh) and 336 (Paris). On the Paris hand, see p. 54; it is not yet excluded that it may be Servetus' own. The Edinburgh MS had to be at least once, but perhaps only once, removed from Servetus' autograph. To fit the gap in the printed book, it had to be recopied on pages of the right size, with the writing area likewise, and the textual continuity from f.10_v to p. 17 just right. This circumstance allows for its text to be very close to Servetus' own.

40. Gordon, "M. Serveto-y-Revés. II," p. 417n.

41. Ibid. Cf. Bainton, *Hunted Heretic,* p. 148: Servetus kept "either copious notes or another draft." The former would have been inadequate.

42. *CO* 8:751 with n. 5.

43. Bainton, "The Present State," pp. 77–78 (with some imprecise references); *CO* 8:xxxiii–xxxiv, 649–714; Alcala, *Treinta cartas,* p. 71 (translation based on Murr, not the 1553 text; note taken of the *Corpus Reformatorum* collations).

44. Alcala and Betes, *Restitución,* p. 382 n. 35 (cf. 374 n. 3).

St. John of the Cross' Poem "Dark Night": The Dark Night of the Soul, or the Senses' Delight?

José C. Nieto

Introduction

The "dark night of the soul" is a well-known mystical motif used to describe the stages of the soul's journey toward purgation and purification in order to achieve union with God. This mystical title was made popular by the Spanish mystic John of the Cross (1542–1591), the name which replaced his family name, Juan de Yepes y Alvarez, when he joined the developing discalced Carmelite Order, at the time struggling to establish itself under the direction of its founder, Teresa of Avila.[1] This essay will discuss John's poem "Dark Night," of which the following English translation is offered:

1. On one dark night,
   Aflame with love's anxiety—
   O happy venture!—
   I slipped out without being noticed,
   My house being already at rest.

2. In darkness and secure
   By the secret ladder, disguised—
   O happy venture!—
   In darkness and in concealment,
   My house being already at rest.

3. On that happy night
   In secret, for nobody saw me,
   Nor did I look at anything,
   Without any other light and guide
   But the one burning in my heart.

4. This one guided me
More certainly than the high noon light,
To where he was expecting me—
Whom so well I knew—
In a place where nobody appeared.

5. O night which so guided!
O night kinder than the dawn!
O night which joined
Lover with his beloved
Transforming the beloved in her lover.

6. Upon my flowering breast,
Which wholly was kept solely for him,
There he fell asleep
While I was caressing him,
And the fanning cedars blew a breeze.

7. The breeze blowing from the turret,
Playing with his locks,
He with his gentle hand
Wounding my neck
And all my senses suspending.

8. I tarried and forgot myself,
Reclining my face on my beloved.
All ceased, and I abandoned myself,
Leaving my care
Forgotten among the lilies.

The Dark Night was the title chosen by John for one of his works describing the mystical stages of the soul. In fact, it is the second theological commentary on his poem "Dark Night," the first of these commentaries being *The Ascent of Mount Carmel.* Two of his other better-known writings, *The Spiritual Canticle* and *The Living Flame of Love,* are also commentaries on poems with the same titles.

All this is well known, and there is nothing unusual about John's writing theological commentaries on his own poems at the request of those who were also members of his religious order. This is the basis on which all scholarship on John's poems and commentaries, including my own, has been grounded.[2] There is, however, something which has puzzled me during the course of my research on this subject, and which has resulted in this attempt to present the whole problem of the relationship between poetry and commentaries in a new light.[3] I shall explain briefly the problem which, once perceived, with its obvious implications, had compelled me to restate research from a new vantage point.

First of all, I came to realize that while John's poems were all religious in their motifs and substance, and therefore justified his commentaries already mentioned, nevertheless there seemed to be an exception, and that is the poem "Dark Night." If this poem was not in fact a mystical, religious poem from the point of view of its literary and aesthetic content, this exception itself needed to be explored and explained from a literary method which cannot assume any longer the mystical nature of the poem unless it is first proved. If this is correct, it will be necessary first to explain the nature of the love which is central to the poem. If it is not divine love, one has to see it as profane love and explore the poem afresh. The implication may at first be startling, but soon one may recognize that with this single poem John reveals his great debt to the secular, Renaissance tradition of love and is firmly rooted in it.

If this be so, then why has it not been obvious before? The answer seems to be that it was the result of a methodological confusion. By this I mean that scholars without exception, myself included, analyzed the poem "Dark Night" not as an independent, self-sufficient, and unique poem in itself, standing alone in the *juancruciano corpus,* but rather as a shorter version of the much larger poem, "The Spiritual Canticle."[4] Thus, the imagery of the "Dark Night" has been understood not for what it said or suggested but rather for what the reader already knew from the content of the larger "The Spiritual Canticle," more complete in its imagery, symbolism, motifs, and theological language. Thus, the identification of "The Spiritual Canticle" and the "Dark Night" as complementary poems created, as a result, a lack of interest in a pure aesthetic and literary analysis of the latter, since it was assumed that "The Canticle" had a more complete, developed vocabulary and theme. Although this is certainly so, it does not warrant the identification of these two poems from a strictly literary and aesthetic analysis.

The telescoping of these two poems into one is the result of a literary analysis which is primarily *synthetic* rather than analytic; that is to say, it does not analyze the imagery and words of the "Dark Night" as self-sufficient and meaningful in themselves but, rather, seeks to explain them as if they in fact belong to the stanzas of "The Canticle" itself. Such a synthetic analysis tends to confuse rather than to clarify the "Dark Night" as a poem. This methodological confusion I call the "cantification" of the "Dark Night."[5]

A second confusion arises from the fact that John himself

interpreted the "Dark Night," as a poem, in his two commentaries on it, as if the poem were not different in its purpose from his other poems "The Canticle" and "The Living Flame." Thus, John himself is the one responsible for the first "cantification" of the "Dark Night" as a poem. John had his own reasons for that. But the fact that he did so cannot be accepted any longer as a paradigm for the literary analysis of the poem of the "Dark Night." Among other reasons, John labored to write a theological, mystical commentary on the poem. He did try twice, and twice he failed to complete the commentaries; yet his other commentaries on the other poems were only tried once and completed.

There is in this twice-failed attempt something more than simple "bad luck." Let us, then, explore some of the problems raised here as methodological inconsistencies, keeping in mind that it is the method itself which is adopted here that will shed light on the "Dark Night" as a poem. To do this, we shall establish the relationship between the "Dark Night" and "The Spiritual Canticle" as poems in order to explore their poetic images and the absence or presence of similar motifs in both poems. Thus it will be possible to understand the poetic intention of the "Dark Night" as a self-consistent and independent aesthetic creation without the need of having to be explained in the light of the "Spiritual Canticle."

The Poetic Limitation of the Images

To begin, the vocabulary of the "Night" is more spontaneous than that of "The Canticle" and does not seek after images, or symbols, derived from sacred sources as is clearly the case in "The Canticle," which is based on the Song of Songs. Of all the images of the "Night," only three can be attributed to biblical sources.[6] The most obvious are the *Amado* and *Amada,* or "male Beloved" and "female Beloved," for which the sources seem to be the Song of Solomon. The same is truc in the usage of the "cedars" as a poetic image recalling the famous "cedars of Lebanon." The third image is the *azucenas,* or lilies, which might recall the "lilies of the field" of the Synoptic Gospels. Yet this last image is more general and cannot be limited only to biblical sources. Furthermore, the "cedars" themselves, although suggesting a biblical landscape, nevertheless do not function within the poem itself as hieratical, as we shall see later. Thus, of these images the *Amado* and *Amada* are the only ones which seem to be biblical in their source and functioning hieratically within the poetic theme. However, under closer analysis this is not so. The internal evidence of the poem itself never discloses the identity of its only two personages, and only by identification with "The Canticle" may they be claimed to be the hieratical characters of the Song of Solomon and, by allegorizations, the human soul and its beloved Jesus.

But it is precisely at this point that the images of the "Night" do not allow themselves to be transformed into such allegorization. This is clear because the *Amado* and *Amada* are never referred to within the poem itself as the "Bride" and the "Bridegroom," something which has been always taken for granted. Besides, there are no suggestions or references to either a previous wedding or a future one, as is the case in Solomon's book and in John's larger poem "The Canticle." Thus, the poetic motifs of the "Night" are clearly removed from the hieratical and mystical symbols which John so obviously and repeatedly describes with poetic images and symbols in his "Canticle."

If John had intended to structure his poem within an allegorical plot for a potential mystical meaning, he would have had only to use *once* either the terms Bridegroom or Bride, and the whole poem would have been transformed into a mystical allegory. This is quite obvious in "The Canticle." A stanza is more than sufficient to show that this is so:

> The bride has entered
> The sweet garden of her desire,
> And she rests in delight,
> Laying her neck
> On the gentle arms of her beloved. (22B)[7]

However, when a similar poetic theme appears in the "Night," John avoids any hieratical images which might function in the mind of the reader, or listeners, as evocative of the Song of Songs or of his own "Canticle." Here is an obvious *would-be* parallel to the theme of the stance of "The Canticle" just quoted above, and which in the "Night" is stated thus:

> Upon my flowering breast,
> Which wholly was kept solely for him,
> There he fell asleep
> While I was caressing him,
> And the fanning cedars blew a breeze. (6)[8]

There are here profound changes besides the obvious inversion of the action of the characters when compared with "The Canticle." In the "Night" the *Amada* caresses her beloved without any hint that such a love-play may be interpreted as the religious divine love between the soul and her Bridegroom

Jesus. Thus, the setting is purely a secular one even though the "cedars" may suggest the biblical cedars of Lebanon. Hence the "Night," although closely resembling "The Canticle," intentionally avoids any images which might be properly identified with its sacred love theme.

Another aspect which is absent in the "Night" when compared with "The Canticle" is that the *Amado* of the "Night" is not described, even with a line or a single word, with any divine qualities or attributes which might suggest his nature or function. The identity of this beloved, never described by his lover, the "narrator" of the poem, is something which cannot be known, but one should not make use of this silence in order to identify him with the divine Bridegroom, as is customary. Again, it is improper to attribute to him transcendent qualities of any sort if they are not warranted by the poem itself. Such a reticence is never present in "The Canticle," which refers often to the beloved Bridegroom with images and symbols of transcendence in such a way that there is no room for doubting the divine-human love of "The Canticle," clearly expressed in theological concepts such as "graces" and "sweet and living knowledge," as the result of her reclining on his breast (5:1–2; 27:1–2) as his Bride. But in the "Night" the beloved is vaguely described in passive actions: "There he fell asleep / While I was caressing him" (6:3–4); but when he is described in action, there is a clear form of love where human eros is explicitly stated without any attempt to disguise it with the face of the divine love. Thus says the "Night":

> The breeze blowing from the turret,
> Playing with his locks,
> He with his gentle hand
> Wounding my neck
> And all my senses suspending. (7)

This love is unambiguously human without any palliated attempts to suggest otherwise. There is here a suspension of the senses as a result of the senses' delight and not as any form of religious or mystical experience. Notice that the beloved *wounds* his lover in her neck, which may have erotic suggestions, but does not wound her in her head, or breast, or limbs; images which easily could be transposed to an allegorical reading of these lines by evocation of Christ's passion or Francis of Assisi's stigmata. Furthermore, he does not show any wounds of Christ's passion.[9] Thus, the only image which might have a religious potential as a redemptive motif is clearly preempted of any religious symbolism. But this is not so in "The Canticle," where the redemptive motif appears with all its theological clarity as well as poetic symbolism:

> Beneath the apple tree:
> There I took you for my wife
> There I offered you my hand
> And restored you
> Where your mother was violated. (28B)[10]

The would-be parallel verses of the "Night" do not explore the same feelings and emotions as this stanza of "The Canticle" does, with its theological and poetical insight of the themes of redemption and restoration of humankind set within the Bride-Bridegroom theological scheme. It is obvious that the "apple tree" is charged with a profound religious symbolism and that its function within the poem and stanza is a hieratical one. Not so with the "cedars" of the "Night" whose poetic function is to "fan" the air to create a breeze which acts as an erotico-aesthetic image, cooling the lovers' bodies. For the mythic apple tree of Paradise, there is intentionally substituted the "cedars," and thus all transcendence is removed from its poetic content.

It seems rather obvious that the *presence* of her beloved, in the stanzas here analyzed, either in his passivity or action, is a nontranscendent one. But why is he there? Again, we do not know; but perhaps it would be more heuristically rewarding to ask why she went there, because as the main character of the poem, she expresses her own feelings, revealing to us her poetic world, although only partially and suggestively. Yet it is enough to realize that it is not a divine, transcendent love expressed as the ascent of the soul climbing up the vertical line to be united with God in a higher plane of transcendence. Rather, she *descends* by a "secret ladder" to go to the outskirts of town, a place well known to both of them. It was, then, a preplanned encounter, a rendezvous, for she knew that he was waiting there for her. This might seem to press too much the meaning of the poem; but this is precisely what has to be done, for it is here that the poem yields its most striking difference from "The Canticle," which opens with the Bride's longing, anxiety, and sense of rejection because while they slept he went away, and she does not know where to find him now. Thus, "The Canticle" from its initial poetic vision reveals the unexpected absence of the beloved Bridegroom, and the poem unfolds the longing and seeking after the Bridegroom by his beloved. This is the quest of the soul for its divine origin after its awakening to transcendent reality and its desire for mystical union with the object of her love. John in "The Canticle" blends the Song of Songs motifs with the mystical, allegorical tradition ranging from Origen of Alexandria to Bernard of Clairvaux, and beyond. The poignancy of the soul's longing for divine union is implicit in the realization that she is divine by nature and thus seeks to be reunited with her absent beloved or Bridegroom. Thus "The Canticle" opens:

> Where have you hidden,
> Beloved, and left me moaning?
> You fled like the stag
> After wounding me;
> I went out calling you, and you were gone. (1B)

But the "Night" opens with a totally different poetic world of feeling and vision. Absent here is the longing for one who had been there with her and while she was asleep had fled away to an unknown place. Rather, in her own house and bedroom, fired by her love's urgent longings, she waits until it is night, and under the cover of darkness she furtively slips away to meet her beloved. There is no experience of unexpected absence, or wondering where he had gone, because he was not supposed to be with her, but rather they had already agreed on a secret rendezvous. This is why they are not Bride and Bridegroom, but lovers, and it is this status which makes the secret rendezvous necessary. Furthermore, the overcoming of the distance between the house and the place where he is to be waiting for her is quickly done, and everything takes place within the same night, and before the dawn. She moves furtively in silence without asking questions of anyone, either people or personified forms of Nature. She does not wander days and nights in search of her absent beloved either, as is the case in "The Canticle." Thus, the "Night" preempts any mystical quest of the soul for her divine Bridegroom, in time and space, with its mythical and fabulous landscapes,[11] as is the case within "The Canticle":

> Shepherds, you that go
> Up through the sheepfolds to the hill,
> If by chance you see
> Him I love most,
> Tell him that I sicken, suffer, and
> die.
>
> Seeking my love
> I will head for the mountains and for
> watersides,
> . . . . (2–3B)

This setting of "The Canticle" is of the pastoral genre typical of the Renaissance. The "Night" does not presuppose anything of this setting but rather indicates that the young girl lives within the confines of the town and not in the bucolic landscapes of "The Canticle." It is impossible, therefore, from an aesthetic and literary analysis of both poems, to presuppose the themes and landscapes of "The Canticle," and what they imply theologically and allegorically, within the aesthetic vision reflected in the "Night." The "Canticle" is clearly opened up to a transcendent, vertical vision which is meant to be understood as an allegory of the soul and Jesus. The "Night" is firmly planted on the horizontal line of human love between lovers longing to meet in a secret place and under the cover of the night. Thus, symbols of transcendence are intentionally avoided, and instead the images predominate not as symbols pointing beyond themselves to a transcendent superior plane of allegorical transposition but rather as images which exhaust their meaning within the limits of the horizontal plane of human love for its own sake and not for the sake of a divine love.

The "night" as a natural phenomenon and not as a symbol of "the dark night of the soul" is what appears to limit the possibilities of the poem as a potential for the way toward purgation, illumination, and union. At first this might seem unacceptable to many, since it has always been assumed that this is so. But under closer scrutiny it can be seen that the night itself, as it functions within the poem, imposes limitation on the mystical night as the mystical way toward the purgation of the soul and its illumination, and ultimately to its realization of substantial union with God. This is because the night in mystical symbolism eventually gives way to the radiance of the sun with its illumination of the soul, after passing through the darkness of the senses, soul, and spirit. That is to say, without the symbol of light the night does not open up possibilities of transcendence for its potential allegorical meaning. This is because in a phenomenology of mysticism the night completes itself in the radiance of light. But paradoxically, it is the image of the night which avoids the mystical meaning of this poem because it does not allow room for the second stage after purgation, which is illumination. However, from the hermeneutical point of view of profane love, night is not required to give way to the morning, because it is the night which the lovers seek to prolong, rather than to await the daybreak when their furtive encounter must terminate. Thus the night of the "Night" exhausts itself as a poetic image which is complete in itself and functions within the structure of the poem with self-evident meaning.

There is, however, the metaphor of "light" in the "Night" which John uses within the poetic imagery of the night itself in order to suggest that it was darkness itself which provided a cover for her to go to meet her beloved. Hence, darkness actually was to her as bright as "the high noon light," because her heart was "burning" with desire for him; and it was this burning in her heart that led her to her lover as surely and clearly as in broad daylight. This light is not, however, a transcendent light, for its source is her love's burning desire for him. It is clearly the girl's eros leading her toward the object of her love. But this image, as metaphor, cannot be made into a symbol of transcendence, because there is not a single word that indicates that she was illuminated from outside, or from God. This light is her own; it is immanent to her because it is latent in every human heart as a potential for experiencing love. Again the image does not point beyond itself as a symbol but does rather exhaust itself within its own metaphor as a human quality and experience. Thus reads the poem:

> On that happy night
> In secret, for nobody saw me,
> Nor did I look at anything,
> Without any other light and guide
> But the one burning in my heart.
>
> This one guided me
> More certainly than the high noon light,
> To where he was expecting me—
> Whom so well I knew—
> In a place where nobody appeared. (3–4)

The horizontal plane of this love is clearly human, and it is rooted in this experience of love. This metaphor of light is susceptible, however, of being perceived as a symbol of transcendence when one assumes that the whole poem is a mystical one. The possibility arises at the point of the next stanza where this "light or guide" burning within her heart gives way to the night itself as a light as lovely as the dawn:

> O night which so guided!
> O night kinder than the dawn!
> O night which joined
> Lover with his beloved
> Transforming the beloved in her lover. (5)

This fifth stanza thus becomes the key to the whole poem, for in it one finds what seems to be indubitably of a mystical nature in its expression. For a close analysis of this it is better to take the first two verses as a unity in their poetic meaning, and then to consider the last three also as a unity in themselves.

The first two lines, by shifting the focus from the light burning in her heart as her passionate love for her beloved, to the night itself as being the guiding light brighter than dawn itself, have truly created a metaphor whereby the heart's desire as guiding light becomes the night itself as a light brighter than daybreak. This metaphor is usually understood as the mystical "Ray of divine Darkness" of *The Mystical Theology* of Dionysius the Areopagite,[12] thus making of this metaphor of the horizontal plane of human love a symbol of transcendence pointing to the vertical plane. But such a confusion of the horizontal metaphor with the vertical symbol creates an awkward problem for the meaning of the poem itself, since it is not a "Ray of Darkness" that makes poetic and aesthetic sense within the structure of the poem but, rather, the more mundane description that the night itself as a natural phenomenon allows her to go under the cover of darkness in a way which she could not have done in broad daylight. This is why night itself is "more lovely than the dawn!" and thus metaphorically functions as light to her heart's desire. Any superimposition of a transcendent symbol of mysticism is extraneous to the aesthetic poetic sense. It is not necessary to explain and understand the self-consistent meaning of the poem.

At this juncture, it is pertinent to say that there is not a single word in the "Night" which, taken by itself, might have an obvious and explicitly theological meaning. For example: God, the soul, Jesus, Christ, faith, hope, redemption, purgation, illumination, as well as other religious terms, are never mentioned; this is not the case with all the other poems of John, without exception. The purely secular nature of the vocabulary of this poem seems, however, to break down just in the next three lines which have to be analyzed now. Again it shall be shown that what is so obviously mystical has, nevertheless, so many ambiguities that a secular or profane understanding of this love makes better sense than if suddenly one were to recast the whole meaning of the poem already explained, into one of mystical love.

The third line of this fifth stanza contains the key word "joined" as a past tense of the verb "to join." This has been translated, almost without exception, into English as "united," thus introducing into its meaning the concept of the verb "to unite" (Spanish, *unir*), rather than its original "to join."[13] This might seem insignificant and the verbs close enough in their respective meanings to warrant validity to such a translation. The problem nevertheless is not a minor one, for it creates obvious ambivalent meanings. Furthermore, from the strict philological and semantic usage of John's terms, it constitutes a most rare exception in his vocabulary. The fact is, John, in his own commentaries to his major poems already mentioned, never uses this verb or its derivative "to join" as a synonym or substitute for the verb "to unite" and its derivatives, union, united, and so forth. There is in his whole corpus only one instance where the verb "to join" *(juntar)* appears, not by itself but as a parallel of the verb "to unite." In this instance, "to unite" appears first, followed by "to join." This is the text: "for love is the only one which unites and joins the soul with God."[14] This usage is an anomaly in John's writings, and one may construe the fact that "joins" appears after "unites" thereby qualifies the former in such a way that whatever else it might mean in this context, it also means "unites." Thus the exception is qualified. If in his commentaries John always uses "to unite" when referring to the substantial union with God, with this one exception, in his poetry he never uses either of the two terms, again with the exception of this poem. This is quite remarkable, since one would expect him to use it, if not in "The Canticle," at least in his poem "Stanzas Concerning an Ecstasy," where the Dionysian motifs of the "Docta ignorantia" are clearly stated from the beginning: "I entered into unknowing, / And there I remained unknowing, Transcending all knowledge." There is not, therefore, any poetic text of John's which might be used for a comparative analysis, while his prose materials very definitely show that "union," and not "joined," is his carefully chosen term to express the experience of mystical union of the soul with God, or Christ. This is also so in other Spanish Mystics.[15]

Granted, there is a certain degree of ambiguity in this term; nevertheless, it points toward a secular rather than a divine joining. Ambiguity is both the suggestiveness and richness of poetry; it makes it more complex and subtle in its meaning. Quite probably John chose this ambiguous term in a very conscious way. But by its context this term strongly suggests the "joining" in a sexual act of intimate love. Yet, the fact that the term "union," or its derivatives, is not used in this context shows John's careful avoidance of an explicit identification of the lovers' experience with that of the mystical experience of union.

Be this as it may, the fact is that the last line of this stanza, "Transforming the beloved in her lover," presses this very issue to its uttermost mystical meaning and might be, after all, the single most crucial text, for its explicit usage of the verb "to transform" qualifies, so it seems, this act of love as the *theopoiesis* or divine transformation of the soul in her Beloved. If this be so, the inescapable conclusion would be that this line is the "clincher" and states without ambiguity the metaphysical, ontological, and psychological transformation of the soul in its experience of union with God, becoming thus divine by the substantial union with God in the experience of mystical love.

The motif of mystical *theopoiesis,* in this line, cannot be lightly brushed aside; and this is the reason why such a word, by itself, has enough aesthetic power to *transform* the whole poem into a mystical one, and this even in spite of all that has been said here so far. This is why it is pertinent here to quote the interpretation which I myself some years ago thought to be the correct one: "The line 'Transforming the beloved into her lover' never has been or can be an erotico-sexual experience. Here John is expressing poetically the *theopoiesis,* or divinization of the soul, being united and transformed into the divine essence."[16]

Some years later, however, I realized that I had introduced the concept of *union* in a verse and poem which never uses it. Thus, a poetic meaning had to be found which, while being faithful to the text itself, would not assume what was not there stated. Could there be other meanings of the word "transforming"? But why use the verb "to transform" while avoiding the verb "to unite," within the same stanza? A critic, Domingo Ynduráin, took care of that.[17] The motif of *transformation,* it now became clear, is not an exclusively mystical one, although it has its semantic and philological roots in it. It is rather commonly used in the Renaissance by secular poets in their envisioning a world of love and affection at the plane of a human love between man and woman and the poet's desire for his object of love. Yet the word, or theme itself, derives from Neoplatonic sources and the whole psychological worldview of Neoplatonism with its love-eros as a theme of transformation of the lover in the object of his love. This motif at the vertical, transcendent plane provides the ontological source for the transformation of the soul into her beloved, or mystical *theopoiesis.*

Ynduráin provided the specific textual evidence in both Spanish and Portuguese Renaissance literature, showing clearly that the theme of *transformation* appears as a motif of profane love in poets such as the Spanish poet Jorge de Montemayor (1520–1561) and the Portuguese Luiz Vaz de Camoëns (1524–1580), among others. Two quotations from these two poets will suffice. First from Montemayor:

> Afterwards when in my breast
> Love abides in me
> And in it I am transformed.

The second one, from Camoëns, is an even better example:

> Transformed is love in the thing it loves
> By virtue of much imagination
> I have then nothing more to desire
> Since within me I have the object desired
> When in her is my own soul transformed.[18]

These quotations, and more which could be added, make it clear that the theme of transformation cannot be claimed to be only a mystical motif. In this respect, then, John's poem appears now as one which might, without doing violence to its text, be understood as a self-consistent poetic creation about human love. But there is in the "Night," as a poem, something which is unique and striking for its apparent novelty in the usage of the motif of transformation. For while in Montemayor and Camoëns, as well as in others, the theme of transformation in their poems is still conceptually structured as a Neoplatonic motif on its way to becoming a secular one, the same theme in John's poem has already been stripped of its Neoplatonic thought forms insofar as the poem itself does not presuppose the ideal world of the other poets with their obviously Platonic references to desire, imagination, within one's breast, soul, and so forth.

John's motif of transformation is not idealized but *realized* in a direct act of human love between male and female who are "joined" in love, but not united, and the love between them is described by the female lover without any hints of embarrassment or palliated with religious language, either of topical theology or the Greco-Roman classical mythology, as was the case in most of the Renaissance poets from Montemayor to Garcilaso and even Cervantes. The personages and landscape of the "Night" are so free from this kind of poetic setting that one does not even notice such an absence, but rather it is taken for granted, and so also is the identification of the "Night" with "The Canticle."[19]

Once this last image is understood as a secular theme, there is nothing else in the poem which might be an obstacle to such an interpretation. If the night is not a symbol of transcendence but an image limited to a clearly confined theme of human love which functions within such limitations imposed by the night itself, then all the other images subordinated to the night are realized within the strict limitations of this natural phenomenon which lovers desire more than the light of dawn. It is because of this that John does not complete his poem with the daybreak, while the lovers experience the wonders of human love as described by "suspending all my senses" in the last line of the seventh stanza. But if there is no reference to "light" at the end of the poem, at least some explicit reference to mystical ecstasy would do. At the end, however, there is neither light nor ecstasy, but a description of the female experience of love:

> I tarried and forgot myself,
> Reclining my face on my beloved.
> All ceased, and I abandoned myself,
> Leaving my care
> Forgotten among the lilies. (8)

This ending may describe the suspension of the senses or the senses' delight, but it does not open up beyond this. One cannot take this for a "mystical ecstasy" when everything else in the poem does not warrant it. It is this directness and self-sufficiency of images, without the need of making them into symbols of transcendence, that gives to this poem a unique place in John's whole corpus.

This stark fact reveals both John's original aesthetic poetic intention and the later necessity of transforming the poem into an allegory of mysticism. This was done first by John in his two commentaries to the poem, and then by all subsequent interpreters. For John the explicit sexuality of the poem, without reference to transcendence, had to be disguised with theological interpretations in his commentaries; for interpreters and critics this quite explicit sexuality was too obvious to be true. It had to have a deeper meaning. Thus the theological motifs and structures of "The Canticle" were superimposed on the "Night," creating confusion in their separate meanings and telescoping both poems into one as a short and long version of the same religious themes.

More detailed analysis of the poetic images of the "Night" as a poem is certainly necessary in order to explore the difference between the images of the "Night" and the symbols of John's other poems, as well as many other complex issues regarding sources and John's creative usage of them. But this has already been done elsewhere.[20] Let us then turn now to the relationship between the poem and its commentaries.

The Commentaries to the Poem

It is pertinent here to explore a little more carefully the relationship between the two incomplete commentaries to the "Night" as a poem. It is rather unusual that in his first commentary to this poem, the *Ascent of Mount Carmel,* John comments only on the first two stanzas; and again in his second commentary, *Dark Night,* after having commented on the same first two stanzas, he further comments only in part on the third stanza—that is to say, the first three lines out of five. As commentaries on the same poem they both cover about the same amount of verses; nevertheless, both commentaries are quite different in methodology. The *Ascent* is not even a commentary, properly speaking, for it does not attempt to write *glosas* to the poem, verse by verse; rather, it is an attempt to write a systematic mystical work, using the poem only indirectly. Thus, the title *Ascent of Mount Carmel* does not fit within the motif, scope, and structure of the poem, for there is no such topic of "ascent" to Mount Carmel in the poem itself. On the contrary, there is only a *descent* or climbing down the secret ladder by the young female on her way to the secret rendezvous with her beloved. In spite of all this, the central theme of the frustrated commentary is the *ascent* to the mountain as the mystical ladder of love at its vertical transcendent plane. There is clearly a transmutation of the images of the "Night" now subordinated to the *inverted* usage of the ladder, which ceases to function as a tool to reach the ground from an upper room. Thus the horizontal space of the poem is metaphysically transformed into its opposite, the vertical, and with it the symbolic language of mysticism with its three *vias: purgativa, illuminativa,* and *unitiva,* and the correspondent three dark nights—of the senses, of the soul, and of the spirit. But what is significant in all this is the fact that John packs all these mystical topics, and thoroughly develops them, within the short scope of the two first stanzas of the poem. This is done in such an arbitrary way that there is no apparent need of dealing with the rest of the stanzas. The commentary on the poem thus ends abruptly, but the mystical topics and theological exposition are rather extensive. This explains why the *Ascent of Mount Carmel* is the most extensive of all John's commentaries on his poems, while at the same time it is the shortest in its coverage of verses. Obviously the poem was not necessary to write this theological work.

The second commentary on this poem bears the same title as the poem *(Dark Night),* clearly indicating his intention to restrict his theological comments to the poem. Yet in spite of this, the commentary is not so different in theological content and hardly covers any more lines. There is a great deal of repetitive material which shows that ultimately both works issue from John's mystical world of thought rather than from the poem itself. It is rather obvious that the poem cannot be the source of John's mystical ideas for his two commentaries on the "Night." This second commentary, although covering three verses more of the poem, nevertheless is much shorter than the first one.

It seems now rather plausible that John's twice-frustrated commentary on this poem is nevertheless not a frustrated mystical treatise, for he covers in both what is at the core of mystical theology and its universal motifs. It can be said, then, that John could have written much better mystical works if he were totally independent from the poem in the first place. The poem thus impaired his attempt to write a truly systematic work on mysticism.

There is something in his two frustrated commentaries on this poem which is rather striking in many respects. By one commentary's stopping at the end of the second stanza, and the other's at the third verse of the third stanza, John completely avoids direct theological commentaries on some of the most crucial images of the poem, such as the "light and guide" (3:4), and the "joining" of the lovers and the consequent "transformation" (5:3–5). And he also eschews commentaries on the very erotic last two stanzas of the poem. Nevertheless, this does not restrict John in his elaboration of mystical themes, which he develops by allegorizing the other verses.

The "Night" creates great difficulties for John as a source of his mystical commentaries and topics, but this is not the case with the other two poems, "The Canticle" and "The Living Flame." Thus, this seems to corroborate what has been already suggested: that the "Night" is a poem about profane love. But if this is so, the poem ought to be looked on not as it always has been—viz., a poetic creation expressing an original mystical experience—but rather as a self-sufficient, self-explained, and unique aesthetic creation which envisions a world at the horizontal plane where profane love is both its motif and aesthetic pleasure. Thus, the "Night," as a poem, cannot be understood as the "Dark Night of the Soul" but rather as the senses' delight; and its contribution is not in the realm of theology but of literature. It is, then, a critique of the aesthetic character of this poem that ought to determine its poetic content.

Conclusion

A literal rendering of the poem in English translation shows neither a theological, mystical worldview, often injected in standard English translations,[21] nor indeed its masterful use of the Castilian language, of which it is, without question, one of the literary gems. It is because of this highest aesthetic quality that his poem is so highly praised in Spanish literature, although always assuming its religious content. It ranks above all the poetry of Teresa of Avila, which is not to say much, but also above Luis de León, and even rivals Garcilaso, the Spanish Renaissance poet par excellence. There is an adroitness in this poem which is indeed unique, and it is because of this that it ranks higher than John's other masterpiece, "The Spiritual Canticle," as a poetic creation.

It is my intention here to give due credit to this aspect of John's poem which has been totally neglected insofar as it has been perceived and envisioned as a mystical poem only. This in no way detracts from John's creativity as a mystical writer of the highest rank, and of his universal recognition as a master of mystical spirituality. On the contrary, it gives to him that which for so long has been denied to him, that place of honor not only among the religious poets of Spain but also among the secular ones. In showing this other, neglected aspect of his creativity, John becomes indeed a more realized, complex, and complete poet in a way which has not been seen before. As for the symbol of the "Dark Night of the Soul," he still remains, if not its poetic creator, certainly the theologian who, by allegorizing his own poetry of the "Night," made of it a universal symbol of mysticism in his twice-frustrated commentary. Thus, the symbol of the "Dark Night of the Soul" also belongs to him, but in a qualified and very different way than it was thought before.

John belongs to the world of the Renaissance through this unique poetic creation, besides his other poems, and to the world of the Counter-Reformation for his intensive search for a more meaningful, and more personal, religious experience which ultimately is freed from the ecclesiastical institutions, even though he remained within them as a Submissive Rebel.[22]

NOTES

1. The standard biographical study on John of the Cross is Silverio de Santa Teresa, O.C.D., *Historia del Carmen Descalzo en España,*

Portugal y América. Volume 5 is devoted to John (Burgos: Tipografía Burgalesa [El Monte Carmelo], 1936). A more recent and updated biography is the one by Crisógono de Jesús, O.C.D., which is included, together with the complete works of St. John of the Cross, in the *Vida y obras de San Juan de la Cruz,* published by the Editorial Católica, Madrid, in the series Biblioteca de Autores Cristianos. There are several editions of this work, with slight revisions and additions. For the English text, *The Collected Works of St. John of the Cross,* tr. Kieran Kavanaugh, O.C.D., and Otilio Rodríguez, O.C.D. (Washington, D.C.: Institute of Carmelite Studies, 1964; paperback 1973), contains his complete works in a more recent translation. Also useful is *John of the Cross: Selected Writings,* Classics of Western Spirituality (Mahwah, N.J.: Paulist Press, 1987), ed. by K. Kavanaugh. It also provides a basic bibliography.

2. Cf. José C. Nieto, *Mystic, Rebel, Saint: A Study of St. John of the Cross* (Geneva: Droz, 1979). This work, revised and enlarged, appeared in Spanish as *Místico, Poeta, Rebelde, Santo: En torno a San Juan de la Cruz* (Mexico City, Madrid: Fondo de Cultura Económica, 1982). Among the new chapters of this edition is a study of John's poem "The Spiritual Canticle."

3. For my views on this, see *Mystic, Rebel, Saint,* pp. 121–123, and *Místico, Poeta, Rebelde, Santo,* pp. 125–144.

4. I deal extensively with this historiographic assumption and my critique of it in the Introduction and chapter 5 of my forthcoming book *San Juan de la Cruz, poeta del amor profano,* to be published in El Escorial, Madrid, by Editorial Swan.

5. By "cantification" I mean the process by which the "Night," as a poem, came to be identified with "The Canticle" as a poem, i.e., to make a canticle out of the "Night."

6. My literal translation of the "Night," provided at the beginning of this essay, makes available for the first time to the English-speaking reader a closer understanding of it, stripped of any theological overlays, of which we shall give some examples later.

7. For the full English text of "The Canticle" see either of Kavanaugh's editions mentioned in note 1. The numbers in parentheses (22B) indicate the stanza of the poem, while "B" stands for the second or final redaction of this poem.

8. The number in parentheses refers to the stanza; if lines or verses are indicated, then the numbers following the stanza will indicate thus. Example (6:2–3). The "Night" has only one redaction of its poetic text.

9. This is shown quite explicitly, however, in the poem "More Stanzas Applied to Spiritual Things of Christ and the Soul," better known as "Un pastorcico," or "Young Shepherd." Here the love between Christ and the soul has both the attributes of transcendence and Christ's passion wounds:

The Shepherd says: I pity the one
Who draws himself back from my
love,
And does not seek the joy of my
presence,
Though my heart is an open wound
with love for him.
After a long time he climbed a
tree,
And spread his beautiful
arms
And hung by them, and died,
His heart an open wound with love. (4–5)

(From *The Collected Works of St. John of the Cross,* translated by Kieran Kavanaugh and Otilio Rodriguez, © 1979 by Washington Province of Discalced Carmelites. ICS Publications, 2131 Lincoln Road, N.E., Washington, DC 20002. Used by permission.) I have kept the original "beautiful" rather than the "shining" of the translation.

10. Kavanaugh's translation, except for the words "wife" and "violated," which I have kept to better reflect the original. This poetic motif is the popular pastoral theme of the Renaissance.

11. For the images of space and time and the mythical and fabulous landscapes of "The Canticle," see Colin P. Thompson, *The Poet and the Mystic* (London: Oxford University Press, 1977); also see Nieto, *Místico, Poeta, Rebelde, Santo,* pp. 76–87.

12. John himself makes reference to the Areopagite's *Mystical Theology* in his commentary *Ascent of Mount Carmel,* which is an indirect commentary on this poem. But his reference does not correspond to this verse, which John never commented on, either in the *Ascent* or in the *Dark Night.* For John's textual reference to *Mystical Theology,* see *Ascent* II.6. It refers to chapter I, paragraph 1 (Migne, *Patrologia Graeca* 3:999). For an English translation, see C. E. Rolt's edition (London: S.P.C.K., 5th impr., 1971), p. 192. The Areopagite's symbol is an obvious one since there is reference to "darkness" and "light." But to do this is to transform the metaphorical image of a human love into a transcendent symbol which is not needed within the motif of the poem itself.

13. Kavanaugh's translation reads, "O night that has united." And even stronger words appear in the now classic translation of E. Allison Peers (London: Burns, Oates & Washbourne, 1934–35). Peers, in his *The Complete Works of St. John of the Cross* (3 vols.), translates this verse thus: "O night that madest us, Lover and lov'd, as one." Scholars analyzing the original Castilian text, of course, do not face this problem; nevertheless they read the Spanish text *as if* in fact this is what it means.

14. This text appears in the commentary *Night* II.18.5.

15. Cf. Melquiades Andres Martin, *Los recogidos. Nueva visión de la mística española (1500–1700)* (Madrid: Fundación Universitaria Español, 1976). The index of subjects does not list "to join," but only "to unite," pp. 836–840.

16. See Nieto, *Místico, Poeta, Rebelde, Santo,* p. 72, in the new material of the Spanish edition.

17. See *San Juan de la Cruz: Poesía,* ed. Domingo Ynduráin (Madrid: Ediciónes Cátedra, 1984). Ynduráin, in commenting on my quotation, makes references to Ficino's *Commentary on Plato's Symposium* (Seventh Oration, Chapters VIII, and II, VIII), as well as León Hebreo's *Dialogues of Love* and Castiglione's *The Courtier.* But it is the Portuguese and Castilian poetic examples which are most significant as paralleling John's usage of this word.

18. Both are from *Cancionero de Gallardo,* as quoted by Ynduráin, p. 210 (translation mine). Ynduráin thus explains that such an affirmation is unwarranted, saying my quotation is "too categorical" (p. 210). This is why he offers those very convincing examples of "transformation" as a secular theme.

19. This is so even in the case of Ynduráin himself, for the fact that he was able to identify the secular sources of the theme of transformation did not alter his vision of the "Night" as a poem. He still assumes that the "Night" and "The Canticle," as poems, share in the same mystical theme. Thus he says: "In the poem 'Night' the same plot is described as in the 'Canticle,' but the circumstantial references have been eliminated, leaving unchanged the process—through internalization—which leads to the encounter and union" (p. 215). It is evident, then, that an understanding of the profane-love motif of the "Night" cannot be derived from the analysis of isolated words, but rather from a thorough rethinking of the poem's structure and its aesthetic motif as a whole. George Tavard, in his *Poetry and Contemplation in St. John of the Cross* (Athens, Ohio: Ohio University Press, 1988, p. 54), links the "Night" as a poem with the theme of the obviously mystical poem "I entered where I knew not," thus superimposing an extraneous theme to it from other of John's poems.

20. This has been done in detail in my forthcoming *San Juan de la Cruz, poeta del amor profano,* chapters 9–12.

21. One last example: Kavanaugh translates the verse: "¡Oh dichosa ventura!" (1.3 and 2.3) as "Ah, the sheer grace!" while a correct translation would be either "O happy venture!" or "O happy chance!"

22. See Nieto, "Two Spanish Mystics as Submissive Rebels," *Bibliothèque d'Humanisme et Renaissance* 33 (1971), 268–419; and *Mystic, Rebel, Saint,* pp. 29–39.

John Wilkins and Galileo Galilei: Copernicanism and Biblical Interpretation in the Protestant and Catholic Traditions

Gary B. Deason

The Bible and the Copernican Revolution

The term "Copernican Revolution" refers to the ideas and events associated with the acceptance of a heliocentric world view in the years between the publication of Copernicus' *De Revolutionibus* in 1543 and Newton's *Principia Mathematica* in 1687. As might be expected of a major revolution in the way human beings conceive of the world, the Copernican Revolution involved complex and far-reaching issues. Among the many subjects debated in the course of the Revolution, heliocentrism and the Bible played only a part in the overall drama. Technical, commonsensical, and philosophical questions left unanswered by Copernicus himself dominated the issues addressed by succeeding generations. If the earth moved in orbit, for instance, why were astronomers unable to detect change in the relative positions of stars (the phenomenon of parallax)? Why does a vertical projectile come back to its point of origin if the earth has moved during the object's flight? How does a marksman ever hit a north-south target without adjusting for the east-west rotation of the earth? On the philosophical side, there were questions as to whether Copernicus had intended heliocentrism as a truth claim about the heavens or merely as a hypothetical model more convenient than geocentrism for the day-to-day work of the astronomer, navigator, or calendar reformer.[1]

None of these questions, to mention only a few, had been answered by the time of the informal injunction against Galileo's teaching of Copernicanism in 1616. Not even

Galileo's telescope—which is commonly assumed to have settled the matter—provided conclusive evidence. Of the four major discoveries announced in *Starry Messenger* (1610), only the phases of Venus appeared directly to support Copernicanism over Aristotelianism, and even this observation could be explained by Tycho Brahe's alternative geocentric model.[2]

The recognition of scientific and philosophical problems surrounding heliocentrism has direct bearing on the assessment of issues related to Copernicanism and scripture. If Copernicanism had had conclusive scientific support and had made sense of everyday phenomena, the persuasiveness of the case for reinterpretation of biblical passages that appeared to conflict with it would have been far stronger than that dictated by the ambiguous evidence available at the time.[3] Unfortunately, modern writing on this subject has assumed conclusive evidence in support of heliocentrism and has seen biblical issues as part of the reactionary response of narrow-minded ecclesiastics.[4] While there was no shortage of stubbornness on any side in the Copernican Revolution, modern writers forget that they have the advantage of three centuries of additional confirmation of the Copernican theory, a luxury not afforded participants in the historical debate. As we turn to discussion of scripture and astronomy, the reader should remember that discussion of this subject in isolation from nonbiblical issues introduces an element of artificiality and raises a flag of caution. With this forewarning in mind, let us review the twentieth-century discussion of biblical issues in the Copernican Revolution.

Contemporary Discussion

History of science texts published since A. D. White's *A History of the Warfare of Science with Theology in Christendom* (1895) that mention Protestant biblical interpretation in connection with Copernicanism almost always present a negative picture. Usually citing remarks of Luther and Melanchthon and attributing to Calvin a statement which subsequently has not been found in his works, they repeat the refrain that the Protestant principle of *sola scriptura* and adherence to the plain meaning (literal reading) of biblical texts set the Reformation in opposition to the new astronomy.[5] For example, Thomas Kuhn's widely read and otherwise valuable *The Copernican Revolution* (1957) takes from White the following remark, which, in turn, was taken from the Aurifaber version of Luther's *Table Talk:*

> People gave ear to an upstart astrologer who strove to show that the earth revolves, not the heavens or the firmament, the sun and the moon. . . . This fool wishes to reverse the entire science of astronomy; but sacred Scripture tells us [Joshua 10:13] that Joshua commanded the sun to stand still and not the earth.[6]

Kuhn continues to depend on White in citing a remark supposedly found in Calvin's *Commentary on Genesis:* "The earth is stablished, that it cannot move or be moved. . . . Who will venture to place the authority of Copernicus above that of the Holy Spirit?"[7] In an excellent piece of detective work, Edward Rosen has shown that White took this from F. W. Farrar, who relied on his prodigious memory for quotation—this time incorrectly.[8]

The citation from Luther, the spurious remark of Calvin, and a citation from Melanchthon have been used repeatedly in support of the conclusion that Protestant biblicism set the Reformation at odds with the new astronomy. For example, Dorothy Stimson writes, "For the absolute authority of the Pope the Protestant leaders substituted the absolute authority of the Bible. It is not strange, then, that they ignored or derided a theory as yet unsupported by proof and so difficult to harmonize with a literally accepted Bible."[9] Herbert Butterfield draws the same conclusion: "When Copernicus's work first appeared it provoked religious objections, especially on Biblical grounds, and since the Protestants were the party particularly inclined to what was called Bibliolatry, some scathing condemnations very soon appeared from their side—for example, from Luther and Melanchthon personally."[10] Alan G. R. Smith, citing Luther, Melanchthon, and the spurious remark of Calvin, observes, "These vehement condemnations by Protestant leaders were not repeated at the time by Catholic dignitaries, who were less immediately ready to resort to literal interpretations than their Protestant counterparts."[11] Thomas Kuhn epitomizes the views of most historians on the subject of Protestant biblical interpretation and Copernican astronomy when he writes:

> The bitterness of official Protestant opposition is, in practice, far easier to understand than its Catholic counterpart. . . . Luther and Calvin and their followers wished to return to a pristine Christianity, as it could be discovered in the words of Jesus and the early Fathers of the Church. To Protestant leaders the Bible was the single fundamental source of Christian knowledge. . . . They abhorred the elaborate metaphorical and allegorical interpretation of Scripture, and their literal adherence to the Bible in matters of

> cosmology had no parallel since the days of Lactantius, Basil, and Kosmas. To them Copernicus may well have seemed a symbol of all the tortuous reinterpretations which, during the later Middle Ages, had separated Christians from the basis of their belief. Therefore the violence of the thunder that official Protestantism directed at Copernicus seems almost natural. Toleration of Copernicanism would have been toleration of the very attitude toward Holy Writ and toward knowledge in general which, according to Protestants, had led Christianity astray.[12]

The works cited above indicate the extent to which the standard view sees Protestant opposition to Copernicus as biblically based, while implying that Catholic approaches to scripture more easily accommodated the new astronomy. These writers depict the early opposition of Luther, Calvin, and Melanchthon as natural or characteristic of Protestantism and suggest that this conflict continued unbroken throughout the Copernican Revolution. Early Catholic neutrality toward Copernicus, on the other hand, made possible by a flexible approach to scripture, gave way after the Council of Trent to the increasing conservatism of the Counter-Reformation and culminated in the unfortunate condemnation of Galileo and the new astronomy. The accepted view, in summary, sees biblical hermeneutics as the key to understanding Protestant attitudes toward Copernicus but emphasizes social, political, and theological repercussions following the division of the church as the primary impetus behind later Catholic opposition.

In this article, I do not reject the accepted view entirely. Instead, I revise it to present a more balanced picture of Protestant and Catholic hermeneutics in relation to Copernicanism. First, by focusing on a leading seventeenth-century Protestant—John Wilkins—writing at a time when knowledge of Copernicanism was more widespread and more accurate than in the early Reformation period, I argue that characteristic Protestant approaches to scripture, including the principle of *sola scriptura* and the emphasis on the literal sense of biblical passages, led by then to an accommodation between Copernicanism and scripture entirely unexpected on the basis of the remarks of early Reformers. Second, by comparing Wilkins' use of the Bible in dealing with the new astronomy to Galileo's, whose hermeneutical principles remained faithful to Catholic tradition, I argue that Galileo had a *far more difficult* task than Wilkins. Galileo's need to (1) reconcile scripture and tradition, (2) employ multiple levels of meaning, and (3) unify scientific truths with biblical truths left him with a significantly greater challenge than his Protestant counterpart. While acknowledging elements of truth in the accepted view, at least for the early period, I argue that closer attention to seventeenth-century writings and an approach comparing Protestants and Catholics suggest that later discussions of Copernicanism and the Bible followed a pattern just the reverse of the accepted view.

Before turning to Galileo and Wilkins, however, we should look more closely at the article of Brian Gerrish (see note 5) because it has added important qualifications to the standard view.[13] Gerrish acknowledges that Luther and Melanchthon (but not Calvin) cited scripture against Copernicus and accepts the claim made by White and others that the early Reformers saw a conflict between heliocentrism and the literal sense of some biblical passages. Gerrish resolutely denounces, on the other hand, the procedure by which White and others jump from citation of a few isolated remarks to the conclusion that Protestant biblical hermeneutics set the entire Reformation against the new science. Numerous passages in the works of Luther, Calvin, and Melanchthon show their recognition of the importance of science for displaying God's handiwork in nature. The Reformers' attitude toward science, Gerrish emphasizes, must be gleaned from a study of all their writings, not just from a few brief quotations.

Gerrish describes several features of Luther's and Calvin's hermeneutics having important implications for our understanding of biblical interpretation and astronomy in the Protestant tradition. What might be called a "theory of multiple discourse" allowed Luther to claim that the same words or phrases may have different meanings in different contexts. The words "God is man" do not mean the same thing for the philosopher and the theologian. Since meanings may differ from discipline to discipline, there can be no real contradiction between disciplines. Real contradiction occurs only *within* a single discipline where the meaning of words ought to be consistent. Thus the astronomer and the biblical exegete, for example, read the same passage of scripture through different eyes. The astronomer, Luther observed, may see the moon as a reflection of the sun, whereas the believer may see it as a token of divine care.[14] Both views are true, but true in separate realms of discourse.

Regarding Calvin, Gerrish reminds us of a point first emphasized in Professor Dowey's *The Knowledge of God in Calvin's Theology* (1952).[15] All of God's revelation to human beings—in scripture, in creation, and through the Holy Spirit—is *accommodated* to their limited capacity for understanding him. Knowledge of God comes from God's self-revelation, not directly as he is in himself but indirectly in forms adapted to human frailty. In addition to the *general* accommodation of God, Calvin speaks of the *specific* accommodation of scripture to limitations of knowledge and culture among the Israelites. The primitive state of Hebrew science at the time of the writing of the Bible, according to Calvin, led God to represent the motion of the heavens as they appear to the unlearned observer, not as they are understood by the astronomer. The purpose of the biblical account of creation, Calvin said, is not to impart technical information about the heavens but to induce thankfulness to God for having created the world. This religious purpose does not conflict with scientific interest, but it does lead to a different manner of speaking, one which the simplest believer can understand. Thus, for example, the expression "great lights" in Genesis 1:16 does not refer to the actual size of the sun and the moon but to their appearance in the eye of the observer.

The importance of Gerrish's article is to remind us that Luther and Calvin held far more complex views of scripture than are implied in the isolated remarks repetitiously cited by historians. When fully elucidated, their biblical hermeneutics had *potential* for resolving apparent conflicts between Copernicanism and the Bible, even if they themselves, because of the upstart character of the new theory or for other reasons, spoke against it (Luther and Melanchthon) or failed to consider it at all (Calvin). It is not within the scope of Gerrish's article to discuss whether this potential is fulfilled among later generations of Protestants or to assess it in relation to Catholic biblical hermeneutics. By examining Wilkins' and Galileo's approaches to the Bible in relation to their views on Copernicanism, I extend several of Gerrish's points into the seventeenth-century discussion and strengthen them by drawing comparisons with Catholicism. In particular, Wilkins' sharp separation of the disciplines of biblical theology and astronomy resembled Luther's theory of multiple discourse and allowed him, unlike Galileo, to advocate the new heliocentric theory without having to concern himself with its scriptural consistency or inconsistency. Moreover, although Wilkins and Galileo employed a principle of accommodation similar to that of Calvin, only Wilkins was able to use the principle fully to his advantage. By limiting the meaning of a text to its literal sense, Wilkins was able to say that the entire text had been accommodated and therefore had no relation to the science of astronomy. By contrast, continuing the Catholic practice of finding several levels of meaning in a single passage of scripture, Galileo could say only that the plain sense of the text had been accommodated to unlearned minds. The deeper meaning still had to be shown consistent with the technical requirements of the astronomer—a remarkably difficult task, even for Galileo.

Galileo's *Letter to the Grand Duchess Christina* (1615)

Public objections to Copernicanism based on scripture were rare in Italy until after the publication in 1612 of Galileo's *Letters on Sunspots.* Written in the vernacular and explicitly endorsing Copernicanism, the *Letters* enhanced popular discussion of the subject and contributed to the growing controversy. A year after their publication Galileo's friend and mathematician at the University of Pisa, Benedetto Castelli, defended heliocentrism after a dinner given by Grand Duke Cosimo II and attended by his mother, the Grand Duchess Christina. Castelli relayed news of the event to Galileo, who immediately drafted and circulated the "Letter to Castelli" (1613), a summary of his views on Copernicanism and scripture and prototype of the *Letter to Christina.* In the period between the two letters, public opposition based on scripture grew. Heliocentrism was attacked from the pulpit of Santa Maria Novella in Florence on December 20, 1614, by the Dominican friar, Father Tommaso Caccini. Not long afterward another Dominican, Father Niccolo Lorini, sent a copy of the "Letter to Castelli" to one of the Inquisitors-General in Rome. Lorini complained, above all, that Galileo and his followers took it on themselves to expound scripture according to their own opinions and contrary to the common interpretation of the Fathers of the church. Thus Lorini associated the specter of Protestantism with Galileo. Had not the Council of Trent already denounced private interpretation of scripture contrary to the teaching of the Fathers?[16] Lorini's accusations and the imposing authority of Trent help to explain Galileo's attention in the expanded letter to the different question of biblical interpretation contrary to the common teaching of the Church Fathers. This issue was a tough hurdle for Catholic Copernicans, since the Fathers, without exception, accepted the geocentric cosmology of their times.

Addressing the issue in a central section of the *Letter to Christina,* Galileo built on a distinction, which he found in Augustine's *De Genesi ad litteram,* between physical propositions in the Bible and propositions teaching faith and morals. Augustine maintained that the authors of the Bible knew the truths of astronomy (and other technical sciences) but did not present them in scripture because they had nothing to do with faith and morals. "The Holy Spirit," Galileo cites Augustine, "did not desire that men should learn things that are useful to no one for salvation." Since it was not the intention of biblical authors to teach physical truths, he adds, the Bible should not be used in deciding scientific controversies, much less in determining "that one belief is required by faith, while the other side is erroneous."[17] Here Galileo followed the long-standing Catholic tradition that physical propositions in the Bible were *adiaphora.* Claims about the nature or structure of the heavens or earth were not matters of doctrine. He concluded that the Fathers, recognizing the irrelevance for faith and morals of physical claims, never bothered to analyze or debate cosmological issues. They simply accepted Aristotelian cosmology as a matter of custom, without discussing its validity or invalidity. If the Fathers never considered the issue, it is inappropriate to use their casual (albeit consistent) references to geocentrism as evidence against heliocentrism.[18]

Finally, Galileo adds, the decree of the Council of Trent against interpretation of biblical passages contrary to the unanimous teaching of the Fathers explicitly applies only to passages pertaining to faith and morals, not to physical propositions. Those who claim that the decree of the Council applies to physical propositions use "an arbitrary simplification of council decrees . . . to favor their own opinions." "All that is really prohibited," Galileo emphasizes, "is the 'perverting into senses contrary to that of the holy Church or that of the concurrent agreement of the Fathers those passages, and those alone, *which pertain to faith and ethics,* or which concern the edification of Christian doctrine.' "[19] Unfortunately for Galileo and his followers, as reasonable and eminent a churchman as Cardinal Robert Bellarmine took issue with this conclusion. Writing to a Carmelite friar, Paolo Antonio Foscarini, who published a book about the same time as Galileo's *Letter* arguing that Copernicanism and scripture were consistent, Cardinal Bellarmine discounted the claim that the unanimous agreement of biblical authors and Church Fathers has authority only in matters of faith and morals. Their authority, he observes, derives not only from the subject matter of their statements but also from their persons. We must acknowledge the veracity of propositions, even physical propositions, on which biblical authors and Church Fathers agree. After all, Bellarmine claims, a statement such as "Abraham had two sons and Jacob twelve" is a physical proposition on which all agree. To deny it would be heretical.[20]

In addition to the problem of the Bible and tradition, a second obstacle arising from Galileo's Catholic hermeneutics involved the practice of finding multiple meanings in biblical passages. Most commentators have assumed that this practice facilitated the reconciliation of problematic passages with the Copernican system. By claiming that another meaning lay behind the literal sense of the text, Galileo could sidestep apparent contradictions between the plain meaning and heliocentrism. At one level, this is true; at another, as we shall see, the use of multiple meanings opened Pandora's box by forcing Galileo to specify the deeper sense of passages and to argue how this sense conformed to Copernicanism.

Throughout the *Letter to Christina,* Galileo affirms that the plain meaning of biblical texts is accommodated to the common reader. Based on his citations of Jerome and Thomas, we have no reason to suppose that Calvin or other Reformers influenced his views on this subject. Galileo writes:

> It is sufficiently obvious that to attribute motion to the sun and rest to the earth was therefore necessary lest the shallow minds of the common people should become confused, obstinate, and contumacious in yielding assent to the principal articles that are absolutely matters of faith. And if this was necessary, there is no wonder at all that it was carried out with great prudence in the holy Bible. I shall say further that not only respect for the incapacity of the vulgar, but also current opinion in those times, made the sacred authors accommodate themselves (in matters unnecessary to salvation) more to accepted usage than to the true essence of things. Speaking of this, St. Jerome writes: . . . "It is the custom for the biblical scribes to deliver their judgments in many things according to the commonly received opinion of their times." And on the words in the twenty-sixth chapter of Job, *He stretcheth out the north over the void, and hangeth the earth above nothing,* St. Thomas Aquinas notes that the Bible calls "void" or "nothing" that space which we know to be not empty, but filled with air. Nevertheless the Bible, he says, in order to accommodate itself to the beliefs of the common people (who think there is nothing in that space), calls it "void" and "nothing." Here are the words of St. Thomas: "What appears to us in the upper hemisphere of the heavens to be empty, and not a space filled with air, the common people regard as void; and it is usually spoken of in the holy Bible according to the ideas of the common people."[21]

If biblical authors withheld direct expression of the truth with respect to the *plenum,* Galileo concludes, "it certainly must appear reasonable that in other and more abstruse propositions they have followed the same policy."[22] Even Copernicus, he observes, sometimes accommodated his language to the ordinary reader. Having demonstrated with enormous technical difficulty the motion of the earth and stability of the sun, he went on to use the language of appearances (e.g., "sunrise," "sunset," and the "rising and setting" of stars), so as "not to increase for us the confusion and difficulty of abstraction." From these biblical and contemporary examples, Galileo concludes, "One may see how natural it is to accommodate things to our customary way of seeing them."[23]

Had Galileo stopped here, he would have been able to say, as Wilkins later said, that the only meaning of the text—its literal sense—did not pretend to present the truths of astronomy but only the appearances of everyday observation. The astronomer and exegete would then be under no obligation to reconcile conflicting views, since they were speaking different languages for different purposes. However, the *Letter to Christina* insists that the literal sense of a passage is not the only sense, or even its most important sense. Following Catholic hermeneutical tradition, Galileo argued that the real essence of the biblical message lay behind the plain sense of texts. Since the true meaning is rarely obvious, it is necessary to probe behind the "unadorned grammatical sense" to discern the "essence" of the text. Ordinarily, this does not have to be done for common people, who are satisfied with the simplicities of the literal sense, but "for the sake of those who deserve to be separated from the herd, it is necessary that wise expositors should produce the true senses." These expositors, Galileo allows, are church-trained theologians in the case of texts teaching faith and morals; but, as he himself exemplified, scientists-turned-biblical exegetes in the case of texts implying claims about the world. In the following passage, some of the major differences between Galileo's approach to scripture and that of the Reformation are accentuated. Whereas the Reformers emphasized the clarity of scripture, the plain sense of texts, and the ability of laypeople to discern the message of the Bible encapsulated in the plain sense, Galileo's remarks are based on the obscurity of scripture, hidden meanings in passages, and the necessity of professionally trained interpreters. These differences are well known to students of Protestant and Catholic hermeneutical theory. What is interesting is to see how they led to surprisingly different ways of—and different capacities for—dealing with the problem of scripture and Copernicanism.

> I think in the first place that it is very pious to say and prudent to affirm that the holy Bible can never speak untruth—whenever its true meaning is understood. But I believe nobody will deny that it is often very abstruse, and may say things which are quite different from what its bare words signify. Hence in expounding the

> Bible if one were always to confine oneself to the unadorned grammatical meaning, one might fall into error. Not only contradictions and propositions far from true might thus be made to appear in the Bible, but even grave heresies and follies. Thus it would be necessary to assign to God feet, hands, and eyes, as well as corporeal and human affections, such as anger, repentance, hatred, and sometimes even the forgetting of things past and ignorance of those to come. These propositions uttered by the Holy Ghost were set down in that manner by the sacred scribes in order to accommodate them to the capacities of the common people, who are rude and unlearned. For the sake of those who deserve to be separated from the herd, it is necessary that wise expositors should produce the true senses of such passages, together with the special reasons for which they were set down in these words. This doctrine is so widespread and so definite with all theologians that it would be superfluous to adduce evidence for it.[24]

In the final sentence, Galileo reveals the degree to which his assumptions lie entirely within Catholic tradition, even to the extent of his apparent ignorance of and disinterest in Protestant hermeneutics. It is ironic, in this light, that Lorini should have accused him of favoring Protestant approaches to the Bible.

Galileo's belief in the hidden meaning of passages, taken together with his emphasis on another traditional feature of Catholic theology, exacerbated the problem of Copernicanism and scripture. By separating the true meaning of a passage from its literal sense, Galileo believed that theologians could pursue one of the important aims of their discipline: the unification of knowledge. With the flexibility of interpretation afforded by the practice of finding hidden truths, theologians could demonstrate consistency between biblical truths and scientific truths. In the case of Copernicanism, however, the theologians needed help. Not only did they refuse to accept its truth but also—or so Galileo maintained—they did not know enough about the new astronomy to detect that scripture, when the hidden meanings of its passages were understood, teaches heliocentrism. Facing this impasse, Galileo took it on himself to show the consistency of the Bible, rightly understood, and Copernicanism. This was a task in keeping with the syncretistic goals of church theology, but outside the boundaries of Galileo's professional training and status. His failure to win an audience had to do not only with professional turf but also with the enormity of his task. As noble as the goal of unifying knowledge was then and is now, the difficulty of achieving it increased exponentially as the new science progressively displaced the Aristotelianism on which medieval theology had been largely built. More than anyone else before Newton, Galileo contributed to the undoing of the medieval synthesis by rejecting its Aristotelian physics and cosmology. But also more than anyone else, he kept alive the unifying *spirit* of medieval theology by insisting that theologians demonstrate anew, in light of Copernicanism, the consistency of biblical faith and empirical science.

In the *Letter to Christina,* Galileo takes up the question of what it means to say theology is "queen of the sciences." It does not mean, he answers, that theology is the source of all truth or even that its methods are the best methods for establishing different truths. It depends on the subject matter. No one who really understands theology would say that "geometry, astronomy, music, and medicine are more excellently contained in the Bible than they are in the books of Archimedes, Ptolemy, Boethius and Galen."[25] Some arrogant theologians may be deluded into thinking this and may try to force their opinions on other sciences, but these small-minded men misconstrue the task of theology. According to Galileo, theology deserves its regal title because of the dignity of its subject. Theology addresses matters of revelation and salvation. It communicates "divine revelation of conclusions which could not be conceived by men in any other way, concerning chiefly the attainment of eternal blessedness." Having regal preeminence by virtue of subject matter and not by virtue of authority or inerrancy, Galileo concludes, theologians should not try to engage in academic imperialism. They "should not arrogate to themselves the authority to decide on controversies in professions which they have neither studied nor practiced."[26]

Instead, theologians must learn about other fields and integrate the information into theology. This synthetic task requires, above all, that the theologian is sufficiently conversant with the content and methods of nontheological disciplines to be able to distinguish between "demonstrated conclusions" and "merely probable opinions." The former cannot contradict the Bible, since the Bible, rightly understood, is true. As Augustine wrote, "It is to be held as an unquestionable truth that whatever the sages of this world have demonstrated concerning physical matters is in no way contrary to the Bible."[27] Biblical interpretation should never fear truth—in whatever discipline it is found—because all truths belong to God and cannot contradict one another. Having determined which conclusions in other fields are demonstrated, the theologian shows their consistency with scripture. In cases where a traditionally accepted interpretation of the Bible contradicts a demonstrated truth, the interpretation will have to be brought into conformity with the truth. Probable opinions, whose truth has not been established in the first place, do not impose the necessity of reinterpretation. Indeed, if these claims are not demonstrated, they should be rejected as false because they contradict the Bible.

> In the books of the sages of this world there are contained some physical truths which are soundly demonstrated, and others which are merely stated; as to the former, it is the office of wise divines to show that they do not contradict the holy Scriptures. And as to the propositions which are stated but not rigorously demonstrated, anything contrary to the Bible involved by them must be held undoubtedly false and should be proved so by every possible means.[28]

Galileo's belief that a major task of theology was to demonstrate the unity of truth, especially the unity of biblical and scientific truths, and his recognition that most theologians in his day were not equipped to do this, led him to take on himself the two tasks that he had outlined for theologians: (1) to establish whether heliocentrism was a demonstrated truth or a probable opinion and (2) if it were a demonstrated truth, to show its consistency with relevant biblical passages, even if this required changing their accepted interpretations. After his telescopic discoveries and certainly after the new physics of the *Dialogues,* Galileo believed that he had demonstrated the truth of Copernicanism. Part of the debate between him and the church rested on the question of whether he had. I have mentioned earlier some of the issues involved in this debate, and there is no need to repeat them here. Rather, I will only emphasize that the way in which Galileo set up the relation of science and biblical interpretation meant that the necessity of reinterpretation rested on the prior, conclusive demonstration of the scientific claim.

Assuming that he had demonstrated Copernicanism, Galileo tried, at the end of the *Letter to Christina,* to show its consistency with scripture by finding the hidden heliocentric teachings of ostensibly geocentric passages. These final pages of the *Letter* have baffled modern readers by their seemingly misdirected and contrived arguments. The reasoning appears entirely improbable, especially when compared to the arguments of earlier pages. I hope that the points made above about Galileo's need to specify hidden meanings in passages and to show their consistency with demonstrated scientific claims clarify his purpose at the end of the *Letter.* By espousing what had always been Catholic tradition—multiple textual meanings and the syncretistic task of theology—Galileo defined his goals and backed himself into a difficult corner.

He focuses on Joshua 10:12–14, which reads:

> Then spoke Joshua to the LORD in the day when the LORD gave the Amorites over to the men of Israel; and he said in the sight of Israel,
>
> "Sun, stand thou still at Gibeon,
> and thou Moon in the valley of Aijalon."
> And the sun stood still, and the moon stayed,
> until the nation took vengeance on their enemies.
>
> Is this not written in the Book of Jashar? The sun stayed in the midst of heaven, and did not hasten to go down for about a whole day. There has been no day like it before or since, when the LORD hearkened to the voice of a man; for the LORD fought for Israel.

In the Ptolemaic system, Galileo argues, the events described in this passage could never happen. In that system the east to west rotation of the *primum mobile* causes day and night. The motion of the sun through the ecliptic, however, is opposite to the *primum mobile.* Therefore, the sun's motion, on a normal day, prolongs the length of the day. If the sun stopped, as in the Joshua passage, the day would shorten! Had Joshua assumed a Ptolemaic worldview, Galileo concludes, he would have commanded the sun to accelerate so that its motion would be equal to the motion of the *primum mobile* (i.e., about 360 times its normal speed and in the opposite direction). This acceleration would appear to stop solar motion by making it coincide with the motion of the stellar sphere.

The Copernican system, Galileo continues, gives a better explanation of how Joshua's command to stop the sun caused the day to lengthen. The command to stop the sun did not simply stop it but also stopped the entire system of celestial spheres. Referring to the *Letter on Sunspots,* in which he argues that the sun rotates in the center of the universe and claims that solar rotation "infuses motion into other bodies which surround it," Galileo concluded, "if the rotation of the sun were to stop, the rotations of the planets would stop too." On the Copernican view, and only the Copernican view, "When God willed that at Joshua's command the whole system of the world should rest and should remain for many hours in the same state, it sufficed to make the sun stand still."[29] By stopping the rotation of the central sun without altering the mutual positions of other celestial bodies, the day could be lengthened. Thus, the Copernican system enables us to interpret the hidden truth of the text in a way consistent with its literal sense. The Ptolemaic system, on the other hand, cannot provide the hidden meaning of the text because its conclusions are contrary to the literal sense; that is, the Ptolemaic day would shorten, not lengthen, if the sun stopped.

Galileo draws similar conclusions when he turns to exegesis of the phrase "in the midst of the heavens." On the heliocentric view this phrase can be easily understood as meaning "in the center of the celestial orbs." Geocentrists, on the other hand, have a hard time interpreting the phrase. They would like it to mean "overhead" or "noonday," except for the fact that, if it meant this, Joshua would have had enough hours left in the day to complete his work and would not have needed a miracle. Moreover, other features of the text, including the long list of accomplishments already occurring on the day in question, suggest that the sun was near setting, not overhead or at noonday. These knotty problems disappear, Galileo maintains, if we recognize that the sun "in the midst of the heavens" refers to heliocentrism.

Galileo does not consider other biblical passages but suggests that he has provided, in the case of the Joshua passage, an example of how theologians could better interpret obscure passages of scripture "if they would add some knowledge of astronomical science to their knowledge of divinity."[30] Given the torturous technicalities of Galileo's exposition of Joshua, we may not be surprised that theologians did not follow his advice. Nonetheless, it is important to recognize that Galileo's exegetical exercise at the end of the *Letter to Christina* was entirely consistent with Catholic hermeneutical theory and with the traditional role of the theologian as one who unifies knowledge by showing the correlation of biblical and extrabiblical truths. As we turn to John Wilkins, we will see very different assumptions at work.

Wilkins' *Discourse Concerning a New Planet* (1640)

The immediate occasion for the publication of Wilkins' *Discourse* was the intention of its author to respond to an earlier attack on the new astronomy by Alexander Ross. An English schoolmaster, Ross had written *Commentum de terrae motu* (1634) on the conviction that acceptance of the Copernican hypothesis would damage religion by undermining the authority of scripture. Ross attempted to show in the *Commentum* that scripture taught geocentrism. He explicitly rejected the claim that geocentrism was merely a way of speaking, arguing that this implies that God misleads his people and that scripture does not communicate truth clearly or directly. That scripture speaks "ad vulgi captum," Ross held, is a pretext used by philosophers to insert their own opinions into the Word of God. To accept heliocentrism when scripture clearly states that the sun moves and the earth stands still is to open the floodgates of private opinion and irreparably damage the Christian faith.

In the *Discourse,* Wilkins mentions Ross as an example of a "hot adversary" who shows more zeal in refuting persons than in constructing sound arguments. Wilkins makes clear that he does not intend to be drawn into mudslinging and that, instead of attacking individuals or specific anti-Copernican pamphlets, he intends to address "common prejudices which usually deter men from taking any argument, tending this way [i.e., in support of Copernicanism], into their consideration."[31] Among the prejudices addressed by Wilkins are fear of novelty, reverence for the authority of the ancients, and judging philosophy by the plain meaning of scripture. These topics are examples of the reasonable approach taken by Wilkins to the question of Copernicanism. His careful, dispassionate style helped to pave the way for heliocentrism in England, particularly in the face of religious challenges. Wilkins' modern biographer, Barbara Shapiro, cites his *Discourse* and the earlier *Discovery of a New World in the Moone* (1638) as the most important English works before Newton contributing to the popularization of the new astronomy.[32]

Successful popularization of Copernicanism is one of the reasons that Wilkins' work has been compared to Galileo's. In addition, Wilkins is known to have borrowed technical arguments and diagrams from Galileo's *Dialogue.* Shapiro writes,

> Galileo appears to have been the chief source for both the *Discovery* and the *Discourse,* though Wilkins also acknowledged great debts to Copernicus, Rheticus, and particularly Kepler. The *Discovery*'s treatment of the earth's similarity to the moon seems to be directly derived from Galileo's *Dialogue Concerning the Two Chief World Systems,* as does the explanation of the brighter and darker spots on the moon's surface. In the *Discourse,* Galileo's influence is even more evident. Many of Wilkins' proofs regarding the movement of the earth and his answers to critics of the heliocentric system are drawn directly from the *Two Chief World Systems,* and several of his diagrams were lifted straight from Galileo's work. Wilkins' broad aims were much the same as Galileo's: to present to the public in an attractive, simple manner the best evidence in favor of Copernicus and the strongest arguments against common anti-Copernican prejudice.[33]

In a more recent work Shapiro includes Galileo and Wilkins, along with Joseph Glanvill, in a select group of Copernicans who argued that "Scripture was not a source of natural truths and that God's penmen accommodated their language to ordinary use." According to these defenders of the new astronomy, "Scripture was intended to provide moral and religious truth, not philosophical speculation and theory."[34]

In addition to Galileo's *Dialogues,* Wilkins apparently depended on Tommaso Campanella's *Apologia pro Galileo* (1622). Written after the injunction of 1616, the *Apologia* sought to vindicate not only Copernicanism but most especially Galileo's specific defense of it in the *Letter to Christina.* Grant McColley has argued that the inspiration of Wilkins' work and specific statements in the *Discovery* and the *Discourse* depended directly on Campanella's *Apologia.*[35]

While Wilkins' dependency on Galileo and Campanella cannot be disputed, McColley and Shapiro leave the impression that these Protestant and Catholic defenders of Copernicanism were like-minded in their approach to Copernicanism and scripture. Their unstated assumption, a frequent one made in discussions of religion and science, seems to be that commitment to science, even a particular scientific theory such as Copernicanism, transcends religious differences. Modern writers usually assume that seventeenth-century scientists took science as primary and that their religious beliefs followed suit. Hence there has been little discussion of how specific Protestant and Catholic differences, such as differences in biblical hermeneutics, affected approaches to new scientific ideas or acceptance of new theories.

Among the important differences between Wilkins and Galileo, the most obvious has to do with scripture and tradition. Galileo delicately addressed the topic of biblical interpretation in agreement with the Church Fathers, distinguishing between the importance of adherence to this principle in matters of faith and morals and its unimportance in physical matters which the Fathers did not discuss. Wilkins, on the other hand, observes no compelling reason to consider the opinions of the Fathers at all. In fact, in discussing what he calls the "common prejudice" of servility to ancient authority, Wilkins cites the need to agree with the Fathers as an anachronism of Catholic doctrine and maintains that the Jesuits would defend Copernicanism were it not for this misplaced principle.[36] Thus Wilkins explicitly points to differences in the relation of scripture and tradition among Protestants and Catholics as a key to their different approaches to Copernicanism.

More similar to Galileo, at least in appearance, is Wilkins' acceptance of the principle of accommodation. His argument under Proposition II in the *Discourse,* for example, is built almost entirely on it. Here he seeks to establish that "there is not any place in scriptures, from which (being rightly understood) we may infer the diurnal motion of the sun or heavens." The key phrase for our purposes is in parentheses. By "rightly understood" Wilkins means understood as accommodated to "the conceit of the vulgar." No passage of scripture teaches geocentrism because, in every place that this cosmology appears, the biblical authors have accommodated their language to everyday observation.

Wilkins classes the relevant passages under these main headings:

> 1. All those scriptures where there is any mention made of the rising or setting of the sun or stars.
> 2. That story in Joshua, where the sun standing still is reckoned for a miracle.
> 3. That other wonder in the days of Hezekiah, when the sun went back ten degrees in the dial of Ahaz.[37]

Discussing each category in turn, Wilkins seeks to show "that the Holy Ghost in the scripture expressions, is pleased to accommodate himself unto the conceit of the vulgar, and the usual opinion."[38] For example, when Joshua said, "Sun, stand thou still upon Gibeon or over Gibeon," he was referring not to the exact point of Gibeon, but to the general *appearance* of the sun overhead. The earth is so small in comparison to the sun that it appears as a point with respect to the solar orbit. Gibeon in turn appears as a point on the globe of the earth. Moreover, it is probable that Joshua was a little east of Gibeon and that the sun was beyond the meridian. All of this adds up to show, Wilkins maintains, that scripture is not speaking exactly. Only with reference to appearances does Joshua command the sun to stand still over Gibeon. Furthermore, when scripture adds, "And the sun stood still in the midst of heaven," it continues the language of appearances. Properly speaking, heaven has no midst but the center. On the geocentric view accepted at the time, the sun does not occupy this center. Therefore, scripture is speaking inexactly. "Midst of heaven" means "such a place as was not very near to either of the ends [horizons], the east or west." By painstaking, if not hairsplitting, analysis of passage after passage, Wilkins establishes that scripture speaks loosely about physical matters and that we must view its language as the inexact language of everyday appearance, not the exact technical language of science.

While Wilkins' discussion recalls Galileo, he most often cites Calvin in support of his views on accommodation. For example, when Moses in Genesis is speaking of the moon as a great light, he is speaking "so as ordinary people without the help of arts and learning, might easily understand him."[39] Moreover, in another place, Wilkins cites Calvin as saying,

> It was not the purpose of the Holy Ghost to teach us astronomy: but being to propound a doctrine that concerns the most rude and simple people, he does (both by Moses and the prophets) conform himself unto their phrases and conceits: lest any should think to excuse his own ignorance with the pretence of difficulty: as men commonly do in those things which are delivered after a learned and sublime manner.[40]

These citations suggest that it is not sufficient simply to refer to Galileo as a source of Wilkins' views on accommodation. Many writers at the time, including Calvin, employed this principle to explain biblical statements implying physical claims. Moreover—and this is the important point for our purposes—Wilkins stops far short of Galileo's view (or Campanella's for that matter). Whereas these Catholics appealed to the "plenitude of Scripture" and employed the practice of finding multiple meanings in texts, Wilkins never moves beyond the plain sense. Once he has established that this sense, the *whole* sense of the text, is accommodated to everyday appearances for religious, not scientific, purposes, there was little else to say. By contrast Galileo, as we have seen, assumed that scripture, in its fullness, had something for everyone. Those "who deserve to be separated from the herd" can move beyond the literal sense of the text, discover its hidden meaning, and establish its consistency with demonstrated scientific truths.

Having been pressed by Ross to explain why the Holy Ghost did not use the most accurate expressions in scripture, so as to inform the people and correct their errors, Wilkins offered the familiar reply that it was not the business of scripture to teach *subtilia* (curiosities of nature) but *utilia* (things profitable for salvation). Had the Holy Ghost inspired biblical writers to state directly the truths of cosmology, the common people would have been confused, skepticism would abound, and the good news of the Bible about salvation would have been lost.

> Though it were, yet it is beside the chief scope of those places, to instruct us in any philosophical points, as hath been proved in the former book; especially when these things are neither necessary

> in themselves, nor do necessarily induce to a more full understanding of that which is the main business of those scriptures. . . .
>
> It is not only besides that which is the chief purpose of those places, but it might happen also to be somewhat opposite unto it. For men being naturally unapt to believe any thing that seems contrary to their senses, might upon this begin to question the authority of that book which affirmed it, or at least to retch scripture some wrong way, to force it to some other sense, which might be more agreeable to their own false imagination. . . .
>
> And besides, if the Holy Ghost had propounded unto us any secrets in philosophy, we should have been apt to be so busied about them, as to neglect other matters of greater importance.[41]

Wilkins' explanation, to this point, does not differ from Galileo's. Nevertheless, as he continues to define his position, profound differences with Galileo emerge. Whereas Galileo held that the authors of scripture knew the truth about the world but expressed it in hidden meanings so as not to confuse common people, Wilkins maintained that the "penmen of scripture . . . might yet be utterly ignorant of many philosophical truths, which are commonly known in these days."[42] According to Wilkins, the calling of biblical authors to reveal truths of salvation did not require that they present in any form—plain or hidden—truths about the world. In fact, biblical authors may have known no more about natural truths than other human beings, since it was not their business to communicate these truths in the Bible. "It is probable," Wilkins writes, "that the Holy Ghost did inform them only with the knowledge of those things whereof they were to be the penmen, and that they were not better skilled in points of philosophy than others."[43] The authors of scripture, although wise and holy men in matters of divinity, did not learn "human arts by any special inspiration, but by instruction and study and other ordinary means."[44] Since human art progresses with time, Wilkins concludes, it is probable that the modern era knows more about the world than did the biblical authors. Their simplemindedness about natural truths, however, has no bearing on their authority in divinity. We should respect their teachings on faith and morals as the revealed truth of God, even while acknowledging that they knew less than we know about the world.

Wilkins' position leads to the *divorce* of philosophy and theology, science and the Bible. If natural truths are not found in the Bible in any form—plain or hidden—no obligation exists to establish consistency between scientific and biblical truths. Whereas Galileo maintained that the Bible *primarily* taught faith and morals and *incidentally* taught truths about the world in concealed language, Wilkins insists that the Bible teaches faith and morals *exclusively* and has nothing to do with truth claims about the world. In divinity, the Bible offers "an infallible rule that does plainly inform us of all necessary truths . . . but for philosophy there is no such reason."[45] In divinity, ancient times were greater than modern times, so we must look to the past for truth; in philosophy, "truth is the daughter of time," so we must look to the future and continue to accumulate knowledge and experience of the world. The belief that divinity looks back to the Bible whereas natural philosophy looks forward to new discoveries is epitomized in Wilkins' revealing question, "Why should we think that Scripture must needs inform us of the earth's motion; whereas neither Pythagoras, nor Copernicus, nor any else, had then discovered it?"[46]

In Wilkins' thought, the important Reformation principle of *sola scriptura* has a double meaning. Scripture is the *only* authority in matters of faith and an authority *only* in matters of faith. It reigns supreme in its realm but has no authority outside that realm. In spite of some differences of language and emphasis, the substance of Wilkins' view does not differ from Luther's "theory of multiple discourse" discussed earlier. Wilkins is as ready as Luther was to isolate areas of discourse by drawing sharp boundaries between them. Whereas Luther primarily cautioned against reason overstepping its boundaries into religion, Wilkins primarily cautioned against extending biblical interpretation into natural philosophy.[47] For both men, the boundary between revelation and reason, the Bible and science, was drawn sharply. Much confusion in religion and in natural philosophy, they claimed, arose out of the failure to draw these boundaries distinctly enough.

It should be clear how the separation of disciplines in Wilkins' thought simplified the problem of Copernicanism and the Bible far beyond Galileo's treatment of the subject. For Wilkins, the astronomer and the theologian do not need to converse at all. Indeed, their attempts at conversation have created problems in the first place. One might say, reminiscent of Wittgenstein, that Wilkins identifies the problem of Copernicanism and scripture as a pseudoproblem, a problem created by the inappropriate mixing of two distinct languages. In his view, the solution of the problem—indeed, the dissolution of the problem—follows once the study of astronomy and the study of scripture are isolated from one another.

This isolation is possible in Wilkins' thought, resting as it does in the Protestant tradition, primarily because the Reformers had already rejected the medieval ideal of theology as the systematization of all truth in favor of theology as the systematization of biblical truth. In a sense, Wilkins' thought represents application of the Protestant spirit of specialization to natural philosophy. Just as the Reformers sought to eliminate philosophy from biblical study so as to arrive at the "pure" discipline of biblical theology, so Wilkins sought to eliminate the Bible from natural philosophy so as to arrive at the "pure" study of nature.[48] By contrast, clinging to the medieval ideal of systematic theology, not biblical theology, neither Galileo nor the Catholic tradition was swept up in specialization. Acknowledging that the Bible *emphasizes* faith and morals, but not to the exclusion of claims about the world, Galileo maintained that incidental biblical remarks about the world must be reconciled with known scientific truths. If theologians are to accept their calling, they must be exegetes and interdisciplinarians. They must be able to discern the often obscure meanings of the Bible and demonstrate their consistency with accepted knowledge in nonbiblical disciplines, whether philosophy, astronomy, geography, or history. Adopting momentarily what he considered to be the task of the theologian, Galileo took on the challenge and tried to discern what he believed must be the hidden Copernican teachings of the Bible. While modern heirs of academic specialization may find his efforts misguided and even amusing, we ought to recognize their appropriateness to Galileo's Catholic tradition and respect his willingness to accept the enormous challenge of theology as defined in that tradition. Even though Wilkins' simplification of the problem of Copernicanism and scripture appeared more successful at the time, the success may have been an illusion. Increasingly aware in the twentieth century of problems caused by specialization, we may be more prepared, even as Protestants, to think again about the unity of knowledge.

NOTES

1. The text of *De Revolutionibus* spoke in realist language, but the "Preface to the Reader" called for conventionalism. We now know that the Lutheran minister Andreas Osiander added the preface after Copernicus' death and without his permission, but to observers at the time, including churchmen such as Cardinal Bellarmine, the preface afforded a convenient middle ground between a rock and a hard place. On Osiander see Bruce Wrightsman, "Andreas Osiander's Contribution to the Copernican Achievement" in *The Coper-*

nican Achievement, ed. Robert Westman (Berkeley: University of California Press, 1975), pp. 213–243.

2. Jupiter's moons, previously unseen stars, and irregularities of the earth's moon questioned Aristotelian claims more than they provided direct evidence for Copernicanism. In general, Tycho's model accounted for the same astronomical observations as those of Copernicus without raising difficult physical questions resulting from moving the earth. See Thomas Kuhn, *The Copernican Revolution: Planetary Astronomy in the Development of Western Thought* (Cambridge, Mass.: Harvard University Press, 1957), chapter 6 passim.

3. In a letter to Paulo Antonio Foscarini, Cardinal Bellarmine confirmed this point: "If there were a real proof that the sun is in the centre of the universe, that the earth is in the third sphere, and that the sun does not go around the earth but the earth round the sun, then we should have to proceed with great circumspection in explaining passages of Scripture which appear to teach the contrary, and rather admit that we did not understand them than declare an opinion to be false which is proved to be true." (Cited in James Brodrick, S.J., *Robert Bellarmine: Saint and Scholar* [London: Burns & Oates, 1961], p. 361.)

4. For example, referring to the above statement of Bellarmine, Kuhn remarks, "Very probably Bellarmine's liberalism is more apparent than real" (Kuhn, *Copernican Revolution,* p. 198).

5. A full discussion of Protestantism and the Bible in recent works is contained in the excellent article by B. A. Gerrish, "The Reformation and the Rise of Science," in *The Impact of the Church Upon Its Culture,* ed. Jerald C. Brauer (Chicago: University of Chicago Press, 1968), pp. 231–265.

6. Kuhn, *Copernican Revolution,* p. 191. Gerrish notes that the Lauterbach version of this passage, which generally is to be considered more reliable, contains no fool clause, although its tone is anti-Copernican (Gerrish, "Reformation," pp. 243–244).

7. Kuhn, *Copernican Revolution,* p. 192.

8. Edward Rosen, "Calvin's Attitude Toward Copernicus," *Journal of the History of Ideas* 21 (July-September 1960), 431–441. There may be an oblique reference to the new astronomy in Calvin's commentary on Psalm 46, but nowhere in Calvin's works is Copernicus mentioned by name (Gerrish, "Reformation," p. 247 n. 47).

9. Dorothy Stimson, *The Gradual Acceptance of the Copernican Theory of the Universe* (1917 ed.; reprint, Gloucester, Mass.: Peter Smith, 1972), p. 41.

10. Herbert Butterfield, *The Origins of Modern Science, 1300–1800,* rev. ed. (New York: Free Press, 1965), p. 68.

11. Alan G. R. Smith, *Science and Society in the 16th and 17th Centuries* (New York: Science History Publications, 1972), p. 97.

12. Kuhn, *Copernican Revolution,* pp. 195–196.

13. In addition to Gerrish, Wrightsman (n. 1 above) and three articles by Robert Westman acknowledge important contributions by Protestants to the growth of the new astronomy. See R. Westman, "The Melanchthon Circle, Rheticus, and the Wittenberg Interpretation of the Copernican Theory," *Isis* 66 (June 1975), 165–193; "Three Responses to the Copernican Theory: Johannes Praetorius, Tycho Brahe, and Michael Maestlin," in *The Copernican Achievement,* ed. by Robert S. Westman (Berkeley: University of California Press, 1975); and "The Copernicans and the Churches" in *God and Nature: Historical Essays on the Encounter Between Christianity and Science,* ed. by David C. Lindberg and Ronald L. Numbers (Berkeley: University of California Press, 1986), pp. 76–113.

14. *WA* 42.31.8ff., quoted in Gerrish, "Reformation," pp. 249–250.

15. Gerrish, "Reformation," pp. 255–262. Edward A. Dowey, Jr., *The Knowledge of God in Calvin's Theology* (New York: Columbia University Press, 1952), pp. 3–17 and passim.

16. The Fourth Session of the Council of Trent decreed: "Furthermore, to check unbridled spirits, it [the Holy Council] decrees that no one relying on his own judgment shall, in matters of faith and morals pertaining to the edification of Christian doctrine, distorting the Scriptures in accordance with his own conceptions, presume to interpret them contrary to that sense which the holy mother Church, to whom it belongs to judge of their true sense and interpretation, has held and holds, or even contrary to the unanimous teaching of the Fathers, even though such interpretations should never at any time be published" (H. J. Schroeder, O.P., *Canons and Decrees of the Council of Trent* [St. Louis: Herder, 1941], pp. 18–19). On Galileo's relation to the Council of Trent, see Olaf Pedersen, "Galileo and the Council of Trent: The Galileo Affair Revisited," *Journal of the History of Astronomy* 14 (1983), 1–29.

17. Galileo Galilei, *Letter to the Grand Duchess Christina,* in *Discoveries and Opinions of Galileo,* tr. with an introduction and notes by Stillman Drake (Garden City, N.Y.: Doubleday & Co., 1957), pp. 184–185. (Galileo cites Augustine, *De Genesi ad litteram* 2.9.) This and subsequent quotations from Drake's translation are used by permission of the publisher, Doubleday, a division of Bantam Doubleday Dell Publishing Group, Inc.

18. "Either the Fathers reflected upon this conclusion [heliocentrism] as controversial, or they did not; if not, then they cannot have decided anything about it even in their own minds, and their incognizance of it does not oblige us to accept teaching which they never imposed, even in intention. But if they had reflected upon it and considered it, and if they judged it to be erroneous, then they would long ago have condemned it; and this they are not found to have done" (ibid., p. 203).

19. Ibid., p. 203.
20. Bellarmine, "Letter to Foscarini," as quoted in Brodrick, *Bellarmine,* p. 361.
21. Galileo, *Letter to Christina,* p. 201. Galileo assumes in this passage, like Aristotle and Thomas, that the heavens are full and that "void" is simply a manner of speaking. Acceptance of a celestial void was not widespread until after Newton's work. See Alexander Koyré, *From the Closed World to the Infinite Universe* (Baltimore: Johns Hopkins Press, 1957).
22. Galileo, *Letter to Christina,* p. 201.
23. Ibid., p. 202.
24. Ibid., pp. 181–182.
25. Ibid., p. 193.
26. Ibid.
27. Augustine, *De Genesi ad litteram* I. 21, as quoted in Galileo, *Letter to Christina,* p. 194.
28. Galileo, *Letter to Christina,* p. 194.
29. Ibid., p. 213.
30. Ibid., p. 215.
31. John Wilkins, "A Discourse Concerning a New Planet," in *The Mathematical and Philosophical Works of the Right Rev. John Wilkins* (London, 1802; reprint, London: Frank Cass & Co., 1970), p. 133.
32. Barbara J. Shapiro, *John Wilkins, 1614–1672* (Berkeley: University of California Press, 1969), p. 38.
33. Ibid., pp. 38–39.
34. Barbara J. Shapiro, *Probability and Certainty in Seventeenth-Century England: A Study of the Relationships Between Natural Science, Religion, History, Law, and Literature* (Princeton, N.J.: Princeton University Press, 1983), p. 158.
35. Grant McColley, "The Debt of Bishop John Wilkins to the *Apologia Pro Galileo* of Tommaso Campanella," *Annals of Science* 4 (1939), 167.
36. Wilkins, "Discourse," p. 147.
37. Ibid., p. 150.
38. Ibid.
39. Calvin, "Commentary on Genesis 1:16," as quoted in Wilkins, "Discourse," pp. 160–161.
40. Calvin, "Commentary on Psalm 136," as quoted in Wilkins, "Discourse," p. 161.
41. Wilkins, "Discourse," pp. 150–151.
42. Ibid., pp. 139–140.
43. Ibid., p. 140.
44. Ibid., p. 141.
45. Ibid., pp. 137–138.
46. Ibid., pp. 165–166.

47. For Luther's views, see B. A. Gerrish, *Grace and Reason: A Study in the Theology of Luther* (1962; reprint, Oxford: Clarendon Press, 1979).

48. In this respect, Wilkins' efforts continued those of Francis Bacon's. See my "The Protestant Reformation and the Rise of Modern Science," *Scottish Journal of Theology* 38, no. 2 (1985), 230–233.

PART FOUR

Reform and Culture in Eighteenth- and Nineteenth-Century Thought

On the Possibility and Perfectibility of Christian Revelation

Jean-Loup Seban

A decade after Reinhold's *Briefe über die Kantische Philosophie* began, in *Teutscher Merkur,* successfully to diffuse criticism all over the German states, and half a decade prior to equally notable attempts by Johann Schultz and Friedrich Born,[1] Christian Wilhelm Flügge diagnosed the crisis of the age in *Versuch einer historisch-kritischen Darstellung des bisherigen Einflusses der Kantischen Philosophie* (1796); he called it "an upsetting of all hitherto known systems, theories, and modes of representation."[2] Throughout history, observed Flügge, who taught at Göttingen, theology has always been receptive to the *Zeitphilosophie,* and it has been a constant desire of the rational being to possess a harmonious, all-encompassing system.

According to Flügge, there are three alternative ways of achieving harmony between philosophical and religious knowledge. One may accommodate one knowledge to the other by allowing a system of philosophy to be the interpreter of the codex of a positive religion. Or one may derive the system of a positive religion from the foundational principles of a philosophical system. Lastly and alternatively, one may verify, expand, and rectify the system of a positive religion by a philosophical system.[3]

Flügge observed that it was, above all, the Kantian practical theory which gave the impetus to a fundamental rethinking of the theory of religion.[4] As one of the purports of the novel *Zeitphilosophie* was assuredly to render the religious reasonable,[5] its followers were divided into those who advocated practical reasonableness and those who gave priority to the miraculous and the mysterious. In other terms, there were

Kantian rationalists and Kantian supernaturalists. Understandably, their disagreement came to the fore as they dealt with immediate revelation, miracles, reconciliation, and the authority of scripture. Moreover, Flügge divided the Kantian influence into two periods: the initial period, which began with the publication of the first *Kritik,* and the later period, which followed the release of *Die Religion innerhalb der Grenzen der blossen Vernunft.* During the initial period the disputed matters were limited to revelation, miracles, proofs of existence, and morality; whereas the entire theological spectrum was passed through the Kantian ordeal during the later period. The transition from one period to the other was caused by a shift of emphasis from the critical to the practical.[6]

I

The *Gottesfrage* was a permanent concern throughout Kant's life. It emerged prominently in his 1755 *Allgemeine Naturgeschichte und Theorie des Himmels,* in which he maintained that the immeasurableness of the universe proved the infinitude of its Creator. It was still very much a focal preoccupation in his *Opus Postumus,* where a conception of a *Deus in nobis* was propounded.[7] In the meantime Kant had disproved the claim to objectivity of the *Verstandesmetaphysik,* refounded rational religion on ethics, and unfolded a philosophy of Christian religion. The distinction, inherited from Wolff through Baumgarten, between *theologia rationalis* and *theologia revelata*—the latter being left aside by the philosopher[8]—the transformation of the metaphysics of nature into a metaphysics of the subject irradicated in the concept of freedom, the definition of religion as recognition of all our duties as divine commands, and the dissociation of theoretical knowledge from practical faith and of both from statutory faith—all these presented to both the neologists and the fideists a stupendous challenge.

As was to be expected, the question of how to secure room for Christian revelation became crucial once again. The Wolffian truce which had produced the neological school was under a serious threat of disruption. The relationship between reason and revelation had to be rethought, since Kant had dissociated faith from revelation by circumscribing the former within the confines of reason. Unlike the Cartesian dichotomy of autarchic reason and theonomic faith, the Kantian dichotomy of theoretical knowledge and practical faith was a matter of distinction inside reason.

In point of fact, Kant placed the problem of the relation of reason to faith on a new footing, removing it from its traditional setting into the sphere of autarchic reason. The doctrine of practical faith, which was unfolded in the three *Kritiken,* as well as in several other writings from 1789 to 1798,[9] constituted the point of departure whence any other faith had to be interpreted. The conclusion Kant reached was that autonomous moral faith set the standards of the truth and divine character of any theonomic tradition or revelation. This was the extent to which Kantian reason could tolerate revelation. Carl Friedrich Stäudlin insightfully observed in his *Geschichte des Rationalismus und Supranaturalismus* of 1826 that the difference between natural and revealed religion was merely a matter of giving precedence to either the moral duties or the divine will.[10] In other terms, the distinction depended on whether the anthropological or the theological aspect of the same concept was given priority.

These fragmentary observations should suffice to clarify the significance of the dual issue of our investigation for the history of the critique of revelation in the 1790s. In the wake of ethical rationalism the possibility of revelation was no longer posed solely in terms of compatibility between natural causality and supernatural agency, but, and above all, in terms of agreement between autonomous and heteronomous truth, autarchic and theonomic moral law, human reason and divine will. The most decisive change in religious matters that ethical rationalism brought about was the displacement of the tension between reason and revelation to a new center of gravity. Our intention in this study is to pass in review some examples of the solutions proffered in the 1790s by philosophers and theologians who claimed the Kantian heritage.

II

Three of Kant's disciples, J. H. Tieftrunk, C. F. Stäudlin, and J. W. Schmid, had begun to apply Kantian principles of criticism to Christian theology.[11] It was, however, Johann Gottlieb Fichte, a recent convert to Kantianism, who had hitherto cultivated Leibnizian and Spinozian views and who found himself taking unexpected delight in reading first the *Kritik der praktischen Vernunft* and then the *Kritik der reinen Vernunft,* who wrote, in July 1791, the first treatise on revelation after the fashion of the new philosophy. Fichte's *Versuch einer Kritik aller Offenbarung,* written with the intent of ingratiating himself with the sage of Königsberg,[12] represents something of a *unicum* in the whole spectrum of his philosophical theology. Fichte's pre-Kantian period, during which he conceived religion as a matter of heart, offers no traces whatsoever of a concept of revelation.

After the publication of the epoch-making *Wissenschaftslehre,* Fichte entertained a different view again. In *Über den Grund unseres Glaubens an eine göttliche Weltregierung* (1798) he identified the moral world order with the Deity, thereby rendering any revelation superfluous. During the *Atheismusstreit* that followed, he was compelled to defend himself against the charge of atheism and thereupon drew a distinction, inspired by Spinoza, between the *ordo ordinatus* and the *ordo ordinans.*[13] With *Die Bestimmung des Menschen* (1799) the *Gottesfrage* eventually superseded the epistemological question as the focal concern. Fichte defined God as *absolutes Sein* and reinstated Kantian practical faith. Finally, he attempted in his *Anweisung zum seligen Leben* (1806) to strike an unattainable balance between his hitherto voluntaristic view and the traditional essentialist conception of God.[14]

The aim of Fichte's *Versuch einer Kritik aller Offenbarung* was to fix the conditions of the possibility of supernatural revelation. The method selected to carry out this ambition was deductive, since philosophy is speculation, as Fichte specified later.[15] The possibility of revelation per se would be inferred from the apriorical principles of practical reason.[16] The point of departure of the whole deductive procedure was the concept of moral law. Notwithstanding this, Fichte also began with a theory of the desire for blissfulness which introduced a theory of what is right, and which as neological legacy happens to be quite incongruous with the Kantian autonomy of moral law. From these incompatible starting points, Fichte proceeded to the concept of a "wholly holy, blessed, and omnipotent Being" who determines nature in conformity with the moral law.[17] Then Fichte derived from the concept of Ruler, Retributor, and moral Legislator the concept of theology, which he differentiates from that of religion. Theology is a mere lifeless science, whereas religion obliges by exerting its influence on the will of the rational being.[18]

To account for the birth of religion, for which Fichte provided several definitions, he had recourse to a concept that wielded a crucial influence on German idealism; namely, that of alienation *(Entäusserung).* The idea of God results from the translation of an intrinsic quality into an extrinsic being who then determines our will.[19] As a matter of course Fichte acknowledged the Kantian equating of moral duties with divine commands. He was therefore anxious to prevent any heteronominization of the moral law. To that effect he maintained that the divine law originated from an alienation of our subjective obligation in the form of the idea of God. And Fichte subjoined to the argument that this very idea of God could in some instances arouse in the rational being respect for the moral law.[20] Religion was conceived *a parte Dei* as the proclamation by God of the moral law as his will, and *a parte hominis* as the fulfillment of the moral law or divine will.

Next to the concept of moral law, proclamation was a pivotal concept in Fichte's reasoning. In order to delineate a space for revelation, Fichte implemented the neological dichotomy of a priori and a posteriori religion. The internal proclamation by God of the moral law as his will forms the supernatural in us; similarly, the external proclamation forms the supernatural outside of us. The former was called natural religion; the latter revealed religion.[21] A further distinction was drawn between form and matter. Although both proclamations convey identical material, the form of the external differs from that of the internal because of its being revealed by the way things are made known in the world of sense. What differentiates revelation from consciousness of the moral law is a question of form.[22] At this stage Fichte was confronted with two questions: Why would God proclaim outwardly what the rational being already knows inwardly? And how can an external proclamation occur in the world of sense? Fichte argued that one ground for the external proclamation lay in the responsibility of the moral Legislator, and another in the nature of the rational being. The theological argument adduced in support of revelation amounts to the idea that it behooves God to advance morality by every means at his disposal.[23] As regards the anthropological argument, which was constructed around the concept of need *(Bedürfnis),* two discordant versions were put forward: one with a hamartiological emphasis, the other with a parenetic purport.[24] The basic idea was that revelation responded to a contingent necessity,[25] inasmuch as it could either induce, by way of sense, depraved individuals or entire people to abide by the moral law, or stimulate awakened moral conscience by way of sensualized moral incitements, thereby advancing natural religion.[26] The latter option stressed the hortatory function of revelation.

To justify the physical possibility of supernatural causality in the world of sense, Fichte advocated a leap of reason which is, unsurprisingly, reminiscent of Spinozism. Such a causality was conceivable provided the whole world is thought of as a supernatural effect of God.[27] The criteria of the divinity of a given revelation had to be fixed rationally and according to form and matter. Albeit faith in revelation is founded in the divine authority, miracles and prophecies are of no avail when it comes to verification. In respect to its form, any revelation which is proclaimed by a moral means is from God. Conversely, any revelation which incites the rational being through other motives is not from God.[28] With regard to its matter, any revelation which proclaims the moral Legislator and conveys the moral law is from God.[29] Interestingly enough, Fichte conceded some room for prayer, because it could enliven one's moral sense.[30] The sole conclusion our cognitive faculty might draw about the fitness of a given supernatural occurrence in the world of sense is neither assertorical nor apodictical, but hypothetical. At best, opined Fichte, one might deduce the possibility, but not the certitude, of a divine origin.[31]

How does rational faith compare with revealed faith? Qualitatively, both are founded on freedom, argued Fichte, yet one is given, the other constructed. The former is a priori, the latter a posteriori. Quantitatively, and only regarding their subjective validity, revealed faith has by contrast with rational faith no universal claim. Relationally, revealed faith refers only to the form of the matter—God and immortality—to which rational faith refers. And finally, modally, rational faith is apodictical whereas revealed faith is categorical.

Stäudlin remarked that Fichte believed he had satisfactorily settled the dispute between the pros and cons by demonstrating that, if revelation were theoretically unestablishable, it was no less conceivable as *Bestimmung des Begehrungsvermögen.*[32] In spite of the significant restriction that the *als ob* speculation of pure practical reason brought about, Fichte's solution offered a constructive alternative to the view sustained earlier by the Leipzig poet and philosopher, Karl Heinrich Heydenreich. The main contention of Heydenreich's 1790 Kantian *Betrachtungen über die Philosophie der natürlichen Religion* was that critical reason could not pronounce either way upon miracles and supernatural revelation.[33] This interpretation later built the line of defense of Kantian theology against the accusation of atheism in Heydenreich's *Briefe über den Atheismus* (1796).

Was Fichte as truly Kantian as he claimed to be? There are notable divarications between Fichte and Kant. First of all, they employed opposite methodologies. In the preface to the second edition of *Die Religion* Kant distinguished two methods, the synthetic and the analytic.[34] By choosing the latter, Kant showed his preference for Stäudlin's *Ideen zur Kritik des Systems der christlichen Religion,* which he read some time after he had perused Fichte's *Versuch.* Kant circumscribed religion within *eine weitere Sphäre des Glaubens,* which encompasses the narrower sphere of rational religion. Because, unlike Fichte, Kant stressed the *innerhalb* instead of the *aus*, his approach was as a result more genuinely phenomenological. One may recall that in the *Streit der Facultäten* Kant had made the well-known distinctions among philosophy, rational theology, and biblical theology, and contended that the rational theologian could pronounce upon the acceptability of scriptural dogmata once he had renounced the deduction of religion from pure reason.[35] As Kant envisioned it, reason functions in this particular instance only regulatively. The Kantian school of theology followed the same path.

A second matter of divarication arises from Kant's recourse to the category of history. Unlike Fichte, Kant showed no interest in determining the inner and outer conditions of revelation, nor did he consider supernatural religion as necessary to true religion, even from a pedagogical point of view. Owing to Semler and Reimarus, Kant liked to contrast true, natural, or rational religion with the historically conditioned, revealed, learned, or statutory religion. The ethical hermeneutics which expressed a disvaluing judgment on history and experience was undoubtedly intended to deter rational beings from enthusiasm, superstition, and atheism as well. Other divarications result from the neological eudaemonism which tinted Fichte's vision of the relation of the moral law to religion, and from the piety which pervades his whole essay. Besides critical epistemology and the overriding normativity of practical reason, what Fichte retained best from Kant was the distinction between subjective and objective validity.

When Friedrich Immanuel Niethammer, whose interest in the topic had been aroused by his teacher, Friedrich Gottlieb Storr, discovered Fichte's *Versuch,* he was convinced by the argumentation. Thereupon Niethammer wrote a Fichtean dissertation in theology. *De Vero Revelationis Fundamento* was published in the vernacular in 1792 under the title *Über den Versuch einer Kritik aller Offenbarung.*[36] At the close of his thesis Niethammer proposed, in the Lessingian vein, that faith could contribute to the betterment of rational beings.[37] He firmly believed in the constructive encounter of theology with education. This accounts for his specific emphasis on the pedagogical office of the Deity.

Niethammer was more concerned than Fichte with establishing the necessity of revelation. In his mind it was not so much an abstract as a concrete issue, insofar as it affected the future of humanity. Owing to Storr's influence, Niethammer had a greater historical awareness than Fichte. Indeed, his thesis opened with a historicized interpretation of the concept of revelation, which reached the conclusion that ignorance was the cause for revelation.[38] The thesis was, however, not Niethammer's last word on the subject. The foundation of a rationally acceptable faith in revelation was the aim that he pursued in his 1798 dissertation in philosophy, entitled in its vernacular edition *Versuch einer Begründung des vernünftmässigen Offenbarungsglaubens.* By that time Niethammer had read Kant's *Religion* and had come closer to the Kantian approach. The question of the absolute necessity of revelation, which is unanswerable from the premises of Kantian epistemology, was relinquished and replaced by the question of a need *(Bedürfnis)* for faith in revelation. Revelation, which as a product of practical reason is subjected to its criteria, has a pedagogic function. Niethammer justified its needfulness by showing, on the basis of that faith in providence which was common to neologists and rationalists, that faith in revelation was an aid to reason, an incitement to morality.[39] Faith in revelation is not superstition so long as its purpose is to lead the rational being to moral self-determination.[40] Having distanced himself from Storr's biblical supernaturalism and from Fichte's hypotheticalism, Niethammer could conclude that religion cleared the path to reason, and thereby announced, as a forerunner, one of the favorite themes of the Kantian school of Marburg.

The leaders of the old Tübingen school deprecated Fichte's solution in their critical reviews. Friedrich Gottlieb Suskind tried laboriously to demonstrate, in the *Neue Deutsche Allgemeine Bibliothek* of 1793, that Fichte failed to solve the conflict between reason and revelation.[41] As for Storr, the founder of the school, he produced one of the most perspicacious analyses. It revealed the division between the conflicting approaches to, and use of, ethical rationalism. Storr's *Bemerkung über den aus Principien der praktischen Vernunft hergeleiteten Überzeugungsgrund von der Möglichkeit und Wirklichkeit einer Offenbarung, in Beziehung auf Fichtes Versuch einer Kritik aller Offenbarung* (1794) treated four major issues: the definition of revelation; its possibility according to practical reason; its content; and the credibility of a particular revelation.

The first issue initiated the divorce from Fichte. Though Storr concurred with Fichte's initial line of argument, he disagreed with the conclusion that the difference between natural and revealed religion is a question merely of form and not therewith of matter. To Fichte, Storr controverted that one could equally well conjecture a priori that God might reveal practical truths hitherto unknown which would have to be counted as religious truths.[42] Storr deplored the restrictiveness of the Fichtean definition of revelation, which was partly caused by a limited definition of the essence of God, and advocated a broader definition. Following Kant, Fichte and Storr concurred that the idea of God as *Bestimmer der Natur* according to the natural law, and Distributor of blissfulness, leads to the idea of a perfect Being; yet whereas Fichte used mainly the concept of moral Legislator, Storr took both into account.[43] In Storr's opinion Fichte's proceeding amounted to a reduction of practical theory to a doctrine of the moral Legislator. Moreover, Storr endorsed the idea of necessity, yet was not at all convinced that revelation was possible only on the condition of human utter depravity. Why would God defer action till it is almost too late?[44] Besides, Storr wondered whether in Jesus' time the world of antiquity was so morally unsound. As a biblical theologian, Storr defended the reliability of historical data for ascertaining that a given occurrence was a divine revelation.[45] Finally, Storr raised the crucial question: Was there any empirical moral need for God to reveal his highest perfections?[46] Assuming that faith in a moral Legislator and Supreme Being was necessary from a practical point of view, Storr envisioned two instances in which a supernatural revelation, in a broader sense than Fichte's, might be expected. In one instance, that natural religion is either unavailable or incommunicable to people; in the other instance, that natural religion, though effectual as *Volksglaube,* is still too wanting in purity, clarity, and certainty to become actually *praktisch-brauchbar.* Nevertheless, in both instances a broader revelation is needed to prevent any moral demise. Fichte's argument is convincing, opined Storr, provided it is assumed that however depraved people might be, they are still capable of discerning a divine revelation.[47]

With regard to the second and third issues, the crux of Storr's argument was that, if revelation be the disclosure of practical truths *überhaupt* by a supernatural means, it must unveil more than just practical postulates. The content of revelation must therefore consist of the postulates as well as all practical truths useful for the advancement of morality even unknown to reason.[48] Storr thereby legitimized the adoption by practical reason of truths pertaining to positive religion. With Storr the confines of practical reason were extended far beyond the Kantian and Fichtean boundaries. To support his view, Storr converted every objection raised by Fichte against such an extension into a reason, be it ethical, gnoseological, or rational. (1) Positive teachings neither hinder freedom nor weaken pure morality, but incite the pursuit of the highest good. (2) Positive teachings are not *physisch unmöglich,* since things-in-themselves or supersensible objects are also intertwined in some kind of causality, and the moral law allows the application of the categories to the intelligible world, thereupon rendering licit its objective knowability. It will be noticed that Storr overstepped the confines of finite knowledge by giving speculative primacy to practical reason in its theoretical usage and thereby objectivized the Kantian and Fichtean *als ob* discourse. (3) Positive teachings successfully stand the test of reasonableness and moral needfulness.[49] Holy Communion and baptism are, for instance, positive teachings unknown to practical reason.[50]

The last issue consummated Storr's divorce from Fichte. Storr pressed his argument to its final conclusion. Although the *positio quaestionis* of the *Versuch* was apposite to its purpose, the conclusion was wanting. Thus Storr proposed to amend the Fichtean noetic principle. Neither theoretical nor practical arguments, on their own, are sufficiently convincing of the possibility of a particular revelation. Only a combination of both can remedy their individual deficiency.[51] Hence Storr considered an association of onto-theology with ethico-theology to be the pertinent procedure for the unfolding of a philosophical theory of revelation.

In the course of his argumentation, Storr referred to his disciple, Johann Friedrich Flatt, a Tübingen, Wolffian theologian, a fervent advocate of positive religion, and a stern adversary of Kantian ethico-theology. In his *Beyträge zur christlichen Dogmatik und Moral,* Flatt incorporated the dogmata of Trinity, resurrection, and incarnation into practical faith.[52]

Fichte's idea of a need for revelation, which Storr basically shared, was robbed of its originality by the *Popularphilosoph,* Friedrich Nicolai, in the damaging recension of Fichte's and Niethammer's essays in his *Neue Deutsche Allgemeine Bibliothek* (1793). Nicolai, who made no secret of his dislike for the novel *Zeitphilosophie,* held that the great figures of Lutheran orthodoxy had, long before Fichte and Niethammer, justified revelation by having recourse to the fall and its aftermath.[53] In a different, yet no less deprecatory, fashion, Flügge tried to enervate Fichte's argument of its *nervus probandi.* Flügge detected four major contradictions: (1) The presupposition that the rational being might lose moral consciousness was anthropologically untenable. (2) How could any religion arouse moral consciousness in supposedly degenerate people? (3) Would God not be expected to prevent such a downfall, which only revelation could rescue? (4) If Fichte were right, the most barbaric nations would have had the benefit of divine revelations.[54]

In the year 1793, Storr had already advocated in his *Doctrinae christianae pars theoretica e sacris litteris repetita* a supernatural revelation founded on the authority of scripture and had adduced a profusion of historical and psychological grounds to support this. In reaction to ethical rationalism, modern supernaturalism drew a hermeneutical circle. Supernatural agency justified the historical data which accounted for the factualness of immediate revelation. Quite understandably, Storr defended at length the legitimacy of the historical argument in his noted *Bemerkungen über Kants philosophische Religionslehre* of 1794. Following an intricate line of reasoning, Storr deduced that historical faith was not contrary to, but complementary to, practical faith.[55] Though historical faith has no claim whatsoever to necessity and universality, it can confirm, support, and enliven practical faith in the same fashion, believed Storr, that the physicoteleological argument of the third *Kritik* confirmed and strengthened the ethical proof of the existence of God. The conclusion Storr drew from his tendentious reading of Kant was that doctrinal and historical faiths come in support of practical faith.[56] Apropos of historical verification, Storr argued that theoretical reason should in historical matters surrender before historical reason, as it already surrendered in other respects to practical reason. Eventually Storr attained his goal, which consisted in demonstrating that Kant could not have objected to supernaturally revealed truths on the basis of his epistemological premises. That questionable ambition was attained by a dual *coup de force.* Indeed, Storr not only exploited unduly Kant's *innerhalb* but also interpreted the tentative synthesis of the third *Kritik* as an opening to a speculative usage of practical reason.[57]

In a similar vein, though less supernaturalistic, the church historian of Rostock, Samuel Gottlieb Lange, released in 1794 to a larger public a *Versuch einer Apologie der Offenbarung,* which followed Fichte's line of argumentation, but concluded apodictically to the incontrovertible possibility and desirability of supernatural revelation.[58] Lange opened his apology with an outline of a dualistic anthropology. The mechanistic laws govern the body, whereas the soul is ruled by freedom.[59] Moral perfection, which consists, as Kant demonstrated, in abiding thoroughly by the highest rational law, is the goal of life.[60] Lange then deduced the idea of religion from the moral nature and destination of the rational being.[61] Kantian in his definition of the "proper, true religion," or rational religion, whose sole requirement is faith in the moral Legislator, Lange contended that religion was necessary because of its connection with morality.[62] Morality and blissfulness, whose association conditions the purpose of humanity, demand both the idea of a Legislator and the hope in a better world to come. Having drawn the current distinction between natural and revealed religion, Lange defined revelation as the immediate divulgence by God himself of religious truths unknown to rational beings.[63] He proceeded to contradistinguish mediate revelation through nature from immediate revelation through the divine Word. Since the former had been deprived of any objectivity by critical epistemology, only the latter was worth considering.[64] In point of fact, Lange used Kant's critique of the physicotheological proof to advocate an immediate, instead of a mediate, revelation. There is here a definite affinity with Storr's procedure.

To the question of the possibility of immediate revelation, Lange answered that reason could object neither to an external revelation through a miracle nor to an internal revelation by divine inspiration.[65] As Fichte and Storr had done, Lange also fixed the conditions for an immediate revelation. As regards its external form, an immediate revelation should be: (1) unequivocal to those concerned; (2) proffered at a propitious time; and, (3) conveyed by a moral means.[66] With respect to its internal form, an immediate revelation should reveal the moral Legislator and stimulate by purely moral means the fulfillment of the moral law. As for the matter disclosed, Lange suggested it be true, hitherto unknown, and useful to the purpose of pure morality.[67] Finally, Lange discerned two reasons to account for the desirability of an immediate revelation; namely, the extension of our theoretical knowledge about the supernatural world and the specification of our duties.[68]

It is small wonder that Schelling, who had given primary attention to the third *Kritik*, directed, though covertly, his *Philosophische Briefe über Dogmatismus und Kriticismus* (1795) against Storr and Flatt, whom he rightly suspected of having appropriated practical reason for a doctrinaire purpose. The *Philosophische Briefe* were aimed at preventing philosophy from lapsing back into what Schelling termed *Schwärmerei* because of the predicament caused by the tension between dogmatism and criticism.[69] They were intended to be a warning against a resurgence of the dogmatic spirit that in post-Kantian times was crowning the theoretical with the practical in its absolutizing and objectivizing process. An advocate of practical idealism, Schelling pleaded for selfhood and freedom of the will.[70] Lest it be overpowered by dogmatism, criticism should renounce the ambition of objectivizing intellectual intuition. Otherwise, passivity would be substituted in the self for activity, and philosophy would lapse into illuminism. How philosophy becomes *Schwärmerei* was exemplified, opined Schelling, by Spinoza.[71] The absolute, as final purpose of our cognitive endeavor, should therefore remain an unattainable ideal, Schelling concluded.[72]

Of all the endeavors made in the 1790s to harmonize ethical rationalism with Christian revelation, none followed more closely the Kantian mode of thought than Johann Heinrich Tieftrunk's. In *Versuch einer Kritik der Religion und aller religiösen Dogmatik* (1790), Tieftrunk made a first, tentative vindication of a superior principle of reason unconstrained by the theologoumena of positive religion. He made another attempt at deducing the plan of Jesus from that principle in *Der einzigmögliche Zweck Jesu,* which induced Stäudlin to warn against the danger of disnaturing Christianity in his *Ideen zur Kritik des Systems der christlichen Religion.*[73] Finally, with his *Censur des christlichen protestantischen Lehrbegriffs nach den Principien der Religionskritik,* Tieftrunk wrote the most comprehensive critical revision of Christian dogmata a Kantian could produce. The *Censur,* which was circumstantially written in 1791 in response to the dogmatics of Döderlein and Morus, was to complete the task undertaken in the sixteenth century by the Reformers by laying the foundation for an unalterable and unpartisan scientific system of theology.[74] Moreover, Tieftrunk intended to end the internecine contest between reason and revelation, exemplified by the conflict between the rationalist demand for understanding and the supernaturalist need for belief. It comes as no surprise, therefore, that the prolegomena fill the first volume of the three-volume *Censur.*

Assuming that the religion of Jesus embodied all the essentials of perfect and universal religion,[75] Tieftrunk chose as a point of departure an anthropological datum: the will. Volition is governed by the law of unconditional autonomy.[76] Like all Kantians, Tieftrunk argued further that the agreement between morality and blissfulness necessitates the idea of a world ruler, and he therefore held as practically necessary what was theoretically impossible.[77] (In passing, it is worth noting that Tieftrunk rightly reproached Fichte for failing to grasp that the moral law was utterly valid and holy regardless of any faith in God.[78]) In true Kantian spirit, Tieftrunk was above all concerned about preserving the intrinsicality of the moral law in his search for a harmony with the extrinsicality of the divine will. Because of the enlightened desire for harmony, he defined religion *überhaupt* as the representation of our law of freedom as that of the will of God.[79] Unlike Storr, Tieftrunk was firmly opposed to founding religion on historical data, because of the religious despotism it brought about.[80]

Tieftrunk's line of reasoning, which proceeded from anthropology to ethics, and from ethics to religion, culminated in the contrast between natural and revealed religion. Natural religion, as deduced from observation and experience of nature, is inconceivable, since in the theory of nature the teleological principle is unfitted to reach, beyond its confines, either ethics or theology. Thus natural religion should be relinquished unless we consider what is revealed to us by the moral law. The moral law indicates a supersensible, intelligible world that we may call nature inasmuch as nature means *das Dasein der Dinge unter Gesetzen.* The law of freedom, which commands access to the intelligible world, is conducive to natural religion, that is better termed *Vernunftreligion.* Natural or rational religion is characterized as immediate, subjective, ethical, and universal.[81]

If natural or rational religion consists of inwardly revealed religion, is revealed religion, as distinct from rational religion, conceivable at all? Two issues were at stake here, and Tieftrunk approached them separately. He dealt first with the conditions and the role of revealed religion, and only after the theological task of reason had been assessed did he treat the probability of revelation which revolved around the question of the credibility of the miraculous. Unlike Fichte, Tieftrunk did not deduce the logical possibility of revelation from pure, practical reason, but, assuming the existence of revealed dogmata, he submitted their alleged specificity and unfathomableness to the test of theoretical and practical reason. This was far more like the Kantian approach of *Die Religion.* From a fastidious scrutiny of the dogmata and mysteries adduced, first by the fideists Döderlein and Morus, and later by some critical reviewers of the first edition of the *Censur,* in support of the exclusiveness of supernatural knowledge—be it the idea of God, human sinfulness, divine benevolence, Jesus' plan, resurrection, incarnation, or redemption—Tieftrunk concluded that none of these theologoumena, apart from the doctrine of recapitulation, was actually impenetrable to reason, and that the difference of knowledge was not a matter of kind but of origin.[82] It ensued, according to Tieftrunk, that revealed religion was acceptable, as heteronomous teaching, on the specific condition, first, that its content not be contrary to reason, and, second, that it be accessible to our cognitive faculty.[83] So as the *principium essendi* of all revealed dogmata is determined by practical reason, the *principium cognoscendi* is determined by theoretical reason. However unique and novel dogmata might be, they cannot be superrational either practically or theoretically. As regards the role played by revealed religion, Tieftrunk discerned a dual function; namely, that of making known hitherto unknown intelligible teachings and coincidental empirical facts.[84]

Following Tieftrunk's view, Heinrich Philipp Konrad Henke proposed in his *Lineamenta institutionum fidei christianae historicocriticarum* (1793) to render the distinction between natural and revealed religion by the dichotomy of rational and authoritarian religion.[85] Whereupon Jacob Christoph Rudolph Eckermann, who altered Tieftrunk's and Schmid's ethicism into full-fledged rationalism which reached its heyday in 1813 with Röhr's *Briefe über den Rationalismus,* objected in his *Handbuch für das systematische Studium der christlichen Glaubenslehre* (1801) that Henke's dichotomy could be understood only as a subdivision of the current distinction.[86] Eckermann argued that the concepts of natural and revealed religion corresponded to a noetic origin. Eckermann's amendment signified a return beyond criticism to the neological formula and foretold as well the crucial shift of ethical rationalism toward the denial of immediate supernatural revelation which Röhr epitomized.[87]

Before tackling the issue of the miraculous, Tieftrunk decided, departing from both Kant and Fichte, to call theology only the doctrine of God, and was imitated by Christoph Friedrich von Ammon.[88] Tieftrunk upheld against Döderlein a regulative and sometimes constitutive function of the employment of reason. Besides the Kantian dichotomy of theoretical and practical, another distinction was drawn between objective and subjective reason, or noetic content and capacity.[89] Moreover, Tieftrunk held that even the most unfathomable dogmata must be subjected to the censorship of reason in its capacity as the superior noetic principle and despite its self-designated confines.[90] To the question of whether such a subjection was acceptable from the point of view of Christian revelation, Tieftrunk answered by advocating a harmony of purpose between revelation and reason. The crux of his argument, strongly disputed by Stäudlin, was that reason and religion had a congruent essence, and that the power and restraint of reason corresponded to the true spirit of the religion of Jesus.[91]

The miraculous was treated at length by Tieftrunk as a catalyst for the material possibility of revelation. Tieftrunk eventually drew thirteen conclusions: (1) Miracles are in the order of the possible logically, physically, and practically; (2) their factuality is unascertainable; (3) their historical credibility depends on the reliability of the narrators; (4) theoretical and practical reason are prejudiced against the miraculous because of its incompatibility with their type of causality; (5) so long as the interests of reason are preserved, certain occurrences might remain unaccountable and still be considered, practically, to serve the purpose of the universe; (6) these occurrences have no significance on their own; (7) they merely attract attention to a person, being signs, testimonies, or manifestations of someone's greatness; (8) the miraculous pertained to the mentality of the world of antiquity; (9) Jesus performed miracles to attain his end; (10) miracles as such do not pertain to the essence of religion; (11) miracles only strengthened Jesus' teaching in order to certify him as sent by God; (12) Jesus reproved the desire for miracles; (13) the apostles themselves disregarded miracles and focused on essentials such as love, faith, and hope.[92]

Tieftrunk's attempt to fit revelation into the larger sphere of rational faith met with resistance from Stäudlin. Though Kantian, Stäudlin apprehended that a systematic rational harmonization might put in jeopardy the theonomic dimension of Christian anthropology and ethics.[93] The alternative solution he proposed in *Ideen zur Kritik des Systems der christlichen Religion* (1791) stands halfway between Tieftrunk's and Storr's. To tackle the issue of revelation, Stäudlin distinguished natural and supernatural revelation. Both are noetic, yet the former originates from our cognitive faculty while the latter is eventual and miraculous.[94] Since the concept of supernatural revelation *(überhaupt)* is inseparable from that of wonder, Stäudlin deduced that, in spite of the empirical unaccountability, miracles were nonetheless possible logically, objectively, and morally and that their finality was either auxiliatory or instructional.[95] Stäudlin then attributed two conceivable functions to supernatural revelation; namely, that of sanctioning truths already known or that of unveiling truths of which the rational being is unaware. Such a dual function presupposes some preconceptions of perfection, good, and duty, as well as a natural capacity or openness to supernatural knowledge.[96] As a true son of the Enlightenment, Stäudlin deplored the fact that supernatural revelation had often been incorporated into systems which promoted despotism.[97] Moreover, Stäudlin addressed three philosophical issues. First, he demonstrated at length that reason was capable of arousing more than a mere religious need and that supernatural revelation contributed to the enhancement and enrichment of reason. Second, he suggested that supernatural revelation be submitted to the same test to which miracles were subjected. Finally, against Kant and Carl C. Schmid, he argued that, far from weakening morality or putting religious awareness to sleep, supernatural revelation served the purpose of humanity.[98] Regarding its content, Stäudlin noted that even if it were unfathomable to the point that it had to be acknowledged on divine authority, it could neither contradict reason nor hinder freedom.[99] The various forms supernatural revelation could take, according to Stäudlin, were a mute symbolic event, a proclamation, or an extraordinary envoy as in Christianity.[100] Eventually narrowing his reflection to Christian revelation, Stäudlin contended that its specificity consisted in teaching, by way of sensible and symbolic forms, monotheism, the immortality of the soul, the fatherhood of God, and the correlation between morality and religion.[101] What can be said of Stäudlin's endeavor to rescue supernatural revelation? As the references which punctuate his *Ideen* testify, Stäudlin proffered a clever combination of fideism with neological ideals and ethical rationalism.

Whereas Kantian philosophers and theologians of the 1790s focused their attention, as they treated revelation, on its possibility, finality, credibility, desirability, and its features, a disciple of Reinhard and Reinhold, Wilhelm Traugott Krug, who later succeeded Kant at Königsberg, raised the issue of the perfectibility of Christian revelation in his *Briefe über die Perfektibilität der geoffenbarten Religion,* collectively released in 1795. It was the reading of Teller and Semler in the winter of 1792 which first gave Krug the idea, and he then became acquainted with criticism. The neological belief in the progress of humanity coupled with practical faith defined the background against which the *Briefe* were drafted. They were intended to unfold the prolegomena to a science of Christian religion. In order to achieve this ambition, Krug proceeded in three stages. First, he evinced the universality and necessity of the principle of the perfectibility of revealed religion; then he answered some objections and showed the practical advantage of revealed religion; lastly, he described its impact on theology and the science of religion. Krug started from Lessing's idea of a progressive education of humanity toward perfection and blissfulness.[102] Likewise, he contended, revealed religion could be elevated to a higher perfection by improving its clarity, purity, completeness, and usefulness. The reason for taking such trouble, argued Krug, lies in the pedagogic strategy implemented by revealed religion, which could be used by wise rulers for the ennoblement of humanity. Do the scriptures not reveal their message progressively from the patriarchs to Jesus, the *Menschenbeglücker?*[103] Notwithstanding this, Krug denied that the latest revelation is the fulfillment of revealed religion. Christian revelation is no final revelation.[104] With Jesus and the apostles a decisive step was taken, but not the final one. According to Krug, there is no mention in the scriptures of any perfect religion. What Jesus did was not much different from what other teachers have done and do: He devised a plan. That his plan was ethical and universal did not imply that he was teaching the most perfect religion. Had Jesus desired to establish a perfect belief, would he not have framed a system? What Jesus actually performed was to give impetus to the inquiry in the fields of morality and religion. By doing so, he became the greatest and wisest *Volkslehrer* of all time.[105]

Krug spent considerable energy refuting criticisms. One of the objections to his thesis had been raised by those who believed in divine inspiration. Such a claim, replied Krug, was disproved by the deficiencies and errors which abound in the scriptures.[106] As the theopneustia is related to Christology and revelation, Krug proceeded further to demonstrate that Jesus was above all a teacher and that the assumption of an immediate revelation was as arbitrary and unfounded as the assumption of a perfect, revealed religion. To decide on the basis of either the concept of revelation or the divine attribute of omnipotence whether revelation was mediate or immediate was impossible. Even if one were to scrutinize the biblical narratives, it might prove as difficult to decide whether the dreams and visions resulted from a natural disposition of the heart or had been effected by a divine agency. Krug conjectured that confirmation could be given by another divine intervention. Yet even then the way God acts on rational beings would remain unfathomable. Miracles and prophecies are of no avail either. Appealing to Hume, among others, Krug insisted that natural and psychological sciences rob the miraculous of its credibility.[107] Krug's refutations discredited ethical supernaturalism and ethical rationalism as well: one on account of its unfoundedness, the other on account of its inconsistency.

Since the theory of the perfectibility of revealed religion constituted a *preambula theologiae,* Christian dogmata would have to be submitted to substantial modifications. These Krugian alterations were carried out by a normative instrument, reason, and by the enlightened method of accommodation.[108] Semler had propounded an exegetical, and Kant a dogmatic, accommodation. It was Krug's contention that the latter was appropriate for extracting the pure rational core of revealed religion and performing afterward the extensive program of perfectibility. Thus Krug proposed to amend Christian dogmatics in four respects. First, the relationship between subjective and objective religion must be redefined. Because subjective religion originates from a universal feeling of dependence on a higher Being, and objective religion is a mere codification of it (the scriptures), the former is superior to the latter. Second, special emphasis should be laid on the perennity, universality, and perfectibility of revealed religion. Third, although theology and religion pursue an identical purpose, the term "theology" should be reserved for the positive theory of religion which embraces not only the scriptures but also philosophy, philology, and history. Fourth, the fundamental articles of faith must be framed accordingly. They are of three sorts: (1) the universal, fundamental articles; namely, God, the immortality of the soul, and freedom, which, as Krug believed, Jesus taught; (2) the dogmatic, fundamental articles or practical teachings of Jesus; and (3) the statutory or historical, fundamental articles, such as the sacraments, which, unlike the other articles, belong properly to Christian faith.[109] It will have been noticed that Krug derived the universal articles from the Wolffian special metaphysics and the Kantian transcendental ideal, the dogmatic from the doctrine of practical faith, and the statutory from the parerga of *Die Religion.* Interestingly enough, Krug drew up his comprehensive, rationalizing program, which basically amounted to correcting objective religion by subjective religion, while denying that he was either a Wolffian or a Kantian,[110] a denial which did not preclude him from writing, in 1798, a sort of apology of Kantian philosophy.[111]

In the year 1797 a follower of Jacobi and Reinhold, Johann Neeb, who taught at Bonn, proffered another kind of solution. In *Vernunft gegen Vernunft oder Rechtfertigung des Glaubens,* Neeb laid the foundations for a theology of subjective revelation on practical reason. Though he did not claim the Kantian heritage directly, he valued the ingeniosity of the moral argument.[112] Neeb's apology for faith, which is reminiscent of Pascal and Jacobi, was based on a subtle combination of Stoicism with a variation of Kantism.[113] Discarding the lifeless *Ens entium,* Neeb stressed the living and loving God of the heart.[114] Then he coupled religion and morality, to the extent that he identified the Word of God or the incarnation with practical reason, and the voice of God with the moral law.[115] In Platonic fashion, Neeb used the artifice of a dialogue between the fideist Gotthold and the rationalist Freymuth to propound his view. In the course of the dialogue, while Spinoza and Leibniz were weighed and contrasted, Freymuth contended that practical reason was God's messenger and advocated the association of moral obedience with spiritual adoration.[116] Neeb concluded that, since religion was unconditional obedience to the Legislator and his law, there was an inner, factual, and eternal divine revelation which bore the same features that any external revelation might possess. Neeb's conclusion has to be understood against the background of Leibniz's immediateness of the soul with God. Unsurprisingly, Neeb altered the Kantian theory of practical reason in two respects: first, when he claimed that Kant had actually described the natural history of the human heart, Neeb systematized ethical criticism by objectivizing the *als ob.*[117] Second, he theonomized the moral law, annihilating thereby the crucial autonomy of practical reason. These corrections renewed the heritage of Leibniz and Wolff, on the one hand, and showed affinity with the ethical, supernaturalist view sustained by Christoph Friedrich von Ammon, among others. The aim of Ammon's *Von dem Ursprunge und der Beschaffenheit einer unmittelbaren göttlichen Offenbarung* was, indeed, to demonstrate that the inner, moral instructions originated from an immediate, divine revelation in the soul. With Ammon freedom meant submission to divine will. Ammon and Storr exemplified two ways in which Kant was reclaimed by the fideists.

III

Who better than Johann Christian August Grohmann could be called on to give the conclusive appraisal of the attempts to justify revelation in the 1790s? In 1799, the very year that Schelling ensured the turn to nature of Fichte's idealism, and Schleiermacher affranchised religion from the dual confines of ethicism and dogmatism, Grohmann's *Über Offenbarung und Mythologie* stigmatized the *leere Lufthimmel* whereon the so-called Kantian theologians and "half-philosophers" founded the possibility of revelation.[118] Grohmann, who taught at Hamburg, first of all deplored the use of the hypothetical concept of noumenon as the foundation stone of realism, dogmatism, supernaturalism, and even mysticism.[119]

Such a usage was illicit, since Kant never suggested that the noumenon was a substratum of the phenomenon.[120] Grohmann wondered how the concept of revelation, which associates the supersensible with the sensible, was logically possible. Such a coalescence sounded quite paradoxical to him. In the second place Grohmann objected that Kant also did not suggest that a revelation of supernature could occur through nature.[121] The dichotomy of theoretical and practical reason provided Grohmann with his third objection. Just as the practical cannot use the theoretical channel, so the supernatural may not use the natural. This applies likewise, noted Grohmann, to supersensible, theoretical dogmata. In Grohmann's opinion, Fichte, Heydenreich, Tieftrunk, Storr, and Ammon all failed to understand the true nature of Kantism.[122] Grohmann argued that since revelation is a transcendent concept, there is little we can do unless we alter the purport of the concept.[123] If we understand revelation as practical instruction, we refer to something every rational being can provide for himself. Though Storr rightly argued, opined Grohmann, that reason could not pronounce upon supersensible objects, he fell short of extending the argument to revelation. Instead, Storr drew a *circulus in demonstrando* by founding the supernatural occurrence on the miraculous.[124]

What Grohmann, like Schelling, dreaded most was a resurgence of the dogmatism and realism of orthodoxy, which could, he believed, be warded off by confining revelation to the realm of utopia.[125] What sort of philosophizing was it which adduced evidences from every available source, be it morality, history, or pedagogy?[126] Finally, Grohmann refuted the assumption that revelation was an aid to morality, because such an idea demeaned human dignity. From the point of view of moral freedom, that Kant defended, revelation was utterly superfluous.[127] The overall conclusion Grohmann drew was that all these endeavors, marred by religious enthusiasm, mysticism, supernaturalism, and absurdity, turned out to be profoundly unphilosophical.[128]

Grohmann's criticism might be well founded. After all, was practical faith not intended to substitute for statutory faith, as the conclusion of the enlightened process of liberation from the bondage of authoritarian truth? Were all these variegated endeavors at rescuing Christian revelation from wreck not unavoidably apologetic, inasmuch as they attempted, often covertly, to elude by every available means the dictates of the natural sciences on the one hand and of practical reason on the other?

NOTES

1. J. Schultz, *Erläuterungen über des Herrn Professor Kant Critik der reinen Vernunft* (Königsberg, 1791); F. G. Born, *Versuch über die ursprünglichen Grundlagen des menschlichen Denkens* (Leipzig, 1791).

2. C. W. Flügge, *Versuch einer historisch-kritischen Darstellung des bisherigen Einflusses der Kantischen Philosophie auf alle Zweige der wissenschaftlichen und praktischen Theologie,* 2 vols. (Hanover, 1796, 1798), 1:6.

3. Ibid., pp. 16–18.

4. Ibid., p. 45.

5. Ibid., p. 48.

6. Ibid., pp. 86–87.

7. *Kants Opus Postumus,* published by Adickes in *Kantstudien* (Berlin, 1920).

8. I. Kant, *Kritik der reinen Vernunft* (Riga, 1781), p. 631; 2nd ed. (Riga, 1787), p. 659.

9. See Kant's essay written on the occasion of the pantheist controversy entitled *"Was heisst: sich im Denken orientieren?"* (*Berliner Monatsschrift,* October 1786; *Werke,* ed. by W. Weischedel, vol. 3, p. 267) and the extensive discussion in relation to statutory faith in *Die Religion* and in *Der Streit der Facultäten* (Königsberg, 1798), pp. 43–63.

10. C. F. Stäudlin, *Geschichte des Rationalismus und Supranaturalismus* (Göttingen, 1826), pp. 148–149.

11. J. H. Tieftrunk, *Einzigmöglicher Zweck Jesu* (Berlin, 1789); *Versuch einer Kritik der Religion und aller religiösen Dogmatik* (Berlin, 1790); C. F. Stäudlin, *Ideen zur Kritik des Systems der christlichen Religion* (Göttingen, 1791).

12. M. Weinhold, *48 Briefe von Fichte und seinen Verwandten* (1862), p. 20 (March 5, 1791); *Briefwechsel von I. Kant,* ed. by H. E. Fischer (Munich, 1912), vol. 2, p. 233 (August 1791).

13. J. G. Fichte, *Sämmtliche Werke* (Berlin, 1845–46), vol. 5, p. 381.

14. Ibid., p. 405.

15. "Der Idealismus kann nie Denken sein, sondern er ist nur Spekulation." (Fichte, *Zweite Einleitung in die Wissenschaftslehre,* 1797/98; *Sämmtliche Werke* 1:455.)

16. Fichte, *Versuch einer Kritik aller Offenbarung; Sämmtliche Werke* 5:16.

17. Ibid., pp. 40–59.

18. Ibid., p. 42.

19. "Die Idee von Gott, als Gesetzgeber durch Moralgesetz in uns, gründet sich also auf eine Entäusserung des unserigen, auf

Übertragung eines Subjektiven in ein Wesen ausser uns" (ibid., p. 55).

20. Ibid., p. 55.
21. Ibid., pp. 58–64, 60.
22. Ibid., p. 62.
23. Ibid., p. 80.
24. Ibid., paras. 6 and 12.
25. "Conceptus non datus, sed ratiocinatus" (ibid., p. 82).
26. Ibid., pp. 80, 155–157.
27. Ibid., p. 109.
28. Ibid., pp. 112, 113.
29. Ibid., pp. 114, 115.
30. Ibid., p. 127.
31. Ibid., pp. 146, 152.
32. Stäudlin, *Geschichte,* p. 189.
33. K. H. Heydenreich, *Betrachtungen über die Philosophie der natürlichen Religion* (1790), vol. 2, pp. 190–193, 197–207.
34. I. Kant, *Die Religion innerhalb der Grenzen der blossen Vernunft,* 2nd ed. (Königsberg, 1794), pp. xxi–xxii.
35. I. Kant, *Der Streit der Facultäten in drey Abschnitten* (Königsberg, 1798), pp. 16–17, 44–63.
36. F. I. Niethammer, *Über den Versuch einer Kritik aller Offenbarung* (Jena, 1792).
37. Ibid., p. 117.
38. Ibid., p. 14.
39. F. I. Niethammer, *Versuch einer Begründung des vernünftmässigen Offenbarungsglaubens* (Leipzig and Jena, 1798), pp. 21, 22.
40. Ibid., p. 25.
41. F. G. Suskind, Review of Fichte's *Versuch,* in *Neue Deutsche Allgemeine Bibliothek* (Keil, 1793), vol. 2, part 1, p. 3.
42. F. G. Storr, *Bemerkungen über den aus Principien der praktischen Vernunft hergeleiteten Überzeugungsgrund von der Möglichkeit und Wirklichkeit einer Offenbarung in Beziehung auf Fichtes Versuch einer Kritik aller Offenbarung* (Tübingen, 1794), p. 138.
43. Ibid., pp. 139, 142, 104.
44. Ibid., p. 147.
45. Ibid., p. 153.
46. Ibid., pp. 155–160.
47. Ibid., p. 164.
48. Ibid., p. 165.
49. Ibid., pp. 166–217.
50. Ibid., pp. 218–223.
51. Ibid., pp. 223–240.

52. J. F. Flatt, *Beyträge zur christlichen Dogmatik und Moral* (Tübingen, 1792), p. 114.
53. F. Nicolai, review of Fichte's and Niethammer's essays, in *Neue Deutsche Allgemeine Bibliothek* (Keil, 1793), vol. 2, part 1, p. 25.
54. C. W. Flügge, op. cit. (note 2), pp. 262–266.
55. F. G. Storr, *Bemerkungen über Kants philosophische Religionslehre* (Tübingen, 1794), pp. 26, 30, 31.
56. Ibid., p. 67.
57. Ibid., pp. 75–76, 78–79; also see Stäudlin's *Geschichte des Rationalismus und Supranaturalismus,* pp. 207–209.
58. S. G. Lange, *Versuch einer Apologie der Offenbarung* (Jena, 1794).
59. Ibid., pp. 40, 61.
60. Ibid., pp. 84, 85.
61. Ibid., p. 101.
62. Ibid., pp. 109, 110, 130.
63. Ibid., p. 145.
64. Ibid., pp. 149–160.
65. Ibid., pp. 166–173.
66. Ibid., pp. 178–190.
67. Ibid., pp. 196, 198, 209.
68. Ibid., p. 215.
69. F. W. J. Schelling, *Philosophische Briefe über Dogmatismus und Kriticismus.* In *Werke,* ed. M. Schroter (Munich, 1927), rev. ed. 1958, 1:256, 263.
70. Ibid., p. 264.
71. Ibid., pp. 245–246.
72. Ibid., p. 255.
73. Stäudlin, *Ideen zur Kritik,* pp. 106–112.
74. J. H. Tieftrunk, *Censur des christlichen protestantischen Lehrbegriffs nach den Principien der Religionskritik,* 3 vols. (Berlin, 1791–95; 2nd ed., vol. 1, 1796), pp. 6–7, 9, 26–33.
75. Ibid., pp. 19, 22.
76. Ibid., p. 48.
77. Ibid., p. 50.
78. Ibid., p. 51.
79. Ibid., p. 55.
80. Ibid., p. 59.
81. Ibid., pp. 71, 73.
82. Ibid., pp. 92–107, 111, 144–172.
83. Ibid., pp. 129, 130.
84. Ibid., pp. 139, 140.
85. H. P. K. Henke, *Lineamenta institutionum fidei christianae historicocriticarum* (Helmstedt, 1793), para. 2.

86. J. C. R. Eckermann, *Handbuch für das systematische Studium der christlichen Glaubenslehre* (Altona, 1801), pp. 161–178.

87. J. F. Röhr, *Briefe über den Rationalismus* (Aachen, 1813), pp. 60–68.

88. C. F. von Ammon, *Entwurf einer Wissenschaftlich-praktischen Theologie* (Göttingen, 1797), pp. 3–4.

89. Tieftrunk, *Censur,* pp. 187–188.

90. Ibid., p. 219.

91. Ibid., p. 220.

92. Ibid., pp. 316, 317.

93. Stäudlin, *Ideen zur Kritik,* p. 172.

94. Ibid., pp. 173, 174.

95. Ibid., pp. 184, 185.

96. Ibid., p. 194.

97. Ibid., p. 205.

98. Ibid., p. 223.

99. Ibid., p. 238.

100. Ibid., p. 243.

101. Ibid., pp. 254–258.

102. W. T. Krug, *Briefe über die Perfektibilität der geoffenbarten Religion* (Jena and Leipzig, 1795), p. 19.

103. Ibid., p. 22.

104. Ibid., p. 43.

105. Ibid., pp. 58, 49.

106. Ibid., p. 65.

107. Ibid., pp. 79–97.

108. Ibid., pp. 45, 149–157; see C. W. Flügge, op. cit. (note 2), pp. 249–260.

109. Ibid., pp. 152–169.

110. Ibid., pp. 209–294.

111. W. T. Krug, *Über das Verhältnis der kritischen Philosophie zur moralischen, politischen, und religiösen Kultur des Menschen* (Jena, 1798).

112. J. Neeb, *Vernunft gegen Vernunft oder Rechtfertigung des Glaubens* (Frankfurt am Main, 1797), p. 362.

113. Ibid., p. 351.

114. Ibid., p. 349.

115. Ibid., pp. 355, 356.

116. Ibid., pp. 332, 333.

117. Ibid., p. 361.

118. J. C. A. Grohmann, *Über Offenbarung und Mythologie* (Berlin, 1799), pp. 144, 134, 140.

119. Ibid., p. 136.

120. Ibid., p. 142.

121. Ibid., p. 143.

122. Ibid., p. 145.
123. Ibid., p. 154.
124. Ibid., pp. 146, 151.
125. Ibid., p. 152.
126. Ibid., pp. 155, 158, 161, 182.
127. Ibid., p. 173.
128. Ibid., p. 202.

Practical Belief: Friedrich Karl Forberg (1770–1848) and the Fictionalist View of Religious Language

B. A. Gerrish

It is *"not a duty to believe"* that a moral world-government, or a God as moral governor of the world, exists. It is simply and solely a *"duty to act as if you believed it."*

Anthropomorphism is the touchstone of all theology. From the way a theologian deals with it . . . you can confidently deduce whether or not he has his principles straight.

—Forberg

Christian theologians have always recognized what John Calvin perceived as a certain "impropriety" in language about God, since nothing at all can be said of the divine majesty except by analogies taken from created things *(nisi similitudine a creaturis mutuo sumpta).*[1] The problem goes back in part to the Bible itself, which, in particular, freely applies *human* characteristics to God while cautioning us that God is God and not a human (Hosea 11:9). Not surprisingly, the way in which the theologians have dealt with the problem of "anthropomorphism," as we call it, has often reflected the prevailing philosophical mentality of their day. Forberg's thoughts on the subject were put together in an atmosphere filled with excitement over the revolutionary ideas of Immanuel Kant (1724–1804). It was an article by Forberg on the concept of religion that sparked the famous Atheism Controversy in 1798, in which, however, he was totally eclipsed by his older colleague and friend Johann Gottlieb Fichte (1762–1814). History has left Forberg in the shadow cast by the greater man. His writings are difficult to obtain, and one scholar who has written on the Atheism Controversy dismisses him as "a philosophical author without philosophical talent" (Fritz Medicus).

More encouraging was the opinion of Hans Vaihinger (1852–1933), who hailed Forberg as a forerunner of fictionalism, or the "philosophy of *as if.*" In Vaihinger's view, Forberg was the only person who really understood Kant's as-if doctrine until Vaihinger himself.[2] And on closer inspection, I think that Forberg's application of the as-if doctrine to religious language can be shown to have philosophical merit. In any case, that is what I shall try to show. Admittedly, the result is not a direct "probing" of the Reformed tradition, but it ought to shed some light on what Forberg identified as the touchstone *(Probierstein)* of *all* theology: the problem of anthropomorphic language about God. It will be as well to begin with at least a provisional definition of "fictionalism," and that can perhaps best be done by contrasting "fictionalism" with Calvin's familiar principle of "accommodation."

I. From Accommodation to Fictionalism

For his solution to biblical anthropomorphism, Calvin turned to an exegetical tradition that went back, beyond medieval Scholasticism, at least to Origen of Alexandria (c. 185–c. 254). Origen stood in the Platonic line that had already been wedded with the Hebrew scriptures by Philo Judaeus (c. 15 B.C.E.–c. 45 C.E.); he held that the language of the Bible is "accommodated" to our limited human capacities. Calvin adopted the principle of accommodation as a comprehensive understanding of revelation, since revelation can come to us solely by an act of divine condescension that has regard for our human limitations. But I am concerned with the principle here only insofar as it provided him with an easy solution to the problem of anthropomorphism whenever he encountered it in his biblical texts.

Take, for example, the notion of God's "anger" or "wrath." It is common enough in the scriptures, and yet we know that we should not attribute human emotions to God. The difficulty is compounded when the scriptures represent God as angry with the very same persons whom his love moves him to save; for here there seems to be a conflict in the mind or heart of God. Calvin disposes of the difficulty (his own confident phrase) by invoking the principle of accommodation. God represents himself to us not as he *is* in himself but as he *seems* to us. "Anger" is an expression taken from our human experience: When God exercises judgment, he gives the *appearance* of a person whose anger is kindled. And this is how he shows himself even to those for whom Christ died, to impress upon them their desperate need for the redemption Christ provides. God is *perceived as* hostile to them *(quodammodo infestus);* and, although this is said by way of accommodation, it is not said falsely.[3]

Calvin goes on to make his point more complicated by agreeing with Augustine (354–430) that God still loves in us what he has made but hates what we sinners have made of ourselves. Clearly, this is a quite different way of solving the problem of God's wrath. But we can set it aside and simply conclude that by "accommodation" (in the context of anthropomorphism) is meant God's representing himself in human terms for the sake of practical ends: to control our attitudes and our behavior. And we may add that this hermeneutic device is fully consistent with Calvin's dominant image of God as a devoted parent. Accommodated language—sometimes at least—is a kind of pretending; indeed, revelation in general is child talk, like the language a nurse uses when playing with a baby.[4]

Now, religious communities are no doubt skilled in making mental adjustments to biblical language without any help from theologians. But one can well imagine the anthropomorphites being troubled even by such modest adjustments as Calvin proposed. For what prevents accommodation from becoming a more or less subtle form of reductionism, which actually loses something that was present in the primary language of faith? Or perhaps the accommodated language still contains *too much,* being in fact no less anthropomorphic than the language it is supposed to interpret. Must it not occur to someone to wonder, sooner or later, whether God is not just without "body, parts, or passions" but not *properly* a person at all? And will he or she perhaps conclude that the language of faith is not prescribed by God's own authority (as, so to say, authorized child talk), but rather created, or at least molded, by our infantile human nature, which Calvin himself aptly described as a "factory of idols"?[5] When that happens, "accommodation" passes over into "fictionalism." And it did in fact happen in the wake of the philosophical revolution brought about by Kant.

Perhaps fictionalism could be described as a radicalized accommodation theory; Kant himself expressly appealed to the principle of accommodation.[6] But it is obvious that Kant's attitude to religious language, or religious ideas (as he would say), was quite different from Calvin's in at least two respects. First, Kant's interest was entirely in the way in which the human reason generates the ideas. He was not offering a doctrine of divine revelation, so that, strictly speaking, the term "accommodation" was no longer appropriate. Secondly, he retained the ideas solely for their practical utility and not because of their objective referent (if any). The revolutionary theory of knowledge in the *Critique of Pure Reason* (1781) led him to conclude that the concept of a Supreme Intelligence is a *mere* idea, justified not by its supposed reference to an actual object but by its usefulness to scientific inquiry insofar as it inspires the quest for a single system of empirical knowledge. We should look on every connection in the world *as if* it had its source in a single, all-sufficient, and necessary first cause. Hence Kant was quite happy to consider the idea of God as a purely mental object; and "belief" was his word for entertaining such an idea—that is, acknowledging its practical utility and permitting oneself to be guided by it.[7]

In the *Critique of Practical Reason* (1788) and *Religion Within the Limits of Reason Alone* (1793), Kant extended the discussion beyond the domain of science and sought to establish the utility of certain religious ideas, including the idea of God, also to morality and religion itself. But it is not my intention to follow him there. That would require me to take up some of the most hotly contested issues in the renewed Kant scholarship of the present day. I turn instead to Forberg, Kant's lesser German disciple and the supposed forerunner of the fictionalist philosophy that Vaihinger espoused. It is true that Vaihinger's generous compliment to Forberg (the only true interpreter of Kant) was not unqualified: He insisted that he was in no way dependent on Forberg for his understanding of Kant, or dependent on Kant for the philosophy of as-if, and he said that Forberg's conception of the Kantian as-if doctrine was inconsistent and contradictory. "The appeal to Forberg was, and is, for me," he wrote, "only an incidental chapter in my book. Forberg is for me not an authority but a curiosity."[8] However, undeterred by that slight (the practical utility of which is only too clear), I hope to show that a look at Forberg may help us to sort out some of the problems that still occupy us. That, I take it, is finally why we read any thinker from the past, not because we seek an authority or a mere historical diversion.

What, then, is the fictionalist theory that Forberg is credited with anticipating? As Vaihinger understands it, the term "fiction" denotes a way of thinking known to be false, or not in accordance with known facts, but retained for the time being because of its usefulness in organizing some aspect of our experience.[9] In other words, if I may venture a paraphrase: to construct a fiction is not to give an imaginative rendering of the way things are, or at least may be, but to create a wholly imaginary object, even an imaginary world, for strictly practical ends. For now, we will take fictionalism in this tough sense, which theologically, of course, is atheistic. My thesis is, then, twofold: first, that Forberg probably was not a fictionalist at all in this sense; and second, that the agnostic position he advocated, though philosophically safe, clearly left him on the threshold of a fresh venture into philosophical theology—that is, a fresh attempt to represent the real world rather than to create another. The way to this double conclusion leads through a brief look at the three most pertinent sources: his autobiography, his article that sparked the Atheism Controversy, and his defense against his accusers.

II. The Career of a Missing Person

Forberg's autobiography, written when he was approaching his seventieth birthday, is a sprightly document of uncommon personal and historical interest despite its brevity (it is only sixty-one pages long).[10] Charming, witty, and often mischievous, he keeps the reader entertained while opening up one corner of eighteenth-century German society at the time of the French Revolution. The excitement of the intelligentsia over Kant's publications is vividly illustrated in an account of discussions held in the residence of Baron Franz Paul von Herbert (1759–1811). Forberg notes the presence of two young ladies, the sisters von Drer, who were Roman Catholic. Since their parents were bigots (as Forberg candidly puts it), the sisters were not permitted to discuss the critical philosophy at home. Ingeniously, they had copies of Kant's forbidden books specially bound in black and took them to Mass with them instead of their missals. Of one of the two sisters, Babette, the aging Forberg says that he still preserves a silhouette of her in his family album and preserves her memory in his heart.

The information given in the autobiography appears to be meticulously accurate: Forberg recalls minute details, gives exact dates, and reports in quotation marks precisely what (he claims) was said. He must surely have kept a diary. For my purposes, what is important is the context he provides for understanding his alleged atheism. He writes as an eighteenth-century "alienated theologian" (to borrow Van Harvey's expression). Brought up in a clergyman's household and himself destined for the Lutheran ministry, he becomes increasingly indifferent to conventional religion. He is captivated by the new philosophy, embroiled in public controversy, renounces even the vocation of the philosopher, and passes quietly from the academic scene. Forberg entitled his autobiography *Ca-*

reer of a Missing Person. (The German word has the legal sense of "pronounced missing" or even "presumed dead.") Whether there is a trace of bitterness in his chosen title, I am not sure. There seems to have been no special occasion for writing—just the sense, perhaps, that time was running out.

His mother, Forberg tells us, was of the melancholic type and very devout. Steeped in pietistic literature, she worried that she was not sufficiently conscious of her sins. "She thought amazingly highly of the Lord Jesus, as she always called him. He was supposed to help her in every need, and in comparison God receded, so to say, into the background of her heart." The father, by contrast, was choleric: short-tempered, but quickly over it. Basically he was orthodox, yet no bigot. Though he spoke disparagingly of Voltaire (1694–1778) and Jean-Jacques Rousseau (1712–1778), their portraits were displayed prominently in the hall. And in later years, Forberg recalls, his father admitted that he did not accept the orthodox belief in immortality. His popular sermons were biblical and—to arouse attention—humorous, although in those days it did not occur to anyone to laugh.

The burden of Forberg's early education fell mostly on his father, who set great store by memory work. Forberg was required to learn a host of biblical passages without any explanation, albeit many of them would have profited from explanation. He professes to have been puzzled, for instance, by a verse from Psalm 147 that was prayed every day at table: "The Lord has no delight in the strength of the horse, and no pleasure in anyone's legs" (v. 10). But then, in 1782, the father had the happy idea of buying Johann Gottfried Eichhorn's (1752–1827) introduction to the Old Testament—"an event," Forberg says, "that marked an epoch in my life." He had been struggling to understand how the Bible could possibly be a divine revelation. Some of the stories it related—Joshua's commanding the sun to stand still, the devil's conversation with Jesus, and so on—were simply incredible. "But if I rejected one [such story], then the credibility of them all collapsed, and with it the credibility of the Bible as divine revelation." Eichhorn said nothing about revelation, and Forberg began to reconceive of the Bible as literature—a very remarkable library of ancient writings, in which the cultivated reader can trace the origins of certain influential ideas. To begin with, Forberg continued to believe in a revelation *in* the Bible (as the theologians of the time liked to say). "But soon the sun of philosophy was to eradicate from my soul even this last vestige of the old faith."

His love of philosophy was first sparked when Forberg became a student, four years later (1786), at the University of Leipzig. Still intending an ecclesiastical career, he studied theological subjects and went to church. (He recalls that later he himself preached occasionally in Jena.) But the skeptical philosopher Ernst Platner (1744–1818) turned his interest to philosophy, and when Forberg moved on to the University of Jena in 1788 he discovered Kant in the classroom of Karl Leonhard Reinhold (1758–1823). "Actually," he says, "I had no desire to study Kantian philosophy. As a pupil of Platner's, I was a strict determinist and eudaemonist, and I was downright shocked when in that class Reinhold spoke of the moral law."

The vividness with which Forberg writes of his relationship with Reinhold is one of the most intriguing features of his narrative. He remembers as though it were yesterday the day when a contemptuous review of one of Reinhold's publications arrived in Jena. With tears in his eyes and speaking in a subdued tone that was quite unlike him, Reinhold gathered his students around him and produced letters in which other scholars had praised his writings; and Forberg was directed to read aloud from them to the embarrassed company. But I must be content to draw attention to just two points in Forberg's reminiscences about Reinhold. First, he represents himself as becoming—in contrast to Reinhold—a genuine Kantian, or at least an authentic interpreter of Kant. Second, he tells of a day in 1792 when Reinhold asked him bluntly: "Are you still a Christian?" Forberg replied that if Christianity is taken to be "nothing but a kind of philosophical morality," he had never stopped being Christian, but he did not feel any need for a Christian revelation. And Reinhold was silent.

By this time, Forberg had become Reinhold's junior colleague: He had begun his first course of lectures in philosophy the previous autumn (on October 24, 1791, as he records with his usual precision). But in 1794 Reinhold left Jena, and amid high expectations Fichte arrived as his successor. Another series of fascinating reminiscences begin in Forberg's autobiography. Once again, only the essentials (for my present purpose) can be noted. Forberg had shown no very deep respect for Reinhold, whose attempts to correct Kant struck him as muddleheaded. Reinhold was not even capable of explaining the difficulties in his own thought, let alone Kant's, and in response to persistent questions he became grouchy. Fichte, by contrast, was a philosophical genius of the highest order—and an immensely powerful personality. He made something original out of Kant's transcendental idealism and proclaimed it with an eloquence that was hard to resist. Forberg was overwhelmed, though I assume no humor is intended when he says that he argued constantly about Fichte's absolute ego. He tired of hearing his students recite the jargon of the latest philosophy. With the modicum of philosophical talent that Nature had bestowed on him, he says, he was no match for these transcendental heroes. His classroom was emptied by the genius and eloquence of the greater man, and Forberg decided to move on.

He did try to put together some critical reflections on "the most recent philosophy" (i.e., Fichte's) and asked Fichte what he thought of them. The reply was: "A waste of good paper." But Forberg took no offense. "Fichte," he says, "was an open, straightforward man, who said everything in such a way and with such a look and tone that it was impossible to be angry with him." From Saalfeld, where in 1797 he had been elected assistant superintendent of a high school, he sent Fichte a token of his undeterred interest in philosophy: It was the article that precipitated the Atheism Controversy, "Development of the Concept of Religion" (1798). The content of the article will occupy my next section; the history of the Atheism Controversy belongs elsewhere. But there are at least two points made in the autobiography that should be stressed here.

First, Forberg tells us expressly what he was trying to do in the article: "My purpose was actually to give a more admissible sense to Kant's practical belief, which had long ceased to satisfy me." Unfortunately, we are left to guess for ourselves *why* he found Kant's notion of practical belief unsatisfactory. But I think we can do so from the article itself and from the subsequent apology.

Second, Forberg is perfectly candid in admitting the implications of his argument:

> If by "God" one means the usual notion of an extramundane, substantial, personal being that created and governs the world by understanding and will, then our doctrine was certainly atheistic, and our accusers were perfectly right. Against the accusation, we could only reply in our defense that we took the concept of God in a totally different sense, which the public at large could not comprehend, and in this sense acknowledged a God. And that is what we did. But we convinced no one of our innocence, and once there was talk of indictment, we could not really expect anything else.[11]

The "we" in this passage is intended to include Fichte. But in fact Fichte's position was different from Forberg's—and so was his personality. Forberg thought the official censure fair enough and accepted it without complaint. Fichte warned in advance that if the state ventured to reprimand him, he would resign.

> This [Forberg comments] was not taken kindly in Weimar. With the censure, Fichte was given his dismissal at the same time. "Why did you do that?" I asked him when I spoke with him soon after in Jena. "You could have remained as quietly in your post as I in mine." "If I were Parmenio," he replied [i.e., if *he* were the second-rate man], "that is what I would have done. But because I am Alexander [Alexander the Great], I could not." "You are right," I said, "and basically I am happy with that. Germany will never forget you." Since then, I never saw him again.[12]

The forgotten member of the team was unhappy at Saalfeld, even though he was promoted to the senior position of superintendent. He felt isolated, and teaching youngsters did not press him intellectually. Enrollment declined as word of his unorthodoxy spread. But he could not give up his ideas, he said, even if he wanted to: They were his existence. In 1801 he moved to Coburg, where he became curator of the ducal library and did the one thing for which he is not *quite* forgotten: He gathered an extensive collection of erotic texts from Latin, Greek, and other literatures and furnished it with illustrations. In the preface he explains: "These trifles engaged our attention first as a mere pastime. We were led to them accidentally, as we roamed from subject to subject, for Philosophy, the garden we had hoped to set up our tent in for life, lies desolate."[13]

There I must leave Forberg's autobiography. It has revealed a man untroubled by those boundary experiences—feelings of guilt, insignificance, and dread—that afflict many who turn to religion, and he therefore had no understanding of the longing for a word from beyond. But, somewhat to his own surprise, he did come to appreciate Kant's sense of a moral imperative, and he tried to understand it within the total system of the critical philosophy. He wanted to be, unlike Reinhold, a sound interpreter of Kant; he also wanted to improve on Kant, though in a way quite different from the path taken by Fichte. What does such a person make of religion? The answer lies in Forberg's controversial essay, "Development of the Concept of Religion," published in 1798. Regrettably, the answer is not unambiguous. But I can turn for further help to Forberg's own commentary: the apology for his alleged atheism, published the following year.

III. Religion as Practical Belief

In an earlier essay, I conceded the ambiguities in Forberg's article but tried to show that his argument, though slippery, was not hopelessly confused. He himself, it must be admitted, did little to encourage the reader to exercise charity, or even to take him seriously. At the end of the article, he added a series of what he called "captious questions," written, as he confessed in his autobiography, out of youthful devilry. The last question asks in effect: Are you kidding? And Forberg's answer is that he will leave it to the reader to decide. In his *Apology,* he noted that anyone who wished to keep some things sacred and safe from humor had better forsake philosophy and go to church and pray. But there was, of course, a serious motive behind all the mischief: He wanted to jolt his readers, if possible, into actually *thinking* about the assumptions of conventional piety. The charitable course is to oblige him by trying to follow his argument.

The aim of the article is clear enough: Forberg wants a new concept of religion that will preserve continuity with the old and yet be free from all the problems of belief in supernatural beings.[14] His task invites confusion, because the old connotations of the words "religion" and "belief" continually return. But the main drift of his argument is by no means unclear. His fundamental definitions of "religion" and "God" sound simple enough: "Religion" is "a practical belief in a moral world government," and by "God" he means "the exalted Spirit who governs the world according to moral laws." Forberg explains that if the way the world goes is calculated to procure the final success of goodness, there is a moral world government; otherwise, there is not. Hence he has no difficulty appropriating the hallowed biblical language of a "kingdom of God" that is to come on earth.

The difficulties begin when Forberg asks: But *will* the kingdom come? Is it a possible goal, or is it an illusion? He has so set up the question that if the kingdom will not come, it follows that there is no moral world government. But his attempt to answer his own question generates three formulas that do not at first seem to be identical in meaning. He variously says that the good man ought either (1) to *believe* that virtue will triumph, or (2) to *act as if* virtue will triumph, or (3) to *act as if he had decided* that virtue will triumph. The ambiguity can be resolved, or almost resolved, if we notice that for Forberg *practical* belief *is* "acting as if." *Theoretical,* or (as we might say) "factual," belief is simply immaterial to this purely practical belief, which is the content of the new religion. As practical belief, religion is commitment to the good, whatever the prospect. Moral commitment is not (theoretically) *believing that* the kingdom will come but (practically) *acting as if* the kingdom were coming. Such indications as Forberg gives suggest that he held an eventual triumph of goodness to be uncertain, even unlikely. But factual belief and factual disbelief in the coming of the kingdom are idle speculation anyhow; they just do not matter to genuine religion. That is the essential point. Forberg saves religion for the educated classes by making it logically independent of claims about the coming of the kingdom, or even claims about the existence of God.

I had to admit, however, in my previous essay, that even the consistency obtained by taking "practical belief" and "acting as if" to be synonymous is jeopardized by the occasional intrusion of what looks like a factual residuum in Forberg's religion. In one place, for instance, he asserts that belief is "the maxim to work for the promotion of good *at least as long as* the impossibility of success has not been clearly proved."[15] Quite what such a proof would look like, he does not say. But it certainly appears that at this point Forberg's practical belief entails a genuine, if very timid, factual claim.

Does the *Apology* dispose of this last vestige of theoretical belief in Forberg's religion? I think it does, although it is not totally free from conceptual problems of its own. At least it reinforces Forberg's basic Kantian strategy of locating religious discourse in the language of morals. And it does something more which is equally Kantian: Having shown that morals cannot *rest on* religious belief as usually understood, Forberg shows how naturally, indeed inevitably (so he thinks), the moral disposition *gives rise to* factual religious beliefs. In his opinion, the assured result of philosophical discussions over the previous two decades is that belief in God cannot be the foundation of morality; rather must morality be the foundation of belief in God.[16] It is this twofold movement of thought that I want to draw out.

First, then, Forberg insists that duty is something absolute, unconditioned, grounded wholly in itself. "One ought because one ought, not because one wants something else, nor because God wants it."[17] A good man, he says, can do his duty as husband, father, or friend just as conscientiously if he holds another explanation of phenomena to be more probable than theism, or even if he prefers not to commit himself to any explanation at all. Forberg had been accused of undermining the morals of students by teaching atheism: His accusers had argued that the only sure way to keep young people virtuous is by holding before them the picture of the divine Judge, who will one day reward the good and punish the wicked. He rejects the charge of atheism, but thinks that an attack of atheism is no bad thing if it helps us to see whether we really are moral. He writes:

> A mild attack of theoretical atheism is accordingly something everyone should actually wish to have at least once in his lifetime, to make an experiment on his own heart: to see whether it wills the good for its own sake, as it should, or solely for the sake of some advantage to be expected—if not in this world, then in another.[18]

In short, if we cannot act rightly without the factual claims of conventional religion, religion (in this sense) is the clearest proof of human corruption: It is powerless to create a genuinely moral disposition.

Conversely, the moral imperative shines most brightly when we do what we ought even if convinced that the world will remain eternally a world of utter rogues and idiots, as hitherto. And if some misanthrope, his gloomy disposition confirmed by experience of human falsehood and stupidity, were to ridicule all hope of a golden age to come *and yet* still acted consistently for the common good, his would be a true and genuine religious disposition. "Religion is not (theoretical) belief that a kingdom of God is coming. The endeavor to make it come *even if* one believes that it will never come—this, and this alone, is religion."[19]

In sum: Forberg's first argument is that because genuine religion is heeding the moral imperative, religion, like the imperative itself, is autonomous: There is nothing more to be said than simply, "I ought because I ought." Nothing at all is added to the moral imperative by asserting that there is a moral order, that its foundation is the will of God, or that virtue will triumph in the end. The point is a strictly logical one: Factual assertions belong in a different class from moral demands. It is, therefore, a matter of total indifference, as far as the moral imperative itself is concerned, whether or not one adopts a theistic worldview: whether one thinks the ultimate success of goodness likely, unlikely, barely possible, or an utter illusion. For, Forberg asks in an eloquent passage:

> What if there were no goal to attain, or—and for the athlete this is the same thing—only a goal at an infinite distance? What if the race were not for the goal, but a goal were supposed for the sake of the race . . . ? What if the commandment of reason by no means had the sense of running *in order to* reach the goal (which is the common good), but only *as if* one wanted to reach it?[20]

That, however, is only the first cadence in Forberg's movement of thought. Second, he recognizes in the *Apology* (though not in his original article) that genuine religion, while not itself theoretical belief, invites or even logically *demands* theoretical belief. The strictly practical belief of Kantian religion is then transformed into *theology,* something that religion as such has not the slightest need to bother itself with.[21] We can fairly paraphrase his point, I think, if we say that while the immediate deliverances of conscience can be stated only as "maxims" or rules of conduct, not as factual assertions, the deliverances of conscience are themselves quite remarkable facts, and as such they invite reflection.

Perhaps Forberg makes the point best when he suggests that acknowledgment of the moral law *appears,* in reflection, as acknowledgment of a deity. Morally disposed individuals do not need to become explicitly conscious of the concept of deity, but they would be if they stopped to think about it. Hence Forberg rests his case in these words:

> I do not understand how I would have to express myself to escape the reproach of atheism. I teach that at a certain point of speculation the moral disposition unavoidably appears as belief in a moral world order, hence also as a belief in a *principle* of this moral world order. I conceive of this principle as a *supreme intelligence,* as an almighty, omniscient, holy being. My God is the God of the Christians.[22]

By way of commentary on this interesting defense, let me go back for a moment to Forberg's misanthrope. On the one hand, the misanthrope's total cynicism about his fellow humans is exactly what enables his moral disposition to shine so brightly, because he is resolved to do what is right anyway, even in a world full of rogues and idiots. His morals are impeccable. But there now appears to be some question about his intelligence if he does not stop to think about his astonishing commitment to virtue. If he did, the grounds for his cynicism ought to vanish: Whatever the present appearance of human wickedness around him, reflection on the moral imperative within should convince him that he is not just doing his duty but affirming a moral order, the condition for the possibility of which is what is meant by "God." The moral disposition, it seems, is most clearly revealed in doubt, but the moral disposition itself tends to generate (theoretical) belief. This, I admit, is not expressly how Forberg puts it; He leaves his misanthrope doubting and grimly doing his duty. But I think I am only drawing out Forberg's own argument.

"Theology"—or, as he sometimes says, "*moral* theology"—is Forberg's word for reflection on genuine religion, or practical belief, or the moral disposition (these three being understood as identical). It is the theologian's task to draw out the concept of God implicit in the concept of morality and to find appropriate ways of representing it. Like Kant, Forberg will not admit that we can have knowledge of God. We can, however, find suitable analogies or symbols, not for picturing God but for representing the relationship of the Unknown to its effects. And since the Unknown is the principle of *moral* effects, no other analogies are open to us than those taken from human life. All theology is therefore bound to be anthropomorphism, and we should not deceive ourselves with the hope of removing everything human from the concept of God. "This, by the way," Forberg adds, "is no new doctrine. . . . I admit that we receive only a *symbol* of a principle, unknown in itself, of the moral course of the world. But have not all theologians, from time immemorial, admitted this?"[23] Well, it is hard to see how Calvin, at least, could disagree with Forberg here, since Calvin states it as a fundamental principle that we should not ask what God is in himself, but what he is like, or how he is disposed, to us.[24]

IV. Toward a Moral Theology

My reading of Forberg's *Apology* has left out some intricate features of his argument, such as the interesting distinction he draws between logical and real possibility. But I believe I have shown, without oversimplification (or willful suppression of any pertinent evidence), that his essential case is fairly represented as twofold, and it is this that justifies my own twofold thesis. His practical, as-if belief denies not the existence of a moral order or God but only the moral pertinence of theoretical belief in them. Hence it was still possible for him, having blocked the route from factual to practical belief, to concede that there is a one-way path in the other direction. Forberg, I conclude, was not a fictionalist in Vaihinger's sense, using modes of thought known to be false; he left the door open to theological hypotheses that may possibly be true.

Vaihinger, of course, noted the many passages in which Forberg's thought sounded agnostic rather than atheistic. But there is no need to infer that Forberg's thinking must therefore have fallen apart into two incompatible doctrines. Two versions of the as-if doctrine, Vaihinger held, lay side by side unreconciled in Forberg's article and defense: a moderate or weaker version, which was agnostic, and a radical version, which—like Vaihinger's own philosophy—was positivistic and pessimistic. The inconsistency was present, he thought, in both the original article and the subsequent apology, but on the whole he saw Forberg making good progress from the weaker to the more radical doctrine: that is, from agnosticism to the fictionalism that knows its fictions are untrue.

In actual fact, it seems to me, Forberg's case is fundamentally consistent throughout but becomes more clearly *non*fictionalist in the later work. What I have characterized as his second logical move emerges only in the defense. In the article, factual belief was said to arise from the *wish* of the good heart; in the apology, it arises also out of *reflection*. But in neither of the two sources is theoretical belief said to be false. Nowhere have I been able to discover evidence for Vaihinger's blunt assertion that "Forberg unequivocally denies the existence of a moral world order."[25] Forberg's point, in the first part of his argument, is that *even if* there is no moral order, that makes no difference to the moral obligation in which genuine religion consists. Vaihinger, by contrast, wanted Forberg to say that I should act as if there were a moral order *although,* in fact, there is not.[26] He transformed the "even if" *("selbst wenn")* into an "although" *("obgleich").* Consequently, he had no interest in the second part of Forberg's argument but thought that for him the concept of a moral order was a mere "accidental way of looking at things" *("eine zufällige Betrachtungsweise").*[27] "Only . . . morality," he says, "is certain, not the moral world order."[28] But Forberg says rather, much more strongly, that the concept of morality *appears as* the concept of a moral order in reflection—inevitably.

It remains entirely possible that in his heart Forberg was a devious atheist. But the historian has only the texts to go by, and what Forberg actually says points toward what he called a "moral theology": not a casuistic theology that tells us *what we ought to do,* but a philosophical theology that reflects on the interesting fact that to be human is, among other things, to feel *that one ought.* If Forberg was right, so to feel is tantamount to believing that humans live in a moral order, and he was therefore willing to admit that we should acknowledge moral order as our distinctively human element.[29] This is the factual or theoretical belief that practical belief leads to, but in no sense needs. And the problem of anthropomorphism is solved in this moral theology by the argument that God-talk is talk about the moral order, or about the principle of its possibility. For there is no other way in which we can conceive of the activity of this unknown principle than by analogy with human moral agency like our own.

His conception of moral theology was certainly not the main burden of Forberg's writing. The fact that he devotes a large section of his *Apology* to it is, in a way, ironic. The reason why he first wrote about Kant's notion of practical belief (in his article on the concept of religion) was that it seemed to provide comfort for those who wished to claim theoretical knowledge of God even after the collapse of the traditional proofs of God's existence. They wanted, as Forberg puts it, to bring back all kinds of nonsense through the back door. His aim was to insulate Kant's notion of practical belief from the abuse to which it was liable.[30] It is all the more remarkable, then, that—on second thought—he found the notion of a moral theology at least viable. Obviously, however, one has to be careful to stress his insistence that moral theology cannot strictly give knowledge of God, and that it belongs to the domain of speculation rather than religion. Indeed, he remained skeptical whether *any* speculative explanations ever really explain things.[31] He remained, in short, an agnostic who looked through the doorway of moral theology but was not much interested in going in.

To criticize, or to correct, or to defend Forberg's conception of a moral theology would require another paper in the constructive, rather than the historical, mode. It is enough to have shown it as part of a philosophical scheme which has the merit of greater coherence than has previously been recognized and which, to this extent, may help in the identification of perennial issues in philosophical theology. I may as well admit that the theologian in me does think that the idea of a moral theology still has possibilities. But the task calls for historical circumspection as well as philosophical wit. I have been at pains to show how the idea arose out of a particular stage in the history of Western philosophy. Forberg's confidence in the assured results of two decades of philosophical discussion proved, like everything else in history, to be transient. The moral law would have to be defended, these days, against subjectivist interpretations of moral experience. In 1943, C. S. Lewis could still end a talk on right and wrong as a clue to the meaning of the universe with this expansive conclusion:

> These, then, are the two points I wanted to make. First, that human beings, all over the earth, have this curious idea that they

> ought to behave in a certain way, and cannot really get rid of it. Secondly, that they do not in fact behave in that way. They know the Law of Nature; they break it. These two facts are the foundation of all clear thinking about ourselves and the universe we live in.[32]

Too expansive, perhaps! Still, Lewis' remarks reflect part of the permanent legacy of the Kantian philosophy: the recognition that the sense of moral obligation is at least *one* clue to the remarkable cosmic experiment going on in *one* small corner of the universe.[33]

NOTES

1. John Calvin, *Comm.* Heb. 1:3, *CO* 55:11–12.
2. Hans Vaihinger, *Die Philosophie des Als Ob: System der theoretischen, praktischen und religiösen Fiktionen der Menschheit auf Grund eines idealistischen Positivismus,* 9th and 10th ed. (Leipzig: Felix Meiner, 1927), pp. 736, 752 n. 2.
3. Calvin, *Inst.* 1.17.13; 2.16.2–4.
4. Ibid. 1.13.1.
5. Ibid. 1.11.8.
6. Immanuel Kant, *Religion Within the Limits of Reason Alone,* tr. by Theodore M. Greene and Hoyt H. Hudson (1934; reprint, New York: Harper & Brothers, 1960), pp. 58–59n.; cf. pp. 100–105.
7. *Immanuel Kant's Critique of Pure Reason,* tr. Norman Kemp Smith (New York: Macmillan Co., 1933), pp. 549–570, 648–650; cf. pp. 318–320, 614–615.
8. Vaihinger, "Die Philosophie des Als Ob und das Kantische System gegenüber einem Erneuerer des Atheismusstreites," *Kant-Studien* 21 (1917), 1–25; p. 21.
9. Vaihinger, *Die Philosophie des Als Ob,* pp. 171–175. More exactly, Vaihinger distinguishes two kinds of fiction: "semi-fictions," which deviate from reality, and "real fictions," which are also *self*-contradictory (pp. 24, 128–129, 153, 172). A "hypothesis," by contrast, *may* be true and is subject to confirmation or disconfirmation (pp. 143–154).
10. Friedrich Carl Forberg, *Lebenslauf eines Verschollenen* (Hildburghausen and Meiningen: Kesselring, 1840).
11. Ibid., pp. 54–55.
12. Ibid., p. 55.
13. Fred. Chas. Forberg, *Manual of Classical Erotology (De figuris Veneris),* Latin text and E.T. by Julian Smithson (1884; facsimile ed., 2 vols. in 1, New York: Grove Press, 1966), p. 5.

14. Forberg's article, "Entwickelung des Begriffs der Religion," first published in *Philosophisches Journal* 8 (1798), 21–46, is most conveniently accessible in Hans Lindau, ed., *Die Schriften zu J. G. Fichte's Atheismus-Streit* (Munich: Georg Müller, 1912), pp. 37–58.

15. Ibid., p. 55 (my emphasis).

16. *Friedrich Carl Forbergs der Philosophie Doctors und des Lyceums zu Saalfeld Rectors Apologie seines angeblichen Atheismus* (Gotha: Justus Perthes, 1799), p. 8.

17. Ibid., pp. 22, 25.

18. Ibid., pp. 35–36.

19. Ibid., pp. 160–163 (my emphasis); cf. p. 105.

20. Ibid., pp. 141–143.

21. Ibid., pp. 91–92, 133; cf. pp. 119–120, 134–135, 164.

22. Ibid., pp. 127–130, 136. The expression "appears as" may be considered another example of Forberg's elusiveness, perhaps even evasiveness. But he certainly must mean *theoretical* belief in this passage; and it is speculation he is talking about, not just wishful thinking. The "appearing as" is purely the result of conceptual analysis (p. 157).

23. Ibid., pp. 132–158; quotation on pp. 154, 156. On the difference between a picture and a symbol, see pp. 168–169.

24. Calvin, *Inst.* 1.2.2, 10.2; 3.2.6.

25. Vaihinger, *Die Philosophie des Als Ob,* p. 751. Vaihinger understands Forberg's use of the expression *als ob* to mean that for him the moral world order was only a fiction (ibid.; cf. p. 748). But that is not what Forberg said. He did think that theology could deduce from the moral consciousness only the *thought* of God (*Apologie,* p. 157), or the *idea* of a kingdom of God (pp. 138–139), and he certainly wanted to guard against the illusion that symbolic language about God is literal (pp. 149–150). That, however, is not to deny the existence of the moral order or its principle, nor does it follow that for him symbolic language was nonreferential—as the fictionalist position maintains.

26. Ibid., p. 751.

27. Ibid., p. 752. What is "accidental," according to Forberg, is *whether* the morally disposed individual decides to reflect or speculate; *if* he does, theoretical belief follows infallibly (*Apologie,* p. 130). This, of course, does not make any particular speculation infallibly correct; speculation is "accidental" also in the sense that systems come and go like fashions in clothing (pp. 20, 91). Nevertheless, speculation is answerable before the forum of logic (pp. 111–112). Forberg takes it seriously as an intellectual enterprise.

28. Vaihinger, *Die Philosophie des Als Ob,* p. 746.

29. Forberg, *Apologie,* p. 145.

30. Ibid., pp. 175–177; cf. pp. 95–98, 110–111.

31. Ibid., pp. 26–27, 96–97, 112.

32. C. S. Lewis, *Mere Christianity* (New York: Macmillan Co., 1954), p. 7. The talk was first published in 1943.

33. See the famous conclusion to Kant, *Critique of Practical Reason,* tr. Lewis White Beck (New York: Liberal Arts, 1956), pp. 166–168.

Schleiermacher's Theology: Ecclesial and Scientific, Ecumenical and Reformed

Terrence N. Tice

A (Reformed) Theology of the Church

Schleiermacher's theology is ecumenical not so much because it reflected his effective efforts toward Lutheran/Reformed union in Prussia[1] but because it is an inclusive theology of the church through and through. It is a theology of the historically existing church, to be sure, and especially for participants in its leadership and governance, both lay and clergy. It is even more basically, however, responsibly geared to the one true church of Christ, visible and invisible, to the church established by the "one eternal divine decree" and manifest from age to age in the continuing redemptive-reconciling work of the divine Spirit.[2] God's self-revelation is a real, objective revelation of God, which comes to the church as a final, yet ever renewed, work of the Holy Spirit within religious self-consciousness, itself socially, corporately mediated and actualized.[3] Moreover, the basic Christian consciousness is directed to, and contained in, fellowship with God, this solely through fellowship with the Redeemer. Finally, it is the Holy Spirit who brings the ideal, one-true-church into the church that now exists, this as its "common spirit."[4] In particular, the divine power of God's Word occurs through preaching, teaching, and learning in the church and in the community of ministries among all Christians.[5]

To understand fully what these propositions mean would require grasping Schleiermacher's entire system of doctrine, constructed as an evolving statement regarding the evangelical church in his time and cultural setting. In *Christian Faith* (1830–1831) this statement culminates in a Christologically formulated discussion of God's love and wisdom with respect to "the divine government of the world" and in a rephrased depiction of the traditional doctrine of the Trinity, viewed as "the coping-stone of Christian doctrine." Although the reference is not to his dogmatics alone but rather to his theology as a whole and in all its parts—philosophical, historical, and practical—the emphasis in this account will be placed on his dogmatics as the place where his doctrine of the church is most systematically explicated.

An even fuller understanding would entail entering into the pain, guilt, and responsibility in realizing how far short of Schleiermacher's ecumenical vision the church's life is today—of how little the "true church" seems to have broken into the church as we know it or into much of its theology. This failure of responsiveness would have to be acknowledged even with respect to much ecumenical discourse, especially given the global context in which the whole church is now surely called to bear witness and to minister. In Schleiermacher's world it was reasonable for a theologian of the church to concentrate on the German situation or on some other provincial setting. Today the entire world, in some basic way, is the proper place of every denomination and of every local congregation. I believe that were Schleiermacher at work today he would readily grasp this global context and responsibility. Transcending external division, he would seek a theology for the whole people of God and for the entire world. Already in *Christian Faith* he presents the Holy Spirit's working through the church as "the ultimate world-shaping power."[6]

In any case, in his situation or ours, Schleiermacher's theological effort would bear the following ecumenically oriented, formal characteristics. As the informed reader would see, substantively his doctrine and ethics—separately presented but inseparable in basic form and content—would still emerge chiefly from a critical study of scripture, from an evangelical, confessional base—though not through literal subscription—and from a Reformed orientation and spirit;[7] but it would also move beyond, drawing from the Christian religious self-consciousness of those parts of the church that have already begun to move beyond. It would emerge out of a listening for God's Word in many places, including those where a theology of liberation has arisen to meet critical need, and out of a dialogue that extends worldwide.

Here, then, also without much immediate elaboration, are seven characteristics to be found in Schleiermacher's ecumenically oriented theology of and for the church. Indirectly these will all be exemplified in the remainder of this account. (1)

First, it is scientific, and it does not claim hermeneutical principles inconsistent with the general requirements of science.[8] (2) Its outlook is also historical, expecting to bear no utterly timeless, unchangeable truth claims though seeking to purvey truth that has currency, that can be validated through experience in the church and by historical, scientific means. (3) Its structure is largely dialectical, notably employing contrasting concepts that hold the dynamic tensions present in experience, avoiding rationalist, supernaturalist, or other speculative rigidity. (4) Accordingly, in its findings it is pluralistic, culturally sensitive, both cognizant of diversity and honoring of that diversity, not expecting total uniformity of life or doctrine. (5) The overall perspective of this theology is developmental, discovering signs of growth in insight, action, and refinement over the centuries and anticipating further growth. (6) Its spirit is open and inclusive, not separatist or exclusive,[9] moving beyond mere tolerance to loving acceptance and critique. It presupposes that no error is absolute and that no truth claim comes unalloyed. (7) Finally, it seeks unity—more, it seeks to find such unity as already exists among the churches and to follow after that ever-forming and ultimate unity to which Christ beckons the church.[10] While I have termed these characteristics formal, they all depend on, and have expression in, material, substantive conditions within Schleiermacher's systematic presentation of doctrine.

Church and World

"Dogmatics," Schleiermacher carefully asserts, "is the science which systematizes the doctrine that has currency in a Christian church at a given time."[11] The primary standpoint effective in this definition is not the world of science, or a speculative, systematic platform, or the status of affairs at a given time, or even a traditional body of doctrine, but the existence of the church itself.[12] Moreover, the essential communal reality to be affirmed in any collocation of Christian doctrine, in his view, is that of the one church, else the science in which one engages is not theological science. In *On Religion* the diversity of religions was shown to be a necessary outcome of the very nature of religion. Exactly the same is true of the relation between the church and the churches. He strongly rejected the possible inferences that any other religion must necessarily exist in its present form, or that the development of one central religion, such as a highly developed Christianity, would be untrue to the nature of religion. He wished only to stress that diversity of apprehension is an essential, not merely an accidental, fact of religion. The true church—taking the same line of argument—is also regarded to be an essential fact underlying all religion, if only as inchoate, suppressed, or as yet unattained.[13]

Viewed historically, according to Schleiermacher's analysis, dogmatic productions may either be rather strict transcriptions of the dominant attitude of the church or more progressive translations of it, depending on the character of the times. His own dogmatics definitely falls within the latter category. Although he is often represented as if he had intended the former—i.e., a purely "empirical" or "descriptive" or "inductive" dogmatics, following some psychological or statistical method for detecting the mind of the contemporary church—nothing could be further from his actual position, for at least two reasons.

In the first place, during times of revolutionary change—called "epochs"—such dogmatics could only be descriptive of chaos. How, for example, would one describe the fundamental mind of the still relatively undivided Western church at the time of the Reformation? Yet, even during such times, he believed, dogmatics has its accustomed role to play, part of which is to mediate between conservative and eruptive doctrine by maintaining scientific procedure.

In the second place, even during the smoother years—called "periods"—the dominant attitude of a particular church may be "variously apprehended."[14] Certainly such a "principle" is likely to be stated and elaborated in a variety of ways. Yet one may still be conscious of a single standpoint from which a perspective on the whole life and career of Christianity is to be gained. Suppose, now, that conditions within the evangelical church of one's own time were conducive toward consolidation of these outlooks, so that all the richness of heritage and present health of this church could be summed up in one vision of its nature and responsibility. Suppose that such a vision had become partially realized in the official consciousness of the church: its publications, its education, its general witness. Then, to the discerning theologian, those various heterogeneous apprehensions of the church's principle might eventually either "present themselves as a new apprehension of the principle already dominant or . . . announce the development of a new one."[15] Obviously, what is involved in such an evaluation would be no mere counting of noses, or any pseudoscientific embellishment of such.

The same citation suggests a third clarification of his view. Genuine dogmatics, for Schleiermacher, represents a knowledge that grows out of the church and is intended only for the purpose of speaking to the church. Thus, a theologian may have to lay one's ear to one's particular church a long time before one catches its most authentic voices.[16] If one's attempt to listen succeeds, and one has fulfilled the formal requirements for doing theology as a whole, then one is in a fair way of producing genuine dogmatics. The more critically gifted one is, on the other hand, the less likely is one's dogmatics merely to echo the representative voices one has heard.[17] In fact, if there is movement in the church of one's time, one may actually contribute toward the development of a new fundamental attitude. Such individual, progressive contributions, however, correct as they may seem, are to go into one's dogmatics as such only if an initial readiness for them is already evident in the church. Thus, the approach remains radically ecclesial.

At the very outset of *Christian Faith,*[18] any founding of dogmatics on general rational principles is strictly disclaimed. To the contrary, one's first methodological task is only to establish the particular character of the Christian church in its broadest outline, as compared with a general conception of "church" derived from ethics.[19] This requirement does not permit defining the Christian church, as such, solely in terms either of some a priori rational conception or of some merely empirical investigation of religious communities. Certain features in its makeup as a human society it does hold in common with other religious communities (a matter also for philosophy of religion),[20] but its essence is determined by unique characteristics that derive from its own distinctive basis (the special concern of Christian apologetics).[21]

Even before "borrowing" concepts from ethics to construct a preliminary definition of "church," Schleiermacher actually began with a prior supposition: that the religious feeling of absolute dependence is an essential element of human nature.[22] Now he adds the further affirmation, from ethics, that every essential element of human nature becomes the basis of a type of community. Community is a satisfaction demanded by the universal "consciousness of kind" *(Gattungsbewusstsein).* It occurs through the expression of inward determinations of consciousness (thought, action, or feeling) and others' perceiving and imitation of these expressions, so that religious consciousness is first awakened "by the communicative and stimulative power of expression or utterance."[23] Consequently, the congeries of fluid relationships between individuals and between families which constitute religious community develop within a church into "well-established relationships." Intercommunication of religious consciousness operates "within certain definite limits," and proper membership may be ascertained by means of "some kind of definite understanding" over "requirements for membership."[24] Thus:

> Religious self-consciousness, like every essential element in human nature, leads necessarily in its development to community which, on the one hand, is variable and fluid, and, on the other hand, has definite limits, i.e. is a church.[25]

From Schleiermacher's ethical works we learn that he does not refer to a church the distinctiveness of which is characterized by such factors as race, nationality, or patriarchical leadership, but one which has an essentially religious basis.[26] He conceives such a church as "the highest individuality," combining within itself the characteristics both of love between man and woman and of friendship, of the family and of the school.[27] Systematic discipline *(Kunstsystem)*, moreover, is bound to develop in such a church as a means of schematizing religious experience *(Schematismen des Gefühls)*.[28] This is sometimes called theology. Insofar as any church originates on genuinely religious grounds, however, its type is already established in the experience of the people who adhere to it; and the particular conception of revelation proclaimed by its priesthood corresponds only to a reality already existing within the mass. All distinctions of office—for example, as between clergy and laity—arise solely out of the original desire to communicate religious feeling. Development of a vocabulary, which each person may appropriate for representing his or her own experience, is "the highest tendency of the church."[29] Out of this develops a cultus and an objective mode or rubric[30] for expressing the identity of feelings over against their differences (the beginnings of *Vernunftreligion* in the good sense) and, eventually, the necessity for critical interpretative disciplines.[31]

This is all that Schleiermacher directly borrows from ethics: a theory of human association, a rough distinction of religious association from other kinds, and an objective indication of various traits belonging to positive, organized religion.[32] The whole is clearly employed merely to give a framework for indicating what he does not mean by "church" and "religion." Of neither are the full definitions given in the introduction to *Christian Faith.* Nor is there the slightest note of classical apologetics at this point. Thinkers in the church themselves, as such, need to be clear as to what church community is in comparison with other kinds.[33]

Three additional relevant points should not be overlooked, because they lie behind Schleiermacher's whole initial conception of church dogmatics. The first is that even his ethical definition of the church is characteristically patterned after the highest ideal of which he could conceive—namely, Christianity. His attempt to lay down general propositions in the ethical works often hides this very concrete source of many of his notions.

In the second place, he is also presupposing what he considered to be the dominant view of the fourth address in *On Religion,* his distinction between "the true church" and "the actually existent religious community."[34] The ideal community of true church has not been entirely lacking to the existing church, for example, in the upper room; but it has never been fully attained. Apart from a truly "cosmopolitan" (i.e., ecumenical) union—egalitarian, at peace, not fundamentally needing progress—"the true church can exist only insofar as there is true life and the production of new forms within existing ecclesial communities."[35] True church community is "the church triumphant," the truly present but only partially realized eschaton.[36] Strictly speaking, the activity of the Holy Spirit is the determinative reality which brings true church into the church that now exists. It is only because this "common spirit" is present in the existing church that it can really be constituted as a church at all.[37]

"The expression 'Holy Spirit,' " Schleiermacher explains in the doctrinal section, "must be understood to mean the vital unity *(Lebenseinheit)* of the Christian fellowship regarded as a moral personality *(Person)* . . . its common spirit . . . the Holy Spirit and the Spirit of God and the Spirit of Christ."[38] The formative reality of the common spirit is "a prolongation of Christ's own activity . . . of his fellowship-forming activity," already present in the preparatory workings of grace (in this sense also present as the common spirit of Judaism),[39] but only fully actualized after Christ was no longer physically present.[40] "The presence of the Spirit . . . is the condition of anyone's sharing in the common life, . . . promised to the whole community."[41] Communal practice, therefore, is said to derive "out of the inner power of their common-indwelling, characteristic spirit."[42] All doctrine "must be traced back" to this common spirit as "the source of all spiritual gifts and good works"—and all genuine proclamation.[43] Finally, it is this "common spirit" by which God becomes present through the action of the Lord's Supper; and the very polity of the church ought to be subject to this same "natural predominance of the common spirit" within the life of individual persons.[44]

Finally, the church in both its aspects is the fullest possible representation of a fundamental fact: that human beings are "set within a world, within a definite order of things and among particular objects."[45] In *Christian Faith,* the doctrine of the church is correspondingly presented as a way of viewing "the constitution of the world in relation to redemption."[46] The church transforms the world by drawing the world to its true fulfillment in itself. There is no question in Schleiermacher's mind, moreover, that this ascent of consciousness which brings human beings into the true fellowship of the church is the work of God. Nonetheless, it is also, on just this account, the self-conscious evolution of the human world.[47]

Again the radicality of such a claim can be discerned only within the doctrinal section. There Schleiermacher asserts that every corporate life which in some way arises out of God-consciousness, "imperfect and sinful as it may be, has yet, in virtue of its presentiments and longing, an inward link with redemption."[48] The Christian church, however, is explicitly defined in terms of Christ's redeeming-reconciling work within and through it, both as to its origin and as to its continued existence.[49] Christ's work is "world-forming" activity.[50] Only in the sense that it is at once "fellowship-forming" and "world-forming" can it also be spoken of as "person-forming" after the analogy of the specifically divine activity in the formation of Jesus' person.[51] If it be said that Christ is Lord and King, moreover, this power of his over the church is not something that began incidentally or in some isolated moment; rather, it is integral to his entire existence as the Redeemer, from start to finish.[52] Regeneration means finding oneself in "transition from the corporate life of sinfulness to a living fellowship with Christ"—and that means ipso facto being a part of the redemptive fellowship of the church through "the mediation of the Word."[53]

Because it is a discipline of the church, therefore, dogmatics is also concerned with the whole life of the human world.[54] It is not only theology but also, as determined by its relation to divine revelation, and only as such, anthropology. And it is anthropology, furthermore, not only because of its determinative center in Jesus the Christ but also because its task is set within the context of the human world,[55] where Christ has been—and is—active. Dogmatics is never theology or anthropology alone; it is always the two together. By this token, both the life of the church and its theology are "related to all else that becomes human around it and out of it" as the fulfillment of what is elsewhere only dimly seen or vaguely understood. The standpoint of dogmatics is unquestionably the revelation of God, which alone constitutes the church; but its landscape is the whole of human reality, and it can safely speak from, to, and for this reality insofar as that touches on the real life of the church.

Living Fellowship with Christ

Although the notion of fellowship *(Gemeinschaft)* is not so ostensible as that of redemption, it exercises an important function in the explication of every single doctrine under the aspect of grace within *Christian Faith.* The doctrines of regeneration and sanctification are set forth to characterize the self-consciousness of "those assumed into living fellowship with Christ" *(Lebensgemeinschaft mit Christo).*[56] This has been achieved at once by the redemptive work of Christ, by which he communicates to us the power of his perfect God-consciousness, unmarred by sin,[57] and by his reconciling work, by which he communicates to us the fruits of his blessedness.[58] Regeneration is correspondingly expanded, on the pattern of this prior Christology, as follows: "Assumption into living fellowship with Christ, regarded as a person's changed relation to God, is one's justification; regarded as a changed form of life, it is one's conversion."[59] This, in turn, signifies the transforming reality of forgiveness and adoption wrought in fellowship with Christ,[60] to which the sacrament of baptism conforms.[61]

> Conversion, the beginning of the new life in fellowship with Christ, makes itself known in each individual by repentance, which consists in the combination of regret and change of heart *(Sinnesänderung);* and by faith, which consists of the appropriation of the perfection and blessedness of Christ.[62]

On the other hand:

> In living fellowship with Christ the natural powers of the regenerate are put at his disposal, whereby there is produced a life akin to his perfection and blessedness; and this is the state of sanctification.[63]

To our sanctifying fellowship with Christ conforms the sacrament of the Lord's Supper.[64] In fact, Schleiermacher's understanding of both sacraments as a corporate act of fellowship with Christ underscores his further affirmation, essential to his entire outlook on Christianity, that there is no truly satisfactory fellowship with God outside the life of mutual sharing in Christian community. Thus, in the doctrine of the church:

> Our attention is at once focused on the most definite thing in our whole self-consciousness, where we always distinguish and com-

> bine both things—our independent *(selbständige)* personality in living fellowship with Christ, and our life as an integral constituent of a whole [i.e., a church].[65]

Here, within the fellowship of Christians, we learn to acknowledge divine predestination as the origin of our fellowship with Christ,[66] and here we may come to understand something of the connection of our election with the divine government of the world. Here, by the Holy Spirit, we enter into the same vital relationship to Christ which the first disciples knew, recognizing the activity of the Holy Spirit as "a prolongation of Christ's own activity" and realizing that "there is no living fellowship with Christ without an indwelling of the Holy Spirit, and vice versa."[67] Within this perspective, no conviction concerning the revelatory content of scripture is of any avail except insofar as it results in fellowship with Christ, and this is impossible unless it rests first on faith and the experience of repentance and change which attends faith.[68] Under the ministry of the Word, therefore, there is no isolated piety; rather, there is an ever-growing consciousness of being members of Christ's body.[69] In the end, our expectation of the consummation of the church and the full answer to prayer

> is rooted in our Christian consciousness as representing the unbroken fellowship of human nature with Christ under conditions wholly unknown and only faintly imaginable, but the only fellowship which can be conceived as wholly free from all that springs from the conflict of flesh and spirit.[70]

Thus it is understandable that it should be the purpose of Christian ethics to consider the task of attaining to "perfect living fellowship with Christ," that this should include not only transformation of ourselves and of the church but of the whole human world as well,[71] and that this transformation may entail "a readiness for and a right to fellowship with the sufferings of Christ."[72]

Fellowship implies communication *(Mittheilung).* Already it is clear that this activity must involve some kind of personal relationship, since it is God's own self that God communicates through the Redeemer and since this divine self-communication cannot be completed unless it is received by us individually and in common.[73] There is no immediate necessity here, however, to conceive God as a person in the ordinary sense—that is, as a particular individual. For this carries with it the limiting notion of the particular, which is extendable at most to the condition of participation. When an individual participates in some thing, group, or action, one may very well retain a distinctive element or contributing power of one's own; but one is still only taking part and is therefore oneself only a part. It is no accident of our present understanding of personality that we use a word, *persona,* which originally denoted the mask that actors once wore to designate the part they were to assume within a drama. Schleiermacher accordingly never speaks of the "personality" of God; he speaks only of that of the Redeemer. This does not at all imply that God is not capable of directly relating to persons and is therefore not capable of personal relationship. It implies only that this capability, as we can know it only within the context of human relations, cannot delimit the total relation of God to the world. Consequently, it cannot wholly delimit the relation of God to persons either, even in the process of redemption.

What is important to assert is, first, that God does convey something of God's own self in such a way that it is actually made known. This does not mean, however, that God's self-revelation is subject to all the conditions of purely objective knowledge. It means only that what God thus imparts can be taken up into consciousness and that such reception is a necessary condition for further communication of divine reality to other human beings.

In the second place, such communication is not simply the distributing of information *(Kunde);* it is the sort of impartation *(Mittheilung)* by which something is shared with another which has been or continues to remain either primarily or entirely one's own—in this case, something which continues to remain God's; namely, God's own being. Nowhere in *Christian Faith,* moreover, is there any mention of being reabsorbed into the divine being or of finally recognizing one's total identification with divine emanation. Within the Christian perspective of sin and grace, each person regards oneself as a unique individual, capable of sustaining one's particularity even beyond death. That each individual is also part of the totality of the human world, and by this token also necessarily takes one's position within the whole divine government of the world, does not cancel out one's unique possession of self; but it does indicate that one is not wholly self-possessed, not wholly under one's own control. Nor in the ultimate sense is one self-possessed at all; that is, capable of escaping the full complex of conditions that constitute the divine government of the world. Yet, consciousness of divine grace does not force one into absolute passivity; instead, it releases one's divinely given freedom for creative self-activity in the world. One realizes that the irrevocable condition of absolute dependence that one shares with the rest of the world includes the possibility of spontaneous personal relationship with God, that it is a dependence within the bounds of which God actually shares God's own being.

In the third place, the Christian religious self-consciousness cannot imply that God is divided up. In essence God is not divisible. Consequently, God cannot be said to distribute God's being out in shares either, whether in three completely distinct persons of the Godhead or in the persons of believers. Nevertheless, God's "sharing" of God's own being in and through the Redeemer does involve a new connection of God with persons of faith of such a nature as can be called a "new creation"; and while this in turn does not involve actual identification *(Gleichartigkeit)* with God, yet God does evoke and effectuate actual union *(Vereinigung)* thereby between human beings and God's own being. This twofold union of God with human nature in Christ and in the common spirit of the church Schleiermacher terms "the essential elements in the doctrine of the Trinity."[74]

Finally, as Schleiermacher makes particularly clear in his doctrine of prayer, the new fellowship with God brought by the divine self-communication and continued in the life of faith is not of such a nature that a new two-way traffic is initiated between God and human beings in the course of which we can, on our side, turn or influence God's will. Grace, however it is established and continued in the affairs of human beings, is still a gift. God remains God. God's will is single, indivisible, and unchangeable. By grace we are brought into the circle of God's will, and only insofar as our requests are in accord with God's will and therefore wholly represent our repentant and thankful surrender to God's will do they become mature Christian prayer. But God's will, while knowable through the Redeemer and through the continued influence of the Holy Spirit, is never wholly scrutable even in relation to ourselves; for we do not possess a perfect consciousness of God and consequently do not enjoy perfect union with God as was true of the Redeemer.

What, then, is the specific role of the Redeemer in the divine self-communication and in the process of redemption in human life? Our relationship with the Redeemer is, first of all, an "inward" thing; that is, it is personally and immediately appropriated, a matter of faith and not primarily one of objective consciousness. Yet, "since faith can rest upon nothing except an impression received," it is also capable of being experienced and in this respect is also a matter of the more public domain which is the church.[75] For Schleiermacher, genuine religious experience always has both an inward and an outward direction. It originates in one's personal relationship of faith to God; but it also necessarily arises within a particular condition of the world and finds its essential external determination within a particular religious community. The person in her- or himself does not constitute her or his own total religious environment. Thus, religious experience, representing the outward aspect (community) and presupposing the inward aspect (faith), is made up of two elements: the impression of the sinless perfection of Jesus received by each individual person from the picture of Christ carried within the common life of the church, which likewise produces a consciousness of sin and of redeeming grace; but also the continuing disposition within the community of the church to carry forth this original "impetus given by his historical life," despite all tendencies toward aberration and corruption.[76] Through the continuing activity of the Holy Spirit, both are genuine, effective communications of Christ's perfection, which is simply the being of God in him.

There is no mixing up of cause and effect here; for his perfection is not merely the result of the divine influence in his consciousness; it itself designates the divinity of his person, describes the fact of this unique person-forming activity of God within Jesus' own nature and existence. What is communicated is the being of God manifest in the person of Christ; and it is only putting the same thing a different way when Schleiermacher refers to the communication of Christ's perfection (with respect to our consciousness of sin) or of his blessedness (with respect to our consciousness of grace).

By the very nature of the case, this communication is not a process by which something in us is simply "incited" or "released" by the Redeemer;[77] rather, it is an influence proceeding from something unique in him. It does not proceed, furthermore, from something that is simply more complete and inclusive in him than in other human beings, or simply by virtue of some peculiar historical position into which he was placed; rather, it is something no one else could accomplish, as the full consequence of "a distinctive spiritual content of his person"—that is, God's completion of the creation of human nature in his person.[78] On just this account, the Redeemer's communication is incapable of extension by mere observation and imitation. It is a truly personal communication aimed not toward the informing of minds but toward the forming of persons, in accordance with, though not in pure repetition of, the forming of his own person, viewed as the coming together of God and humanity.[79] Since the substance of Jesus' self-proclamation is his own self-communication, his person and work cannot be abstracted from each other so that Christ might be in some way distinguishable from others by his person but not by his work, or vice versa.

Thus Schleiermacher proposes a new formula in place of the old doctrine of the two natures. Christ is distinguished from other human beings by that which constituted the innermost determination of his existence; namely, God's being in him in such a manner that (using the old language) "the divine nature alone was active or self-communicating and the human alone passive or in process of being taken up."[80] Therefore, in order to express the simultaneous uniting of God and humanity in the person of Christ, Schleiermacher proposed the formula already mentioned, that "in Christ the creation of humanity first reaches completion."[81] In these terms, redemption is at once the activity of God and of the human Jesus, and the peculiarly divine dignity of the Redeemer in no way excludes the humanity of Jesus.

The complete character of the divine communication in Christ, therefore, can be apprehended only if "the total content" of the doctrines of Christ's person and of his work is taken to be "the same" and if all doctrines of the Christian life and of the church are regarded solely as "that which came to pass through Christ."[82] As for Calvin, the doctrine of the Holy Spirit falls wholly under the aegis of the doctrine of redemption and, viewed as representing the continued influence of God in Christ, is substantially identical in scope with the doctrines of the church and of the Christian life. The "communication of the Holy Spirit" within the new corporate life of the church founded by Christ is experienced not as a private but as a "common spirit," an activity of God's Spirit bent to the regeneration and sanctification of human beings in and through community. The entire doctrine of the church, therefore, is a direct extension and indispensable completion of the doctrines of regeneration and sanctifiction, which are described as "the manner in which fellowship with the perfection and blessedness of the Redeemer expresses itself in the individual soul."[83] "Life in Christ" is a continual theme of *Christian Faith;* but being "led by the Spirit" is the same theme.[84] It is only in this way that the all-wise God "orders and determines the world for the divine self-communication which is evinced in redemption."[85] That is, God does this in such a way that God's Word becomes a "self-representation" *(Selbstdarstellung)* of God through the lips and actions of the community.[86] This does not occur, however, without the prior condition and final goal of church proclamation, which is the work of divine love in redemption, whereby God "communicates" God's own self to persons of faith in and through the church.[87]

Schleiermacher also has a fully developed doctrine of sin, presented as the need of each and every human being for redemption, whether within the new or within the old creation. After the fact, the Christian may become aware that one's own need for redemption is a universal need, that the preparatory activity of divine grace within one's own life is going on everywhere according to the divine good pleasure, and that the existence of sin is itself "among the preparatory and introductory elements of the divine government of the world."[88] The traditional joining of divine holiness and justice to reprobation, moreover, must be rejected; for under the presupposition that "God regards all human beings only in Christ," every human being must be looked upon as bearing within him- or herself the divine predestination to blessedness.[89] The manner of God's final disposition of grace is a subject not of faith but of hope, not of doctrine proper but of prophecy, not given to religious consciousness but hidden in the sacred counsels of God. Within Schleiermacher's perspective there are two aspects of grace—preparatory and under the direct conditions of redemption—but there is no natural grace and no separate kind attached to sanctification.[90]

Schleiermacher accordingly divides the divine government of the world into only two periods: before and after the historical appearance of Christ. Before Christ, "humanity was in a condition of living under preparatory grace—the whole of humanity." In Israel there existed some vague, rudimentary presentiment of the church, some approximation to faith, some partial instrumentality of grace, and in this regard at least some appropriation of Christ's blessedness, though not of his perfection—some degree of sanctification and, by this token, even justification for Christ's sake. But Israel was—and is—not the only object of preparatory grace. We are not obliged to teach either that God first started loving human beings when Christ appeared or that God restricted the divine love to Israel. We must only testify that this appearance was the first "temporal manifestation" of God's redeeming love. Regarded in this way, the true church can be held to have existed since the beginning of the human race and yet one may maintain that there is no truly visible church except in Christ and on the condition of faith in Christ.[91]

The same holds true of every individual. From our birth we fall under the operation of preparatory grace; but only by faith in Christ are we conscious of God's redeeming love. Only then, moreover, is our capacity for an active, living relationship to God released.[92] Christ's production of responsible activity in the individual furnishes the bridge from Christology to the doctrine of the Christian life and constitutes its teleological character.[93] Since this productivity is actualized only within the corporate life of the church, it is also at the same time the bridge from Christology to the doctrine of the church. We are enabled by grace to do good because we are not only forgiven but are also adopted, not only redeemed but also sent forth. Fellowship with Christ, therefore, "is always a fellowship with his mission to the world";[94] and full conduct of the Christian life in and through the church has the same aim as prayer: in reflecting on the image of Christ to become better "organs of the divine Spirit for rightly discovering and introducing whatever may be necessary for the increase and progress of the Kingdom of God."[95]

To the extent that Christ's presence determined the activity of the early disciples, their attitude was predominantly receptive; but once he was gone, their "reminiscent apprehension of Christ must grow into a spontaneous imitation *(Nachbildung)* of him." Within the redemptive fellowship, they took active responsibility for themselves and for each other. This is where the activity of the Holy Spirit came in: as the continued "fellowship-forming activity" of Christ, as the "common spirit" by which "this common spontaneous activity" is still produced as the act of the Redeemer become our own act. Individual purpose is to be formed in view of the reality and potential support of the fellowship.[96] Because of this common, interpersonal reality of the Christian life, admittance of any purely sensuous—empirical, magical, merely symbolic, strictly imaginative or legalistic—determinants of Christian purpose is severely opposed everywhere in *Christian Faith;* for within the aesthetic perspective responsible self-activity is bound to yield to the passive absorption or the mechanical imitation of mere externals.

At no point is the doctrinal ground for Schleiermacher's entire dogmatic procedure more evident than in this representation of the manner in which Christ's activity is realized in the individual life. Church dogmatics is subject to the same rigorous ethical requirements as is the rest of the Christian life. Ultimately, moreover, the same is to be said of every other part of Christian theology. Insofar as it is itself Christian conduct, deeply and pervasively directed toward the kingdom of God as its essential environment, it is also Christian prayer. Insofar as its activity is centered in Christ, it is also centered in the church and in the Holy Spirit. Finally, insofar as its concern reflects awareness of the one divine government of the world, it never isolates its presentation of Christ from the whole reality of God in relation to humanity. Teleology never gets impaled on the eccentricities of law. It is always a reflection of monotheistic faith; yet, just because it is the whole Christ Schleiermacher attempts to keep in mind, and the whole reality of God, proclamation is never set apart from ethics, gospel from the life in Christ. Gospel, nonetheless, comes first: grace before fellowship, *Glaubenslehre* before *Sittenlehre;* and this means, for Schleiermacher, that Christian ethics like Christian dogmatics is preferably indicative rather than imperative. Law can be a means of grace, but only insofar as it is itself a good work, itself having its basis in love and arising as a fruit and not a rigid condition of sanctification.[97] Only the inner determination of faith can be considered ultimately regulative of Christian thought and action, however necessary the outer accoutrements of faith may be for its development and expression. This attitude is decisive for Schleiermacher's position over against previous dogmatic method and accounts more than any other factor for the distinctive, revolutionary character and productive power of his dogmatic system.[98]

Concluding Remarks

I have attempted to demonstrate that Schleiermacher's theology is ecumenical at its very core. It is so preeminently as a theology of and for the church, which can only truly exist, according to him, in fellowship with God in and through fellowship with the Redeemer. It is also true that his ecumenical engagements were greatly limited by the conditions of his time. His own perspective would demand more widely inclusive interactions, within a global context, today. No one has yet adequately laid out his specific indebtedness to Reformed tradition, borrowings which were selective though considerable.[99] An adequate account would have to present his theology comparatively and in its entirety, not being restricted to his explicit references to materials from the Reformed tradition. Unquestionably, moreover, he grew up in that tradition—with an important sojourn among the Herrnhuter Brethren as a youth; he served as a Reformed minister for over forty years. Most that John McNeill has stated about Calvin in the ecumenical role could easily be claimed of Schleiermacher.[100] Gottfried Locher's emphasis on Zwingli's Christ-centered view of the church's catholicity and on his strong emphasis on the rule of God's kingdom in Christ beyond the church could be extended to Schleiermacher.[101] More striking yet, however, are parallels that can be drawn with Bullinger. Mark Burrows has emphasized six features in Bullinger's distinctly Reformed theology[102] that are certainly reflected in Schleiermacher's: (1) "the pastoral depth" *(pietatis praxis),* (2) God's communication to human beings in Christ through the presence of the Holy Spirit (though, unlike Schleiermacher, he thinks of this as *gratia infusa*), (3) the direct participation of Christ in the Christian life (the *Christus in nobis* theme of the Second Helvetic Confession), (4) the "real" presence of Christ as something expected in the life of faith, not relegated to the sacraments, (5) soteriology as Christology and vice versa, and finally (6) seeing his efforts as a *via media* between Roman Catholic and Anabaptist positions, critiquing and in some respects rejecting, yet honoring, both. The circumstances of the church and therefore the tasks that Bullinger confronted were different from those in Schleiermacher's case. Nevertheless, the parallels suggest strong lines of connection between aspects of sixteenth-century Reformed theology and Schleiermacher's own efforts.

Without making any direct comparisons, Hans Grass,[103] among many others, has recently indicated some features which Schleiermacher modified, enlarged, or added in relation to earlier Evangelical-Reformed positions. These came into the picture, I believe, not only because Schleiermacher keenly listened for the Word of God within the conditions of his own church and world, but also because he had come to understand, utilize, and contribute to new methods of science. He always encouraged his students to grasp the theology of the church for themselves, in their own way, to own it through careful listening and critical study. This is what he eminently achieved himself.

NOTES

1. A number of studies have focused on his church union activities. For a brief early statement of my own, see "Schleiermacher as Ecumenical Theologian," *Ecumenical Review* 17, no. 3 (July 1965), 273–274.

2. See my companion essay, "Themes in Schleiermacher's Later Theology," *Papers of the Schleiermacher Seminar, American Academy of Religion 1988 Annual Meeting,* ed. by John E. Thiel (Fairfield, Conn.: Fairfield University, 1988). Other works on themes discussed in these essays can be found in my successive bibliographical compilations: *Schleiermacher Bibliography* (Princeton, N.J.: Princeton University Press [for Princeton Theological Seminary],

1966, 1985) and in *New Athenaeum/Neues Athenäum* (beginning with the first annual issue, 1988). In the references that follow, *K.D.* is the conventional abbreviation for *Kurze Darstellung* ("Brief Outline"); my new translation and edition of this work by Schleiermacher includes fresh interpretive essays: *Brief Outline of Theology as a Field of Study* (Lewiston, N.Y.: Edwin Mellen Press, 1988, 234 pp.). *OR* refers to Schleiermacher's work *On Religion,* tr. T. Tice (Richmond, Va.: John Knox Press, 1969); *R* refers to the critical German edition of these *Reden* by Pünjer. With occasional adjustments, *The Christian Faith* (Edinburgh: T. & T. Clark, 1928; also in later printings) is followed and its pagination referred to here. However, since the entire work is organized numerically by propositions (using the # sign here) and subsections, the conventional abbreviation for *Glaubenslehre* is also used, e.g., *Gl.* #128:3,538. *Gl.1* refers to the first edition of 1821–22; the second edition appeared in 1830–31 and is the one translated. The title, as Wilfred Cantwell Smith has helpfully argued—"On Mistranslated Booktitles," *Religious Studies* 20, no. 1 (March 1984), 27–42—should be simply *Christian Faith.*

3. This and the themes that immediately follow will be treated below. On corporate mediation, e.g., see *Gl.* ##87:3; 108:5,492; 113. On the church's interaction with the rest of the world, e.g., see *Gl.* ##115 and 121–125.

4. E.g., see *K.D.* #234; *Gl.* #121:1,560.

5. E.g., see *Gl.* #108:5,490 and #121:1,561.

6. *Gl.* #169:3,737.

7. Recently the beginning of an approach to Schleiermacher's use of the confessions has been made by Wolfgang Sommer, "Schleiermachers Stellung zu den reformatorischen Bekenntnisschriften, vor allem nach seiner Schrift 'Über den eigenthümlichen Wert und das bindende Ansehen symbolischer Bücher' (1819)," in *Internationaler Schleiermacher-Kongress Berlin 1984,* ed. Kurt-Victor Selge, vol. 2 (Berlin: Walter de Gruyter, 1985), pp. 1061–1074.

8. All these characteristics and allied principles are presented in *Brief Outline* (note 2 above); some of them I discuss in the Introduction and Postscript there. See also my essay "Schleiermacher on the Scientific Study of Religion," in Albert Blackwell et al., *Friedrich Schleiermacher and the Founding of the University of Berlin: The Study of Religion as a Scientific Discipline* (Lewiston, N.Y.: Edwin Mellen Press, 1988). Still other features were developed at length in my 1960 Princeton Theological Seminary dissertation, *Schleiermacher's Theological Method,* from which portions of the present essay are derived.

9. E.g., see *K.D.* ##54–61, 234; *Gl.* #108:5,492.

10. E.g., see *Gl.* ##121:1; 126:1.

11. *Gl.* #19 (in the first ed., #1). A similar definition is given in *K.D.* ##97 and 195. The English translation of #19 has "preva-

lent," which is misleading since prevalence is not an adequate selective criterion for Schleiermacher. "Current" would be too loose and "valid" too tight.

12. *K.D.* #1.
13. *Gl.* ##148–156.
14. *K.D.* #200.
15. *K.D.* #200. On heterodoxy as a desired accompaniment of orthodoxy see *K.D.* ##203–208, 210.
16. In his *Concept of Dread* (Princeton, N.J.: Princeton University Press, 1946), p. 18, Søren Kierkegaard praises Schleiermacher's "immortal services" to dogmatics, emphasizing that he was "in the beautiful Greek sense a thinker who could talk of what he had known," in contrast to Hegel, who had to explain everything.
17. *K.D.* #202: A dogmatics is the more complete the more successfully it combines these "divinatory" and "assertory" features.
18. *Gl.* #2.
19. See *K.D.* #29.
20. See *K.D.* #23.
21. See *K.D.* ##24, 43.
22. *Gl.* #6:1. Compare *K.D.* #22, also *Gl.* ##33:1 and 61:4,352.
23. *Gl.* #6:2,27.
24. *Gl.* #6:4,29.
25. *Gl.* #6.
26. *Schleiermachers Werke in Auswahl,* vol. II, 2. A., ed. by Otto Braun (Leipzig: Meiner, 1927), pp. 101f., 359f.
27. Ibid., pp. 190f.
28. Ibid., p. 360.
29. Ibid., p. 362.
30. Ibid., p. 190.
31. Ibid., pp. 359–365.
32. Compare *K.D.* ##8, 238.
33. Karl Barth regularly attacked Schleiermacher for purportedly making the church and much else a product of human rather than divine action. In itself, nothing even among Schleiermacher's introductory propositions, however, precludes God's having originated such actions or causing them to continue. See my chapter, "Interviews with Karl Barth and Reflections on His Interpretations of Schleiermacher," in *Barth and Schleiermacher: Beyond the Impasse?* by James O. Duke et al. (Philadelphia: Fortress Press, 1988), pp. 43–60.
34. Note #11 to the fourth address, *OR* 253–255.
35. Ibid., 255.
36. *OR* 218 (*R* 191); *Gl.* #157:1,697.
37. *Gl.* #122:3,568f. The common spirit *(Gemeingeist)* is never absolutely identified with the consensus of the community *(Gemeinsinn);* e.g., see *K.D.* #313.

38. *Gl.* #116:3,535.
39. *Gl.* #132:2,609. See also *Gl.* ##71:3,290; 74:3–4; 113:4,527f.
40. *Gl.* #122:3.
41. *Gl.* #121:2; see ##123–125 for a fuller definition.
42. *Gl.* #110:2,507. See also ##122:1,565; 127:1; 129:1–2,595.
43. *Gl.* ##130:2,598; 133:1.
44. *Gl.* ##141:1,652; 144:1,661.
45. *OR* 296 (*R* 266).
46. Already in Schleiermacher's 1806 dialogue *Christmas Eve,* Eduard reflects much of Schleiermacher's mature view of the relation of church and world. See my translation (Richmond, Va.: John Knox Press, 1966), p. 83.
47. Compare *Gl.* #164.
48. *Gl.* #80:2,328; compare ##87–88.
49. *Gl.* ##113:2,526; 101:2,433.
50. *Gl.* #100:2,427f.
51. *Gl.* ##101:2,433; 132:2,609.
52. *Gl.* #105:1,467.
53. *Gl.* ##107:1,478; 108:5,490f.; 105:1,467.
54. Compare *K.D.* ##4, 22, 48.
55. Compare *K.D.* ##167, 173.
56. *Gl.* #106.
57. *Gl.* #100:1,425 and #100:2,428.
58. *Gl.* #101:1–2,432.
59. *Gl.* #107.
60. *Gl.* #109:2.
61. *Gl.* #136.
62. *Gl.* #108.
63. *Gl.* #110.
64. *Gl.* #139:1,639; #141.
65. *Gl.* #114:2,531.
66. *Gl.* #119:1,547.
67. *Gl.* #122;3,568f.; #124.
68. *Gl.* #128:1,592; #108.
69. *Gl.* #134:3,617.
70. *Gl.* #157:2,698.
71. *Gl.* #169:3,737.
72. *Gl.* #109:2,499; see also #104:4,461.
73. See especially ##63:2; 91:1.
74. *Gl.* #170:1.
75. *Gl.* #88:3,364f.
76. *Gl.* #88:3,364f.
77. *Gl.* #92:1,374.
78. *Gl.* #92:1,374.
79. See *Gl.* ##97:2,400f.; 100:2,427; 101:2,433; 101:4,437; and especially the warning in #123:3,573.

80. *Gl.* #97.
81. Note also *Gl.* #97:4,411.
82. *Gl.* #92:3,376.
83. Title, Division II.
84. *Gl.* #124:2,575f. See also *Gl.* #127:2,587 and ##133–135.
85. *Gl.* #168.
86. *Gl.* #168:1,733
87. *Gl.* #166.
88. *Gl.* #164:3,726. See also ##79–82; 66:2,273; 72:4,300; 111:1–3.
89. *Gl.* ##83–85; 118; 120:P.S.
90. On preparatory grace see *Gl.* ##73:2,306; 83–84; 86:2,356; 89:2,367; 108:6,495; 133:2,526; 156:2,694. On sanctification, see #112:2,520.
91. *Gl.* #156:1–3.
92. *Gl.* #108:6,494f.
93. *Gl.* #63:1–2; *Gl.1* #79. See also ##62:2,261; 100:1–2; 101:1.
94. *Gl.* #112:4.
95. *Gl.* #146:2,671; compare #121. Among recent treatments, see Eilert Herms, "Reich Gottes und menschliches Handeln," in *Friedrich Schleiermacher, 1768–1834,* ed. Dietz Lange (Göttingen: Vandenhoeck & Ruprecht, 1985), pp. 163–192.
96. *Gl.* #122:2,568f.; compare #168:2.
97. *Gl.* #112:4–5.
98. See *Gl.* #128:3,593.
99. Much of this essay is intended to be an implicit contribution to this question. The most notable article so far displays abysmal misreadings of Schleiermacher, reminiscent of Barth's: Wilhelm Niesel, "Schleiermachers Verhältnis zur reformierten Tradition," *Zwischen den Zeiten* 8 (1930), 511–525. Several of Brian A. Gerrish's books and essays from 1978 to 1984 (in my 1985 bibliography, cited in note 2, ##2105–2109), deal with aspects of this question, as does his article, "Nature and the Theater of Redemption: Schleiermacher on Christian Dogmatics and the Creation Story," *Ex Auditu* 3 (1987), 120–136.
100. John T. McNeill, "Calvin as an Ecumenical Churchman," *Church History* 57, Supplement (1988), 43–55.
101. Gottfried W. Locher, "Die reformatorische Katholizität Huldrych Zwinglis," *Theologische Zeitschrift* 42, no. 1 (1986), 1–13.
102. Mark S. Burrows, " 'Christus intra nos Vivens': The Peculiar Genius of Bullinger's Doctrine of Sanctification," *Zeitschrift für Kirchengeschichte* 98, no. 1 (1987), 48–69.
103. Hans Grass, "Grund und Grenzen der Kirchengemeinschaft," in the 1985 volume cited in note 95, pp. 217–235. See also Dietz Lange's essay there, "Neugestaltung christlicher Glaubenslehre," pp. 85–105.

Philip Schaff at Chur, 1819–1834[1]

Ulrich Gäbler

Philip Schaff is a well-known figure in the history of the Protestant churches in North America. Born in Switzerland in 1819, he left his hometown of Chur in 1834, attended school in Württemberg, then took his theological training at the universities of Tübingen, Halle, and Berlin. From 1844 he taught in Mercersburg, Pennsylvania, at the Seminary of the German Reformed Church in the United States. Together with his colleague John H. Nevin, he became responsible for the shaping of the so-called Mercersburg Theology, one of the most remarkable theological movements in nineteenth-century American Protestantism.[2] In 1870 Schaff moved to New York, where he held a chair at Union Theological Seminary until his death in 1893. Among his numerous works are *Church and State in the United States, Amerika, The Creeds of Christendom,* and the massive *History of the Christian Church.* Schaff tried to bring European and American Protestants together not only through his published works but also by keeping up a broad correspondence with European scholars and churchmen and by extensive travel on both sides of the Atlantic. His special concern was the Evangelical Alliance, for which he chaired the General Conference in New York in 1873.

The main source for studying Schaff's life until now has been the hagiographic biography by his son David, *The Life of Philip Schaff.*[3] On the occasion of the centennial celebration of the American Society of Church History, George Shriver added new material and wrote a fine and comprehensive account of his life.[4] Concerning Schaff's early years at Chur, the biographers relied on "Autobiographical Reminiscences,"[5] which seemed to be trustworthy. Schaff began to write down these remarks on the very last day of the year 1871, more than thirty-five years after he had left Switzerland.[6] Besides the fact that David Schaff did not render his father's text in its entirety, and that he made minor changes, the manuscript itself reveals that the father was not always sure how to tell his own life's story. He continued to work on the text, as is proved by the great number of changes, corrections, and deletions in his handwriting. The care he took is appropriate, for publication of the text was not out of the question for him.

A recent search for source material on Schaff in the Swiss Archives turned out to be successful. Generally speaking, the material still preserved in Chur does not contradict Schaff's own "Reminiscences," but it reveals that the celebrated churchman and theologian did not even mention decisive elements of his early biography. For reasons which are understandable from the character of these facts, he passed over them in silence. I will tell here, in three parts, the story of Schaff's time at Chur: his family, the religious situation at Chur, especially the activities of his patron, Paul Kind; and Schaff's life from 1819 to 1834.

I

In Switzerland the name "Schaff" appears for the first time in the middle of the eighteenth century. On June 27, 1759, a Johannes Schaf was baptized in Zizers, a small village in the Rhine valley in the Grisons.[7] His parents were Johannes Schaf senior from Lindau on Lake Constance in Germany and Anna Maria Jenni from Chur, the capital of the Grisons. It is not surprising that a man from Lindau came to Zizers, for there were very close connections between the Alpine territory and the South German city. The stagecoach from Lindau to Milan in Italy ran through Zizers and Chur. Johannes Schaf, born in 1759, left Zizers and settled in Chur. He is the grandfather of our Philip Schaff.

From about 1781, at the latest, until his death in 1837 Johannes Schaf lived permanently in Chur.[8] Besides his immediate family there were no other Schaffs in Chur. Johannes Schaf was married to Anna Barbara Bender in 1781. On their wedding day a child was born to them, a daughter. Five more children followed, including Philipp senior, the father of the church historian, born in 1789.

Grandfather Johannes Schaf worked as a tailor employed by other craftsmen. In 1805 he was able to buy a small house in Chur and a piece of land outside the town.[9] Owing to the fact that he had immigrated to Chur, he did not have full citizenship; therefore, an administrator had to sign the purchase contract. None of the members of the Schaff family ever received full citizenship in Chur. All of them remained "alien residents."

At the beginning of the nineteenth century the immigration of foreign people formed a very urgent problem for the Grison authorities. Foreigners settled in both the rural areas and the towns. An official report from 1820 estimated that there were about 2,000 homeless people in the Grisons—more than half the population of the capital, Chur. There were different forms of "alien residency." Though Johannes Schaf did not have any political or economic rights in Chur, he was entitled to stay as long as he wished. Against the eventuality that these aliens would run into economic troubles, they were legally obligated to pay an annual fee in support of a general relief fund; thus the town reduced the potential financial risk involved in the admission of large numbers of strangers. In 1815 Johannes Schaf was one of fifteen alien residents in Chur who did not pay this annual fee and consequently had his property mortgaged to the municipality of Chur. His administrator was obliged to report regularly to the city about the economic status of Schaf's property. These reports show that Schaf was not able to enlarge his property and, furthermore, that his real estate underwent devaluation between 1823 and 1837. Though J. Schaf held property, the family was regarded to be poor by the Chur authorities. When in 1820 J. Schaf was found to have failed to maintain proper precautionary fire measures, the penalty was waived "due to his poverty."[10] Considering the social and economic status of the Schaff family, one can justly conclude that they belonged to the marginally poor within the society of Chur.

In 1815 all the noncitizens of Chur were registered for purposes of more accurate control. The entry of J. Schaf's household indicates that the family lived in a small house near St. Martin's church, and consisted of the tailor himself, his wife, two daughters, and one son, Philipp, at the time twenty-six years old, employed as a carpenter and still living at home.[11] Philipp and Anna Schindler later became parents of the church historian.

About Anna Schindler we know very little. She was born in the same year as was Philipp, 1789, and curiously in the same place where the Schaffs first settled, Zizers,[12] near Chur. She is known to have arrived in Chur for the first time on January 26, 1818. Because she was a stranger in Chur, she had to apply for permanent-residence permission. The commission of the

Town Council which was in charge of all alien residence affairs refused her request. Surprisingly enough, the minutes of the committee meeting not only state that Anna's application was refused but also that she was married—but not to Philipp Schaff. Nothing is said about her husband or her family.[13] At any rate, it seems fair to say that the married woman, Anna Schindler, had come to Chur from another place and lived there as a subtenant without her husband. These, then, were the parents of Philip Schaff, the church historian: his mother was a thirty-year-old married woman, residing in Chur illegally; his father, of the same age, was living in his own father's household together with two sisters, their mother having already died in 1817. Both parents belonged to the marginal members of society.

When Anna Schindler became pregnant, Philipp denied being the child's father. Therefore, Schindler was forced to sue him for paternity support. In October 1818 the lawsuit began. There were three unsolved problems: first, the paternity of the unborn baby; second, the illegal status of the mother in Chur; third, both Anna and Philipp had transgressed the law—she was under suspicion of having committed adultery and he, of promiscuous behavior.

On October 27 the Municipal Court handed down a decision. Both Anna and Philipp were found guilty and fined; also the landlords had to pay a penalty for not having made this violation of law impossible. Additionally, the court decided that Philipp was to be regarded as the father of the child and required him to pay the midwifery costs and regular child support. Before the judge closed the case, Philipp took the floor and asked the court to make Anna return four rings and a clock which he had presented to her as a seal to their engagement. Obviously the engagement had taken place without Anna's having mentioned her married state. The judge was a wise man. Anna, he declared, had to return the rings, for they were considered to be a seal of the engagement, whereas she was allowed to keep the clock, which was viewed as an ordinary gift.

Withal, one might say that the baby, who was born around two months later, came into the world under rather unpleasant circumstances. The exact date of Schaff's birth is unknown.[14] Surprisingly enough, at his baptism on January 7, 1819, he was given the name of his father, Philip. Anna Schindler was required to reapply for residence status and did so at the end of January 1819. The answer was brief: because the request had already been refused a year earlier and because she had behaved in an improper manner, the applicant was ordered to leave town within eight days. But according to the legislation of the Grisons, the committee was obliged to accept the baby as an inhabitant of the town of Chur. Anna Schindler was entitled to receive the appropriate residence certificate for her child. Philip Schaff junior became an *Angehöriger* of Chur, which meant that, while he still did not have full citizenship status, in contrast to mere alien residents, he did not have to pay the aforementioned regular residence fee. In the event of his incurring economic difficulties, the city would be obliged to support him. Philip Schaff the church historian was not a full citizen of Chur and did not have any political rights in Switzerland.

We do not know with complete certainty what happened to Anna Schindler and her child after the decision of the City Commission. If we can trust Schaff's autobiographical notes, the mother left Chur and the baby stayed.[15] One can assume that little Philipp was accepted into the family of his grandfather Johannes Schaf. His grandmother had already died in 1817, and his father passed away in February 1820. One of his two aunts left the house in 1824 to get married. Clearly, when Anna Schindler had to leave her baby behind, the odds for him could not have been worse. One can draw the conclusion that Philip Schaff came from a socially and economically depressed family and that he began life under tragic circumstances.

II

When Napoleon remodeled the Swiss Confederacy, the Grisons became the sixteenth canton of Switzerland.[16] Some years later, in 1814, the Grisons accepted this connection with the Confederacy by passing a new democratic constitution. This constitution officially acknowledged two Christian churches in the canton, the Reformed and the Catholic. Within the Grisons, the capital, Chur, with about 3,200 inhabitants, formed the political, economic, and cultural center. Though Chur was regarded as a Protestant town, the see of the Catholic bishop formed an eminent enclave within the town precincts.

At the time Protestant Chur worshiped in two churches, St. Martin's and St. Regula's. The minister of St. Martin's also held the honorary function of Antistes of the entire Grisons Church. The peaceful arrangement of religious affairs was also mirrored in the organization of the cantonal education system. From the time of its establishment in 1804, the state secondary school at Chur had two branches, one for Catholic and another for Protestant pupils. There was no university, but the Reformed church had the right to train ministers at a theological institute which was closely connected with the regular secondary school *(Kantonsschule).*[17]

In the eighteenth century the Grisons Reformed Church[18] was shaken by a fervent and long-lasting conflict between an orthodox party and the Moravians. Though eventually the Moravians were defeated and the Reformed ministers had to promise to stay away from Moravian gatherings, the spirit of pietism was not extinguished and continued until well into the nineteenth century. Rationalistic and "awakened" ministers cooperated with one another peacefully. There were no real clashes at that time.

The two leading theologians in Chur during the time of Philip Schaff were the Antistes Simon Dominik Benedikt at St. Martin's and his colleague Paul Kind, professor at the aforementioned theological seminary and simultaneously preacher at St. Regula's. In his autobiographical notes Philip Schaff remarked that he had close ties with Paul Kind,[19] and, indeed, original sources in Chur confirm Schaff's statement. Since he strongly influenced the spiritual climate in which Schaff grew up, it is worth taking a closer look at Paul Kind.

Kind was born in Chur in 1873 as the son of a lawyer. His uncle, the theologian, Paul Kind the Elder (1734–1802), opposed Enlightenment ideas and had close connections with the Deutsche Christentumsgesellschaft in Basel. This anti-Enlightenment society had aims similar to those of the British Society for Promoting Christian Knowledge. In fact, there were close ties between these two associations. Paul Kind the Younger inherited his uncle's contacts. After attending the universities of Tübingen and Heidelberg, he returned to Chur in 1808 to become professor at the Theological Institute, where he was responsible for a large share of the courses. In 1832 Kind left the Theological Institute to accept the ministry at St. Martin's as a successor to Antistes Benedikt. His personal relations with southern Germany can be seen by the fact that his second wife was the daughter of a Württemberg minister.[20] They had seven children, one of whom, Immanuel, was about the same age as Schaff; it is likely that Immanuel and Philip studied theology together in Tübingen. One of Kind's descendants was Theophil Wurm, the famous bishop of Württemberg during the time of the Nazi regime. Besides his tasks at the Theological Institute and at St. Regula's, Kind fulfilled a number of honorary offices; he functioned, for example, as the supervisor of the Chur schools.

Kind's many activities made him one of the leading figures of the Upper-German-Swiss revival in the Grisons. In close cooperation with the Christentumsgesellschaft and the Basel Missionary Society (BMS), Kind tried to create local agencies in Chur which would be responsible for missionary, educational, and welfare projects.

Since 1813 there had been a Bible Committee in Chur, which distributed Bibles, produced in Basel, to the different language groups in the Grisons—to the German, Romansh, and Italian populations. Initially, there were only six members, but later on the society flourished. The secretary of the association was the Council member Jacob Papon, who had served the elder Johannes Schaf as estate administrator. He was the executor of Schaf's legacy.[21] Kind worked closely with him.

A special effort was made by Kind in 1820 to establish a local chapter of the BMS. In August of that year Kind published an appeal "to all who want to spread the Kingdom of God."[22] Pointing to the success of Christian missions overseas and at home, he asked for money to support the education of a candidate from the Grisons at the Basel Missionary Seminary. A local chapter of the BMS should be established, he argued, in order to raise funds and interpret reports from the missionary fields. Kind made a very optimistic report to Basel about the first steps of his undertaking. But this was a miscalculation. A formal society could not be established, and by as early as 1823 giving had fallen off to almost nothing. Kind was forced to admit that his efforts had failed.[23]

Kind's unshakable optimism is illustrated by the intention he expressed in the same period to set up a school for poor or orphaned children in Chur. In his opinion these poor children were not receiving adequate care at the Municipal Hospital. The first step, he thought, might be to let these children live with local families but to have them financially supported by others.[24] This plan was never realized. As in the case of the Bible Committee and the missionary activities plan, this later concept, too, was influenced by similar projects among the Basel societies. It was not entirely a question of one-way traffic from Basel to Chur, however. Kind was asked, for example, to mail a hundred copies of his printed sermons to Basel to have them distributed there.[25] It is clear that in Paul Kind, Schaff met a more-than-average theologian with a rather broad vision of church and society, and with excellent connections in Basel and Württemberg. In my opinion Kind opened the door to Schaff to the world of *Erweckung* or *réveil.*

III

Philip Schaff probably spent the whole period of his primary education at Chur. It is tempting to suppose that Kind developed his plans concerning the care of orphans in part with an eye to young Philip, who was supported by the municipal relief institutions for the poor. The primary school at Chur was fairly good.[26] During the first three years the children were taught reading, writing, and arithmetic. In the last two grades there were also German, music, and religion. It is very likely that Schaff attended that school from 1826 to 1831.

Schaff was an excellent pupil at the primary school and was therefore allowed to apply for admission to the *Kantonsschule* (secondary school) located in Chur, in order to be trained as a schoolteacher. In September 1831 he was admitted for study at the *Kantonsschule,* with the stipulation that the school would waive all fees in his case. During the entire time he spent at this school, he lived in the home of one Wilhelm Weck. Unfortunately, I have not yet succeeded in uncovering any information on Wilhelm Weck. It is certain, however, that during the period Schaff lived with a family other than his own, at the city's expense.[27] Interestingly, this arrangement corresponded precisely with Paul Kind's proposed plan for the care and nurture of orphans. The Schaff family, including Philip's grandfather and aunt, is not mentioned in the sources at all, which does not necessarily mean that young Philip had no contact with them. His family played no official part in Schaff's education or in his contacts with the municipal authorities.

The *Kantonsschule*[28] had a good name, with excellent teachers from the Grisons and from abroad. Within the teaching staff both the spirit of political liberalism and of religious *réveil* was present. It is fair to say that the intellectual and religious climate at Chur during Schaff's time can by no means be characterized as obscurantist or backward. In fact, the situation at Chur was certainly better than in some other larger European towns.

In his first year at the *Kantonsschule* Schaff studied,[29] among other subjects, religion, geography, mathematics, music, writing, and German. Though he received a fairly good report card at the end of his first year, the Commission for Relief of the poor was not entirely satisfied. Schaff was admonished to work harder in the future in order to prove himself worthy of the benefits he had received. The following entry in the minutes of the Commission reads: "He promised to do so."

In the next grade he began to study Latin. That year (1832–33) Schaff finished at the very head of the group of thirteen-year-old pupils. It was in Latin, not religion, that he got the highest marks. At the end of that year the Commission made no remarks concerning his work; on the contrary, they permitted him to buy cloth in order to have six shirts made. This success was repeated in the 1833–34 school year. Again, Philip was one of the thirteen pupils out of 150 to be exempted from paying tuition. His performance was not as excellent as before, but obviously he still enjoyed full support from the teachers, the school, and the Relief Commission.

In July 1834 Philip's fortunes were radically altered. On July 19, 1834, a meeting of the school board was held under the chairmanship of the board president, Jakob Ulrich Sprecher (1765–1841), one of the leading statesmen of the Grisons and a figure of national prominence, who himself had attended Moravian schools in Germany and had studied law in Jena and Wittenberg. The board had received an extensive report from the faculty, in which it was revealed that a number of pupils had been proved guilty of the "vice of masturbation." This fact came to light through an accusation and was confirmed by an investigation carried out by two teachers. Twelve boys were mentioned by name. The faculty suggested that special measures be taken against them. Others whose identities were not revealed were to be placed under close observation. The report stated that Philip Schaff was one of the chief offenders. He had encouraged fellow students to participate in the trespass. For that reason, the report recommended his expulsion from the *Kantonsschule* for the period of one year. A minority of the faculty found that penalty too severe, and two teachers offered to take personal supervision of those concerned. When one compares Schaff's trespasses to those of the others, it is striking that one reads nary a word about bad habits or failing grades. Thus the impression is correct that Schaff had outstanding talents.

Nevertheless, the board agreed with the majority of the teachers and decided that Schaff and four other students were to be expelled for one school year. In 1834 one of the entries in the register of the *Kantonsschule* reads: "Philip Schaff, dismissed in July." It seems that the masturbation issue had badly shaken the six members of the board. After having made this painful decision, one of its members asked permission to start a weekly devotional service in order to bring to the attention of the students the vices of youth and the consequences thereof. In fact, such meetings had already been held at the school, but now it was decided that the minister in charge should get an increase in salary of one hundred gulden, which, one might expect, would have given him some little incentive to pursue his task rather diligently.

Surprisingly enough, the municipality of Chur did not abandon Schaff to his fate. Just as the minority of the faculty had not agreed with the severe punishment of the boys, the Relief Commission tried to prevent the interruption of Schaff's career. Especially Paul Kind did his best to provide a solution. Fortunately, he had been a member of the Commission for some time. On September 1, 1834, the Commission met and discussed Schaff's situation. Its chairman, the former mayor of Chur, Von Albertini, opened the meeting by giving a report. Schaff, he argued, was well equipped for continuing his education. He should be helped to get academic training. His sin had not been so far-reaching that one could speak of serious damage to his body or his soul. There was hope for the boy's successful future provided that he was looked after closely. Obviously, Von Albertini did not agree with the school board.[30] Furthermore, it is worth noting that Schaff's vocational goal had been changed. When he entered the *Kantonsschule* in 1831, he intended to become a teacher; now he wanted to continue his education at a university.

Von Albertini went on to state that contact had already been made with the boarding school at Korntal in Württemberg. The director there had been informed about Schaff's situation and had been asked to admit him as a student. Shortly before, Von Albertini continued, Antistes Kind had received a positive reply: the said director was willing to accept Schaff on the condition that the usual tuition be paid. If it were discovered, however, that he continued to indulge in "the hidden sin," he would be removed from school immediately. After this opening statement by the chairman, Paul Kind made a number of supplementary remarks. He revealed his personal acquaintance with the director of the Korntal School and praised the merits of that institution, which had been established by Moravians and was indeed highly esteemed among the upper German and Swiss pietists. This plea by the chairman and the Antistes convinced the Commission. It was decided that Schaff would be granted a scholarship for one year in Korntal. After that period he was supposed to reenter the *Kantonsschule* in Chur.

In September 1834 Schaff had to leave his hometown. In a poem authored at that time and titled "Friendship,"[31] he expressed his feelings. There he describes the final hours of two young men. Friedrich visits Conradin, who is expecting execution. The two friends are praising their relationship. When fifteen-year-old Philip left Chur on September 10, 1834, he carried with him a letter of introduction, written by Antistes Kind.[32] There is no evidence that he or his superiors did not expect his return on completion of the year in Württemberg. But the course of his life soon changed again.

After Schaff had spent some months in Korntal, an epidemic broke out and the school had to be closed. The young Grisonian moved to Stuttgart in order to continue his education. At the conclusion of this year, however, he did not return to Chur, for what reasons we are not able to ascertain. It is probable that he found the general mentality in Stuttgart more congenial than that in Chur, where he had been marked as an outsider. In September 1835 the Relief Commission in Chur had to face a new and rather difficult situation. On the one hand Schaff's move from Korntal to Stuttgart considerably increased the cost of his maintenance and, moreover, it became apparent that he was not willing to return home. On the other hand, he still clearly needed financial support. It is remarkable that even in these new circumstances the Chur authorities were still inclined to help the boy. Though they were not willing to underwrite all the costs Schaff had incurred or was going to incur, a suitable solution was found: The savings bank in Chur offered him credit to finance his education. Obviously the Relief Commission succeeded in presenting Schaff's case convincingly to the Chur bankers.

After having finished school in Stuttgart, Schaff decided to pursue theological studies at the University of Tübingen. He had not given up the idea of returning to the Grisons, however, for he planned to become a minister there. To that end in 1838 he had a go-between investigate the possibilities of receiving a scholarship in Chur. The very same school board which had expelled him four years earlier had to make a decision on this application, which, strictly speaking, it would not have been possible to honor: The church order of the canton stated that a requirement for the ministry was legitimate parentage.[33] It is very unlikely that Schaff was not aware of this stipulation.

The reaction of the board is surprising. The go-between was told that an alteration of the church order on this point was imminent and that therefore Schaff should be invited to submit a formal application. It is very likely that Schaff followed that advice but his application was refused.[34] The expectations of the board regarding the revision of the church order were not fulfilled until the year 1854. It was only then that the requirement of legitimate parentage for the ministry, which had been in effect since the seventeenth century, was dropped.[35] In the meantime Schaff had become a well-known theologian who was in contact with European churches and therefore also not forgotten in the Grisons. The church leaders there were well aware that his emigration had been prompted by the strictures of the church order. As a kind of act of compensation he was made honorary member of the Grisons Synod[36] in 1859. This was an extraordinary distinction, for he seems to have been the only person to have been so honored during the nineteenth century. By the time he reached the age of forty, the disgrace of Philip Schaff's origins had been definitely redeemed.

NOTES

1. The original version of this essay was presented at the Centennial Meeting of the American Society of Church History, Lancaster, Pennsylvania, April 1988. I am grateful to P. Roberts and J. D. Gort for polishing up my English.

The original spelling of the name was Philipp Schaf (or Schaff), which Schaff himself changed into Philip Schaff after a couple of years in the United States.

2. James H. Nichols, ed., *The Mercersburg Theology* (New York, 1966).

3. David S. Schaff, *The Life of Philip Schaff* (New York, 1897).

4. George H. Shriver, *Philip Schaff: Christian Scholar and Ecumenical Prophet* (Macon, Georgia: Mercer University Press, 1987).

5. "Autobiographical Reminiscences for My Children, commenced Dec. 31, 1871 in N. York," preserved at Lancaster Theological Seminary, Lancaster, Pa. (hereafter abbreviated LTS).

6. "Autobiographical Reminiscences," p. 3.

7. Chur, Staatsarchiv (hereafter abbreviated: StA), Zizers, Tauf-, Ehe- und Totenregister, protestantisch, 1646–1804, Mikrofilm 87, sub 1759.

8. The following information on the Schaf family at Chur is based on the local church registers, preserved in Chur, Stadtsarchiv (hereafter abbreviated: Sta), S 13,7, pp. 91, 137, 282; S 13.8, pp. 19, 29, 39, 335; S 13.9, pp. 125; S 13.10, pp. 60, 76; S 13.22, pp. 12, 22, 686.

9. On the economic status of the Schafs, cf. Sta F 12.2, p. 170; F 18.36, p. 13; P 4.3, p. 187; P 43.0, pp. 54, 89, 127, 162, 191, 239, 270, 308, 342, 390, 433; P 43.1, pp. 36, 86, 188, 216, 265, 336; P 43.2, p. 147.

10. Sta, G 7.3, p. 1291.

11. Sta, F 18.36, pp. 13, 16; G 7.1, p. 486.

12. StA, Mikrofilm 87 (n. 7 above), sub 1789. Her father, Johann Heinrich Schindler (1756–1830), had his home originally in Mollis (Kanton Glarus), where on April 30, 1783, he was married to her

mother Anna Schatzi (1756–1838) from Zizers. Between 1785 and 1787 the couple moved to Zizers, where five of their seven children, including Anna, were born. (Glarus, Landesarchiv, Genealogiebände, Mollis, sub Schindler, Nr. 257.)

13. The information on Anna Schindler's stay at Chur and her relationship with Philipp Schaff is based on Sta, G 7.3, pp. 1101s., 1115, 1118–1120; P 4.3, pp. 311, 374. Only the name of the husband "Louis" is mentioned in the manuscript sources in Chur. It is very likely that this "Louis" was Heinrich Louis, a tailor and alien resident in Malans (about five kilometers north of Zizers). There he died from an inflammation of the chest on October 22, 1823, at sixty-four years of age. He was earlier married to Menga Danuser from Chur, but she had died on July 31, 1813 (Chur, StA, Altes Kirchenbuch Malans [Schreibmaschinentranskription], II, AB IV 6 145 b, Totenrodel sub 1813 resp. 1823). This church register does not mention Anna Schindler at all, but her marriage to a certain Louis in Malans is recorded in Glarus (Landesarchiv, Genealogiebände, Mollis, sub Schindler, Nr. 257). The date of the marriage is unknown.

14. Sta, S 13.9, p. 125; 13.22, p. 12. The remark of the legitimate birth in the parish register has later been scratched out. The date of birth is not recorded. Schaff himself says in his "Autobiographical Reminiscences" (p. 15): "I was born January 1, 1819, at Coire." The following sentence he crossed out: "I was baptized on the day of my birth, according to the rite of the Reformed Church, to which all my ancestors belonged as far as I can know" (p. 16). D. Schaff, *Life* (n. 3 above), says: "He was born January 1, 1819, at Chur . . . and was baptized a week later" (p. 1). It is possible that he was born on January 1 and was baptized a week later, but it is more likely that Schaff's original phrase "baptized on the day of my birth" is correct, so that his remark 'born January 1' is an error maybe stemming from misreading of the '7' in the baptismal paper" (D. Schaff, p. 2) which was in the possession of the Schaffs but is no longer extant.

15. It is very unlikely that A. Schindler returned to her husband in Malans after these dramatic events in Chur. Otherwise, her name would have been mentioned in the entry concerning her husband's death in the church register. It might be that she went to Mollis in Glarus, where she had, by way of her father, full citizenship. Philip Schaff says in his "Autobiographical Reminiscences," p. 16, that soon after the death of his own father (1820), his mother moved to Glarus and was married to a widower with several children. Contrary to this statement it is more likely that Anna went back to her birthplace, Zizers, for there, on January 14, 1829, she was married for a second time. Her husband, Peter Kubli (1773–1832), like her father, came originally from Glarus but, leaving behind his legitimate wife, he had left the canton in 1812–1813 and settled beyond the borders in Zizers in order to be able to enter into a second marriage. With his

second wife Elisabeth Leuzinger (1783–1828), he had six children (born between 1810 and 1822), who, however, were regarded as illegitimate. Schaff is right in saying that his mother was married to a widower, but the marriage took place ten years after she had left Chur. The second husband died within a few years. The contacts with Glarus did not cease, for after a couple of years A. Schindler was married in Glarus on July 20, 1841, to Andreas Stüssi (1782–1867). For him also it was the third marriage. His first wife had died in the year of their marriage, 1813, leaving behind an infant son. The second wife died in 1838 after a marriage of almost twenty-five years. As Schaff says ("Autobiographical Reminiscences," p. 17), Anna Schindler lived with A. Stüssi near the town of Glarus. This place was very probably Riedern, the native village of her husband Stüssi. In 1867 Anna Schindler became a widow for the third time. She had to witness a drama around the only child born of the first marriage of her third husband. In 1870 Fridolin Stüssi committed suicide in prison after having been indicted for homicide of his drunken wife (Glarus, Landesarchiv, Genealogiebände, Glarus, sub Stüssi, Nr. 88; Netstal, sub Kubli, Nr. 153). In the same year, 1870, A. Schindler moved to Fürstenau (Kanton Graubünden). Two years later, accompanied by her son, Philip Schaff, she moved to Chur, and eventually to Glarus, where she died on May 25, 1876 ("Autobiographical Reminiscences," p. 17; D. Schaff, *Life,* p. 3).

16. On the history of the Grisons in general cf. Friedrich Pieth, *Bündnergeschichte,* 2nd ed. (Chur, 1982), passim, esp. pp. 330f., 370–372.

17. Janett Michel, *Hundertfünfzig Jahre Bündner Kantonsschule 1804–1954. Festschrift zur 150-Jahrfeier im Auftrag des Kleinen Rates des Kantons Graubünden* (Chur, 1954).

18. Peter Niederstein, *Bündner Kirchengeschichte, 4. Teil: Die letzten drei Jahrhunderte. Bewahrung und Wandlung* (Chur, 1987).

19. "Autobiographical Reminiscences," p. 18; D. Schaff, *Life,* pp. 7, 8f. On Kind cf. Niederstein, *Bündner Kirchengeschichte,* pp. 117–121; Ernst Stähelin, ed., *Die Christentumsgesellschaft in der Zeit von der Erweckung bis zur Gegenwart. Texte aus Briefen, Protokollen und Publikationen* (Basel, 1974), p. 86.

20. StA, B/N 333; cf. Basel, Staatsarchiv PA 653, V, 20 (16 letters from Kind to theologians and churchmen in Basel, 1803–1852).

21. Fritz Montigel, "Graubünden und die Bibelgesellschaften," in *Bündnerische Monatsblatt Zeitschrift für bündner. Geschichte, Landes- und Volkskunde* (1946), p. 273; Sta, P 43.1, pp. 188, 216, 265, 336.

22. Sta, B 1217.

23. Basel, Staatsarchiv PA 653, V, 20, Kind to Christian Gottlieb Blumhardt, June 20, 1824.

24. Ibid.

25. Basel, Staatsarchiv PA 653, V, Johann Christian Schircks to Christian Friedrich Spittler, October 16, 1831.

26. Joh. Ulrich Maier, *Geschichte des bündnerischen Volksschulwesens in der ersten Hälfte des 19. Jahrhunderts* (Chur, 1919), p. 16f.

27. The minutes of the Commission for Relief of the poor mention the case of Philip Schaff, Sta, P 6, pp. 293, 296f., 354, 430, 449f., 452, 501f.

28. Pieth, pp. 376–381; Michel, pp. 11–62.

29. Schaff's stay at the *Kantonsschule* is documented in the school's register StA, CB III 478, year 1832 (No. 145); 1833 (No. 89); 1834 (No. 66) and in the minutes of the school board StA, CB II 391, pp. 95, 96, 164, 189, 194–202; CB II 392, p. 195.

30. In Western civilization masturbation had not been an issue before the middle of the eighteenth century. Especially pedagogues started to indicate that "the hidden sin" endangers the harmonious development of the juvenile body and soul. Since their assertion could not be proved by enlightened medical science it was by no means generally accepted (J. M. W. van Ussel, *Geschiedenis van het seksuele problem,* 6th ed., Meppel, 1978). The Schaff case reflects this different attitude toward masturbation. The school board, guided by pedagogic principles, naturally asked for severe punishment, whereas the members of the Commission for Relief of the poor, including the theologian Kind, tried to preserve the proportions. Another indication that such a severe punishment as Schaff and his fellows had to undergo was not unquestioned is seen in the fact that in October of the same year (1834) a second case of masturbation at the *Kantonsschule* was revealed. No difference from Schaff's transgression is to be seen, but this time the trespassers were treated more kindly, for they were only threatened with exclusion (StA CB II 391, pp. 205f).

31. LTS; on the cover Schaff wrote "Ein schwacher poetischer Versuch. Chur im Sept. 1834," f. 2[r] gives the title "Die Freundschaft." No earlier work by Schaff has been preserved.

32. In his "Autobiographical Reminiscences" (p. 18) he says: "The greatest service for which I am indebted to Antistes Kind was that he sent me to a Christian institution in Kornthal, near Stuttgart, where moral and religious interests were much better provided for than in the College of my native place, *which was controlled by rationalistic influence.*" The italicized phrase later on was scratched out by Schaff. D. Schaff docs not give this quote but remarks only, "Following the advice of Antistes Kind, young Schaff left Chur in 1834, and entered the boys' academy in Kornthal, Württemberg" (pp. 8f.).

33. *Leges synodales ecclesiae rhaeticae reformatae, emendatae et restauratae in synodo Curiae celebrata anno MDCCXCIII,* Chur

1825, caput III, s 10: "Qui illegitimo toro nati, et quorum parentes seu avi commerito supplicio affecti fuerunt a sacro Ministerio arceantur" (p. 10).

34. There is no evidence of such an application and refusal in the Chur archives, but this procedure might be inferred from a letter by Theodore Passavant to Schaff dated September 29, 1839 (LTS, ZD S 14, Box 2). Passavant confirms the receipt of a letter by Schaff from Halle and, referring to 2 Samuel 12:24, he says: "Nun, wenn Sie Bündten verstösst, andere werden Sie nicht verstossen [Now, if the Grisons repel you, others will not repel you]."

35. *Kirchliche Gesetzessammlung des Kantons Graubünden, enthaltend sämmtliche gegenwärtig geltenden kirchlichen Verordnungen und Gesetze, zusammengestellt durch den evangel. Kirchenrath* (Chur, 1854).

36. Chur, Archiv des Evangelischen Kirchenrates des Kantons Graubünden, "Protokoll des evangelischen Kirchenrates des Kantons Graubünden, 1853–1871," pp. 236, 264; "Synodalprotokoll, 1843–1879," pp. 166f.; "Synodalmatrikel," p. 3.

James Henley Thornwell and the Shaping of the Reformed Tradition in the South

John H. Leith

James Henley Thornwell qualifies as a representative Reformed theologian and churchman in the South on at least three grounds. First of all, his influence on culture was greater than that of any other churchman in South Carolina, if not in the South. As professor, president, and trustee of the South Carolina College, he shaped the life of an important institution as well as the intellectual life of society. He took vigorous positions on public issues, and at the close of his life he spoke effectively for both slavery and secession. Some judged him to be to social ethics what John C. Calhoun was to politics.[1]

Thornwell was also a churchman who shaped the institutional life of the Presbyterian Church in the United States (Southern) as did no other person. He attended nine General Assemblies, including five of the six Assemblies from 1855 to 1860. He was elected Moderator of the 1847 General Assembly at the age of thirty-four. Twenty years after his death John B. Adger, a highly knowledgeable churchman, declared:

> How often his name . . . is named in our Church courts and Church papers. What Thornwell held, what Thornwell said, is always felt to be a most potent argument for or against any debatable position. As long as our Church lives, James Henley Thornwell will live in our hearts and his name dwell on our lips.[2]

Others have judged that the polity and theology of the Presbyterian Church U.S. were the embodiment of James Henley Thornwell.[3] These were the views of friends, but there was no lack of substantiating evidence, particularly until 1940, after which his influence waned.

Thornwell was also a thinker whose thought shaped the

dominant theology and polity of southern Presbyterianism for at least eighty years after his death. The Synod of South Carolina voted to celebrate the centennial of his birth in 1912 because of his "most eminent service to our Church in defining her theological views and in expounding, organizing, and applying her ecclesiastical polity."[4] Thornwell used the *Institutes of the Christian Religion* as the basic textbook in theology, but a student exclaimed that Thornwell found more in the *Institutes* than Calvin did.[5] And the student was right, for Thornwell read the *Institutes* in the light of the developing Reformed tradition and in the light of his own particular theological frame of reference. The Calvinism and the Reformed tradition that would dominate theological teaching at Columbia Theological Seminary for the next eighty years would be that which had been filtered through the person of James Henley Thornwell. What was true for theology was also true for polity. Again Thornwell believed that his ecclesiastical views were rooted in the Reformed tradition, and particularly in the fourth book of the *Institutes,* but he did not hesitate to elaborate and to clarify the traditional polity of the church, just as he confidently and boldly dealt with theological issues. Thornwell's powers were sharpened and his influence enhanced by his theological associates in a radius of about fifty miles of Columbia; namely, Benjamin M. Palmer, John B. Adger, Charles Colcock Jones, George Howe, Thomas Smyth, J. Leighton Wilson, Joseph R. Wilson, along with younger ministers John L. Girardeau and James Woodrow. It is not likely that any abler group of Presbyterian ministers was ever congregated in so small an area in the history of American Presbyterianism.

Thornwell's influence was diminished by his early death at fifty years of age and by the public support he gave to the losing causes of slavery and secession. Yet the actual achievements of his life merit for him a significant place in the history of the Reformed tradition in America as well as in the culture of the South.

I. Life and Work

Thornwell was born in Marlborough District in South Carolina in 1812, the son of a plantation overseer.[6] His father died in 1819, leaving James to the care of his mother, a devout Welsh Baptist. His education began in one of the old field schools, but James was fortunate to come to the attention of a traveling teacher, Peter McIntyre, who was impressed with his student's ability. His reputation as a scholar impressed General

James Gillespie, a planter, and W. H. Robbins of Cheraw, a lawyer with broad intellectual interests. They sponsored his further study at Cheraw Academy and his studies at the South Carolina College. Thornwell entered the junior class at college with a reputation for brilliance, but a fellow student who became the renowned physician J. Marion Sims described him on entrance as a "dirty looking, malarial looking" youth of one hundred pounds.[7] In the end his scholarship proved itself. He established himself as the best debater on the campus and was graduated as the best scholar in his class.

South Carolina College had an able faculty and a very remarkable president in Thomas Cooper while Thornwell was a student.[8] Cooper had studied chemistry at Oxford but probably did not receive his degree because of his refusal to sign the Thirty-nine Articles. He investigated the French Revolution firsthand and then practiced law and medicine in Pennsylvania. He became a friend of Jefferson and Madison and hoped to have a position at the University of Virginia when it opened. In the meantime, he took the position of professor of chemistry at South Carolina College. After one year he was elected president pro tempore and then president. Thomas Cooper was a Deist and an unashamed man of the Enlightenment. As such, he left some important legacies in the state. He advocated a medical school and better hospitals for the mentally ill, and he taught one of the first courses anywhere on political economy. In 1830 he brought to white heat his war with the church, and especially with Presbyterians, with a pamphlet, *An Exposition of the Doctrine of Calvinism.* In the subsequent investigations, Thornwell as a student reported that Cooper taught that Moses was not the author of the Pentateuch, but that he (Cooper) had never made an attack on the Sabbath. He had no clear recollection of an attack on prayer, but he had a vague feeling that Cooper was hostile to it.[9] Thornwell's own attitude is not clear. Once Cooper was described as Thornwell's idol,[10] but as a senior Thornwell refused to support a petition in support of Cooper.[11] The important point is that Cooper is sufficient evidence that Thornwell could not have been uninformed about the issues the Enlightenment and modern science were raising for Christian faith.

Thornwell never really left the South Carolina College. After graduation, he remained for further study, supporting himself as a tutor. This did not turn out to be financially possible, and Thornwell had to begin teaching at Sumterville. In 1837 he returned to the college as professor of Belles Lettres and rhetoric. The department of metaphysics, more to his liking, was soon committed to his care. Thornwell left South

Carolina College for a pastoral charge in January 1840, but he returned in January 1841 as chaplain and professor of sacred literature and evidences of Christianity, a position he held until May 1851 when he left for another brief pastorate.

In December of the same year he returned to the college as president, discharging that responsibility until he became professor of theology at Columbia Theological Seminary in 1854. In a short time he now became a trustee of the college and served in this position until his death in 1862. Thus he was connected with the college from his graduation to his death, except for intervals adding up to a little more than five years.

The sesquicentennial historian of the University of South Carolina entitled his chapter on Thornwell, "Thornwell and the Status Quo."[12] This was a good title, but it must not obscure Thornwell's contributions to education in the state. He regarded the college as a means whereby he as a Christian could mightily influence society. He restored for the church people of the state the confidence in the college that had been forfeited by Cooper. Not all church people were happy, however. One prominent Episcopalian exclaimed, "I know the chaplain of the college well, and I know of no man under whose influence I should place a man with more reluctance."[13] Thornwell did maintain the ideal of superior, classical education in the college. His letter to Governor Manning on the state's responsibility became a classic document in the policy of South Carolina. In this letter he makes explicit his ideal of education as the training of the human mind and his conviction that this training would contribute to the common good.

> Devoted to the interests of general, in contradistinction from professional, education, its design is to cultivate the mind without reference to any ulterior pursuits. "The student is considered an end to himself; his perfection as a man simply, being the aim of his education." The culture of the mind, however, for itself, contributes to its perfection as an instrument; so that general education, while it directly prepares and qualifies for no special distinction, indirectly trains for every vocation in which success is dependent upon intellectual exertion. It has taught the mind the use of its powers, and imparted those habits without which those powers would be useless. It makes *men,* and consequently promotes every enterprise in which *men* are to act.[14]

A university maintaining this ideal would, Thornwell believed, influence the entire culture of the state.

Thornwell was a man of action. Hence he was never totally happy as an academician. He could write of his work in bitter despair.

> From long experience, I am satisfied that the possibilities of usefulness in such a situation are largely overrated. The influence which a good man can exert is rather negative than positive; it consists more in preventing evil, than in directly doing good. This negative sort of usefulness has never been enough to fill up my desires. But Providence seems to have cast my lot where my labour is drudgery, and my reward is disappointment. My time is so frittered away by the constant intervention of external duties, that I can pursue no consecutive plans of study; and what little writing I am able to perform, and it is little enough, must be done at the expense of sleep or recreation. But here I am, mysteriously shut up to a position which is not the object of my choice, discouraged, mortified, distressed at the fruitlessness of my efforts, toiling day after day without hope, worn down by a constant pressure of responsibility, and unsustained, for the most part, by sympathy, cooperation, or approval, on the part of those around me. If there are any who envy me my chair, they would gladly relinquish to me all its honours after six months' experience of its cares.[15]

Thornwell was also a churchman. As an ordained minister, he was always facing the question of whether his work at South Carolina College fulfilled the responsibilities of his ordination.[16] This question was made acute by Thornwell's views on ordination.[17] All the time he was at the South Carolina College, he was also engaged in an active vocation as a churchman, if not as pastor of a church.

Thornwell was not born a Presbyterian, and material is not available to trace in detail his religious and theological development. Unquestionably, acquaintance with the Westminster Confession, which he bought for twenty-five cents in a secondhand bookstore, played its part. On May 13, 1832, he became a member of the Concord Presbyterian Church near Sumterville, and shortly thereafter he decided to become a minister. He applied to the Presbytery of Harmony to become a candidate for the ministry in the fall of 1833, but his examination was so unsatisfactory in the area of personal experience and reasons for seeking the office that the Presbytery doubted that it should accept him.[18]

When his obligation at Cheraw Academy, where he was then teaching, was finished, he went to the theological seminary at Andover, Massachusetts. He was not pleased with it and transferred to Harvard. He found Harvard stimulating, but for reasons of health he returned to South Carolina within the year. He became pastor of the Presbyterian Church in Lancaster, and he served this congregation for three years (1835–1837) before returning to the college. He later served as pastor of the First Presbyterian Church of Columbia from January 1 to December 31, 1840, and a decade later as pastor of the Glebe Street Church, a small congregation in Charleston, for a brief time (May 18 to December 31, 1851). On another occasion (1845) Thornwell accepted the call from the Second Presbyterian Church of Baltimore, but the actions of the board of the college and of Charleston Presbytery in a rare exercise of presbyterial power prevented his leaving the college.

Thornwell's work in the church, however, cannot be defined in terms of his brief pastorates. He first attended the General Assembly of the Presbyterian Church in 1837 when he was twenty-four years of age. This was the Assembly that accomplished the Old School–New School division, and it plunged Thornwell immediately into debate, though in this he never needed encouraging. He was elected Moderator of the Assembly in 1847, when he was thirty-four years of age, probably the youngest man ever to hold this office in American Presbyterianism. From this point on, he was frequently elected to the Assembly and became known as its preeminent debater.

In addition to his work in the Assemblies, Thornwell was a vigorous protagonist in the debates of the church. In the debates on church boards, he argued for committees that were immediately answerable to the Assembly. On the elder question, he insisted that the ruling elder is the basic office to which the teaching and preaching function is added. He engaged in vigorous debates with the Roman Catholics, and in the Presbyterian Church courts he opposed the validity of Roman Catholic baptism. He became an advocate of the doctrine of the church as a spiritual institution that does not engage as a corporate body in such activities as temperance societies, hospitals, education, and abolition. He also became the theological and ethical justifier of slavery and a hardy supporter of secession, though as a young man he had written against nullification.

Thornwell was one of the principal architects of the Presbyterian Church in the Confederate States. As soon as the division in the nation became apparent, Thornwell began working toward an organizing assembly. When this Assembly met in December 1861 in Augusta, Georgia, Thornwell was one of its most active members. He was responsible for "The Address to All the Churches of Jesus Christ Throughout the Earth," which the Assembly adopted as a statement of its reasons for coming into existence.[19] Thornwell also prepared a "Farewell Letter to the General Assembly of the Presbyterian Church in the United States," but the opposition in the Assembly was so great that he withdrew his motion. In this letter Thornwell gave three reasons for the separation, which he hoped could be accomplished without a break in love. Thornwell believed that political differences would exacerbate the discussions of church courts, that as a general rule church organizations should follow national lines, and that the efforts to evangelize the "slave population" would be impeded by a Northern alliance.[20] Thornwell's views in the field of polity were later written into the *Book of Church Order* of the Southern church.

A resumé of Thornwell's work must also mention his editorship of the *Southern Quarterly Review* as a service to the culture of the area. He took on this work with enthusiasm, but public support was insufficient to sustain the publication. He was also one of the founders and editors of the *Southern Presbyterian Review,* a journal that made a significant contribution to churchmanship and scholarship. He wrote concerning this enterprise:

> The editors of the concern are Dr. Howe, brother [B. M.] Palmer and myself. We intend to make it a free journal on the subject of Eldership, Boards, Agencies, *et id omne genus.* We shall not, like Princeton, put an extinguisher upon any candle that emits any light.[21]

Thornwell died on August 1, 1862. His friend and colleague John B. Adger took as the text for the funeral sermon the watchword of his friend, "Shall not the Judge of all the earth do right?" (Gen. 18:25).

II. Theological Formation

An analysis of the sources of, and influences on, Thornwell's theological development provides clues to Thornwell's place in the theological tradition and the character of the Reformed theology that he established in Southern Presbyterianism. Thornwell's theology was not simply a compilation of sources, for his own individuality and genius contributed to the theology he formulated. Some sources are elusive, but Thornwell leaves little doubt about those that were obvious to him.

The first theological influence that shaped Thornwell was that of his Welsh Baptist mother, Martha Terrell Thornwell. Thornwell was always deeply attached to her. In his inaugural address as professor of theology at the Presbyterian Theological Seminary he declared that he had been taught from the cradle, thanks to a noble mother, those eternal principles of grace which the Westminster Confession contained.[22] It is not likely that Martha Thornwell had studied the Confession or even Baptist versions of it. It is more likely that the theology that informed her life was that of the Protestant community.

It is reasonable to assume that Thornwell's early formation grew out of the Protestant piety and popular theology that had been mediated in the culture generally, not only by the Presbyterians but also by the heirs of the dissenting and Puritan traditions of British Protestantism.

A second documentable source of Thornwell's theology is the Westminster Confession. This Confession played a significant role in Thornwell's first Christian commitment. While Thornwell had been reared under the tutelage of a Christian mother, he was exposed to the influence of those who made no Christian commitment. One such influence was Thomas Cooper, a man of the Enlightenment. Another was his patron and sponsor, W. H. Robbins, who was also touched by Enlightenment thought. B. M. Palmer reports on the basis of personal conversation with Thornwell that Deism or at least Enlightenment versions of Christian faith had a great attraction for Thornwell while he was a student at the South Carolina College.[23] Yet he turned away from Socinianism with the exclamation, "I found it a system that would not hold water."[24] Thornwell had a conviction, apparently dating from his early training, that the Bible was the revelation of God, and he maintained this view through college. While in college he read the Bible through, even though he was under Dr. Cooper's influence.[25] Yet he did not make a confession of faith or identify with the church.

Thornwell was a man of deep religious sensitivities and in old age could say, "I can take you to the very spot, where I stood and gnashed my teeth, and raised my hand, and said, 'Well, I shall be damned, but I will demonstrate to the assembled universe that I am not to blame. God made me as I am, and I can't help my wickedness.' "[26] A student remembered his once saying:

> My own experience was the most mysterious thing I know of. From a boy, I was so constituted that I could rest in no opinion, unless I saw the first principles on which it hung, and into which it could be resolved. . . . God never had a more rebellious subject. Feeling guilty, condemned, and miserable, I was determined to fight it out to the last, that it was not my fault, and that I was born without any agency or consent of my own. . . . At last, light began gradually to break in upon me; and by degrees I came out, as I believe, a Christian.[27]

On May 13, 1832, he made his decision and united with the Concord Presbyterian Church near Sumterville, South Carolina.

The discovery of the Westminster Confession of Faith lying

on the counter of a bookstore was an important factor in his decision. He bought it for twenty-five cents and read it through that night. "For the first time," he declared, "I felt that I had met with a system which held together with the strictest logical connection; granting its premises, the conclusions were bound to follow."[28] In his inaugural as professor of theology at the Theological Seminary of the Synods of South Carolina and Georgia, he declared:

> I was not born in your department of the kingdom of God; it was that Confession which first drew me to you. . . . I am not ashamed of that Confession of Faith. . . . Ashamed of the Westminster Confession of Faith? the inspiration of Heroes and Sages, of Martyrs and Philosophers?—a faith that has founded states, immortalized kingdoms and redeemed countless multitudes of souls from the thraldom of slavery and sin? No, never! I love it, sir, and love it with all my heart, and bless God that in His providence I was permitted to see that book with a knowledge of which my earlier years had not been blessed as yours were.[29]

In his diary he once wrote:

> Saturday night, May 22d.—It is now Saturday night, and I must prepare for the holy Sabbath. My Bible and my Confession of Faith are my travelling companions, and precious friends they have been to me. I bless God for that glorious summary of Christian doctrine contained in our noble standards. It has cheered my soul in many a dark hour, and sustained me in many a desponding moment. I love to read it, and ponder carefully each proof-text as I pass along.[30]

Again, Thornwell writes:

> I have read the creeds of most Christian bodies; I have been rejoiced at the general harmony of Protestant Christendom in the great doctrines of the gospel; but I know of no uninspired production, in any language, or of any denomination, that, for richness of matter, clearness of statement, soundness of doctrine, scriptural expression, and edifying tenderness, can for a moment enter into competition with the Westminster Confession and Catechisms. It was a noble body of divines, called by a noble body of statesmen, that composed them; and there they stand, and will stand for ever, the monuments alike of religious truth and civil freedom.[31]

In London, Thornwell would visit with satisfaction the place where "our noble standards were compiled."[32] These passages have been quoted in detail because they indicate that Thornwell's attachment to the Confession was deeply personal and devotional as well as intellectual. They also indicate that it was a document with which he lived not occasionally but continually.

Thornwell was too Protestant to assign to the Confession any absolute authority, though practically he may have come close to that. In a document adopted by the Synod of South Carolina in 1861, Thornwell proposed that the Presbyterian Church in the seceding states should set up machinery for changing its constitution.

> A Protestant Church, with an unchanging creed, is an anomaly. Its very name is a confession of its liability to err; and that no provision should be made for correcting its errors seems not a little extravagant. In the old Assembly, it was a disputed point whether we could modify, in the slightest degree our doctrinal Standards, and the plan of adding new constitutional rules was awkward and inefficient. We say this, not because we desire to make any changes in our creed. The Westminster Confession and Catechisms we cordially receive as the mind of the Spirit. We believe them to be faithful expositions of the Word of God. The great system which they teach can never be altered by those who love the Truth; but there are incidental statements, not affecting the plan of salvation and the doctrines of grace, about which our children may not be as well satisfied as ourselves.[33]

This statement reaffirms Thornwell's commitment to the Confession, but it also documents greater theological flexibility than he would later be credited with. Moreover, the procedure he proposed for constitutional change, requiring a three-fourths vote of three Assemblies but not of the presbyteries, was more liberal than the church would later adopt.[34]

A third source of Thornwell's theology was the writing of John Calvin. As in the case of the Westminster Confession, Thornwell's writings reveal an emotional as well as an intellectual attachment to Calvin. John L. Girardeau speaks of Thornwell's passion for Calvin.[35] From Geneva Thornwell wrote his wife:

> Here I am in Geneva, the city of Calvin, of Beza, of Farel, of Viret, of Turretin, and of Pictet. I have stood under the same canopy which covered the head of Calvin three hundred years ago. . . . I visited also his grave. There is no monument to mark the spot. He gave orders in his will against all ostentation. There is nothing but a little stone, with the letters "J. C." marked upon it; but I felt the inspiration of his genius, of his learning, and of his piety, as I stood over the earth which contained his mortal remains.[36]

He would write General Gillespie:

> I . . . have paused, in grateful meditations, over the humble grave, without a stone or monument, which covers his mortal remains. I bless God for the labors and sufferings of His honoured servant. Indeed, for the last six weeks, every inch of the ground beneath my feet has been hallowed ground.[37]

These statements from letters to those closest to him reveal, perhaps better than his formal theology, the direction and passion of his theology.

Thornwell read Calvin's commentaries for his own spiritual refreshment as well as for theological learning.[38] He assigned Calvin's *Institutes* as the basic text in theology along with the Confession.[39] His notes contained an elaborate outline of part of the *Institutes* as well as questions on the *Institutes* that he prepared for his students.[40] He urged his colleague, John B. Adger, to use Calvin's *Institutes,* Book 4, as the basic text in polity.[41] There can be little question that Thornwell intended to continue the theological tradition that Calvin had shaped in the sixteenth century.

A fourth source of Thornwell's theology was the Reformed confessions and the theologies of the tradition. He found the confessions convenient summaries of the Reformed faith and frequently used them when he attempted to identify the tradition, as for example in establishing infralapsarianism over supralapsarianism.[42] Another indication of the importance he attached to them is his recommendation of them as basic data for theological education. In advising a young friend, he wrote, "You will find it interesting to study the Confessions and Apologies of the Reformed Churches. This will show you the substantial unity of faith that has prevailed among God's people; and these Confessions are, besides, most valuable compends of theology. The *Corpus et Syntagma,* etc., and Niemeyer's *Collectio* will be sufficient for your purpose."[43]

Thornwell was well acquainted with the theologians of the Reformed tradition of the seventeenth and eighteenth centuries as well as those of the sixteenth century. He refers to Edwards, Owens, Turretin, Witsius, and Cocceius among others. He apparently did not read the theologians of the early church, but he knew Thomas. Butler's *Analogy* fascinated him even though he found it defective, and he was likewise concerned with Paley. Post-Barthian commentators may judge that Thornwell had too much in common with Butler to deal adequately with him, but the same judgment can be made concerning most Reformed theologians of the seventeenth and eighteenth centuries.

A fifth source of Thornwell's theology was the Scottish "common sense" philosophy. While he was engaged in college preparatory studies, his patron, W. H. Robbins, found him reading Locke's *Essay on Human Understanding* and badgered him about reading so difficult a book.[44] This only incited Thornwell to master the book. Shortly thereafter he found Dugald Stewart's *Elements of the Philosophy of the Human Mind* in General Gillespie's library. Palmer quotes Thornwell as saying that he "felt that his fortune was now made."[45] Thus, at the very beginning of his academic career he came into contact with British empiricism and responded to it with affirmative vigor.

Thornwell has left very little writing in the field of philosophy, but his metaphysical ability and achievements ought not to be overlooked or minimized. As a college student he displayed both ability and interests in metaphysics. As a professor at South Carolina College he lectured in metaphysics and the history of philosophy. He had in his library the finest editions of Plato and Aristotle, and he read and quoted them in the original language.[46] He boasted that he had the finest private collection of books on logic in America.[47] He was an avid reader of the philosophers, such as Schelling and Hegel, with whom he very much disagreed.

Thornwell was an open adherent of the Scottish school of Common Sense philosophy, frequently expressing admiration for Thomas Reid, Dugald Stewart, and William Hamilton.[48] All knowledge, Thornwell believed, begins in experience; but he distinguished his own beliefs from those who, in corruption of Locke's principles, represent the mind "as a *tabula rasa* or a sheet of blank paper, upon which, from without, are written the characters which, contemplated by itself, constitute the sole materials of cognition."[49] "Experience," Thornwell contended, "must include conditions in the subject which make it capable of intelligence."[50] These conditions are laws of belief, implicitly contained in the mind, existing apart from experience but remaining dormant apart from experience. Over against Kant he maintained that these fundamental laws of belief by which the order of existence is made capable of detection by human intelligence are not merely regulative principles, which adjust "the relations of our thoughts without any objective validity or any power to certify that things really were as we thought them. Every law of thought is at the same time a law of existence. If our thoughts represent real beings, the connections of our thoughts will answer to the connection of the things."[51]

Thornwell insisted that all human knowledge is phenomenal and relative, and that science transcends its sphere when it seeks to penetrate into the region of substances or into that of efficient causes, two things which rationalists are perpetually attempting to do.[52] "From Locke to Hamilton, English and Scotch philosophy has been for the most part a confession of human ignorance; from Leibnitz to Hegel, German philosophy has been for the most part an aspiration to omniscience."[53]

Thornwell also insisted that the human mind has been constituted with special reference to God.

> It contains elements of faith, or laws of intelligence, which, when normally applied to the phenomena of experience, necessitate the inference that there is a God, and, apart from all disturbing influences, would conduct to a just apprehension and a true worship of His name. The very principles by which man is capable of knowing anything have their proper termination in God. . . . This knowledge . . . is not a remote deduction but an immediate inference.[54]

Thornwell's individuality and genius also contributed to the shaping of his theology. He was a friend of Joseph LeConte, the geologist, and John C. Calhoun noted the breadth of his knowledge. He was without question a person of high intelligence with real sensitivity for philosophical and theological nuances. This can be documented from his record as a student and from his writings. Beyond this an analysis of his personality and its bearing on his theology must be left to the psychohistorians, except for his remarkable capacity for identification. Like Calvin, Thornwell's keen intelligence and sharp way with language alienated people; but also, like Calvin, he had deep and lasting friends. A remarkable capacity for camaraderie and friendly banter is revealed in his letters to close friends.[55] More important for Thornwell's theological task was his capacity to identify with communities and institutions and to become their spokesman.

This capacity is first of all evident in his deep attachment to Presbyterianism. As has been indicated, he was not born a Presbyterian, but no one in the history of Presbyterianism has excelled Thornwell in his passionate espousal of Presbyterian polity. This also carried over into his concern for the organized life of the church, to which Thornwell devoted much time and energy. He debated the issues of church life not as an observer but as a participant.

Thornwell's capacity for identification is also apparent in his commitment to the nation. The nation was first the United

States. In 1832 he opposed nullification,[56] and in the early 1850s he spoke passionately for the preservation of the union.

> We have always associated the idea of a high and glorious vocation with the planting of this Republic. . . . We have looked upon it as destined to be a blessing to mankind. Placed between Europe and Asia, in the very center of the earth . . . entering upon its career at the very period of the history of the world, most eminently adapted to accelerate its progress, and to diffuse its influence, it seems to us to be commissioned from the skies as the apostle of civilization, liberty, and Christianity to all the races of men.[57]

His biographer declares that he could never have been elected to public office in his state because he so frequently opposed the interests of the state.[58] Yet in 1861 he became an ardent defender of secession, and the ardor that he had expressed for the union he now transferred to the Confederacy.

Thornwell's attitude toward slavery likewise reveals the same capacity for identification. Thornwell owned slaves, and he did not regard slavery as necessarily an evil.[59] Indeed, he found that in the providence of God it played a positive role in the education and development of people.[60] Thornwell's innocence or blindness to the brutality or inhumanity of slavery that historians record and that must have been apparent is difficult to understand and impossible to justify. Yet he did have the capacity to oppose the slave trade and to resolve in 1861, when in Europe, to work for the gradual emancipation of slaves when he returned.[61] Many factors contributed to his defense of slavery, including his nonhistorical reading of the Bible and his doctrine of providence. Yet his writings leave the reader with the impression that he is writing from within the community and culture with which he had identified.

Thornwell's powerful capacity to identify with his church, his nation, and his culture was a source of his strength. It made him a power to be reckoned with in church, culture, and state. There is no gainsaying that he provided leadership in all three areas, such as few men do. Yet this capacity was also his undoing, for it contributed to the culturalization of the faith.

III. Reformed Theologian

Thornwell was by intention a Reformed theologian standing especially in the tradition of Calvin and the Westminster Confession. He was also a brilliant thinker, if not a genius, and he had personal courage. He did not repeat what others had said but assimilated it into his own person and articulated it with marks of his own individuality. His lectures on theology, even more than his own polemical writings, reveal his willingness to challenge the positions of the ablest of philosophers and theologians.

Thornwell's definition of theology was comprehensive. In his inaugural lecture as professor at the Theological Seminary, he declared, "Theology, then, is precisely and definitely the science of true religion, or the science of the life of God in the soul of man."[62] This is a broader definition than that of Hodge: Theology "is the science of the facts of divine revelation so far as those facts concern the nature of God and our relation to him, as his creatures, as sinners, and as the subjects of redemption."[63] The breadth of Thornwell's definition of the theological task is seen in his objection to the exclusively "objective" theology of Breckinridge. "Theological truth," Thornwell contended, "may be contemplated absolutely as it is in itself, relatively as it is in effects, and elenchtically in its contrast to error. In the first case it is merely a matter of thought; in the second, of experience; and in the third, of strife. The result, in the first case, is a doctrine; in the second, a life; in the third, a victory. In the first case the mind speculates; in the second, it feels; in the third, it refutes."[64] Theology properly blends all three dimensions of its task in a unity. Thornwell followed Calvin in insisting that every statement about God must also be a statement about humanity and vice versa. He vigorously protested the separation of truth from its effects or the revelation of God from the application of revelation by the Holy Spirit.[65] Theology is lived before it is a work of reflection. It is a life, not a system. Thornwell was aware of Schleiermacher, but how much this emphasis on experience or the work of the Holy Spirit is a consequence of Schleiermacher's work or of Thornwell's philosophical orientation remains to be investigated.[66] In any case Thornwell insisted that theology must always be concrete, rooted in the actual facts of experience and revelation.[67]

Thornwell admired the logical precision of Scholastic theology, but he deplored its neglect of experience.

> Its great defect was not its logical method, nor its contempt of the embellishments of rhetoric, but the manner in which it used its method. It gave no scope to the play of Christian feeling; it never turned aside to reverence, to worship or adore. It exhibited truth, nakedly and baldly, in its objective reality, without any reference to the subjective conditions which, under the influence of the Spirit, that truth was calculated to produce. It was a dry digest of theses and propositions—perfect in form, but as cold and lifeless as a skeleton. What it aimed at was mere knowledge, and its ar-

> rangements were designed to aid intelligence and memory. A science of *religion* it could not be called.[68]

Thornwell also underscored Calvin's teaching that true knowledge of God is productive of piety. "Truth is in order to goodness." Theology is both practical and theoretical; and while these elements may be distinguished, they cannot be disjoined. "It pertains neither to intelligence, emotions nor will but is a peculiar state, a condition of life in which all are blended in indissoluble unity."[69] Spiritual cognition knows by loving and loves by knowing. Theology has to do with the life of God in the souls of men and women, and this involves knowing, feeling, and doing.

Thornwell's definition of the theological task not only included experience and ethics but also made a significant place for human reason. His theology gave a positive place to natural theology. It "is the instrument of spiritual cognition. It is the seed which the Holy Spirit quickens into vital godliness. We must first know as men before we can know as renewed man."[70] Thornwell becomes eloquent when he writes of the presence of God in nature.

> We should see Him in the stars, hear Him in the winds, catch His smile in the calm serenity of the sky, and in the gayety of the fields discern the dim reflection of His goodness. Every dumb thing should become gifted with a tongue to proclaim its Maker's name. In the light of these discussions nature becomes an august temple which God dwells in and irradiates with His light; all created things a vast congregation of worshippers; and the glory of God, as it shines over all and upon all, is the burden of that mighty chorus of praise and doxology which is ever sounding in the ears of the Almighty from all above and all below.[71]

Theology not only puts life in science; it is also the key that unlocks its meaning.

> Of all beings the blindest is that burlesque upon his species who can dwell in a world that is full of the Divine riches, where God surrounds him at every step and permeates with His influence every department of being, and yet he cannot see Him. He may congratulate himself upon his wisdom, but it is the wisdom of the dog, which sees only bright points in the firmament or green spots on the globe. The incapacity of the brute for science is precisely analogous to the incapacity of the fool for Theology.[72]

Thornwell believed that all truth is from God and that all truth fits together in one coherent pattern, even though this is beyond the power of the mind to grasp. Insofar as human reason can, it has the task of integrating Christian faith with all knowledge. Reason must show that "the eternal principles which are exemplified in Nature are exemplified in Grace." "God is one, and however manifold His works, they must all bear the marks of the same hand. They are all really, though in different degrees, impressions of Himself. They are all, in a certain sense, His word."[73] Thornwell belongs in the tradition of those who believe in order to understand and who in faith seek understanding.

Reason also has certain powers in the testing of an alleged revelation. An accredited revelation puts an end to controversy. On this Thornwell had no doubt. But he was equally certain that revelation cannot be contradictory of reason "without committing an act of suicide." A revelation that contradicted reason would destroy the very condition under which it can be known and received as revelation.[74]

Revelation may also embrace data that are purely natural, such as matters of history, geography, and political institutions. Human understanding when furnished with proper sources of knowledge is fully competent to judge these matters.[75]

Revelation, however, goes beyond reason. Reason "cannot say beforehand what revelation ought to contain; it cannot even prescribe the form in which it should be given; and therefore cannot object to it for containing things contrary to arbitrary opinion."[76]

Thornwell combined this profound respect for reason as a gift of God with an adamant affirmation of the authority of the Bible. He could say with Chillingworth that the Bible is the religion of Protestants.[77] He was convinced that the Bible was inerrant and that it had nothing to fear from any contradiction by science. The Bible stood the test.[78] In theological methodology he intended for every theological assertion to be based on, and in accord with, the Bible.

Thornwell's theology can be properly understood only if the Bible and reason are held together in harmony. He did not go the way of the revivalist with his emphasis on experience, or the way of the rationalist, or the way of the biblicist. Neither was he as shaken by the absurdities of life as is the modern existentialist. In holding together revelation and reason, Thornwell believed that he was in the tradition of Calvin and Reformed theology generally. Those who read Thornwell as a biblicist cannot account for his amazingly positive attitude toward science and culture. Those who read him as a rationalist cannot account for the Christian and biblical depth of his theology. Thornwell's theology may be challenged by Marx's analysis of the ideological factor in all reasoning, by the development of historical consciousness and method, and by the achievements of modern science. It is interesting, but dangerous, to speculate how Thornwell's theology would have developed if he had lived another twenty years, but it is too simple to conclude that he would have become a fundamentalist.

Thornwell's organization of his theology bears the imprint of his personality and his mind. He rejected the doctrine of the covenants and of the person of Christ as the organizing principle of theology. In their place he put justification, for "every Divine system of religion is only the answer which Divine wisdom gives to the question, How shall a moral creature be justified?"[79] This is true of the religions of nature as of grace. Under the rubric of this principle, Thornwell organized theology into three parts.

> The first part treats of God and of moral government in its essential principles; the second part treats of moral government as modified by the Covenant of Works; the third part treats of moral government as modified by the Covenant of Grace. The point of unity between the two covenants is their concurrence in a common end; the point of divergence, the different states in which man is contemplated. Both are answers to the question, How shall man be adopted into the family of God? But the Covenant of Works answers it with reference to man as a moral creature, in a state of integrity; the Covenant of Grace answers it with reference to man as a sinner, under the condemnation of the law. These three divisions seem to me to exhaust the whole subject of Theology.[80]

Thornwell never lived to complete his systematic theology. He left lecture notes, which were in continual process of revision, covering less than the first two divisions of his projected theology. The dominance of the moral government theme and the insistence on the question, How shall a moral creature be justified? gave Thornwell's theology its individuality. The problem of justification was so pressing that its origins must be sought in considerable measure in Thornwell's own experience.[81] It was also nourished by the covenant theology, though Thornwell had too many intellectual questions and interests ever to be a covenant theologian. The organizing principle inevitably gave Thornwell's theology a distinctly moral and rational character.

It is too simple to conclude that Thornwell was a biblicist, an exponent of Westminster theology, or a disciple of Calvin. He intended to be all three, and in some measure succeeded. It is also too simple to explain him in terms of the Enlightenment. Thornwell was aware of the "gospel of the Age of Reason," and he rejected it.[82] The theological emphases that may be attributed to Enlightenment sources can also be traced to sources in the Reformed tradition, as, for example, his emphasis on natural theology, on the role of reason, and on providence. It is probably more correct to conclude that these characteristics of his theology were nourished and encouraged by the Enlightenment, even in his rejection of it. Thornwell's theology is best understood as a development of the Reformed tradition that runs from Calvin through the Westminster Confession and Catechisms in the context of the Scottish Common Sense philosophy and of Southern culture; and it must be noted that this theology never faced the challenge of Marx or Darwin, or the emergence of historical consciousness and critical methodology.

IV. Churchman

Thornwell was never content to be an academician. He was always involved, particularly in the life of the church even while on college and seminary faculties. The man of action and the thinker came to focus in ecclesiology. John B. Adger, one of Thornwell's best informed contemporaries, believed that Thornwell's greatest contribution to the church was not in theology but in polity.[83] Thornwell's interests centered on the nature of the church and on the nature of Presbyterianism.

Thornwell was insistent that the "Church of Jesus Christ is a spiritual body," and as such it is not the business of the church to build asylums for the insane and blind, or to promote temperance societies or to serve as "a contrivance for every species of reform—individual, social, political."[84] Thornwell did not deny that the church must speak on such issues, but he insisted that the church speak only when there is a clear Word of God. The church, for example, "has no hesitation in cordially approving of abstinence from intoxicating drinks as a matter of Christian expediency, according to the words of the Apostle in Romans XIV:21."[85] The church, however, cannot go beyond the proclamation of the Word of God. Temperance societies, philanthropic causes, and moral reform movements must appeal to church members, not to church courts. The church must limit itself to its spiritual mission and through the fulfillment of this mission transform society.

The doctrine of the spirituality of the church is easily confused with indifference to, or retreat from, the problems of society. Thornwell was himself blind to certain problems, especially in connection with slavery, to an extent that is difficult to understand and impossible to defend. Nevertheless, he did not intend to retire as a Christian from politics or from culture. He opposed, for example, the church's establishment of colleges, but he understood his work at the South Carolina College as a Christian vocation. Thornwell regarded "a godless education as worse than none," but he believed that creeds and confessions should be left to the fireside and the church. Yet colleges need not be atheistic or unchristian. Religion and the Christian character of the university can be maintained not by indoctrination in the catechism but by the character and the demeanor of the professors, by worship in the sanctuary, and by the "vindication of those immortal records which constitute the basis of our faith."[86] Thornwell operated on the basis of a Christian society[87] and gives evidence of some disdain for the sectarian, denominational pattern of church life. In fact, he believed that the Christian society would more likely maintain the Christian character of the state school than the sectarian group would the church college.[88] At the organizing meeting of the General Assembly of the Presbyterian Church in the Confederate States, Thornwell favored an overture to the Confederate Congress in support of an article in the constitution recognizing the Christian religion.[89] Thornwell insisted on the spiritual character of the church, but he did not isolate Christian faith from public life.

Closely related to Thornwell's doctrine of the spirituality of the church was his contention that the church must carry out its mission directly and not indirectly through boards. Thornwell could find no biblical warrant for boards, and he also opposed them on the grounds that the work assigned to boards was the work of the church itself. "God gave the Church a work to do *in her organized capacity;* she refuses to do that work in that organized capacity, but appoints another organization to do it *in its organized capacity.*"[90] The church is a missionary society, and every member is to have a part and to be responsible for a share in the work.[91] The General Assembly voted against Thornwell but embodied much of his argument in the modification of its practice concerning boards. In the Southern church executive committees replaced boards.

Thornwell's ecclesiology was also characterized by a careful refinement of Presbyterianism, which he believed was the scriptural form of church government. Charles Hodge called it hyper-hyper-hyper-High-Presbyterianism.[92] "The cornerstone in Thornwell's polity is the office of the eldership."[93] The pastor, bishop, and presbyter are the same office in scripture, and the ruling elder is the presbyter of scripture. Teaching and preaching are superadded functions to this basic office. The practical consequence for polity is that a ruling elder should share in the ordination of ministers and that church courts cannot be properly held without the presence of ruling elders. The preacher has a right to rule not as a preacher but as an elder.[94]

Thornwell's Presbyterianism was distinguished by his emphasis on government by representative assemblies and on the headship of Christ in the church. Elders are representatives of the people—the right of the people to elect officers being inalienable—but they are delegates of God.[95] This emphasis was closely related to the doctrine of the spirituality of the church, for the church can only declare the Word of God and cannot as such speak on political and social issues or engage in partisan activities.

Thornwell obviously intended that his polity should be in the tradition of Calvin. It is also clear that in seeking a pure and biblical Presbyterianism, he was not exceeded even by a Melville or Cartwright. While much of Thornwell's Presbyterianism was written into the *Book of Church Order* of the Southern Presbyterian church, his conception of a Christian society was undercut by a pluralism and a secularism that he did not anticipate. He was fully aware of the voluntary character of the church, and the contemporary church may be able to learn from him.[96] There is no doubt that he took the organized church and its work seriously and that even his opponents respected him as a churchman.

V. Influence

Thornwell was by intention a Reformed theologian in the tradition of Calvin and the Westminster Confession and Catechisms. It was also his intention to do his theological work with the aid of the Common Sense philosophy. It was furthermore his intention to be a churchman and also a Christian man in a Christian society. He succeeded in significant measure in all these intentions. But in each case his intention was modified by his own peculiar genius, by the Enlightenment culture he rejected, and by his identification with his communities: church, state, and culture. His achievements were aborted by his early death at fifty and by his involvement with the losing causes of slavery and secession. Nevertheless, his influence was dominant in the Southern Presbyterian church for the eighty years after his death. In his time he influenced culture as well as the church more than any other theologian Presbyterianism has yet produced in the South.

NOTES

1. H. Shelton Smith, "The Church and the Social Order in the Old South as Interpreted by James Henley Thornwell," *Church History* 7, no. 2 (June 1938), 115.

B. M. Palmer, *The Life and Letters of James Henley Thornwell, D.D., LL.D.* (Richmond, Va.: Whittet & Shepperson, 1875), pp. 527ff. (Hereafter cited as *Life and Letters*.)

2. *Memorial Volume of the Semi-Centennial of the Theological Seminary at Columbia, South Carolina* (Columbia, S.C.: Presbyterian Publishing House, 1884), p. 188.

3. *Centennial Addresses, Commemorating the Birth of the Reverend James Henley Thornwell, D.D., LL.D.,* printed by the authority of the Synod of South Carolina (Spartanburg, S.C.: Band & White Printers, 1913).

William C. Robinson, *Columbia Theological Seminary and the Southern Presbyterian Church* (Decatur, Ga., 1931), pp. 69ff., 193ff.

4. *Centennial Addresses,* p. 3.

5. *Centennial Addresses,* p. 19.

6. The writer is dependent for biographical data chiefly on Palmer, *Life and Letters.*

7. Quoted by Daniel Walker Hollis, *University of South Carolina,* vol. 1, *South Carolina College* (Columbia, S.C.: University of South Carolina Press, 1951), p. 162.

8. Ibid., pp. 74–118.

9. Ibid., p. 162.

10. *Life and Letters,* p. 61.

11. Ibid., p. 82.

12. Hollis, *University of South Carolina,* vol. 1, p. 160.

13. Ibid., p. 166.

14. *Life and Letters,* p. 356.

15. Ibid., pp. 300–301.

16. Ibid., p. 153.

17. John B. Adger, ed., *The Collected Writings of James Henley Thornwell, D.D., LL.D.,* 4 vols. (Richmond, Va.: Presbyterian Committee of Publication, 1870–73), vol. 4, pp. 25ff. (Hereafter *Collected Writings.*)

18. *Life and Letters,* p. 113.

19. *Collected Writings* 4:446ff.

20. *Life and Letters,* p. 113.

21. Ibid., p. 296.

22. *Collected Writings* 1:576.

23. *Life and Letters,* p. 78.

24. Ibid., p. 79.

25. Ibid., p. 96.

26. Ibid., p. 97.

27. Ibid., p. 96.
28. Ibid., p. 80.
29. *Collected Writings* 1:576–577.
30. *Life and Letters,* p. 162.
31. Ibid., p. 165.
32. Ibid., p. 172.
33. *Collected Writings* 4:442.
34. Ibid., p. 443.
35. John L. Girardeau, *The Will in Its Theological Relations* (Columbia, S.C.: W. J. Duffie, 1891), p. 178. Cf. *Life and Letters,* p. 534.
36. *Life and Letters,* p. 458. Calvin's actual grave is unknown. Cf. Williston Walker, *John Calvin* (1906; reprint, New York: Schocken Books, 1969), p. 440.
37. *Life and Letters,* p. 462.
38. Ibid., p. 445.
39. Ibid., pp. 532, 535.
40. *Collected Writings* 1:597–650.
41. John B. Adger, *My Life and Times, 1810–1899* (Richmond, Va.: Presbyterian Committee of Publication, 1899), p. 232.
42. *Collected Writings* 2:23.
43. *Life and Letters,* p. 322.
44. Ibid., p. 44.
45. Ibid., p. 45.
46. Ibid., pp. 152, 536.
47. *Collected Writings* 4:232, 266.
48. *Life and Letters,* p. 410.
49. *Collected Writings* 3:80.
50. Ibid.
51. *Collected Writings* 1:57.
52. *Collected Writings* 3:95–96.
53. Ibid., pp. 85–86. In a footnote Thornwell made an exception of Kant.
54. *Collected Writings* 1:74.
55. *Life and Letters,* p. 496.
56. Ibid., pp. 93, 469.
57. Ibid., p. 576; cf. *Collected Writings* 4:477.
58. *Life and Letters,* p. 469.
59. *Collected Writings* 4:398ff.
60. Ibid., pp. 430ff.
61. *Life and Letters,* p. 482.
62. *Collected Writings* 1:578.
63. Charles Hodge, *Systematic Theology* (New York: Scribner, Armstrong & Co., 1872), p. 21.
64. *Collected Writings* 1:451.
65. Ibid., pp. 579, 49.
66. Ibid., p. 582.

67. Ibid., p. 88.
68. Ibid., p. 34.
69. Ibid., p. 38.
70. Ibid., p. 37.
71. Ibid., p. 467.
72. Ibid., p. 468.
73. Ibid., p. 52.
74. Ibid., p. 50.
75. Ibid., p. 51.
76. Ibid., p. 51; 3:198–199.
77. *Collected Writings* 1:48; cf. *Life and Letters,* p. 545.
78. *Collected Writings* 3:218–220.
79. *Collected Writings* 1:580.
80. Ibid., pp. 42–43.
81. *Life and Letters,* pp. 80, 96–97.
82. *Collected Writings* 1:47.
83. *Memorial Volume of the Semi-Centennial of the Theological Seminary at Columbia,* pp. 188ff.
84. *Collected Writings* 2:47.
85. *Collected Writings* 4:471.
86. *Life and Letters,* pp. 335ff.
87. Ibid., p. 507. Cf. *Collected Writings* 4:549ff.
88. *Life and Letters,* p. 336.
89. Ibid., p. 507.
90. *Collected Writings* 4:221.
91. Ibid., p. 223.
92. Ibid., p. 232.
93. Robinson, *Columbia Theological Seminary and the Southern Presbyterian Church,* p. 71.
94. *Collected Writings* 4:43ff.
95. Ibid., pp. 62ff.
96. Jeffrey K. Hadden, *The Gathering Storm in the Churches* (Garden City, N.Y.: Doubleday & Co., 1969), p. 231.

APPENDIX

Edward A. Dowey, Jr. *Semper Reformanda* in the Twentieth Century

Elsie Anne McKee

I fled Him, down the nights and down the days;
I fled Him down the arches of the years;
I fled Him down the labyrinthine ways
Of my own mind;
. . . .
From those strong Feet that followed, followed after.

—Francis Thompson,
"The Hound of Heaven"

The Sea of Faith
Was once, too, at the Full, and round earth's shore
Lay like the folds of a bright girdle furl'd.
But now I only hear
Its melancholy, long, withdrawing roar,
Retreating,
. . . .
And we are here as on a darkling plain
Swept with confused alarms of struggle and flight,
Where ignorant armies clash by night.

—Matthew Arnold,
"Dover Beach"[1]

Looking back over seventy years, Edward A. Dowey, Jr., called on these poems to express in impressionistic fashion something of his life. Both images evoked here rang true to at least some of the hearers. Though these allusions do not capture all the facets of the churchman and scholar, the family man and friend, there is a sense in which the driving, intense spirit of the person is clearly illumined by the haunting words of the poetry.

The formative years of childhood often pose the questions pursued throughout life. For Edward A. Dowey, Jr., life in the world of theological debate antedated consciousness. When he was born, on February 21, 1918, his father, Edward A. Dowey, Sr., and mother, Margaret Turner Dowey, were living in their native Philadelphia, Pennsylvania, where the elder Dowey was pastor of the South United Presbyterian Church. A younger brother, William, came to join Edward in the various manses, where arguments over "fundamentalist-modernist" issues and the new continental theology dominated the religious scene. Although conservative, the elder Dowey was never extreme or bad tempered, his son remembers. In his high school years, the latter considered following his father's profession; and when the time came to go to the university, young Edward applied for financial aid as a prospective minister.

University experience, first at Keystone, a junior college, and then at Lafayette College, changed certain things for Edward, Jr. Encounter with the lively philosophical debates at the university led Dowey to question his belief in God, something which, in his own words, "caused fireworks at home."[2] The two years at Keystone during the Depression, however, provided an excellent liberal arts education. Moving on to Lafayette, from which he graduated *summa cum laude* in philosophy in 1940, Edward Dowey met biblical criticism, British philosophical theology, neo-Thomism, and American pragmatism and naturalism.

Nonetheless, drawn by John Mackay, who was in the process of revitalizing Princeton Theological Seminary, Dowey entered on his formal theological studies in 1940. Many of his professors at Princeton seem to have been considerably less than exciting, but some, like Mackay himself, were bringing new life. Dowey's own memories name Tim Kerr, John Mackay, and especially Joseph Hromádka as critically important. In Hromádka's courses and Mackay's example, the young Dowey began to find the compatibility of religious faith with social awareness, a link he had almost unconsciously felt missing. For Dowey, seminary was a time of existential questioning; perhaps one hears the baying of the hounds of heaven? This period culminated for Dowey in the conviction, reached with the aid of Karl Barth's *Romans,* that he was, indeed, called to the ordained ministry.

Following graduation from Princeton in 1943, Dowey entered the United States Navy as a chaplain. He spent two of the next three years with the Marines in the Pacific theater of World War II. The third year he served as a hospital chaplain, among the Navy's wounded. Whether or not the hounds still gave tongue, it seems probable that the atmosphere of Arnold's poem was again making itself felt at this time.

After the war it was back to more formal theological education. On finishing Princeton, Dowey had been awarded the Newberry Fellowship for Graduate Study. Now he took up those studies. First he went to Columbia University, where he had the opportunity to work in philosophy and the history of religions as well as with some of the great names of the time, Paul Tillich and especially Reinhold Niebuhr at Union Theological Seminary. Having written a thesis on the noetic effects of sin according to Calvin—his first real acquaintance with the reformer—Dowey received the M.A. degree from Columbia in 1947.

In August 1947 Dowey left for Europe. Although his own position was closer to that of Karl Barth, for various reasons, including some acquaintances in Zurich, Dowey elected to study with Emil Brunner. The young American's first choice for a dissertation topic was the nineteenth-century French Swiss pastor and theologian of religious liberty, Alexandre Vinet. Discussion with Brunner led Dowey to the realization that it was John Calvin who really fired his imagination—Brunner's rule of thumb for a thesis topic being something that excites the researcher passionately. How Dowey came to study with Brunner must be told in his own words.

> I had a surprising debate with Brunner over whether he would supervise my dissertation. I had given him my master's thesis to read, and I asked him what he thought of it and he said that it was not very good. We had a pitched battle for about a half an hour. And then he said, now I call Mrs. Brunner and we'll have some tea. And I said, I didn't come over here to drink tea. And so we went at it again. It was intense on the relation of philosophy and theology. There was finally some tea but I decided I had better pack my bags. The next day Brunner wrote a note urging me to stay in Zurich and write a dissertation there. He said it takes fire to make a real theologian.[3]

After Brunner accepted him as a doctoral candidate, Dowey spent the next eighteen months in Zurich. Despite some acquaintances, it was a relatively lonely time, well captured in the images of Arnold's poem. (Dowey once spoke of walking along one of the bridges in Zurich, looking over at the water, and reciting Arnold to himself.) One fruit of the Swiss period was Dowey's competent command of German. More obviously, in 1949 the University of Zurich awarded him the degree of Doctor of Theology. Dowey's dissertation, *The Knowledge of God in Calvin's Theology,* was published in 1952 and reprinted in 1965, evidence of the impression made by this penetrating theological treatment of Calvin's doctrine of faith, the law, and the twofold knowledge of God. Indeed, Dowey's well-known work is often considered one of the best introductions to the study of Calvin.

On his return from Europe, Edward A. Dowey, Jr., began the professional work which was to be his chief occupation until retirement. From 1949 until 1951 Dowey was Instructor at his alma mater, Lafayette College, teaching in the field of religion, including biblical topics and philosophy of religion. In 1951 the pastor-professor moved to New York. There, the first year, 1951–52, he was Counsellor to Protestant Students for the Westminster Foundation, and Lecturer in Religion at Columbia University. From 1952 to 1954, Dowey was Assistant Professor at Columbia, chiefly engaged in the history of religions.

The period in New York was notable for other than academic reasons; in 1954 Edward A. Dowey and Lois Elaine Montgomery were married. Two years later, in 1956, their first child, Edward M., was born, followed in 1958 by his sister, Elizabeth. In the following years the family developed a number of special interests and traditions. One great delight was hiking together, most often in the Swiss mountains during various sabbaticals or in New England on weekends. The treks became even more extensive in time, extending to six weeks in West Africa in the summer of 1977, when Dowey joined his wife, who was studying in Ghana. The African art and culture enjoyed on this trip were only a continuation of another long family tradition guided by the broad interests and wide knowledge of Lois Dowey.

In 1954 Dowey the teacher shifted from the university setting to teaching in theological seminaries. First he spent three years in Chicago, as Associate Professor of Church History at McCormick Theological Seminary. In 1957 John Mackay invited him to return to Princeton, where he served as professor until retirement in 1988. Although he began by seeing himself as a theologian, and "backed into history later,"[4] Dowey was an exciting teacher in both fields. Indeed, his courses on Calvin and Luther soon became a legend in Princeton circles. Presbyterians were not the only ones to feel that they could not properly graduate without having given themselves the pleasure and challenge of at least one of these classes, complete with Dowey's inimitable humor, charm, and occasional fascinating digressions.

Something of the same breadth of interest manifested by the combination of theology and history is evident in Dowey's perspective on the strengths and disadvantages of teaching in university and seminary settings. Dowey the Renaissance scholar emphasizes the stimulation of working with specialists in the humanities in the college context, where the scientists were the Christians and the liberal arts scholars, who shared the theologians' concern with life issues, were the skeptics. In the university, then, Dowey the theologian found himself a "kind of a preacher," while in the divinity faculty, among his "own crowd," he felt compelled to be "sort of a gadfly."[5] The *semper reformanda* of the tradition has always been much more than a phrase for Dowey, to the considerable enrichment of his colleagues and students as well as the church at large. Although from 1957 until retirement he was occupied primarily with the history of theology, Dowey's continued interest in university education is evident in the occasions he spent as visiting professor: at Princeton University in 1958 and 1965, at Drew University in 1963 and 1964, and at Bryn Mawr College in 1965–66. The appreciation of those in the liberal arts for Dowey's contributions is manifested in the honorary degrees given him by Lafayette, Lewis and Clark, and Coe colleges.

Professor Dowey's own continuing, rich appreciation for the liberal arts, especially the fine arts, was notable in his teaching. For example, Dowey often went to New York City art galleries to choose paintings for a class expedition, paintings intended to illustrate the themes of a course such as "sin and evil." One favorite story is related to the Guggenheim fellowship Dowey received for research on Heinrich Bullinger. It had been suggested that sometimes a foundation, when faced with a very strong application, is pleased to find some superfluous items that might be eliminated before awarding the grant. Architecture being one of Dowey's passions, as a part of his sabbatical proposal he requested funds to visit baroque churches in southern Europe. He fully expected to have this luxury cut from the fellowship budget. But no! With a slightly sheepish grin, Dowey told his Calvin class that he got the whole of his request, baroque churches and all. Furthermore, he profited deeply from it.

The Guggenheim fellowship, awarded for 1961–62, was not Dowey's only honor or the only extensive traveling in his academic career. Far from it. Twice Dowey was a fellow of the

American Association of Theological Schools, in 1967–68 and in 1978. Most periods of extended research were spent in Europe, centered in Zurich, Switzerland. Major speaking engagements in various places in the United States included the Moore Lectures at San Francisco Theological Seminary and the Todd-Dickey Lectures at the Synod of Illinois; the Couillard Lectures at Moravian College in 1974; and the Pitcairn-Crabbe Foundation Lectures in 1976. In 1964 Dowey was Remson Bird Lecturer at Occidental College, and in 1971, Danforth Regional Lecturer. On a worldwide tour in 1971, Dowey gave lectures and addresses in theological seminaries and universities in Lebanon, Egypt, Japan, Korea, Hong Kong, and Thailand. Dowey's interest in the wider world has always been strong, and his concern for the church in many lands has continued, finding expression also in his welcome to students from around the world.

Dowey's involvement in ecclesiastical affairs extends much farther than lecturing in theological faculties at home and abroad. The best-known of the churchman's contributions is the work on the Confession of 1967. Dowey was the chairman of the Committee on a Brief Contemporary Statement of Faith of The United Presbyterian Church in the U.S.A. With others, Dowey devoted years to this vital part of the church's life, manifesting wisdom and humor, intelligence and tact, in the sometimes extremely painful and stressful process of drafting and winning approval of the text at the General Assembly of 1967. There are many stories of the skill and patience with which Dowey led his colleagues in the effort to educate and persuade, an effort that culminated in the acceptance not only of the Confession but also of the incorporation of a book of confessions into the constitution of the UPCUSA. In this connection, the professor also reappeared, publishing *A Commentary on the Confession of 1967 and an Introduction to The Book of Confessions.*

Work with the Confession of 1967 was far from Edward Dowey's only important role in church life. He also served on the Joint Committee on Church Union, the Task Force on the Confessional Nature of the Church, and committees of the Synod of New Jersey. Beyond the bounds of North America, Dowey was also a member of the Faith and Order Commission of the World Council of Churches.

Professor Dowey's participation in the scholarly world, as in the ecclesiastical, has included a variety of activities as consultant and leader. He has been a member of the Board of Trustees of Lafayette College and has served on the Board of Directors of the Westminster Foundation and the Advisory

Council of the Department of Religion of Princeton University. Long a member of the American Society of Church History, Dowey has also been much involved in international circles of Reformation studies. His continuing vigorous and very rich contributions to Calvin studies include a distinguished and forceful presence in the guiding Praesidium of the International Congress for Calvin Research, the foremost gathering of Calvin scholars, which meets at regular four-year intervals in various places around the world.

Edward A. Dowey, Jr.: pastor and scholar, theologian and historian, churchman and teacher, husband, father, and friend, lover of poetry, architecture, and music. Edward A. Dowey: quietly devout and loyally devoted to being a gadfly in the face of racism and all the other corporate sins of his church and his people. Edward A. Dowey, Jr.: an unforgettable character.

NOTES

1. Francis Thompson, *The Hound of Heaven,* in *Conversions,* ed. H. T. Kerr and J. M. Mulder (Grand Rapids: Wm. B. Eerdmans Publishing Co., 1983), p. 145. Used by permission. Matthew Arnold, "Dover Beach," *The Norton Anthology of English Literature,* ed. M. H. Abrams et al., 3rd ed. (New York: W. W. Norton & Co., 1975), pp. 2183–2184.
2. See Daniel L. Migliore, "A Conversation with Edward A. Dowey," *Princeton Seminary Bulletin,* n.s., 9, no. 2 (1988), 89.
3. Ibid., pp. 92–93.
4. Ibid., p. 92.
5. Ibid., p. 93.

Chronological Bibliography of the Works of Edward A. Dowey, Jr.

Mark S. Burrows

Books

The Knowledge of God in Calvin's Theology. New York: Columbia University Press, 1952; reprint 1965.

A Commentary on the Confession of 1967 and an Introduction to The Book of Confessions. Philadelphia: Westminster Press, 1968.

Chapters of Books

"Calvinism" and "Predestination," in *Handbook of Christian Theology: Definition Essays in Concepts and Movements of Thought in Contemporary Protestantism.* Ed. by M. Halverson. New York: Meridian Books, 1958.

"Redeemer and Redeemed as Persons in History," in *The Theology of Emil Brunner.* Ed. by Robert W. Bretall and Charles W. Kegley. New York: Macmillan Co., 1962.

"But Is It Barth?" in *Faith and the Philosophers.* Ed. by John Hick. New York: St. Martin's Press, 1964.

"Introduction to The Second Helvetic Confession," in *Reformed Confessions of the Sixteenth Century.* Ed. by Arthur C. Cochrane. Philadelphia: Westminster Press, 1966.

"Das Wort Gottes als Schrift und Predigt im Zweiten Helvetischen Bekenntnis," in *Glauben und Bekennen: Vierhundert Jahre Confessio Helvetica posterior. Beiträge zu ihrer Geschichte und Theologie.* Ed. by Joachim Staedtke. Zurich: Zwingli Verlag, 1966.

"Der theologische Aufbau des Zweiten Helvetischen Bekenntnis," in *Glauben und Bekennen: Vierhundert Jahre Con-*

fessio Helvetica posterior. Beiträge zu ihrer Geschichte und Theologie. Ed. by Joachim Staedtke. Zurich: Zwingli Verlag, 1966.

"The Structure of Calvin's Thought as Influenced by the Twofold Knowledge of God," in *Calvinus Ecclesiae Genevensis Custos. Die Referate des Congrès International des Recherches Calviniennes vom 6.–9. September 1982 in Genf.* Ed. by Wilhelm Neuser. Frankfurt: Peter Lang, 1984.

"Always to Be Reformed," in *Always Being Reformed: The Future of Church Education.* Ed. by John C. Purdy. Philadelphia: Geneva Press, 1985.

Articles

"New Life Among German Laymen." *Union Seminary Quarterly Review* 7, no. 2 (1952) 33–37.

"Love and Sacrifice." *Christianity and Crisis* 13, no. 15 (1953) 38–39.

"Poling and the Presbyterian Letter." *Christianity and Crisis* 14, no. 16 (1954) 124–127.

"Continental Reformation: Works of General Interest, Studies in Calvin and Calvinism Since 1948" (Bibliographical essay). *Church History* 24, no. 4 (1955) 1–8.

"Calvin on Church and State." *The Reformed and Presbyterian World* 24, no. 6 (1957) 244–252.

"Tillich, Barth, and the Criteria of Theology." *Theology Today* 15, no. 1 (1958) 43–58.

"The Third Use of the Law in Calvin's Theology." *Social Progress* 49, no. 3 (1958) 20–27.

"Continental Reformation: Works of General Interest. Studies in Calvin and Calvinism Since 1955." *Church History* 29, no. 2 (1960) 3–20.

"Communism and the Churches." *Princeton Seminary Bulletin* 54, no. 3 (1961) 57–59.

"Revelation and Faith in the Protestant Confessions." *Pittsburgh Perspective* 2, no. 1 (1961) 9–27.

"From Guilt to Grace." *Christian Round Table* 15, no. 1 (1964) 53–80.

"Confessions of the Church: Types and Functions." *Report of the Special Committee on a Brief Contemporary Statement of Faith.* Philadelphia: Office of the General Assembly, 1965.

"The Confession of the Church," *Presbyterian Life* 18, no. 4 (1965) 15–17.

"A Comment on 'Questions and Answers,' " *Presbyterian Life* 18, no. 22 (1965) 13–15, 37.

Encyclopedia articles on "Theodore Beza," "John Calvin," "Johannes Cocceius," "Helvetic Confessions," "Charles Hodge," and "Westminster Confession," in *The Encyclopaedia Britannica,* 1967 edition.

"Black Manifesto: Revolution, Reparation, Separation." *Theology Today* 26, no. 3 (1969) 288–293.

"Presbyterian Plan of Reunion." *Monday Morning* 36, no. 10 (1971) 12–14.

"Two Plans Examined." *Presbyterian Life* 25, no. 5 (1972) 48–50.

"Reconciliation Militant." *Trends* 5, no. 2 (1972) 2–6.

"The Confessing Church, Then and Now: The Bicentennial and the Confessions of Westminster and of 1967." *A Report on the United States Bicentennial.* New York: Office of the General Assembly, 1975.

"A Viewpoint on Miller Chapel." *Viewpoints* 15, no. 4 (1977) 2–4.

"Confessional Documents as Reformed Hermeneutic." *Journal of Presbyterian History* 61 (1983) 90–98.

"Law in Luther and Calvin." *Theology Today* 41, no. 2 (1984) 146–153.

Unpublished Papers

(Cataloged and available in Speer Library, Princeton Theological Seminary)

"A Docetism of the Spirit? Some Theses Offered for Discussion" (paper presented to faculty colloquium, PTS).

"Critique of the Report on Biblical Authority and Interpretation."

"Grounds for Amending the Plan of Reunion Before Adoption."

"The Problem of Revelation in Several Protestant Confessional Documents" (paper presented to faculty colloquium, PTS).

"The Word of God as Scripture and Preaching."